CHARLES SPURGEON

ON JOY
AND REDEMPTION

CHARLES SPURGEON

ON JOY
AND REDEMPTION

WHITAKER
HOUSE

Unless otherwise indicated, all Scripture quotations are taken from the King James Version of the Holy Bible. Scripture quotations marked (RV) are taken from the Revised Version of the Holy Bible.

CHARLES SPURGEON ON JOY AND REDEMPTION

Titles included in this anthology:
God's Grace to You
ISBN: 978-0-88368-432-0 © 1997 by Whitaker House
Key to Holiness
ISBN: 978-1-60374-494-2 © 1997 by Whitaker House
Joy in Praising God
ISBN: 978-0-88368-566-2 © 1995 by Whitaker House
Joy in Your Life
ISBN: 978-0-88368-763-5 © 1998 by Whitaker House
Soulwinner
ISBN: 978-0-88368-709-3 © 1995 by Whitaker House
When Christ Returns
ISBN: 978-1-60374-493-5 © 1997 by Whitaker House
How to Have Real Joy
ISBN: 978-0-88368-662-1 © 1998 by Whitaker House
The Fullness of Joy
ISBN: 978-0-88368-412-2 © 1997 by Whitaker House

ISBN: 978-1-60374-836-0
Printed in the United States of America
© 2013 by Whitaker House

Whitaker House
1030 Hunt Valley Circle
New Kensington, PA 15068
www.whitakerhouse.com

3 4 5 6 7 8 9 10 11 12 13 **ய** 25 24 23 22 21 20 19 18 17

CONTENTS

1. God's Grace to You 7

2. Key to Holiness 105

3. Joy in Praising God 161

4. Joy in Your Life 255

5. Soulwinner 359

6. When Christ Returns 555

7. How to Have Real Joy 649

8. The Fullness of Joy 759

About the Author 863

GOD'S GRACE TO YOU

CONTENTS

1. The Wondrous Covenant 11

2. God in the Covenant 24

3. Christ in the Covenant 40

4. The Holy Spirit in the Covenant 55

5. The Blood of the Covenant 72

6. Pleading the Covenant of Grace 91

1

THE WONDROUS COVENANT

For this is the covenant that I will make with the house of Israel after those days, saith the Lord; I will put my laws into their mind, and write them in their hearts: and I will be to them a God, and they shall be to me a people.
—Hebrews 8:10

The doctrine of the divine covenant lies at the root of all true theology. It has been said that the person who understands the distinction between the covenant of works and the covenant of grace is a master of divinity. I am persuaded that most of the mistakes that men make concerning the doctrines of Scripture are based upon fundamental errors with regard to the covenants of law and of grace. May God grant me the power to impart instruction on this vital subject, and may He give you the grace to receive it.

In the order of history, so far as this world is concerned, the human race first stood in subjection to God under the covenant of works. Adam was the representative man. A certain law was given to him. If he kept it, he and all his posterity would be blessed as the result of obedience. If he broke it, he would incur the curse himself and subject all those represented by him to the same curse. Our first father broke that covenant. He fell; he failed to fulfill his obligations.

11

In his fall, Adam involved us all, for all people descended from him and all were physically present in his seed, just as Levi *"payed tithes in Abraham, for he was yet in the loins of his father, when Melchisedec met him"* (Hebrews 7:9–10). The first Adam thus represented us before God in the Fall. Our ruin, then, was complete before we were ever born. We were ruined by the failure of the first Adam, who stood as our first representative. To be saved by the works of the law is now impossible, for under that covenant we are already lost. If we are to be saved at all, it must be according to quite a different plan, not under the plan of doing and being rewarded for it. That has been tried, and the representative man upon whom it was tried has failed for us all. We have all failed in his failure; it is hopeless, therefore, to expect to win divine favor by anything that we can do or to merit divine blessing by way of reward.

However, divine mercy has intervened and provided a plan of salvation from the Fall. That plan is another covenant, a covenant God the Father made with His Son Jesus Christ, who is appropriately called the Second Adam because He also stood as the representative of men.

As far as Christ was concerned, the second covenant was quite as much a covenant of works as the first one was. The plan went something like this: Christ was to come into the world and perfectly obey the divine law. Inasmuch as the first Adam had broken the law, He was also to suffer the penalty of sin. If He would do both of these, then all whom He represented would be blessed in His blessedness and saved because of His merit. Do you see that, until our Lord lived and died on this earth, it was a covenant of works on His part? He had certain works to perform; upon condition of His performance, certain blessings would be given to us.

Our Lord has kept that covenant. His part of it has been fulfilled to the last letter. There is no commandment that He has not honored; there is no penalty of the broken law that He has not endured. He became a servant and was *"obedient unto death, even the death of the cross"* (Philippians 2:8). He has thus done what the first Adam could not accomplish, and He has retrieved what the first Adam forfeited by his transgressions. He has established the covenant, and now it ceases to be a covenant of works, for the works have all been completed.

> Jesus did them, did them all,
> Long, long ago.

And now, what remains to be fulfilled of the covenant? On His part, God has solemnly pledged Himself to give undeserved favor to everyone whom Jesus represented on the cross. For all whom the Savior died, there are stored up bountiful blessings that will be given to them, not through their works, but as the sovereign gift of the grace of God, according to His covenant promise by which they are saved.

Beloved, behold the hope of the sons of men. The hope of their saving themselves is forever crushed, for they are already lost. The hope of their being saved by works is a fallacious one, for they cannot keep the law; they have already broken it. Yet, there is a way of salvation opened that can be explained this way: whosoever believes in the Lord Jesus Christ receives and partakes of the bliss that Christ has bought. All the blessings that belong to the covenant of grace through the work of Christ will belong to every soul who believes in Jesus. Whoever "*worketh not, but* [rather] *believeth on him that justifieth the ungodly*" (Romans 4:5), unto that person will the blessing of the new covenant of grace be undoubtedly given.

I hope that this explanation is clear enough. If Adam had kept the law, we would have been blessed by his keeping it. He broke it, and we have been cursed through him. Now the Second Adam, Christ Jesus, has kept the law. Therefore, if we are believers, we are represented in Christ and blessed with the results of the obedience of Jesus Christ to His Father's will. Through the ancient Scriptures Christ said, "*Lo, I come to do thy will, O God*" (Psalm 40:7–8). He has done that will, and the blessings of grace are now freely given to the sons of men.

Now, first we will reflect on the privileges of the covenant of grace as found in our wondrous text. Secondly, I will direct your attention to the parties concerned in the covenant. This will be quite enough for consideration in this chapter, I am sure, because of the depth of the subject at hand.

The Privileges of the Covenant of Grace

The first privilege is that illumination of their minds will be given to as many as are interested in receiving it. "*I will put my laws into their mind.*" By nature our minds are dark toward God's will. Conscience keeps up in us a sort of broken recollection of what God's will is. It is a monument of God's will, but it is often hardly legible. People do not care to read it; they are averse to what they read there. "*Their foolish heart was darkened*" (Romans 1:21) is the expression Scripture gives with regard to the mind of man.

However, the Holy Spirit is promised to those interested in the covenant. He will come upon their minds and shed light instead of darkness, illuminating them as to what the will of God is. The ungodly man has some degree of light, but it is merely intellectual. It is a light that he does not love. *"Men loved darkness rather than light, because their deeds were evil"* (John 3:19). Nevertheless, where the Holy Spirit comes, He floods the soul with a divine luster in which the soul delights and desires to participate to the fullest degree.

> Beloved, the renewed man, the man who is under the covenant of grace, does not need to resort constantly to his Bible to learn what he ought to do, nor does he have to go to some fellow Christian to ask instruction. For him, the law of God is no longer written just on a tablet of stone or on parchment or on paper; rather, the law is written upon his own mind and heart. There is now a divine, infallible Spirit dwelling within him who tells him right and wrong. By this Spirit, he speedily discerns between good and evil. No longer is he of those *"that call evil good, and good evil; that put darkness for light, and light for darkness; that put bitter for sweet, and sweet for bitter!"* (Isaiah 5:20). His mind is enlightened as to the true holiness and the true purity that God requires.

Just watch the people to whom this light comes. By nature some of them are deeply depraved. All of them are depraved, but by practice some of them become still further dark. Is it not marvelous that a poor heathen, who scarcely seemed to recognize the distinction between right and wrong before the Spirit of God entered his mind, has afterward received at once the light of a responsive and tender conscience without needing to be taught all the precepts individually? This new mind has led him to know what is right and to love it, to recognize evil and to shun it.

If you want to civilize the world, it must be by preaching the gospel. If you want to have men well instructed as to right and wrong, it must be by this divine instruction that only the Spirit of God can impart. He says, *"I will put my laws into their mind."* Then, how blessedly He does this when He takes a man, who previously had loved evil and called it good, and sheds a divine ray of light into his soul in such a way that, from that time, the man cannot be perverse or obstinate, but submits himself willingly to the divine will. That is one of the first blessings of the covenant—the illumination of the understanding.

The next blessing is *"I will write them in their hearts."* This is more than knowing the law—infinitely more. God is saying, "I Myself will write the law, not merely on their understandings, where it may guide them, but in their hearts, where it will lead them." Beloved, the Holy Spirit makes men love the will of God, delight in all in which God delights, and abhor what God abhors. It is well said in the text that God will do this, for certainly it is not what a man can do for himself. *"Can the Ethiopian change his skin, or the leopard his spots? then may ye also do good, that are accustomed to do evil"* (Jeremiah 13:23). A minister cannot do this for a person; although he may preach to the ear, he cannot write God's law on the heart.

I have marveled at the expression used in the text: *"I will write them in their hearts."* To write *on* a heart must be difficult work, but to write *in* a heart, in the very center of the heart—who could do this but God? A man may cut his name in the bark of a tree, and there it will stand, the letters growing with the tree. But, to cut his name in the heart of the tree—how could he accomplish this? And yet, God divinely engraves His will and His law in the very heart and nature of man!

The notion the world has about Christian people is that we do not conform to certain customs because we are afraid of God's punishment; they think we would like to revel in the vanities of the world, but we do not do so because we might encounter the harsh penalties that the Almighty could justly impose on us. Sons of this age, you do not comprehend the mysterious work of the Spirit! He does nothing of this sort. He does not make the children of God to be slaves in fear of bondage, but He so changes the nature of men that they do not love what they once loved. They turn away with loathing from the things they once delighted in; they can no more indulge in the sins that were once pleasurable to them than an angel could plunge himself down and wallow in the mire with the swine. This is a gracious work of God, and this is a blessed covenant in which it is promised that we will be taught what is right, to know and love what is right, and to do what is right with willing minds and hearts.

I may be addressing someone reading this who has been saying, "I wish I could be saved." What do you mean by that? Do you mean that you wish you might escape from hell? I would rather you had another wish, namely, "Oh, that I could escape from sin! Oh, that I could be made pure! Oh, that my passions could be bridled! Oh, that my longings and my lusts could be changed!" If that is your wish, what a glorious gospel I have to present to you. I do not come and command you, "Do this, but do not do that." Moses gave the commandments in that way, and the legalistic preacher speaks in that fashion. However, as an ambassador of Christ who is unveiling the covenant of grace, I write to you that Jesus Christ has done such a work for sinners that God now comes to them for Christ's sake, makes them see what is right, and by a divine work upon them and in them makes them love holiness and follow after righteousness.

I consider this one of the greatest blessings that I could ever address. I would sooner be holy than happy, if the two things could be divorced. Were it possible for a man always to sorrow and yet to be pure, I would choose the sorrow if I might win purity. Beloved, to be free from the power of sin, to be made to love holiness, is true happiness. A man who is holy is at peace with the creation, and he is in harmony with God. It is impossible for that man to suffer for long. He may for a while endure suffering for his lasting good; but as certainly as God is happy, the person who is holy must be happy. This world is not so constituted that in the long run holiness goes with sorrow. In eternity God will show that to be pure is to be blessed, to be obedient to the divine will is to be eternally glorified. In writing to you, then, about these two blessings of the covenant, I have essentially presented to you the open kingdom of heaven, open to all whom God's grace looks upon with an eye of mercy.

The next blessing of the covenant is "*I will be to them a God.*" If anyone should ask me what this means, I might reply, "Give me a month to consider it." When I had considered the text for a month, I would ask for another month; when I had waited a year, I would ask for another; and when I had waited until I grew gray, I would still ask the postponement of any attempt to fully explain it until eternity.

"*I will be to them a God.*" Now, please understand that where the Spirit of God has come to teach you the divine will and make you love the divine will, what does God become to you? A father? Yes, a loving, tender Father. A shepherd? Yes, a watchful Guardian of His flock. A friend? Yes, "*a friend that sticketh closer than a brother*" (Proverbs 18:24). A rock? A hedge? A fortress? A high tower? A castle of defense? A home? A heaven? Yes, all of these and more. When the Lord said, "*I will be their God*" (Jeremiah 32:38), He said more than all of these put together, for "*I will be to them a God*" encompasses all gracious titles, all blessed promises, and all divine privileges.

"I will be to them a God" includes—and now I hesitate, for what I am writing about here is infinite, and the infinite embodies all blessings. Do you want provision? The cattle on a thousand hills are His. (See Psalm 50:10.) It is nothing for Him to give; it will not impoverish Him; He will give to you like a God. Do you want comfort? He is the God of all consolation (see 2 Corinthians 1:3); He will comfort you like a God. Do you want guidance? There is infinite wisdom waiting at your beck and call: *"If any of you lack wisdom, let him ask of God, that giveth to all men liberally, and upbraideth not; and it shall be given him"* (James 1:5). Do you want strength? There is eternal power, the same that upholds the everlasting hills, waiting to strengthen you. (See Philippians 4:13.) Do you want grace? He *"delighteth in mercy"* (Micah 7:18), and all His mercy is yours.

Every attribute of God belongs to His people who are in covenant with Him. All that God is or can be (and what is not included in that?); all that you can imagine; all that the angels have; all that heaven is; all that is in Christ, even the boundless fullness of the Godhead (see Colossians 2:9)—all this belongs to you, if you are in covenant with God through Jesus Christ. How rich, how blessed, how majestic, how noble are those who are in covenant with God! You who are allied with heaven, infinity belongs to you! Lift up your head, O child of God, and rejoice in a promise that I cannot expound and you cannot explore. There I must leave it; it is too deep to comprehend; we strive in vain to fathom it.

Notice the next blessing: *"And they shall be to me a people."* All flesh belongs to God in a certain sense. All men are his by rights of creation, and He has an infinite sovereignty over them. But He looks down upon the sons of men, selects some, and says, "These are Mine; these will be My special people."

When the hymnwriter set to music the historic battle of the king of Navarre, who was fighting for his throne, he penned these lyrics:

> He looked upon the foemen,
>   And his glance was stern and high;
> He looked upon his people,
>   And the tear was in his eye.

And when the king saw some of the French in arms against him,

> Then out spoke gentle Henry,
>   "No Frenchman is my foe;

Down, down, with every foreigner,
But let your brethren go."

The king took care of his people even if they were in rebellion against him. He had different thoughts toward them than he had toward others. "Let them go," he seemed to say, "because they are my people." Therefore, take note that in the great battles and strife of this world, when God lets loose the terrifying artillery of heaven, His glance is stern toward His enemies, but a tear is in His eye for His people. He is always tender toward them. "Spare My people," He says, and the angels intervene, lest any of His chosen should "*dash* [his] *foot against a stone*" (Psalm 91:12).

People have their treasures—their pearls, their jewels, their rubies, their diamonds—these are their special valuables. Likewise, all who are in the covenant of grace are "*a peculiar treasure*" (Exodus 19:5) of God. He values them above all other beings. In fact, He keeps the world spinning for them. The world exists only to serve as a scaffold for His church. He will send creation packing once His children no longer live on earth. Sun, moon, and stars will pass away like worn-out rags once He has gathered together His own elect and enclosed them forever within the safety of the walls of heaven. Time goes on for the sake of the elect; for them the world exists. He measures the nations according to their number, and He makes the very stars of heaven fight against their enemies and defend them against their foes.

"*They shall be to me a people.*" The favor that is contained in such love cannot be expressed in earthly language. Perhaps on some of those quiet resting places prepared for the saints in heaven, a part of our eternal enjoyment will be to contemplate that love. May we "*be able to comprehend with all saints what is the breadth, and length, and depth, and height*" (Ephesians 3:18) of these precious, golden thoughts.

The Beneficiaries of the Covenant

Just now, I have a practical consideration to discuss, which is to inquire, For whom has God made this covenant? I have already stated that He made it with Christ, but He made it with Christ as the Representative of His people. Each one of us must answer for himself certain questions, which are: Do I have a personal interest or a share in *"the inheritance of the saints in light"* (Colossians 1:12)? Did Christ Jesus specifically represent me in fulfilling the covenant?

Now, if I were to say that Christ is the Representative of the whole world, you would not find any substantial advantage in that. Since the great proportion of mankind is lost, whatever interest they may have in Christ is certainly of no beneficial value to them as to their eternal salvation.

The question I ask is, Do I have such a special interest in Christ that this covenant holds good toward me, so that I will have, or so that I now have, an enlightened mind and sanctified affections, and so that I possess God as my own God? Be not deceived, my friends, not one of us can turn over the pages of the book of destiny. It is impossible for us to force our way into the council chamber of the Eternal. I hope you are not deluded by superstitious ideas that a special revelation has been given to you, or that you have had some unique dream that makes you think that you are a Christian.

It is on sounder premises that I will try to help you a little. Have you already obtained any of these covenant blessings? Has your mind been enlightened? Do you now find that your spirit tells you what is right and what is wrong? Better still, do you have a love for what is good and a hatred for what is evil? (See Amos 5:15.) If so, since you have one covenant blessing, all the rest go with it.

Dear one, has your nature undergone a great change? Have you come to hate what you once loved and to love what you once hated? If you have, the covenant lies before you like Canaan before the enraptured eyes of Moses, as he stood on the mountaintop. Look now, for it is yours. It flows with milk and honey, and it belongs to you. You have inherited it.

However, if there has been no such change in you, I cannot hold out any congratulations to you, but I thank God I can do what may serve to bring about this change in your heart. I can hold out divine direction to you; the way to obtain an interest in this covenant and to secure your interest in it is simple. It is contained in just a few words. Pay attention to these three words: "Believe and live." Whoever believes in Christ Jesus has everlasting life, which is the blessing of the covenant. The argument is obvious. Having the blessing of the covenant, you must be in the covenant; and being in the covenant, Christ evidently must have stood as your Representative or Sponsor.

"But," someone asks, "what does it mean to believe in Christ?" There is another word that is a synonym for *believe*—it is *trust*. "How do I know whether Christ died for me in particular?" Trust Him whether you know that or not. Jesus Christ is lifted up upon the cross of Calvary as the atonement for sin; and the proclamation has been given that everyone who looks upon Him will live. (See Numbers 21:8.) Whoever will cast away his self-righteousness, who will cast away everything upon which he now depends, and who will come and trust in the finished work of our exalted Savior, has in that very faith the indication that he is one of those who were in Christ when He went to the cross and obtained eternal redemption for His elect.

I do not believe that Christ died on the tree to render men salvable, but to save them, really to redeem them. He then and there gave Himself as a ransom. He there paid their debts, there *"cast all their sins into the depths of the sea"* (Micah 7:19), and there made a clean sweep of everything that could be laid to the charge of God's elect. You are one of His elect if you believe. Christ died for you if you believe in Him, and your sins are all forgiven.

"But," somebody says, "what about that change of nature that needs to come about?" It always comes with faith. It follows true faith. Wherever there is genuine faith in Christ, faith works in love. (See Galatians 5:6.) A sense of mercy breeds affection; affection for Christ breeds hatred of sin; hatred of sin purges the soul; and, the soul being purged, the life is changed.

The Work of the Covenant of Grace

You must not begin by trying to mend yourself externally. Rather, you must begin with receiving the new internal life, which is found only in this way: *"it is the gift of God"* (Ephesians 2:8) through simply believing in Jesus. That faith in Christ is given to you according to the working of the covenant of grace, for *"it is God which worketh* [faith] *in you"* (Philippians 2:13).

A man who had been for some time attending a certain place of worship had embraced the idea—and a very natural one, too—that he was saved because he had been baptized. He had been to one of those churches where they teach little children to repeat something like this: "In my baptism, wherein I was made a member of Christ, a child of God, and an inheritor of the kingdom of heaven." "Now," said he, very simply and very plainly, according to what that catechism teaches (and a gross delusion it is), "I am saved because I have been baptized; that has made me a child of God."

The good elder who sought to instruct him more soundly and scripturally could find no metaphor that would suit his intellect better than to take a black inkwell and show it to him. "Now," said the mature Christian, "I will wash it." Having washed the outside of that ebony, ink-filled bottle, he invited the man to drink out of it because it was clean. "No," said the man, "it is black, all black; it is not clean just because you have washed the outside." "Oh," came the elder's reply, "and so it is with you; all that those drops of water could do, all that your baptism could do for you, was to wash the outside; but that does not make you clean, for the filth is all within."

The work of the covenant of grace is not to wash the outside, not to cleanse the flesh, not to impose rites and ceremonies and the laying on of hands. Instead, it is to wash the inside, to purge the heart, to cleanse the inner being, to renew the soul. This is the only salvation that will ever enable a man to enter heaven. You may right now renounce all your outward vices, and I hope you will. You may go and practice all of the church rites and ceremonies, and if they are scriptural, I wish you would. However, they will do nothing for you, nothing whatever to enable you to enter heaven, if you miss one other essential thing—that is, obtaining the covenant blessing of the renewed nature, which can only be received as a gift of God through Jesus Christ and as the result of a simple faith in Him who died upon the tree.

I press the work of self-examination upon you. I earnestly urge any church member to apply yourself to this task. It is of no avail that you have joined a religious institution. It is of no avail that you have been baptized. It is of no avail that you take the sacrament of communion. Avail? Indeed, it will bring a greater responsibility and a curse upon you unless your heart has been made new by the Holy Spirit according to the covenant of promise. If you do not have a new heart, go to a quiet place, fall upon your knees, and cry to God for it. May the Holy Spirit constrain you so to do. While you are pleading, remember that the new heart comes from the bleeding heart, and the changed nature comes from the suffering nature. You must look to Jesus, and looking to Jesus, know this:

> There is life in a look at the crucified One,
> There is life at this moment for thee.

The Blessings of the Covenant of Grace

These blessings of the covenant seem to me to be a great consolation and inspiration. Their comfort comes in different ways to believers everywhere.

A Source of Consolation

The covenant blessings can be a great source of consolation for you. You are in the covenant, my dear friend, but you tell me you are very poor. God has said to you, "*I will be your God*" (Jeremiah 7:23). Why, then, you are very rich! A man may not have a penny to his name, but if he has a diamond, he is rich. Therefore, even though a man may have neither penny nor diamond, if he has his God, he has the "*one pearl of great price*" (Matthew 13:46), and he is rich beyond measure.

Yet, you tell me that your coat is threadbare, and you do not see where you are going to obtain the money to buy a new one.

Why take ye thought for raiment? Consider the lilies of the field, how they grow; they toil not, neither do they spin: and yet I say unto you, That even Solomon in all his glory was not arrayed like one of these.

(Matthew 6:28–29)

Remember, you have the same God as the lilies have:

Wherefore, if God so clothe the grass of the field, which to day is, and to morrow is cast into the oven, shall he not much more clothe you, O ye of little faith? Therefore take no thought, saying, What shall we eat? or, What shall we drink? or, Wherewithal shall we be clothed? (For after all these things do the Gentiles seek:) for your heavenly Father knoweth that ye have need of all these things. But seek ye first the kingdom of God, and his righteousness; and all these things shall be added unto you.   (Matthew 6:30–33)

Therefore, console yourself with the remembrance of these covenant blessings, but especially that "*my God shall supply all your need according to his riches in glory by Christ Jesus*" (Philippians 4:19).

A Source of Inspiration

I also stated that the covenant of grace should be a great source of inspiration for believers, and I think it is. The covenant is an inspiration for us all to work for Christ, because we are sure to have some results.

Therefore said he unto them, The harvest truly is great, but the labourers are few: pray ye therefore the Lord of the harvest, that he would send forth labourers into his harvest.   (Luke 10:2)

Say not ye, There are yet four months, and then cometh harvest? behold, I say unto you, Lift up your eyes, and look on the fields; for they are white already to harvest. And he that reapeth receiveth wages, and gathereth fruit unto life eternal: that both he that soweth and he that reapeth may rejoice together.

(John 4:35–36)

In due season we shall reap, if we faint not. (Galatians 6:9)

I desire, indeed, I desire that the nations would be converted to Christ. I long for all of London to belong to my Lord and Master and every street to be inhabited by those who love His name. Yet, when I see sin abounding and the gospel often in retreat, I fall back upon this: *"Nevertheless the foundation of God standeth sure, having this seal, The Lord knoweth them that are his"* (2 Timothy 2:19).

Christ will have His own. The infernal powers of hell will not rob our Redeemer. *"He shall see of the travail of his soul, and shall be satisfied"* (Isaiah 53:11). Calvary does not mean defeat. Gethsemane, a defeat? Impossible! The mighty Man who went up to the cross to bleed and die for us, being also the Son of God, did not go down in defeat there, but achieved a victory. *"He shall see his seed, he shall prolong his days, and the pleasure of the LORD shall prosper in his hand"* (Isaiah 53:10).

If some are not saved, others will be. If, being invited, some do not consider themselves worthy to come to the feast, others will be brought in, even the blind and the deaf and the lame, and the supper will be furnished with guests. If they do not come from our great country, *"these shall come from far: and, lo, these from the north and from the west; and these from the land of Sinim"* (Isaiah 49:12). *"Though Israel be not gathered, yet shall [Christ] be glorious in the eyes of the LORD"* (Isaiah 49:5), for then the heathen will be gathered unto Him. Then Egypt will yield herself to the Redeemer, and Ethiopia will stretch out her arms to God (see Psalm 68:31); the desert nomad will bow the knee, and the far-off stranger will seek Christ.

Oh, no, beloved, the purposes of God are never frustrated; the eternal will of God is not defeated. Christ has died a glorious death, and He will have a full reward for all of His pain.

Therefore, my beloved brethren, be ye stedfast, unmoveable, always abounding in the work of the Lord, forasmuch as ye know that your labour is not in vain in the Lord. (1 Corinthians 15:58)

2

GOD IN THE COVENANT

I will be their God.
—Jeremiah 32:38

What a glorious covenant the second covenant is! Well might it be called *"a better covenant, which was established upon better promises"* (Hebrews 8:6). It is so glorious that the very thought of it is enough to overwhelm our souls when we discern the amazing condescension and infinite love of God in having framed a covenant for such unworthy creatures, for such glorious purposes, with such impartial motives. It is better than the other covenant, the covenant of works, which was originally made with Adam, but which was renewed with Israel, and spelled out in detail for them, when they came out of Egypt. The covenant of grace is far better than the covenant of works, for it is founded upon a better principle.

The old covenant was founded on the principle of merit. Essentially, the covenant conditions were these: "Serve God, and you will be rewarded for it; if you walk perfectly in the fear of the Lord, God will deal well with you, and all the blessings of Mount Gerizim (see Deuteronomy 11:29; 27:12) will come upon you, and you will be exceedingly blessed in this world and in the world that is to come." However, the old covenant fell by the wayside. Although it was just that man should be rewarded for his good works or punished for his evil ones, yet the covenant of works was not suitable for man's happiness, nor could it promote his eternal welfare, since man was sure to sin and invariably tended toward iniquity since the Fall.

However, the new covenant is not founded on works at all. It is a covenant of pure, unmingled grace. You may read it from its first word to its last, but you will not find a solitary syllable as to anything to be done by us. The whole covenant is a covenant, not so much between man and his Maker, as it is between the Almighty and man's Representative, the Lord Jesus Christ. The human side of the covenant has been already fulfilled by Jesus, and there remains nothing now but the covenant of giving. The requirements as to the human part of the covenant no longer exist.

The entire covenant of grace, in regard to us as the people of God, now stands this way: "I, your Lord, will give this; I will bestow that; I will fulfill this promise; I will grant that favor." We have to do nothing to merit this grace, for there is nothing we can do. God will work all our works in us, and the very graces that are sometimes represented as being stipulations of the covenant are promised to us. He gives us faith. (See Ephesians 2:8.) He promises to give us the law in our *"inward parts"* and to *"write it on* [our] *hearts"* (Jeremiah 31:33).

It is a glorious covenant, because it is founded on simple mercy and absolutely pure grace. It stands, quite irrespective of any past actions on our part or anything that could yet be performed by man. Hence, this covenant surpasses the other in stability. Where there is anything of man, there is always a degree of inconstancy. Anywhere you have anything to do with created beings, there you have something to do with change, for created beings and change and uncertainty always go together. But, since this new covenant now has nothing whatever to do with mankind—in the sense that mankind does not have to do anything except receive—the idea of change is utterly and entirely gone.

It is God's covenant, and therefore it is an unchanging covenant. If there is something that I am to do in the covenant, then I have no security in the covenant. However, if the covenant is dependent only on God's works, then as long as my name is in that covenant, my soul is as secure as if I were now walking the streets of gold in heaven. (See Revelation 21:21.) If any blessing is in the covenant, I am as certain to receive that blessing as if I had already grasped it in my hands, because the promise of God is sure to be followed by fulfillment. The promise never fails; it always brings with it everything that it is intended to convey. The moment I receive it by faith, I am sure of the blessing itself. How infinitely superior is this covenant to the other in its manifest security! It is beyond the risk or hazard of the least uncertainty.

I have been thinking for the last two or three days that the covenant of grace excels the other covenant most marvelously in the mighty blessings that it confers. What does the covenant of grace convey? Earlier, I even considered entitling this chapter, "The Blessings That the Covenant of Grace Gives to God's Children." Yet, when I began to think of it, I realized that there is so much in the covenant that if I only made a catalog of all of the great and glorious blessings wrapped up within its folds, I would need to occupy nearly an entire library in making a few simple observations about each one.

Consider the great things God has given in the covenant. He sums them up by saying He has "*given unto us all things that pertain unto life and godliness*" (2 Peter 1:3). He has given you eternal life in Christ Jesus; yes, He has given Christ Jesus to be yours. He has made Christ "*heir of all things*" (Hebrews 1:2), and He has made you one of His "*joint-heirs with Christ*" (Romans 8:17). Hence, He has given you everything.

Were I to sum up the vast amount of unutterable treasure that God has conveyed to every elect soul through this glorious covenant, space would fail me. Therefore, I will commence with the greatest benefit conveyed to us by the covenant. This singular blessing is enough to startle us by its immense value. In fact, unless it had been written in God's Word, we never could have dreamed that such a blessing could be ours. By the terms of the covenant, God Himself becomes the believer's own portion and inheritance: "*I will be their God.*"

I will begin with the subject in this way. I will show you first that this is a special blessing: "*I will be their God.*" God is the special possession of the elect, whose names are in the covenant. Secondly, I will discuss this as being an exceedingly precious blessing: "*I will be their God.*" Thirdly, I will dwell upon the security of this blessing: "*I will be their God.*" Then, I will endeavor to encourage you to make good use of this blessing, which has been so freely and liberally conveyed to you by the eternal covenant of grace: "*I will be their God.*"

Stop a moment, and think about this promise before we go on. In the covenant of grace, God conveys Himself to you and becomes yours. May you comprehend this truth and take it personally to heart. All that is meant by the word GOD: eternity, infinity, omnipotence, omniscience, perfect justice, infallible integrity, eternal love; all that is meant by GOD: Creator, Guardian, Preserver, Governor, Judge; all that the word GOD can mean: all of goodness and of love, all of bounty and of grace—all that and more this covenant gives you to be your absolute property as much as anything you can call your own. "*I will be their God.*" Reflect on that thought. If this truth is opened up and applied by the all-glorious Spirit to your heart and life, there is enough in it to excite your joy for all eternity: "*I will be their God.*"

> My God! How cheerful is the sound!
>   How pleasant to repeat!
> Well may that heart with pleasure bound,
>   Where God hath fixed His seat.

The Universal Powers of God

How is God especially the God of His own children? God is the God of all men, of all creatures; He is the God of the lowly worm, of the flying eagle, of the bright star, and of the billowy cloud; He is God everywhere. How then is He more my God and your God than He is the God of all created things? In some ways God is the God of all His creatures, but even in these ways a special relationship exists between Himself and His chosen ones, whom He has loved "*with an everlasting love*" (Jeremiah 31:3). In addition, there are certain ways of relating that do not exist between God and His creatures, except with His own children.

As Sovereign

First, God is the God of all His creatures in that He has the sovereign right to deal with them as He pleases. He is the Creator of all; as such, He is the supreme Sovereign of the universe. He is the Potter and has "*power over the clay, of the same lump to make one vessel unto honour, and another unto dishonour*" (Romans 9:21). However men may sin against God, He is still their God in the sense that their destinies are immovably in His hand. He can do with them exactly as He chooses. However they may resent His will or spurn His good pleasure, yet He makes the wrath of man to praise Him, and the remainder of that wrath He restrains. (See

Psalm 76:10.) He is the God of all creatures, and absolutely so in the matter of predestination, seeing that He is their Creator and has an absolute right to do with them as He wills.

However, God the Father has a special regard for His children. He is their God in this way: while He exercises the same sovereignty over them, He exercises it in grace and grace only. He makes them the vessels of His mercy, who will be to His honor forever. He has chosen them out of the ruins of the Fall and has made them heirs of everlasting life, while He allows the rest of the world to continue in sin and to fulfill their guilt by well-deserved punishment. Thus, while His relationship with all His creatures is the same as far as His sovereignty and His right of determination are concerned, there is something special in the aspect of His love toward His people. In this sense, He is their God.

As Governor

Further, He is the God of all His creatures in that He has a right to command obedience of all. He is the God of every person who was ever born into this earth, because everyone is bound to obey Him. God can command the homage of all of His creatures because He is their Creator, Governor, and Preserver. All men are, by the fact of their creation, so placed in subjection to Him that they cannot escape the obligation of submission to His laws.

Even in this aspect, however, there is something special regarding His relationship with His child. Although God is the Ruler of all men, yet His rule is special toward His children. He lays aside the sword of His rulership; in His hand He grasps the rod of correction for His child, not the sword of punitive vengeance. While He gives the world a law written on stone, He gives to His children laws written in their hearts. (See Jeremiah 31:33.)

God is my Governor and yours, but if you are unregenerate, He is your Governor in a different sense than He is mine. He has ten times as much claim to my obedience as He has to yours. Seeing that He has done more for me, I am bound to do more for Him. Seeing that He has loved me more, I am bound to love Him more. However, should I disobey, the vengeance on my head will not fall as heavily as it would on yours, if you are outside of Christ. The vengeance incurred by me has already fallen upon Christ, my Substitute, and only the chastisement will remain for me. Here again, we see that while God's relationship to all men is universal, there is something special in it in reference to His children.

As Judge

Next, God has a universal power over all His creatures in His office of Judge. *"With righteousness shall he judge the world, and the people with equity"* (Psalm 98:9). It is true that He will judge all men with righteousness. However, as if His people were *"not of the world"* (John 15:19), the additional statement is added, *"and [His] people with equity."* God is the God of all creatures, I repeat, in the sense that He is their Judge. He will summon them all before His bar to condemn or acquit each and every one of them.

However, even at the judgment seat, there is something exceptional regarding His children, for to them the condemnation sentence will never come, only the acquittal. While He is Judge of all, He especially is their Judge. He is the Judge whom they love to reverence, the Judge whom they long to approach, because they know His lips will confirm that which their hearts have already felt—the sentence of their full acquittal through the merits of their glorious Savior. Our loving God is the Judge who will acquit our souls, and in that respect we can say He is our God.

So then, whether as Sovereign in determining outcomes, as Governor in enforcing the law, or as Judge in punishing sin, God is the God of all men. Yet, in each of these aspects of God's divine character, there is something special in the way He relates to His people, so that they can say, "He is our God, even in these relationships."

Our God in Special Ways

But now, beloved, there are other aspects of the way God relates to His children that the rest of His creatures cannot benefit from, and here the great crux of the matter lies. Here the very heart of this glorious promise dwells. God is our God in a sense that the unregenerate, the unconverted, the unholy, can never know, and in a way in which they have no part whatever. We have just considered other points with regard to what God is to man generally. Let us now consider what He is to His children, as He is to no one else.

In Election

First of all, God is my God in that He is the God of my election. If I am His child, then He loved me from before the creation of the universe, and His infinite mind made plans for my salvation long before He ever framed the worlds by His word (see Hebrews 11:3):

> *According as he hath chosen us in him before the foundation of the world, that we should be holy and without blame before him in love: having predestinated us unto the adoption of children by Jesus Christ to himself, according to the good pleasure of his will.* (Ephesians 1:4–5)

If He is my God, He has seen me when I have wandered far from Him. When I have rebelled, His mind has determined when my path would be blocked and I would be turned from the error of my ways. He has been providing for me the means of grace. He has applied those means of grace in due time, but His everlasting purpose has been the basis and the foundation of it all. Thus, He is my God as He is the God of no one else besides His own children. He is my glorious, gracious God in eternal election, for He thought of me and chose me from *"before the foundation of the world, that* [I] *should be holy and without blame before him in love."*

Looking back, then, I see election's God, and election's God is my God if I am in election. However, if I do not fear God or even have any thoughts of Him, then He is another man's God and not mine. If I have no claim and participation in election, then I am compelled to look upon Him as being the God of a great body of people whom He has chosen, but not my God. If I can look back and see my name *"written in the Lamb's book of life"* (Revelation 21:27), then indeed He is my God in election.

In Justification

Furthermore, the Christian can call God his God from the fact of his justification. A sinner can call God, "God," but he must always put in an adjective and speak of God as an angry God, an incensed God, or an offended God. In contrast, the Christian can say, "my God," without putting in any adjective except a sweet one with which to extol Him, for now we *"who sometimes were far off are made nigh by the blood of Christ"* (Ephesians 2:13). We who were enemies of God because of our wicked states are now His friends. Looking up to Him, I can say, "my God," for He is my Friend, and I am His friend. Enoch could say, "my God," because he walked with Him. (See Genesis 5:24.) Adam could not say, "my God," when he hid himself in the Garden after he had sinned. So, while I, as a sinner, run from God, I cannot call Him mine; but when I have peace with God and am brought near to Him, then indeed He is my God and my Friend.

By Adoption

God the Father is also the believer's God by adoption, and in that the sinner has no part. I have heard people represent God as the Father of the whole universe. It surprises me that any reader of the Bible would talk like that. Paul once quoted a heathen poet, who said that *"we are also his offspring"* (Acts 17:28); and it is true in some sense that we are, as having been created by Him. But in the high sense in which the term *children* is used in Scripture to express the holy relationship of a regenerate child toward his Father, none can say, "my Father," except those who have *"Abba, Father"* (Romans 8:15) imprinted on their hearts by the Spirit of Adoption. By the Holy Spirit, God becomes my God in a way in which He is not the God of others. The Christian has a special claim to God, because God is his Father in ways He is not the Father of anyone except a person who is His child.

Beloved, these things are quite enough to show you that in special ways God is the God of His own people. I must leave this to your own meditations, which will suggest twenty different ways in which God is specially the God of His own children more than He is of the rest of His creatures. "God," say the wicked, but "my God," say God's children.

As Covering

Then, if God is your God personally, let Him clothe and cover you according to your position as His child. Be adorned with *"the Sun of righteousness"* (Malachi 4:2). *"Put ye on the Lord Jesus Christ"* (Romans 13:14). *"The king's daughter is"*—and so let all the King's sons be—*"all glorious within: her clothing is of wrought gold"* (Psalm 45:13). *"Be clothed with humility"* (1 Peter 5:5). Put on love, compassion, gentleness, and meekness; and say as you do so, *"He hath clothed me with the garments of salvation, he hath covered me with the robe of righteousness"* (Isaiah 61:10).

Let your company and conversation be according to your clothing. Live among the excellent, among the generation of the just; go *"to the general assembly and church of the firstborn and to the spirits of just men made perfect"* (Hebrews 12:23). Live in the courts of the great King. Behold His face, wait at His throne, bear His name, show forth His virtues, set forth His praises, advance His honor, uphold His interests. Let vile persons and vile ways be condemned in your eyes; be of a more noble spirit than to be companions with them. Regard not their associations or their scorns, their flatteries or their frowns. Rejoice not with their joys, fear not their fears, care not their cares, eat not their dainties. Go out from among them to your country, your city, where no unclean thing can enter or annoy. Live by faith, in the power of the Spirit, in the beauty of holiness, in the hope of the gospel, in the joy of your God, in the magnificence and the humility of the children of the great King.

Exceedingly Precious Grace

Now, for a moment, let us consider the exceeding preciousness of this great mercy: "*I will be their God.*" I imagine that God Himself could say no more than that. I do not believe if the Infinite were to stretch His powers and magnify His grace by some stupendous promise that could outdo every other, that it could exceed in glory this promise: "*I will be their God.*" Oh, Christian, do consider what it is to have God as your own! Consider what it is, especially in comparison with anything else.

> Jacob's portion is the Lord;
>> What can Jacob more require?
> What can heaven more afford,
>> Or a creature more desire?

Compare your life with the lot of your fellowmen. Some of them have their portion in the fields; they are "*rich, and increased with goods, and have need of nothing*" (Revelation 3:17); their yellow harvests are even now ripening in the sun. But what are harvests compared with your God, the Lord of the Harvest? Or, what are full granaries compared with God who is your Husbandman (see John 15:1) and feeds you with "*the true bread from heaven*" (John 6:32)?

Some have their portion in the city; their wealth is superabundant; it flows to them in constant streams, until they become a very reservoir of gold. But what is gold compared with your God? You could not live on it; your spiritual life could not be sustained by it. If you applied it to your aching head, would it afford you any ease? If you put it on a troubled conscience, would your gold assuage its pangs? If you put it on your despondent heart, would it soothe even one solitary groan or give you one less grief? But you have God, and in Him you have more than gold or riches could ever buy, more than heaps of brilliant ore could ever purchase for you.

Some have their portion in this world, in what most men love, applause and fame. Yet, ask yourself, is not your God more to you than that? If a thousand trumpets would proclaim your praise, and if a myriad of cornets would loudly resound with ovations for you, what would it all mean to you if you had lost your God? Would this calm the turmoil of your soul that is ill at ease with itself? Would this prepare you to pass through the Jordan and to encounter those stormy waves that finally must be forded by every man, when he is called from this world to lands beyond? Would a puff of wind serve you then, or would the clapping of the hands of your fellow creatures bless you on your deathbed? No, there are griefs here with which men cannot meddle, and there are griefs to come with which men cannot interfere to alleviate the pangs and pains and agonies and dying strife.

However, when you have this—"*I will be your God*" (Jeremiah 11:4)—you have as much as all other men can have put together, for earthly things are all they have. How little ought we to estimate the value of the treasures of this world, especially when we consider that God frequently gives the most riches to the worst of His creatures! As Martin Luther said, "God gives food to His children and husks to His swine; and who are the swine that get the husks?" It is not often that God's people get the riches of this world; this only proves that material riches are of little real worth, or else God would give them to us. Abraham gave the sons of Keturah "*gifts, and sent them away*" (Genesis 25:6). Let me be Isaac and have my Father in heaven, and the world may take all the rest. Oh, Christian, ask for nothing in this world, except that you may live and die on this: "*I will be their God.*" This exceeds all the world has to offer.

Compare this with what you need, Christian. What do you require? Is there not here all that you need? To make you happy, you want something that will satisfy you. Come now, is not this enough? Will not this fill your pitcher to its very brim, until it runs over? If you can put this promise inside your cup, will you not be forced to say, with David, "*My cup runneth over*" (Psalm 23:5); I have more than any heart can wish"? When this is fulfilled, when the Lord says to you, "*I am your God*" (Ezekiel 34:31), let your cup be completely empty of earthly things.

Suppose you have not one solitary drop of earthly happiness, yet is not His promise enough to fill your cup until your unsteady hand cannot hold it because of its fullness? Are you not complete when God is yours? Do you want anything except God? If you think you do, it would be good for you to remain without it, for all you want, apart from God, is only to gratify your lust. Christian, is not the fact that God is your God enough to satisfy you, even if all else should fail?

However, you want more than quiet satisfaction. Sometimes you desire rapturous delight. Come, soul, is there not enough here to delight you? Put this promise to your lips. Did you ever drink wine half as sweet as this: "*I will be their God*"? Did trumpet or harp ever sound half as sweet as this: "*I will be their God*"? Not all the music blown from harmonious instruments or drawn from living strings could ever give such melody as this sweet promise: "*I will be their God.*" Oh, here is a sea of bliss, an ocean of delight. Come, bathe your spirit in it; you may swim to eternity and never find a shore. You may dive to the very infinite depths and never find the bottom. "*I will be their God.*" If this does not make your eyes sparkle, if this does not make your feet dance for joy and your heart soar with bliss, then assuredly your soul is not in a healthy state.

However, you want something more than present delights. You desire something concerning which you may exercise hope. What more could you ever hope to get than the fulfillment of this great promise: "*I will be their God*"? Oh, hope, you are a great- handed thing; you lay hold of mighty things that even faith does not have the power to grasp. Yet, although your hand may be very large, this blessing fills it, so that you can carry nothing else.

I declare before God that I have not a hope beyond this promise: "*I will be their God.*" "Oh," you say, "you have a hope of heaven." Yes, I have a hope of heaven, but this is heaven: "*I will be their God.*" What is heaven, but to be with God, to dwell with Him, to realize that God is mine and I am His? I say I have not a hope beyond that. There is not a promise beyond that, for all promises rest on this, and all hopes are included in this: "*I will be their God.*"

"*I will be their God*" is the masterpiece of all promises. It is the capstone of all the great and precious things that God has provided for His children. If we could really grasp it, if it could be applied to our souls so that we could understand it, we might clap our hands and say, "Oh, the wonder! Oh, the glory! Oh, the graciousness of that promise!" It makes a heaven below, and it must make a heaven above. Nothing else will ever truly be needed except this: "*I will be their God.*"

The Certainty of the Promise

Now, let us briefly consider the certainty of this promise. It does not say, "I may be their God," but, "*I will be their God.*" Nor does the text say, "Perhaps I will be their God." No, it says, "*I will be their God.*"

Let us suppose there is a sinner who says he will not have God for his God. He will have God to be His preserver, to take care of him and keep him from harm. He does not object to God feeding him, giving him his bread and water and clothing. Nor does he mind making God somewhat of a showpiece that he may take out on Sundays and bow before. However, he will not have God for his God; he will not take Him to be his all. He makes his belly his god (see Philippians 3:19), gold his god, the world his god. How is God's promise to be fulfilled in this sinner?

Here is one of God's chosen people, but he does not know that he is chosen yet, and he says he will not have God. How then is this promise to be carried out? "Oh," say some, "if the man won't have God, then, of course, God cannot win him." We have heard it preached, and we read it frequently, that salvation entirely depends upon man's will: that if man stands back and resists God's Holy Spirit, the creature can be the conqueror of the Creator, and finite power can overcome the Infinite.

Frequently, I take up a book and read this: "Sinner, be willing, for unless you are, God cannot save you." Sometimes the question is asked: "How is it that a certain person is not saved?" Often, the answer is given: "He is not willing to be; God strove with him, but he would not be saved." But, suppose God had striven with him as He has done with those who are saved. Would he have been saved then? The usual reply is this: "No, he would have resisted." Instead, I answer, "It is not dependent on man's will; it is '*not of blood, nor of the will of the flesh, nor of the will of man, but of God*'" (John 1:13). We should never entertain such absurd ideas as the notion that man can conquer Omnipotence or the thought that the might of man is greater than God's might.

I believe, indeed, that certain usual influences of the Holy Spirit may be withstood. I believe that there are general operations of the Spirit in many men's hearts that are resisted and rejected. However, I believe that the effectual working of the Holy Spirit, with the determination to save, cannot be resisted, unless you suppose that God can be overcome by His creatures and that the purpose of

Deity can be frustrated by the will of man, which would be to suppose something akin to blasphemy.

Beloved, God has power to fulfill the promise, "*I will be their God.*"

The sinner cries, "I will not have You for a God."

"Is that so?" says He, and He gives him over to the hand of Moses. Moses takes the person for a little while and applies the club of the law, dragging him to Sinai, where the mountain towers over his head as lightning flashes and thunder bellows.

Then the sinner cries, "O God, save me!"

"I thought you would not have me for a God," He replies.

"O Lord, You shall be my God," says the poor, trembling sinner. "I have stripped myself of all my ornaments. (See Exodus 33:6.) O Lord, what will you do to me? Save me! I give myself to You. Oh, take me!"

"Yes," says the Lord, "I knew it. I said that '*I will be their God,*' and I have made you '*willing in the day of* [My] *power*'" (Psalm 110:3). "*I will be their God, and they shall be my people*" (Ezekiel 37:27).

Making Use of This Blessing

Now, lastly, I urge you to make use of God, if He is yours. It is strange that spiritual blessings are our only possessions that we do not use. We get a great spiritual blessing, and we let it rust away for many a day. There is the mercy seat, for instance. My friends, if you had a cash box as full of riches as that mercy seat is, you would go often to it, as often as your necessities require. Yet, you do not go to the mercy seat half as often as you need to go. Most of the precious things God has given to us we never overuse. The truth is, they cannot be overused. We cannot wear a promise threadbare. We can never burn out the incense of grace. We can never use up the infinite treasures of God's lovingkindness.

If the blessings God gives us are not used, perhaps God Himself is the least used of all. Although He is our God, we turn to and seek Him less than we turn to any of our kindred human beings or seek any of His mercies that He bestows upon us.

Look at the example of the poor heathen; they use their gods, although they are no gods. They put up a piece of wood or stone and call it God. And how they use it! They want rain: the people assemble and ask for rain in the firm but foolish hope that their god can give it. There is a battle, and their god is lifted up. He is brought out from the house where he usually dwells, so that he may go before them and lead them on to victory.

Receive Guidance

Yet, how seldom God's children ask counsel at the hands of the Lord! How often we go about our business without asking His guidance! In our troubles, do we not constantly strive to bear our burdens, instead of casting them upon the Lord, in order that He may sustain us? This is not because we may not, for the Lord says, *"Come unto me, all ye that labour and are heavy laden, and I will give you rest"* (Matthew 11:28). I am yours, My child; come and make use of Me as you will. You may freely come to My storehouse, and the more often, the better. Welcome." Have you set God in the background, having no purpose in your life? Do not let your God be as other gods, serving only for show. Do not let your relationship with God be in name only. Since He allows you, and since you have such a Friend, use Him daily for caring, wise guidance.

Have Your Needs Met

"My God shall supply all your need according to his riches in glory by Christ Jesus" (Philippians 4:19). Never lack anything while you have God; never fear or faint while you have God. Go to your treasure chest, and take whatever you need. There you will find bread and clothing and health and life and all that you need. Beloved, learn the divine skill of making God all things; learn to make bread of your God, and water and health and friends and ease. He can supply you with all of these. Better still, He can be your food, your clothing, your friend, your life. All this He said to you in this promise: *"I am your God"* (Ezekiel 34:31).

Find Companionship

From here on, you may say, as a heaven-born saint once did, "I have no husband, and yet I am no widow, for my Maker is my husband (Isaiah 54:5). I have no father or friend, and yet I am neither fatherless (see Psalm 68:5) nor friendless; my God is both my Father and my Friend. I have no child, but He is better to me than ten children. (See 1 Samuel 1:8.) I have no house, but yet I have a home; I have made the Most High my habitation. (See Psalm 91:9.) I am alone, yet I am not by myself, for my Father has not left me alone (see John 8:29) and is good company for me. With Him I can walk; with Him I can take sweet counsel and sweet repose. When I go to bed, when I arise, while I am in my house, and as I conduct my daily business, my God is always with me. (See Matthew 28:20.) With Him I travel, I dwell, I lodge, I live, and I will live forever."

Be Comforted in Prayer

Oh, child of God, let me urge you to make use of your God. Make use of Him in prayer. I implore you to go to Him often, because He is your God. If He were another man's God, you might weary Him; but He is your God. If He were my God and not yours, you would have no right to approach Him. However, He is your God. He has "made Himself over" to you like a bank check, if I may use such an expression. He has become the incontestable property of all His children, so that all He has and all He is, is theirs. O child, will you let your treasury lie idle, when you need it? No, go and draw from it by prayer.

Run to Him in Times of Trouble

To Him in every trouble flee,
Thy best, thy only, Friend.

Run to Him. Tell Him all your needs at all times. I plead with you, if some dark cloud as a sun, for He is *"the Sun of righteousness"* has come against you, use your God for a shield, for He is a shield to protect you. (See Psalm 3:3.) If you have lost your way in the maze of life, use Him as your guide, for the great Jehovah will direct you. If you are in the midst of storms, use Him as your pilot, for He is the God who stills the raging of the sea and says unto the waves, *"Peace, be still"* (Mark 4:39). If you are a poor thing, not knowing which way to turn, use Him for your shepherd; remind yourself that *"the LORD is my shepherd; I shall not want"* (Psalm 23:1). Whatever you are, wherever you are, remember that God is just what you need, and He is just where you need Him to be.

I urge you to make use of your God for all your wants and needs. Do not forget Him in your trouble, but flee to Him in the midst of your distresses, crying,

When all created streams are dried,
   Your fullness is the same;
May I with this be satisfied,
   And glory in Thy name!

No good in creatures can be found,
   But may be found in Thee.
I must have all things, and abound,
   While God is God to me.

Take Delight in Your God

Beloved, let me persuade you to allow God to be your delight this day. If you have trials, or if you are free from them, I urge you, make God your delight. Be happy right now in the Lord. Remember, it is a commandment: *"Rejoice in the Lord alway: and again I say, Rejoice"* (Philippians 4:4). Do not be content to be moderately happy; seek to soar to the heights of bliss and to enjoy a heaven below. Get near to God, and you will get near to heaven. It is not as it is here on earth where the higher you go, the colder you find it, because on the mountain there is nothing to reflect the rays of the sun. Instead, with God, the nearer you go to Him, the brighter He will shine upon you, and the warmer you will be. When there are no other creatures to reflect His goodness, His light will be all the brighter. Go to God continually, persistently, confidently.

> *Delight thyself also in the* LORD; *and he shall give thee the desires of thine heart. Commit thy way unto the* LORD; *trust also in him; and he shall bring it to pass.*　　　　　　　　　　　　　　　　　(Psalm 37:4–5)

> *Thou shalt guide me with thy counsel, and afterward receive me to glory.*
> 　　　　　　　　　　　　　　　　　　　　　　　　　(Psalm 73:24)

"I will be their God" is the first blessing of the covenant; the second is equal to it. We will consider that in the next chapter.

3

CHRIST IN THE COVENANT

I will give thee for a covenant of the people.
—Isaiah 49:8

We all believe that our Savior has very much to do with the covenant of eternal salvation. We have learned to regard Him as the Mediator of the covenant, as the Surety of the covenant, and as the Substance of the covenant.

We consider Him to be the Mediator of the covenant, for we are certain that God could make no covenant with man unless there were a mediator, a middleman who could stand between them both. We hail Him as the Mediator, who, with mercy in His hands, came down to tell sinful man the good news that grace was promised in the eternal counsel of the Most High.

We also love our Savior as the Surety of the covenant. On our behalf, He undertook to pay our debts. On His Father's behalf, He also undertook to see that all of the souls of His elect would be secure and safe, and that every one of the Father's children would ultimately be presented unblemished and complete before Him.

Moreover, I do not doubt that we also rejoice in the thought that Christ is the Substance of the covenant. We believe that when we sum up all spiritual blessings, we must say, *"Christ is all, and in all"* (Colossians 3:11). He is the matter, He is the essence, of it. Although much might be said concerning the glories of the covenant, yet nothing could be said that is not to be found in that one word *Christ*.

However, at this time I will dwell on Christ, not as the Mediator, nor as the Surety, nor as the Substance of the covenant, but as the one great and glorious Bequest of the covenant that God has given to His children. It is our firm belief that Christ is ours and has been given to us by God. We know *"that [God] spared not his own Son, but delivered him up for us all,"* and we therefore believe that He will *"with him freely give us all things"* (Romans 8:32). We can say, with the spouse, *"My beloved is mine, and I am his"* (Song of Solomon 2:16). We feel that we have a personal share in our Lord and Savior Jesus Christ. It will therefore delight us, in the best manner possible, without the garnishment of eloquence or the trappings of flowery rhetoric, just to meditate upon this great thought: in the covenant Jesus Christ is the portion of every believer.

First, we will undertake to examine this bestowed inheritance. Secondly, we will notice the purpose for which it was conveyed to us. And then, we will explore one principle of relationship with Christ that may well be affixed to such a great blessing as this, and is indeed an inference from it.

The Believer's Great Inheritance

First, here is every Christian's great possession: Jesus Christ is the portion of each believer by the terms of the covenant. By this, we must understand Jesus Christ in many different senses.

We will begin, first of all, by declaring that Jesus Christ is ours in all His attributes. He has a double set of attributes, seeing that there are two natures joined in glorious union in one Person. He has the attributes of very God, and He has the attributes of perfect Man. Whatever these may be, they are each one of them the perpetual property of every believing child of God.

In All of His Attributes As God

I do not need to dwell on Christ's attributes as God. You already know how infinite His love is, how vast His grace, how firm His faithfulness, how unswerving His veracity! You know that He is omniscient, you know that He is omnipresent, and you know that He is omnipotent.

It would be a great consolation to you if you could realize that all these great and glorious attributes that belong to God are yours. Does He have power? His power is yours—yours to support and strengthen you, yours to overcome your enemies, yours to keep you firmly secure. Does He have love? There is not a particle of love in His great heart that is not yours; all His love belongs to you. You may dive into the immense, bottomless ocean of His love, and you may say of it all, "It is mine." Does He have justice? This may seem a stern attribute, but even that is yours; by His justice He will see to it that all that is covenanted to you by the oath and promise of God will be most certainly granted to you. Believer, mention whatever you please that is a characteristic of Christ as the ever glorious Son of God, and you may put your hand upon it and say, "It is mine."

Your arm, O Jesus, upon which the pillars of the earth do hang, is mine. Those eyes, O Jesus, which pierce through the thick darkness and behold the future—Your eyes are mine, to look on me with love. Those lips, O Christ, which sometimes speak words louder than ten thousand thunders or whisper syllables sweeter than the music of the harps of the glorified—those lips are mine. And that heart, which beats high with such unselfish, pure, and genuine love—that heart is mine. The whole of You, in all Your glorious nature as the Son of God, as God over all, blessed forever, is mine—positively, actually, without metaphor, in reality mine.

In All of His Attributes As Man

Consider Him as a man, too. All that He has as perfect Man is yours. As perfect Man, He stood before His Father, *"full of grace and truth"* (John 1:14), full of favor, and accepted by God as a perfect being. O believer, God's acceptance of Christ is your acceptance. Do you not know that the same love that the Father set on a perfect Christ, He now sets on you? All that Christ did is Yours. The perfect righteousness that Jesus lived out, when through His stainless life He kept the law and made it honorable, is yours. There is not a virtue Christ ever had that is not yours; there is not a holy deed He ever did that is not yours. There is not a prayer He ever sent to heaven that is not yours. There is not one solitary thought toward God, which it was His duty to think and which He thought as a man serving His God, that is not yours. All His righteousness, in its vast extent and in all the perfection of His character, is imputed to you.

Oh, believer, think of all that you have obtained in the word *Christ*. Come, consider that word *God*, and think how mighty it is. Then meditate upon the idea of the perfect man: all that Christ, as the man-God and the glorious God-man, ever had or ever can have, as the characteristic of either of His natures, is yours. It all belongs to you. It is given out of pure, free favor and is beyond the fear of revocation, passed on to you to be your actual property—and that forever.

In All of His Offices

Then, consider, believer, that not only is Christ yours in all His attributes, but He is yours in all His offices. Great and glorious these offices are; I scarcely have space to mention them all. Is He a prophet? Then He is your Prophet. Is He a priest? Then He is your Priest. Is He a king? Then He is your King. Is He a redeemer? Then He is your Redeemer. Is He an advocate? Then He is your Advocate. Is He a forerunner? Then He is your Forerunner. Is He a surety of the covenant? Then He is your Surety. In every name He bears, in every crown He wears, in every vestment in which He is arrayed, Christ is the believer's own.

Child of God, if you had grace to gather up this thought into your soul, it would comfort you marvelously to think that in all Christ is in His offices, He is most assuredly yours. Do you see Him there, interceding before His Father, with outstretched arms? Do you see His ephod and His golden crown on His brow, inscribed with "HOLINESS TO THE LORD" (Exodus 39:30)? Do you see Him as He lifts up His hands to pray? Do you hear His marvelous intercession such as man never prayed on earth, that authoritative intercession such as He Himself could not use in the agonies of the Garden of Gethsemane?

> With sighs and groans, He offered up
>   His humble suit below.
> But with authority He pleads,
>   Enthroned in glory now.

Do you see how He asks and how He receives, as soon as His petition is lifted up? Can you, dare you, believe that His intercession is all your own, that on His heart your name is engraved, that in His heart your name is stamped in marks of indelible grace, that all the majesty of His surpassing intercession is yours, and that it would all be expended for you if you needed it? Can you comprehend that He has no authority with His Father that He will not use on your behalf, if you require it, and that He has no power to intercede that He would not employ for you in all times of necessity? Come now, words cannot set this forth—it is only your meditations that can teach you this. It is only God the Holy Spirit bringing home the truth that can set this rapturous, transporting thought in its proper position in your heart: that Christ is yours in all He is and has.

Do you see Him on earth? There He stands, the Great High Priest, offering His bloody sacrifice. See Him on the tree: His hands are pierced, His blood gushes forth from His wounds. Oh! Do you see that pale countenance and those languid eyes filled with compassion? Do you observe that crown of thorns? Do you behold that mightiest of sacrifices, the sum and substance of them all? Believer, all that is yours: those precious drops plead and claim your peace with God; that open side is your refuge; those pierced hands are your redemption; that groan, He groans for you; that cry of a forsaken heart, He utters for you; that death, He died for you.

Come, I urge you to consider Christ in any one of His various offices. However, when you do consider Him, lay hold of this thought: in all these things He is your Christ, given unto you in the eternal covenant as your possession forever.

In All of His Works

Notice next that Christ is the believer's in every one of His works. Whether they are works of suffering or of duty, they are the property of the believer. As an infant, He was circumcised, and is that bloody rite ours? Yes, *"in whom also [we] are circumcised with the circumcision made without hands, in putting off the body of the sins of the flesh by the circumcision of Christ"* (Colossians 2:11). As an adult, He was baptized, and is that spiritual sign of watery baptism ours? Yes, we are *"buried with him by baptism into death"* (Romans 6:4). We share Jesus' baptism when we lie interred with our Best Friend in the same watery tomb. See, there He dies, but is His death ours? Yes, we are *"dead with Christ"* (verse 8). He is buried, and is that burial ours? Yes, we are buried with Christ. He rises. See Him startling the guards and rising from the tomb! And is that resurrection ours? Yes, we *"are risen with him through the faith of the operation of God, who hath raised him from the dead"* (Colossians 2:12).

Notice this also: *"When he ascended up on high, he led captivity captive"* (Ephesians 4:8). Is that ascension ours as believers? Yes, for He has *"raised us up together*" (Ephesians 2:6). And see, He sits on His Father's throne; is that place ours? Yes, He has made us to "*sit together in heavenly places*" (verse 6).

All Christ did is ours. By divine decree, there exists such a union between Christ and His people that all Christ did, His people did. All Christ has performed, His people performed in Him, for they were in His loins when He lay in the tomb, and in His loins they have "*ascended up on high*" (verse 8). With Him they entered into bliss, and with Him they sit in heavenly places. Represented by Him, their Head, all His people even now are glorified in Him—even in Him who is "*the head over all things to the church*" (Ephesians 1:22). Remember, believer, that you have a covenant interest in all the deeds of Christ, either in His humiliation or His exaltation, and that all those acts are yours.

In All the Fullness of the Godhead

I would for one moment hint at a sweet thought, which is this: you know that in the person of Christ "*dwelleth all the fulness of the Godhead bodily*" (Colossians 2:9). Now, remember that the Scripture says, "*And of his fulness have all we received, and grace for grace*" (John 1:16).

All the fullness of Christ! Do you know what that is? Do you understand that phrase? I assert that you do not comprehend it, and will not just yet. All the fullness of Christ—the abundance of which you may infer from the depth of your own emptiness—all that fullness is yours to supply your multiplied necessities. All the fullness of Christ is yours—to restrain you, keep you, and preserve you. All that fullness of power and love and purity, which is stored up in the Lord Jesus Christ, is yours. Do treasure that thought, for then your emptiness will never be a cause of fear. How can you be lost while you have all that fullness to go to?

In His Very Life

Now I come to something even sweeter: the very life of Christ is the property of the believer. This is a thought into which I cannot dive, and I feel I have outdone myself in only mentioning it. The life of Christ is the property of every believer. Can you conceive what Christ's life is? "Of course," you say, "He poured it out upon the cross." He did, and it was His life that He then gave to you. However, He took that life up again; even the life of His body was restored.

Yet, the life of His great and glorious divinity had never undergone any change, even at the time of His death. Now, you know He is immortal, for "*only*

[He] *hath immortality"* (1 Timothy 6:16). Can you conceive what kind of life it is that the second person of the Trinity possesses? Can He ever die? No, far sooner may the harps of heaven be stopped and the chorus of the redeemed cease forever, far sooner may the glorious walls of paradise be shaken and its foundations be removed, than that God the Son should ever die. As immortal as His Father, Christ now sits at the Father's right hand (see Colossians 3:1), the Eternal One.

Christian, that life of Christ is yours. Hear what Jesus said: *"Because I live, ye shall live also"* (John 14:19). *"Ye are dead, and your life is hid with Christ in God"* (Colossians 3:3). The same blow that would strike us dead, spiritually, would have to slay Christ at the same time. The same sword that would take away the spiritual life of a regenerate man would also have to take away the life of the Redeemer. Our lives and His life are intricately linked together—they are not two lives, but one. We are but the rays of the great Sun of Righteousness, our Redeemer—sparks that must return to the great orb again. If we are indeed the true heirs of heaven, we cannot die until He from whom we take our life dies also. We are the stream that cannot stop until the fountain dries up; we are the rays that cannot cease until the sun ceases to shine. We are the branches, and we cannot wither until the trunk itself dies. *"Because I live, ye shall live also."* The very life of Christ is the possession of every one of His own.

In His Person

Best of all, the person of Jesus Christ is the property of the Christian. I am persuaded, beloved, that we think a great deal more of God's gifts than we do of God, and we preach a great deal more about the Holy Spirit's influence than we do about the Holy Spirit. I am also certain that we talk a great deal more about the offices and works and attributes of Christ than we do about the person of Christ.

The reason that few of us can understand the metaphors that are used in Solomon's Song concerning the person of Christ is because we have seldom sought to see Him or desired to know Him. But, believer, you have sometimes been able to behold your Lord. Have you not seen Him, who *"is white and ruddy, the chiefest among ten thousand, [and] altogether lovely"* (Song of Solomon 5:10, 16)? Have you not been lost in pleasure sometimes when you have seen His head, which is *"as the most fine gold"* (verse 11)? Have you not beheld Him in His dual character: the white and the red; the lily and the rose (see Song of Solomon 2:1); the God and yet the man; the dying and yet the living; the perfect One and yet the One who bears *"about in [His] body the dying"* (2 Corinthians 4:10)? Have you ever beheld the Lord with the nail prints in His hands and the scar still on His side? And have you ever longed to behold His loving smile or to hear His sweet voice? (See Song of Solomon 2:14.) Have you ever had love visits from Him? Has He ever put His banner of love over you? (See verse 4.) Have you ever gone with Him into the fields and the villages (see Song of Solomon 7:11) and the garden of nuts? (See Song of Solomon 6:11.) Have you ever *"sat down under his shadow with great delight"*? Have you ever found that *"his fruit was sweet to [your] taste"* (Song of Solomon 2:3)? Yes, you have. His person, then, is yours.

A wife loves her husband. She loves his house and his property. She loves him for all that he gives her, all the bounty he confers, and all the love he bestows. But, his person is the object of her affections. So it is with the believer: he blesses Christ for all He does and all He is, but it is Christ that is everything to him. The believer does not care as much about Christ's offices as he does about Christ Himself.

Imagine a child on his father's knee. The father is a professor at the university, a learned man with many titles. Perhaps the child knows that these are honorable titles and esteems him for them; but the chid does not care as much about the professor and his dignity as he does about the person of his father. It is not the collegiate square cap or the gown that the child loves. Further, if the child is loving, the meals the father provides or the house in which the child lives will not be as important to the child as is the father whom the child loves. It is the father's dear person that has become the object of true and hearty affection for the child.

Likewise, I am sure it is so with you, if you know your Savior. You love His mercies, you love His offices, you love His deeds, but you love His person best. Take a moment to reflect, then, that the person of Christ is conveyed to you in the covenant: *"I will give thee for a covenant of the people."*

The Purposes of Christ in the Covenant

Now, let us turn our attention to the second point of consideration: For what purposes did God put Christ in the covenant?

To Provide Comfort for Repentant Sinners

In the first place, Christ is in the covenant in order to comfort every repentant sinner. "Oh," says the sinner who is coming to God, "I cannot lay hold of such a great covenant as that. I cannot believe that heaven is provided for me. I cannot conceive that that robe of righteousness and all these wondrous things can be intended for such a wretch as I am." Comfort comes in the thought that Christ is in the covenant. Sinner, are you able to lay hold of Christ and His cross? You are if you can say,

> Nothing in my hand I bring,
> Simply to Your cross I cling.

If you have laid hold of Christ, then He was put into the covenant on purpose so that you would be able to hold on fast to Him. God's covenant mercies all go together, and if you have laid hold of Christ, you have gained every blessing in the covenant. That is one reason why Christ was put there.

Why, if Christ were not there, the poor sinner would say, "I dare not seize upon that mercy. It is a godly and a divine one, but I dare not fasten my hope on it, because it is too good for me. I cannot receive it; it staggers my faith." However, the man sees Christ with all the great atonement in the covenant. Christ looks so lovingly at Him and opens His arms so wide, saying so kindly, *"Come unto me, all ye that labour and are heavy laden, and I will give you rest"* (Matthew 11:28), that the sinner comes and wraps his arms around Christ in response. Then Christ whispers, "Sinner, in laying hold of Me, you have laid hold of all." The sinner cries, "Lord, I dare not think I could have any other mercies. I dare to trust You, but I dare not take the others." And Christ replies, "Oh, sinner, in that you have taken hold of Me, you have taken all the other mercies, too."

The mercies of the covenant are linked together as in a chain. The one link of Christ is an enticing one. The sinner can lay hold of Him, and God has purposely put Him there to entice the sinner to come and receive the mercies of the covenant. For when the sinner has once grasped hold of Christ—and here is the comfort—he has everything that the covenant can give.

To Reassure the Doubting Saint

Christ was also put in the covenant to confirm the doubting saint. Sometimes the wavering one cannot comprehend his share in the covenant. He cannot imagine that his allotment is with those who are sanctified. He is afraid that God is not his God and that the Spirit has no dealings with his soul. But then,

> Amid temptations, sharp and strong,
> His soul to that dear refuge flies;
> Hope is his anchor, firm and strong,
> When tempests blow and billows rise.

And so, that poor, uncertain child lays hold of Christ. Were it not for that, even the believer would not dare to come at all. He could not lay hold of any other mercy than that with which Christ is connected. "Oh," he says, "I know I am a sinner, and Christ came to save sinners." Therefore, he holds fast to Christ. "I can hold fast here," he says; "My black hands will not blacken Christ; my filthiness will not make Him unclean." So the saint holds on tightly to Christ, as tightly as if his grip were the death-clutch of a drowning man. And what then? Why, he has got every mercy of the covenant in his hand.

God, in His wisdom, has put Christ in the covenant of grace. Thus, any poor sinner or any doubting saint, who might be afraid to lay hold of any other, but who knows the gracious nature of Christ, is not afraid to lay hold of Him. Thus, even though he might be totally unaware of it, he grasps the whole of the covenant to himself.

To Give Substance to Many Blessings

Further, it was necessary that Christ should be in the covenant, because there are many things there that would be nothing without Him. Our great redemption is in the covenant, but we have no redemption except through His blood. It is true that my righteousness is in the covenant, but I can have no righteousness apart from that which Christ has won for me, and which is imputed to me by God. It is very true that my eternal perfection is in the covenant, but the elect are only perfect in Christ. They are not perfect in themselves, nor will they ever be, until they have been washed and sanctified and perfected by the Holy Spirit. Even in heaven, the perfection of the saints in glory does not consist so much in their sanctification as it does in their justification in Christ.

> Their beauty this, their glorious dress,
> Jesus the Lord their righteousness.

In fact, if you were to take Christ out of the covenant, you would do the same as if you would break the string of a necklace: all the jewels or beads or pearls would drop off and scatter all over, separating from each other. Christ is the golden string on which the mercies of the covenant are threaded, and when you lay hold of Him, you have obtained the whole string of pearls. However, if Christ were to be taken away, it is true that the pearls would still be there, but we would not be able to wear them or grasp them. They would be separated, and poor faith would never know how to get hold of them. Oh, this is a mercy that is worth worlds: Christ is in the covenant!

To Be Used by the Saints

Notice once more—just as I wrote concerning God in the covenant—Christ is in the covenant to be used. God never gives His children a promise that He does not intend for them to use. There are some promises in the Bible that I have never yet availed myself of. However, I am sure that there will come times of trial and trouble when I will find that a long-neglected promise, which I thought was never meant for me, will be the only one on which I can rest. I also know that the time is coming when every believer will know the worth of every promise in the covenant. God has not given His children any part of the inheritance that He did not intend for them to make use of. Christ has been given to us to use. Believer, use Him!

I tell you again, as I told you before, that you do not use your Christ as you ought to do. When you are in trouble, why do you not go and tell Him? Has He not a sympathizing heart, and can He not comfort you and alleviate your pain? No, you are gadding about to all your friends except to your Best Friend, and telling your tale everywhere except into the heart of your Lord. Oh, use Him, use Him.

Are you black with yesterday's sins? Here is a fountain filled with blood; use it, saint, use it. Has your guilt returned again? Well, His power has been proved again and again; come, use Him! Use Him! Do you feel naked? Come near, soul, and take *"the robe of righteousness"* (Isaiah 61:10). Do not stand there staring at it; put it on. Strip your own righteousness off, and your own fears, too. Put this on instead. Wear it, for it was meant to be worn.

Do you feel sick? Will you not go and pull the night-bell of prayer to wake up the Great Physician? I urge you to go and appeal to Him, and He will give the medicine that will revive you. What? Are you sick, with the Great Physician next door to you, *"a very present help in [time of] trouble"* (Psalm 46:1), and will you not go to Him?

Oh, dearly beloved, remember that you may be poor, but then you have *"a kinsman [Redeemer], a mighty man of wealth"* (Ruth 2:1). What! Will you not go to Him and ask Him to give you of His abundance, when He has given you this promise: that as long as He has anything, you will share with Him, for all He is and all He has is yours?

Oh, believer, do use Christ, I urge you. There is nothing Christ dislikes more than for His people to make a showpiece of Him and not to use Him. He loves to be worked. He is a great laborer; He always was for His Father, and now He loves to be a great laborer for His sheep.

The more burdens you put on His shoulders, the better He will love you. *"Cast all your care upon him; for he careth for you"* (1 Peter 5:7). You will never know the sympathy of Christ's heart and the love of His soul so well as when you have heaved a mountain of trouble from yourself to His shoulders and have found that He does not stagger under the weight. Are your troubles like huge mountains weighing upon your spirit? Command them to rumble like an avalanche upon the shoulders of the Almighty Christ. He can bear all of your troubles away and cast them *"into the depths of the sea"* (Micah 7:19), just as He does with your sins.

Do cry out to your Lord and Master, and use Him. For this very purpose Christ was put into the covenant, that you might use Him whenever you need Him.

A Principle of Reciprocal Relationship

Finally, here is a principle that can be inferred from what we have learned, and what is that precept? Since Christ is yours, then you are Christ's, beloved. You are Christ's, you know very well. You are His by your Father's gift when He gave you to the Son. You are His by His bloody purchase, when He paid the price for your redemption. You are His by dedication, for you have dedicated yourself to Him. You are His by adoption, for you were brought to Him and made one of His siblings and a joint-heir with Him.

Therefore, dear friend, I urge you to endeavor to show the world that you are His in practice. When tempted to sin, reply, "I cannot do this great wickedness. I cannot, for I am one of Christ's." When wealth is before you to be won by sin, touch it not. Say that you are Christ's; otherwise, you would take it, but now you cannot. Tell Satan that you would not gain the world if you had to love Christ less.

Are you exposed to difficulties and dangers in the world? Stand fast in the evil day (see Ephesians 6:13), remembering that you are one of Christ's. Are you working in a job where much is to be done, but others are sitting around idly and lazily, doing nothing? Go to your work, and when the sweat stands upon your brow and you are tempted to stop, say, "No, I cannot; I am one of Christ's. He had a baptism to be baptized with, and so have I, and I am distressed until it is accomplished. (See Luke 12:50.) I am one of Christ's. If I were not one of His and purchased by blood, I might be like Issachar, crouching '*between two burdens*' (Genesis 49:14); but I am one of Christ's." When the siren song of pleasure would tempt you from the path of righteousness, reply, "Hush your strains, O temptress. I am one of Christ's. Your music cannot affect me; I am not my own, for I am bought with a price."

When the cause of God needs you, give yourself to it, for you are Christ's. When the poor need you, give yourself away, for you are one of Christ's. When at any time there is something to be done for His church and for His cross, do it, remembering that you are one of Christ's. I urge you, never repudiate your profession of faith. Do not go where others could say of you, "He cannot be Christ's." Rather, always be one of those whose dialect is Christian, whose every idiom is Christlike, whose conduct and conversation are so scented with heaven that all who see you will know that you are the Savior's and will recognize in you His features and His lovely countenance.

Now, dearly beloved, I must direct a word to those of you who have not laid hold of the covenant. I sometimes hear it whispered, and sometimes I read it, that there are men who are trusting in the "uncovenanted" mercies of God. Let me solemnly assure you that there is now no such thing in heaven as uncovenanted mercy; there is no such thing beneath God's sky or above it, as uncovenanted grace toward men. All you can receive, and all you ever can hope for, must be through the covenant of free grace, and that alone.

Perhaps, poor convicted sinner, you do not dare to take hold of the covenant today. You cannot say the covenant is yours. You are afraid it never can be yours, because you are such an unworthy wretch. Listen, can you lay hold of Christ? Do you dare to do that? "Oh," you say, "I am too unworthy." No, that is not true. Soul, do you dare to touch the hem of His garment today? Do you dare to come near enough to Him just to be able to touch the very bottom of His robe that is trailing on the ground? "No," you say, "I dare not." Why not, poor soul, why not? Can you not trust Christ?

Are not His mercies rich and free?
Then say, poor soul, why not for thee?

"I dare not come; I am so unworthy," you say. Hear to this, for my Master invites you to come: "*Come unto me, all ye that labour and are heavy laden, and I will give you rest*" (Matthew 11:28). Are you still afraid after that? "*This is a faithful saying, and worthy of all acceptation, that Christ Jesus came into the world to save sinners*" (1 Timothy 1:15).

Why, then, do you not come to Christ? Oh, are you afraid He will turn you away? Listen, then, to what He said: "[Whoever] *cometh to me I will in no wise cast out*" (John 6:37). You say, "But I know He would cast me out." Come, then, and see if you can prove Him a liar. I know you cannot, but come and try. Christ has said that He will not reject anyone who comes to Him. "But I am the blackest." Nevertheless, He has said "*him that cometh*" (verse 37), and that includes you, as long as you come to Him, no matter what condition you are in. Come along, blackest of the black. "Oh, but I am so filthy!" Come along, filthy one, come and try Him. Come and prove Him; remember that He has said He will cast out none that come to Him by faith.

Come and try Him. I am not asking you to lay hold of the whole covenant right now—you will do that soon enough—but just to lay hold of Christ. If you will do that, then you will have the covenant. "Oh, I cannot lay hold of Him," says one poor soul. Well then, lie prostrate at His feet and beg Him to lay hold of you. Groan one groan, and say, "*God be merciful to me a sinner*" (Luke 18:13). Sigh one sigh, and say, "*Lord, save me, or I will perish*" (Matthew 8:25). Let your heart say it, even if your lips cannot. If grief, long smothered, burns like a flame within your bones, at least let one spark out.

Now pray one prayer, and—I am telling you the truth—that one sincere prayer will most assuredly prove that He will save you. One true groan, when God has put it in your heart, is a deposit of His love. One true wish for Christ, if it is followed by a sincere and earnest seeking of Him, will be accepted by God, and you will be saved.

Come, soul, lay hold of Christ. "Oh, but I dare not!" Now, I was about to express a foolish thing: I was going to write that I wish I were a sinner like you now, because I would run before you, lay hold of Christ, and then say to you, "Take hold of Him, too." However, I am a sinner like yourself, and no better than yourself. I have no merits, no righteousness, no works. I will be damned in hell unless Christ has mercy on me, and I should have been there now if I had been given what was rightfully due me.

Here am I, a sinner once as black as you are. Yet, I can say, "O Christ, these arms embrace You." Sinner, come and take your turn after me. Have I not embraced Him? Am I not as vile as you are? Come, and let my case assure you. How did He treat me when I first laid hold of Him? Why, He said to me, *"I have loved thee with an everlasting love: therefore with lovingkindness have I drawn thee"* (Jeremiah 31:3). Come, sinner, come and try. If Christ did not drive me away, He will never spurn you. Come along, poor soul, come along.

> Venture on Him ('tis no venture),
> Venture wholly,
> Let no other trust intrude;
> None but Jesus
> Can do helpless sinners good.

He can do for you all the good you need. Oh, trust my Master, trust my Master. He is a precious Lord Jesus, He is a sweet Lord Jesus, He is a loving Savior, and He is a kind and condescending forgiver of sin. Come, you black; come, you filthy; come, you poor; come, you dying; come, you lost—you who have been taught to feel your need of Christ—come, all of you. Come now because Jesus invites you to come! Come quickly! Lord Jesus, draw them, draw them by Your Spirit!

4

THE HOLY SPIRIT IN
THE COVENANT

And I will put my spirit within you.
—Ezekiel 36:27

The Holy Spirit is the third person of the Trinity and in the covenant. We have already considered "God in the Covenant" and "Christ in the Covenant." At this time, we will consider God the Holy Spirit's involvement in the covenant. Remember, it was necessary that the Triune God should work out the salvation of the elect, if they were to be saved at all. It was also absolutely requisite that, when the covenant was made, all that was necessary should be put into it. This included, among the rest, the Holy Spirit, without whom all things done even by the Father and by Jesus Christ would have been ineffectual. The Spirit is as much a part of the covenant as the Savior of men or the Father of spirits.

Today, when the Holy Spirit is too much forgotten, and when only a little honor is accorded to His sacred person, I know that there is a deep responsibility upon me to endeavor to magnify His great and holy name. I almost tremble, right now, in entering on so profound a subject, for which I feel myself so insufficient. But, nevertheless, relying on the aid, the guidance, and the witness of the Holy Spirit Himself, I will venture to explain our text: "*I will put my spirit within you.*"

In the covenant of grace, the Holy Spirit is given to all the children of God and is received by each, in due course. Yet, upon our Lord Jesus Christ did the Holy Spirit first descend, resting upon Christ (see Matthew 3:16) as our covenant Head, "*like the precious ointment upon the head, that ran down upon the beard, even Aaron's beard: that went down to the skirts of his garments*" (Psalm 133:2). The Father gave the Holy Spirit without measure to His Son. (See John 3:34.)

From Jesus, in a measured amount, although still in abundance, all the "*brethren* [who] *dwell together in unity*" (Psalm 133:1), or union with Him, partake of the Holy Spirit. This holy anointing of the Spirit flows down from Christ, the Anointed One, to every part of His body, to every individual member of His church. The Father's declaration concerning Christ was this: "*Behold my servant, whom I have chosen; my beloved, in whom* [I am] *well pleased: I will put my spirit upon him*" (Matthew 12:18). And Christ said,

> *The Spirit of the Lord is upon me, because he hath anointed me to preach the gospel to the poor; he hath sent me to heal the brokenhearted, to preach deliverance to the captives, and recovering of sight to the blind, to set at liberty them that are bruised, to preach the acceptable year of the Lord.*
>
> (Luke 4:18–19)

Thus, the Holy Spirit was first poured out upon our covenant Head, Jesus Christ. From Him, then, the Spirit descends to all those who are in union with Christ. Let us bless the name of Jesus if we are united with Him, and let us look up to our covenant Head, expecting that from Him will flow down the heavenly ointment that will consecrate our souls—the anointing of the Spirit.

Our text is one of the unconditional promises of Scripture. There are many conditional promises in the Word of God given to certain biblical characters, although even those promises are in some sense unconditional, since the very condition of the promise is by some other promise secured as a gift. However, this one has no conditions whatever. It does not say, "I will put My Spirit within you if you ask for Him or if you seek Him with all your heart." Rather, it says plainly, without any reservations or stipulations, "*I will put my spirit within you.*"

The reason is obvious. Until the Spirit is put within us, we cannot feel our need of the Spirit, and neither can we ask for or seek Him.

Therefore, it is necessary that there should be an absolutely unconditional promise, made to all the chosen of God, that they should have given to them the waiting grace, the desiring grace, the seeking grace, the receiving grace, the believing grace, that will make them pant and hunger and thirst after Jesus. To everyone who is *"chosen of God, and precious"* (1 Peter 2:4), to every redeemed soul, however much he is now condemningly sunk in sin, however much he is now lost and ruined by the Fall, however much he may hate God and despise his Redeemer at the present moment, this promise still holds true: *"I will put my spirit within you."* In due course, all of the redeemed will be instilled with the Holy Spirit, who will quicken their spirits from spiritual death, lead them to seek pardon, induce them to trust in Jesus Christ, and adopt them into the living family of God.

The promise also concerns an internal blessing that will be bestowed: *"I will put my spirit within you."* Remember, we have the Spirit of God in His written Word. We also find the Spirit in the ordinances of baptism and the Lord's Supper, which are administered by every faithful minister of the gospel. God is perpetually giving the Spirit to us by these means. However, it is in vain for us to hear of the Spirit, to talk of Him, or to believe in Him, unless we have a realization of His power within us. Here, therefore, is the promise of such an internal blessing: *"I will put my spirit within you."*

We will now consider this promise in all of its comprehensiveness. May the Holy Spirit Himself assist us in doing this! We will take the various works of the Holy Spirit, one by one, and we will remember that, in all the works that He performs, the Holy Spirit is put in the covenant to be possessed by every believer.

The Holy Spirit As Our Quickener

In the first place, Christ told us, *"It is the spirit that quickeneth"* (John 6:63). Until the Holy Spirit is pleased to breathe upon a soul, that person is dead to any spiritual life. It is not until the Holy Spirit, like some heavenly wind, breathes upon the dry bones and puts life into them (see Ezekiel 37:6) that they can ever live. You may take a corpse and dress it in all the garments of external decency. You may wash it with the water of morality. You may adorn the corpse with the crown of glory and put upon its brow a tiara of beauty. You may paint its cheeks until you make it appear lifelike. But, remember, unless its spirit is alive, corruption will seize the body before too long.

Therefore, beloved, it is the Holy Spirit who is the Quickener. You would have been as *"dead in trespasses and sins"* (Ephesians 2:1) now as you ever were, if it had not been for the Holy Spirit who made you alive. You were not simply lying, *"cast out in the open field"* (Ezekiel 16:5), but, worse than that, you were the very prey of mortality. Corruption was your father; the worm was your mother and your sister. (See Job 17:14.) You were noxious in the nostrils of the Almighty.

It was as the Savior beheld you in that deplorable state, in all your loathsomeness, that He said to you, *"Live"* (Ezekiel 16:6). In that moment, you were *"begotten again unto a lively hope by the resurrection of Jesus Christ from the dead"* (1 Peter 1:3). Life entered into you at His command. Then it was that the Holy Spirit quickened your spirit. As Jesus told His disciples, *"The words that I speak unto you, they are spirit, and they are life"* (John 6:63). You were made alive entirely through the might and power of the quickening Spirit.

> The Spirit, like some heavenly wind,
>   Blows on the sons of flesh;
> Creates a new—a heavenly mind,
>   And forms the man afresh.

If, then, you feel at any time death working in you, as doubtless you will, withering the bloom of your piety, chilling the fervor of your devotions, and quenching the ardor of your faith, remember that He who first quickened you must keep you alive. The Holy Spirit's quickening power is the sap that flowed flowed into your poor, dry branch, when you were grafted into Christ. (See Romans 11:16–17.) Just as, by that sap, you were first made green with life, so it is by that sap alone you can ever bring forth fruit unto God. By the Spirit you drew your first breath when you cried out for mercy, and from the same Spirit you must draw the breath to praise that mercy in hymns and anthems of joy.

"Having begun in the Spirit" (Galatians 3:3), you must be made perfect in the Spirit, for perfection cannot come from the flesh. *"The flesh profiteth nothing"* (John 6:63); the works of the law will not help you; your own heart's thoughts and devices are of no avail. You would be cut off from Christ; you would be more depraved than you were before your conversion; you would be more corrupt than

you were prior to your being regenerated—*"twice dead, plucked up by the roots"* (Jude 1:12)—if God the Holy Spirit were to withdraw from you. You must live in His life, trust in His power to sustain you, and seek of Him fresh supplies when the tide of your spiritual life is running low.

The Holy Spirit As Our Helper

We need the Holy Spirit as our able Helper in all the duties we have to perform. We all need *"to be strengthened with might by his Spirit"* (Ephesians 3:16) to do the *"good works, which God hath before ordained that we should walk in them"* (Ephesians 2:10). *"I will pray the Father, and he shall give you another* [Paraclete or Helper], *that he may abide with you for ever; even the Spirit of truth; he dwelleth with you, and shall be in you"* (John 14:16–17). *"Likewise the Spirit also helpeth our infirmities"* (Romans 8:26).

An Aide in Prayer

The most common Christian duty is that of prayer, and the most insignificant child of God must be a praying child. Remember that the passage in Romans continues this way:

> *Likewise the Spirit also helpeth our infirmities: for we know not what we should pray for as we ought: but the Spirit itself maketh intercession for us with groanings which cannot be uttered. And he that searcheth the hearts knoweth what is the mind of the Spirit, because he maketh intercession for the saints according to the will of God.*   (Romans 8:26–27)

The Spirit of God is in the covenant as the great Aide to us in all our petitions to the throne of grace. Child of God, you do not know what to pray for; depend on the inspiration of the Holy Spirit, who will teach you how to pray. Sometimes you do not know how to express what you desire; rely upon the Spirit, then, as the One who can touch your lips with the *"live coal from off the altar"* (Isaiah 6:6), because then you will be able to pour out your fervent wishes before the throne. Sometimes, even when you have life and power within you, you cannot express your inward emotions; then rely upon that Spirit to interpret your feelings, for He *"maketh intercession for us with groanings which cannot be uttered."* When, like Jacob, you are wrestling with the angel and are nearly thrown down, ask the Holy Spirit to strengthen your arms.

The Holy Spirit is the chariot wheel of prayer. Prayer may be the chariot, and desire may pull it forward, but the Spirit is the wheel by which it moves. He propels the desire and causes the chariot to roll swiftly on, carrying to heaven the supplication of the saints, when the desire of the heart is *"according to the will of God."*

An Aide in Preaching

Another duty to which some of the children of God are called is that of preaching. Here also we must have the Holy Spirit to enable us. Those whom God calls to preach the gospel are assisted with might from on high. He has said, *"Lo, I am with you alway, even unto the end of the world"* (Matthew 28:20). It is a solemn thing to enter into the work of the ministry.

I will just make an observation here, for there are young men who are striving to enter into the ministry before they scarcely know the alphabet of the gospel. They set themselves up as preachers of God's Word, when the first thing they ought to do is to join the kindergarten class in a school and learn to read properly.

I know there are some to whom God has given the desire thus to seek the glory of His name and the welfare of souls, and they humbly wait until He has opened the way. May God bless them and speed them in answering His call. But—would you believe it?—I know a young man who was baptized and received into the church one Sunday, and who went off to a seminary the next day to ask if they would accept him! I asked him whether he had ever preached before or addressed a half-dozen Sunday school students. He said that he had not. But what surprised me most was that he said he was called to the work before he was converted! I truly believe this was a call from the Enemy—not a call from God in the slightest sense.

Be careful that you do not touch God's ark of the covenant with unholy fingers. You may preach if you can, but take care that you do not set yourself up in the ministry without having a solemn conviction that the Spirit from on high has set you apart for that vocation. If you do, *"in thy skirts [will be] found the blood of the souls of the poor innocents"* (Jeremiah 2:34). Too many have rushed into the Holy Place without being called by God; and if they could have rushed out of it on their deathbeds, they would have had eternal cause for gratitude. However, they ran presumptuously, then preached unsent, and therefore unblessed. When dying, they felt a greater condemnation from the fact that they had taken on themselves an office to which God had never appointed them. Beware of doing that.

But, if God has called you, however little talent you may have, do not fear anyone's frown or rebuke. If you have a solemn conviction in your soul that God has really ordained you to the work of the ministry, and if you have obtained a seal to your commission in the conversion of even one soul, do not let death or hell stop you. Go straight on, and never think you must have certain endowments to become a successful preacher.

The only endowment necessary for success in the ministry is the endowment of the Holy Spirit. As I was addressing a number of ministers recently, I told the brothers there, when one of them asked how it was that God had been pleased to bless me so much in my ministry, "There is not one of you whom God could not bless ten times as much, if you had ten times as much of the Spirit." It is not any ability of the preacher nor any human qualification that brings the blessing; it is simply the influence of God's Spirit that is necessary.

I have been delighted to find myself labeled as ignorant, unlearned, and devoid of eloquence, all of which I knew long before those titles were given to me. But so much the better, for then all the glory belongs to God. Let men say what they please, I will always confess to the truth of it: I am a fool. *"I am become a fool in glorying"* (2 Corinthians 12:11), if you please. I will take any contemptible title that worldlings like to put upon me. However, they cannot deny the fact that God blesses my ministry, that prostitutes have been saved, that drunkards have been reclaimed, that some of the most forsaken characters have been changed, and that God has produced such a work in their midst as my critics have never seen before in their lives. Therefore, give all the glory to His holy name. Cast as much reproach as you like on me, you worldlings; it only brings more honor to God, who works as He pleases and with whatever instrument He chooses, irrespective of man's opinions.

An Aide in Every Endeavor

Again, dearly beloved, whatever your vocation is, whatever God has ordained you to do in this world, you are equally certain to have the assistance of the Holy Spirit in it. If it is the teaching of a nursery class in the Sunday school, do not think that the Holy Spirit will not help you. His support will be granted as freely to you as to the person who addresses a large assembly. Are you sitting down by the side of some poor, dying woman? Believe that the Holy Spirit will come to you there, as much as if you were administering the sacred elements of the Lord's Supper. Seek strength from God as much for the humblest work as for the loftiest. Spiritual plowman, sharpen your plowshare with the Spirit! Spiritual sower, dip your seed in the Spirit, so it will germinate, and ask the Spirit to give you grace to scatter it so that it may fall *"into good ground"* (Matthew 13:8)! Spiritual warrior, sharpen your sword with the Spirit, and ask Him, whose Word is a two-edged sword (see Hebrews 4:12), to strengthen your arm to wield it!

The Holy Spirit As Our Revealer

The next point we will discuss is that the Holy Spirit is given to the children of God as *"the spirit of wisdom and revelation in the knowledge of* [God]*"* (Ephesians 1:17). The Spirit brings us *"out of darkness into his marvellous light"* (1 Peter 2:9). By nature, we are ignorant, extremely so, but the Holy Spirit teaches the family of God and makes them wise. *"Ye have an unction from the Holy One, and ye know all things"* (1 John 2:20).

Student in the school of Christ, do you want to be wise? Then, do not ask the theologian to expound to you his system of divinity. Instead, sitting down meekly at the feet of Jesus, ask that His Spirit may instruct you. For I tell you, student, that although you might read the Bible for many years and turn over its pages continually, you will not learn anything of its hidden mysteries without the revelation of the Holy Spirit. Yet, in a solitary moment of your study, when suddenly enlightened by the Spirit, you may learn a truth as swiftly as you see the lightning flash.

Young person, are you striving to understand the doctrine of election? It is the Holy Spirit alone who can reveal it to your heart and make you comprehend it. Are you struggling to grasp the doctrine of human depravity? The Holy Spirit must reveal to you the depth of the wickedness of the human heart. Do you really desire to know the secret of the life of the believer, as he lives *"by the faith of the Son of God"* (Galatians 2:20), and the mysterious fellowship with the Lord that he enjoys? It will always be a mystery to you unless the Holy Spirit unfolds it to your heart.

Whenever you read the Bible, cry to the Spirit, *"Open thou mine eyes, that I may behold wondrous things out of thy law"* (Psalm 119:18). The Spirit gives heavenly eye salve to those who are spiritually blind. If your eyes are not open now, seek the eye salve, and you will see—yes, and see so clearly that he who has only been educated in man's school will ask, *"How knoweth this man letters, having never learned?"* (John 7:15).

Those who are taught by the Holy Spirit often surpass those who are taught by man. I once met an entirely uneducated country bumpkin who never went to school for one hour in his life, yet who knew more about the Holy Scriptures than many clergymen who have received advanced training at the finest seminaries. I have been told that it is a common practice for men in Wales, while they are at work breaking stones in the quarries, to discuss difficult points in theology, which many a theologian cannot master. Their understanding is enlightened because they humbly read the Scriptures, trusting only in the guidance of the Holy Spirit and believing that *"when he, the Spirit of truth, is come, he will guide [them] into all truth"* (John 16:13). And the Holy Spirit is pleased to do so.

All other instruction is very good. Solomon said, *"That the soul be without knowledge, it is not good"* (Proverbs 19:2). We should all seek to know as much as can be known. Yet, let us remember that in the work of salvation, real knowledge must be obtained by the teaching of the Holy Spirit. If we would learn in the heart, and not merely in the head, we must be taught entirely by the Holy Spirit. What you learn from man, you can unlearn; but what you learn from the Spirit is fixed indelibly in your heart and your conscience, and not even Satan himself can steal it from you. Go, you ignorant ones, who often shy away from the truths of revelation. Go, and ask the Spirit, for He is the Guide of unenlightened souls and the Guide of His own enlightened people. Without His aid, even when they have been *"once enlightened, and have tasted of the heavenly gift"* (Hebrews 6:4), they could not understand all truth unless the Spirit led them into it.

The Holy Spirit As Our Applier

God also gives the Holy Spirit to us as the Spirit of Application. Thus it was that Jesus said to His disciples, *"He shall glorify me: for he shall receive of mine, and shall show it unto you"* (John 16:14). To make the matter clearer still, our Lord added, *"All things that the Father hath are mine: therefore said I, that he shall take of mine, and shall show it unto you"* (verse 15). Let me remind you how frequently Jesus impressed on His disciples the fact that He spoke to them the words of His

Father: *"Jesus answered them, and said, My doctrine is not mine, but his that sent me"* (John 7:16). Again, He said, *"The words that I speak unto you I speak not of myself: but the Father that dwelleth in me, he doeth the works"* (John 14:10).

As Christ thus made known the will of God the Father to His people, so the Holy Spirit makes known to us the words of Christ. I could almost affirm that Christ's words would be of no use to us if they were not instilled in us by the Holy Spirit. Beloved, we need this application to assure our hearts that His words belong to us, that they are intended for us, and that we have a share in their blessedness. Further, we need the anointing of the Spirit to make them bedew our hearts and refresh our souls.

Did you ever have a promise applied to your heart? Do you understand what is meant by *application* as the exclusive work of the Spirit? Just as Paul said the gospel came to the Thessalonians, it comes to you *"not in word only, but also in power, and in the Holy Ghost, and in much assurance"* (1 Thessalonians 1:5).

Sometimes the Spirit's application comes suddenly. Your heart may have been the scene of a thousand distracting thoughts, wave after wave crashing upon your mind, until the tempest rose beyond your control. And then, some text of Scripture, like a mighty decree from the lips of Jesus, has stilled your troubled soul. Immediately, there has been a great calm, and you have wondered where it came from. The sweet passage has rung like music in your ears; like a wafer made of honey, the Scripture has moistened your tongue; like a charm, it has quelled your anxieties. It has stayed uppermost in your thoughts all day long, reining in all your lawless passions and restless strivings. Perhaps it has continued in your mind for weeks; wherever you went, whatever you did, you could not dislodge it, nor did you wish to do so, because it was so sweet and so savory to your soul. Have you not thought of such a text that it is the best in the Bible, the most precious in all the Holy Scriptures? That was because it was so graciously applied to you by the Holy Spirit.

Oh, how I love applied promises! I might read a thousand promises as they stand recorded on the pages of the Sacred Volume, and yet get nothing from them. My heart would not burn within me, even for all their richness. Yet, one promise, brought home to my soul by the Spirit's application, has such *"marrow and fatness"* (Psalm 63:5) in it that it would be food enough for forty days for many of the Lord's Elijahs. How sweet it is, in times of deep affliction and trial, to have this promise applied to one's heart:

When thou passest through the waters, I will be with thee; and through the rivers, they shall not overflow thee: when thou walkest through the fire, thou shalt not be burned; neither shall the flame kindle upon thee. (Isaiah 43:2)

Perhaps you are saying, "Oh, that is all just emotionalism." Of course, it appears that way to you, if you, in the natural, cannot discern the things of the Spirit. But we are talking about spiritual things to spiritually-minded men. (See 1 Corinthians 2:13–14.) To them this is not merely emotionalism; it is often a matter of life or death. I have known numerous cases where the only plank on which a poor, troubled believer was able to float was just one verse, on which he had, somehow or other, so tightened his grasp that nothing could take it away from him.

Nor is it only the Word of our Lord that needs to be applied to our hearts. *"The Spirit of truth shall receive of mine, and shall show it unto you"* (John 16:13–14) may likewise refer to our Savior's precious blood. We sometimes sing,

> There is a fountain filled with blood
> Drawn from Immanuel's veins.

We talk of bathing in that blood-filled reservoir. Now, faith does not apply the blood of Christ to the soul; that is the work of the Spirit. Yes, it is true that I seek it by faith, but it is the Spirit who washes me in the *"fountain opened for sin and for uncleanness"* (Zechariah 13:1).

It is the Holy Spirit who receives the things of Christ and shows them to us. We would never have a drop of blood sprinkled on our hearts if it were not sprinkled there by the Holy Spirit. So, too, the robe of Christ's righteousness is fitted on us entirely by the Spirit. We are not invited to appropriate the obedience of Christ for ourselves, but the Spirit brings everything to us that Christ has made available for us. Ask the Spirit, then, that you may have the Word applied, the blood applied, pardon applied, and grace applied. You will not be asking in vain, because God Almighty has promised, *"I will put my spirit within you."*

The Holy Spirit As Our Sanctifier

Now, we need to note another very important point: we must receive the Spirit as our Sanctifier. Perhaps this is one of the greatest works of the Holy

Spirit—sanctifying the soul. It is a great work to purge the soul from sin: it is greater than if one could wash a leopard until all his spots were obliterated, or an Ethiopian until his sable skin became white. (See Jeremiah 13:23.) Our sins are more than skin-deep—they have entered into our very nature. If our exteriors were washed pure and clean right now, we would be polluted before tomorrow; and if all the spots were taken away today, they would grow again tomorrow, for we are sin-stained all the way through. You may scrub the flesh, but we are filthy to the core; our sinfulness is a leprosy that lies deep within.

However, it is the Holy Spirit who sanctifies the soul. He enters the heart, beginning the work of sanctification with conversion. He retains possession of the heart and preserves sanctification by perpetually pouring in the fresh oil of grace, until at last He will perfect sanctification by making the soul pure and spotless, fit to dwell with the blessed inhabitants of glory.

The way the Holy Spirit sanctifies a person is this: first, He reveals to the soul the evil of sin and makes that soul hate it; the Spirit shows sin to be a deadly evil, full of poison. Then, when the soul begins to hate the evil of sin, the next thing the Holy Spirit does is to show that the blood of Christ takes all the guilt away, and, from that very fact, to lead the soul to hate sin even more than he did when he first knew his blackness. The Holy Spirit takes that soul to *"the blood of sprinkling, that speaketh better things than that of Abel"* (Hebrews 12:24). There He tolls the death knell of sin as He points to the blood of Christ and says, "Jesus shed this for you, in order that He might purchase you for Himself, to be one of His *'peculiar people, zealous of good works'"* (Titus 2:14).

Afterward, the Holy Spirit may, at times, allow sin to break out in the heart of the redeemed child of God so that he may be more strongly restrained by greater watchfulness and carefulness in the future. When an heir of heaven does indulge in sin, the Holy Spirit sends a sanctifying chastisement upon his soul until, his heart being broken with deep grief by the pain of the wound, evil is cleansed away. The soul's conscience, feeling uneasy, propels his heart to Christ, who removes the chastisement and takes away the guilt.

Remember, believer, all your holiness is the work of the Holy Spirit. You do not have one grace that the Spirit did not give you, not a solitary virtue that He did not work in you, no goodness that was not given to you by the Spirit. Therefore, never boast of your virtues or of your graces. Are you even-tempered now, where once you were easily angered? Do not brag about it; you will be angry again if the Spirit leaves you. Are you now pure, whereas you were once unclean? Do not flaunt your purity, the seed of which was brought to you from heaven. It never grew within your heart by nature; it is God's gift alone.

Is unbelief prevailing against you? Do your lusts, your evil passions, and your corrupt desires seem likely to master you? Then, I will not say, "Up and at 'em!" but I urge you to cry out mightily to God that you would be filled with the Holy Spirit. Then you will conquer at last and become more than a conqueror (see Romans 8:37) over all your sins, because the Lord has promised, "*I will put my spirit within you.*"

The Holy Spirit As Our Guide

The Spirit of God is promised to the heirs of salvation as a directing Spirit, to guide them in the path of providence. "*When he, the Spirit of truth, is come, he will guide you into all truth*" (John 16:13). "*In all thy ways acknowledge him, and he shall direct thy paths*" (Proverbs 3:6).

If you are ever in a position in which you do not know what road to take, remember that true strength is found in your being at rest, and true wisdom is discovered when you wait for the directing voice of the Spirit, as He says to you, "*This is the way, walk ye in it*" (Isaiah 30:21). I trust that I have learned this principle myself, and I am sure every child of God who has been placed in difficulties must have felt, at times, the reality and blessedness of the Holy Spirit's guidance.

Have you ever prayed that He would direct you? If you have, did you ever find that you went wrong afterward? I do not mean the sort of prayers that are presented by those who ask for counsel, but not of the Lord:

> Woe to the rebellious children, saith the LORD, that take counsel, but not of me; and that cover with a covering, but not of my spirit, that they may add sin to sin: that walk to go down into Egypt, and have not asked at my mouth; to strengthen themselves in the strength of Pharaoh, and to trust in the shadow of Egypt!   (Isaiah 30:1–2)

Those rebellious souls ask God to bless them in ways that He never sanctioned. Instead, you must start by renouncing every other trust. Only then can you find proof of His promise: "*Commit thy way unto the LORD; trust also in him;*

and he shall bring it to pass" (Psalm 37:5). Child of God, take an open confession with you as you *"come boldly unto the throne of grace"* (Hebrews 4:16). Say, "Lord, I desire, like the wind, to be moved by the breath of the Spirit. Here I am, Lord, passive in Your hand. Happily would I know only Your will. Joyfully I would act according to Your will alone. Show me *"what is [Your] good, and acceptable, and perfect, will"* (Romans 12:2), Lord! Teach me what to do and what to refrain from doing."

To some of you, this may seem to be complete fanaticism; you do not believe that God the Holy Spirit ever guides men in the way they should take. And this is the perspective you would be expected to have if you have never experienced His guidance. I have heard that, when an English traveler in Africa told the inhabitants about the intense cold that sometimes prevailed in his country, by which water became so hard that people could skate and walk upon it, the king threatened to put him to death if he told any more lies, for he had never felt or seen such things. What one has never seen or felt is certainly an appropriate subject for doubt and contradiction.

However, regarding those of the Lord's people who tell you that they are led by the Spirit, I advise you to give careful consideration to their words and seek to be so led yourself. It would be a good thing if you were just to go to God as a child in all your distresses. Remember that, as an Advisor whom you may safely consult, as a Guide whose directions you may safely follow, as a Friend on whose protection you may safely rely, the Holy Spirit is personally present in the church of Christ and with each of the disciples of Jesus. And there is no fee to pay except your heartfelt gratitude and praise for His wise direction to you.

The Holy Spirit As Our Comforter

The Holy Spirit is given to God's children as a comforting Spirit. This is distinctively His office. Have you never felt that, immediately before a great and grievous trouble, you have had a most unaccountable season of joy? You scarcely knew why you were so happy or so tranquil; you seemed to be floating upon the Sea of Paradise. There was not a breath of wind to ruffle your peaceful spirit; all was serene and calm. You were not agitated by the ordinary cares and anxieties of the world; your whole mind was absorbed in sacred meditation. Later on, when the trouble came, you could say, "Now I understand it all; I could not before comprehend the meaning of that pleasant lull, that quiet happiness; but I see now that it was designed to prepare me for these trying circumstances. If I had been low and dispirited when this trouble burst upon me, it would have broken my heart. But now, thanks be to God, I can perceive through Jesus Christ how this *"light affliction, which is but for a moment,* [is working for me] *a far more exceeding and eternal weight of glory"* (2 Corinthians 4:17).

I do believe that it is worthwhile to have the troubles in order to get the comfort of the Holy Spirit; it is worthwhile to endure the storm in order to realize the joys.

Sometimes, my heart could have been shaken by derision, shame, and contempt: a fellow minister, of whom I had thought better things, reviled me; a Christian in my congregation turned on his heel and walked away from me because I had been misrepresented to him, and he hated me without cause. However, it has so happened that, at the very time of these incidents, if the whole church had turned its back on me and the whole world had hissed at me, it would not have greatly moved me. Some bright ray of spiritual sunshine filled my heart, and Jesus whispered to me those sweet words, *"I am my beloved's, and my beloved is mine"* (Song of Solomon 6:3). At such times, the consolations of the Spirit have been neither few nor small with me.

O Christian, if I were able, I would bring you yet further into the depths of this glorious passage; but, as I cannot, I must leave it with you. It is full of honey; only put it to your lips, and get the honey from it. *"I will put my spirit within you."*

The Holy Spirit As Our Grace

Finally, do you not see here the absolute certainty of the salvation of every believer? Or rather, is it not absolutely certain that every member of the family of God's Israel must be saved? For it is written, *"I will put my spirit within you."* Do you think that when God puts His Spirit within men, they could possibly be damned? Can you dare to think God puts His Spirit into them, and yet they could perish and be lost? You may think so if you please, but I will tell you what God thinks: *"I will put my spirit within you, and cause you to walk in my statutes, and ye shall keep my judgments, and do them"* (Ezekiel 36:27). Sinners are far from God because of their wicked works, and they will not come unto Him that they may have life. (See John 5:40.) Yet, when God says, *"I will put my spirit within you,"* He compels them to come to Him.

What a vain pretense it is to profess to honor God by a doctrine that makes salvation depend on the will of man! If it were true, you might say to God, "We thank you, O Lord, for what You have done; You have given us a great many things, and we offer You Your reward of praise, which is justly due to Your name; but we think we deserve more, for the deciding point was in our free will." Beloved, do not swerve from the free grace of God, for the babblings about man's free agency are neither more nor less than lies, absolutely contrary to the truth of Christ and the teachings of the Spirit.

How certain, then, is the salvation of every elect soul! It does not depend on the will of man; he is made *"willing in the day of* [God's] *power"* (Psalm 110:3). He will be called at the appointed time, and his heart will be completely changed, in order that he may become a trophy of the Redeemer's power. The fact that he was unwilling before then is no hindrance; God gives him the will, so that he is then of a willing mind. Thus, every heir of heaven must be saved, because the Spirit is put within him, and thereby his disposition and affections are molded according to the will of God.

How useless is it for any person to suppose that he can be saved without the Holy Spirit! Dear friend, men sometimes go very near to salvation without being saved, like the poor man who lay beside the pool of Bethesda for thirty-eight years, always close to the water, but never getting in. (See John 5:2–7.) How many changes in outward character there are that very much resemble conversion, yet, these people, not having the Spirit within them, fail after all! Deathbed repentances are often looked upon as very sincere, although too frequently, I fear, they are but the first gnawings of *"their worm* [that] *shall not die"* (Isaiah 66:24).

I have recently read an extraordinary anecdote of a woman who, many years ago, was condemned to death for murdering her child and was hanged in the Grass Market at Edinburgh. She very diligently reformed during the six weeks that were allowed her by Scottish law, previous to her execution. The ministers who were with her continually stated as their opinion that she would die in the sure and certain hope of salvation. The appointed day came, and she was hanged. But, because it was very rainy that day and no awning had been prepared, those who were in charge of her execution were in a great hurry to complete it and get themselves under shelter, so her body was cut down before the legally set time had elapsed. As the custom was, the body was given up to her friends to be buried. A coffin was provided, and she was transported in it to East Lothian, where her husband was going to bury her. Her friends stopped at an inn on the road to refresh themselves, when, to their great surprise and alarm, in rushed a boy who said he heard a noise in the coffin. They went out and found that the woman was alive. Her vital powers had been suspended, but her life was not extinct, and the jolting of the cart had stimulated her to arousal. After a few hours, she was quite revived. She and her husband moved their residence and went to another part of the country.

The sad part of this tale is that the woman was as bad a character after she recovered as she ever had been before, and, if anything, she was worse. She lived just as openly in sin, despising and hating religion even more than she had previously done. Hers was a most remarkable case. Nevertheless, I believe that you can see from it that the great majority of those who profess to repent on their deathbeds, if they could rise again from their graves, would live a life as profane and godless as ever.

Rely on this: it is nothing but the grace of the Spirit of God that makes sure work of your souls. Unless He transforms you, you may be changed, but it will not be a change that will endure. Unless He puts His hand to the work, the work will be marred, the pitcher spoiled on the potter's wheel.

Therefore, cry unto the Lord that He may give you the Holy Spirit, and that you may have the evidence of a real conversion and not a cheap counterfeit. Take heed, sinner, take heed! Natural fear, natural love, natural feelings are not conversion. In the first place, and by all subsequent edification, conversion must be the work of the Holy Spirit, and of Him alone. Never rest comfortably, then, until the Holy Spirit's operations are most surely working in your heart!

5

THE BLOOD OF
THE COVENANT

*Now the God of peace, that brought again from the dead our Lord Jesus,
that great shepherd of the sheep, through the blood of the everlasting
covenant, make you perfect in every good work to do his will, working in
you that which is wellpleasing in his sight, through Jesus Christ; to whom be
glory for ever and ever. Amen.*
—Hebrews 13:20–21

What we ask others to do we should be prepared to do ourselves. Instruction fails unless it is followed by clear example. The writer had just exhorted the Hebrew believers to *"pray for us"* (Hebrews 13:18). Then, as if to show that he did not ask of them what he was not himself willing to give, he penned this most wonderful prayer for them. The pastor who prays genuinely from his heart for his congregation may confidently say to them, "Pray for me."

The prayer of the writer, as you observe, has overtones of the subject in which he had been engrossed. This epistle to the Hebrews is full of distinctions between the old covenant and the new one. The main idea of Hebrews is that the former covenant was only a foreshadowing of the dispensation that was to follow; it had only the shadow, and not the very image, of heavenly things. The writer's subject had been the covenant. When he prayed, his garments smelled sweetly of the myrrh and aloes and cassia (see Psalm 45:8) among which his meditations had conducted him. He prayerfully expressed his desires according to his thought patterns. He wove into the texture of his prayer the meditations of his heart.

This is a very good method, especially when the prayer is public, for it ensures variety, it encourages unity, and it promotes edification. In fact, as the bee gathers nectar from many flowers to make honey, and the honey is often flavored with wild thyme or some other special flower that abounds in the region from where the bee collects its sweets, so do our souls gather dainty stores of the honey of devotion from all sources; but that upon which we linger the longest in our meditations yields a paramount savor and flavor to the expression and the spirit of our prayers. Nothing could have been more natural than that this discourse on the covenant was followed by this covenant prayer: *"The God of peace, that brought again from the dead our Lord Jesus, that great shepherd of the sheep, through the blood of the everlasting covenant, make you perfect in every good work to do his will."*

The subject of the epistle to the Hebrews is very deep, for it moves from the superficial fundamentals of the faith to those underlying truths that are more mysterious and profound. It is a book for the higher grade levels in Christ's school. Hence, this prayer is not for babes, but for men of understanding. Concerning this prayer, we could not say to all believers, *"After this manner therefore pray ye"* (Matthew 6:9), for they would not understand what they were asking. They would need to begin with something simpler, such as that beautiful *"Our Father which art in heaven"* (verse 9), which was Christ's original model of prayer, and which suits all believers alike.

Mature men eat strong meat, think sublime thoughts, and offer mighty prayers. As we may admire the prayer of the child in its simplicity, and the prayer of the young man in its vitality, so we may rejoice in the depth, extent, and sublimity of the prayer of one who has become a father in Christ (see 1 Corinthians 4:15) and feeds upon the covenant. All of these characteristics we find in this prayer, and thus we may safely infer that the writer was a spiritually mature father in the faith.

I invite those who want to understand the deep things of God to ask the Holy Spirit's assistance while we follow the writer of Hebrews in his covenant prayer—a prayer of which the covenant is the thread, the substance, and the plea. Our broader subject, therefore, is the covenant of grace, as it is referred to here.

The Names of the Covenant

I will begin by first reviewing the covenantal names the writer used. He called the ever blessed Father, who is one party of the covenant, "*the God of peace*." To the Redeemer, who has taken responsibility for fulfilling the other half of the covenant, he gave the title, "*our Lord Jesus, that great shepherd of the sheep*."

Dear friends, those of us who have believed in the Lord Jesus Christ are in Christ. He is our Head and Representative, our Shepherd and Sponsor. On our behalf, He made a covenant with the Father along these lines: since we "*were dead in* [our] *trespasses and sins*" (Ephesians 2:1), Christ promised that He would make full recompense to injured justice, so that the law of God would be fully honored; and the Father stipulated that He would grant full pardon, acceptance, adoption, and eternal life to us. The covenant has been completely satisfied on our part by Christ. Our text assures us of that, because, in fulfillment of His promise, Jesus has shed His blood.

"The God of Peace"

Now, the covenant only needs to be fulfilled on God's part by the eternal Father. In that aspect of the covenant, the writer of Hebrews called the Father, "*the God of peace*." What a precious name! Under the covenant of works, He is the God of vengeance: "*For the LORD thy God is a jealous God*" (Deuteronomy 4:24), who will "*execute vengeance upon the heathen, and punishments upon the people*" (Psalm 149:7). To sinners He is the thrice-holy God, "*terrible out of* [His] *holy places*" (Psalm 68:35), and even "*a consuming fire*" (Hebrews 12:29). Yet to us, seeing that the covenant has been fulfilled on our side by our great Head and Representative, He is "*the God of peace*."

Christian, all is peace between you and God. No previous grounds for quarreling remain, nor should you ever fear that a new one can arise. The everlasting covenant secures everlasting peace between you and God. He is not the God of a hollow truce, not the God of a patched-up forgetfulness of unforgiven injuries, but "*the God of peace*" in the very deepest sense. He is Himself at peace, for there is a "*peace of God, which passeth all understanding*" (Philippians 4:7).

Moreover, by reason of His mercy, His people are made to enjoy peace of conscience within themselves. Thus, you feel that God is reconciled to you. Your heart rests in Him. Your sins, which separated you, have been removed. Perfect love has cast out all fear, which has torment. (See 1 John 4:18.)

While the Lord is at peace with Himself, and you are made to enjoy inward peace through Him, He is also at peace with you, for He loves you with a love unsearchable; He sees nothing in you but that which He delights in. In the covenant of grace, He does not look at you as you are in and of yourself, but as you are in your Surety, Christ Jesus. To the eye of God, there is no sight in the universe as lovely as His own dear Son, and His people in His Son. There is enough beauty in Jesus to make God forget our deformities, enough merit in Jesus to engulf our demerits, and sufficient efficacy in the atoning blood of our Great High Priest to wash away all our transgressions.

As for us, our souls, recognizing Christ's atoning blood and perceiving the love of God toward us, no longer experience war with God. We rebelled once, for we hated Him. Even now, when our old natures champ at the bit, and the Lord's will runs counter to our desires, we do not find it easy to bow before Him and say, *"I thank thee, O Father, Lord of heaven and earth, because it seemed good in thy sight"* (Matthew 11:25–26). But yet, the new nature that has come to the forefront rules and governs, and all heart-contests between the soul and God have ended. In the broadest and most perfect sense, the Lord is to us, *"the God of peace."*

Oh, how I love that name, *"the God of peace."* He is Himself the peaceful, joyful God, unruffled, undisturbed; and we within ourselves are made to enjoy *"the peace of God, which passeth all understanding,* [which keeps our] *hearts and minds through Christ Jesus"* (Philippians 4:7). God is at peace with us, declaring that He will never be wrathful toward us or rebuke us, and we are rejoicing in Him, delighting in His law, and living for His glory. Henceforth, may it be that in every anxious hour, we look to the Lord by this cheering name, *"the God of peace,"* for as such the covenant reveals Him.

"Our Lord Jesus"

The writer of Hebrews had a view of the other great party to the covenant; he named Him *"our Lord Jesus."* We must know the Redeemer first as *"Jesus,"* our Savior, who leads us into the promised eternal *"rest"* (Hebrews 4:1), the spiritual Canaan that has been given to us by the covenant (see Exodus 6:4): *"there remaineth therefore a rest to the people of God"* (Hebrews 4:9).

Our Redeemer is also the *"Lord Jesus,"* in all the dignity of His nature, exalted *"far above all principality, and power"* (Ephesians 1:21), to be obeyed and worshipped by us. Moreover, He is *"our Lord Jesus"*: ours because He has given Himself to us, and we have accepted and received Him with holy delight as the Lord whom we cheerfully serve; ours because He saved us; ours because, by bringing us into His kingdom, He rescued us; and ours because we have a special relationship both to His sovereignty and His salvation.

We are not generally observant of the appropriateness of our Lord's names. We do not notice the instruction that was intended by the writers who used them, nor do we exercise enough discretion in our employment of them. Yet, there is great force in these titles when they are appropriately employed. Other names may be relatively insignificant, but in the titles of Jesus there is a wealth of meaning.

"That Great Shepherd of the Sheep"

Further, our Lord is called *"that great shepherd of the sheep."* In the covenant we are the sheep, and the Lord Jesus is the Shepherd. You cannot make a covenant with sheep; they do not have the ability to covenant. However, you can make a covenant with their Shepherd. Thus, glory be to God, although we like lost sheep had gone astray (see Isaiah 53:6), we belonged to Jesus, and He made a covenant on our behalf and stood for us before the living God.

Now, I want to explain to you that in His death our Lord is the Good Shepherd: *"the good shepherd giveth his life for the sheep"* (John 10:11), and so He shows His goodness. In His resurrection He is the *"great shepherd,"* as we have it in the text, for His resurrection and return to glory display His greatness. Moreover, in the Second Advent He is the Chief Shepherd, and in this He shows His superior sovereignty: *"when the chief Shepherd shall appear"* (1 Peter 5:4), *"then shall ye also appear with him in glory"* (Colossians 3:4).

Our Lord was the "good" Shepherd in that He laid down His life for the sheep. There are other shepherds to whom He imparts His own goodness, who in His name feed His lambs and sheep. When He comes again the second time, He will appear with His undershepherds, as the Chief among them all. Yet, in His resurrection for our justification, in connection with the covenant, He is alone and bears the name of *"that great shepherd,"* of whom all prophecy has spoken, in whom all the divine decrees are fulfilled, before whom all others shrink away. He stands alone in that covenant capacity as the one and only Shepherd of the sheep.

It is very beautiful to trace the shepherds through the Old Testament. We can see Christ represented in Abel, the witnessing shepherd, pouring out the *"blood [that] crieth unto [God] from the ground"* (Genesis 4:10); in Abraham, the separating shepherd, leading his family flock into a strange country where they dwelt alone (Hebrews 11:9); in Isaac, the quiet shepherd, digging wells for his flock (see Genesis 26:18) and feeding them in peace in the midst of his enemies; and in Jacob, the shepherd who was the surety for his sheep, who earned them by long toil and weariness. (See Genesis 29:20, 30.)

There, too, we see our Lord in Joseph, the head shepherd over Egypt for the sake of Israel, of whom his dying father said, *"From thence is the shepherd, the stone of Israel"* (Genesis 49:24). Our Lord Jesus is now *"the head over all things [for] the church"* (Ephesians 1:22), the King who governs all the world for the sake of His elect, *"that great shepherd of the sheep"* who has all power committed into His hands for their sakes.

We can see Christ in Moses, the chosen shepherd, who led his people through the Red Sea, into the wilderness (see Exodus 15:22), and up to the Promised Land (see Exodus 16:35), feeding them with manna and giving them water from the rock that he struck. (See Exodus 16:32; 17:6.) What a grand theme for reflection we have here! And then, there is David, the shepherd king and another type of Jesus, as he reigned in the covenanted inheritance over his own people, as a glorious king in the midst of them all. All these together enable us to see the varied glories of *"that great shepherd of the sheep."*

While we rest in the covenant of grace, we should view our Lord as our Shepherd and find solace in the fact that sheep have nothing to do with their own feeding, guidance, or protection. They have only to follow their shepherd to the pastures that he prepares, and all will be well with them. *"He maketh me to lie down in green pastures: he leadeth me beside the still waters"* (Psalm 23:2).

Beloved, this is a great subject, and I can only hint at it. Let us rejoice that our Shepherd is *"great,"* because He will be able to preserve all of His large flock from the great dangers that they will have to face. *"Yea, though I walk through the valley of the shadow of death, I will fear no evil: for thou art with me; thy rod and thy staff they comfort me"* (verse 4). He will be able to perform for them the great transactions with the great God that are demanded of a Shepherd of such a flock as that which Jesus calls His own. Under the covenant of grace, Jesus is Prophet, Priest, and King—a shepherd should be all this to his flock—and He is great in each of these offices.

The Seal of the Covenant

The second major point for our consideration is the writer's reference to the covenant seal in our text: *"The God of peace that brought again from the dead our Lord Jesus, that great shepherd of the sheep, through the blood of the everlasting covenant."* The seal of the covenant is the blood of Jesus.

In ancient times, when men made covenants with one another, they generally used some kind of ceremony or exchange to bind and seal the bargain, as it were. Now, covenants with God are always confirmed with blood. As soon as blood has been shed and the victim has died, the agreement is forever established.

The Binder of the Covenant

When our heavenly Father made a covenant with Jesus Christ on our behalf, that covenant was true and firm: *"I will make an everlasting covenant with you, even the sure mercies of David"* (Isaiah 55:3). However, to make it stand eternally, blood had to be shed. Now, the blood ordained to seal the covenant was not *"the blood of bulls and of goats"* (Hebrews 10:4), but the blood of the Son of God Himself. This has made the covenant so binding that *"it [would be] easier for heaven and earth to pass, than one tittle of the [covenant] to fail"* (Luke 16:17).

God must keep His own promises. He is a free God, but He bound Himself:

> *When God made promise to Abraham, because he could swear by no greater, he sware by himself, for men verily swear by the greater: and an oath for confirmation is to them an end of all strife. Wherein God, willing more abundantly to show unto the heirs of promise the immutability of his [promise], confirmed it by an oath: that by two immutable things, in which it was impossible for God to lie, we might have a strong consolation.*
>
> (Hebrews 6:13, 16–18)

As soon as Christ's blood was shed to seal the covenant of grace, God was bound by His oath to bestow covenant blessings upon the flock that the Great Shepherd represented.

Beloved, as honest people, you and I are bound by our word. If we were to take an oath, which I trust we would not, we would certainly feel doubly bound by it. Moreover, if we had lived in the old times and blood had been sprinkled on a contract that we had made, we would respect the solemn sign and never even think of turning back from it.

Consider, for a moment, how impossible it would be for God to ever break that covenant of grace, which He voluntarily made with His own Son, and with us in Him, after it had been sprinkled with blood from the veins of His own beloved Son. No, the covenant is everlasting. It stands true forever, because it is confirmed by blood that is none other than the blood of the Son of God.

The Satisfaction of the Covenant Terms

Remember, too, that in our case, Christ's blood not only confirmed the covenant, but actually satisfied its terms. The stipulations of the covenant went like this: Christ must suffer for our sins and honor the divine law. He had kept the law in His life, but it was necessary, if He were to completely fulfill His part of the covenant, that He should also be *obedient unto death, even the death of the cross*" (Philippians 2:8). Therefore, the shedding of His blood was the carrying out of His promised obedience to its utmost. It was the actual satisfaction of Christ's part of the covenant on our behalf. Thus, the whole covenant must now stand firm, for that upon which it depended is finished forever. It is not only ratified with that bloody signature, but by that blood it is actually accomplished on Christ's part. It cannot be that the eternal Father should turn back from His side of the compact, since our part of it has been carried out to the letter by *"that great shepherd of the sheep"* who laid down His life for us.

The Blood of the New Testament

By the shedding of blood, the covenant was turned into a testament. As the Scriptures say, *"For this is my blood of the new testament, which is shed for many for the remission of sins"* (Matthew 26:28), and, *"For where a testament is, there must also of necessity be the death of the testator"* (Hebrews 9:16).

In some Bibles, the marginal notes give "testament" as an alternate translation for *covenant*. We scarcely know how to translate the word in some Scripture passages, whether to say the new testament or the new covenant. Certainly it is now a testament: since Christ has kept His part of the covenant, He wills to us what is due to Him from God. Further, He bequeaths to us by His death all that comes to Him as His reward, making us His heirs by a testament that is rendered valid by His death. So, you may say "testament" if you please, or "covenant" if you will; but do not forget that His shed blood has made both testament and covenant sure and everlasting to all the sheep of whom Jesus is the Shepherd.

The Eternal Seal of the Covenant

Dwell with pleasure upon that phrase *"everlasting covenant."* Certain men in these days declare that *"everlasting"* does not mean everlasting, but indicates a period to which an end will come sooner or later. I have no sympathy with them whatever. Neither do I have any inclination to renounce the eternal nature of heaven and other divine blessings in order to gratify the tastes of wicked men who wish to deny the eternity of future punishments. Human nature leans in that direction, but the Word of God does not. Following its unerring direction, we rejoice in the everlasting covenant, which will abide forever and ever.

The covenant of works is gone. Since it was based on human strength and ability, it necessarily dissolved as a dream. Given the nature of mankind, it could not be everlasting. Man could not keep its conditions, and so it fell by the wayside. However, the covenant of grace depended only upon the power and love and faithfulness of Christ, who has obediently fulfilled His part of the covenant. Therefore, the covenant now rests only upon God, who remains *"faithful: he cannot deny himself"* (2 Timothy 2:13). Since *"he sware by himself"* (Hebrews 6:13), His word cannot fail.

> As well might He His being quit,
> As break His promise, or forget.

"His mercy is everlasting; and his truth endureth to all generations" (Psalm 100:5). He has said, *"I will make an everlasting covenant with them, that I will not turn away from them, to do them good"* (Jeremiah 32:40). Therefore, do them good He must, for *"God is not a man, that he should lie; neither the son of man, that he should repent"* (Numbers 23:19). So then, the covenant seal of Christ's blood makes all things sure.

The Fulfillment of the Covenant

Now, let us explore the fulfillment of the covenant, for God has begun to carry out His part in it. *"The God of peace, that brought again from the dead our Lord Jesus, that great shepherd of the sheep, through the blood of the everlasting covenant."*

First, Jesus Christ has been brought back from the dead by the Almighty through the blood of the covenant. Here is the story. Jesus was the Covenanter on our behalf; He took our sin upon Himself and undertook to suffer for it. Having been crucified, He yielded up His life. From the cross He was taken to the grave, and there He lay, imprisoned in death. Now, it was a term of the covenant on God the Father's part that He would not leave Christ's *"soul in hell, neither suffer [His] Holy One to see corruption"* (Acts 2:27); this agreement has been faithfully kept.

Christ on the cross represented all of us who believe in Him, for we were crucified in Him. Jesus in the tomb also represented us, for we were buried with Him. Whatever happened to Him also happened to His flock. Now, then, what occurred to the body of Jesus? Did God keep His covenant? Did the worm devour that lovely frame, or did it defy corruption? Did it come to pass that He who descended into the earth never returned?

Wait for the dawning of the third day! Now, the promised time has come. As yet no worm dared to feed upon that godlike form, yet it lay among the dead. But on that glorious morning, the Slumberer awakened like one who has been refreshed with sleep. He arose. The stone was rolled away. Angels escorted Him to liberty. He came into the open air of the garden and spoke to His disciples.

Jesus who bled left the dead, no more to die. He waited for forty days so that He might let His friends see that He was really risen, but He had to rise higher still to be brought fully back to His former honors. Would God be faithful to Him and bring Him back from the dead, all the way from where He once had descended? Yes, for on the Mount of Olives, when the time came, He started to ascend. Cleaving the atmosphere, He mounted from amid His worshipping disciples, until a cloud received Him. But, did He rise fully to the point from which He had come? Did He in His own person gain for His church a full recovery from all the ruin of the Fall? Oh, see Him as He entered the gates of pearl! How He was welcomed by the Father! See how He climbed aloft and sat upon the Father's throne, for *"God also hath highly exalted him, and given him a name which is above every name: that at the name of Jesus every knee should bow"* (Philippians 2:9).

Now note by what means our Lord returned from the dead to all this glory. It was because He had presented the blood of the everlasting covenant. When the Father saw that Jesus had kept His part of the covenant, even to death, then He began to fulfill His portion of the contract by bringing back His Son from the grave to life, from shame to honor, from humiliation to glory, from death to immortality. And so, Jesus Christ *"sat down on the right hand of God; from hence-forth expecting till his enemies be made his footstool"* (Hebrews 10:12–13).

Now, what has been done to Jesus has been virtually done to all His people, because *"the God of peace brought again from the dead,"* not the Lord Jesus as a private person only, but *"our Lord Jesus,"* as *"that great shepherd of the sheep."* The sheep are with the Shepherd. Shepherd of the sheep, where is Your flock? We know that You have loved them even to the end, but You are gone. Have You left them in the wilderness? It cannot be, for thus it is written: *"Who shall separate us from the love of Christ?"* (Romans 8:35). Hear the Shepherd say, *"Father, I will that they also, whom thou hast given me, be with me where I am"* (John 17:24). *"Because I live, ye shall live also"* (John 14:19). *"Where I am, there shall also my servant be"* (John 12:26). Beloved, the sheep never are away from *"that great shepherd of the sheep."* They are always in His hand, and none can snatch them out of His hold. (See John 10:28.) They were on earth with Him, and they are risen with Him.

If Jesus had remained in the grave, all His sheep would have perished there, too. However, when the Father brought Him back by the blood, He brought us back by the blood. In this He gives us the *"lively hope"* (1 Peter 1:3) that our souls will never die and the joyous expectation of resurrection for our bodies.

> For though our inbred sins require
> Our flesh to see the dust,
> Yet as the Lord our Shepherd rose,
> So all His followers must.

Jesus in heaven is there as our Representative, and His flock is following Him. I wish you could get a picture in your mind of the hills of heaven rising up from these lowlands called earth. We are feeding here a while under His watch-ful eye, and at a distance is a river that flows at the foot of the celestial hills and separates us from the heavenly pastures. One by one, our beloved ones are being called across the waters by the Good Shepherd's voice, and they cross the river pleasantly at His bidding, so that a long line of His sheep may be seen going over the stream and up the hillside to where the Shepherd stands and receives them. This line joins the upper flock to the lower and makes them all one company. Do you not see them continually streaming up to Him and proceeding under the direction of God, who tells them to be fed by the Lamb and to lie down forever where wolves can never come?

Thus, the one flock is even now with the Shepherd, for it is all one pasture to Him, although to us it seems divided by Jordan's torrent. Every one of the sheep is marked with the blood of the everlasting covenant. Every one of them has been preserved because Jesus lived. And as He was brought again from the dead by the Almighty through His shed blood, even so must they be, for so the covenant stands.

Remember, then, dear friends, that the punishment of the flock was borne by the Shepherd, that the flock died in the Shepherd, and that the flock now lives because the Shepherd lives. The life of the flock is consequently a new life. Remember, also, He will bring all His sheep that as yet are not called, out of their death in sin, even as He was brought out of His own death; He will lead onward and upward those who are called, even as He went onward and upward from the grave to the throne; He will preserve them all their journey through, even as He was preserved by the blood of the everlasting covenant; and He will perfect them even as He is perfect. Even as the God of peace has glorified His Son, so also will He bring all His chosen to eternal glory with Him.

The Great Blessing of the Covenant

Next, let us delve into the blessing of the covenant that we find in on our text. What is one of the greatest of the covenant blessings? The writer of this epistle pleaded for it: *"Now the God of peace make you perfect in every good work to do his will, working in you that which is wellpleasing in his sight."* Notice that one of the principal blessings of the new covenant is the power and will to serve God. The old covenant said, "There are the tablets of stone; make sure that you obey every word that is written on them. If you do, you will live, and if you do not, you will die." Man never did obey, and consequently no one ever entered heaven or found peace by the law.

However, the new covenant is drawn up this way: *"I will put my laws into their hearts, and in their minds will I write them; their sins and iniquities will I remember no more"* (Hebrews 10:16–17), and, *"I will put my fear in their hearts, that they shall not depart from me"* (Jeremiah 32:40). The prophets enlarged on this new covenant most instructively. It is not a covenant of "If you will, I will," but rather, "I will do, and you shall be."

As a covenant, this exactly suits me. If there were something to be performed by me, I could never be sure that I had fulfilled its terms, but since it is finished, I am at rest. God sets us working, and we work; but the covenant itself depends wholly upon that great promise: *"I will not turn away from them, to do them good"* (Jeremiah 32:40).

Thus, it was right for the writer of Hebrews to pray that God would *"make* [us] *perfect in every good work to do his will,"* because from ancient times this was the master promise: that those for whom Jesus died should be sanctified, purified, and equipped to serve their God. *"For we are his workmanship, created in Christ Jesus unto good works, which God hath before ordained that we should walk in them"* (Ephesians 2:10). Great as the prayer is, it is only asking what the covenant itself guarantees.

Fully Equipped for Service

Taking the text word by word, I see that the first blessing asked for by the writer is the ability for divine service. The Greek word *katartizo*, translated here as *"make you perfect,"* does not have the same meaning of *perfect* in the sense that we use it today; rather, it means "equipped," "fit," "prepared," "able." With this observation, I am not making any reference to the persistent debate about the doctrine of perfection. No one text could decide that controversy. I simply am stating a matter of fact. The expression should be rendered, "make you fully complete," or "fully equipped" to do His will. We ought to request earnestly that we may be qualified, adapted, and suited to be used by God for the performance of His will.

After a man, once dead in sin, is made alive again, the question arises, Who should be his master? To whom should we, having died in our Great Shepherd and having been brought again from the dead, yield ourselves? Certainly unto God alone. Our prayer is that we may be fully enabled to do His will. Our Shepherd did His Father's will, for He cried, *"I delight to do thy will, O my God"* (Psalm 40:8). *"By the which will we are sanctified"* (Hebrews 10:10), and each one of us is henceforth sanctified so that we may do that same will.

It is a grand desire, but it burns in every Christian's heart, that he may be prepared to serve his God, may be a vessel such as God can use, an instrument fit for the divine hand—weak and feeble, but not impure; unsuitable due to a lack of innate strength, but suitable through having been cleansed by the blood of the covenant. Dear brothers and sisters, ask for ability for service. Pray day and night that you may be *"meet for the master's use, and prepared unto every good work"* (2 Timothy 2:21).

An Inward Work of Grace

The writer of Hebrews was praying not merely for the ability for service, but moreover for an inward work of grace: *"working in you that which is wellpleasing in his sight."* I long above everything to possess more clearly in myself the inworking of the Holy Spirit. There is so much superficial religion, and we are so apt to be contented with it. Thus, it will enrich us to pray for deep heart work. We need to have our affections elevated, our wills subdued, our minds enlightened, and our entire beings deeply spiritualized by the presence of the Holy Spirit.

This is the promise of the covenant: *"God hath said, I will dwell in them, and walk in them"* (2 Corinthians 6:16). Remember, God worked in Christ in the grave by quickening His body to life, and He must work in us, *"according to the working of his mighty power, which he wrought in Christ, when he raised him from the dead"* (Ephesians 1:19–20).

Ask the Lord to do it in you. Do not be satisfied with a little, weak, almost imperceptible pulse of religion, of which you can hardly judge whether it is there or not. Instead, ask to feel the divine energies working within you. Keep asking to experience the eternal omnipotence of God, struggling and striving mightily in your spirit, until sin is conquered and grace gloriously triumphs. This is a covenant blessing. Seek for it.

An Outward, Visible Change

However, we need to be worked on outwardly as well as inwardly by God's Spirit. *"Working in you that which is wellpleasing in his sight"* is no small matter when you remember that nothing but perfect holiness can please God. Paul wanted each of us to be *"a vessel unto honour, sanctified, and meet for the master's use, and prepared unto every good work"* (2 Timothy 2:21).

Jesus expressed His desire to equip us to be versatile people who can do *"every good work,"* in this way: *"Verily, verily, I say unto you, He that believeth on me, the works that I do shall he do also; and greater works than these shall he do"* (John 14:12). He wishes us to be qualified for any station and every position.

When Jesus Christ rose from the dead, He was seen. There was not merely a secret quickening in Him, but a visible life. He was seen by angels and by men. Here on earth He lived for a period of time, being observed by all eyewitnesses. Just so, dearly beloved, there ought to be in us not only an inner resurrection that we feel, but also such a quickening that we are clearly alive to *"walk in newness of life"* (Romans 6:4). We must know the power of our Lord's resurrection and exhibit it in every action of our lives. May God grant us this, and may you know it by experience.

The Completeness of the Blessing

Next, let us observe the completeness of this covenant blessing. Just as Jesus has been fully restored to the place from which He came and has lost no dignity or power by having shed His blood, but rather has been exalted higher than ever, so God's design is to make us as pure and holy as Adam was initially. Likewise, He intends to add to our characters a force of love that never would have been there if we had not sinned and been forgiven—an energy of intense devotion, a strength of perfect self-sacrifice that we never could have learned if it had not been for *"Christ [who] hath loved us, and hath given himself for us"* (Ephesians 5:2).

God means to make us princes of the royal bloodline of the universe and court attendants of the Lord of Hosts. He desires to fashion an order of beings who will come very near to Him, and yet will feel the humblest reverence for Him. They will be like Himself, *"partakers of the divine nature"* (2 Peter 1:4), and yet the most obedient of servants; perfectly free agents, and yet bound to Him by bonds that will never let them disobey in thought, in word, or in deed.

This is how He is fashioning the central battalion who will obey His eternal marching orders forever: He is forgiving us great sins; He is bestowing upon us great blessings; He is making us one with His dear Son; and when He has entirely freed us from our shrouds of death, He will call us up to where Jesus is, and we will serve Him with an adoration superior to all the rest of His creatures. Angels and seraphim cannot love as much as we will be able to, for they have never tasted His redeeming grace and His dying love. This high devotion is the Lord's aim for us.

God did not raise the Lord Jesus from the dead so that He might live a common life. He lifted Him up so that Christ might *"be the head over all things* to the church," and that "*all things* [might be] *under his feet*" (Ephesians 1:22). Even so, the destiny of Christians is mysteriously sublime. They will not be lifted up from their natural deaths to a mere morality; they are destined to be something more than philanthropists and men esteemed by their peers. They are to exhibit to angels and principalities and powers the wonderful grace of God, showing in their own persons what God can do with His creatures through the death of His Son.

The Doxology of the Covenant

We conclude this study with the covenant doxology: "*To whom be glory for ever and ever. Amen.*" If anything in the world can make a man praise his God, it is the covenant of grace, and the knowledge that he is included in it.

I ask you to think over the love of God in the covenant. It does not belong to all of you. Christ is not the Shepherd of the whole flock of men; He is only the Shepherd of the sheep, and He has not entered into any covenant for all mankind, but for His sheep alone. The covenant is for His own people. If you believe in Him, it is a covenant for you; but if you reject Him, you can have no participation in this covenant, for you are under the covenant of works, which condemns you.

But now, believer, for a moment think over this exceeding mercy. Your God, the everlasting Father, has entered into a solemn compact with Christ on your behalf, that He will save you, keep you, and make you perfect. He has saved you; in that act He has performed a large part of the covenant in you already. He has placed you in the path of life and kept you there to this day.

Further, if you are indeed His, He will keep you to the end. The Lord is not as the foolish man who began to build but was unable to finish. He does not commence to carry out a design and then turn from it. He will continue His work until He completes it in you: "*Being confident of this very thing, that he which hath begun a good work in you will perform it until the day of Jesus Christ*" (Philippians 1:6).

Can you really believe it? With you, a poor puny mortal, who will soon sleep in the grave—with you He has made an everlasting covenant! Will you not say with our text, "*To whom be glory*"? Like David on his deathbed, you can say, "*Although my house be not so with God; yet he hath made with me an everlasting covenant, ordered in all things, and sure*" (2 Samuel 23:5). I am sure you will joy-fully add, "Glory be to His name."

Exclusive Glory

Our God deserves exclusive glory. Covenant theology glorifies God alone. There are other theologies everywhere that magnify men. They give him a finger in his own salvation, and so leave him a reason for throwing his cap up in the air and saying, "Well done, self!" But covenant theology puts man aside and makes him a debtor and a receiver. It does, as it were, plunge him into the sea of infinite grace and unmerited favor. It makes him give up all boasting, stopping the mouth that could have boasted by filling it with floods of love, so that it cannot utter a conceited word. A person saved by the covenant must give all the glory to God's holy name, for to God all the glory belongs. In salvation by the covenant, the Lord has exclusive glory.

Endless Glory

God also has endless glory. "*To whom be glory for ever and ever.*" Have you glo-rified God a little, dear friends, because of His covenant mercy? Go on glorifying Him. Did you serve Him well when you were young? Oh, not as well as you wish you had, I know, but serve Him better now in these riper days. Throw yourself into the glorifying of God.

The task of saving yourself is not yours, for Jesus has done it all. You may sing,

> A charge to keep I have,
> A God to glorify—

However, you will not need to add these lines:

> A never-dying soul to save,
> And fit it for the sky.

That soul of yours is saved: He "*hath saved us and called us with an holy call-ing*" (2 Timothy 1:9). You have been made fit for the sky by the blood of the ever-lasting covenant: "*Thanks [be] unto the Father, which hath made us meet to be par-takers of the inheritance of the saints in light*" (Colossians 1:12). All you have to do is to glorify the Lord who has saved you, *"set [your] feet upon a rock"* (Psalm 40:2), and established your ways. Now, glorify Him with all your might.

Are you getting gray, dear brother? With all your experience, you ought now to glorify the Lord more than ever. You will soon be up in the land of the living. Do not praise the Redeemer any longer in a poor feeble way, for you have but a short time to remain here. When we ascend above the clouds, how we will magnify our covenant God! I am sure I will not feel my powers extensive enough, even in heaven, to express my gratitude for His amazing love. I do not wonder that the poet said,

> Eternity's too short
> To utter half His praise.

People find fault with that expression and say it is an exaggeration. How would you have the poets write? Is not hyperbole allowable to them? I might even plead that it is not an extravagant exaggeration, for neither time nor eternity can utter all the praises of the infinite Jehovah.

> Oh, for a thousand tongues to sing
> Our great Redeemer's praise.

Covenant Glory

This will be the sweetest note of all our music: that He made with us *"an everlasting covenant, ordered in all things, and sure"* (2 Samuel 23:5), the covenant with *"that great shepherd of the sheep,"* by which every sheep was preserved, kept, and brought into the rich pastures of eternal glory. We will sing of covenant love in heaven. Our last song on earth and our first in paradise will be of the covenant, the covenant sealed with blood.

How I wish Christ's ministers would increasingly spread this covenant doctrine throughout the world. He who understands the two covenants has found the heart of all theology, but he who does not know the covenants knows next to nothing of the gospel of Christ. You would think, to hear some ministers preach, that salvation is all of works, that it is still uncertain who will be saved, that it is all a matter of *ifs* and *buts* and *maybes*. If you begin to give them *shalls* and *wills* and purposes and decrees and pledges and oaths and blood, they call you Calvinistic.

Why, this doctrine was true long before Calvin was born! Calvin loved it as we do, but it did not come from him. Paul had taught it long before—no, the Holy Spirit taught it to us in the Word, and therefore we hold to it. Bringing this truth again to the forefront will be a grand thing for the church.

By God's good grace, we must live this doctrine as well as preach it. May *"the God of peace, that brought again from the dead our Lord Jesus, that great shepherd of the sheep, through the blood of the everlasting covenant, make you perfect in every good work to do his will."* Then He will have glory through the covenant and through you, both now and forever.

6

PLEADING THE COVENANT OF GRACE

Have respect unto the covenant.
—Psalm 74:20

Themes the person who understands the science of pleading with God will
succeed in prayer. *"Put me in remembrance: let us plead together"*
(Isaiah 43:26) is His divine command. *"Come now, and let us reason together"*
(Isaiah 1:18) is His sacred invitation. *"Produce your cause, saith the LORD; bring
forth your strong reasons"* (Isaiah 41:21) is His accommodating direction as to
how to become victorious in supplication. Pleading is wrestling: arguments
are the holds, the feints, the throes, the struggles with which we grip and van-
quish the covenant angel, as Jacob did long ago until he received of God. (See
Genesis 32:24–28.)

The humble statement of our desires is not without its value, but to be able to
give reasons and arguments why God should hear us is to offer potent, prevailing
prayer. Among all the arguments that can be used in pleading with God, perhaps
there is none stronger than this: *"Have respect unto the covenant."* Like Goliath's

sword, we may say of it, *"There is none like that"* (1 Samuel 21:9). If we have God's word regarding something, we may well pray, "Do as You have said, for as a good man only needs to be reminded of his own word in order to be brought to keep it, even so is it with You, our faithful God. We only need to put You in remembrance of these things, because You will do them for us." Since He has given us more than His word—namely, His covenant, His solemn compact—we may surely, with the greatest composure of spirit, cry to Him, *"Have respect unto the covenant."* Then we may both hope patiently and wait quietly for His salvation.

I trust that I need not explain to you, for you are by this point well-grounded in the matter, that the covenant spoken of here is the covenant of grace. There is a covenant that we could not plead in prayer, the covenant of works, a covenant that destroys us, because we have broken it. The first Adam sinned, and the covenant was broken. We have continued in his perverseness, and that covenant condemns us. By the covenant of works none of us can be justified, because we still continue to break our portion of it and thus to bring upon ourselves wrath to the uttermost degree.

However, God has made a new covenant with the Second Adam, our federal Head, Jesus Christ our Lord. This covenant is without conditions, except such conditions as Christ has already fulfilled; *"an everlasting covenant, ordered in all things, and sure"* (2 Samuel 23:5); a better covenant that now consists only of promises, which are after this fashion:

I will be to them a God, and they shall be to me a people.   (Hebrews 8:10)

A new heart also will I give you, and a new spirit will I put within you.
(Ezekiel 36:26)

I will cleanse them from all their iniquity, whereby they have sinned against me; and I will pardon all their iniquities, whereby they have sinned, and whereby they have transgressed against me.   (Jeremiah 33:8)

This covenant of grace, which once had conditions in it, all of which our Lord Jesus fulfilled when He paid the penalty for our transgressions, made an end of sin, and brought in everlasting righteousness. Now the covenant is all of promise, and it consists of infallible and eternal *shalls* and *wills*, which remain the same forever.

We will first contemplate what is meant by the plea of our text: *"Have respect unto the covenant."* Next, we will consider from where it derives its force. Thirdly, we will discuss how and when we may plead it. Then, we will determine the practical inferences that we can draw from it.

The Meaning of the Plea

First of all, what is meant by the plea: *"Have respect unto the covenant"*? It must mean something like this: "Fulfill Your covenant, O God; let it not be null and void. You have said this and that; now do as You have said. You have been pleased by the solemn sanction of oath and blood to make this covenant with Your people. Now be pleased to keep it. *"Hath he said, and shall he not do it? or hath he spoken, and shall he not make it good?"* (Numbers 23:19). We are persuaded of Your faithfulness; let our eyes behold Your covenant commitments fulfilled."

This plea means, "Fulfill all the promises of the covenant," for indeed all the promises in the covenant are now available. *"For all the promises of God in* [Christ Jesus] *are yea, and in him Amen, unto the glory of God by us"* (2 Corinthians 1:20). They are all *"yea"* and *"Amen"* in Christ Jesus, to the glory of God by us; and I may say without being unscriptural that the covenant contains within its sacred charter every gracious word that has come from the Most High, either by the mouth of prophets or apostles, or by the lips of Jesus Christ Himself.

The meaning in this case would be: "Lord, keep Your promises concerning Your people. We are in need. Now, O Lord, fulfill Your promise that we *"shall not want any good thing"* (Psalm 34:10). Here is another of Your promises: *"When thou passest through the waters, I will be with thee"* (Isaiah 43:2). We are in rivers of trouble. Be with us now. Redeem Your promises to Your servants. Let them not stand in the Book as letters that mock us, but prove that You meant what You wrote and said. Let us see that You have power and will make good every jot and tittle of all You have spoken. Have You not said, *"Heaven and earth shall pass away, but my words shall not pass away"* (Matthew 24:35)? O Lord, have respect for the promises of Your covenant."

In the context of our text there is no doubt that the petitioner meant, "O Lord, prevent anything from turning aside Your promises." The people of God were then in a very terrible state. The temple was burnt, the assembly was broken up, the worship of God had ceased, and idolatrous emblems stood even in the

Holy Place where once the glory of God had been manifested. The supplicant was pleading, "Do not allow the power of the enemy to be so great as to frustrate Your purposes or to make Your promises void." Likewise, we may pray: "O Lord, do not allow me to endure such temptation that I would fall. Do not permit such affliction to come upon me that I would be destroyed. Did You not promise that no temptation would overtake us but such as we are able to endure and that, with the temptation, there would be a way of escape? (See 1 Corinthians 10:13.) Now, *"have respect unto the covenant,"* and so order Your providence that nothing will happen to us contrary to Your divine pledge."

This plea also means, "So order everything around us that the covenant may be fulfilled. Is Your church at a low ebb? Raise up in her midst men who will preach the gospel with power, who will be the means of her uplifting. Creator of men, Master of human hearts, You who can circumcise human lips to speak Your word with power, do this. Let Your covenant with Your church—that You will never leave her—be fulfilled. The kings of the earth are in Your hands. All events are controlled by You. You order all things, from the minute to the immense. Nothing, however small, is too small for Your purpose. Nothing, however great, is too great for Your rule. Manage everything so that, in the end, each promise of Your covenant will be fulfilled to all Your chosen people."

That, I think, is the meaning of the plea, *"Have respect unto the covenant."* "Lord, keep the covenant, and see that it is kept. Fulfill the promise, and prevent Your foes from doing evil to Your children." This is a most precious plea, assuredly.

The Source of the Power of the Plea

Let us see where this plea, *"Have respect unto the covenant,"* derives its forcefulness. Because it pleads the covenant, which is based in God's character, it has all of the power of the Almighty behind it.

The Truth of God

It derives its force, first, from the veracity of God. If a man makes a covenant, we expect a man to keep it; and a man who does not keep his covenant is not esteemed among his peers. If a man has given his word, that word is his bond. If a thing is solemnly signed and sealed, it becomes even more binding. The person who would go back on a covenant would be thought to have forfeited his character among men.

God forbid that we should ever think the Most High could be false to His word! It is not possible. He can do all things except this—He cannot lie. (See Numbers 23:19.) It is not possible that He could ever be untrue. He cannot even change: *"I am the LORD, I change not"* (Malachi 3:6). *"The gifts and calling of God are without repentance"* (Romans 11:29); His word is irrevocable. He will not break His covenant or alter anything that has gone out of His lips. (See Psalm 89:34.)

Thus, when we come before God in prayer for a covenant mercy, we have His truthfulness to support us. "O God, You must do this. You are sovereign: You can do as You will, but You have bound Yourself by bonds that hold Your majesty. You have said it, and it is not possible that You should go back on Your own word." How strong our faith ought to be when we have God's fidelity to lean on. What dishonor we do to our God by our weak faith, for it is virtually a suspicion of the faithfulness of our covenant God.

His Jealous Guarding of His Honor

Next, to support us in using this plea, we have God's sacred jealousy for His honor. He has revealed to us that He is a jealous God: *"The LORD, whose name is Jealous, is a jealous God"* (Exodus 34:14). He has great respect for His honor among the sons of men. Hence, this was Joshua's plea: *"What will the enemy say? 'And what wilt thou do unto thy great name?'"* (Joshua 7:9).

Now, if God's covenant could be trifled with, and if it could be proven that He had not kept the promise that He made to His chosen ones, it would not only be a dreadful thing for us, but it would bring grievous dishonor upon His name. That will never happen. God is too pure and holy, and He is completely too honorable ever to go back on the word that He has given to His servants.

If I feel that my strength is almost gone and I am about to fall into the pit, I may still be assured that He will not allow me to perish utterly, or else His honor would be stained, for He has said, *"They shall never perish, neither shall any man pluck them out of my hand"* (John 10:28). He could easily give me up to my enemies so far as my just deserts are concerned, for I deserve to be destroyed by them. However, His honor is engaged to save the lowliest of His people, and He has said, *"I give unto them eternal life"* (verse 28). He will not, therefore, for His honor's sake, allow me to be the prey of the Adversary, but will preserve me, even me, unto the end, so that I may be found blameless in the day of my Lord. (See 1 Corinthians 1:8.) Here is a solid foundation for faith.

The Enduring Quality of the Covenant

The next reflection that should greatly strengthen us is the enduring character of the covenant. This venerable covenant was no transaction of yesterday; before the earth ever existed, this covenant was made. We may not refer to first or last in regard to God, but humanly speaking, we may express it this way: the covenant of grace was God's first thought. Although we usually put the covenant of works first since it was revealed first in order of time, yet the covenant of grace is indeed the older of the two. God's people were not chosen yesterday, but *"before the foundation of the world"* (Ephesians 1:4). The Lamb, slain to ratify that covenant, although slain many centuries ago, was actually slain in the divine purpose from before the foundation of the world. (See Revelation 13:8.) It is an ancient covenant: there is no other covenant as ancient.

It is to God a covenant that He holds in high esteem. It is not one of His light thoughts, not one of those thoughts that led Him to create the morning dew that melts before the day has run its course, or to make the clouds that light up the setting sun with glory but which soon lose their radiance. Rather, it is one of His great thoughts; yes, it is His eternal thought, the thought out of His own innermost being—this covenant of grace.

And because it is so ancient, and to God a matter so important, when we come to Him with this plea in our mouths, we must not stagger *"at the promise of God through unbelief"* (Romans 4:20). Instead, we may open our mouths wide, for He will assuredly fill them. "Here is Your covenant, O God. By Your own purposeful, sovereign will, You did ordain of old a covenant in which Your very heart is laid bare and Your love, which is Yourself, is manifested. O God, have respect for it. Do as You have said, and fulfill Your promise to Your people."

The Endorsement of God's Word

Nor is this all. It is but the beginning. In one chapter or even one book, I would not have the space to show you all the reasons that give force to the plea, but here is one more. The covenant has upon it a solemn endorsement. There is the stamp of God's own word—that is enough. The very word that created the universe is the word that spoke the covenant. But, as if that were not sufficient, seeing we are so prone to unbelief, God has added to it His oath, and *"because he could swear by no greater, he sware by himself"* (Hebrews 6:13). It would be blasphemy to dream that the Eternal could be perjured. He has set His oath to His covenant, in order *"that by two immutable things, in which it was impossible for God to lie,"* He might give to the heirs of grace *"strong consolation"* (verse 18).

Sealed with the Blood of the Lamb

Moreover, this venerable covenant, having been confirmed by God's oath, was sealed with blood. Jesus died to ratify it. His heart's blood was sprinkled on that Magna Charta of the grace of God to His people. It is a covenant that the just God must now keep. Jesus has fulfilled our side of it by having executed to the letter all the demands of God upon man. Our Surety and Substitute simultaneously kept the law and suffered all that was due by His people on account of their breach of it. Now, will not the Lord be true to His own word and the everlasting Father be faithful to His own Son? How can He refuse to His Son *"the joy that* [He] *set before him"* (Hebrews 12:2) and the reward that He promised Him? *"He shall see his seed. He shall see of the travail of his soul, and shall be satisfied"* (Isaiah 53:10–11).

Beloved, the faithfulness of God to His covenant is not so much a matter between you and God as it is between Christ and God. It now stands that Christ, as the unblemished Advocate, puts in His claim before the throne of infinite justice for the salvation of every soul for whom He shed His blood, and He must have what He has purchased. Oh, what confidence there is in this! The rights of the Son, blended with the love and the veracity of the Father, cause the everlasting covenant to be *"ordered in all things, and sure"* (2 Samuel 23:5).

The Unfailing Nature of the Covenant

Further, keep in mind that nothing in the covenant has ever failed up until this very moment. The Lord's word has been tried by ten thousand times ten thousand of His people. They have been in perplexing emergencies and serious difficulties. Yet, it has never been reported in the gates of Zion that the promise has been invalidated; neither have any said that the covenant is null and void. Ask those who were before you, who passed through deeper waters than you. Ask the martyrs who gave up their lives for their Master, "Was He with you to the end?"

The peaceful smiles upon their faces while enduring the most painful deaths were evident testimonies that God is true. Their joyous songs when being burned alive, their exaltation even while on the rack, and the clapping of their hands and their high praises when rotting away in loathsome dungeons—all these have proved how faithful the Lord has been.

And have you not heard with your own ears the testimony of God's people as they were dying? They were in conditions in which they could not have been sustained by mere imagination or buoyed up by delirium, and yet they were as joyful as if their dying day had been their wedding day. Death is too solemn a matter for a man to sustain a masquerade at that time. What did your wife say in death? Or your mother, who is now with God? Or your child, who had learned the Savior's love? Can you not recall their testimonies even now? I think I hear some of them. Among the things of earth that are most like the joys of heaven, I think this is one of the foremost—the joy of departing saints when they already hear the voices of angels hovering near, when they attempt to tell us in broken language of the joys that are bursting in upon them, as their sight is blinded by the excess of brightness and their hearts are enraptured with the bliss that floods them. Oh, it has been sweet to see true believers depart from this world!

I mention these things now, not merely to refresh your memories, but to establish your faith in God. He has been true so many times and never false. Should we now experience any difficulty in depending on His covenant? No, by all these many years in which the faithfulness of God has been put to the test and has never failed, let us be confident that He will still regard us, and let us pray boldly, "*Have respect unto the covenant.*" Remember, "As it was in the beginning, it is now and ever shall be, world without end." It will be to the last believer as it was with the first. The testimony of the last soldier of the host will be this: "*According to all that he promised: there hath not failed one word of all his good promise*" (1 Kings 8:56).

The Gift of Faith in the Covenant

I have one more reflection here. Our God has taught many of us to trust in His name. We were long in learning the lesson, and nothing but Omnipotence could have made us willing to "*walk by faith, not by sight*" (2 Corinthians 5:7). With much patience the Lord brought us at last to have no reliance on ourselves, but only on Him. Now we depend solely on His faithfulness and His truth. Is that your case, beloved? What then? Do you think that God has given you this faith to mock you? Do you believe that He taught you to trust in His name and brought you thus far to put you to shame? Has His Holy Spirit given you confidence in a lie? Has He developed in you a false faith? God forbid! Our God is no demon that would delight in the misery that a groundless confidence would be sure to bring to us.

If you have faith, He gave it to you. (See Ephesians 2:8.) He who gave it to you knows His own gift and will honor it. He has never been false yet, even to the feeblest faith. If your faith is great, you will find Him greater than your faith, even when your faith is at its greatest. Therefore, "*be of good cheer*" (Matthew 14:27). The fact that you believe should encourage you to say, "Now, O Lord, I have come to rest upon You; can You fail me? I, poor worm, know no confidence but in Your dear name; will You forsake me? I have no refuge but Your wounds, O Jesus, no hope but in Your atoning sacrifice, no light but in Your light; can You cast me off?"

It is not possible that the Lord would cast away one who thus trusts Him. "*Can a woman forget her sucking child, that she should not have compassion on the son of her womb? yea, they may forget, yet will I not forget thee*" (Isaiah 49:15). Can any of us forget our children when they fondly trust us and are dependent on us? No, we cannot, and neither can our heavenly Father. The Lord is no monster: He is tender and full of compassion, faithful and true. Moreover, Jesus is our "*friend that sticketh closer than a brother*" (Proverbs 18:24). The very fact that He has given us faith in His covenant should help us to plead, "*Have respect unto the covenant.*"

Applications of the Covenant Plea

Having thus shown you, dear friends, the meaning of the plea and the source from which it derives its power, I will now discuss some of the practical considerations in pleading, "*Have respect unto the covenant*," such as how and when that covenant may be pleaded.

When Being Convicted of Sin

First, it may be pleaded when you are under a sense of sin, when your soul feels the weight of its guiltiness. The author of the book of Hebrews reiterated the words of Jeremiah when he wrote this about the covenant of grace:

For this is the covenant that I will make with the house of Israel after those days, saith the Lord; I will put my laws into their mind, and write them in their hearts: and I will be to them a God, and they shall be to me a people: and they shall not teach every man his neighbour, and every man his brother, saying, Know the Lord: for all shall know me, from the least to the greatest. For I will be merciful to their unrighteousness, and their sins and their iniquities will I remember no more. (Hebrews 8:10–12)

Now, dear friend, suppose that you are under a sense of sin, a burden of conviction. Perhaps something has revived in you a recollection of past guilt, or it may be that you have sadly stumbled this very day. Satan is whispering, "You will surely be destroyed, for you have sinned." Go to your heavenly Father, open your Bible to this passage, put your finger on that twelfth verse, and say, "Lord, You have in infinite, boundless, inconceivable mercy entered into covenant with me, a poor sinner, seeing that I believe in the name of Jesus. Now I plead with You, *'Have respect unto [Your] covenant.'* You have said, *'I will be merciful to their unrighteousness.'* O God, be merciful to mine. *'Their sins and their iniquities will I remember no more.'* Lord, remember no more my sins; forget forever my iniquity." This is the way to use the covenant: when you are under the conviction of sin, plead the clause in the covenant that meets your case.

When Desiring Holiness

But suppose, beloved brother or sister, you are striving to overcome inward corruption, with the intense desire that holiness be developed in you. Then, read the covenant again as you find it in the book of Jeremiah. This is just another version of the same covenant of grace:

This shall be the covenant that I will make with the house of Israel; after those days, saith the LORD, I will put my law in their inward parts, and write it in their hearts. (Jeremiah 31:33)

Now, can you not plead that and say, "Lord, Your commandments upon stone are holy, but I forget them and break them. O my God, write them on the fleshy tablets of my heart. Come now, and make me holy; transform me; write Your will upon my very soul, so that I may live it out and, from the warm impulses of my heart, serve You as You would be served. *'Have respect unto the covenant,'* and sanctify Your servant."

When Resisting Temptation

Or, suppose that you desire to be upheld when you are under strong temptation, lest you should slip back and return to your old ways. Take the covenant as you find it in the thirty-second chapter of Jeremiah. Meditate on these verses and learn them by heart, for they may be a great help to you one of these days.

And they shall be my people, and I will be their God: and I will give them one heart, and one way, that they may fear me for ever, for the good of them, and of their children after them: and I will make an everlasting covenant with them, that I will not turn away from them, to do them good; but I will put my fear in their hearts, that they shall not depart from me. (Jeremiah 32:38–40)

Now, "*come boldly unto the throne of grace*" (Hebrews 4:15), and say, "O Lord, I am almost gone, and people are telling me I will inevitably fall. But, O my Lord and Master, here stands Your word. Put a godly fear of You in my heart, and fulfill Your promise, so that I will not depart from You." This is the sure road to final perseverance.

In Any Kind of Need

In a similar way, I might take you through all the various needs of God's people and show that, in seeking to have them supplied, they may aptly cry, "*Have respect unto the covenant.*" For instance, suppose you were in great distress of mind and needed comfort. You could go to Him with that covenant promise, "*As one whom his mother comforteth, so will I comfort you*" (Isaiah 66:13). Go to Him with that and say, "Lord, comfort Your servant."

If there happens to be trouble plaguing the church, how sweet it is that we are able to go to the Lord and say, "Your covenant says this: '*The gates of hell shall not prevail against* [Your church]' (Matthew 16:18). O Lord, it seems as though they would prevail. Interpose Your strength, and save Your church."

Whenever you are seeking the conversion of the ungodly, desiring to see sinners saved, and the world seems so dark, look at our text again—the entire verse—"*Have respect unto the covenant: for the dark places of the earth are full of the habitations of cruelty*" (Psalm 74:20). To this you might add, "But, Lord, You have said that '*the earth shall be filled with the knowledge of the glory of the* LORD, *as the waters cover the sea*' (Habakkuk 2:14), and that '*all flesh shall see the salvation* of God' (Luke 3:6). '*Have respect unto the covenant,*' Lord. Help our missionaries, speed Your gospel, command the mighty angel to fly through the midst of heaven to preach the everlasting gospel to all who dwell on earth, to every nation and kindred and tongue and people." (See Revelation 14:6.) Why, this is a grand missionary prayer: "*Have respect unto the covenant.*"

Beloved, the covenant plea is a two-edged sword, to be used in all conditions of strife, and it is a holy balm of Gilead that will heal all conditions of suffering.

The Obvious Inference of the Plea

And now, let us conclude with this last question, What is the obvious, practical inference for our lives from this plea, "*Have respect unto the covenant*"? Why, is it not that, if we ask God to have respect unto it, we ought to have respect for the covenant ourselves? There are several aspects of respect for the covenant that we each need to develop in our own lives.

A Grateful Respect

First, we need to have a grateful respect for it. Bless the Lord that He ever condescended to enter into covenant with you. What could He see in you even to give you a promise, much more to make a covenant with you? Blessed be His dear name that He condescended to covenant eternally with sinners such as we are. This is the sweet theme of our hymns on earth, and it will be the subject of our songs in heaven.

A Believing Respect

Next, we need to have a believing respect for it. If it is God's covenant, do not dishonor it with your doubt. The "*everlasting covenant* [stands], *ordered in all things, and sure*" (2 Samuel 23:5). May you be like Abraham, who "*staggered not at the promise of God through unbelief; but was strong in faith, giving glory to God*" (Romans 4:20).

> His every work of grace is strong
> As that which built the skies;
> The voice that rolls the stars along
> Speaks all the promises.

A Joyful Respect

Next, we need to have a joyful respect for the covenant. Get out your harps, and join in praise with David: *"Although my house be not so with God; yet he hath made with me an everlasting covenant, ordered in all things, and sure"* (2 Samuel 23:5). Here is enough to make a heaven in our hearts while we are yet on earth: the Lord has entered into a covenant of grace and peace with us, and He will bless us forever.

A Jealous Respect

Then, we need to have a jealous respect for it. Never allow the covenant of works to be mixed with the covenant of grace. Hate that preaching—I say no less than that—hate the preaching that does not discriminate between the covenant of works and the covenant of grace, for it is deadly preaching and damning preaching. You must always draw a straight, clear line between what is of man and what is of God, for *"cursed be the man that trusteth in man, and maketh flesh his arm"* (Jeremiah 17:5).

If you have begun with the Spirit under this covenant, do not think of being made perfect in the flesh under another covenant. Be holy under the precepts of the heavenly Father, but do not be legalistic under the taskmaster's lash. Do not return to the bondage of the law, for *"ye are not under the law, but under grace"* (Romans 6:14). *"Stand fast therefore in the liberty wherewith Christ hath made us free, and be not entangled again with the yoke of bondage"* (Galatians 5:1).

A Practical Respect

Finally, we need to have a practical respect for the covenant. Let others see that the covenant of grace, while it is your reliance, is also your delight. Be ready to speak of it to others. Be ready to show that the effect of its grace upon you is one that is worthy of God, since it has a purifying effect upon your life. *"Every man that hath this hope in him purifieth himself, even as he is pure"* (1 John 3:3). Thus, *"have respect unto the covenant"* by conducting yourself in a way that one of God's elect should conduct himself.

The covenant says, *"Then will I sprinkle clean water upon you, and ye shall be clean: from all your filthiness, and from all your idols, will I cleanse you"* (Ezekiel 36:25). Do not love idols, then. Be clean, you covenanted ones.

May the Lord preserve you and make His covenant to be your boast on earth and your song forever in heaven. Oh, may the Lord bring us all into the bonds of His covenant and give us a simple faith in His dear Son, for that is the mark of the heirs of the covenant!

KEY TO HOLINESS

CONTENTS

1. Perfection in Faith..109
2. Threefold Sanctification 121
3. Perfect Sanctification..139

Appendices

    Appendix A 157
    Appendix B 159

1

PERFECTION IN FAITH

The LORD will perfect that which concerneth me: thy mercy, O LORD, endureth for ever: forsake not the works of thine own hands.
—Psalm 138:8

For by one offering he hath perfected for ever them that are sanctified.
—Hebrews 10:14

Think for a moment about the preceding Scriptures. In the first Scripture, Psalm 138:8, David went from bold faith to meek prayer. After having said in confidence, *"The LORD will perfect that which concerneth me,"* he was inclined to ask the Lord, *"Forsake not the works of thine own hands,"* sinking, as it were, to a lower note in the scale of music. We, also, are often inclined in this way. We often behold perfection in the dim obscurity of the future, like the sun veiled behind a cloud. Our faith rests on it as a thing unseen at the present time; our hearts yearn for it as an inheritance still in reserve for us.

Yet, this perfection is brought near to us as a thing accomplished, as an ever present fact, whose eternal reality shines upon us with unclouded luster. It is because of this that I quote the verse, "*By one offering* [our Lord Jesus Christ] *hath perfected for ever them that are sanctified*" (Hebrews 10:14). Is it not incredibly pleasing to observe that what is presented to us in one part of Scripture as a matter of *faith*, is stated in another place as a matter of *fact*? He has perfected us forever.

I have been turning this text over and over in my mind, and praying about it, and looking into it, and seeking illumination from the Holy Spirit; but it has taken me a long time to be clear about its exact meaning. It is very easy to select a meaning, and then to say, "That is what the text means"; and it is very easy also to look at something that lies upon the surface. However, I am not quite so sure that, after several hours of meditation, any believer would be able to ascertain what is the Spirit's mind in this particular verse, "*By one offering* [Christ] *hath perfected for ever them that are sanctified.*"

When I was trying to find out what this meant, I thought I would simply read the chapters before it, and if I should happen to find any word that seemed to be the key to this verse, I would then, under the Spirit's guidance, seek to open this lock and mystery with the key that was there provided for me. Well, I read the chapters in Hebrews, and I did find something that seemed to explain the meaning of this verse. Now, as I write this chapter, I will try to show you what I think it means; and then I think it will stand out in a very clear and glorious light.

Sanctified as a Child of God

First, I will discuss the condition of the child of God—what he is. He is a sanctified person. The term *sanctified* is wholly intended for the children of God; they are described as sanctified people. What does this mean?

We usually say there are two meanings to the term *sanctified*. One is "set apart." God has set apart His people from before the foundation of the world (see Ephesians 1:4), to be His chosen and peculiar inheritance (see Psalm 33:12), and we are sanctified by God the Father. The other meaning implies not the decree of the Father, but the work of the Holy Spirit. We are sanctified in Christ Jesus, by the Holy Spirit, when He subdues our corruptions, imparts graces to us, and leads us onward in the divine walk and life of faith. Even so, the verse here, I think, includes both of these senses; and I must try, if I can, to find an illustration that will embrace them both.

What was the apostle writing about? In the ninth chapter of Hebrews, he wrote about the tabernacle, the candlestick, the table, the showbread, the sanctuary, the golden censer,[1] the ark of the covenant overlaid with gold, and the golden pot of manna (see Hebrews 9:2–4). He also wrote about priests, and about priestly things and holy things (see verses 6–7). He declared that all these were sanctified things, but even though they were sanctified, they still needed to be made perfect by the sprinkling of blood (see verse 7).

Now, I believe that the sanctification referred to in our text is to be understood in this sense. There were certain golden vessels that were used in the sanctuary, that were never used for anything else except the service of God. They were set apart; they were made holy; and they were kept strictly to be the vessels of the sanctuary of the Lord God. They were sanctified things.

In the sanctuary, there were people who did nothing else but wait upon the Lord. These people were chosen, and then they were prepared. God chose the tribe of Levi, and out of the tribe of Levi, He chose the house of Aaron. The members of Aaron's family were consecrated to their offices. They underwent certain ceremonies and various washings, and so they were made ceremonially holy; and these priests were therefore sanctified people because they were set apart, dedicated, and reserved for the special service of the Lord God. Now, that is just what you and I are, and what we ought to be: we are sanctified persons. That is to say, we are chosen by God to be the particular vessels that He will use in pouring out His mercy, and to be the special priests whom He will employ in His divine worship in this world.

No man had any right to take wine, for his own drinking, out of the golden cups of the sanctuary. If he did so, he did it to his own destruction—witness what happened to Belshazzar. (See Daniel 5.) He took the cups and the golden candlesticks, and so forth, and used them in his debaucheries, and lo! he was swept away, and the handwriting on the wall foretold his doom. In the same manner, Christian men are not to be used for anything but for God. They are a people set apart (see Psalm 4:3); they are vessels of mercy (see Romans 9:23); they are not for the devil's use, not for their own use, not for the world's use, but for their Master's use. He has purposefully made them to be used entirely, solely, and wholly for Him.

Now, that is what is meant in this text by the word *sanctified*. We are sanctified people, set apart for God's use, consecrated just as the vessels, the cups,

---

1. Censer: a vessel for burning incense.

the candlesticks, the tables, and the altars of the sanctuary, were sanctified unto God and set apart for His service. We are priests, and we are sanctified, but not because of any holiness in our character, just as there were some of those early priests who were not holy in their character.

My text does not concern character. Rather, it concerns our position in the sight of God. We are not perfect in character, any one of us; we are only perfect in position. There were two men who officiated as priests before God, namely, the sons of Eli, who committed sin and iniquity before God. (See 1 Samuel 2:22.) And yet, they were set apart for God's service, for when they offered the sacrifices as priests, they were officially accepted as being sanctified persons because they had been washed with water and sprinkled with blood.

Now, dear reader, the children of God are sanctified people, sanctified to offer spiritual sacrifices to God through Jesus Christ, and we have no right to do anything else but serve God. "What," you say, "am I not to attend to my business?" Yes, and you are to serve God in your business. "Am I not to look after my family?" Assuredly, you are, and you are to serve God in looking after your family, but still you are to be set apart.

You are not to wear the white robe nor the breastplate (see Exodus 28:4), but still you are to think of yourself as being as much a priest as if the breastplate were on your breast, and the white robe about your loins; for you are *"priests unto God and his Father"* (Revelation 1:6). He has made you a peculiar generation and a royal priesthood (see 1 Peter 2:9), and He has set you apart for Himself (see Psalm 4:3).

Now, I think that this first point has given you an idea of what the rest must mean. I have already hinted at what I think is the sense of the text. I have explained clearly enough, I suppose, in what sense God's people are sanctified people, as understood in this verse. They are chosen and set apart and reserved to be God's instruments and God's servants, and, therefore, they are sanctified.

Perfected in Christ's Blood

Now comes the second thing. *"He hath perfected for ever them that are sanctified"* (Hebrews 10:14). In what sense are we to understand that Christ has perfected these who are sanctified? Why, in the sense of what Christ has done for them. When the golden vessels were brought into the temple or into the sanctuary, they were sanctified the very first moment that they were dedicated to God. No one dared to employ them for anything except holy uses. Even so, they were not perfect. What did they need, then, to make them perfect? They needed to have blood sprinkled on them; and, as soon as the blood was sprinkled on them, those golden vessels were perfect vessels, officially perfect. God accepted them as being holy and perfect things, and they stood in His sight as instruments of an acceptable worship.

It was the same with the Levites and the priests. As soon as they were set apart to their office—as soon as they were born, in fact—they were consecrated; they belonged to God; they were His peculiar priesthood. However, they were not perfect until they had passed through many washings, and had had the blood sprinkled upon them. Then God looked upon them, in their official priestly character, as being perfect. I repeat, they were not perfect in character; they were only perfect officially, perfect in the sight of God, and they stood before Him to offer sacrifice as acceptably as if they had been as pure as Adam himself.

Now, then, how does this refer to us, and what is the meaning of this text, that *"by one offering he hath perfected for ever them that are sanctified"* (Hebrews 10:14)? Turn back to Hebrews 9:6–7, where you will read,

> *Now when these things were thus ordained, the priests went always into the first tabernacle, accomplishing the service of God. But into the second went the high priest alone once every year, not without blood, which he offered for himself, and for the errors of the people.*

Note that the first meaning of my text is this: the child of God is a priest, and as a priest he is sanctified to enter within the veil. He is now permitted to go into the place that was once within the veil, but that is not so now because the veil is torn in two. (See Matthew 27:51.)

The high priest, on the contrary, could not go within the veil, because he was not perfect. He had to be sprinkled with the blood, and that made him officially perfect. It would not make him perfect merely to put on the breastplate, or to wear the ephod; he was not perfect until the blood had been sprinkled upon him, and then he went within the veil. Even so, when the next year came around, he was not fit to go within the veil until blood was sprinkled on him again. The same would happen every year, for although he was always a sanctified man, he was not always, officially, a perfect man. He had to be sprinkled with blood again. And so, year after year, the high priest who went within the veil needed afresh to be made perfect, in order to obtain access to God.

A Position of Perfection

Therefore, this is one sense of Hebrews 10:14. The apostle said that we who are the priests of God have a right as priests to go to God's mercy seat, which is within the veil; but it would mean our death to go there unless we were perfect. However, we are perfect, for the blood of Christ has been sprinkled on us, and, therefore, our standing before God is the standing of perfection. Our standing, in our own conscience, is imperfection, just as the character of the priest might be imperfect. But that has nothing to do with it. Our standing in the sight of God is a standing of perfection; and when He sees the blood—as of old, when the destroying angel passed over Israel (see Exodus 12:3–13)—so this day, when He sees the blood, God passes over our sins and accepts us at the throne of His mercy, as if we were perfect.

Therefore, let us come boldly to His throne. (See Hebrews 4:16.)

Let us draw near with a true heart in full assurance of faith, having our hearts sprinkled from an evil conscience, and our bodies washed with pure water.
(Hebrews 10:22)

In this twenty-second verse of Hebrews 10, the apostle brought in one infer-ence that I have just drawn from my text: in having access to God, perfection is absolutely necessary. God cannot talk with an imperfect being. He could talk with Adam in the Garden, but He could not talk with you or with me, even in Paradise itself, as imperfect creatures.

How, then, are we to have fellowship with God, and access to His throne? Why, simply through the blood of Christ, which *"hath perfected for ever them that are sanctified"* (Hebrews 10:14). As a consequence of His offering, we can come boldly to the throne of heavenly grace, and may come boldly in all our times of need. (See Hebrews 4:16.) And, what is better still, we are always perfect, always fit to come to the throne, whatever our doubts, whatever our sins.

I say this not of the priest's character; we have nothing to do with that at present. We come before God in our position, in our standing, not in our char-acter; and therefore, we may come as perfect men at all times, knowing that God sees no sin in Jacob, and no iniquity in Israel. (See Micah 3:8.) For in this sense, Christ has perfected forever every consecrated vessel of His mercy.

Is this not a delightful thought, that when I come before the throne of God, I feel that I am a sinner, but God does not look upon me as one? When I approach Him to offer my thanksgivings, I feel that I am unworthy in myself, but I am not unworthy in that official standing in which He has placed me. As a sanctified and perfected being in Christ, I have the blood upon me. God regards me in my sacrifice, in my worship, yes, and in myself, too, as being perfect.

Oh, how joyful this is! And there is no need to repeat this perfecting a second time. It is an everlasting perfection; it allows a constant access to the throne of heavenly grace. That is one meaning of the text.

Perfected Forever

A little further on, the apostle, in Hebrews 9:21, wrote, *"He sprinkled with blood both the tabernacle, and all the vessels of the ministry."* They were all sanctified vessels, as you know, but they were not perfect vessels until they were sprinkled with the blood.

And almost all things are by the law purged with blood; and without shedding of blood is no remission. It was therefore necessary that the patterns of things in the heavens should be purified with these; but the heavenly things themselves with better sacrifices than these. (Hebrews 9:22–23)

Now, the vessels of the sanctuary, as I have said, were sanctified the moment they were put there, but they were not perfect. God could not therefore accept any sacrifice that was touched with the golden tongs or that lay upon the bronze altar, as long as those golden tongs and the bronze altar were imperfect. What was done to make them perfect? Why, they were sprinkled with blood; but they had to be sprinkled with blood many, many times—once, twice, three times, multitudes of times—because they continually needed to be made perfect.

You and I, if we are consecrated people, are presently like the vessels of the sanctuary. Sometimes we are like the censer: God fills us with joy, and then the smoke of incense ascends from us. Sometimes we are like the slaughter knife that the priest used: we are enabled to deny our lusts, to deny ourselves, and to put the knife to the neck of the victim. And sometimes we are like the altar: upon us God is pleased to lay a sacrifice of labor, and there it smokes acceptably to heaven. We are made like sanctified things of His house.

But, beloved, although we are sanctified and He has chosen us to be the vessels of His spiritual temple, we are not perfect until the blood is on us. Yet, blessed be His name, that blood has been put upon us once, and we are perfected for eternity. Is it not delightful to think that when God uses us in His service, He could not use unhallowed instruments? The Lord God is so pure that He could not use anything but a perfect tool to work with.

"Then surely He could never use you or me," you say. No! Do you not see? The blood is on us, and we are the sanctified instruments of His grace; moreover, we are the perfect instruments of His grace through the blood of Jesus. Oh! I take delight in just thinking about it! I am imperfect in my own estimation and, rightly enough, in yours; yet, when God makes use of me, He does not make use of an imperfect man. No, He looks upon me as being perfect in Christ, and then He says, "I can use this tool. I could not put My hand to an unholy thing, but I will look upon him as being perfected forever in Christ, and therefore I can use him."

Oh, Christian, do try to digest this precious thought. It has indeed been precious to my soul since I first laid hold of it. You cannot tell what God may do with you, because if He uses you at all, He does not use you as a sinner. Rather, He uses you as a sanctified person; no, more than that, He uses you as a perfect person. I will repeat it: I do not see how a holy God could use an unholy instrument; but He puts the blood on us, and then He makes us perfect—He perfects us for eternity—and then He uses us.

And so, we may see the work of God carried on by men who we think are imperfect, but, in reality, we never see God doing any of His deeds except with a perfect instrument. If you were to ask me how He has done it, I would tell you that all His consecrated ones, all whom He has sanctified to His use, He has first of all perfected forever through the sacrifice of Jesus Christ.

A Perfect Justification before God

And now we will examine one more thought, and then I will have given you the full meaning of Hebrews 10:14. In Hebrews 7:19, there is a word that is a key to the meaning of my text, and that helped me through it:

*For the law made nothing perfect, but the bringing in of a better hope **did**; by the which we draw nigh unto God.*   (emphasis added)

Compare Hebrews 10:1:

The law having a shadow of good things to come, and not the very image of the things, can never with those sacrifices which they offered year by year continually make the comers thereunto perfect.

There is the word *perfect*, which is implied in the verse that follows: *"For then* [if they had been perfect] *would they not have ceased to be offered?"* (verse 2). Why offer any more, if you are already a perfect man? Because, if the sacrifice is perfect, *"the worshippers once purged should have had no more conscience of sins"* (verse 2).

Note that the Jewish sacrifice was never intended to make the Jews' moral character any better, and it did not. It had no effect upon what we call a person's sanctification. All the sacrifice dealt with was his justification; and after that, the perfection would be sought. The perfection is not of sanctification, which the Arminian[2] talks about. Rather, it is the perfection of official standing, as a person stands justified before God.

Now, that is the meaning of the word *perfect* here. It does not mean that the sacrifice did not make the man perfectly holy, perfectly moral, and so forth, because the sacrifice had no tendency to do that, for it was quite another matter. Rather, it means that it did not perfectly make him justified in his own conscience and in the sight of God, because he had to come and offer again.

Suppose a man who is troubled in his conscience comes sighing to the temple, and he must speak to the priest. He says to the priest, "I have committed such and such a sin."

"Ah!" says the priest. "You will never have any ease in your conscience unless you bring a sin offering." So the man brings a sin offering, and it is offered, and the man sees it burn, and he goes away. He has faith—faith in the great Sin Offering that is to come—and his conscience is easy.

A day or two later, the same feelings arise; and what does he do? He goes to the priest again. "Ah!" says the priest. "You must bring another offering; you must

---

2. Arminian: one who is opposed to the absolute predestination of strict Calvinism and who maintains the possibility of salvation for all.

bring a trespass offering." So, he brings the trespass offering, and his conscience grows easier for a time; but the more his conscience comes alive, the more he sees the unsatisfactory character of the offering he brings. At last, he says, "I am so uneasy; how I wish that I could have a sacrifice every hour! For when I put my hand on the head of the victim, I feel so happy; when I come to see it slaughtered, and the blood flowing, I feel so easy; but I do not feel perfect. I will go up to the temple again, so that I may live."

So he sees a lamb slaughtered in the morning, and tears of joy are in his eyes. "Oh!" he says. "I have seen that lamb; and when I saw the blood of that lamb flowing, I felt so glad." Noon comes. "Ah!" he says. "My sins arise again; where can I get relief for my conscience?" So off he goes to the temple. And there is another lamb in the evening, because God well knew that the sacrifices were themselves imperfect—only a shadow of the great Substance—and that His people would need to have the service renewed, not only every year, but every day—no, every morning and every evening.

But now, beloved, behold the glory of Christ Jesus as revealed to us in our text. Those sacrifices could not *"make the comers thereunto perfect"* (Hebrews 10:1). They could not feel in their own conscience that they were perfectly justified, and they wanted fresh offerings; but today we see the slaughtered Lamb on Calvary. It may have been just yesterday that you rejoiced in Him, but you can rejoice in Him again today.

Years ago, I sought Him, and I found Him. I do not want another Lamb. I do not want another sacrifice. I can still see that blood flowing, and I can feel continually that I have no more consciousness of sin. The sins are gone. I have no more remembrance of them; I am purged from them; and as I see the perpetually flowing blood of Calvary, and the ever rising merits of His glorious passion, I am compelled to rejoice in this fact, that He has perfected me forever. (See Hebrews 10:14.) He has made me completely perfect through His sacrifice.

And now, Christian, try to lay hold of this meaning of the text. Christ has set your conscience at ease forever; and if it disturbs you, recall that it has no cause to do so, if you are a believer in Christ. For has He not given you that which will put away all consciousness of sin? Oh, rejoice! His sacrifice has purged you so entirely that you may sit down and rest. You may sing with the poet—

Turn, then, my soul unto thy rest;
The merits of thy great High Priest

Speak peace and liberty.
Trust in his efficacious blood,
Nor fear thy banishment from God,
Since Jesus died for thee.

Look again at Hebrews 10:14. Once again, I am going to repeat the same things, lest I should not be quite understood. We, as believers, cannot have access to God unless it is on the footing of perfection; for God cannot walk and talk with imperfect creatures. But, we are perfect—not in character, of course, for we are still sinners—but we are perfected through the blood of Jesus Christ, so that God can allow us as perfected creatures to have access to Him. We may come boldly to the throne of grace (see Hebrews 4:16), because, being sprinkled with the blood, God does not look on us as unholy and unclean. Otherwise, He could not allow us to come to His mercy seat. However, He looks upon us as being perfected forever through the one sacrifice of Christ.

That is one thing. Another is this: we are the vessels of God's temple; He has chosen us to be like the golden pots of His sanctuary. Those vessels, remember, were made perfect by being sprinkled with blood. God could never accept a worship offered to Him in unholy vessels. Likewise, God could not accept the praise that comes from your unholy heart; He could not accept the song that springs from your uncircumcised lips, nor the faith that arises from your doubting soul, unless He had taken the great precaution to sprinkle you with the blood of Christ. And now, whatever He uses you for, He uses you as a perfect instrument, regarding you as being perfect in Christ Jesus. That, again, is the meaning of the text, and the same meaning, only a different phase of it.

The last meaning is that the sacrifices of the Jews did not give believing Jews peace of mind for any length of time; they had to come again and again and again, because they felt that those sacrifices did not give them a perfect justification before God. But, behold, beloved, you and I are complete in Jesus (Colossians 2:10). We have no need for any other sacrifice. All others we disclaim. *"He hath perfected [us] for ever"* (Hebrews 10:14). We may set our consciences at ease, because we are truly, really, and everlastingly accepted in Him. *"He hath perfected for ever them that are sanctified"* (verse 14).

Now, what is left, except to ask you, "Are you a sanctified person?" I have known a man to say sometimes to a believer, "Well, you look so sanctified. Ah! You must be one of those sanctified people!" Well, if they said that to me, I would reply, "I wish you would prove it, then." What can be more holy than to be a sanctified man?

Let me ask you, then, "Are you sanctified?" You may say, "I feel so sinful." But I do not ask you that. Rather, I ask you whether you are set apart to God's service. Can you say,

> Dear Lord, I give myself away,
> 'Tis all that I can do?

Can you say, "Take me just as I am, and make use of me; I desire to be wholly thine"? Do you feel that for you to live is Christ (see Philippians 1:21); that there is not any reason for which you are living except for Christ; that Christ is the great aim of your ambition, the great objective of all your labors; that you are like Samson, a Nazarite, consecrated to God? Oh, then, remember that you are perfected in Christ. (See Hebrews 10:14.)

But, dear reader, if you are not sanctified to God in this sense—if you live unto yourself, unto pleasure, and unto the world—then you are not perfected in Christ. And what will become of you? God will give you no access to Him. God will not use you in His service; you will have no rest in your conscience; and in the day when God will come to separate the precious from the vile, He will say, "Those are My precious ones, who have the blood on them. But these have rejected Christ; they have lived unto themselves; they were dead while they lived, and they are damned now that they are dead."

Take heed of that! May God give you grace to be sanctified to God, and then you will be forever perfected through Christ.

2

THREEFOLD SANCTIFICATION

Sanctified by God the Father.
—Jude 1:1

Sanctified in Christ Jesus.
—1 Corinthians 1:2

Through sanctification of the Spirit.
—1 Peter 1:2

As we study the Scriptures, we come to recognize the union of the three divine persons of the Trinity, in all their gracious and glorious acts. Although we rejoice to recognize each person of the Trinity, they are always most distinctly a Trinity in unity. We believe in one God, and our watchword still remains: *"Hear, O Israel: the LORD our God is one LORD"* (Deuteronomy 6:4).

Many young believers talk very unwisely when they claim to have preferences in the persons of the Trinity. They think of Christ as if He were the embodiment of everything that is lovely and gracious, while the Father they regard as severely just, but destitute of kindness. And how foolish are those who magnify the decree of the Father, or the atonement of the Son, thereby depreciating the work of the Spirit! In deeds of grace, not one of the three persons of the Trinity acts apart from the rest. They are as united in their deeds as they are in their essence. In their love toward the chosen, they are one; and in the actions that flow from that great central source, they are still undivided.

I want you to notice this in the case of sanctification. While we may, without the slightest mistake, speak of sanctification as the work of the Spirit, yet we must take heed that we do not view it as if the Father and the Son had no part in it. It is correct to speak of sanctification as the work of the Father, of the Spirit, and of the Son. God still says, "*Let **us** make man in our image, after our likeness*" (Genesis 1:26, emphasis added), and thus we are…

> …**his** *workmanship, created in Christ Jesus unto good works, which God hath before ordained that we should walk in them.*
> (Ephesians 2:10, emphasis added)

Dear reader, I beg you to notice and carefully consider the value that God sets upon real holiness, since the three persons are represented as coworking to produce a church without "*spot, or wrinkle, or any such thing*" (Ephesians 5:27). Those men who despise holiness of heart are in direct conflict with God. Holiness is the architectural plan upon which God builds up His living temple. (See 1 Peter 2:5.)

We read in Scripture of the "*beauties of holiness*" (Psalm 110:3); nothing is beautiful before God except that which is holy. All the glory of Lucifer, that "*son of the morning*" (Isaiah 14:12), could not screen him from divine abhorrence when he had defiled himself by sin. "*Holy, holy, holy*" (Revelation 4:8), the continual cry of the cherubim, is the loftiest song that that creature can offer, and the noblest that the Divine Being can accept.

Notice that God considers holiness to be His choice treasure. It is like the seal upon His heart (see Song 8:6), and like the signet upon His right hand. (See Jeremiah 22:24.) He could as soon cease to exist as cease to be holy, and sooner renounce the sovereignty of the world than tolerate anything in His presence contrary to purity, righteousness, and holiness.

You who profess to be followers of Christ, I pray that you will set a high value upon purity of life and godliness of conversation. Consider the blood of

Christ as the foundation of your hope, but never speak disparagingly of the work of the Spirit, which makes you fit for *"the inheritance of the saints in light"* (Colossians 1:12). Yes, prize it; prize it so heartily that you dread the very appearance of evil. Prize it so that, in your most ordinary actions, you may be…

> …*a royal priesthood, an holy nation, a peculiar people; that ye should show forth the praises of him who hath called you out of darkness into his marvellous light.* (1 Peter 2:9)

At first, I intended to use the word *sanctification* in the way in which it is understood among theologians; for you must know that the term *sanctification* has a far narrower meaning in schools of theology than it has in Scripture. I decided, however, that I want you to notice that sanctification is treated in Scripture in various ways. It may in some way illuminate the understanding of many believers, if I simply draw attention not to the theological, but to the scriptural, uses of the term *sanctification*, and show that, in God's holy Word, it has a much wider meaning than is agreed upon by systematic theologians.

It has been well said that the Book of God, like the works of God, is not systematically arranged. How different is the freedom of nature from the orderly precision of the scientific museum! If you were to visit the British Museum, you would see all the animals there, placed in cases according to their respective classifications. On the other hand, you go into God's world and find dog and sheep, horse and cow, lion and vulture, elephant and ostrich, all roaming abroad as if no zoology had ever ventured to arrange them in classes. The various rocks are not laid in the order in which the geologist draws them in his books, nor are the stars marked off in the sky according to their sizes.

The order of nature is variety. Science simply arranges and classifies, in order to assist the memory. In the same manner, systematic theologians, when they come to deal with God's Word, find scriptural truths arranged, not in order for the classroom, but for common life. The theologian is as useful as the analytical chemist, or the anatomist, but still, the Bible is not arranged as a body of theology. It is a handbook to heaven; it is a guide to eternity, meant for the man at the plow as much as for the scholar at his table. It is a primer for babes, as well as a classic for sages. It is the humble, uneducated man's book; and though there are depths in it, in which the elephant may swim, there are shallows where the lamb may wade. We bless God that He has not given us a body of theology in which we might lose ourselves, but that He has given us His own Word, put into the very best practical form for our daily use and edification.

Set Apart unto God

It is a recognized truth among us, that the Old Testament very often helps us to understand the New, while the New also expounds the Old. With God's Word, self-interpretation is the best. "Diamond cuts diamond" is a rule with jewelers; so must it be with students of Scripture. Those who wish to know best God's Word, must study it in its own light.

Now, in the Old Testament we find the word *sanctify* very frequently indeed, and it is used there in three senses. Let me call your attention to the first one.

The word *sanctify* in the Old Testament frequently has the meaning of "setting apart." It signifies the taking of something that was common before, that might legitimately have been put to ordinary uses, and setting it apart for God's service alone. It was then called sanctified or holy.

Take, for instance, the passage in Exodus 13:2: "*Sanctify unto me all the firstborn.*" On account of the destruction of the firstborn of Egypt, God claimed the firstborn of men and the firstborn of cattle to be His. Members of the tribe of Levi were set apart to be the representatives of the firstborn, to stand before the Lord to minister day and night in His tabernacle and in His temple. Those who were set apart to be priests and Levites were, as a result, said to be sanctified.

There is an earlier use of the term *sanctified* in Genesis 2:3:

And God blessed the seventh day, and sanctified it: because that in it he had rested from all his work which God created and made.

The seventh day had been an ordinary portion of time before, but He set it apart for His own service, that on the seventh day man should do no work for himself, but rest and serve his Maker. That is why, in Leviticus 27:14, you read, "*And when a man shall sanctify his house to be holy unto the LORD,*" and so on. This particular verse was meant as a direction to devout Jews who set apart a field or house to be God's, intending that either the produce of the field or the occupation of the house should be wholly given either to God's priests or to the Levites, or that, in some other way, it should be set apart for holy uses. Now, nothing was done to the house; there were no ceremonies; we do not read that it was cleansed or washed or sprinkled with blood; but the mere fact that it was set apart for God was considered to be a sanctification.

Likewise, in Exodus 29:44, we read that God said, "I will sanctify the tabernacle of the congregation, and the altar," by which, plainly enough, He meant that He would set it apart to be His house, the special place of His abode, where, between the wings of the cherubim, the bright light of the Shekinah might shine forth—the glorious evidence that the Lord God dwelt in the midst of His people.

The following verses are to the same effect:

+ The sanctification of the altar, instruments, and vessels, in Numbers 7:1

+ The setting apart of Eleazer, the son of Abinadab, to keep the ark of the Lord while it was at Kirjathjearim, in 1 Samuel 7:1

+ The establishment of cities of refuge, in Joshua 20:7, where we find in the original manuscripts that the word rendered "appointed" is the same that elsewhere is translated "sanctified"

It is clear from the Old Testament that the word *sanctify* sometimes has the meaning simply and only of "setting apart for holy uses."

This explains the text in John 10:36, which reads,

Say ye of him, whom the Father hath sanctified, and sent into the world, Thou blasphemest; because I said, I am the Son of God?

Jesus Christ here speaks of Himself as having been "sanctified" by His Father. Now, He was not purged from sin, for He had no sin in Him. Immaculately conceived, and gloriously preserved from all touch or stain of evil, He needed no sanctifying work of the Spirit within Him to purge Him from dross or corruption. All that is here intended is that He was set apart.

Likewise, in that notable and well-known passage in John 17:19, He meant only that He gave Himself up especially to God's service, to be occupied only with His Father's business: "*And for their sakes I sanctify myself, that they also might be sanctified through the truth.*" As a result, He could also say, "*My meat is to do the will of him that sent me, and to finish his work*" (John 4:34).

Dear friend, you now understand our first text, "*Sanctified by God the Father*" (Jude 1:1). Surely it means that God the Father has specially set apart or sanctified His people. This does not mean that God the Father actively works in the believer's heart, although Paul tells us *"it is God which worketh in* [us] *both to will and to do"* (Philippians 2:13)—that task belongs directly and effectively to the Holy Spirit—but that He, in the decree of election, separated unto Himself a people who were to be sanctified to Himself forever and ever. By the gift of His Son for them, He redeemed them from among men so that they might be holy; and, by continually sending forth the Spirit, He fulfills His divine purpose that they should be a separate people, sanctified from all the rest of mankind.

In this sense, every Christian is perfectly sanctified already. We may speak of believers as those who are sanctified by God the Father; that is to say, they are set apart. They were set apart before they were created; they were legally set apart by the purchase of Christ; they are manifestly and visibly set apart by the effectual calling of the Spirit of grace. They are, in this sense, at all times sanctified; and, speaking of the work as it concerns God the Father, they are completely sanctified unto the Lord forever.

Is this doctrine not clear enough to you? Then leave the doctrine for a moment, and look at it practically. Dear readers, have we ever realized this truth as we ought to? When a vessel, cup, altar, or instrument was set apart for divine worship, it was never used for common purposes again. No man except the priest could drink out of the golden cup; the altar could not be trifled with; God's bronze laver was not for ordinary ablution;[3] even the tongs upon the altar and the snuffers for the lamps were never to be profaned for any common purpose whatsoever.

What a solemn and meaningful fact this is! If you and I are, indeed, sanctified by God the Father, we should never be used for any purpose but for God. "What," you say, "not for ourselves?" No, not for ourselves. *"Ye are not your own... ye are bought with a price"* (1 Corinthians 6:19–20). "But," you say again, "must we not work and earn our own bread?" Truly, you must, but not with that as your chief purpose. You must still be diligent *"in business; fervent in spirit; serving the Lord"* (Romans 12:11). And, if you are servants, you are to serve *"not with eyeservice, as menpleasers; but as the servants of Christ"* (Ephesians 6:6).

If you think you can say, "I have an occupation in which I cannot serve the Lord," then leave it; you have no right in it. I think there is no calling—certainly no lawful calling—in which man can be found, in which he may not be able to

---

3. Laver: a large basin used for ceremonial ablutions, or washings, in the ancient Jewish tabernacle and temple worship.

say, "Whether I eat or drink, or whatsoever I do, I do all to the glory of God." (See 1 Corinthians 10:31.) The Christian is no more a common man than the altar was a common place. It is as great a sacrilege for the believer to live unto himself, or to live unto the world, as if you and I had profaned the Most Holy Place, used the holy fire for our own kitchen, the censer for a common perfume, or the candlestick for our own bedroom. These things were God's; no one could venture to make use of them without the right to do so. And we are God's and must be used only for Him.

Oh, Christians, if only you would know this, and know it fully! You are Christ's men and women, God's men and women, servants of God through Jesus Christ. You are not to do your own works; you are not to live for your own objectives. You are to say at all times, *God forbid that I should glory, save in the cross of our Lord Jesus Christ*" (Galatians 6:14). You are to take for your motto, *"For to me to live is Christ, and to die is gain"* (Philippians 1:21).

Sometimes I fear that nine out of ten professing Christians have never recognized this fact. They think that if they were to devote a part of their possessions, a part of themselves, or a part of their time, that would be enough. Oh, but Christ did not buy a part of you! He bought you entire—body, soul, and spirit—and He must have you, the whole man. Oh, if you are to be saved partly by Him and partly by yourselves, then live to yourselves; but if God has wholly set you apart to be vessels of mercy (see Romans 9:23) fitted for His use, oh, do not rob the Lord; do not treat as common cups those things that are as the bowls of the altar.

There is another practical thought to be considered here. It was a crime that brought destruction upon Babylon when Belshazzar, in his drunken frolic, cried, "Bring forth the cups of the Lord, the goodly spoil of the temple at Jerusalem." (See Daniel 5:2–3.) They brought the golden candlestick, and there it stood, flaming high in the midst of the marble hall. The despot, surrounded by his wives and his concubines, filled high the bowl with the foaming drink. He then commanded them to pass around the cups of Jehovah, and the heathen and the worshippers of idols drank confusion to the God of heaven and earth.

In that moment, just as the sacred vessel touched the sacrilegious lip, a hand was seen mysteriously writing out his doom: *"Thou art weighed in the balances, and art found wanting"* (Daniel 5:27). This was the crime that filled up the *ephah* of his sin.[4] The measure of his iniquity was fully accomplished. He had used, for

---

4. Ephah: an ancient Hebrew unit of dry measure equal to about .65 of a bushel.

lascivious and drunken purposes, vessels that belonged to Jehovah, the God of the whole earth.

Oh, take heed, take heed, you who profess to be sanctified by the blood of the covenant, that you do not consider the covenant an unholy thing. See to it that you do not make your bodies, which you profess to be set apart for God's service, slaves of sin (see Romans 6:6), or *"your members servants...[of] iniquity unto iniquity"* (Romans 6:19)—lest you should hear in that hour the voice of the recording angel as he cries, "Thou art weighed in the balances and found wanting."

"Be ye clean, that bear the vessels of the LORD" (Isaiah 52:11). And you who hope that you are Christ's, and have a humble faith in Him each morning, see that you walk circumspectly (see Ephesians 5:15), that by no means you prostitute, to the service of sin, that which was set apart in the eternal covenant of grace to be God's alone. If you and I are tempted to sin, we must reply, "No, let another man do that, but I cannot. I am God's man; I am set apart for Him. *'How then can I do this great wickedness, and sin against God?'* (Genesis 39:9)." Let dedication enforce sanctification.

Think of the dignity to which God has called you—Jehovah's vessels, set apart for the Master's use. May everything that would make you impure, be far, far away. When Antiochus Epiphanes offered a sow on the altar of the Lord in the temple at Jerusalem, his awful death might have been easily foretold.[5] Oh, how many there are who profess to be sanctified servants of the Lord, who have offered unclean flesh upon the altar of God, who have made religion a stalking-horse to their own advantage, and who have adopted the faith in order to gain respect and applause among men!

What does the Lord say concerning such things? *"Vengeance belongeth unto me, I will recompense, saith the Lord"* (Hebrews 10:30). For many, their god is their stomach; they glory in their shame; they mind earthly things; and they die justly accursed. (See Philippians 3:19.) They are spots in your solemn feasts (see Jude 1:12), *"wandering stars, to whom is reserved the blackness of darkness for ever"* (verse 13). But you, beloved, do not become carried away with the error of the wicked (see 2 Peter 3:17), but keep yourselves *"unspotted from the world"* (James 1:27).

---

5. Antiochus Epiphanes: ruler of Syria and the Seleucid Dynasty from 175 to 164 b.c. See Appendix A.

Declared and Regarded as Holy

Secondly, in the Old Testament, the word *sanctify* is sometimes used in another sense—one that I do not think is hinted at in our biblical encyclopedias, but that is needed to make the subject complete. The word *sanctify* is used, not only to signify that the thing is set apart for holy uses, but also that it is to be *regarded, treated, and declared as a holy thing.* I will give you an example from Isaiah 8:13.

In this passage we read, *"Sanctify the LORD of hosts himself."* You may clearly understand that the Lord does not need to be set apart for holy uses; the Lord of Hosts does not need to be purified, for He is holiness itself. However, what the sense of the word actually means is that we are to adore and reverence the Lord; with fear and trembling we must approach His throne and regard Him as the Holy One of Israel. Let me give you other instances of this.

When Nadab and Abihu, as recorded in Leviticus 10, offered a sacrifice to God and put strange fire on the altar, the fire of the Lord went forth and consumed them, and this was the reason given: *"I will be sanctified in them that come nigh me"* (Leviticus 10:3). By this He did not mean that He would be set apart, nor that He would be made holy by purification, but that He would be treated and regarded as a Most Holy Being, with whom such liberties were not to be taken.

Another example is found in Numbers 20, on that unfortunate occasion when Moses lost his temper and smote the rock twice, saying, *"Hear now, ye rebels; must we fetch you water out of this rock?"* (Numbers 20:10). Then the Lord said that Moses would see the Promised Land, but would never enter it, the reason being, *"Because ye believed me not, to sanctify me in the eyes of the children of Israel"* (verse 12). By this He meant that Moses had not acted so as to honor God's name among the people.

An even more familiar instance occurs in what is commonly called the Lord's Prayer: *"Our Father which art in heaven, hallowed be thy name"* (Matthew 6:9). The word *hallowed* is simply an English variation of *sanctified*, because the Greek reads, "Sanctified be thy name." Now, we know that God's name does not need purifying or setting apart, so the sense here can only be "Let thy name be reverenced and adored throughout the whole earth, and let men regard it as being a sacred and holy thing."

Beloved, do we not have some light here concerning our second text, "*Sanctified in Christ Jesus*" (1 Corinthians 1:2)? If the word *sanctified* may mean "regarded as holy and treated as such," can you not see how in Christ Jesus the saints are regarded by God as being holy, and are treated as such? Surely, we do not lay that down as being the only meaning of the text, for another sense may yet be attached to it.

There have been certain believers who have elaborated on our being sanctified in Christ, and have almost forgotten the work of the Spirit. Now, if they only speak of our being sanctified in Christ, in the sense of being treated as holy (or, in fact, as being justified), we have no quarrel with them; but if they deny the work of the Spirit, they are guilty of deadly error.

I have sometimes heard the term *imputed sanctification* used, which is sheer absurdity. One cannot use the term *imputed justification* and be at all correct. *Imputed righteousness* is correct enough and implies a glorious doctrine, but justification is neither imputed nor attributed; it is actually conferred, or given. We are justified through the imputed righteousness of Christ, but as to being "imputedly sanctified," no one who understands the use of language can speak this way. The term is inaccurate and unscriptural.

I know it is said that the Lord Jesus is made "*of God…unto us wisdom, and righteousness, and sanctification, and redemption*" (1 Corinthians 1:30), but this sanctification is not by imputation, nor does the text say so. Why, you might as readily prove imputed wisdom or imputed redemption by this text, as force it to teach imputed sanctification.

It is a fact that for the sake of what Jesus Christ did, God's people—though in themselves they are only partially sanctified because they are yet subject to sin—are for Christ's sake treated and regarded as if they are perfectly holy. But this, according to theological definitions, is justification rather than sanctification, although it must be admitted that the Scripture sometimes uses the word *sanctification* in such a manner so as to make it tantamount to justification. By this, however, we can clearly see that God's people have access with boldness to the Lord (see Hebrews 4:16), because they are regarded, through Christ, as though they are perfectly holy.

Oh, Christian, think about this for a moment! A holy God cannot have dealings with unholy men. A holy God—and is not Christ Jesus God?—cannot have communion with unholiness, and yet you and I are unholy. How, then, does

Christ receive us to His bosom? How does His Father walk with us and find Himself yielding His consent? Because He views us, not in ourselves, but in our great covenantal Head, the Second Adam. He looks at us,

> Not as we were in Adam's fall,
> When sin and ruin covered all;
> But as we'll stand another day,
> Fairer than sun's meridian ray.

He looks on the deeds of Christ as ours, on His perfect obedience and sinless life as ours, and thus we may sing in the language of Hart—

> With thy spotless garments on,
> Holy as the Holy One.

We may boldly enter into that which is within the veil, where no unholy thing may come, yet where we may venture because God views us as holy in Christ Jesus.

This is a great and precious doctrine; yet the use of the term *sanctification* in any other sense than that in which it is commonly employed, as meaning "the work of the Spirit," tends to foster confused ideas, and really does, I fear, lead some to despise the work of the Spirit of God. I think it is better, in ordinary conversation between Christians, to speak of sanctification without confusing it with what is quite a distinctly different act, namely, justification through the imputed righteousness of our Lord and Savior Jesus Christ. Yet, if we hear a brother talk in this manner, we must not be too severe with him, as though he had certainly strayed from the faith, for in Scripture, the terms *sanctification* and *justification* are frequently used interchangeably, and Christ's righteousness made the subject matter of both works of grace.

Purified and Made Holy

We now come to the usual sense in which the word *sanctification* is employed. It means actually "to purify or make holy," not merely to set apart or to account holy, but to make really and actually so in nature. You have the word in this sense in many places in the Old Testament. Let us examine it in Exodus 19:10–12.

On the third day of the third month, God was about to proclaim His holy Law on top of Mount Sinai, and the mandate went forth, "*Sanctify* [the people] *to day and to morrow*" (verse 10). This sanctification consisted of certain outward deeds by which their bodies and clothes were put into a state of cleanliness and their souls were brought into a reverential state of awe.

Likewise, in the third chapter of Joshua, you find, when the children of Israel were about to cross the Jordan, it was said, "*Sanctify yourselves: for tomorrow the* LORD *will do wonders among you*" (verse 5). They were to prepare themselves to be beholders of a scene so grand: when the Jordan was driven back and the river was utterly dried up before the feet of the priests of God. There was, in this case, an actual purification. Men in the old times were sprinkled with blood, and they were thus sanctified from defilement and considered to be pure in the sight of God. This is the sense in which we view our third text, "*Through sanctification of the Spirit*" (1 Peter 1:2), and this, I repeat, is the general sense in which we understand it in common conversation among Christians.

Sanctification begins in regeneration. The Spirit of God infuses into man the new element called the spirit, which is a third and higher nature, so that the believing man becomes body, soul, *and spirit*. In this he is distinct and distinguished from all other men of the race of Adam. This work, which begins in regeneration, is carried on in two ways: by vivification and by mortification; that is, by giving life to that which is good, and by sending death to that which is evil in the man.

Mortification is the process whereby the lusts of the flesh are subdued and kept under; and vivification, the process by which the life that God has put within us, is made to be "*a well of water springing up into everlasting life*" (John 4:14). This is carried on every day in what we call perseverance, by which the Christian is preserved and continued in a gracious state, and is made to abound in good works (see 2 Corinthians 9:8) unto the praise and glory of God. And it culminates, or comes to perfection, in glory, when the soul, being thoroughly purged, is caught up to dwell with holy beings (see 1 Thessalonians 4:17) at "*the right hand of the Majesty on high*" (Hebrews 1:3).

Now, this work, though we commonly speak of it as being the work of the Spirit, is quite as much the work of the Lord Jesus Christ as of the Spirit. In looking for texts on the subject, I have been struck with the fact that where I found one verse speaking of it as the Spirit's work, I found another in which it was treated as the work of Jesus Christ. I can well understand that my second text,

"*Sanctified in Christ Jesus*" (1 Corinthians 1:2), has as great a fullness of meaning as the third, "*Through sanctification of the Spirit*" (1 Peter 1:2). Oh, that you may yet know how precious to a believer is the purifying work of sanctification!

Sanctification is a work *in* us, not a work *for* us. It is a work in us, and there are two agents: one is the worker who works this sanctification effectually—that is the Spirit; and the other, the efficacious means by which the Spirit works this sanctification—Jesus Christ and His most precious blood.

Imagine, to put it as plainly as we can, there is a garment that needs to be washed. There is a person to wash it, and there is a bath in which it is to be washed. In terms of sanctification, the person is the Holy Spirit, but the bath is the precious blood of Christ. It is entirely correct to speak of the person cleansing as being the sanctifier. It is quite as accurate to speak of that which is in the bath and which makes the garment clean, as being the sanctifier, too. So, the Spirit of God sanctifies us; He works it effectively; but He sanctifies us through the blood of Christ, through the water that flowed with the blood from Christ's side.

I repeat my illustration: imagine a garment that is black. A fuller,[6] in order to make the garment white, uses nitre and soap;[7] and both the fuller and the soap are cleansers. Likewise, both the Holy Spirit and the atonement of Christ are sanctifiers. This should be enough of an explanation of my point. Now, let us look further into this doctrine.

The Spirit of God is the great worker by whom we are cleansed. I will not cite the texts here. Perhaps you have read the Baptist Confession of Faith[8] and the Catechism.[9] They will furnish you with an abundance of texts on this subject, for this is a doctrine that is generally accepted—that it is the Spirit of God who creates in us a new heart and a right spirit, according to the whole tone of the covenant:

A new heart also will I give you, and a [right] spirit will I put within you....
And I will put my spirit within you, and cause you to walk in my statutes.
(Ezekiel 36:26–27)

---

6. Fuller: one who shrinks and thickens cloth (especially woolen cloth) by moistening, heating, and pressing.

7. Nitre: also known as *niter*, is an oxidizing agent that is often white, gray, or colorless.

8. The Baptist Confession of Faith: adopted by the Ministers and Messengers of the general assembly that met in London in 1689. See Appendix B.

9. Catechism: Many evangelical churches of Spurgeon's time copied some of the teaching methods of the High Church. The basic doctrinal beliefs of the church were written as small books and then taught in Sunday school classes, instead of catechism classes.

The Spirit renews and changes the nature, turns the bias of the will, and makes us seek that which is good and right, so that every good thing in us may be described as *"the fruit of the Spirit"* (Galatians 5:22), and all our virtues and all our graces are efficiently worked in us by the Spirit of the living God. Never, never, never forget this. Oh, it will be an evil day for any church when the members begin to think lightly of the work of the Holy Spirit within us! We delight to magnify the work of Christ *for* us, but we must not depreciate the work of the blessed Spirit *in* us.

In the days of my venerable predecessor, Dr. Gill, who was fully of the opinion of ultra-Calvinists, this vicious evil broke out in the Metropolitan Tabernacle. There were some who believed in "imputed sanctification," and denied the work of the blessed Spirit. Recently, I read a note written in our old church book, in the doctor's own handwriting, concerning the deliberate opinion of the church in those days. It went as follows:

> Agreed: That to deny the internal sanctification of the Spirit, as a principle of grace and holiness wrought in the heart, or as consisting of grace communicated to and implanted in the soul, which, though but a begun work, and as yet incomplete, is an abiding work of grace, and will abide, notwithstanding all corruptions, temptations, and snares, and be performed by the Author of it until the Day of Christ, when it will be the saints' meetness [fitness] for eternal glory; is a grievous error, which highly reflects dishonor on the blessed Spirit and His operations of grace on the heart, is subversive of true religion and powerful godliness, and renders persons unfit for church communion. Wherefore, it is further agreed, that such persons who appear to have embraced this error be not admitted to the communion of this church, and should any such who are members of it appear to have received it and continued in it, that they be forthwith excluded from it.

Two members, who were then present, declared themselves to be of the opinion condemned in the above resolution; and a third person, who was absent, was well known to have been under this awful delusion. All three of them were consequently excluded, that very evening, from fellowship. In addition, a person of another church, who held the opinion thus condemned, was forbidden to receive Communion. His pastor at Kettering was written to upon the subject, and was warned not to allow so great an errorist to remain in fellowship. Dr. Gill thought the error to be so deadly, that he used the pruning knife at once; he did not stop until it spread, but he cut off the very twigs.

This is one of the benefits of church discipline, when we are enabled to carry it out under God: that it does destroy the growth of error in its very early stages, and that through such discipline, those who are not infected as yet, are kept from it by the blessed providence of God through the instrumentality of the church. I have always believed, and still believe and teach, that the work of the Spirit in us, whereby we are conformed unto Christ's image, is as absolutely necessary for our salvation as is the work of Jesus Christ, by which He cleanses us from our sins.

Pause here for a moment, but do not allow me to distract you from the substance of this chapter. While the Spirit of God is said in Scripture to be the Author of sanctification, yet there is a visible agent that must not be forgotten. *"Sanctify them,"* said Christ, *"through thy truth: thy word is truth"* (John 17:17).

Look up all the passages of Scripture that prove that the instrument of our sanctification is the Word of God. You will find that there are very many. It is the Word of God that sanctifies the soul. The Spirit of God brings to our minds the commands and precepts and doctrines of truth (see John 14:26), and applies them with power. These are heard in the ear, and, being received in the heart, they work in us to will and to do of God's good pleasure. (See Philippians 2:13.) How important, then, that the truth should be preached! How necessary that you never tolerate a ministry that leaves out the great doctrines or the great precepts of the gospel! The truth is the sanctifier, and if we do not hear the truth, we will certainly not grow in sanctification.

We only progress in sound living as we progress in sound understanding. *"Thy word is a lamp unto my feet, and a light unto my path"* (Psalm 119:105). Do not say of such-and-such an error, "Oh, it is merely a matter of opinion," for if it is a mere matter of opinion today, it will be a matter of practice tomorrow. No man commits an error in judgment, without sooner or later committing an error in practice. Every grain of truth is like a grain of diamond dust; you would do well to prize it all.

> *Therefore, brethren, stand fast, and hold the traditions which ye have been taught, whether by word, or our epistle.* (2 Thessalonians 2:15)

"*Hold fast the form of sound words*" (2 Timothy 1:13), and in this day when doctrines are ridiculed, when creeds are despised, hold fast to that which you have received, that you may be found faithful among the faithless. For by so holding the truth, you will be sanctified by the Spirit of God. The agent, then, is the Spirit of God working through the truth.

But, now, let me bring you back to the substance of this matter. We are sanctified, in another sense, through Christ Jesus, because it is His blood—and the water that flowed from His side—in which the Spirit washes our hearts from the defilement of and the tendency toward sin. It is said of our Lord,

> *Christ also loved the church, and gave himself for it; that he might sanctify and cleanse it with the washing of water by the word, that he might present it to himself a glorious church, not having spot, or wrinkle, or any such thing.*
> (Ephesians 5:25–27)

There are hundreds of texts of this kind. Remember these verses:

> *Jesus also, that he might sanctify the people with his own blood, suffered without the gate.*
> (Hebrews 13:12)

> *He that sanctifieth and they who are sanctified are all of one: for which cause he is not ashamed to call them brethren.*
> (Hebrews 2:11)

> *Thou shalt call his name JESUS: for he shall save his people from their sins.*
> (Matthew 1:21)

> *God forbid that I should glory, save in the cross of our Lord Jesus Christ, by whom the world is crucified unto me, and I unto the world.* (Galatians 6:14)

In that memorable passage where Paul, struggling with corruption, exclaimed, "*O wretched man that I am! who shall deliver me from the body of this death?*" (Romans 7:24), the answer does not concern the Holy Spirit, but he said, "*I thank God through Jesus Christ our Lord*" (verse 25). I do not have room enough here to write all the texts that would apply, but there are many passages to the effect that our sanctification is the work of Jesus Christ. He is our sanctifier, for

He filled the sacred laver of regeneration in which we are washed, filled it with the blood and with the water that flowed from His side, and in this we are washed by the Holy Spirit.

There is no sanctification through the law, for the Spirit does not use legal precepts to sanctify us. There is no purification by mere dictates of morality, for the Spirit of God does not use them, either. No, for just as when Marah's waters were bitter (see Exodus 15:23), Moses, in order to make them sweet, commanded the people to take a tree and cast it into the waters, and they were sweet (verse 25), so the Spirit of God, finding our natures bitter, takes the tree of Calvary, casts it into the stream, and makes everything pure. He finds us lepers, and to make us clean, He dips the hyssop of faith into the precious blood and sprinkles it upon us, and we are clean. (See Leviticus 12:5–7.)

There is a mysterious efficacy in the blood of Christ, not merely to make satisfaction for sin, but to bring about the death of sin. The blood appears before God, and He is well pleased. It falls on us: lusts wither, and old corruptions feel the death stroke. Dagon falls before the ark of the Lord (see 1 Samuel 5:2–3), and although its stump is left (see verse 4) and corruptions still remain, Christ will put an end to all our inbred sins, and through Him we will mount to heaven, *"perfect, even as* [our] *Father which is in heaven is perfect"* (Matthewe 5:48).

Just as the Spirit only works through the truth, so the blood of Christ only works through faith. Again I say, turn to your Bibles at your leisure, and find the many passages that speak of faith as sanctifying the soul and purifying the mind. Our faith lays hold of the precious atonement of Christ. It sees Jesus suffering on the tree, and it says, "I vow revenge against the sins that nailed Him there." His precious blood works in us an extreme contempt for all sin; and the Spirit, through the truth, working by faith, applies the precious blood of sprinkling, and we are made clean, and are *"accepted in the beloved"* (Ephesians 1:6).

I am afraid that I have confused and obscured this matter with words. Even so, I think I may have suggested some trains of thought that will lead you to see that Holy Scripture teaches us a sanctification that is not narrow and concise, so as to be written down with a short definition, as in our creed books, but wide, large, and expansive—a work in which we are sanctified by God the Father, sanctified in Christ Jesus, and yet have our sanctification through the Spirit of God. Oh, my dear readers, strive after practical holiness! You who love Christ, do not let anyone say of you, "There is a Christian, but he is worse than other men." It is not our eloquence, our learning, our fame, or our wealth that can ever commend Christ to the world; it is only the holy living of Christians.

Just the other day, I was talking with a fellow minister about a current movement that I fear will be an immense injury to Christ's church. I said that I feared, lest it should be made an opportunity for strife among believers; error must be corrected, but love must not be wounded. He remarked—and I thought it was so truthful—that the only way by which the dissent from the established church flourished in earlier times, was by the then superior holiness of the dissenting ministers. It would often happen that, while the clergyman of the established church was off hunting, the dissenting minister would visit the sick. And then he said, "If our ministers become political and worldly, it will be all over with us. This is the way in which we will lose power."

I have never avoided rebuke, when I thought it necessary, but I hate contention. The only allowable strife is to see who can be the most holy, the most earnest, the most zealous; who can do the most for the poor and the ignorant; and who can lift Christ's cross the highest. This is the way to lift up the members of any denomination—by the members of that body being more devout, more sanctified, more spiritually minded than the others. All infighting will only create strife and animosities and bickering, and is not of the Spirit of God; but to live unto God and to be devoted to Him—this is the strength of the church; this will give us the victory, God helping us, and all the praise will be to His name.

As for those of you who are not converted, and are unregenerate, I cannot write to you concerning sanctification. I have opened a door, but you cannot enter. Only, remember, if you cannot enter into this, you cannot enter into heaven, for

> Those holy gates for ever bar,
>   Pollution, sin, and shame;
> None shall obtain admission there,
>   But followers of the Lamb.

May it be your privilege to come humbly and confess your sin, to ask and find forgiveness; for then, but not until then, there is hope that you may be sanctified in the spirit of your mind. The Lord bless you for Jesus' sake. Amen.

3

PERFECT SANCTIFICATION

By the which will we are sanctified through the offering of the body of Jesus Christ once for all.
—Hebrews 10:10

Dear friends, ever since the Lord has quickened us by His grace, we have begun to look into ourselves and to search our hearts to see our condition before God. As a result, many things that once caused us no disquietude, now create great anxiety in us. We thought that we were all right, and we felt it was enough to be as good as others were. We dreamed that, if we were not quite as good as we should be, we would certainly grow better, though we did not stop to inquire how or why. We took stock of our condition and concluded that we were *"rich, and increased with goods, and* [had] *need of nothing"* (Revelation 3:17).

Even so, a change has come over the spirit of the scene; the grace of God has made us thoughtful and careful. We dare not take things haphazardly now. We test and prove things, for we are very anxious not to be deceived. We look upon eternal realities as being of the utmost consequence, so we dare not take for granted that we are right about them. We are afraid of being presumptuous; we desire to be sincere. We hold an examination within our spirits, and we are so afraid that we may be partial (although we probably are so), that we ask the Lord to search us and try us, to "*see if there be any wicked way*" in us, that He may lead us out of such a way, into the way of everlasting (Psalm 139:23–24).

This is all very wise and very proper, and I would not for a moment try to take the people of God away from a proper measure of this state of heart. And yet, may it never be forgotten that, in the sight of God, we are different in some respects than we will ever see ourselves to be if we look through the glass of feeling and consciousness. There are other matters to be taken into consideration, matters that our anxiety may lead us to overlook, and that our inward search may cause us to forget.

Faith reveals to us another position for the people of God besides that which they occupy in themselves. Some call it an evangelical fiction, and the like; but, thank God, it is a blessed fact that, sinners as we are in ourselves, yet we are saints in God's sight; and sinful as we feel ourselves to be, yet we are washed, cleansed, and sanctified in Jesus Christ. Notwithstanding all that we mourn over, the very fact that we do mourn over it becomes evidence that we are no longer what we once were, and do not stand now where we once stood.

We have passed from death unto life. (See 1 John 3:14.) We have escaped from underneath the dominion of law and into the kingdom of grace. We have come from being under the curse, and we dwell in the region of blessing. We have believed "*on him that justifieth the ungodly,* [and our] *faith is counted for righteousness*" (Romans 4:5). Therefore, there is no condemnation for us, because we are in Christ Jesus our Lord, and we walk no longer after the flesh, but after the Spirit. (See Romans 8:1.) Think of the noble position into which the grace of God has lifted all believers—the condition of sanctification that is spoken of in the text—for by the will of God "*we are sanctified through the offering of the body of Jesus Christ once for all*" (Hebrews 10:10).

In this chapter, I will point out, first, the nature of the eternal will; second, the effectual sacrifice by which that will has been carried out; and, third, the everlasting result accomplished by that will through the sacrifice of the body of Christ. May the Holy Spirit, who has revealed the grand doctrine of justification, enable you to understand it and to feel its comforting power.

The Eternal Will

By "the eternal will," I mean the will by which we are sanctified. (See Hebrews 10:10.) This will must, first of all, be viewed as the will ordained from all eternity by the Father.

Ordained by the Father

The eternal decree of the infinite Jehovah was that a people whom He chose should be sanctified and set apart unto Himself. (See Deuteronomy 7:6.) The will of Jehovah stands fast forever and ever; and we know that it is altogether unchangeable, and that it has no beginning. It is an eternal will; we have no vacillating Deity, no fickle God. He wills changes, but He never changes His will.

> *He is in one mind, and who can turn him? and what his soul desireth, even that he doeth.* (Job 23:13)

The will of God is invincible as well as eternal. We are told in the epistle to the Ephesians that He *"worketh all things after the counsel of his own will"* (Ephesians 1:11). Who can *"stay his hand, or say unto him, What doest thou"* (Daniel 4:35)? The good pleasure of His will is never defeated: there cannot be such a thing as a vanquished God. *"My counsel shall stand, and I will do all my pleasure"* (Isaiah 46:10), says the Lord. In fact, the will of God is the motive force of all things. *"He spake, and it was done; he commanded, and it stood fast"* (Psalm 33:9). His Word is omnipotent because His will is behind it, and puts force into it.

"God said, Let there be light: and there was light" (Genesis 1:3), because He willed that there should be light. He commanded creatures to come forth, as numerous as the drops of dew, to inhabit the world that He had made; and they came forth, flying, leaping, swimming, in varied orders of life, because He created them by His own will. His will is the secret power that sustains the universe, threads the starry orbs, and holds them like a necklace of light about the neck of nature. His will is the alpha and the omega of all things.

It was according to this eternal, invincible will of God that He chose, created, and set apart a people that should show forth the glory and riches of His grace, a people that should bear the image of His only begotten Son, a people that should joyfully and willingly serve Him in His courts forever and ever, a people who should be His own sons and daughters, to whom He would say, *"I will dwell in them, and walk in them; and I will be their God, and they shall be my people"* (2 Corinthians 6:16). Thus stood the eternal will from ages past.

> *For whom he did foreknow, he also did predestinate to be conformed to the image of his Son, that he might be the firstborn among many brethren.*
>
> (Romans 8:29)

Even so, the people concerning whom this will was set forth were dead in sin, defiled with evil, polluted by transgression. The old Serpent's venom was in their veins. They were in a condition to be set apart for the curse, but not to be set apart for the service of the thrice-holy God. And the question was, "How, then, can the will of the Immutable Invincible ever be carried out? How will these rebels become absolved of sin? How will these fountains of filth become clear as crystal, pouring forth floods of living water and divine praise? How will these unsanctified and defiled ones become sanctified unto the service of God? It must be, but how will it happen?"

Then came the priests, with smoking censers, and with basins full of blood, steaming because it had just come fresh from the slaughtered victims; and they sprinkled this blood upon the Book and upon the people, upon the altar and upon the mercy seat, and upon all the hangings of the tabernacle, and upon all the ground on which the worshippers walked; for almost all things under the law were sanctified by blood. This blood of bulls and of goats was everywhere—fresh every morning and renewed every evening.

Still, God's will was not done; the chosen were not thus sanctified; and we know they were not, because it is written, *"Sacrifice and offering thou wouldest not"* (Hebrews 10:5). His will was not fulfilled in such sacrifices; it was not His will that they should sanctify the people. They were inefficacious to accomplish such an end, for, as the Scriptures say, it *"is not possible that the blood of bulls and of goats should take away sins"* (verse 4). And so, if these offerings had been all there was, generations upon generations of the house of Aaron and of the priests of the tribe of Levi might have come and gone, and yet the will decreed by the eternal Father would not have been an accomplished fact.

Performed by the Son

Thus we come to our second point concerning the eternal will, which is that this will by which we are sanctified was performed by the ever blessed Son. It was the will of God the Father, but it was carried out by the divine Son when He came into the world. A body was prepared for Him; He entered into that body in a manner that we will not attempt to conceive of; and He was the incarnate God. This incarnate God, by offering His own blood, by laying down His own life, by bearing in His own body the curse, and by enduring in His own spirit the wrath, was able to carry out the purpose of the everlasting Father in the purging of His people, in the setting apart of His chosen, and in making them henceforth holy unto the Lord.

Do you not see what the will of the Father was—that He should have a people that should be sanctified unto Himself? But that will could not be carried out by the blood of bulls and of goats; it had to be achieved by *the offering of the body of Jesus Christ once for all* (Hebrews 10:10). Our Lord Jesus Christ has done what the will of the Father required for its perfect achievement. This is our satisfaction.

We will not enter at this time into a detailed account of our Lord's active and passive obedience, by which He magnified the law and set apart His people. However, I hope that you will never fall into the error of dividing the work of Christ, as some do, and saying, "Here He made atonement for sin, and there He did not." In these modern times, some believers have invented fancy ways of saying the most trivial things—things that are not even worth the trouble of thinking about—and yet, like babes with a new rattle, they make noise with them all day long.

It is amusing how so many wise professors make grave points out of mere hairsplitting distinctions; and if we do not agree with them, they put on a show of haughtiness, pitying our ignorance and glorying in themselves as superior persons who have an insight into things that ordinary Christians cannot see. God save us from having eyes that are so sharp that we are able to spy out new occasions for argument, and fresh reasons for making men into offenders for their mere words. I believe in the life of Christ as well as in His death, and I believe that He stood for me before God as much when He walked the acres of Palestine as when He hung on the cross at Jerusalem.

You cannot divide and split Him in two and say, "Only in these cases is He an example, and only in these cases is He an atonement." Instead, you must take the entire Christ, and look at Him from the very first as *the Lamb of God, which taketh away the sin of the world* (John 1:29). "Oh," they say, "but He made no atonement except in His death." This is surely an absurdity in language. Ask yourself, "When does a man die?" There is the minute in which the soul separates from the body; but all the time that a man may be described as dying, he is still alive, is he not?

A man does not suffer once he is actually dead. What we call the pangs of death are truly and accurately the pangs of life. Death does not suffer; it is the end of suffering. A man is still alive while he suffers; and if they say, "It is Christ's death that makes an atonement, and not His life," I reply that death, alone and by itself, makes no atonement. Death in its natural sense, and not in this modern, unnatural sense of severance from life, does make atonement; but it cannot be viewed apart from life by any unsophisticated mind. If they must have distinctions, we could certainly make enough distinctions to worry them, but we have nobler work to do.

To us, our Lord's death seems to be the consummation of His life, the finishing stroke of a work that His Father had given Him to do among the sons of men. We view Him as having come in a body prepared for Him, to do the will of God *once*, and that "once" lasted throughout His one life on earth. We will not, however, dwell on any moot point, but genuinely rejoice that whatever was needed to make God's people wholly sanctified unto God, Christ has carried it out. *"By the which will we are sanctified through the offering of the body of Jesus Christ once"* (Hebrews 10:10).

"It is finished" (John 19:30). Does the divine law require, in order for us to be accepted, perfect submission to the will of the Lord? He has rendered it. Does it ask for complete obedience to its precepts? He has presented the same. Does the fulfilled will of the Lord call for abject suffering, a sweat of blood, pangs unknown, and death itself? Christ has presented it all, whatever that "all" may be. When God created, His Word carried forth all His will. Likewise, when God redeemed, His blessed and incarnate Word accomplished all His will.

Applied by the Spirit

Just as God looked on each day's work and said, "It is good" (see Genesis 1:4), so, as He looks upon each part of the work of His dear Son, He can say of it, "It is good." The Father joins in the verdict of His Son, that it is finished (see John 19:30): all the will of God for the sanctification of His people is accomplished.

Dear Christian, this work must be applied to us by the Holy Spirit. It is the Holy Spirit who brings us to know that Jesus Christ has sanctified us, or set us apart, and made us acceptable with God. It is the Holy Spirit who has given us the New Testament, and shed a light upon the Old. It is the Holy Spirit who speaks to us through the ministers of Christ when He blesses them to help us to our conversion. It is especially the Holy Spirit who takes away from us all hope of being sanctified before God by any means of our own, brings us to see our need of cleansing and reconciliation, and then takes of the things of Christ and reveals them to us. Not without the going forth of His sacred power are we made to take the place of separation and dedication, to which the Lord ordained us from eternity.

Thus it is by the will of the Father, carried out by the Son, and applied by the Holy Spirit, that the church of God is regarded as sanctified before God, and is acceptable to Him.

I will not dwell any longer on this point, because these great things are best written of with few words: they are subjects that are better to be meditated upon by quiet thought than exhibited in writing.

The Effectual Sacrifice

In the second place, I invite you to consider the effectual sacrifice by which the will of God, with regard to the sanctity of His people, has been carried out. *"By the which will we are sanctified through the offering of **the body of Jesus Christ**"* (Hebrews 10:10, emphasis added). What does this mean?

The Incarnation of God as Man

First of all, this implies His incarnation, which, of course, includes His eternal deity. We can never forget that Jesus Christ is God. The church has given forth many a valiant confession to His deity; and woe be to her should she ever hesitate on that glorious truth! Yet, sometimes she has great need to earnestly insist upon His humanity. As you bow before your glorious Lord and adore Him with all the sanctified, remember that He whom you worship was truly and really a man.

The gospel of His incarnation is not a spiritual idea, nor a metaphor, nor a myth. In very deed and truth, the God who made heaven and earth came down to earth and hung upon a woman's breast as an infant. That child, as He grew *"in wisdom and stature"* (Luke 2:52), was as certainly God as He is at this moment in glory. He was as surely God when He was here hungering and suffering, sleeping, eating, and drinking, as He was God when He hung up the morning stars and kindled the lamps of night, or as He will be when sun and moon shall grow dim at *"the brightness of His coming"* (2 Thessalonians 2:8).

Jesus Christ, very God of very God, certainly did stoop to become such as we are, and He was made in the likeness of sinful flesh. This is a truth you undoubtedly know, but I want you to grasp it and realize it; for it will help you to trust Christ if you clearly understand that, divine as He is, He is bone of your bone and flesh of your flesh (see Genesis 2:23)—your kinsman, though He is the Son of God.

All this is implied in the text, because it speaks of the offering of the *body* of Christ. But why did the author of Hebrews speak especially of the body? I think he did this in order to show us the reality of that offering: His soul suffered, and His soul's sufferings were the soul of His sufferings; yet, to make it palpable to you, to record it as a sure historical fact, he mentioned that there was an offering of the body of Christ.

The Whole of Christ

I take it, however, that the word *body* means "the whole of Christ"—that there was an offering made of all of Christ, the body of Him, or that of which He was constituted. It is my solemn conviction that His deity coworked with His humanity in the wondrous passion by which He has sanctified His elect.

I am told that Deity cannot suffer. I am expected to subscribe to that because theologians say so. Well, if it is true, then I will content myself with believing that the deity of Christ helped the humanity of Christ, by strengthening it to suffer more than it could otherwise have endured.

Yet, I believe that Deity can suffer, unorthodox as that notion may seem to be. I cannot believe in a God who is insusceptible to pain. If He pities and sympathizes, surely He must have some sensibilities. Is He a God of iron? If He wills it, He can do anything, and therefore He can suffer if He pleases.

It is not possible for God to be made to suffer; that would be a ridiculous supposition. Yet, if He wills to do so, He is certainly capable of doing that as well as anything else, for all things are possible to Him. (See Matthew 19:26.) I look upon our Lord Jesus as, in His very Godhead, stooping down to bear the weight of human sin and human misery, sustaining it because He was divine, and able to bear what otherwise would have been too great a load. Thus, the whole of Christ was made a sacrifice for sin. It was the offering, not of the spirit of Christ, but of the very body of Christ—the essence, substance, and most manifest reality and personality of Jesus Christ, the Son of the Most High.

A Complete Offering

And Christ was wholly offered. I do not know how to explain my own thought here; but in order to accomplish the will of God in sanctifying all His people, Christ must be the offering, and He must be wholly offered. There were certain sacrifices that were only presented to God in part, so far as the consumption by fire was concerned. A part was eaten by the priest or by the offerer, and in that sense it was not a whole burnt offering. In this there was much precious truth set forth, of which I will not write here; but as our sin offering, making expiation for guilt, our blessed Lord and Master gave Himself wholly for us, as an atoning sacrifice and offering for sin.

That word *Himself* sums up all you can conceive to be in and of the Christ of God; and the pangs and griefs that went through Him like a fire, did consume Him and everything that was in Him. He bore all that could be borne, stooped to the lowest place to which humility could come, descended to the utmost abyss to which a descent of self-denial could be made. He *"made himself of no reputation"* (Philippians 2:7); He emptied Himself of all honor and glory, and *"was made in the likeness of men"* (verse 7). He gave up Himself without reserve. He saved others, though He did not save Himself. (See Luke 23:35.)

He spares us in our chastisements, but Himself He did not spare. He says of Himself, in the twenty-second Psalm, *"I am a worm, and no man; a reproach of men, and despised of the people"* (verse 6). You do not know, you cannot imagine, how fully the sacrifice was made by Christ. It was not only a sacrifice of all of Himself, but a complete sacrifice of every part of Himself for us. The blaze of eternal wrath for human sin was focused upon His head! The anguish that must have been endured by Him who stood in the place of millions of sinners, to be judged of God and stricken in their stead, is altogether inconceivable.

He Himself was perfectly innocent, yet in His own person He offered up a sacrifice that could honor the divine justice on account of a myriad of sins of the sons of men. This was a work far beyond all human realization! You may let go of your reason and your imagination, and rise into the seventh heaven of sublime conception as with eagles' wings, but you can never reach the utmost height. Here is the sum of the matter: "*Thanks be unto God for his unspeakable gift*" (2 Corinthians 9:15), for unspeakable and inconceivable it certainly is when we view the Lord Jesus as a sacrifice for the sins of men.

A Singular Offering

This offering was made once, *and only once*. The meaning of our text lies in the finishing words of it: "*through the offering of the body of Jesus Christ once for all*" (Hebrews 10:10). Those words, *for all*, are very properly put in by the translators, but you must not make a mistake as to their meaning. The text does not mean that Christ offered Himself up once for *all*—that is, for all mankind. That may be a doctrine of Scripture, or it may not be a doctrine of Scripture, but it is not the teaching here. The passage means "once for all" in the sense of—all at once, or only once, for all time.

Just as a man might say, "I gave up my whole estate once for all to my creditors, and there was an end of the matter," so, here, our Lord Jesus Christ is said to have offered Himself up as a sacrifice once for all—that is to say, only once, and there was an end of the whole matter. His sacrifice on behalf of His people was for all the sins before He came. Think of what they all were. Ages had succeeded ages, and among the various generations of men had been found criminals of the blackest hue, and crimes had been multiplied; but the prophet Isaiah said in vision concerning Christ, as he looked on all the multitude,

> All we like sheep have gone astray; we have turned every one to his own way; and the LORD hath laid on him the iniquity of us all.   (Isaiah 53:6)

That was before He came. Reflect that there has been no second offering of Himself ever since, and never will be, but it was once, and that "once" did the deed. Let your mind ponder the nearly two thousand years that have passed since the offering. If the prophet were to stand here this day and look back through those many years, he would still say, "All we like sheep have gone astray; we have turned every one to his own way; and the LORD hath laid on him the iniquity of us all."

Oh, it is a wonderful concept! The sacrifice of the Lord Jesus was the reservoir into which all the sin of the human race ran, from this quarter, and that, and that, and that. All the sin of His people rolled in a torrent unto Him, and gathered as in a great lake. In Him was no sin, and yet the Lord made Him to be sin for us. (See 2 Corinthians 5:21.)

You may have seen a deep mountain tarn that has been filled to the brim by innumerable streamlets from all the hillsides round about. From one side comes a torrent gushing down, and from another side there trickles from the moss that has overgrown the rock a little drip, drip, drip, that falls perpetually. Great and small tributaries all meet in the black tarn, which, after the rain, is full to the brim and ready to burst its banks. That lone lake portrays Christ, the meeting place of the sins of His people. It was all laid on Him, that from Him the penalty might be exacted. At His hands the price must be demanded for the ransom of all this multitude of sins.

The Blotting Out of Sin

And it is said that He did this *once for all*. I have no language with which to describe it, but when I look around me, I see the great load of sin, the huge, tremendous world of sin. No, no, it is greater than the world. Atlas might carry *that*,[10] but this is a weight in comparison with which the world is but the head of a pin. Mountains upon mountains, alps upon alps, are nothing, to the mighty mass of sin that I see before my mind's eye; and lo, it all falls upon the Well Beloved.

He stands beneath it, and bows under it, until the bloody sweat springs from every pore, and yet He does not yield to its weight in order to get away from the burden. It presses more heavily; it bows Him to the dust; it touches His very soul; it makes Him cry in anguish, *"My God, my God, why hast thou forsaken me?"* (Matthew 27:46); and yet, at the last, He lifts Himself up and flings it all away and cries, *"It is finished"* (John 19:30), and it is gone. There is not a wreck of it left; no, not an atom of it left. It is all gone at once, and once for all. He has borne the immeasurable weight and cast it off from His shoulders forever; and as it lies no more on Him, so also it lies no more on His people. Sin will never be mentioned against them anymore, forever. Oh, wondrous deed of Deity! Oh, mighty feat of love accomplished once for all! The Redeemer never offered Himself to death before. He never will do it again.

Look at it this way: the reason that it never will be done again is there is no need for it. All the sin that was laid upon Jesus is gone; all the sin of His people

---

10. Atlas: in Greek mythology, a Titan who, because of his part in a revolt against the gods, was condemned by Zeus to support the heavens upon his shoulders.

is forever discharged. He has borne it; the debt is paid. The handwriting of ordinances against us is nailed to His cross; the Accuser's charge is answered forever.

What, then, will we say of those who come forward and pretend that they perpetually present the body of Christ in the unbloody sacrifice of the mass? We say that no profane jest from the lip of Voltaire[11] ever had even the slightest degree of God-defiant blasphemy in it compared with the hideous insult of this horrible pretense. It is infernal. There can be nothing more intolerable than that notion, for our Lord Jesus Christ has offered Himself for sin once, and once for all; and he who dares to think of offering Him again, insults Him by acting as if that once were not enough. There would be no language of abhorrence too strong if the performers and attendants at the mass really knew what is implied in their professed act and deed. In the judgment of Christian charity we may earnestly pray, "*Father, forgive them; for they know not what they do*" (Luke 23:34).

Our words fail and our ideas falter at the thought of the great Substitute, with all the sins of His people condensed into one black liquid and set before Him, for Him to drink. Can we think of Him as putting that cup to His lips, and drinking, drinking, drinking all the wrath, until He had drained the cup to the bottom and filled Himself with horror? Yet, He has finished the death-drink and turned the cup upside down, crying, "It is finished" (John 19:30). In one tremendous drink, the loving Lord has drained destruction dry for all His people, and there is no dreg nor drop left for any one of them, for now is the will of God accomplished—"*by the which will we are sanctified through the offering of the body of Jesus Christ once for all*" (Hebrews 10:10). Glory be to God! Again, glory be to our God!

> He bore on the tree the sentence for me,
> And now both the Surety and sinner are free.
> In the heavenly Lamb thrice happy I am;
> And my heart doth rejoice at the sound of his name.

The Everlasting Result

At last I come to my third point: the everlasting result. There are several glorious results that have come about through God's eternal will and by Christ's effectual sacrifice.

---

11. Voltaire: French writer, 1694–1778.

The Expiation of Our Sin

The first everlasting result of this effectual carrying out of the will of God, is that now God regards His people's sin as expiated, and their persons as sanctified. Our sin is removed by expiation. Atonement has been offered, and its efficacy abides forever. There is no need for any other expiation. Believers repent bitterly, but this is not expiation. There is no penance to be exacted of them through putting away guilt. Their guilt is gone; their transgression is forgiven. The covenant is made with them, and it goes like this: *"Their sins and iniquities will I remember no more"* (Hebrews 10:17). Their sins have, in fact, been ended, blotted out, and annihilated by the Redeemer's one sacrifice.

We Are Reconciled to God

Next, His people are reconciled to Him. There is no quarrel now between God and those who are in Christ Jesus. Peace is made between them. The middle wall that stood between them is taken away. Christ, by His one sacrifice, has made peace for all His people, and has effectually established a union that will never be broken.

> Lord Jesus, we believing
>   In thee have peace with God,
> Eternal life receiving,
>   The purchase of thy blood.
> Our curse and condemnation
>   Thou bearest in our stead;
> Secure is our salvation
>   In thee, our risen Head.

We Are Purified in Him

Moreover, they are not only accepted and reconciled, but they are also purified. The taint that was upon them is taken away. In God's sight they are regarded no more as unclean; they are no longer shut outside the camp. (See Numbers 5:1–4.) They may come to the throne of the heavenly grace when they desire to do so. God can have communion with them. He regards them as fit to stand in His courts and to be His servants, for they are purified, reconciled, and expiated through the one offering of Christ. Their admission into the closest intimacy with God could never be allowed if He did not regard them as purged from all uncleanness, and this has been effected not at all by themselves, but alone by the great sacrifice.

> Thy blood, not mine, O Christ,
> Thy blood so freely spilt,
> Has blanched my blackest stains,
> And purged away my guilt.

> Thy righteousness, O Christ,
> Alone does cover me;
> No righteousness avails
> Save that which is in thee.

Living as a Sanctified Christian

Again, what has come of this offering of Christ's body? That is the point. Let us now leave the doctrine and try to bring out the practical experience arising from it. What Christ has done in the carrying out of the great will of God has brought about salvation for all His chosen people. However, this is applied to them actually and experientially by the Holy Spirit dwelling in them, by which indwelling they know they are God's people. The Israelites were God's people, after a fashion; the Levites were especially so; and the priests were still more especially so; and these had to present perpetual sacrifices and offerings, that God might be able to look upon them as His people, for they were a sinful people.

Truly His People

You and I are not a type, but we are truly and really His people. Through Jesus Christ's offering of Himself once for all, we are really set apart to be the Lord's people, henceforth and forever. And He says of us—of as many as have believed in Jesus, and to whom the Holy Spirit has revealed His finished work—"*I will be their God, and they shall be my people*" (2 Corinthians 6:16).

You, believers, are sanctified in this sense: you are now the ones set apart unto God, and you belong wholly to Him. Will you think that over? "I am now not my own. I do not belong now to the common order of men, as all the rest of men do. I am set apart. I am called out. I am taken aside. I am one of the Lord's own. I am His treasure and His portion. He has, through Jesus Christ's death, made me one of those of whom He says, '[They] *shall dwell alone, and shall not be reckoned among the nations*' (Numbers 23:9)."

I want you to feel it, so that you may live under the power of that fact; I want you to feel, "My Lord has cleansed me. My Lord has made expiation for me. My Lord has reconciled me unto God, and I am God's man, or I am God's woman. I cannot live as sinners do. I cannot be one among you. I must come out, and I must be separate. (See 2 Corinthians 6:17.) I cannot find my pleasure where you find yours. I cannot find my treasure where you find yours. I am God's, and God is mine. That wondrous transaction on the cross—that wondrous unspeakable deed upon the cross—that wonderful life and death of Jesus, has made me one of God's people, set apart unto Him, and I must live as such."

Fit for His Service

When you realize that you are one of God's people, the next thing is to reflect that God, in sanctifying a people, set them apart for His service, and He made them fit for His service. You, beloved, through Christ's one great offering of His body for you, are permitted now to be a servant of God.

You know it is an awful thing for a man to try to serve God until God gives Him that right: otherwise, there is a presumption about it. Well, suppose that one of the enemies of this country, who has sought the life of our leader and has always spoken against him, were to say, "My intention is to be one of his servants; I will go into his house, and I will serve him," having all the while in his heart a rebellious, proud spirit. His service could not be tolerated; it would be sheer impudence. Even so, "*Unto the wicked God saith, What hast thou to do to declare my statutes?*" (Psalm 50:16).

A wicked man, pretending to serve God, does what Korah, Dathan, and Abiram tried to do when they rebelled against Moses (see Numbers 16): he will try to offer incense, yet he is not purified and not called to the work, and he has no fitness for it. But now, beloved, you who are in Christ are called to be His servant. You have permission and leave to serve Him. It ought to be your great joy to be an accepted servant of the living God. If you are only the Lord's chimney sweep, you have a greater privilege than if you were an emperor on earth.

If the highest thing you ever will be allowed to do, should be to untie the laces of your Master's shoe, or to wash His servants' feet—if the master is Christ, then you are favored above the mightiest of the mighty. Men of renown may envy you; their Order of the Garter[12] is nothing compared with the high dignity of being a servant of King Jesus. Look upon this as being the result of Christ's death upon the cross, that a poor, sinful creature like you, who was once a slave of the devil, is now allowed to be the servant of God. On the cross my Master bought for us a sanctification that has made us the Lord's people, and has enabled us to engage in His service. Do we not rejoice in this?

Acceptable in His Sight

Next to that we have this privilege, that what we do can now be accepted. Because Jesus Christ, by the offering of His body once, has perfected the Father's will and has sanctified us, what we do is now acceptable to God. Previously, we might have done whatever we wanted to, but God would not have accepted it from a sinner's hands—from the hands of one who was out of Christ. Now He accepts anything from us.

You dropped a penny into the offering: it was all that you could give, and the Lord accepted it. It dropped into His hand. You offered a little prayer in the middle of business this afternoon because you heard an ill word spoken, and your God accepted that prayer. You went down the street and spoke to a poor sick person: you did not say much, but you said all you could, and the great God accepted it.

Acceptance by the Beloved, not only for our persons, but also for our prayers and our work, is one of the sweetest things I know. We are accepted. That is the joy of it. Through that one great, bloody sacrifice, once for all offered, God's people are forever accepted, and what His people do for Him is accepted, too. And now we are privileged to the highest degree, being sanctified—that is to say, made into God's people, God's servants, and God's accepted servants. Every privilege that we could have had if we had never sinned, is now ours, and we are in Him as His children. We have more than would have come to us by the covenant of works; and if we will but know it, and live up to it, even the very privilege of suffering and the privilege of being tried, the privilege of being in need, should be looked upon as a great gift.

---

12. Order of the Garter: the highest English Order of Chivalry, and one of the most important of all such Orders throughout the world.

An angel spirit, seated high alone there, meditating and adoring, might say to himself, "I have served God: these swift wings have borne me through the heavens on His errands, but I have never suffered for Him. I have never been despised for Him. Drunkards have never called me evil names. I have never been misrepresented as God's servant. After all, though I have served Him, it has been one perpetual joy. He has set a hedge about me and all that I have." (See Job 1:10.)

If an angel could envy anybody, I think he would envy the martyr who had the privilege of burning to death for Christ. Or, he would envy Job, who, when stripped of everything and covered with sores, could sit on a dunghill and still honor his God. Such men as these achieved a service unique within itself, which has sparkling diamonds of the finest clarity and luster glittering about it—the kind that cannot be found in a ministry without suffering, complete as it may be. You are favored sons of Adam, you who have become sons of God. You are favored beyond cherubim and seraphim in accomplishing a service for the manifestation of the riches of the grace of God, which unfallen spirits never could accomplish. Rejoice and be exceedingly glad that this one offering has put you there!

Eternally Secure

And now you are eternally secure. No sin can ever be laid at your door, for it is all put away; and sin being removed, every other evil has lost its fang and sting. Now you are eternally beloved, for you are one with Him who can never be other than dear to the heart of Jehovah. That union never can be broken, for nothing can separate us from the love of God (see Romans 8:38–39); and therefore, your security can never be imperiled.

You are now in some measure glorified, for *"the spirit of glory and of God resteth upon you"* (1 Peter 4:14), and *"our conversation is in heaven; from whence also we look for the Saviour, the Lord Jesus Christ"* (Philippians 3:20), who *"hath* [already] *raised us up together, and made us sit together in heavenly places"* (Ephesians 2:6). Heaven is already ours in promise, in price, and in principle, and the preparation for it has also begun.

> All that remains for me
> Is but to love and sing,
> And wait until the angels come
> To bear me to their King.

In such a spirit would I always live.

Brother or sister, are you discouraged at this time? Do you have a great trouble upon you? Are you alone in the world? Do others misjudge you, or does the sword of scandal pierce your very soul? Do fierce coals of juniper (see Psalm 120:4) await those vicious tongues that wrong you? Do you feel *"bowed down to the dust"* (Psalm 44:25)? Yet, what position are you in to be despairing? Child of God, and heir of all things, *"why art thou cast down"* (Psalm 42:5)? Joint heir with Christ, why do you abase yourself? Why do you lie among the pots (see Psalm 68:13) when you already have angels' wings upon you?

Get up! Your heritage is not here among the dragons and the owls. (See Job 30:29.) Up! You are one of God's eagles, born for brighter light than earth could bear—light that would blind the bleary-eyed sons of men if they were once to get a veiled glimpse of it. You, a twice-born man, one of the imperial family, one who will sit upon a throne with Christ as surely as Christ sits there (see Revelation 3:21), what position are you in, that you are moaning and groaning?

Wipe your eyes and smooth your brow, and in the strength of the Eternal, go to your life battle. It will not be long. The trumpet of victory almost sounds in your ears. Will you now retreat? No, for you can win the day. *"Trust in the LORD, and do good; so shalt thou dwell in the land, and verily thou shalt be fed"* (Psalm 37:3), until He comes to catch you away. There you will see what Jesus did for you when He made His body once for all a sacrifice, that He might fulfill the will of the eternal Father, and sanctify you and all His people unto God forever and ever.

May the best of blessings rest upon all who are in Christ Jesus. Amen.

APPENDIX A

Antiochus Epiphanes, ruler of Syria and the Seleucid Dynasty from 175 to 164 BC, intervened rather brutally in the fighting that had been troubling Jerusalem during that time. He made a great attempt to hellenize the Jews, or to assimilate the Jews into Greek culture and views, by, among other things, destroying all the Old Testament books he could find.

According to *Great Themes of the Book, Part 3*, of the *Living by the Book* series, Antiochus became virtually the Antichrist to the writer of the book of Daniel. He

> sacked Jerusalem; stripped the temple of its gold, implements, and secret treasures; and took ten thousand people into captivity as slaves. He compelled the Jews to cease worshipping God, placed idols on the altar, and sacrificed swine (an unclean animal according to Jewish dietary law) to them. He erected similar shrines in every Jewish city and village and forbade the practice of circumcision. Mothers who disobeyed were tied to crosses, strangled, and had their sons hung about their necks.

Because offering a sow on the altar was the sacrificing of an unclean animal for a sin offering, Antiochus desecrated the purity of the temple with his sacrifice.

His action is considered by many to be the initial historical fulfillment of the first prophecies regarding the abomination of desolation. (See Daniel 11:31.) The "awful death" of Antiochus, of which Spurgeon writes, was due to an illness in the year 164 BC.

APPENDIX B

C hapter 13 of the Baptist Confession of Faith, entitled, "Of Sanctification," concerns the work of the Holy Spirit in sanctification. The following are the three points from that chapter.

A. They who are united to Christ, effectually called, and regenerated, having a new heart and a new spirit created in them through the virtue of Christ's death and resurrection, are also further sanctified, really and personally, through the same virtue, by His Word and Spirit dwelling in them; the dominion of the whole body of sin is destroyed, and the several lusts thereof are more and more weakened and mortified, and they [are] more and more quickened and strengthened in all saving graces, to the practice of all true holiness, without which no man shall see the Lord. (See Acts 20:32; Romans 6:5–6; John 17:17; Ephesians 3:16–19; 1 Thessalonians 5:21–23; Romans 6:14; Galatians 5:24; Colossians 1:11; 2 Corinthians 7:1; Hebrews 12:14.)

B. This sanctification is throughout the whole man, yet imperfect in this life; there abideth still some remnants of corruption in every part, whence ariseth a continual and irreconcilable war; the flesh lusting against the Spirit, and the Spirit against the flesh. (See 1 Thessalonians 5:23; Romans 7:18, 23; Galatians 5:17; 1 Peter 2:11.)

C. In which war, although the remaining corruption for a time may much prevail, yet through the continual supply of strength from the sanctifying Spirit of Christ, the regenerate part doth overcome; and so the saints grow in grace, perfecting holiness in the fear of God, pressing after an heavenly life, in evangelical obedience to all the commands which Christ, as Head and King, in His Word, hath prescribed them. (See Romans 7:23; 6:14; Ephesians 4:15–16; 2 Corinthians 3:18; 7:1.)

JOY IN PRAISING GOD

CONTENTS

1. Awakening Praise 165

2. Heavenly Adoration 178

3. A Pattern for Praise 194

4. A New Song for New Hearts 209

5. Ethan's Song in the Night... 225

6. Praise for the Gift of Gifts 239

1

AWAKENING PRAISE

Awake, awake, Deborah: awake, awake, utter a song: arise, Barak, and lead
thy captivity captive, thou son of Abinoam.
—Judges 5:12

Many of the saints of God are as mournful as if they were captives in Babylon, for their lives are spent in tears and sighing. They will not chant the joyous psalm of praise. If anyone requires of them a song, they reply, "How can we sing the Lord's song in a strange land?" However, we are not captives in Babylon. We do not sit down to weep by Babel's streams. The Lord has broken our captivity. He has brought us up out of our house of bondage. We are free men, not slaves. We have not been sold into the hand of cruel taskmasters, but *"we which have believed do enter into rest"* (Hebrews 4:3).

Moses could not give rest to Israel. He could bring them to Jordan, but he could not conduct them across the stream. Joshua alone could lead them into the lot of their inheritance. Likewise, Jesus, our Joshua, has led us into the land of promise. He has brought us into a land which the Lord our God reflects, a land of hills and valleys, a land that flows with milk and honey. Though the Canaanites are still in the land and plague us sorely, yet is it all our own. God has said unto us, "*All things are yours, whether Paul, or Apollos, or Cephas, or the world, or life, or death, or things present, or things to come, all are yours, and ye are Christ's, and Christ is God's*" (1 Corinthians 3:21–23).

We are not captives, sold under sin. We are a people who "*sit every man under his vine and his fig tree, and none shall make [us] afraid*" (Micah 4:4). "*We [dwell in] a strong city; salvation will God appoint for walls and bulwarks*" (Isaiah 26:1). We have come to "*Zion, the city of our solemnities*" (Isaiah 33:20). Babylon's mourning is not suitable in Zion, which is "*beautiful for situation, the joy of the whole earth…the city of the great King*" (Psalm 48:2). "*Serve the LORD with gladness: come before his presence with singing*" (Psalm 100:2).

Many of God's people live as if their God were dead. Their conduct would be quite consistent if "*all the promises of God in him are [not] yea, and in him Amen*" (2 Corinthians 1:20) and if God were a faithless God. If Christ were not a perfect Redeemer, if the Word of God might after all turn out to be untrue, if He had not power to keep His people, and if He had not love enough with which to hold them even to the end, then might they give way to mourning and to despair. Then might they cover their heads with ashes and wrap their loins about with sackcloth. But while God is just and true, while His promises stand as fast as the eternal mountains, while the heart of Jesus is true to His spouse, while the arm of God is unpalsied and His eye undimmed, while His covenant and His oath are unbroken and unchanged, then it is not proper or fitting for the upright to go mourning all their days. You children of God, refrain from weeping and make a joyful noise unto the Rock of your salvation. Let us come before His presence with thanksgiving, expressing our gladness in Him with psalms.

> Your harps, ye trembling saints
> Down from the willows take;
> Loud to the praise of love divine
> Bid every string awake.

First, I will urge you to stir up all your powers for sacred praise, to "*awake, awake, utter a song.*" In the second place, I will persuade you to practice the sacred leading of your captivity captive. "*Arise Barak, and lead thy captivity captive, thou son of Abinoam.*"

Let us look to stirring up all our powers to praise God, according to the words of the holy woman in the text, *"Awake, awake,"* repeated yet again, *"Awake, awake."* What is there that we need to awaken if we would praise God? I reply, we ought to arouse all the bodily powers. Our flesh is sluggish. We have been busy with the world. Our limbs have grown fatigued. But there is power in divine joy to arouse even the body itself, to make the heavy eyelids light, to reanimate the drowsy eye, and quicken the weary brain. We should call upon our bodies to awake, especially our tongues. Let it put itself in tune like David's harp of old.

A toil-worn body often makes a mournful heart. The flesh has such a connection with the spirit that it often bows down the soul. Come, then, my flesh, I charge you, awake. Blood, leap in my veins. Heart, let your pulsing be as the joy-strokes on Miriam's timbrel! Oh, all my bodily frame, stir yourself now. Begin to magnify and bless the Lord, who made you, and who has kept you in health, and preserved you from going down into the grave.

Surely we should call on all our mental powers to awaken. Wake up, memory, and find matter for the song. Tell what God has done for me in days gone by. Fly back, thoughts, to my childhood. Sing of cradle mercies. Review my youth and its early favors. Sing of long-suffering grace, which followed my wandering and bore with my rebellions. Revive before my eyes that glad hour when first I knew the Lord. Tell again the matchless story of the never ceasing streams of mercy, which have flowed to me since then and which call for songs of loudest praise. Wake up, my judgment, and give measure to the music. Come forth, my understanding, and weigh His loving-kindness in scales and His goodness in the balances. See if you can count the small dust of His mercies. See if you can understand the unsearchable riches which He has given to you in that unspeakable gift of Christ Jesus. Count His eternal mercies to you, the treasures of that covenant which he made on your behalf, even before you were born. Sing, my understanding, sing aloud of that matchless wisdom which contrived, of that divine love which planned, and of that eternal grace which carried out the scheme of your redemption.

Awake, my imagination, and dance to the holy melody. Gather pictures from all worlds. Bid sun and moon stay in their courses and join in your new song. Constrain the stars to yield the music of the spheres. Put a tongue into every mountain and a voice into every wilderness. Translate the lowing of the cattle and the scream of the eagle. Hear the praise of God in the rippling of the rills, the dashing of the waterfalls, and the roaring of the sea, until all His works in all places of His dominion bless the Lord.

But especially let us cry to all the graces of our spirits, *"awake."* Wake up, my love, for you must strike the keynote and lead the strain. Awake and sing unto your beloved a song touching your Well-beloved. Give to Him choice canticles, for He in the fairest among ten thousand and altogether lovely. Come forth then with your richest music and praise the name which is an ointment poured forth. Wake up, my hope; join hands with your sister, love, and sing of blessings yet to come. Sing of my dying hour, when He will be with me on my couch. Sing of the rising morning when my body will leap from its tomb into its Savior's arms! Sing of the expected advent, for which you look with delight! And, O my soul, sing of that heaven which He has gone before to prepare for you, that where He is, there may His people be. (See John 14:3.)

Awake my love, awake my hope, and you my faith, awake also! Love has the sweetest voice; hope can thrill forth the higher notes of the sacred scale; but you, faith, with your deep resounding bass melody, you must complete the song. Sing of the promise sure and certain. Rehearse the glories of the covenant ordered in all things, and sure. Rejoice in the sure mercies of David! Sing of the goodness which will be known to your in all your trials yet to come. Sing of that blood which has sealed and ratified every word of God. Glory in that eternal faithfulness which cannot lie, and of that truth which cannot fail. You, my patience, utter your gentle but most joyous hymn. Sing today of how He helped you to endure in sorrow's bitterest hour. Sing of the weary way along which He has borne your feet and brought you at last to lie down in green pastures beside the still waters. Oh, all my graces, heaven-begotten as you are, praise Him who did beget you. You children of His grace, sing unto your Father's name and magnify Him who keeps you alive. Let all that is in me be stirred up to magnify and bless His holy name.

Let us wake up the energy of all those powers—the energy of the body, the energy of the mind, the energy of the spirit. You know what it is to do a thing coldly and weakly. We might as well not praise at all. You know also what it is to praise God passionately, to throw energy into the song and so to exalt His name. Do so, each one of you, this day. Should someone like Michal, Saul's daughter, look out of the window and see you dancing before the ark with all your might and chide you as though your praise were unseemly, say unto her, *"It was before the LORD, which chose me before thy father, and before all his house...therefore will I play before the LORD"* (2 Samuel 6:21). Tell the enemy that the God of election must be praised, that the God of redemption must be extolled, that if the very heathen leaped for joy before their gods, surely they who bow before Jehovah must adore Him with rapture and with ecstasy. Go forth with joy then, with all your energies thoroughly awakened for His praise.

But you say unto me, "Why should we this day awake and sing unto our God?" There are many reasons. If your hearts are right, one will well satisfy you. Come, you children of God, and bless His dear name.

Does not all nature around you sing? If you were silent, you would be an exception to the universal adoration. Does not the thunder praise Him as it rolls like drums in the march of the God of armies? Does not the ocean praise Him as it claps its thousand hands? Does not the sea roar with the fullness thereof? Do not the mountains praise Him when the shaggy woods upon their summits wave in adoration? Do not the lightnings write His name in letters of fire upon the midnight darkness? Does not this world, in its unceasing revolutions, perpetually roll forth His praise? Has not the whole earth a voice, and yet will we be silent? Will man—for whom the world was made, and suns and stars were created—will he be dumb? No, let him lead the chorus. Let him be the world's high priest. While the world will be as the sacrifice, let him add his heart to it, and thus supply the fire of love which will make that sacrifice smoke towards heaven.

But, believer, will your God be praised? I ask you, will your God be praised? When men behold a hero, they fall at his feet and honor him. Garibaldi emancipated a nation, and they bowed before him and did him homage. You, Jesus, the Redeemer of the multitudes of Your elect, shall You have no song? Shall You have no triumphal entry into our hearts? Shall Your name have no glory? Shall the world love its own, but the church not honor its own Redeemer? Our God must and will be praised.

If no other heart should ever praise Him, surely mine must. If creation should forget Him, His redeemed must remember Him. Do you tell us to be silent? Oh, we cannot. Do you bid us restrain our holy mirth? Indeed you ask us to do an impossibility. He is God, and He must be extolled. He is our God, our gracious, tender, faithful God. He must have the best of our songs.

Believer, you ask, "Why should I praise Him?" Let me ask you a question, too: "Is it not heaven's employment to praise Him?" What can make earth more like heaven than to bring down from heaven the employment of glory and to be occupied with it here? Come, believer, when you pray, you are but a man, but when you praise, you are as an angel. When you ask favor, you are but a beggar, but when you stand up to extol, you become next of kin to cherubim and seraphim.

Happy, happy day, when the glorious choristers will find their numbers swelled by the addition of a multitude from earth! Happy day when you and I will join the eternal chorus! Let us begin the music here. Let us strike some of the first notes at least. If we cannot sound the full thunders of the eternal hallelujah, let us join in as best we can. Let us make the wilderness and the solitary place rejoice, and bid the desert blossom as the rose. (See Isaiah 35:1.)

Besides, Christian, do you not know that it is a good thing for you to praise your God? Mourning weakens you. Doubts destroy your strength. Your groping among the ashes makes you of the earth, earthy. Arise, for praise is pleasant and profitable to you. "*The joy of the* LORD *is your strength*" (Nehemiah 8:10). "*Delight thyself also in the* LORD *and he shall give thee the desires of thine heart*" (Psalm 37:4). You grow in grace when you grow in holy joy. You are more heavenly, more spiritual, more Godlike, as you get more full of joy and peace in believing on the Lord Jesus Christ. I know some Christians are afraid of gladness, but I read, "*Let the children of Zion be joyful in their King*" (Psalm 149:2). If murmuring were a duty, some saints would never sin. If mourning were commanded by God, they would certainly be saved by works, for they are always sorrowing, and so they would keep His law. Instead, the Lord has said, "*Rejoice in the Lord alway, and again I say, Rejoice*" (Philippians 4:4). To make it still stronger, He has added, "*Rejoice evermore*" (1 Thessalonians 5:16).

But I ask you one other question, believer. You say, "Why should I awake this morning to sing to my God?" I reply to you, "Do you not have overwhelming reasons?" Has He not done great things for you, and are you not grateful? Has He not taken you out of the horrible pit and out of the miry clay? Has He not set your feet on the Rock and established your goings, and is there no new song in your mouth? What, are you bought with blood and yet still have a silent tongue? Were you not loved of God before the world began, but you cannot sing His praise? Are you His child, an heir of God and joint heir with Jesus Christ, and yet you have no notes of gratitude? Has He fed you this day? Did He deliver you yesterday out of many troubles? Has He been with you these thirty, forty, fifty years in the wilderness, and yet have you no mercy for which to praise Him? Shame on your ungrateful heart and your forgetful spirit. Come, pluck up courage. Think of your mercies and not of your miseries. Forget your pains awhile and think of your many deliverances. Put your feet on the neck of your doubts and fears, and stand on the Rock of your salvation. May God the Holy Ghost be your Comforter, and may you begin from this hour to utter a song of gratitude.

Someone asks, "When should I praise my God?" The answer is that all His people should praise the Lord at all times, and give thanks at every remembrance of Him. Extol Him even when your souls are drowsy and your spirits are inclined to sleep. When we are awake, there is little cause to say to us four times, *"Awake, awake...awake, awake, utter a song."* But when we feel most drowsy with sorrow and our eyelids are heavy, when afflictions are pressing us down to the very dust, then is the time to sing psalms to our God and praise Him in the very depths. But this takes much grace, and I trust that you know that there is much grace to be had. Seek it of your divine Lord, and do not be content without it. Do not be easily cast down by troubles, nor quickly made silent because of your woes.

Think of the martyrs of old, who sang sweetly at the stake. Think of Ann Askew, of all the pains she bore for Christ, and then of her courageous praise of God in her last moments. Often she had been tortured most terribly. She lay in prison expecting death, and there she wrote a verse in old English words and rhyme:

> I am not she that lyst
> > My anker to let fall,
> For every dryslynge myst;
> > My shippe's substancyal.

She meant in the verse that she would not stop her course and cast her anchor for every drizzling mist, because she had a ship that could bear a storm, one that could break all the waves that beat against it and joyously cut through the foam. So it will be with you. Do not give God only fair-weather songs; give Him black-tempest praises. Give Him not merely summer music, as some birds will do and then fly away; give Him winter tunes. Sing in the night like the nightingales. Praise Him in the fires. Sing His high praises even in the shadow of death, and let the tomb resound with the shouts of your sure confidence. So may you give to God what God well claims from you.

When should you praise Him? Why, praise Him when you are full of doubts, even when temptations assail you, when poverty hovers round you, and when sickness bows you down. They are cheap songs which we give to God when we are rich. It is easy enough to kiss the hand of a giving God, but to bless Him when He takes away is to bless Him indeed. To cry like Job, *"though he slay me yet will I trust in him"* (Job 13:15), or to sing like Habukkuk, *"Although the fig tree shall not blossom, neither shall fruit be in the vines; the labor of the olive shall fail, and the fields shall yield no meat; the flocks shall be cut off from the fold, and there shall be no herd in the stalls: yet will I rejoice in the* Lord, *I will joy in the God of my salvation*" (Habukkuk 3:17–18). Christian, you ask when you should rejoice. Today, "*Awake, awake, Deborah: awake, awake, utter a song.*"

Yet once more, you reply to me, "But how can I praise my God?" I will be a teacher of music to you, and may the Comforter be with me. Will you think right now how great your mercies are? You are not blind, deaf, or dumb. You are not a lunatic. You are not decrepit. You are not vexed with piercing pains. You are not full of agony caused by disease. You are not going down to the grave. You are not in torment, not in hell. You are still in the land of the living, the land of love, the land of grace, the land of hope. Even if this were all, there were enough reason for you to praise your God. You are not this day what you once were, a blasphemer, a persecutor, and an injuror. The song of the drunkard is not on your lips. The lascivious desire is not in your heart. And is not this a theme for praise? Remember but a little while ago, for many of you, all these sins were your delight and joy. Must not you praise Him, you chief of sinners, whose natures have been changed, whose hearts have been renewed? Think of your iniquities, which have been put away, and your transgressions, which have been covered and not laid to your charge. Think of the privileges you enjoy: you are elect, redeemed, called, justified, sanctified, adopted, and preserved in Christ Jesus. Why, if a stone or rock could but for a moment have such privileges as these, the very hardest would melt and the dumb rock give forth "hosannas."

Will you still be silent when your mercies are so great? Let them not remain "forgotten in unthankfulness, and without praises die." Think yet again how little are your trials after all. You have not yet resisted unto blood while striving against sin. You are poor, it is true, but then you are not sick; or you are sick, but still you are not left to wallow in sin. All afflictions are but small when once sin is put away. Compare your trials with those of many who live in your own neighborhood. Put your sufferings side by side with the sufferings of some whom you have seen on their death beds. Compare your lot with that of the martyrs who have entered into their rest. Then, you will be compelled to exclaim with Paul, "*I reckon that the sufferings of this present time are not worthy to be compared to the glory which shall be revealed in us*" (Romans 8:18).

Come, now, I implore you, by the mercies of God, to be of good cheer and rejoice in the Lord your God, if it were for no other reason than that of the brave-hearted Luther. When he had been most slandered, when the Pope had launched out a new edict against him, and when the kings of the earth had threatened him fiercely, Luther would gather together his friends and say, "Come let us sing a psalm and spite the devil." He would sing the most psalms when the world roared the most. Let us now join the great German in recalling his favorite psalm:

God is our refuge and strength, a very present help in trouble. Therefore will not we fear, though the earth be removed, and though the mountains be carried into the midst of the sea; though the waters thereof roar and be troubled, though the mountains shake with the swelling thereof. (Psalm 46:1–3)

So, sing to make Satan angry. He has vexed the saints. Let us vex him.

Praise the Lord to put the world to shame. Never let it be said that the world can make its devotees happier than Christ can make His followers. Let your songs be so continual and so sweet, that the wicked are compelled to say, "That man's life is happier than mine. I long to exchange with him. There is a something in his religion which my life and my wicked pleasures can never afford me." Praise the Lord, saints, that sinners' mouths may be set watering after the things of God. Especially praise Him in your trials, if you would make the world wonder. Strike sinners silent and make them long to know and taste the joys of which you are a partaker.

"Alas!" says one, "I cannot sing. I have nothing to sing of, nothing external for which I could praise God." It is remarked by old commentators that the windows of Solomon's temple were narrow on the outside, but that they were broad within, and that they were so cut, that though they seemed to be only small openings, yet the light was well diffused. (See the Hebrew text of 1 Kings 6:4.) So is it with the windows of a believer's joy. They may look very narrow without, but they are very wide within. There is more joy from that which is within us than from that which is outside us. God's grace within, God's love, the witness of His Spirit in our hearts, these are better themes of joy than all the corn, wine, and oil with which God sometimes increases His saints. So if you have no outward mercies, sing of inward mercies. If the water fails without, go to that perpetual fountain which is within your own soul. *"A good man shall be satisfied from himself"* (Proverbs 14:14). When you see no cheering providence without, yet look at grace within. *"Awake, awake, Deborah! awake, awake, utter a song."*

I do not know whether you feel as I do, but in teaching about this theme, I lament over my scantiness of words and slowness of language. If I could let my heart express itself without speech or written prose, I think with God's Spirit, I could move you indeed with joy. But I find that the language of the heart is beyond them. My mind has discovered that it cannot express the fullness of joy that is within me through the confines of human language.

I now turn to the second part of this subject, very briefly and inadequately. *"Arise, Barak, and lead thy captivity captive, thou son of Abinoam."* Understand the exact picture here. Barak had routed Sisera, Jabin's captain, and all his hosts. Deborah now exhorts Barak to celebrate his triumph. as if she were saying, "Mount your chariot, Barak, and ride through the midst of the people. Let the corpse of Sisera with Jael's nail driven through its temples be dragged behind your chariot. Let the thousand captives of the Canaanites walk with their arms bound behind them. Drive before you the ten thousand flocks of sheep and herds of cattle that you have taken as a spoil. Let their chariots of iron and all their horses be led captive in grand procession. Bring up all the treasures and the jewels of which you have stripped the slain, with their armor, shields, and spears bound up as glorious trophies. Arise, Barak, lead captive those who led you captive, and celebrate your glorious victory."

Beloved, this is a picture which is often used in Scripture. It is written of Christ that, *"when he ascended up on high, he led captivity captive"* (Ephesians 4:8). He led principalities and powers captive at His chariot wheels. But here is a picture for us, not concerning Christ, but concerning ourselves. We are exhorted to lead captivity captive today.

Come up, come up, you great hosts of sins, once my terror and dismay. Long was I your slave, you Egyptian tyrants. Long did this back smart beneath your lash when conscience was awakened. Long did these members of my body yield themselves as willing servants to obey your dictates. Come up, sins, come up, for you are prisoners now. You are bound in fetters of iron—no, even more than this—you are utterly slain, consumed, destroyed. You have been covered with Jesus' blood. You have been blotted out by His mercy. You have been cast by His power into the depths of the sea. Yet would I bid your ghosts come up, slain though you be, and walk in grim procession behind my chariot. Arise, people of God, celebrate your triumph. Your sins are many, but they are all forgiven. Your iniquities are great, but they are all put away. Arise and lead captive those who led you captive—your blasphemies, your forgetfulness of God, your drunkenness, your lust, all the vast legion that once oppressed you. They are all completely destroyed. Come and look upon them, sing their death psalm, and chant the life psalm of your grateful joy. Lead your sins captive this very day.

Bring here, bound in chains, another host who once seemed too many for us, but whom by God's grace we have totally overcome. Arise, my trials. You have been very great and very numerous. You came against me as a great host, and you were tall and strong like the sons of Anak. O my soul, you have beaten down their strength. By the help of our God have we leaped over a wall. By His power have we broken through the troops of our troubles, our difficulties, and our fears. Come now, look back and think of all the trials you have ever encountered—death in your family, losses in your business, afflictions in your body, despair in your soul. Yet here you are, more than conquerors over them all. Come, bid them all walk now in procession. To the God of our deliverances, who has delivered us out of deep waters, who has brought us out of the burning, fiery furnace, so that the smell of fire has not passed upon us—to Him be all the glory, while we lead our trials captive.

Arise and let us lead captive all our temptations. You, dear believers, have been foully tempted to the vilest sins. Satan has shot a thousand darts at you and hurled his javelin multitudes of times. Bring out the darts and snap them before his eyes, for he has never been able to reach your heart. Come, break the bow, and cut the spear in two. Burn the chariot in the fire. *"Thy right hand, O Lord, is become glorious in power: thy right hand, O Lord, hath dashed in pieces the enemy; And in the greatness of thine excellency, thou hast overthrown them that rose up against thee"* (Exodus 15:6–7). Come, children of God, kept and preserved where so many have fallen, lead now this day your temptations captive.

I want to give you hope in the example of how the Metropolitan Tabernacle congregation has indeed led captivity captive. No single church of God existing in England for the past fifty years has had to pass through more trial than we have done. We can say, *"'Thou hast caused men to ride over our heads; we went through fire and through water.'"* What has been the result of it all? *"'But thou broughtest us out into a wealthy place'* (Psalm 66:12) and set our feet in a large room. All the devices of the enemy have been of no effect."

Scarcely a day rolls over my head in which the most villainous abuse, the most fearful slander is not uttered against me both privately and by the public press. Every device is employed to put down God's minister; every lie that man can invent is hurled at me. But thus far the Lord has helped me. I have never answered any man, nor spoken a word in my own defense, from the first day until now. The effect has been this: God's people have believed nothing against me. They who fear the Lord have said as often as a new falsehood has been uttered, "This is not true concerning that man. He will not answer for himself, but God will answer for him." They have not checked our usefulness as a church. They have not thinned our congregation. That which was to be but a spasm—an enthusiasm which it was hoped would only last an hour—God has daily increased, not because of me, but because of that gospel which I preach; not because there was anything in me, but because I came out as the exponent of straightforward, honest doctrine; and not because I speak according to the critical dictates of man, but because I seek to speak the Word simply, so that the poor may comprehend what I have to say.

The Lord has helped us as a church. Everything has contributed to help us. The great and terrible catastrophe, invented by Satan to overturn us, was only blessed of God to swell the stream. Now I would not shut a liar's mouth if I could, nor would I stop a slanderer if it were in my power, except so that he might not sin. All these things only aid our profit, and all these attacks do but widen the stream of usefulness. Many a sinner who has been converted to God in our church was first brought to us because of some strange anecdote, some lying tale which had been told of God's servant, the minister. I say it boasting in the Lord my God. Though I become a fool in glorying, I do lead in God's name my captivity captive. Arise! Arise! You who have followed the son of Barak, and have gone up as the thousands at his feet, arise and triumph for God is with us, and His cause will prosper. His own right arm is made bare in the eyes of all the people, and all the ends of the earth will see the salvation of our God.

As it is in this one church and in our own individual spheres, so it will be in the church at large. God's ministers are all attacked; God's truth is everywhere assailed. A terrible battle awaits us. O church of God, remember your former victories. Awake, ministers of Christ, and lead your captivity captive. Sing of how the idols of Greece tottered before you. Say, "Where is Diana now? Where are the gods that made glad ancient Ephesus?" Was not Rome's arm broken before the majesty of the church's might? Where is Jupiter, where Saturn, where Venus? They have ceased to be. And you Vishnu, you Brahma, you gods of China and India, you too must fall, for this day the sons of Jehovah arise and lead their captivity captive.

Come, behold the works of the Lord, *what desolations he hath made in the earth. He maketh wars to cease unto the end of the earth; he breaketh the bow, and cutteth the spear in sunder; he burneth the chariot in the fire. Be still, and know that I am God: I will be exalted among the heathen, I will be exalted in the earth.* (Psalm 46:8–10)

Church of God, come forth with songs. Come forth with shouting to your last battle. Behold the battle of Armageddon draws near. Blow the silver trumpets for the fight, soldiers of the cross. Come on, come on, you besieged hosts of hell. Strong in the strength of God Almighty, we will dash back your ranks as the rock breaks the waves of the sea. We will stand against you triumphantly and tread you down as ashes under the soles of our feet. *"Arise, Barak, and lead thy captivity captive, thou son of Abinoam."*

I pray to God that the joy of heart which I feel may entice some soul to seek the same. That peaceful, joyous inner state is to be found only in Christ at the foot of His dear cross. Believe on Him, sinner, and you shall be saved.

Beloved believer, may the triumphant joy to be found in the victories of winning the battle ring in your hearts today. May the Lord of Hosts grant you the ability to praise Him bountifully even in the thick of warfare when the enemy has yet to be overcome. Amen.

2

HEAVENLY ADORATION

I will extol thee, my God, O king; and I will bless thy name for ever and ever.
Every day will I bless thee; and I will praise thy name for ever and ever.
—Psalm 145:1–2

I f I were to put to you the question, "Do you pray?" the answer would very quickly given by every Christian, "Of course I do." Suppose I then added, "And do you pray every day?" the prompt reply would be, "Yes, many times in the day. I could not live without prayer." This is no more than I would expect.

However, let me change the inquiry and ask, "Do you bless God every day? Is praise as certain and constant a practice with you as prayer?" I am not sure that the answer would be quite so certain, so generous, or so prompt. You would have to stop a little while before you gave the reply. I fear in some cases, when the reply did come, it would be, "I am afraid I have been negligent in praise." Well, dear friend, have you not been wrong? Should we omit praise any more than we omit prayer? Should not praise come daily and as many times in the day as prayer does? It strikes me that to fail in praise is as unjustifiable as to fail in prayer. I will leave it with your own heart and conscience, when you have answered the question, to see to it in the future that far more of the sweet frankincense of praise is mingled with your daily offering of prayer.

Praise is certainly not at all so common in family prayer as other forms of worship. We cannot all of us praise God in the family by joining in song, because we are not all able to carry a tune, but it would be well if we could. I agree with Matthew Henry when he says, "They that pray in the family do well; they that pray and read the Scriptures do better; but they that pray, and read, and sing do best of all." There is a completeness in that kind of family worship which is much to be desired.

Whether in the family or not, let us endeavor to be filled personally and privately with God's praise and honor all the day. Let this be our resolve: *"I will extol thee, my God, O king; and I will bless thy name for ever and ever. Every day will I bless thee; and I will praise thy name for ever and ever."*

Praise cannot be a second-class business for it is evidently due to God, and that in a very high degree. A sense of justice and duty ought to make us praise the Lord. It is the least we can do, and in some senses it is the most that we can do, in return for the multiplied benefits which He bestows upon us. What, no harvest of praise for Him who has sent the sunshine of His love and the rain of His grace upon us? What, no revenue of praise for Him who is our gracious Lord and King? He does not exact from us any servile labor, but simply says, *"Whoso offereth praise glorifieth me"* (Psalm 50:23). Praise is good, pleasant, and delightful. Let us rank it among those debts which we would not wish to forget, but are eager to pay at once.

Praise is an act which is preeminently characteristic of the true child of God. The man who only pretends piety will fast twice a week, and stand in the temple and offer something like prayer. But to praise God with all the heart, this is the mark of true adoption, this is the sign and token of a heart renewed by divine grace. We lack one of the surest evidences of the pure love of God if we live without presenting praise to His blessed name.

Praising God is singularly beneficial to ourselves. If we had more of it, we would be greatly blessed. What would lift us so much above the trials of life, what would help us to bear the burden and heat of the day, as well as songs of praise to the Most High? The soldier marches without weariness when the band is playing spirited strains. The sailor, as he pulls the rope or lifts the anchor, utters a cheery cry to aid his toil. Let us likewise try the animating power of hymns of praise.

Nothing would oil the wheels of the chariot of life so well as more praising of God. Praise would end murmuring and nurse contentment. If our mouths were filled with the praises of God, there would be no room for grumbling. Praise throws a halo of glory around the head of toil and thought. In its sunlight the basest duties of life are transfigured. Sanctified by prayer and praise, each duty is raised to a hallowed worship, akin to that of heaven. It makes us more happy, more holy, and more heavenly, when we say, "*I will extol thee, my God, O King.*"

Besides, unless we praise God here, are we preparing for our eternal employment? All is praise in heaven. If we are strangers to that exercise, how can we hope to enter in? This life is a preparatory school, and in it we are preparing for the high calling of the perfected. Are you not eager to rehearse the everlasting hallelujahs?

> I would begin the music here,
>> And so my soul should rise:
> Oh, for some heavenly notes to bear
>> My passions to the skies!

Learn the essential elements of heavenly praise by the practice of joyful thanksgiving, adoring reverence, and wondering love. Then, when you step into heaven, you may take your place among the singers and say, "I have been practicing these songs for years. I have praised God while I was in a world of sin and suffering, and when I was weighed down by a feeble body. Now that I am set free from earth, sin, and the bondage of the flesh, I take up the same strain to sing more sweetly to the same Lord and God."

I wish I knew what to say that would stir up every child of God to praise. As for you that are not His children—oh, that you were such! You must be born again. You cannot really praise God till you are. "*Unto the wicked God saith, What hast you to do to declare my statutes, or that you shouldest take my covenant in thy mouth?*" (Psalm 50:16). You can offer Him no real praise while your hearts are at enmity with Him. Be reconciled to God by the death of his Son, and then you will praise Him. Let no one that has tasted that the Lord is gracious, let no one that has ever been delivered from sin by the atonement of Christ, ever fail to pay to the Lord His daily tribute of thanksgiving.

To help us in this joyful duty of praise, we will examine our text and keep to it. May the Holy Spirit instruct us by it! We have first of all the resolve of personal loyalty: "*I will extol thee, my God, O king...for ever and ever.*" David personally comes before his God and King and utters this deliberate resolution that he will praise the divine Majesty forever.

Note here, first, that he pays homage to God as his King. There is no praising God correctly if we do not see Him upon the throne, reigning with unquestioned sway. Disobedient subjects cannot praise their sovereign. You must take up the Lord's yoke—it is easy—and His burden, which is light. You must come to Him, touch His scepter, receive His mercy, and own Him as your rightful Monarch, Lawgiver, and Ruler. Where Jesus comes, He comes to reign. Where God is truly known, He is always known as supreme. Over the united kingdom of our bodies, souls, and spirits the Lord must reign with undisputed authority. What a joy it is to have such a King!

"*O king,*" says David, and it seems to have been a sweet morsel in his mouth. He was himself a king after the earthly fashion, but to him God alone was King. Our King is no tyrant, no maker of cruel laws. He demands no crushing tribute or forced service. His "*ways are ways of pleasantness, and all* [His] *paths are peace*" (Proverbs 3:17). His laws are just and good, and "*in the keeping of them there is great reward*" (Psalm 19:11). Let others exalt that they are their own masters; our joy is that God is our King. Let others yield to this or that passion or desire; as for us, we find our freedom in complete subjection to our heavenly King. Let us praise God by loyally accepting Him as our King. Let us repeat with exaltation the hymn:

> Crown him, crown him
> King of kings, and Lord of lords.

Let us not be satisfied that He reigns over us only, but let us long for the whole earth to be filled with His glory. Let this be our daily prayer: "*Thy kingdom come. Thy will be done, in earth as it is in heaven*" (Matthew 6:10). Let us constantly ascribe to Him this praise: "*For thine is the kingdom, and the power, and the glory, forever. Amen*" (Matthew 6:13).

Also note that the psalmist, in this first sentence, praises the Lord by a personal appropriation of God to himself by faith: "*I will extol thee, my God.*" That word "*my*" is a drop of honey. Even more, it is like Jonathan's wood, full of honey; it seems to drip from every bough. He that comes into it stands knee-deep in sweetness. "*My God*" is as high a note as an angel can reach. What is another man's God to me? He must be my God, or I will not extol Him. Dear heart, have you ever taken God to be your God? Can you say with David in another place, "*This God is our God forever and ever; he shall be our guide, even unto death*" (Psalm 48:14)?

Blessed was Thomas when he bowed down, touched his Master's wounds with his finger, and cried, "*My Lord and my God*" (John 20:28). That double-handed grip of appropriation marked the death of his painful unbelief. Can you say, "Jehovah is my God"? To us there are Father, Son, and Holy Spirit; but these are one God, and this one God is our own God. Let others worship whom they will, this God our souls adore, love, and claim to be our personal possession. O beloved, if you can say, "*My God,*" you will be bound to exalt Him! If He has given Himself to you so that you can say, "*My Beloved is mine*" (Song of Solomon 2:16), you will give yourself to Him, and you will add, "*And I am his.*" Those two sentences, like two covers of a book, shut within them the full score of the music of heaven.

Observe that David is firmly resolved to praise God. This text has four "*I will's*" in it. Frequently it is foolish for us poor mortals to say "*I will*" because our will is so feeble and fickle. But when we resolve to praise our God, we may say, "*I will…I will…I will…I will,*" until we make a solid footing of determinations. Let me tell you that you will need to say "*I will*" a great many times, for many obstacles will hinder your resolve. There will come depression of spirit, and then you must say, "*I will extol thee, my God, O King.*" Poverty, sickness, losses, and crosses may assail you, and then you must say, "*I will praise thy name forever and ever.*" The devil will come to tell you that you have no interest in Christ, but you must say, "*Every day will I bless thee.*" When death comes, perhaps you will be in fear of it. Then it will be incumbent upon you to cry, "*I will praise thy name forever and ever.*"

> Sing, though sense and carnal reason
>   Fain would stop the joyful song:
> Sing, and count it highest treason
>   For a saint to hold his tongue.

A bold man took this motto: "While I live, I'll crow," but our motto is, "While I live, I'll praise." An old motto was, "*Dum spiro spero,*" but the saint improves upon it and cries, "*Dum expiro spero.*" Not only while I live, will I hope; but when I die, I will hope. The believer even gets beyond all that and determines,

"Whether I live or die, I will praise my God. O God, my heart is fixed; I will sing and give praise."

While David is thus resolute, I want you to notice that the resolution is strictly personal. He says, "*I will extol thee.*" Whatever others do, his own mind is made up. David was very glad when others praised God. He delighted to join with the great congregation that kept holy days, but still he was attentive to his own heart and his own praise. There is no selfishness in looking well to your own personal state and condition before the Lord. He cannot be called a selfish citizen who is very careful to render his own personal suit and service to his King. A company of persons praising God would be nothing unless each individual was sincere and earnest in the worship. The praise of the great congregation is precious in such proportion as each individual, with all his heart, is saying, "*I will extol thee, my God, O King.*"

Come, my soul, I will not sit silent because so many others are singing. However many songsters there may be, they cannot sing for me. They cannot pay my personal debt of praise. Therefore awake, my heart, and extol your God and King. What if others refuse to sing, what if a shameful silence is observed in reference to the praises of God? Then, my heart, I must stir you even more to a double diligence, that you may with even greater zeal extol your God and King! I will sing a solo if I cannot find a choir in which I may take my part. Anyhow, my God, "*I will extol thee.*" At this hour men go off to other lords and set up this and that newly made god. But as for me, my ear is bored to God's doorpost as a sign of my being His bond slave. I will not go out from His service forever. Bind the sacrifice with cords, even with cords to the horns of the altar. Whatever happens, "*I will extol thee, my God, O King.*"

Now, brothers and sisters, have you been losing your own personality in the multitude? As members of a church, have you thought, "Things will continue very well without me"? Correct that mistake. Each individual must have its own note to bring to God. Let Him not have to say to you, "*Thou hast bought me no sweet cane with money; neither hast thou filled me with the fat of thy sacrifices*" (Isaiah 43:24). Let us not be slow in His praise, since He has been so swift in His grace.

Once more observe that, while David is thus loyally resolving to praise God, he is praising all the time. The resolution to praise can only come from the man who is already praising God. When he says, "*I will extol thee,*" he is already extolling. We go from praise to praise. The heart resolves and so plants the seed. Then the life is affected, and the harvest springs up and ripens. Do not let us say, "I will extol You tomorrow," or, "I will hope to praise You when I grow old, or when I have less business on hand." No, you are this day in debt. This day admit your obligation. We cannot praise God too soon.

Our very first breath is a gift from God, and it should be spent in the Creator's praise. The early morning hour should be dedicated to praise. Do not the birds set us the example? In this matter, he gives twice who gives quickly. Let your praise follow quickly your receiving of benefits, lest even during the delay you are found guilty of ingratitude. As soon as a mercy touches our coasts, we should welcome it with acclamation. Let us copy the little chick, which lifts up its head as it drinks as if to give thanks. Our thanksgiving should echo the voice of divine loving-kindness. Before the Lord our King, let us continually rejoice as we bless Him and speak well of His name.

Thus, I have set before you the resolve of a loyal spirit. Are you loyal to your God and King? Then I charge you to glorify His name. Lift up your hearts in His praise, and in all manner of ways make His name great. Praise Him with your lips. Praise Him with your lives. Praise Him with your substance. Praise Him with every faculty and capacity. Be inventive in methods of praise: *"Sing unto the Lord a new song"* (Psalm 96:1). Bring forth the long-stored and costly alabaster box. Break it open, and pour the sweet nard upon your Redeemer's head and feet. With penitents and martyrs, extol Him! With prophets and apostles, extol Him! With saints and angels. extol Him! *"For the Lord is great, and greatly to be praised"* (Psalm 96:4).

Now let us examine the second clause of the text which is equally full and instructive. We have in the second part of the verse the conclusion of an intelligent appreciation: *"And I will bless thy name forever and ever."* Blind praise is not fit for the all-seeing God. God forbade of old the bringing of blind sacrifices to His altar. Our praise ought to have brains as well as a tongue. We ought to know who the God is whom we praise. Hence David says, *"I will bless thy name,"* by which he meant God's character, His deeds, His revealed attributes.

First, observe that David presents the worship of inward admiration. He knows, and therefore he blesses the divine name. What is this act of blessing? Sometimes *"bless"* would appear to be used interchangeably with *"praise."* Yet there is a difference, for it is written, *"All thy works shall praise thee, O Lord;*

and thy saints shall bless thee" (Psalm 145:10). You can praise a man, and yet you may never bless him. For instance, you may praise a great artist, but he may be so ungenerous to you and others that it may never occur to you to bless him. Blessing has something in it of love and delight. It is a nearer, dearer, heartier thing than praise. Saying, *"I will bless thy name,"* is to say, "I will take an intense delight in Your name. I will lovingly rejoice in it."

The very thought of God is a source of happiness to our hearts. The more we meditate on His character, the more joyous we become. The Lord's name is love. He is merciful and gracious, tender and pitiful. Moreover, He is a just God, righteous, faithful, true, and holy. He is a mighty God, wise and unchanging. He is a prayer-hearing God, and He keeps His promise evermore. We would not have Him other than He is. We have a sweet contentment in God as He is revealed in Scripture. Not everybody can say this, for a great many of those who profess faith nowadays desire a god of their own making and shaping. If they find anything in Scripture concerning God that grates on their tender susceptibilities, they cannot abide it. The God that casts the wicked from His presence forever— they cannot believe in Him. They therefore make unto themselves a false deity who is indifferent to sin.

All that is revealed concerning God is to me abundantly satisfactory. If I do not comprehend its full meaning, I bow before its mystery. If I hear anything of my God which does not yield me delight, I feel that there I must be out of order with Him, either through sin or ignorance, and I say, "What I know not, teach me, Lord."

I do not doubt that perfectly holy and completely informed beings are fully content with everything that God does and are ready to praise Him for all. Do not our souls even now bless our Lord God, who chose us, redeemed us, and called us by His grace? Whether we view him as Maker, Provider, Savior, King, or Father, we find in Him an unfathomable sea of joy. He is God, our exceeding joy. Therefore, we sit down in holy quiet and feel our souls saying, "Bless the Lord!" He is what we would have Him to be. He is better than we could have supposed or imagined. He is the crown of delight, the climax of goodness, the sum of all perfection. As often as we see the light or feel the sun, we desire to bless the Lord's name.

I believe that when David said, *"I will bless thy name,"* he meant that he wished well to the Lord. To bless a person means to do that person good. By blessing us, what untold benefits the Lord bestows! We cannot bless God in such a sense as that in which He blesses us, but we would if we could. If we cannot give anything to God, we can desire that He may be known, loved, and obeyed by all men. We can wish well to His kingdom and cause in the world. We can bless Him by blessing His people, by working for the fulfillment of His purposes, by obeying His precepts, and by taking delight in His ordinances. We can bless Him by submission to His chastening hand and by gratitude for His daily benefits. Sometimes we say with the psalmist, "*O my soul, thou hast said unto the* LORD, *thou art my Lord: my goodness extendeth not to thee; but to the saints that are in the earth, and to the excellent, in whom is all my delight*" (Psalm 16:2–3).

If only I could wash Jesus Christ's feet! Is there any believer, man or woman, who would not aspire to that office? It is not denied you. You can wash His feet by caring for His poor people and relieving their wants. You cannot provide a feast for your Redeemer. He is not hungry, but some of His people are. Feed them! He is not thirsty, but some of His disciples are. Give them a cup of cold water in the Master's name, and He will accept it as given to Himself. Do you not feel today, you that love Him, as if you wanted to do something for Him? Arise, do it, and so bless Him. It is one of the instincts of a true Christian to wish to do something for his God and King, who has done everything for him. He loved me and gave Himself for me. Should I not give myself for Him? Oh, for perfect consecration! Oh, to bless God by laying our all upon His altar and spending our lives in His service!

It seems, dear friends, that David studied the character and actions of God and thus praised Him. Knowledge should lead our song. The more we know of God, the more acceptably will we bless Him through Jesus Christ. I exhort you, therefore, to acquaint yourselves with God. Study His holy Book. As in a mirror you may there see the glory of the Lord reflected, especially in the person of the Lord Jesus, who is in truth the Word, the very name of the Lord. It would be a pity that we should spoil our praises by ignorance.

They that know the name of the Lord will trust Him and will praise Him. It appears from this text that David discovered nothing after a long study of God which would be an exception to this rule. David does not say, "I will bless Your name in all but one thing. I have seen some point of terror in what you have revealed of Yourself, and in that thing I cannot bless You." No, without any exception he reverently adores and joyfully blesses God. All his heart is contented with all of God that is revealed. Is it so with us, beloved? I earnestly hope it is.

I beg you to notice how intense he becomes over this: "*I will bless thy name forever and ever.*" You have heard the quaint saying of "forever and a day." Here you have a gain on it: it is "forever" and then another "forever." David says, "*I will bless thy name forever.*" Is not that long enough? No, he adds, "*and ever.*" Are there two forevers, two eternities? If there were fifty eternities, we would spend them all in blessing the name of the Lord our God. "*I will bless thy name forever and ever.*" It would be absurd to explain this hyperbolic expression. It runs parallel with the words of Addison, when he says:

> Through all eternity to thee
>   My song of joy I'll raise;
> But oh, eternity's too short
>   To utter all thy praise!

Somebody found fault with that verse the other day. He said, "Eternity cannot be too short." Ah, my dear friend was not a poet, I can see. But if he could get just a spark of poetry into his soul, literalism would vanish. Truly, in poetry and in praise, the letter kills. Language is a poor vehicle of expression when the soul is on fire. Words are good things for our cool judgment, but when thoughts are full of praise, they break the back of words. How often have I felt that if I could throw my tongue away and let my heart speak without syllables and arbitrary sounds, then I might express myself! David speaks as if he scorned to be limited by language. He must leap even over time and possibility to find room for his heart. "*I will bless thy name forever and ever.*" How I enjoy these enthusiastic expressions! It shows that when David blessed the Lord, he did it heartily. While he was musing, the fire burned. He felt like dancing before the ark. He was in much the same frame of mind as Dr. Watts when he sang:

> From thee, my God, my joys shall rise
>   And run eternal rounds,
> Beyond the limits of the skies
>   And all created bounds.

But I must move on to the third sentence of our text, which is, the pledge of daily remembrance. On this I would dwell with great earnestness. If you forget my teaching, I would like you to remember this part of the text: "*Every day will I bless thee.*" This does not mean that I will do it now and be done with it, or I will take a week of the year in which to praise Him and leave the other fifty-one weeks silent, but rather *"every day will I bless thee."*

All through the year I will extol my God. Why should it be so? The greatness of the gifts which we have already received demands it. We can never fully express our gratitude for saving grace, and therefore we must keep at it. A few years ago we were lost and dead, but we have been found and made alive again. We must praise God every day for this. We were black as night with sin, but now we are washed whiter than snow. When can we cease praising our Lord for this? He loved me and gave Himself for me. When can the day come that I will stop praising Him for this? Gethsemane and the bloody sweat, Calvary and the precious blood, when will we ever be done with praising our dear Lord for all He suffered when He bought us with His own heart's blood? No, if it were only the first mercies—the mercy of election, the mercy of redemption, the mercy of effectual calling, the mercy of adoption—we have had enough to begin with to make us sing unto the Lord every day of our lives. The light which has risen on us warms all our days with gladness. It will also light them up with praise.

Today it becomes us to sing of the mercies of yesterday. The waves of love as well as of time have washed us up on the shore of today, and the beach is strewn with love. I find myself on Sunday morning exalting because another six days' work is done, and strength has been given for it. Some of us have experienced a world of loving-kindness between one Sunday and the next. If we had never had anything else from God but what we have received during the last week, we have overwhelming reason for extolling Him today. If there is any day in which we would refrain from praising God, it must not be the Lord's day, for:

> This is the day the Lord hath made,
>   He calls the hours his own.
> Let heaven rejoice, let earth be glad,
>   And praise surround the throne.

Oh, let us magnify the Lord on the day of which it can be said:

> Today he rose and left the dead,
>   And Satan's empire fell.
> Today the saints his triumphs spread,
>   And all his wonders tell.

When we reach Monday, will we not praise God for the blessing of Sunday? Surely you cannot have forgotten the Lord as quickly as Monday! Before you go out into the world, wash your face in the clear crystal of praise. Bury each yesterday in the fine linen and spices of thankfulness.

Each day has its own mercies and should return its praise. When Monday is over, you will have something to praise God for on Tuesday. He that watches for God's hand will never be long without seeing it. If you will only spy out God's mercies, with half an eye you will see them every day of the year. Fresh are the dews of each morning, and equally fresh are its blessings. "Fresh trouble," says one. Praise God for the trouble, for it is a richer form of blessing. "Fresh care," says another. *"Cast all your care on him, for he careth for you"* (1 Peter 5:7), and that act will in itself bless you. "Fresh labor," says another. Yes, but fresh strength, too. There is never a night that a day does not follow it, never an affliction without its consolation. Every day you must utter the memory of His great goodness.

If we cannot praise God on any one day for what we have had that day, let us praise Him for tomorrow. It will be better than before. Let us learn that quaint verse:

> And a new song is in my mouth,
>   To long-lived music set;
> Glory to thee for all the grace
>   I have not tasted yet.

Let us forestall our future and draw upon the promises. What if today I am down? Tomorrow I will be up! What if today I cast ashes on my head? Tomorrow the Lord will crown me with loving-kindness! What if today my pains trouble me? They will soon be gone! It will be all the same a hundred years from now, so let me praise God for what is within measurable distance. In a few years I will be with the angels and be with my Lord Himself. Blessed be His name! Begin to enjoy heaven now. What does Paul say? *"For our citizenship is in heaven"* (Philippians 3:20 RV), not is going to be, but is. We belong to heaven now. Our names are enrolled among its citizens. The privileges of the new Jerusalem belong to us at this present moment. Christ is ours, and God is ours!

> This world is ours,
>   And worlds to come;

> Earth is our lodge,
> And heaven our home.

Therefore let us rejoice and be exceeding glad, and praise the name of God this very day. *"Every day,"* said David, *"will I bless thee."*

There is a seasonable sense about the praising of God every day. Praise is in season every month. When you awoke, the sunlight streamed into the windows and touched your eyelids, and you said, "Bless God. Here is a charming summer's day." Birds were singing, and flowers were pouring out their perfume. You could not help praising God. But another day it was dark at the time of your rising. You groped in the dark to find the light. A thick fog hung like a blanket over all. If you were a wise man, you said, "Come, I will not get through the day if I do not make up my mind to praise God. This is the kind of weather in which I must bless God, or else go down in despair." So you woke yourself up and began to adore the Lord. One morning you awoke after a refreshing night's rest, and you praised God for it; but on another occasion, you had tossed about through a sleepless night, and then you thanked God that the weary night was over.

You smile, dear friends, but there is always some reason for praising God. Certain fruits and meats are in season at special times, but the praise of God is always in season. It is good to praise the Lord in the daytime. How charming is the lark's song as it carols up to heaven's gate! It is good to bless God at night. How delicious are the liquid notes of the nightingale as it thrills the night with its music! Therefore I say to you very heartily, "Come, let us praise the Lord together, in all sorts of weather and in all sorts of places."

Sometimes I have said to myself, "During this last week I have been so full of pain that I am afraid I have forgotten to praise God as much as I should have done, and therefore I will have a double portion of it now. I will get alone and have a special time of thankful thought. I want to make up some of my debts and magnify the Lord above measure." I do not like feeling that there can ever be a day in which I have not praised Him. That day would surely be a blank in my life.

Truly the sweetest praise that ever ascends to God is that which is poured forth by saints from beds of languishing. Praise in sad times is praise indeed. When your dog loves you because it is dinnertime, you are not sure of him; but when somebody else tempts him with a bone and he will not leave you, though just now you struck him, then you feel that he is truly attached to you. We may learn from dogs that true affection is not dependent upon what it is just now receiving. Let us not have a cupboard love for God because of His kind providence, but let us love Him and praise Him for what He is and what He has done. Let us follow hard after Him when He seems to forsake us, and praise Him when He deals hardly with us, for this is true praise. For me, though I am not without affliction for very long, I have no fault to find with my Lord. I desire to praise Him, and praise Him, and only to praise Him. Oh, that I knew how to do it worthily! Here is my resolve: *"I will extol thee, my God, O King; and I will bless thy name forever and ever. Every day will I bless thee."*

The last sentence of the text sets forth the hope of eternal adoration. David here exclaims, *"And I will praise thy name forever and ever."* I am quite sure when David said that, he believed that God is unchangeable. If God could change, how can I be sure that He will always be worthy of my praise? David knew that what God had been, He was, and what He was, then He always would be. He had not heard the sentence, *"Jesus Christ the same yesterday, and today, and forever"* (Hebrews 13:8), nor this, *"I am the LORD, I change not; therefore ye sons of Jacob are not consumed"* (Malachi 3:6). However, he knew the truth contained in both these verses, and therefore he said, *"I will praise thy name forever and ever."* As long as God is, He will be worthy to be praised.

Another point is also clear: David believed in the immortality of the soul. He says, *"I will praise thy name forever and ever."* That truth was very dimly revealed in the Old Testament, but David knew it very well. He did not expect to sleep in oblivion, but to go on praising. Therefore he said *"I will praise thy name forever and ever."* No cold hand fell upon him, and no killing voice said to him, "You shall die and never praise the Lord again." Oh, no, he looked to live forever and ever, and praise forever and ever! Such is our hope, and we will never give it up. We feel eternal life within our souls. We challenge the cold hand of death to quench the immortal flame of our love or to silence the ceaseless song of our praise. The dead cannot praise God. *"God is not the God of the dead, but of the living"* (Matthew 22:32). Among the living we are numbered through the grace of God, and we know that we will live because Jesus lives.

When death comes, it will bring no destruction to us. Though it will change the conditions of our existence, death will not change the object of our existence. Our tongues may be silenced for a little while, but our spirits, unaffected by the diseases of our bodies, will go on praising God in their own fashion. By and by, in the resurrection, even this poor tongue will be revived. Then body, soul, and spirit will together praise the God of resurrection and eternal glory. *"I will praise thy name forever and ever."* We will never grow weary of this hallowed exercise forever and ever. It will always be new, fresh, delightful. In heaven they never require any change beyond those blessed variations of song, those new melodies which make up the everlasting harmony. On and on, forever telling the tale which never will be fully told, the saints will praise the name of the Lord forever and ever.

Of course, dear friends, David's resolve was that he would never cease to praise God as long as he was here below. This is our resolve also. We may have to suspend some cherished engagements, but we will never cease from praise. At a certain period of life, a man may have to stop preaching to a large congregation. Good old John Newton declared that he would never cease preaching while he had breath in his body. I admire his holy perseverance, but it was a pity that he did not suspend his preaching, for he often wearied the people and forgot the thread of his sermon. He might have done better in another place.

Well we may cease preaching, but we must never suspend praising! The day will come when you, my dear friend, cannot go to Sunday school. I hope you will go as long as you can toddle there, but it may be that you will not be able to interest the children or that your memory will begin to fail. Even then you can go on praising the Lord. And you will, never fear. I have known old people almost forget their own names and their own children, but I have known them still to remember their Lord and Master. I have heard of one who lay dying, and his friends tried to make him remember certain things, but he shook his head. At last one said, "Do you remember the Lord Jesus?" Then the mind came into full play, the eyes brightened, and the old man eloquently praised his Savior. May our last gasp be given to the praise of the Lord.

When once we have passed through the iron gate and forded the dividing river, then we will begin to praise God in a manner more satisfactory than we can reach at present. After a nobler sort, we will sing and adore. What soaring we will attempt upon the eagle wings of love! What plunges we will take into the crystal stream of praise! I think, for a while, when we first behold the throne, we will do no more than cast our crowns at the feet of Him that loved us, and then bow down under a weight of speechless praise. We will be overwhelmed with wonder and thankfulness. When we rise to our feet again, we will join in the chorus of those redeemed by blood. We will only drop out of the song when again we feel overpowered with joyful adoration and are constrained again in holy silence to shrink to nothing before the infinite, unchanging God of love. Oh, to be there!

To be there soon! We may be much nearer than we think. I cannot tell what I will do, but I know this, I want no other heaven than to praise God perfectly and eternally. Is it not so with you? A heart full of praise is heaven in the bud. Perfect praise is heaven full-blown.

Let us ask for grace from God that, if we have been deficient in praise, we may now mend our ways and put on the garments of holy adoration. This day and onward may our watchword be, "Hallelujah! Praise the Lord!"

3

A PATTERN FOR PRAISE

*And when he was come nigh, even now at the descent of the mount of Olives,
the whole multitude of the disciples began to rejoice and praise God with a
loud voice for all the mighty works that they had seen; saying, Blessed be the
King that cometh in the name of the Lord: peace in heaven, and glory in the
highest. And some of the Pharisees from among the multitude said unto him,
Master, rebuke thy disciples. And he answered and said unto them, I tell you
that, if these should hold their peace, the stones would immediately cry out.*
—Luke 19:37–40

The Savior was truly *"a man of sorrows,"* but every thoughtful person
has discovered the fact that down deep in His innermost soul He
must have carried an inexhaustible treasury of refined and heavenly joy. I suppose
that of all the human race, there was never a man who had a deeper, purer, or
more abiding peace than our Lord Jesus Christ. He was *"anointed with the oil of
gladness above* [his] *fellows"* (Psalm 45:7).

Benevolence is joy. From the very nature of things, the highest benevolence
must have afforded the deepest possible delight. To be engaged in the most

blessed of all errands, to foresee the marvelous results of His labors in time and in eternity, and even to see around Him the fruits of the good which He had done in the healing of the sick and the raising of the dead, all must have given to such a sympathetic heart as that which beat within the bosom of the Lord Jesus Christ much secret satisfaction and joy. There were a few remarkable seasons when this joy manifested itself. *"At that hour Jesus rejoiced in spirit and said, I thank you, O Father, Lord of heaven and earth"* (Luke 10:21). Christ had His songs though it was night with Him, though His face was marred and His countenance had lost the luster of earthly happiness. Yet sometimes it was lit up with a matchless splendor of unparalleled satisfaction, as He thought upon the recompense of the reward and, in the midst of the congregation, sang His praise unto God.

In this, the Lord Jesus is a blessed picture of His church on earth. It is the day of Zion's trouble. At this hour the church expects to walk with her Lord along a thorny road. She is *"without the camp"* (Hebrews 13:13). Through much tribulation she is forcing her way to the crown. She expects to meet with reproaches. To bear the cross is her office, and to be scorned and counted an alien by her mother's children is her lot.

Yet the church has a deep well of joy, from which none can drink but her own children. There are stores of wine, oil, and corn hidden in the midst of our Jerusalem, upon which the saints of God are evermore sustained and nurtured. Sometimes, as in our Savior's case, we have our seasons of intense delight, for *"there is a river, the streams whereof shall make glad the city of our God"* (Psalm 46:4). Exiles though we are, we rejoice in our King. Yes, in Him we exceedingly rejoice, while in His name we set up our banners.

For each local assembly there is a season when we are peculiarly called upon to rejoice in God. The Lord Jesus, in the narrative before us, was going to Jerusalem. His disciples fondly hoped that He would take the throne of David and set up the long-expected kingdom. Well might they shout for joy, for the Lord was in their midst in state, riding amid the acclamations of a multitude who had been glad partakers of His goodness. Jesus Christ is in our midst today, too. The kingdom is securely His. We see the crown glittering upon His brow. He has been riding through our streets, healing our blind, raising our dead, and speaking words of comfort to our mourners. We, too, attend Him in state today. The acclamations of little children are not lacking, for from the Sunday school there have come songs of converted youngsters who sing gladly, as did the children of Jerusalem long ago, *"Hosanna! Blessed is he that cometh in the name of the Lord!"* (Mark 11:9).

I want, dear friends, to stir up in all of us the spirit of holy joy, because our King is in our midst. We need to welcome Him and rejoice in Him, so that He will not lack such music as our feeble lips can produce. Therefore, I invite your attention to these four verses, by way of example, that we may take a pattern for our praise from this inspired description. We will observe four things: first, delightful praise; secondly, appropriate song; thirdly, intrusive objections; fourthly, an unanswerable argument.

First, observe the delightful praise found here in the thirty-seventh verse. Every word is significant in this passage and deserves the careful notice of all who would learn the lesson of how to magnify the Savior. To begin with, the praise given to Christ was speedy praise. The happy choristers did not wait until He entered the city, but *"when he was come nigh, even now, at the descent of the mount of Olives, the whole multitude of disciples began to rejoice."* It is well to have a quick eye to perceive occasions for gratitude. Blind unbelief and bleary-eyed thanklessness allow the favors of God to lie forgotten in unthankfulness and die without praises. They walk in the noonday of mercy and see no light to sing by. But a believing, cheerful, grateful spirit detects at once the rising of the Sun of mercy and begins to sing, even at the break of day. Christian, if you sing of the mercy you have already, you would soon have more. If twilight has made you glad, you would soon have the bliss of noon. I am certain that the church in these days has lost much by not being thankful for little blessings.

We have had many prayer meetings, but very few praise meetings. It is as if the church believes she is able to cry loud enough for her own needs to be answered, but is dumb as to music for her Lord. Her King acts to her very much as He did with the man with the one talent. That man did not lend the money for interest, and therefore it was taken away. We have not thanked Him for little mercies, and therefore even these have been removed. Churches have become barren and deserted by the Spirit of God.

Let us lift up the voice of praise to our Master because He has blessed us. We have had a continual stream of revival. The cries of sinners have sounded in our ears; every day we have seen souls converted. Benjamin's mess (see Genesis 43:34) has been set near our place at the table, we have been made to feast on royal dainties, and we have been filled with bread until we have been completely sated. Shall we not praise God? Let us not require being told twice, but let our souls begin to praise Him even now, because He has come to Jerusalem.

It strikes us at once, also, that this was unanimous praise. Observe not only the multitude, but *"the whole multitude of the disciples"* rejoiced and praised Him. There was not one silent tongue among the disciples, not one who withheld his song. Yet, I suppose, those disciples had their trials as we have ours. There might have been a sick wife at home, or a child withering with disease. They were doubtless poor—we know they were, indeed—and poverty is never without its pinches. They were men of like passions as ourselves. They had to struggle with inbred sin and with temptation from without. Yet there seems to have been not one who, on those grounds, excluded himself from the choir of singers on that happy day. Oh, my soul, whatever you have about you which might bow you down, be glad when you remember that Jesus Christ is glorified in the midst of His church.

Beloved, why is that harp of yours hanging on the willows? (See Psalm 137:1–2.) Have you nothing to sing about? Has He done nothing for you? If you have no personal reason for blessing God, then lend us your heart and voice to help us, for we have more praise work on hand than we can get through alone; we have more to praise Him for than we are able to discharge without extra aid. Our work of praise is too great for us, so come and help us. Sing on our behalf, if you cannot on your own. Then, perhaps, you will catch the flame and find something after all for which you, too, must bless Him.

I know there are some of you who do not feel as if you could praise God at this moment. Ask the Master to put your harp in tune. Be not silent! Do bless Him! If you cannot bless Him for temporal gifts, bless Him for the spiritual ones. If you have not of late experientially enjoyed many of these, then bless Him for what He is. For that dear face covered with the bloody sweat, for those pierced hands, for that opened side, will you not praise Him? Surely, if He had not died for me, yet I must love Him, to think of His goodness in dying for others. His kindness and the generosity of His noble heart in dying for His enemies might well provoke the most unbelieving to a song. I am, therefore, not content unless all of you will contribute your note. I would have every bird throw in its note, though some cannot imitate the lark or nightingale. Yes, I would have every tree of the forest clap its hands, and even the hyssop on the wall wave in adoration. Come, beloved, cheer up. Let dull care and dark fear be gone. Up with harps and down with doubts.

Next, it was multitudinous. It must be praise from *"the whole multitude."* The praise must be unanimous—not one chord out of order to spoil the tune. There is something most inspiring and exhilarating in the noise of a multitude singing

God's praises. Sometimes, when the congregation has been in good tune and has sung, "Praise God from whom all blessings flow," our music has rolled upward like thunder to the dome and has reverberated peal on peal. These have been the happiest moments some of us have ever known, when every tongue was praise and every heart was joy. Oh, let us renew those happy times; let us anticipate the season when the dwellers in the East and in the West, in the North and in the South, of every age and of every climate, will assemble on the celestial hilltops and join the everlasting song, extolling Jesus as Lord of all. Jesus loves the praise of many. He loves to hear the voices of all the bloodwashed.

> Ten thousand thousand are their tongues,
> But all their joys are one.

Each local church is not as many as that, but we are counted by thousands. Therefore, let us, "*the whole multitude*," praise His name.

Still it is worthy of observation that, while the praise was multitudinous, it was quite select. It was the whole multitude "*of the disciples.*" The Pharisees did not praise Him; they were murmuring. All true praise must come from true hearts. If you do not learn of Christ, you cannot render to Him acceptable song. These disciples, of course, were of different sorts. Some of them had but just enlisted in the army, just learned to sit at His feet. Some had worked miracles in His name and had preached the word to others, having been called to the apostolic office. But they were all disciples. I trust that in today's church congregations, a vast majority of the people are disciples. Well, all of you—you who have lately come into His school, you who have long been in it, you who have become fathers in Israel and are teaching others, you the whole multitude of disciples—I hope, will praise God. May God grant my prayer that those of you who are not disciples might soon become so. "*Take my yoke upon you,*" He said, "*and learn of me, for I am meek and lowly in heart*" (Matthew 11:29).

A disciple is a student. You may not know much, but you need not know anything in coming to Christ. Christ begins with ignorance and bestows wisdom. If the only thing you know is that you know nothing, you know enough to become a disciple of Jesus. There is no matriculation necessary in order to enter into Christ's college. He takes fools and makes them know the wonders of His dying love. Oh, that you may become a disciple! "Write my name down, sir," say you to the writer with the inkhorn by his side. Henceforth, you are a humble follower of the Lamb.

Now, though I would not have those who are not disciples close their mouths whenever others sing, yet I do think there are some hymns in which they would behave more honestly if they did not join, for there are some expressions which hardly ought to come from unconverted lips. Better far would it be is they would pray, *"O Lord, open thou my lips, and my mouth shall show forth thy praise"* (Psalm 51:15). You may have a very sweet voice, my friend, and may sing with admirable taste and in exquisite harmony any of the parts, but God does not accept the praise where the heart is absent. The whole multitude of the disciples whom Jesus loves are the proper persons to extol the Redeemer's name. May you, dear hearer, be among that company!

Then, in the next place, you will observe that the praise they rendered was joyful praise. *"The whole multitude of the disciples began to rejoice."* I hope the doctrine that Christians ought to be gloomy will soon be driven out of the universe. There are no people in the world who have such a right to be happy, nor have such cause to be joyful as the saints of the living God. All Christian duties should be done joyfully, but especially the work of praising the Lord. I have been in congregations where the tune was dolorous to the very last degree; where the rhythm was so dreadfully slow that one wondered whether they would ever be able to sing through Psalm 119, and whether, to use the expression, eternity would not be too short for them to get through it. In those places, the spirit of the people has seemed to be so damp, so heavy, so dead, that we might have supposed that they had met to prepare their minds for hanging rather than for blessing the ever-gracious God.

True praise sets the heart ringing its bells and hanging out its streamers. Never hang your flag at half-mast when you praise God. No, run up every color, let every banner wave in the breeze, and let all the powers and passions of your spirit exalt and rejoice in God your Savior. We are really most horribly afraid of being too happy. Some Christians think cheerfulness a very dangerous folly, if not a ruinous vice. That joyous hymn has been altered in all the English versions:

> All people that on earth do dwell
> > Sing to the Lord with cheerful voice,
> Him serve with fear, his praise forth tell,
> > Come ye before him and rejoice.

"Him serve with fear," says the English version, but the Scotch version has less thorniness and far more rose in it. Listen to it, and catch its holy happiness:

Him serve with mirth,
His praise forth tell;
Before Him exceedingly rejoice.

How do God's creatures serve Him out of doors? The birds do not sit on a Sunday with golden wings, dolefully silent on the boughs of the trees, but they sing as sweetly as may be, even though the rain drops fall. As for the newborn lambs in the field, they skip to His praise, though the season is damp and cold. Heaven and earth are lit up with gladness, so why not the hearts and houses of the saints? "Him serve with mirth." The hymnologist said it well. "Before Him exceedingly rejoice." It was joyful praise.

The next point we must see is that it was demonstrative praise. They praised Him with their voices and with a loud voice. Propriety very greatly objects to the praise which is rendered by Primitive Methodists at times. Their shouts and hallelujahs are thought by some delicate minds to be very shocking. I would not, however, join in the censure, lest I should be numbered among the Pharisees who said, *"Master, rebuke thy disciples."* I wish more people were as earnest and even as vehement as the Methodists used to be. In our Lord's day we see that the people expressed the joy which they felt. I am not sure that they expressed it in the most melodious manner, but at any rate they expressed it in a hearty, lusty shout. They altogether praised with a loud voice.

It is said of Mr. Rowland Hill that, on one occasion, someone sat on the pulpit stairs, who sang in his ears with such a sharp shrill voice that he could endure it no longer, but said to the good woman, "I wish you would be quiet." When she answered, "It comes from my heart." "Oh," said he, "pray forgive me. Sing away: sing as loudly as you will." Truly, dear friends, though one might wish there were more melody in it, yet if your music comes from the heart, we cannot object to the loudness, or we might be found objecting to that which the Savior could not and would not blame. Must we not be loud? Do you wonder that we speak out? Have not His mercies a loud tongue? Do not His kindnesses deserve to be proclaimed aloud? Were not the cries upon the cross so loud that the very rocks were rent thereby? Yet should our music be a whisper? No, as Watts declares, we should:

Loud as his thunders shout his praise,
And sound it lofty as his throne.

If not with loud voices of actual sound, yet we should make the praise of God loud by our actions, which speak louder than any words. We should extol Him by such great deeds of kindness, love, self-denial, and zeal that our actions may assist our words. *"The whole multitude of the disciples began to rejoice and praise God with a loud voice."* Let me ask every Christian to do something in the praise of God to speak in some way for his Master. I would say, speak today. If you cannot with your voice, speak by act and deed, but do join in the hearty shout of all the saints of God while you praise and bless the name of our ever-gracious Lord.

The praise rendered, though very demonstrative, was very reasonable. The reason is given: *"for all the mighty works that they had seen."* My dear friends, we have seen many mighty works which Christ has done. I do not know what these disciples happened to have seen. It is certain that after Christ entered Jerusalem, He was lavish with His miracles. The blind were healed, the deaf had their ears opened, many of those possessed with devils were delivered, and incurable diseases gave way at His word.

We have a similar reason in a spiritual sense. *"What hath God wrought?"* (Numbers 23:23). Recently at Metropolitan Tabernacle, it has been marvelous—as the elders would tell you if they could recount what God has done—the many who have come forward during the last two weeks to tell what God has done for their souls. The Holy Spirit has met with some whom hitherto no ministry had reached. Some have been convinced of sin who were wrapped up in self-righteous rags. Others have been comforted whose despondent hearts were near despair. I am sure those men who sat with inquirers must have been astonished when they found hundreds coming to talk about the things that make for their peace. It was blessed work, I doubt not, for them. They, therefore, would lead the praise. But you have all in your measure seen something of it.

During the meetings we have held we have enjoyed an overpowering sense of the divine presence. Without excitement there has been a holy bowing of spirit, and yet a blessed lifting up of hope, joy, and holy fervor. The Master has cast sweet smiles upon His church. He has come near to His beloved; He has given her the tokens of His affection and made her rejoice with joy unspeakable. Any joy which we have towards Christ will be reasonable enough, for we have seen His mighty works.

The reason for their joy was a personal one. There is no praise to God so sweet as that which flows from the man who has tasted that the Lord is gracious. Some of you hare been converted during the last two or three months. You must bless Him, and you will. You must take the front row now and bless His name for the mighty work which you have seen in yourself. The things which once were dear you now abhor, and those things which seemed dry and empty are now sweet and full of savor. God has turned your darkness into light. He has brought you up out of the horrible pit, out of the miry clay, and has set your feet upon a rock. Will not your established goings yield Him a grateful song? You will bless Him.

Others have had their own children saved. God has looked on one family and then another, and has taken one, two, or three. He has been pleased to lay His hand on many parents and bless their families. Oh, sing unto His name! Sing praises for the mighty works which we have seen. This will be unimpressive talk enough to those of you who have not seen it. But those who have will feel the tears starting to their eyes as they think of son and daughter, of whom they can say, "*Behold, he prayeth*" (Acts 9:11).

Saints of God, I wish I could snatch a firebrand from the altar of praise that burns before the great throne of God with which to fire your hearts, but it is the Master's work to do it. May He do it now. May every one of you feel as if you could cast your crown at His feet, as if you could sing like the cherubim and the seraphim, as if you could not yield even the first place of gratitude to the brightest spirit before the eternal throne. Right now may it be truly said, "*The whole multitude of the disciples rejoiced with a loud voice for all the mighty things which they had seen.*"

> O come, loud anthems let us sing
>   Loud thanks to our Almighty King;
> For we our voices high should raise,
>   When our salvation's rock we praise.
>
>
> Into his presence let us haste
>   To thank him for his favors past;
> To him address, in joyful songs
>   The praise that to his name belongs.

We will now go on to the second point: their praise found expression in an appropriate song: "*Blessed be the King that cometh in the name of the Lord. Peace in heaven, and glory in the highest.*"

It was an appropriate song, if you will remember that it had Christ for its subject. *"My heart is indicting of a good matter: I speak of the things which I have made touching the king"* (Psalm 45:1). No song is so sweet from believing lips as that which tells of Him who loved us and who gave Himself for us. This particular song sings of Christ in His character of King—a very royal song then—a melody fit for a coronation day. Crown Him! Crown Him Lord of all! This was the refrain: *"Blessed be the King."* It sang of that King as commissioned by the Most High, *"who cometh in the name of the Lord."* To think of Christ as bearing divine authority, as coming down to men in God our Father's name, speaking what He has heard in heaven, fulfilling no self-willed errand, but a mission upon which the divine Father sent Him according to His purpose and decree—all this is matter for music. Bless the Lord, saints, as you remember that your Savior is the Lord's anointed: He has set Him on His throne. Jehovah, who was pleased to bruise Him, has said, *"Yet have I set my king upon my holy hill of Zion"* (Psalm 2:6). See the Godhead of your Savior. He whom you adore, the son of Mary, is the Son of God. He who rode upon a colt, the foal of an ass, did also ride on a cherub and on the wings of the wind. They spread their garments in the way and broke down branches. It was a humble triumph, but long before this, the angels had strewn His path with adoring songs. Before Him went the lightnings, coals of fire were in His track, and up from His throne went forth hailstones and coals of fire. Blessed be the King! Praise Him this day. Praise the King, divine and commissioned by His Father.

The focus of their song was, however, of Christ present in their midst. I do not think they would have rejoiced so loudly and sweetly if He had not been there. That was the source and center of their mirth: the King riding upon a colt, the King triumphant. They could not but be glad when He revealed Himself. Beloved, our King is here. Many times has the hymn been sung, "Arise, O King of grace, arise, and enter to thy rest!" Remember the verse:

> O thou that art the Mighty One
> Thy sword gird on thy thigh.

And King Jesus has done so in state. He has ridden prosperously, and out of the ivory palaces His heart has been made glad. The King's daughter, all-glorious within, standing at His right hand, cannot but be glad, too. Loud to His praise wake every string of your heart, and let your souls make the Lord Jesus the focus of your song.

This was an appropriate song, in the next place, because it had God for its object. They extolled God, God in Christ, when they thus lifted up their voices. They said, *"Peace in heaven, and glory in the highest."* When we extol Christ, we desire to bless the infinite majesty that gave Christ to us. *"Thanks be unto God for his unspeakable gift"* (2 Corinthians 9:16). O eternal God, we your creatures in this little world do unfeignedly bless You for that great purpose and decree by which You did choose us to be illustrious exhibits of Your majesty and love. We bless You that You did give us grace in Christ Your Son before the starry sky was spread abroad. We praise You, O God, and magnify Your name as we inquire, *"What is man, that thou art mindful of him, or the son of man, that thou visitest him?"* (Psalm 8:4). How could You lower Yourself to stoop from all the glory of Your infinity, to be made man, to suffer, to bleed, to die for us?

"Give unto the LORD*, O ye mighty, give unto the* LORD *glory and strength. Give unto the* LORD *the glory that is due unto his name"* (Psalm 29:1–2). Oh, that I could give place to some inspired bard, some poet of old who, standing before Him, mouth streaming with holy eloquence, would extol Him who lives but once was slain, and bless the God who sent Him here below that He might redeem unto Himself a people who would show forth His praise.

I think this song to have been very appropriate for another reason, namely, because it had the universe for its scope. It was not praise inside walls as generally ours are: the multitude sang in the open air with no walls but the horizon, with no roof but the unpillared arch of heaven. Their song, though it was from heaven, did not stay there, but enclosed the world within its range. It was, *"Peace in heaven, glory in the highest."* It is very singularly like that song of the angels, that Christmas carol of the spirits from on high when Christ was born. But it differs, for the angels' song was, *"On earth, peace"* (Luke 2:14), and this at the gates of Jerusalem was, *"Peace in heaven."*

It is the nature of song to expand and spread itself. From heaven the sacred joy began when angels sang, and then the fire blazed down to earth in the words, *"On earth, peace."* But in this case the song began on earth, and so it blazed up to heaven with the words, *"Peace in heaven; glory in the highest."* Is not it a wonderful thing that a company of poor beings, such as we who are here below, can really affect the highest heavens? Every throb of gratitude which moves our hearts glows through heaven.

God can receive no actual increase of glory from His creatures, for He has infinite glory and majesty. Yet the creature manifests that glory. A grateful man here below, when his heart is all on fire with sacred love, warms heaven itself. The multitude sang of peace in heaven, as though the angels were established in their peaceful seats by the Savior, as though the war which God had waged with sin was over because the conquering King was come. Let us seek music which will be fitted for other spheres! I would begin the music here, and so my soul should rise. Oh, for some heavenly notes to bear my passions to the skies!

This praise was appropriate to the occasion, because the universe was its sphere. It seems also to have been most appropriate because it had gratitude for its spirit. They cried aloud, *"Blessed!" "Blessed be the King."* We cannot bless God, and yet we do bless Him, in the sense in which He blesses us. Our goodness cannot extend to Him, but we reflect the blessedness which streams from Him as light from the sun. Blessed be Jesus! Have you ever wished to make Him happier? Have you wished that you could really extol Him? Let Him be exalted! Let Him sit on high! I have almost wished selfishly that He were not so glorious as He is, so that we might help to lift Him higher. If the crushing of my body, soul, and spirit would make Him one atom more glorious, I would not only consent to the sacrifice, but bless His name that He counted me worthy to do so. All that we can do brings nothing to Him. Yet, I desire that He had His own glory.

Praise Him that He rode over our great land in triumph! If only King Jesus were as well known here now as He was once in puritanical times! If only Scotland were as loyal to Him now as in covenanting periods! Would that Jesus had His majesty visible in the eyes of all men! We pray and for this. Among the chief joys, the most joyous is to know that God has highly exalted Him and given Him a name which is above every name, that at the name of Jesus every knee should bow.

We have thus said something about the appropriateness of the song. May each of you discover such hymns as will serve to set forth your own case and show forth the mercy of God in saving you. Do not be slack in praising Him in such notes as may be most suitable to your own condition.

Thirdly—and very briefly because I am not going to give much time to these men—we have intrusive objections. *"Master, rebuke thy disciples."* We know that voice, the old grunt of the Pharisee. What could he do otherwise? Such is the man, and such must his communications be. While he can dare to boast, *"God, I thank thee that I am not as other men are"* (Luke 18:11), he is not likely to join in praises such as other men lift up to heaven.

But why did these Pharisees object? I suppose it was first of all because they thought there would be no praise for them. If the multitude had been saying, "Oh, these blessed Pharisees! These excellent Pharisees! What broad phylacteries! What admirable hems to their garments! How diligently and scrupulously they tithe their mint and their anise and their cumin! What a wonder that God should permit us poor vile creatures to look upon these super-excellent incarnations of virtue," there would not have been a man among them who would have said, "*Master, rebuke thy disciples.*" A proud heart never praises God, for it hoards up praise for itself.

Also, the Pharisees were jealous of the people. They did not feel so happy themselves, and they could not bear that other people should be glad. They were like the elder brother who said, "*Yet you never gavest me a kid, that I might make merry with my friends*" (Luke 15:29). Was that a reason why nobody else should be merry? A very poor reason truly! Oh, if we cannot rejoice ourselves, let us stand out of the way of other people. If we have no music in our own hearts, let us not wish to stop those who have.

But I think the main point was that they were jealous of Jesus. They did not like to have Christ crowned with majesty. Certainly this is the drift of the human heart. It does not wish to see Jesus Christ extolled. If you preach morality, dry doctrine, or ceremonies, many will be glad to hear your words. However, if you preach Jesus Christ, some will say, "*Master, rebuke thy disciples!*" It was not bad advice of an old preacher to a young beginner, when he said, "Preach nothing down but sin, and preach nothing up but Christ." Let us praise nothing up but Christ. Have nothing to say about your church, say nothing about your denomination, hold your tongue about the minister, but praise Christ. The Pharisees will not like it, but that is an excellent reason to give them more of it. That which Satan does not admire, he ought to have more of. The preaching of Christ is the whip that flogs the devil; the preaching of Christ is the thunderbolt, the sound of which makes all hell shake. Let us never be silent then. We will put to confusion all our foes, if we do but extol Christ Jesus as Lord.

"*Master, rebuke thy disciples!*" There is not much occurring in the Christian church in the present day to elicit this kind of request from critics for Jesus Christ to rebuke. There used to be; there used to be a little of what the world calls fanaticism. A consecrated cobbler once set forth to preach the gospel in Hindustani regions. There were men who would go preaching the gospel among the heathen, counting not their lives dear to them. The day was when the church was so foolish as to fling away precious lives for Christ's glory. She is more prudent now. Alas for your prudence! She is so calm and quiet—no Methodist's zeal now. Even that denomination which did seem alive has become most proper and cold, and we are so bent too.

We let the most abominable doctrines be preached, and then put our fingers to our lips and say, "There are so many good people who think so." Nothing is to be rebuked nowadays. My soul is sick of this! Oh, for the old fire again! The church will never prosper until it becomes once more on fire. Oh, for the old fanaticism, for that indeed was the Spirit of God transforming men's spirits in earnest! Oh, for the old doing and daring that risked everything and cared for nothing, except to glorify Him who shed His blood upon the cross! May we live to see such bright and holy days again! The world may murmur, but Christ will not rebuke.

We come now to the last point, namely, an unanswerable argument. Jesus said, "If these should hold their peace, the very stones would immediately cry out." I think that is very much our case. If we were not to praise God, the very stones might cry out against us. We must praise the Lord. Woe unto us if we do not! It is impossible for us to hold our tongues. Saved from hell, and be silent? Secure of heaven, and be ungrateful? Bought with precious blood, and hold our tongues! Filled with the Spirit, and not speak? From fear of feeble man, restrain the Spirit's course within our souls? God forbid. In the name of the Most High, let such a thought be given to the winds. We watch our children being saved, the offspring of our loins brought to Christ! We see them springing up like willows by the water's edge, and yet have no awakening of song, no gladness, no delight! Oh, then we would be worse than brutes, and our hearts would have been steeled. We must praise God!

What, the King in our midst, King Jesus smiling into our souls, feasting us at His table, making His word precious to us, and we do not praise Him? If Satan could know the delight of Christ's company, He might begin to love. But we were worse than devils if we did not praise the name of Jesus! What! The King's arm made bare, His enemies subdued, His triumphant chariot rolling through our streets, and yet no song? Oh Zion, if we forget to sing, if we count not the King's triumph above our chief joy, let our right hand forget her cunning. The King is coming, His advent is drawing near, the signs of blessing are in the sky and air around, and yet no song? Oh, we must bless Him! *"Hosanna! Blessed is he that cometh in the name of the Lord!"*

But could the stones ever cry out? Yes, that they could, and if they were to speak they would have much to talk of even as we have this day. If the stones were to speak, they could tell of their Maker. Will we not tell of Him who made us anew, and out of stones raised up children unto Abraham? They could speak of ages long since gone. The old rocks could tell of chaos and order and the handiwork of God in various stages of creation's drama. Cannot we talk of God's decrees, of God's great work in ancient times, and all that He did for His church? If the stones were to speak, they could tell of their breaker, how he took them from the mine and made them fit for the temple. Cannot we tell of our Creator and Maker, who broke our hearts with the hammer of His word so that He might build us into His temple? If the stones were to speak, they would tell of their builder, who polished them and fashioned them after the similitude of a palace. Will not we talk of our Architect and Builder, who has put us in our place in the temple of the living God? Oh, if the stones could speak, they might have a long story to tell by way of memorial, for many times has a great stone been rolled as a memorial to God. We can tell of stones of help, stones of remembrance. The broken stones of the law cry out against us, but Christ Himself, who has rolled away the stone from the door of the sepulcher, speaks for us.

The stones might well be able to cry out, but we will not let them. We will hush their noise with ours. We will break forth into sacred song and bless the majesty of the Most High all our days. Let this day and all of our days be especially consecrated to holy joys. May the Lord in infinite mercy fill your souls with rejoicing, both in practical deeds of kindness and benevolence and works of praise! Blessed be His name who lives forever and ever!

4

A NEW SONG FOR
NEW HEARTS

And in that day thou shalt say, O LORD, I will praise thee: though thou wast angry with me, thine anger is turned away, and thou comfortedst me.
—Isaiah 12:1

This prophesy is said by some to relate to the invasion by Sennacherib. That calamity threatened to be a very terrible display of divine anger. It seemed inevitable that the Assyrian power would make an utter desolation of Judea. But God promised that He would interpose for the deliverance of His people and punish the stout heart of the king of Assyria. Then His people would say, "We will praise You: though You were angry with us, and thus sent the Assyrian monarch to chastise us, Your anger is turned away, and You comforted us."

If this is the meaning of it, it is an instance of sanctified affliction. It is a lesson to us that whenever we smart under the rod, we may look forward to the time when the rod will be withdrawn. It is also an admonition to us that when we escape from trial, we should take care to celebrate the event with grateful praise.

Let us set up the pillar of memorial, let us pour the oil of gratitude upon it, and let us garland it with song, blessing the Lord whose anger endures but for a moment, but whose mercy is from everlasting to everlasting.

Others think that this text mainly relates to the latter days. It would be impossible to read Isaiah 11 without feeling that such a reference is clear. There is to be a time when the wolf will dwell with the lamb, the lion will eat straw like the ox, and the weaned child will put his hand on the viper's den. The Lord will set His hand the second time to recover the remnant of His people and repeat his wondrous works in Egypt and at the Red Sea. Then the song of Moses will be rehearsed again: "*The LORD is my strength and song, and he is become my salvation: he is my God, and I will prepare him an habitation: my father's God, and I will exalt him*" (Exodus 15:2). In that day the Jewish people, on whose head the blood of Christ has come, who these many centuries have been scattered and sifted as in a sieve throughout all nations, will be restored to their own land, the dispersed of Judah gathered from the four corners of the earth. They will participate in the glories of the millennial reign. With joy will they draw water out of the wells of salvation. In those days, when all Israel will be saved and Judah will dwell safely, the jubilant thanksgiving will be heard, "*O LORD, I will praise you, for though thou wast angry with me, thine anger is turned away, and thou comfortedst me.*" All people will sing with such unanimity and undivided heart that they will sound as though they were one man and will use the singular where their numbers might require the plural. "*I will praise thee*" will be the exclamation of the once divided but then united people.

Although both of these interpretations are true, and both instructive, the text is many-sided and bears another reading. We will find out the very soul of the passage if we consider it as an illustration of what occurs to everyone of God's people when he is brought out of darkness into God's marvelous light, when he is delivered from the spirit of bondage beneath divine wrath and led by the spirit of adoption into the liberty in which Christ makes him free. In that day I am sure that these words are fulfilled. The believer then says very joyously, "*O LORD, I will praise thee: though thou wast angry with me, thine anger is turned away, and thou comfortedst me.*"

Regarding the text from this point of view, we will first observe the prelude of this delightful song, and then we will listen to the song itself. First, consider the prelude of this charming song. Here are certain preliminaries to the music. They are contained in the first line of the text. *"In that day thou shalt say…"* We have the tuning of the harps, the notes of the music following after in the succeeding sentences. Much of instruction is couched in these six words of prelude.

Note that there is a time for that joyous song which is here recorded, *"In that day."* The term, *"that day,"* is sometimes used for a day of terror, and often for a period of blessing. The common factor to both is this, they were both days of the manifestation of divine power. *"That day,"* a day of terrible confusion for God's enemies. *"That day,"* a day of great comfort for God's friends. The day in either case is the time of the making God's arm bare and the manifestation of His strength.

Now, the day in which a man rejoices in Christ is the day in which God's power is revealed on his behalf in his heart and conscience, and the Holy Spirit subdues him to the reign of Christ. It is not always that God works with such effectual power as this in the human heart. He has His set times. Oftentimes the work of human ministry proves ineffectual: the preacher exhorts, the hearer listens, but the exhortation is not obeyed. It sometimes happens that even desires may be excited, yet nothing is accomplished: these aroused feelings prove to be as those spring blossoms on the trees which do not pollinate and fall fruitless to the ground. There is, however, an appointed time for the calling of God's elect, a set time in which the Lord visits His chosen with a power of grace which they cannot effectually resist. He makes them willing in the day of His power. It is a day in which not only is the gospel heard, but the report is believed, because the arm of the Lord is revealed.

For everything, according to Solomon, there is a season: a time to break down and a time to build up; a time of war and a time of peace; a time to kill and a time to heal. (See Ecclesiastes 3:1–3.) Just so, there is a time for conviction and a time for consolation. With some who are in great distress of spirit, it may be God's time to wound and to kill. Their self-confidence is too vigorous, their carnal righteousness yet too lively. Their confidence must be wounded, and their righteousness must be killed; otherwise, they will not yield to grace. God does not clothe us until He has stripped us; He does not heal till He has wounded. How could He make alive those who are not dead?

There is a work of grace in the heart of digging out the old foundations before grace begins to build up our hopes. Woe to that man who builds without having the foundation dug out, for his house will fall. Woe to that man who leaps into a sudden peace without ever having felt his need of pardon, without repentance, without brokenness of spirit. He will see his hasty fruit wither before his eyes. The time when God effectually blesses is sometimes called "a time of love." It is a time of deep distress to us, but it is a time of love with God, a time wisely determined in the decree and counsel of the Most High, so that healing mercy arrives at the best time to each one who is interested in the covenant.

Someone may inquire, "When do you think will be the time when God enables me to say, '*Thine anger is turned away*'?" Beloved, you can easily discern it. I believe God's time to give us comfort is usually when we are brought low, so as to confess the justice of the wrath which He is pouring on us. Humbleness of heart is one sure indication of coming peace.

A German nobleman years ago inspected the galley ships at Toulon. He saw many men condemned by the French government to perpetual toil at the galley oars for their crimes. Being a prince in much repute, he obtained the favor that he could give liberty to one of the captives. He went among them and talked to them, but found they all thought themselves wrongly treated, oppressed, and unjustly punished. At last he met with one who confessed, "In my case my sentence is a most just and even a merciful one. If I had not been imprisoned in this way, most likely I would have been executed for some still greater crime. I have been a great offender, and the law is doing nothing more than it ought in keeping me in confinement for the rest of my life." The nobleman returned to the manager and said, "This is the only man in all this gang that I would wish to set free. I elect him for liberty."

So it is with our great Liberator, the Lord Jesus Christ, when He meets with a soul that confesses its demerit, admits the justice of divine wrath, and has not a word to say for itself, then He says, "*Thy sins, which are many, are forgiven*" (Luke 7:47–48). The time when His anger is turned away is the time when you confess the justice of His anger, and bow down and humbly entreat for mercy. Above all, the hour of grace has struck when you look alone to Christ. While you are looking to any good thing in yourself, and hoping to grow better or to do better, you are making no advances towards comfort. But when you give up in despair any hope that is grounded in yourself, and instead look away to those dear wounds of His, to that suffering humanity, the Son of God, who stooped from heaven for you, then has the day dawned in which you will say, "*O Lord, I will praise thee.*" I pray earnestly that this set time to favor you may now come—the time when the rain is over and gone, and the voice of the turtle is heard in your land.

Looking at the preliminaries of this song again, notice that a word indicates the singer. *"In that day thou shalt say."* *"Thou"* is a singular pronoun and points out one individual. One by one we receive eternal life and peace. "You, the individual, singled out to feel in your conscience God's wrath, you are equally selected to enjoy Jehovah's love." Beloved, it is never a day of grace to us until we are taken aside from the multitude and set by ourselves. Our individuality must come out in conversion, if it never appears at any other time. So many of you fancy that it is all right with you because you live in a Christian nation. I tell you it is woe unto you, if having outward privileges, they involve you in responsibilities, but bring you no saving grace. Perhaps you believe that your family religion may help you. The erroneous practices of certain Christian churches may foster this delusion, but it is not so. There is no birthright godliness: *"Ye must be born again"* (John 3:7). The first birth will not help you, because *"That which is born of the flesh is flesh; and that which is born of the Spirit is spirit"* (John 3:6). I know you imagine that if you mingle in godly congregations, sing as they sing, and pray as they pray, it will go well with you, but it is not so. The gate of eternal life admits but one at a time. Is it not written, *"Ye shall be gathered one by one, O ye children of Israel"* (Isaiah 27:12)? Know that when the fountain is opened in the house of David for sin and for uncleanness at Christ's coming, it is declared by the prophet Zechariah:

> *The land shall mourn, every family apart; the family of the house of David apart, and their wives apart; the family of the house of Nathan apart, and their wives apart; the family of the house of Levi apart, and their wives apart; the family of Shimei apart, and their wives apart; all the families that remain every family apart, and their wives apart.* (Zechariah 12:12–14)

Each one of you must be brought to feel the divine anger in your souls and to have it removed from you, so that you may rejoice in God as your salvation. Has it been so with you, dear one? Are you that favored singer? Are you one of that chosen throng who can say, *"Thine anger is turned away, and you comfortedst me"*? Away with generalities. Do not be satisfied except with particulars. Little it matters to you that Christ died for millions of men, if you have no part in His death. Little blessing is it to you that there should be joy from myriads of pardoned hearts, if you should die unpardoned. Seek a personal interest in Christ. Do not be satisfied unless it has been satisfactorily revealed in your heart that your own sin has been put away by an act of grace.

Remember that the word, "*thou,*" is spoken to those who have been brought into the last degree of despair by sorrow. "*In that day you shalt say, though thou wast angry with me, thine anger is turned away.*" You poor down-trodden heart, where are you? Woman of sorrowful spirit, rejoice, for in that day of mercy you will sing. Broken-hearted sinner, ready to destroy yourself from anguish of conscience, in the day of God's mercy, you will rejoice. Your note will be all the sweeter because you have had the most sin to be forgiven and felt most the anger of God burning in your soul. Dwell on that. May God grant that this is realized personally by all of us.

The next thing to be noted in the preliminaries is the Teacher. "*In that day you shalt say…*" Who says this? It is God alone who can so positively declare, "*thou shalt say.*" Who but the Lord can thus command man's heart and speech? It is the Lord alone. He who has made us is Master of our spirits. By His omnipotence He rules in the world of mind as well as matter, and all things happen as He ordains. He states, "*In that day,* [that is, in God's own time] *thou shalt say,*" and He who so declares will make good the word. Here is revealed God's will. What the Lord wills shall be accomplished, and what He declares will be spoken assuredly shall be spoken.

Here is consolation to those feeble folk who fear the word will not be fulfilled in them. "*Thou shalt say,*" is a divine word and cannot fail. The Lord alone can give a man the right to say, "*Thine anger is turned away.*" If any man presumes to say, "God has turned His anger from me," without a warrant from the Most High, he lies to his own confusion. However, when it is written, "*Thou shalt say,*" God has said, "I will make it true, so that you will be fully justified in the declaration."

Yet more comfort is found here, for even when the right to such a blessing is bestowed, we are often unable to enjoy it because of weakness. Unbelief is frequently so great that many things which are true we cannot receive. Under a sense of sin we are so despondent that we think God's mercy too great for us. Therefore we are not able to appropriate the blessing presented to us, though it be inexpressibly delightful. Blessed be God, the Holy Ghost knows how to chase away our unbelief and give us power to embrace the blessing. He can make us accept the covenant favor and rejoice in it, so as to declare the joy.

I have tried to induce many to believe comfortable truths about themselves, but they have fairly defeated me. I have put the gospel plainly to them, feeling sure that its promises were meant for them, and have said within my heart, "Surely they will be comforted. Certainly their broken hearts will be bound up by that gracious word." But I cannot make anyone say, "Lord, I will praise You." I am unable to lead them to faith and peace.

However, my joy is that my Master can do what His servant cannot. He can make the tongue of the dumb sing. He delights to look after desperate cases. Man's impossibility becomes His opportunity. Where the most affectionate words of people fail, the consolations of the blessed Spirit are divinely efficacious. He does not merely bring oil and wine, but He knows how to pour them into wounds and heal the anguish of contrite spirits. I pray that the Master, who alone can teach us to sing this song, may graciously instruct those who have been seeking rest, but finding none. *"I am the LORD thy God which teacheth thee to profit"* (Isaiah 48:17). He can put a song in your heart, for nothing is beyond the range of His grace.

Notice another preliminary, namely, the tone of the song. *"Thou shalt say, O LORD, I will praise thee."* The song is to be an open one, avowed, vocally uttered, heard by men, and published abroad. It is not to be a silent feeling, the kind of soft music whose sweetness is spent within the spirit. Rather in that day you will say, you will speak it forth, you will testify and bear witness to what the Lord has done for you. When a man gets his sins forgiven, he cannot help revealing the secret. *"When the LORD turned again the captivity of Zion, we were like them that dream. Then was our mouth filled with laughter, and our tongue with singing"* (Psalm 126:1–2). Even if the forgiven one cannot speak with his tongue, he can say it with his eye. His countenance, his manner, his very gait will betray him. The gracious secret must ooze out in some fashion. Spiritual men, at any rate, will find it out, and with thankfulness mark the joyful evidences.

I know that, before I found the Savior, had you known me, you would have observed my solitary habits. If you had followed me to my bed chamber, to my Bible, and to my knees, you would have heard groans and sighs which revealed a sorrowful spirit. Ordinary amusements of youth had few attractions for me then. Conversation, however cheerful, yielded me no comfort. But the very morning that I really heard the gospel message, *"Look unto me, and be ye saved, all the ends of the earth"* (Isaiah 45:22), I am certain that no person who knew me could have helped remarking the difference even in my face. A change came over my spirit, which as I remember was even indicated in the way I walked, for the heavy step of melancholy was exchanged for a more cheerful pace. The spiritual condition affects the bodily state, and it was evidently so with me. My delight at being forgiven was no ordinary sensation. I could have fairly leaped for joy.

> All through the night I wept full sore
>   But morning brought relief;
> That hand which broke my bones before,
>   Then broke my bonds of grief.

> My mourning he to dancing turns,
>   For sackcloth joy he gives
> A moment, Lord, thine anger burns
>   But long thy favor lives.

If I had not declared my deliverance, the very stones must have cried out. It was not in my heart to keep it back, but I am sure I could not have done so if I had desired. God's grace does not come into the heart as a beggar into a barn and lie hidden away as if it stole a night's lodging. No, its arrival is known all over the house. Every chamber of the soul testifies to its presence. Grace is like a bunch of lavender: it discovers itself by its sweet smell. Like the nightingale, it is heard where it is not seen. Like a spark which falls into the midst of straw, it burns, blazes, and consumes until it reveals itself by its own energetic operations.

O soul, burdened with sin, if Christ comes to you and pardons you, I am certain that before long all your bones will say, "LORD, *who is like unto thee?*" (Psalm 35:10). You will be of the same mind as David when he cried, "*Deliver me from bloodguiltiness, O God, thou God of my salvation: and my tongue shall sing aloud of thy righteousness*" (Psalm 51:14). You will gladly say with him, "*Thy vows are upon me, O God: I will render praise unto thee, for thou have delivered my soul from death*" (Psalm 56:12–13). Not only will you soberly tell what great things grace has does for you, but more than likely your exuberant joy may lead you beyond the boundaries of solemn decorum.

The precise and slow going will condemn you, but you need not mind, for you can offer the same excuse for it as David made to Michal when he danced before the ark. Far be it from me to condemn you if you cry, "Hallelujah," or clap your hands. It is our cold custom to condemn every demonstration of feeling, but I am sure Scripture does not warrant us in our condemnation. We find such passages as these: "*O clap your hands, all ye people; shout unto God with the voice of triumph*" (Psalm 47:1). "*Praise him upon the loud cymbals: praise him upon the high sounding cymbals*" (Psalm 150:5). If the overflowing of holy joy seems to be disorderly, does it matter since God accepts it? He who gets his liberty from a long confinement in prison may well take a skip or two with an extra leap for joy. Who would begrudge him? He who has long been hungry and famished, when he sees the table spread, may be excused if he eats with more eagerness than politeness. Yes, they say, "*I will praise thee, O LORD.*" In the very disorderliness of their demonstration, they more emphatically say, "*I will praise thee: though thou wast angry with me, thine anger is turned away.*"

Now let us turn our attention to the song itself. Notice the fact that all of the song concerns the Lord. It is all addressed to Him. "*O LORD, I will praise thee: though thou wast angry, thine anger is turned away.*" When a soul escapes from the bondage of sin and becomes consciously pardoned, it resembles the apostles on the Mount Tabor who saw no man except Jesus. While you are seeking grace, you think much of the minister, the service, the outward form; but the moment you find peace in God through the precious blood of Christ, you will think of your pardoning God only. How small everything becomes in the presence of that dear cross, where God the Savior loved and died! When we think of all our iniquity being cast into the depths of the sea, we can no more boast of anything that was once our glory. The instrumentality by which peace came to us will be always dear to us. We esteem the preacher of the gospel who presented salvation to us as our spiritual father, but still we would never think of praising him. We will give all the glory to our God. As for each of us personally, self will sink like lead amid the waters when we find Christ. God will be all in all when iniquity is pardoned.

I have often thought that if some of my fellow pastors, who preach a gospel in which there is little of the grace of God, had felt a little more conviction of sin in being converted, they would be sure to preach a clearer and more gracious gospel. Now many appear to leap into peace without any conviction of sin. They do not seem to have known what the guilt of sin means, but they scramble into peace before the burden of sin has been felt. It is not for me to judge, but I must confess I have my fears of those who have never felt the terrors of the Lord. I look upon conviction of sin as a good ground work for a well-instructed Christian. I observe as a rule that when a man has been put in the prison of the law, made to wear the heavy chains of conviction, and at last obtains his liberty through the precious blood, he is sure to proclaim the grace of God and magnify divine mercy. He feels that in his case salvation must be of grace from first to last, and magnifies most the grace of God.

Those who have not experienced the anger of God over their sinfulness, whose conversion has been of the easy kind, produced more from excitement than by depth of thought, seem to me to choose a flimsy divinity in which man is more prominent and God is less regarded. I am sure of this one thing, that I personally desire to ascribe conversion in my own case entirely to the grace of God and to give God all the glory for it. I dread any conversion which in any way may deprive God of being, by His everlasting word, the cause of it; by the effectual sacrifice of His Son, the direct agent of it; and by His continued working through the Holy Ghost, the perfecter of it. Give God all the praise. You must do so, if you have thoroughly experienced the weight of God's anger and what the turning away of it means.

The next thing in this song is, that it includes repentant memories. "O LORD, *I will praise thee: though thou wast angry with me.*" There was a time when we were conscious that God was angry with us. When was that, and how did we know that God was angry with us? Outsiders think that when we talk about conversion we are merely talking sentimental theories, but let me assure you that it is as much matter of fact to us with regard to our spiritual nature as feelings of sickness and of recovery are real and actual.

As some of us read the Word of God, believing it to be an inspired book, we perceived that it contained a law, holy and just, the breach of which was threatened with eternal death. As we read it, we discovered that we had broken that law, not in some points, but in all. We were obliged to feel that all the sentences of that book against sinners were sentences against us. Perhaps we had read these chapters before, but we gave them no serious thought until on one occasion we were led to see that we stood condemned by the law of God as contained in holy Scripture. Then we knew that God was angry with us. It was not a mere idea of our own conjecture: we had this Book as evidence of it. If that Book were indeed true, we knew we were condemned. We dared not try to convince ourselves that the old Book was a cunningly-devised fable; we knew it was not. Therefore, from its testimony, we concluded that God was angry with us.

At the same time we learned this terrible truth from the Book, our conscience suddenly awoke and confirmed the fact. It said, "What the Book declares is correct. The just God must be angry with such a sinful being as you are." Conscience brought to our recollection many things which we would have preferred to forget. It revealed to us the evil of our hearts which we had no wish to remember. As we looked at Scripture by the light of conscience, we concluded that we were in a very dreadful plight, because God was angry with us. Then there entered into us at the same time, above all the rest, a certain work of the Holy Spirit called conviction of sin, "*When he, the Spirit of truth is come…he shall reprove the world of sin*" (John 16:13, 8). He has come and convinced us of sin in a way in which the Scripture and conscience would not have done apart from Him. But His light shone in on us, and we felt as we never felt before. Sin appeared exceeding sinful, as it was committed against infinite love and goodness. Then it seemed as though hell must swallow us up and the wrath of God must devour us. Oh, the trembling and the fear, the dismay and the alarm which then possessed our spirits! Yet now, the remembrance of it is cause for thankfulness.

In the Hebrew, the wording of our text is slightly different from what we get in the English. Our English translators have very wisely put in the word "*though,*" a little earlier than it occurs in the Hebrew. The Hebrew would run something like this, "O Lord, I will praise thee; thou wast angry with me." Now we can praise God that He made us feel His anger. You ask, "Is a sense of anger cause for praise?" No, not if it remains alone, but because it drives us to Christ. If wrath had been laid up for us hereafter, it would be a cause of horror, deep and dreadful. However, because it was let loose in a small measure upon us here, we were thus condemned in conscience so that we might not be condemned at the last. Therefore, we have reason for much thankfulness.

We would never have felt His love if we had not felt His anger. We laid hold on His mercy because of necessity. No soul will accept Christ Jesus until it must. It is not driven to faith until it is driven to self-despair. God's angry face makes Christ's loving face dear to us. We could never look at the Christ of God, unless first of all the God of Christ had looked at us through the tempest and made us afraid. "I will praise You, that You let me feel Your anger, in order that I might be driven to discover how that anger could be turned away." So you see, the song in its deep bass note includes plaintive recollections of sin pressing heavily on the spirit.

The song of our text contains blessed certainties. "*I will praise thee; though thou wast angry with me, thine anger is turned away.*" Can a man know that and be quite sure that he is forgiven? Yes, he can. He can be as sure of pardon as he is of his existence, as infallibly certain as he is of a mathematical proposition.

Someone asks, "How?" Surely, this is a matter for spiritual men, yet at the same time it is a matter of certainty as clearly as anything can be humanly ascertained.

The confidence of a man's being pardoned, and God's anger being turned away from him, is not based upon his merely feeling that it is so or his merely believing that it is so. You are not pardoned because you work yourself up into a comfortable frame of mind and think you are pardoned. That may be a delusion. You are not necessarily delivered from God's anger because you believe you are. You may be believing a lie, and may believe what you like, but that does not make it true. There must be a fact going before, and if that fact is not there, you may believe what you choose, but it is pure imagination, nothing more.

On what ground does a man know that God's anger is turned away? I answer this way: on the truth of the Bible. "*It is written*" (Matthew 4:4) is our basis of assurance. I turn to that Book and discover that Jesus Christ the Son of God came into this world and became the substitute for a certain body of men; that he took their sin and was punished in their stead in order that God, without the violation of His justice, might forgive as many as are washed in Christ's blood. My question then is, for whom did Christ die? The moment I turn to the Scriptures, I find very conspicuously on its page this declaration, that "*Jesus Christ came into the world to save sinners*" (1 Timothy 1:15). I am a sinner—of that I am certain—which gives me some hope. I next find that "*he that believeth on him is not condemned*" (John 3:18). Looking into myself, I find that I do really believe, that is, I trust Jesus. Very well, then I am sure I am not condemned, for God has declared I am not. I read again, "*He that believeth and is baptized shall be saved*" (Mark 16:16). I know that I have believed. I trust my salvation with Christ and have, in obedience to His command, been baptized. Then I am saved and will be saved, for the Word says so.

Assurance is simply a matter of testimony which we receive. He that believes in Christ receives the testimony of God, and that is the only testimony he needs. I know it has been thought that you get some special revelation in your own soul, some flash as it were of light, some extraordinary intimation, but nothing of the kind is absolutely necessary. I know that "*the Spirit itself beareth witness with our spirits, that we are the children of God*" (Romans 8:16), but the first essential matter is God's witness in the Word. "*He that believeth not God, hath made him a liar; because he believeth not the record that God gave of his Son*" (1 John 5:10). God's witness concerning His Son is that if you trust His Son, you are saved. His Son suffered for you. His Son bore the punishment that was due you for your sins. God declares that you are forgiven for Christ's sake. He cannot punish twice for offenses, first His Son and then you. He cannot demand retribution from His law to vindicate His justice, first from your Substitute and then from you.

Was Christ your substitute? That is the question. He was if you trust Him. Trusting Him is the evidence that He was a substitute for you. Now see then that the moment have come to trust my soul forever in the hands of Christ, God's anger is turned away from me because it was turned upon Christ. I stand, guilty sinner as I am in myself, absolved before God. None can lay anything to my charge, for my sins were laid on Christ and punished through Christ, and I am clear. Now, what will I say to the Lord but, "*I will praise thee, for though thou wast angry with me, thine anger is turned away, and thou comfortedst me.*" It is a matter of certainty. It is not a matter of "ifs," "ands," or "buts," but of fact. At this moment you are either forgiven or you are not; you are either clean in God's sight or else the wrath of God abides on you. I urge you, do not rest until you know which it is. If you find out that you are unforgiven, seek the Savior. "*Believe in the Lord Jesus Christ, and thou shalt be saved*" (Acts 16:31). But if you believe in Him, you are no longer guilty—you are forgiven. Do not sit down and fret as if you were guilty, but enjoy the liberty of the children of God. "*Therefore being justified by faith, we have peace with God through our Lord Jesus Christ*" (Romans 5:1).

I must add that our song includes holy resolutions: "*I will praise thee.*" I will do it with my heart in secret. I will get alone and make my expressive silent hymn His praise. I will sit and pour out liquid songs in tears of gratitude, welling up from my heart. I will praise Him in the church of God. I will search out other believers, and I will tell them what God has done for me. I will cast in my lot with His people: if they are despised, I will bear the shame with them and count it honor. I will unite myself to them and help them in their service. If I can magnify Christ by my testimony among them, I will do it. I will praise Him in my life. I will make my business praise Him. I will make my parlor and my drawing room, my kitchen and my field praise Him. I will not be content unless all I am and all I have praises Him. I will make a harp of the whole universe. I will make earth and heaven, space and time to be strings on which my joyful fingers play lofty tunes of thankfulness. I will praise my God. My heart is fixed. I will sing and give praise. When I die—or rather pass from this life to another—I, who have been forgiven so much sin through such a Savior, will continue to praise Him.

Oh, how I long to join the choir
Who worship at his feet!

Lord, grant me soon my heart's desire!
Soon, soon thy work complete!

Note that this is a song which is peculiar in its character and appropriate only to the people of God. I may say of it, "No man could learn this song but the redeemed." Only he who has felt his own vileness and has had it washed away in the "fountain filled with blood," can know its sweetness. It is not a Pharisee's song: it has no likeness to "*God, I thank thee that I am not as other men*" (Luke 18:11). Rather, it confesses, "*Thou wast angry with me,*" admitting that the singer was just like others, but it glories that through infinite mercy, the divine anger is turned away. Here it leans on the Savior. It is not a Sadducean song: doubting does not mingle with the lyrics. It is not the philosopher's query, "There may be a God, or there may not be." It is the voice of a believing worshipper. It is not, "I may or may not be guilty." Every note of it is positive. I know and feel that "*thou wast angry with me,*" yet I am sure too that "*thine anger is turned away.*" I believe it by the witness of God, and I cannot doubt His Word.

It is a song of strong faith and of humility. Its spirit is a precious incense made up of many costly ingredients. We have here not only one characteristic, but many rare virtues. Humility confesses, "*Thou wast angry with me.*" Gratitude sings, "*Thine anger is turned away.*" Patience cries, "*You comfortedst me,*" while holy joy springs up and says, "*I will praise thee.*" Faith, hope, and love all have their notes here; from the bass of humility to the highest soprano of glorious communion, all the different parts are represented. It is a full song, the symphonic swelling of the heart.

I conclude with some words on the practical results from the subject. One is a word of consolation, consolation to you who are under God's anger right now. My heart goes out to you. I know what your heartache is. I knew it for a period of five long years while I mourned the guilt and curse of sin. Poor soul, you are in a sad plight indeed, but be of good cheer. You have in your heart a key which will open every lock in the doubting castle in which you are now confined. If you but have the heart to take it out of your bosom and out of the Word of God, and use it, liberty is near. I will show you that key. Look at it: "*Him that cometh to me, I will in no wise cast out*" (John 6:37). "Oh, but that does not happen to fit," you say. Well, here's another: "*The blood of Jesus Christ his Son cleanseth from all sin*" (1 John 1:7). Does not that meet your case? Then let me try again: "*He is able also to save them to the uttermost that come unto God by him*" (Hebrews 7:25). "*To the uttermost"*—dwell on that and be comforted. I never knew God to shut a soul in the prison of conviction, but that sooner or later He released the captive. The Lord will surely bring you out of that low dungeon. The worst thing in the world is to go unchastised. To be allowed to sin and eat honey with it is the precursor of damnation; but to sin and have the wormwood of repentance with it is the prelude of being saved. If the Lord has embittered your sin, He has designs of love towards you. His anger will yet be turned away. *"When the poor and needy seek water, and there is none, and their tongue faileth for thirst, I the* LORD *will hear them, I the God of Israel will not forsake them"* (Isaiah 41:17).

The next is a word of admonition. Some of you hare been forgiven, but are you praising God as you should? I have heard say, that in our churches there are not more than five percent who are doing any real work for Christ. I would be very sorry if that were true of the church I pastor, but I fear there are more than five percent who are doing nothing. Where are you who have felt His anger pass away, and yet are not praising Him? Come, stir yourself, and seek to serve Jesus. Do you not know that you are meant to be the winners of souls? The American beekeeper, when he wants to collect a hive, first catches a single bee, puts it in a box with a piece of honeycomb, and then shuts the door. After awhile, when the bee is well fed, he lets it out. It comes back again after more of the sweet, bringing companions with it. When they have eaten the honey, they always bring yet more bees. Thus eventually there is a goodly assembly for the hive.

In this same fashion you ought to act. If you have found mercy, you ought to praise God and tell others, so that they may believe and in their turn lead others to Jesus. This is the way the kingdom of God grows. I am afraid you are guilty here. See to it, dear ones, and who can tell of what use you yet may be? There was a dear servant of Christ who was just on the verge of the grave, very old and ill, frequently delirious. The doctors said no one must go into the chamber except the nurse. A little Sunday-school boy, who was rather curious, peeped in at the door to look at the minister. The poor dying servant of God saw him, and the ruling passion was strong even in death. He called him. "David," said he, "did you ever close in with Christ? I have done so many a time, and I long that you may." Fifty years later, that boy was living and bearing testimony that the dying words of the good man had brought him to Jesus, for by them he was led to seek Christ.

You do not know what a word might do if you would but speak it. Do not keep back the good news that might bring salvation to your wife, to your husband, to your child, to your servant. If you have indeed felt the Lord's anger pass away from you, right now, on your knees repeat this vow, "My God, I will praise You! I have been a sluggard. I have been very silent about You. I am afraid I have not given You of my substance as I ought. I am sure I have not given You of my heart as I should. But oh, forgive the past, and accept your poor servant yet again. Then '*I will praise thee; for though thou wast angry with me, thine anger is turned away, and you comfortedst me.*'"

God bless you, for Christ's sake.

5

ETHAN'S SONG IN THE NIGHT

I will sing of the mercies of the LORD for ever: with my mouth will I make known thy faithfulness to all generations. For I have said, Mercy shall be built up for ever: thy faithfulness shalt thou establish in the very heavens.
—Psalm 89:1–2

This psalm is one of the choicest songs in the night. Amid a stream of troubled thoughts, there stands an island of rescue and redemption which supplies standing room for wonder and worship, while the music of the words sounds sweetly in our ears like the murmuring of a river. Read the entire psalm carefully and it will arouse your sympathy, for the author was bearing bitter reproach and was almost broken-hearted by the grievous calamities of his nation. Yet his faith was strong in the faithfulness of God. So he sang of the stability of the divine covenant when the outlook of circumstances was dark and cheerless. Nor did he ever sing more sweetly than he sang in that night of his sorrow. Greatly does it glorify God for us to sing His high praises in storms of adversity and on beds of affliction. It magnifies His mercy if we can bless and adore Him when He takes as well as when He gives. It is good that out of the very mouth of the burning fiery furnace there should come a more burning note of grateful praise.

I am told that there is a great deal of relief from sorrow in complaining, that our murmuring may sometimes tend to relieve our pain. I suppose it is so. Certainly it is a good thing to weep, for I have heard it from the mouth of many witnesses. Most of us have felt that there are griefs too deep for tears, and that a flood of tears proves the sorrow has begun to abate.

However, I think the best relief for sorrow is to sing. This man tried it, at any rate. When mercy seems to have departed, it is well to sing of departed mercy. When no present blessing appears, it is a present blessing to remember the blessings of past years and to rehearse the praises of God for all His former mercies towards us. Two sorts of songs we ought to keep up, even if the present appears to yield us no theme: the song of the past for what God has done, and the song of the future for the grace we have not tasted yet—the covenant blessings held in the pierced hand, safe and sure against the time to come.

Beloved, I want you to feel the spirit of gratitude within your heart. Even though your mind may be heavy, your countenance sad, and your circumstances gloomy, still let the generous impulse kindle and glow. Come, let us sing unto the Lord. It is not much for us to sing God's praises in fair weather. The shouts of "harvest home" over the loaded hay wagon are proper, but they are only natural. Who would not sing then? What bird is silent when the sun is rising and the dews of spring are sparkling? But the choicest choir charms the stars of night, and no note is sweeter, even to the human ear, than that which comes from the bare bough amid the snows of dark winter. Sorrowful ones, your hearts are tuned to notes the joyful cannot reach. Yours is the full range of tone and volume. You are harps on which the chief Player of stringed instruments can display His matchless skill to a larger degree than on the unafflicted. May He do so now.

Some will not readily yield in this holy exercise. Like Elijah, we will try to run before the king's chariot in the matter of praise. Accounting ourselves the greatest debtors of all to the grace and mercy of God, we must and will sing loudest of the crowd and make even:

> Heaven's resounding arches ring
> With shouts of sovereign grace.

I invite your attention to two things. First, we will look at the work of the eternal Builder: *"Mercy shall be built up forever."* Secondly, we will listen to the resolve of an everlasting singer: *"I will sing of the mercies of the LORD forever."* For the best handling of the subject, I will discuss the second verse first. In the book of common prayer, the canon prescribes that a certain form of words is "to be said or sung." From the text we are to do both. The second verse begins *"I have said,"* and then the first verse begins *"I will sing."* We will say and sing, too. God grant we may say it in the depth of our hearts, and afterwards that our mouths may sing it and make it known unto all generations.

First, let us contemplate the eternal Builder and His wonderful work. *"I have said, Mercy shall be built up forever: thy faithfulness shalt thou establish in the very heavens."* I can see a vast mass of ruins. Heaps upon heaps lie around me. A stately edifice has tumbled down. Some terrible disaster has occurred. There it lies— cornice, pillar, pinnacle, everything of ornament and of utility, broken, scattered, dislocated. The world is strewn with the debris. Journey wherever you will, the desolation is before your eyes. Who has done this? Who has cast down this temple? What hand has ruined this magnificent structure? Manhood has been destroyed, and sin was the agent that effected the fall. It is man broken by his sin. Iniquity has done it. Oh, devastation, what destruction have you wrought in the earth! What desolation you have made unto the ends of the world! Everywhere is ruin. Futile attempts are made to rebuild this temple upon its own heap. The Babel tower arises out of the rubbish and abides for a season, but it is soon broken down. The mountain of decay and corruption becomes even more hopeless of res- toration. All that man has done with his greatest effort is but to make a huge dis- play of his total failure to recover his position, to realize his ostentatious plans, or to restore his own fleeting memories of better things. They may build; they may pile stone upon stone and cement them together with mortar. However, their rude structure will all crumble to dust again, for the first ruin will be perpetuated even to the end. So must it be, because sin destroys all. I am vexed in my spirit and very troubled as I look at these ruins, fit habitations for the bittern and the dragon, the mole and the bat. Alas, that manhood should be thus destroyed!

But what else do I see? I behold the great original Builder coming forth from the ivory palaces to undo this mischief. He comes not with implements of destruction to cast down every vestige, but He advances with plummet and line so that He may set up and establish on a sure foundation a noble pile that will not crumble with time, but endure throughout all ages. He comes forth with mercy.

Thus I said as I saw the vision, *"Mercy shall be built up forever."* There was no material but mercy with which a temple could be constructed among men. What can meet the guilt of human crimes but mercy? What can redress the misery occasioned by wanton transgression but mercy? Mere kindness could not do it. Power alone—even omnipotence—could not accomplish it. Wisdom could not even commence until mercy stood at her right hand. But when I saw mercy intervene, I understood the meaning. Something was to be done that would change the dreary picture that made my heart groan. At the advent of mercy, the walls would soon rise until the roof ascended high and the palace received within its renovated glory the sublime Architect who erected it. I knew that now there would be songs instead of sighs, since God had come, and come in mercy.

Blessed was that day when mercy, God's Benjamin, His last-born attribute, appeared. Surely it was the son of our sorrow, but it was also the son of His right hand. There would have been no need for mercy if it had not been for our sin. From direst evil the Lord displayed the greatest good. When mercy came— God's darling, for He said, *"he delighteth in mercy"* (Micah 7:18)—then was there hope that the ruins of the fall would no longer be the perpetual misery of men. *"Mercy shall be built up."*

If you closely scan the passage, you will clearly perceive that the psalmist has the idea of God's mercy being manifest in building, because a great breach has to be repaired and the ruins of mankind are to be restored. As for building, it is a very substantial operation. A building is something which is palpable and tangible to our senses. We may have plans and schemes which are only visionary, but when it comes to building, as those who have to build know, there is something real being done—something more than surveying the ground and drawing the plans. What real work God has done for men! What real work in the gift of His dear Son! The product of His infinite purpose now becomes evident. He is working out His great designs after the counsel of His own will. What real work there is in the regeneration of His people. That is no fiction. Mercy is built, and the blessings that you and I have received have not mocked us. They have not been the dream of fanatics nor the fancy of enthusiasts. God has done real work for you and for me, as we can testify.

"For I have said, Mercy shall be built." That is no sham, no dream; it is the act and deed of God. Mercy has been built. A thing that is built is a fixed thing. It exists—exists really, and exists according to a substantial plan. It is presumed to be permanent. True, all earthly structures will eventually deteriorate and decay,

and man's buildings will dissolve in the last great fire. Still, a building is much more durable than a tent. *"I have said, Mercy shall be built."* It is not a movable berth, but a fixed habitation! I have found it so, have you? Some of you began to perceive God's mercy many years ago when heads that are now bald or gray had locks bushy and black as a raven, when you were curly-headed boys and girls that clambered on your father's knee. You remember the mercy of your God, and it has continued with you—a fixed, substantial, real thing. Your old family house has not been more fixed than the mercy of God. There has been a warm place for you by the fireside from your childhood until now, and a mother's love has not failed. But more substantial than a house has been the mercy of God to you. You can endorse the declaration of Ethan: *"I have said, Mercy shall be built."*

A building is an orderly thing as well as a fixed thing. There is a scheme and design about it. *"Mercy shall be built."* God has gone about blessing us with designs that only His own infinite perfection could have completed. We have not seen the design yet in the full proportion. We will be lost in wonder, love, and praise when we see it all carried out. Now, however, we can already perceive some lines, some distinct traces of a grand design.

As I caught first one thought of God and then another, I said of His mercy toward me, *"Mercy shall be built."* I see that it definitely will be. This is no load of bricks. It is polished stones built one upon another. God's grace and goodness toward me have not come to me by chance, or as the blind distribution of a God who cared for all alike, and for none with any special purpose. No, there has been as much a specialty of purpose for me as if I were the only one He loved, though, praise His name, He has blessed and is blessing multitudes of others beside me. As I discovered that in His dealings of mercy there was a plan, I said, *"Mercy shall be built,"* and so it has been.

If I had the space, I would like to picture for you the digging of that foundation of mercy in past times, the marking out of the lines of mercy in the predestining purpose and the ancient covenant of God. I would appeal to your experience and entreat you to observe how progressively, line upon line, the many promises have been verified to you up until now. With what alacrity you would say, "Yes, the figure may run on all fours, if it likes, and may go on as many legs as a centipede. Yet there will be no spoiling of it; the metaphor is so good. Mercy has been in the course of construction and is now being built." So the song begins, *"Mercy shall be built."*

Notice now that the psalmist says, "*Mercy shall be built up.*" Will you try to think for a minute upon these words, "*built up*"? It is not merely a long, low wall of mercy that is formed to make an enclosure or to define a boundary, but a magnificent pile of mercy, whose lofty heights will draw admiring gazes, that is being built up. God piles mercy on top of mercy. He gives one favor so that we may receive another.

There are some covenant blessings that you and I are not ready to receive yet. They would not be suitable to our present capacities. "*I have yet many things to say unto you, but ye cannot bear them now*" (John 16:12). Weak eyes that are gradually recovering their use must not have too much light. A man half-starved must not be fed at once upon substantial meat: he must have the nutriment gently administered to him. An excess of rain might inundate the land and wash up the plants, while gentle showers refresh the thirsty soil and invigorate the vegetation.

Likewise, mercy is bestowed on us in measure. God does not give us every spiritual blessing at once. There are the blessings of our childhood in grace, which we perhaps will not so much enjoy when we come to be strong men. Just so, the blessings of the strong man and of the father would crush the child. God abounds toward us in all wisdom and prudence in distributing His gifts. I said, "Yes, '*Mercy shall be built up.*' There will be one mercy on another."

If I only had a vivid imagination and a tongue gifted with eloquence, then I would try to portray the twelve courses of the new Jerusalem and show how the stones of fair colors came one next to the other, so that the colors set each other off and blended into a wondrous harmony. I can clearly see that the mercy of the azure will not come first, but there will be the mercy of the emerald underneath it. There will be a progression made in the preciousness of the stones with which God will build us up. We cannot tell what the next is to be; certainly not what the next after that is to be, nor the next after that. But as I saw half-a-dozen of the courses of God's mercy, I said, "*Mercy shall be built up.*" As I see it rising tier on tier, course on course, it gathers wonders. The longer I gaze, the more I am lost in contemplation. Silent with astonishment, spell-bound with the fascinating vision, I think, I believe, and I know that "*Mercy shall be built up.*"

Further, mercy awakens expectations. I am waiting eagerly for the next scene. The designs of mercy are not exhausted. The deeds of mercy are not all told. The display of mercy must reach higher than has ever yet dawned upon my imagination. Its foundations were laid deep. In great mercy He gave me a broken heart.

That was pure mercy, for God accepts broken hearts. They are very precious in His sight. But it was a greater mercy when He gave me a new heart which was wrapped up in His love and filled with His joy. Let us remember how He showed us the evil of sin and caused us to feel a sense of shame. That was a choice mercy, but it was a clearer mercy when He gave us a sense of pardon. It was a blessed day when He gave us the little faith that tremblingly touched His garment's hem. It was better when He gave us faith as a grain of mustard seed that grew. It has been better still when by faith we have been able to do mighty works for Him. We know not what we will do in the future when He gives us more faith.

Far less can we imagine how our powers will develop in heaven, where faith will come to its full perfection. It will not die, as some idly pretend. There we will implicitly believe in God. With the place of His throne as the point of our survey, we will see nothing but His sovereign will to shape events. Thus, with joyful assurance of hope, we will look onward to the advent of our Lord Jesus Christ and the glory that is to follow. We will sit in heaven and sing that the Lord reigns. We will gaze on the earth and behold how it trembles at the coming of the King of Kings. With radiant faces we will smile at Satan's rage. We do not know what any one of our graces may be built up into, but if you are conscious of any growth in any grace, you have learned enough to appreciate the voice that speaks in this manner, "*I have said, Mercy shall be built up forever.*"

Once again read this verse with very great emphasis. Notice how it rebukes the proud and the haughty, and how it encourages the meek and lowly in spirit. "*I have said, Mercy shall be built up forever.*" In the edification of the saints, there is nothing else but mercy.

Some people seem to imagine that when we get to a certain point in grace, we do not need to petition for mercy. Dear ones, if any of you get into the frame of mind in which you believe that you need not make any confession of sin nor ask pardon of sin, you are trifling with the very truths of which you seem to hold dear. I do not care what doctrine it is that brings you to that point. You are in a dangerous state if you stay there. Get back to the truth quickly. Your right position is at the throne of grace, and a throne of grace is meant for people that want grace. You need grace now, more than ever. Without mercies new every morning, as the manna that fed the Israelites of old, your days will be full of misery.

Your Lord and Master taught you to say not only "*Our Father which art in heaven*" and "*Thy kingdom come,*" but He instructed you constantly to pray,

"Forgive us our trespasses as we forgive them that trespass against us" (Matthew 6:9, 10, 12). "But I have no trespasses," someone says. Dear one, look at your own heart. I will have no argument with you. Take the bandage off your eyes. You are about as full of sin as an egg is full of protein. Among the rest of your many sins is this rotten egg of an accursed pride about your own state of heart. Whatever you say, *"I said, Mercy shall be built up forever."*

I expect God to deal with me on the basis of mercy as long as I live. I do not expect that He will build me up in any way but according to His grace, compassion, and forgiving love. If there are any creatures in this world that can boast of having progressed beyond the need of asking for mercy, I have not learned their secret of self-deception. I do know of some professors of the faith who climb so high up the ladder that they come down the other side. It is very much like the wonderful growing in perfection of which they talk so foolishly. Often it means climbing so high that they are pure saints in their own estimation, but before long they have sunk so low that they are poor lost sheep in the eyes of the church. God grant that you may not fall by any such delusion.

"I have said, Mercy shall be built up forever." If we get to the gate of heaven and stand at the alabaster doorstep with our finger on the glittering latch, unless the mercy of God carries us over the threshold, we will be dragged down to hell even from the gates of paradise. Mercy, mercy, mercy! *"His mercy endureth forever"* (Psalm 118:1) because we always need it. As long as we are in this world, we will have to make our appeal to mercy and cry, "Father, I have sinned. Blot out my transgressions." That is, as I have said, what the text declares, *"I have said, Mercy shall be built up,"* and nothing else but mercy. There will not come a point when the angelic masons will stop and say, "Now then, the next course is to be merit. So far it has been mercy, but the next course is to be perfection in the flesh. The next course is to be no need of mercy." Absolutely not! Mercy only, until the topstone is brought forth with shouts of *"Grace, grace unto it"* (Zechariah 4:7). *"Mercy shall be built up."*

Further cast your eyes on the Scripture. *"I said, mercy shall be built up forever."* Forever? Well, I have been peering back into the past, and I discover that nothing else but mercy can account for my being or my well-being. By the grace of God, I am what I am. The psalm of my life, though filled with varied stanzas, has but one chorus, *"His mercy endureth forever."* Will you look back, beloved, on all the building of your life and character? Any of it that has been real building—gold and silver and precious stones—has all been mercy, and so the building will go on.

The operation is proceeding slowly but surely. Even though at this present hour you may be in grievous trouble, mercy is being built up for you. "Oh, no," say you, "I am tottering, my days are declining, and I feel I will be utterly cast down." Yes, you may be very conscious of your own weakness and infirmity; but the mercy of the Lord is steadfast, its foundation abides firm, not a single stone can be moved from its setting. The work is going on, storm or tempest notwithstanding.

Nothing is precarious about the fact that *"mercy shall be built up forever."* Let not the murky atmosphere that surrounds you blind the eyes of your understanding to this glorious word *"forever."* Rather, realize that if you are well set in this fabric of mercy, your castings down are often the way in which God builds up His mercy. You will be built up forever by His mercy. And if it goes on being built up forever—I am ravished with the thought, though I cannot give expression to it—what will it grow to? If it is going to be built up in the case of any one of you, for seventy years or so, it will be a grand pinnacle, an everlasting monument to the eternal Builder's praise. But you see it will continue, for it will be built up forever. What! Never cease? No, never. But will it ever come to a pause? No, *"mercy shall be built up forever."* It will go on towering upward. Do you imagine that eventually it will slow down? That is not likely. It is not God's way. He generally hastens His speed as He ripens His purposes.

I suspect that God will go on building up His mercy tier on tier forever. Someone asks, "Will its colossal altitude pierce the clouds and rise above the clear azure of the sky?" It will. Read the text: *"Thy faithfulness shalt thou establish in the very heavens"*—not in the heavens only, but in the *"very heavens,"* the heaven of heavens. He will continue building you up in mercy, dear brother or sister, until He gets you to heaven. He will build you up until He makes a heavenly man of you; until where Christ is, you are; and what Christ is, as far as He is man, you are also. With God Himself you will be allied, a child of God, an heir of heaven, a joint heir with Jesus Christ.

Again I wish I had an imagination, bold and clear, uncramped by all ideas built up by men, free to expand, and still able to cry, "Excelsior." Palaces, I think, are paltry, and castles and cathedrals are only grand in comparison with the little cottages that nestle on the plain. Even mountains, high as the Himalayan range or broad as the Andes, though their peaks are very lofty from our perspective, are mere specks on the surface of the great globe itself. Our earth is small among the celestial orbs, a little sister of the larger planets.

Figures quite fail me: my description must take another turn. I try and try again to realize the gradual rising of this temple of mercy which will be built up forever. Within the limits of my feeble vision, I can discern that it has risen above death, above sin, above fear, above all danger. It has risen above the terrors of the judgment day. It has out-soared the wreck of matter and the crash of worlds. It towers above all our thoughts. Our bliss ascends above angels' enjoyments. They have pleasures that were never checked by a pang of guilt, but they do not know the indescribable delight of free grace and undying love. It has ascended above all that I dare to speak of, for even the little I know has about it the idea that it is not lawful for a man to utter. It is built up into the very arms of Christ, where His saints will lie in paradise forever. *"I said, Mercy shall be built up forever."* The building-up process will go on throughout eternity.

Further, what is once built will never fall down, in whole or in part. That is the mercy of it. God is such a Builder that He finishes what He begins, and what He accomplishes is forever. *"The gifts and calling of God are without repentance"* (Romans 11:29). He does not do and undo, or build for His people after a covenant fashion and then cast down again because the counsel of His heart has changed. So let us sing and praise and bless the name of the Lord. I do hope that, from what our experience has taught us already, we are prepared to cry, like the psalmist, *"I have said, Mercy shall be built up forever: thy faithfulness shalt thou establish in the very heavens."*

Now let us examine the first verse. There are first that shall be last, and last that shall be first; so is it with our text. We have looked at the eternal Builder, let us listen to an everlasting singer. *"I will sing of the mercies of the LORD forever: with my mouth will I make known thy faithfulness to all generations."*

Here is a good and godly resolution: *"I will sing."* The singing of the heart is intended, and the singing of the voice is expressed, for the psalmist mentions his mouth. Equally true is it that the singing of his pen is implied, since the psalms that he wrote were for others to sing in generations that should follow. He says, *"I will sing."* I do not know what else he could do. God is building with mercy. We cannot assist Him in that. We have no mercy to contribute, and what is built is to be all of mercy. We cannot impart anything to the great temple which He is building. However, we can sit down and sing. It seems delightful that there should be no sound of hammer or noise of ax; that there should be no other sound than the voice of song, as when the ancient fabled instrument player was said to have built temples by the force of song. So will God build up His church, and so will He build us as living stones into the sacred structure. So will we sit and muse on His mercy until the music breaks forth from our mouths as we rise to stand and sing about it. I will sing of the mercy while the mercy is being built up. "*I will sing of the mercies of the* LORD."

But will not the psalmist soon quit these sweet notes and relapse into silence? No, he says, "*I will sing of the mercies of the* LORD *forever.*" Will he not grow weary and wish for some other occupation? No, for true praise is a thirsty thing: when it drinks from a golden chalice, it soon empties it and yearns for deeper draughts with strong desire. It could drink up Jordan at a gulp. Singing praise to God is a spiritual passion. The saved soul delights itself in the Lord and sings on and on tirelessly. "*I will sing...forever,*" says he. Not, "I will get others to perform and then I will retire from the service," but rather, "I will myself sing. My own voice will take the solo, whoever may refuse to join in the chorus. I will sing, and with my mouth will I make known His faithfulness."

That is blessed—that singing personally and individually. It is a blessed thing to be one of a choir in the praise of God, and we like to have others with us in this happy employment. Yet, for all that, Psalm 103 is a most beautiful solo. It begins, "*Bless the* LORD, *O my soul,*" and it finishes up with "*Bless the* LORD, *O my soul.*" There must be personal, singular praise for we have received personal, singular mercies. I will sing, "*I will sing of the mercies of the* LORD *forever.*"

Now note the subject of his song: "*I will sing of the mercies of the* LORD." What, not of anything else? Are the mercies of the Lord his exclusive theme? *Arma virumque cano*—"Arms and the man, I sing," says the Latin poet. "Mercies and my God, I sing," says the Hebrew lyricist. "I will sing of mercies," says the devout Christian. If a man drinks from this fountain of mercy, he will sing far better than he who drinks of the Castalian fountain and on Parnassus begins to tune his harp.

> Praise the mount, oh, fix me on it,
>   Mount of God's unchanging love.

Here we are taught a melodious sonnet, "sung by flaming tongues above." "I will sing of mercies, I will sing of mercies forever," he says, and I suppose the reason is because he knew God's mercies would be built up forever. The morning stars sang together when God's work of creation was completed. Suppose God created a world every day. Surely the morning stars would sing every day. God gives us a world of mercies every day: therefore, let us sing of His mercies forever. Any one day that you live, beloved, contains enough mercy to make you sing not only through that day but through the rest of your life. I have thought sometimes when I have received great mercies of God that I almost wanted to stop, rest, and be thankful, and say to Him, "My blessed Lord, do not send me anything more for a little while. I really must take stock of these. Come, my good secretaries, take down notes and keep a record of all His mercies."

Let us gratefully respond for the manifold gifts we have received and return our heartiest praise to God who is the giver of every good thing. But, dear me, before I can put the basketfuls of present mercies away on the shelf, there come wagons loaded with more mercy. What am I to do then, but to sit on the top of the pile and sing for joy of heart? So let us lift each parcel, look at each label, store them in the cupboard, and say, "It is certainly full of mercy." As for me, I will go and sit before the Lord like David, and say, "*Who am I, O Lord* God? *and what is my house, that thou hast brought me hitherto?…And is this the manner of man, O Lord* God?" (2 Samuel 7:18–19). "*I will sing of the mercies of the* Lord *forever,*" because I will never reach the end of them.

As Addison put it, "Eternity's too short to utter all thy praise." You will never accomplish the simple task of acknowledgments, because there will be constantly more mercies coming. You will always be in arrears. In heaven itself you will never have praised God sufficiently. You will want to begin heaven over again and have another eternity, if such a thing could be, to praise Him for the fresh benefits that He bestows. "*For I have said, mercy shall be built up forever.*" Therefore, "*I will sing of the mercies of the* Lord *forever.*" What a spectacle it will be as you sit in heaven and watch God building up His mercies forever, or, if it be the case, wander over all the worlds that God has made. I suppose we may do that and yet still have heaven for our home. Heaven is everywhere to the heart that lives in God. What a wonderful sight it will be to see God going on building up His mercy.

We have not acquired an idea of the grandeur of the plan of mercy. The grandeur of His justice no thought can conceive, no words can paint. Although there have been expressions and metaphors used about the wrath to come which cannot be found in Scripture, and are not justified, yet I am persuaded that there is no exaggeration possible of the inviolability of God's law, of the truthfulness of His threatening, of the terror of His indignation, or of the holiness of the Lord, a holiness that will compel universal homage.

Nevertheless, you must always take care that you balance your thoughts. In the requital of His wrath, there will be a revelation of His righteousness. No sentence of His majesty will ever cast a shadow over His mercy, and every enemy will be speechless before the equity of His award. They that hate Him will hide their faces from Him, In burning shame they will depart to perpetual banishment from His presence. Their condemnation will not dim the purity of His attributes. The glory of the redeemed will also reveal the righteousness of Jehovah, and His saints will be perfectly satisfied when they are conformed to His likeness. On the summit of the eternal hill, you will sit down and survey the built-up mercy city which is now in the course of construction. It lies four square: its height is the same as its breadth, ever towering, ever widening, ever coming to that divine completion which, nevertheless, it has already attained, in another sense. We know that God in His mercy will be all in all. *"I will sing of the mercy of the LORD forever,"* because I will see His mercy built up forever.

This singing of Ethan was intended to be instructive. How large a class did he want to teach? He intended to make known God's mercy to all generations. Dear me, if a man teaches one generation, is not that enough? Modern thought does not venture beyond a decade, and it gets tame and tasteless before half that tiny span of sensationalism has given it time to evaporate. But the echoes of truth are not so transient. They endure, and by means of the printing press we can teach generation after generation, leaving books behind us. This good man has bequeathed this psalm, which is teaching us now, perhaps more so than it taught any generation closer to him. Will you transmit blessed testimonies to your children's children? It should be your desire to do something in the present life that will live after you are gone. It is one proof to us of our immortality that we instinctively long for a sort of immortality here. Let us strive to get it, not by carving our names on some stone, or writing our epitaphs upon a pillar, as Absalom did when he had nothing else by which to commemorate himself. (See 2 Samuel 18:18.) Rather, let us get to work to do something which will be a testimony to the mercy of God, that others will see when we are gone. Ethan said, *"Mercy shall be built up forever,"* and he is still teaching us that blessed fact.

Suppose you cannot write and your sphere of influence is very narrow. Still you will go on singing of God's praise forever, and you will go on teaching generations yet to come. You Sunday-school teachers, you will be Sunday-school teachers forever. "Oh, no," you say, "I cannot put stock in that." Well, but you will. You know it will always be Sunday when you get to heaven. There will never be any other day there, but one everlasting Sabbath. Through you and by you will be made known to angels, principalities, and powers, the manifold wisdom of God.

I often think some of you old, experienced saints could better teach me than I can teach you. You will teach me by and by. When we are in glory we will all be able to tell one another something of God's mercy. Your view of it, you know, differs from mine, and mine from another's. You, my dear friend, see mercy from one perspective; but even though you two are one together, your spouse sees it from another point of view and detects another facet of it which your eye has never caught. So we will barter and exchange our knowledge in heaven, and trade together and grow richer in our knowledge of God there. *"I have said, mercy shall be built up forever: thy faithfulness shalt thou establish in the very heavens."*

Then I said, *"I will sing of the mercies of the* LORD *forever: with my mouth will I make known thy faithfulness to all generations."* We will go on exalting in God's mercy as long as we have any being, and that will be forever and ever. When we have been in heaven millions of years, we will not desire any other subject to speak of but the mercy of our blessed God. We will find an audience with charmed ears to sit and listen to the matchless tale, and some that will ask us to tell it yet again. They will come to heaven as long as the world lasts, some from every generation. We will see them streaming in at the gates more numerously, I hope, as the years roll by, until the Lord returns. We will continue to tell to newcomers what the Lord has done for us. We never can cease it. The heavens are continually telling the glory of God, and every star declares His praise in wondrous diversity. Just as the stars differ from one another in the glory of God above, so the saints will forever tell the story which yet will remain untold—the love we knew, but which surpassed our knowledge; the grace of which we drank, but yet was deeper than our draughts; the bounty in which we swam until we seemed to lose ourselves in love; the favor which was greater than our utmost conceptions and rose above our most eager desires.

God bless you, beloved, and send you out singing:

> All that remains for me
>   Is but to love and sing,
> And wait until the angels come,
>   To bear me to my King.

6

PRAISE FOR THE GIFT OF GIFTS

Thanks be unto God for his unspeakable gift.
—2 Corinthians 9:15

In the chapter from which the text is taken, Paul is stirring up the Christians at Corinth to be ready with liberal gifts for the poor saints at Jerusalem. He finishes by reminding them of a greater gift than any they could bring. By this one short word of praise, *"Thanks be unto God for his unspeakable gift,"* he sets all their hearts singing. Let men give as liberally as they may, you can always proclaim the value of their gift: you can appraise it and add up its worth. But God's gift is unspeakable, unreckonable. You cannot fully estimate the value of what God gives.

The gospel is a gospel of giving and forgiving. We may sum it up in those two words. Hence, when the true spirit of it works upon the Christian, he forgives freely and also gives freely. The large heart of God breeds large hearts in men, and they who live upon His bounty are led by His Spirit to imitate that bounty, according to their power.

However, I am not going to say anything further right now on the subject of liberality. I must get to the text immediately, hoping that we may really drink in the spirit of it, and out of full hearts use the apostle's language with more intense meaning than ever as we read his words: "*Thanks be unto God for his unspeakable gift.*" I will begin by showing that salvation is altogether the gift of God, and as such is to be received by us freely. Then I will try to show that this gift is unspeakable, and, thirdly, that for this gift thanks should be rendered to God. Though it is unspeakable, yet we should speak our praise of it.

We start with the thought that salvation is totally the gift of God. Paul said, "*Thanks be unto God for his unspeakable gift.*" Over and over again, we have to proclaim that salvation is wholly of grace—not of works, nor of wages, but the gift of God's great bounty to undeserving men. Often as I have preached this truth, I must keep on doing so, as long as there are men in the world who are self-righteous, and as long as there are minds in the world so slow to grasp the meaning of the word *grace*—that is, "free favor"—and as long as there are memories that find it difficult to retain the idea of salvation being God's free gift.

Let us say, simply and plainly, that salvation must come to us as a gift from God, for salvation comes to us by the Lord Jesus, and what else could Jesus be? The essence of salvation is the gift of God's only-begotten Son to die for us, that we might live through Him. I think you will agree with me that it is inconceivable that men have ever merited God giving His only-begotten Son to them. To give Christ to us, in any sense, must have been an act of divine charity; but to give Him up to die on that cruel and bloody tree, to yield Him up as a sacrifice for sin, must be a free favor that surpasses the limits of human thought. It is not plausible that any man could deserve such love.

It is plain that if man's sins needed a sacrifice, he did not deserve that a sacrifice should be found for him. The fact of his need proves his lack of merit and his guiltiness. He deserves to die. He may be rescued by another dying for him, but he certainly cannot claim that the eternal God should take from His bosom His only-begotten, well-beloved Son and put Him to death. The more you look that thought in the face, the more you will reject the idea that, by any possible sorrow, or by any possible labor, or by any possible promise, a man could put himself into the position of deserving to have Christ to die for him. If Christ came to save sinners, it must have been as a gift, a free gift of God. The argument to me is conclusive.

Besides, over and over again in God's Word, we are told that salvation is not of works. Although there are many who cling to the notion of man's works as grounds for salvation, yet as long as this Book stands and there are eyes to read it, it will bear witness against the idea of human merit, and it will speak out plainly for the doctrine that men are saved by faith, and not by works. Not just once, but often, it is written, "*The just shall live by faith*" (Habakkuk 2:4; Romans 1:17; Galatians 3:11; Hebrews 10:38). Moreover, we are told, "*Therefore it is of faith, that it might be by grace*" (Romans 4:16). The choice of salvation by believing, rather than by works, is made by God purposefully so that He might show that grace is a gift. "*Now to him that worketh is the reward not reckoned of grace, but of debt: but to him that worketh not, but believeth on him that justifieth the ungodly, his faith is counted for righteousness*" (Romans 4:4–5).

Faith is that virtue, that grace, which is chosen to bring us salvation, because it never takes any of the glory to itself. Faith is simply the hand that takes. When the beggar receives alms, he does not bless the hand that takes, but blesses the hand that gives. Therefore we do not praise the faith that receives, but the God who gives the gift. Faith is the eye that sees. When we see an object, we delight in the object, rather than in the eye that sees it. Thus we glory in the salvation which God bestows, not in faith. Faith is appointed as the porter to open the gate of salvation, because that gate turns on the hinges of free grace.

Additionally, may we always remember that we cannot be saved by the merit of our own works, because holy works are themselves a gift, the work of the grace of God. If you have faith, joy, and hope, who gave them to you? These did not spring up spontaneously in your heart. They were sown there by the hand of love. If you have lived a godly life for years, if you have been a diligent servant of the church and of your God, in whose strength have you done it? Is there not One who works all our works in us? Could you work out your own salvation with fear and trembling if God did not first work in you both to will and to do of His good pleasure? How can that, which is itself the gift of God, claim a reward? I think the ground is cut right out from under those who would put confidence in human merit, when we show, first of all, that, in Scripture, salvation is clearly said to be "*not of works, lest any man should boast*"; and, secondly, that even the good works of believers are the fruit of a renewed life, "*for we are his workmanship, created in Christ Jesus unto good works, which God hath before ordained that we should walk in them*" (Ephesians 2:9–10).

> All that I was, my sin, my guilt,
>   My death, was all mine own;
> All that I am, I owe to thee,
>   My gracious God, alone.

Further, if salvation were not a free gift, how else could a sinner get it? I will pass over some of you, who imagine that you are the best people in the world. It is sheer fantasy, mark you, without any truth in it. But I will say nothing about you. There are, however, some of us, who know that we were not the best people in the world—we who sinned against God and knew it, and who were broken in pieces under a sense of our guilt. Personally, I know that there would have been no hope of heaven for me if salvation had not been the free gift of God to the undeserving. After ministering for thirty-seven years, I stand exactly where I stood when first I came to Christ: a poor sinner, nothing at all, but taking Christ as the free gift of God to me, just as I took Him when I was a lad and fled to Him for salvation.

Ask any of the people of God who have been abundant in service and constant in prayer, whether they deserve anything from the hand of God. Those who have most to be thankful for will tell you that they have nothing that they have not received. Ask great soul winners, whom God has honored to participate in the conversion of many, whether they lay any claim to the grace of God, whether they have any merit, or whether they dare bring a price, seeking to buy God's love; they will loathe the very thought. There is no way to heaven for you and me, my friend convinced of sin, unless all the way we are led by grace, and unless salvation is the gift of God.

Once more, look at the privileges which come to us through salvation! I cannot, as I value those privileges, conceive that they are purchasable, or that they come to us as the result of our deserving them. They must be a gift. They are so numerous and glorious as to be totally outside the limits of our furthest search and beyond the height of our utmost reach. We cannot encompass any salvation of any sort by our own efforts; but if we could, it certainly would not be a salvation such as this.

Let us look, then, at our privileges. Here comes, first, *"the forgiveness of sins, according to the riches of his grace"* (Ephesians 1:7). He that believes in Christ has no sin. His sin is blotted out. It has ceased to be. Christ has finished it, and he is to God as though he had never sinned. Can any sinner deserve that?

> Here's pardon for transgressions past
> It matters not how black their cast
> And oh, my soul, with wonder view
> For sins to come, here's pardon too.

Can any sinner bring a price that will purchase such a blessing? No, such mercy must be a gift.

Next, everyone that believes in Christ is justified and looked upon by God as being perfectly righteous. The righteousness of Christ is imputed to him, and he *is "accepted in the beloved"* (Ephesians 1:6). By this he becomes not only innocent, that is, pardoned, but he becomes praiseworthy before God. This is justification. Can any guilty man deserve that? Why, he is covered with sin, defiled from head to foot! Can he deserve to be arrayed in the sumptuous robe of the divine righteousness of Christ, and *"be made the righteousness of God in him"* (2 Corinthians 5:21)? It is inconceivable. Such a blessing must be the gift of infinite bounty, or it can never come to man.

Furthermore, beloved, remember that *"now are we the sons of God"* (1 John 3:2). Can you realize that truth? Others are not, but believers are the sons of God. He is their Father, and the Spirit of adoption breathes within their hearts. They are children of His family, and come to Him as children come to a father, with loving confidence. Think of being made a son of God, a son of Him that made the heavens, a son of Him who is God over all, blessed forever. Can any man deserve that? Certainly not. This also must come as a gift.

Sonship leads to heirship. *"If children, then heirs; heirs of God, and joint-heirs with Christ"* (Romans 8:17). If you are a believer, all things are yours—this world and worlds to come. Could you ever desire all that? Could such an inheritance have come to you through any merits of your own? No, it must be a gift. Look at it, and the blaze of its splendor will strike all idea of merit blind.

Further than that, we are now made one with Christ. Oh, tell everywhere this wonder which God has done for His people! It is not to be understood; it is an abyss too deep for a finite mind to grasp. Every believer is truly united to Christ: *"For we are members of his body, of his flesh, and of his bones"* (Ephesians 5:30). Every believer is married to Christ, and none of them will ever be separated from Him. Seeing, then, that there is such a union between us and Christ, can you suppose that any man can have any claim to such a position apart from the grace of God? By what merit, even of a perfect man, could we deserve to become one with Christ in an endless unity? Such a privilege is out of the realm of purchase. It can only be the gift of God. Oneness with Christ cannot come to us in any other way.

Listen again. In consequence of our union with Christ, God the Holy Spirit dwells in every believer. Our bodies are His temple. God dwells in us, and we dwell in God. Can we deserve that? Even a perfect keeping of the law would not have brought to men the abiding of the Holy Ghost in them. It is a blessing that rises higher than the law could ever reach, even if it had been kept.

Let me say, further, that if you possess a blessed peace, as I trust you do, you can say:

> My heart is resting, O my God;
> I will give thanks and sing;
> My heart is at the secret source
> Of every precious thing.

That divine peace must surely be the gift of God. If there is a great calm within your soul, an entire satisfaction with Christ your Lord, you never deserved that priceless blessing. It is the work of His Holy Spirit and must be His free gift.

When you come to die—unless the Lord comes, as He will—the grace that will enable you to face the last enemy fearlessly will not be yours by any right of your own. If you fall asleep, as I have seen many a Christian pass away, with songs of triumph, with the light of heaven shining on your brow, almost in glory while yet you are in your bed, why, you cannot deserve that! Such a deathbed must be the free gift of God's almighty grace. It cannot be earned by merit. Indeed, it is just then that every thought of merit melts away, and the soul hides itself in Christ and triumphs there.

If this does not convince you, look once more. Let a window be opened in heaven. See the long lines of white-robed saints. Hark to their hallelujahs. Behold, their endless, measureless delight. Did they deserve to come there? Did they come to their thrones and to their palms of victory by their own merits? Their answer is, they *"have washed their robes, and made them white in the blood of the Lamb"* (Revelation 7:14). From them all comes the harmonious anthem, *"Non nobis, Domine"*: "Not unto us, O Lord, not unto us; but unto thy name give glory, for thy mercy and for thy truth's sake." From first to last, then, we see that salvation is all the gift of God. And what can be freer than a gift, or more glorious than the gift of God? No prize can approach it in excellence, no merit can be mentioned in the same hour. We are indeed debtors to the mercy of God! We have received much, and there is more to follow. It is all of grace from first to last. We know but little at what cost these gifts were purchased for us, but we will know it better by and by, as McCheyne so sweetly sings:

> When this passing world is done,
>   When has sunk you glaring sun;
> When I stand with Christ in glory,
>   Looking o'er life's finished story,
> Then, Lord, shall I fully know
>   Not till then, how much I owe.

> When I stand before the throne.
>   Dressed in beauty not my own;
> When I see thee as thou art
>   Love thee with unsinning heart;
> Then, Lord, shall I fully know,
>   Not till then, how much I owe.

Now, I would like to direct your thoughts in another direction as we consider that this gift is unspeakable. Do not think it means that we cannot speak about this gift. Ah, how many times have I, for one, spoken about this gift during the last forty years! I have spoken of little else. I heard of someone who said, "I suppose Spurgeon is preaching that old story again." Yes, that is what I keep doing. If I live another twenty years, it will be "the old, old story" still, for there is nothing like it. It is inexhaustible, like an artesian well that springs up forever and ever. We can speak about it, yet it is unspeakable. What is meant, then, by saying it is unspeakable? Well, as I have said already, Christ Jesus our Lord is the sum and substance of salvation and of God's gift. O God, this gift of Yours is unspeakable, and it includes all other gifts beside!

> Thou didst not spare thine only Son,
>   But gav'st him for a world undone;

And freely with that Blessed One,
    Thou givest all.

Consider, first, that Christ is unspeakable in His person. He is perfect man and glorious God. No tongue of seraph or cherub can ever describe the full nature of Him whose name is *"Wonderful, Counselor, The mighty God, The everlasting Father, The Prince of Peace"* (Isaiah 9:6). This is He whom the Father gave for us and for our sakes. He was the Creator of all things, for *"without him was not any thing made that was made"* (John 1:3), yet He was *"made flesh and dwelt among us"* (John 1:14). He filled all things by His omnipresence, yet He came and tabernacled on the earth. This is that Jesus, who was born of Mary, yet who existed before all worlds. He was that Word, who was *"in the beginning...with God, and the Word was God"* (John 1:1). He is unspeakable. It is not possible to put into human language the divine mystery of His sacred being, truly man and yet truly God. But how great is the wonder of it! Soul, God gave God for you! Do you hear it? To redeem you, O believer, God gave Himself to be your Savior. Surely, that is an unspeakable gift.

Christ is unspeakable, next, in His condescension. Can any one measure or describe how far Christ stooped, when, from the throne of splendor, He came to the manger to be swaddled and lie where the oxen fed. Oh, what a stoop of humility was that! The Infinite became an infant. The Eternal was cradled on a woman's knee. He was there in the carpenter's shop, obedient to His parents. There in the temple sitting among the doctors, hearing them and asking them questions. There in poverty, crying, *"The Son of man hath not where to lay his head"* (Matthew 8:20). There, in thirst, asking of a guilty woman a drink of water. It is unspeakable that He, before whom the hosts of heaven veiled their faces, should come here among men, and among the poorest of the poor; that He, who dwelt amid the glory and bliss of the land of light, should deign to be a Man of sorrows and acquainted with grief. It surpasses human thought! Such a Savior is a gift unspeakable.

But if unspeakable so far, what shall I say of Christ in His death? Beloved, I cannot speak adequately of Gethsemane and the bloody sweat, nor of the Judas kiss, nor of the traitorous flight of the disciples. It is unspeakable. That binding, scourging, plucking of the beard, and spitting in the face! Man's tongue cannot utter the horror of it. I cannot tell you truly the weight of the false accusations, slanders, and blasphemies that were heaped on Him; nor would I wish to picture the old soldier's cloak flung over His bleeding shoulders, the crown of thorns, the buffeting, and the shame and sorrow He endured, as He was thrust out to execution. Do you wish to follow Him along the streets, where weeping women lifted up their hearts in tender sympathy for the Lord of love about to die? If you do, it must be in silence, for words but feebly tell how much He bore on the way to the cross.

> Well might the sun in darkness hide,
>   And shut his glories in
> When God, the mighty Maker, died
>   For man, the creature's sin.

Oh, it was terrible that He should be nailed to the tree, that He should hang there to be ridiculed by all the mob of Jerusalem! The debased flouted Him, the meanest thought Him meaner than themselves. Even dying thieves upbraided Him. His eyes were choked; they became dim with blood. He must die. He cried, "*It is finished*" (John 19:30). He bowed His head. The glorious Victim yielded up His life to put away His people's sin. This is God's gift, divine and unspeakable, to sons of men!

But that is not all. Christ is unspeakable in His glory. When we think of His resurrection, of His ascending to heaven, and of His glory at the right hand of God, words languish on our lips. However, in every one of these positions, He is the gift of God to us. When He comes with all the glory of the Father, He will still be to His people the *Theo Dora*, the gift of God, the great unspeakable benediction to the sons of men. I wish that the people of Christ had this aspect of the Lord's glory more consciously on their hearts, for though He seems to tarry, yet will He come again the second time, as He promised.

> With that blessed hope before us,
>   Let no harp remain unstrung;
> Let the mighty Advent chorus
>   Onward roll on every tongue.
>   Maranatha,
> Come, Lord Jesus, quickly come!

To me, one of the most wonderful aspects of this gift is Christ in His chosen. All the Father gave Him, all for whom He died, these He will glorify with Himself, and they will be with Him where He is. Oh, what a sight will that be when we see the King in His beauty, and all His saints beautiful in His glory, shining like so many stars around Him who is the Sun of them all! Then, indeed, will we see what an unspeakable gift God gave to men, when, through that gift, He makes His saints all glorious, even as He predestined them, *"to be conformed to the image of his Son, that he might be the firstborn among many brethren"* (Romans 8:29).

But we do not need to wait until we see His face to know His glory. Christ is unspeakable as the gift of God in the heart here. "Oh," you say, "I trust I have felt the love of God shed abroad in my heart!" I rejoice with you, but could you speak it? Often, when I have tried to preach the love of Christ, I have not been able to preach it well, because I did not feel it as I ought; but more often, I have not been able to tell it because I felt it so much. I would rather preach in that manner always, and feel Christ's love so much that I could speak of it but little. Child of God, if you have known much of Christ, you have often had to weep out your joys instead of speaking them, to lay your finger on your mouth and be silent because you were overpowered by His glory. See how it was with John: *"When I saw him, I fell at his feet as dead"* (Revelation 1:17). If John were to try to explain what happened, he would say, "I could not speak then; the splendor of the Lord made me dumb. I fell at His feet as though I were dead."

This is one reason why the gift of God is unspeakable, because, the more you know about it, the less you say about it. Christ overpowers us. He makes us tongue-tied with His wondrous revelations. When He reveals Himself fully, we are like men that are blinded with excess of vision. Like Paul, on the Damascus road, we are forced to confess, *"I could not see for the glory of that light"* (Acts 22:11). We cannot speak of it fully. All the apostles and prophets and saints of God have been trying to speak of the love of God as manifested in Christ, but yet they have all failed.

I say, with great reverence, that the Holy Ghost Himself seems to have labored for expression, and, as He had to use human pens and mortal tongues, even He has never spoken to the full measure and value of God's unspeakable gift. It is unspeakable to men by God Himself. God can give it, but He cannot make us fully understand it. We need to be like God Himself to comprehend the greatness of His gift when He gave us His Son.

Though we make constant effort, it is unspeakable, even throughout a long life. Ministers, especially those who have been in one place a long time, sometimes think that they will eventually run out of sermon subjects. If they preach

Christ, however, they never will run short. If they have preached ten thousand sermons about Christ, they have not yet left the shore and are not out in the deep sea yet. With splendor of thought, they need to plunge into this great mystery of free grace and dying love. When they have dived the deepest, they will perceive that they are as far from the bottom as when they first broke the surface of the water. It is an endless, unspeakable theme!

> Oh, could I speak the matchless worth,
>   Oh could I sound the glories forth
> Which in my Savior shine!
>   I'd soar and touch the heavenly strings,
> And vie with Gabriel while he sings
>   In notes almost divine.

But I can neither speak it nor sing it as I ought. Yet I would finish Medley's hymn:

> Well, the delightful day will come
>   When my dear Lord will bring me home,
> And I shall see his face;
>   Then with my Savior, Brother, Friend,
> Blest eternity I'll spend
>   Triumphant in his grace.

Even in heaven, Christ will still be forever a gift unspeakable. Perhaps we will have a talk together, friends, on this subject when we get there. One good woman said to me, "We will have more time in eternity than we have now." To that I replied, "I do not know whether there is any time in eternity, the words look like a contradiction." "Oh," said she, "I will at least get to talk with you, anyhow. I have never had the chance yet." Well, I dare say we will commune up there about these blessed things when we will know more about them. As we are to be there forever and ever, we will need some great subjects with which to keep up the conversation. What vaster theme could we have than this? In one of his verses, Addison has said:

> But, oh! eternity's too short
>   To utter half thy praise.

I have heard simpletons say that the couplet was very faulty. "You cannot make eternity short," they say. That shows the difference between a poet and a critic. A critic is a being with all teeth, without any heart; and a poet is one who has much heart, and who sometimes finds that human language is not sufficient to express his thoughts. We will never be finished with Christ in heaven. Oh, my Lord, Your presence will make my heaven!

> Millions of years my wondering eyes,
>   Shall o'er thy beauties rove;
> And endless ages I'll adore
>   The glories of thy love.

This wondrous gift of God is an utterly inexhaustible, unspeakable subject.

Now, I come to the final point, that for this gift, thanks should be rendered. The text says, "*Thanks be unto God for his unspeakable gift.*" By this the apostle not only meant that he gave thanks for Christ, but he thus calls upon the church and upon every individual believer to join him in his praise. Here I adopt his language, and praise God on my own behalf, and exhort all of you who know the preciousness of Christ, the gift of God, to join in the thanksgiving. Let us as with one heart say it now, "*Thanks be unto God for his unspeakable gift.*"

Some cannot say this, for they never think of the gift of God. You who never think of God, how can you thank God? There must be "think" at the bottom of "thank." Whenever we think, we ought to thank. But some never think, and therefore never thank. Beloved friend, where are you? That Christ should die—is it nothing to you? That God "*gave his only begotten Son, that whosoever believeth in him should not perish, but have everlasting life*" (John 3:16)—is that nothing to you? Let the question drop into your heart. Press it home upon yourself. Will you say that you have no share in this gift? Will you deliberately give up any hope you may have of ever partaking of the grace of God? Are you determined now to say, "I do not care about Christ"? Well, you would hardly like to say that. But why do you practically declare this to be your intention, if you do not want to say it? Oh, that you might now so think of Christ as to trust Him at once, and begin to raise this note of praise!

Some, on the other hand, do not thank God because they are always delaying. In attendance at almost any church service are those who were there ten years ago, and were rather more hopeful then than they are now. "There is plenty of time," you say, but you do not say this about other matters. I admired the children, the other day, when the teacher said, "Dear children, the weather is unsettled. You can go out next Wednesday. But do you not think that it would be better to stop for a month, so that we could go when the weather is better?" There was not a child that voted for stopping for a month. All the hands were up for going next Wednesday. Now, imitate the children in that. Do not make it seem as if you were in no hurry to be happy. As he that believes in Christ has eternal life, to postpone having it is an unworthy and an unwise thing to do. No, you will have it, I hope, at once.

There is a man who is going to be a very rich man when his old aunt dies. He does not wish that she should die, I am sure, but he sometimes wonders why some people are spared to be ninety. He is very poor now and wishes that some of this money could come to him at once. He is not for putting that off. Why should you put off heavenly riches and eternal life? I urge you to believe in Christ now. Then you will be filled with thankfulness and joy.

Some cannot say, "*Thanks be unto God for his unspeakable gift,*" because they do not know whether they have it or not. They sometimes think that they have; more often they fear that they have not. Never tolerate a doubt on this subject, I implore you. Get full assurance. "*Lay hold on eternal life*" (1 Timothy 6:12). Get a grip it. Know Christ, trust Christ wholly, and you have God's word for it: "*He that heareth my word, and believeth on him that sent me, hath everlasting life and shall not come into condemnation, but is passed from death unto life*" (John 5:24). Then you can say, "*Thanks be unto God for his unspeakable gift.*"

Now, dear friends, let me ask you to enter into this exercise. Let us first thank God for this gift. Put out of your mind the idea that you ought to thank Christ, but not thank the Father. It was the Father who gave Christ. Christ did not die to make His Father love us, as some say. I have always preached the very opposite. This idea was well expressed by Kent in verse:

> 'Twas not to make Jehovah's love
>   Towards the sinner flame,
> That Jesus, from his throne above,
>   A suffering man became.
> 'Twas not the death which he endured,
>   Nor all the pangs he bore,
> That God's eternal love procured
>   For God was love before.

God gave his Son because He already loved us. Christ is the exhibition of the Father's love, and the revelation of Christ is made because of *"the love of the Spirit"* (Romans 15:30). Therefore, *"thanks be unto God* [the Father, the Son, and the Holy Ghost] *for his unspeakable gift."*

While you that are saved raise your note of gratitude, be very careful to thank God only. Do not be thinking by whose means you were converted and begin to thank the servant instead of the Lord whom he serves. Let the man who was used as the instrument in God's hand be told, for his comfort, of the blessing God sent you through him; but thank God, and thank only God, that you were led to *"lay hold on Christ,"* who is His unspeakable gift.

Moreover, thank God spontaneously. Look at the apostle Paul and imitate him. When he sounded this peal of praise, his mind was occupied at the time about the collection for the poor saints; but, collection or no collection, he thanked God for his unspeakable gift. I like to see thanks to God come up at what might seem to be an untimely moment. When a man does not feel just as happy as he might, and yet says, "Thank God," it sounds refreshingly real.

I like to hear such a bubbling up of praise as in the case of old Father Taylor of New York, when he broke down in the middle of a sentence. Looking up at the people, he said, "There now! The nominative has lost its verb; but, hallelujah! I am on the way to glory;" and so he went on again. Sometimes we ought to do just like that. Take an opportunity, when there comes a little interval, just to say, "Whether this is in tune or not, I cannot help it: *'thanks be unto God for his unspeakable gift.'*"

Lastly, as you receive the precious gift, thank God practically. Thank God by doing something to prove your thanks. It is a poor gratitude which only effervesces in words, but shirks deeds of kindness. Real thankfulness will not be in word only, but in deed too, and so it will prove that it is in truth. "Well, what could I do that would please God?" you ask. First, I think you could look for His lost children. That is sure to please Him. Go and see whether you can find one of the erring whom you might bring back to the fold. Would you not please a mother if you set to work to find her lost baby? We want to please God. Seek the lost ones and bring them in.

If you want to please God, succor His poor saints. If you know anything of them, help them. Do something for them for Christ's sake. I knew a woman who always used to relieve anybody that came to her door in the dress of a sailor. I do not think that half those who came to her ever had been to sea at all. But, still, if they came to the door as sailors, she would say, "My dear boy was a sailor. I have not seen him for years. He is lost somewhere at sea. But for dear Jack's sake, I always help every sailor that comes to my door." It is a right feeling, is it not? I remember, when I first came to London from my country charge, I thought that if I came across a dog or a cat that came from Waterbeach, I would like to feed it. So, for love of Christ, love Christ's poor people. Whenever you find them, say, "My Lord was poor, and so are you. For His dear sake, I will help you."

If you want to thank God by bearing with the evil ones. Do not lose your temper. By that I mean, do not get angry with the unthankful and the evil. Let your anger be lost in praise for the gift unspeakable. Please God by bearing with evil men, as He bears with you. But if you have a bad temper, in another sense, I hope that you may lose it and never find it again.

Lastly, if you want to please God, like the Thessalonians, *"wait for his Son from heaven"* (1 Thessalonians 1:10). The Lord Jesus is coming again in like manner as He departed. (See Acts 1:11.) There is no attitude with which God is more delighted in His saved people than with that of watching for the time when *"unto them that look for him shall he appear the second time, without sin unto salvation"* (Hebrews 9:28).

Beloved, may God enable you to magnify His Son. To Him be all the praise! Let us again lift up our glad hallelujah: *"Thanks be unto God for his unspeakable gift."* Amen.

JOY IN YOUR LIFE

CONTENTS

1. Sons of Jacob 259

2. Faith versus Fear 262

3. Liberty from the Fear of Death 267

4. Suffering and Consolation 271

5. The Saints Are Kings 275

6. The Holy Spirit, Another Comforter 280

7. Promises for the Bruised and Broken 285

8. Against the World 290

9. The Divine Refuge 295

10. The Use of Chastisement 299

11. Responsibility and Success 305

12. Devotions in the Night 310

13. All Joy and Peace 316

14. Mr. Ready-to-Halt and His Companions 320

15. Joy in Life's Hard Times 325

16. Cure for Heartache 329

17. A Word to the Troubled 333

18. All Things Work Together for Good 337

19. An Ever Present Help 343

20. Deliverance from Surrounding Troubles 348

21. A Harp's Sweet Note 354

1

SONS OF JACOB

For I am the Lord, *I change not;*
therefore ye sons of Jacob are not consumed.
—Malachi 3:6

The phrase *"sons of Jacob"* means persons who enjoy particular rights and titles. Jacob had no rights by birth, but he soon acquired them. He exchanged a mess of pottage with his brother Esau and thus gained the birthright. I do not justify the means, but he also obtained the blessing and so acquired unique rights.

"Sons of Jacob" also includes Christians who have unusual rights and titles, too. Unto those who believe, the Lord has given the right and power to become sons of God. They have an interest in the blood of Christ. They have a right to enter in through the gates into the city. They have a title to eternal honors. They have a promise of everlasting glory. They have a right to call themselves sons of God. Yes, there are unique rights and privileges belonging to the *"sons of Jacob."*

But these *"sons of Jacob"* were men of unusual manifestations. Jacob had experienced unusual manifestations from his God, and thus he was highly honored.

Once, at night, he lay down and slept. He had the hedges for his curtains, the sky for his canopy, a stone for his pillow, and the earth for his bed. Then he had an extraordinary manifestation. He saw angels of God ascending and descending a ladder from heaven to earth. He thus had a manifestation of Christ Jesus, as the ladder that reaches from earth to heaven, by which angels came up and down to bring us mercies.

And then, what a manifestation there was at Mahanaim, when the angels of God met Jacob! Again at Peniel, when Jacob wrestled with God, he saw Him face to face. Those were all unique, unusual manifestations. This passage refers to those who, like Jacob, have had remarkable manifestations.

The "*sons of Jacob*" have had unusual manifestations. They have talked with God as a man talks with his friend. They have whispered in the ear of Jehovah. Christ has been with them to eat with them, and they with Christ. The Holy Spirit has shone into their souls with such a mighty radiance that they could not doubt about special manifestations. The "*sons of Jacob*" are the men who enjoy these manifestations.

Then, they are men of unusual trials. Oh, poor Jacob! I would not choose Jacob's lot even if I did not have the prospect of Jacob's blessing, for a hard lot his was. He had to run away from his father's house to Laban's. Then that surly old Laban cheated him all the years he was there—cheated him of his wife, cheated him in his wages, cheated him in his flocks, and cheated him all through the story. By and by, he had to run away from Laban, who pursued him and overtook him. Next came Esau with four hundred men to cut him up, root and branch. Then there was a season of prayer, after which he wrestled and had to go the rest of his life with his thigh out of joint. However, a little later, his dearly beloved Rachel died. His daughter Dinah was led astray, and his sons murdered the Shechemites. Then his favored dear Joseph was sold into Egypt, and a famine came. Reuben went up to his bed and polluted it, Judah committed incest with his own daughter-in-law, and all his sons became a plague to him. At last Benjamin was taken away and the old man, almost broken-hearted, cried, "*Joseph is not, and Simeon is not, and ye will take Benjamin away*" (Genesis 42:36). Never was a man more tried than Jacob, all because of the one sin of cheating his brother. All through his life, God chastised him.

I believe there are many who can sympathize with dear old Jacob. They have had to pass through trials very much like his. Well, cross-bearers! God says, "*For*

I am the LORD, I change not; therefore ye sons of Jacob are not consumed." Poor tried souls! You are not consumed because of the unchanging nature of your God. Now do not start fretting and say with the self-conceit of misery, *"I am the man who hath seen affliction"* (Lamentations 3:1). The Man of Sorrows was afflicted more than you; Jesus was indeed a mourner. You only see the skirts of the garments of affliction. You never have had trials like His. You do not understand what troubles mean. You have hardly sipped the cup of trouble. You have only had a drop or two, but Jesus drank the dregs. *"Fear not,"* says God, *"I am the LORD, I change not; therefore ye sons of Jacob,"* men of unusual trials, *"are not consumed."*

Then, *"sons of Jacob"* are men of exceptional character. Though there were some things about Jacob's character that we cannot commend, there are traits that God commends. There was Jacob's faith, by which Jacob had his name written among the mighty worthies who did not obtain the promises on earth, but will possess them in heaven. Are you a person of faith, beloved? Do you know what it is to walk by faith, to live by faith, to get your temporary food by faith, to live on spiritual manna—all by faith? Is faith the rule of your life? If so, you are a *"son of Jacob."*

Jacob was a man of prayer—a man who wrestled, groaned, and prayed. "Ah, you poor heathen, don't you pray?" "No!" you say, "I never thought of such a thing. For years I have not prayed." Well, I hope you may before you die. Live and die without prayer, and you will pray long enough when you get to hell.

I knew a woman who was so busy sending her children to Sunday school that she said she had no time to pray. No time to pray? Had she time to dress? There is a time for every purpose under heaven, and if she had purposed to pray, she would have prayed.

Sons of God cannot live without prayer. They are wrestling Jacobs. They are men in whom the Holy Spirit so works that they can no more live without prayer than I can live without breathing. They must pray. Mark you, if you are living without prayer, you are living without Christ; and, dying like that, your portion will be in the lake that burns with fire. May God redeem and rescue you from such a lot! But you who are *"the sons of Jacob"* take comfort, for God is immutable.

2

FAITH VERSUS FEAR

He would put strength in me.
—Job 23:6

When the believer is brought into peace with God, he does not tremble at the thought of God's power. He does not ask, "Will He plead against me with His great power?" But he says, "No, that very power, once my terror and fear, is now my refuge and my hope, for He will put that very power in me. I rejoice that God is almighty, for He will lend me His omnipotence. *'He would put strength in me.'* The very power that would have damned my soul saves my soul. The very power that would have crushed me God puts into me, so that the work of salvation may be accomplished. No, He will not use it to crush me, but He will put that very strength into me."

Do you see the Mighty One upon His throne? "Dread Sovereign, I see Your ominous arm. What, will You crush this sinner? Will You utterly destroy me with Your strength?" "No," says He, "come here, child." If you do go to His almighty throne, He says, "There, the same arm that made you quake, see there, I give it to you. Go out and live. I have made you mighty as I am, to do My works.

262

I will put strength into you. The same strength that would have broken you to pieces on the wheel will now be put into you, so that you may do mighty works."

Now, this great strength sometimes goes out in prayer. Did you ever hear the prayers of a man in whom God had put strength? I venture to say, you have heard some of us poor puny souls pray, but have you ever heard a man pray that God had made into a giant? Oh, if you have, you will say it is a mighty thing to hear such a man in supplication.

I have seen such a man as if he had seized the angel and would pull him down. I have seen him now and then slip in his wrestling. But, like a giant, he has recovered his footing and seemed, like Jacob, to hurl the angel to the ground. I have marked the man lay hold of the throne of mercy and declare, *"I will not let thee go, except thou bless me"* (Genesis 32:26). I have seen him, when heaven's gates have been apparently barred, go up to them and say, "Gates, open wide in Jesus' name." Then I have seen the gates fly open before the man as if he were God himself, for he is armed with God Almighty's strength. I have seen that man discover in prayer some great mountain in his way and pray it down until it became a tiny molehill. He has beaten the hills and made them like chaff by the immensity of his might in prayer.

Some of you think I am talking enthusiasm, but such cases have there been and are now. Oh, to have heard Luther pray! When Melanchthon was dying, Luther went to his deathbed and said, "Melanchthon, you must not die!" "Oh," said Melanchthon, "I must die! It is a world of such toil and trouble." Luther said, "I have need of you, and God's cause has need of you, and as my name is Luther, you shall not die!" The physician said he would.

Well, down went Luther on his knees and began to tug at death. Old Death struggled mightily for Melanchthon, and he had got him well-nigh on his shoulders. "Drop him," said Luther, "I want him." Death replied, "No, he is my prey. I will take him!" "Down with him," commanded Luther, "Down with him, Death, or I will wrestle with you!" And he seemed to take hold of the grim monster and hurl him to the ground. Luther came away victorious, like Orpheus with his wife, up from the very shades of death. He had delivered Melanchthon from death by prayer!

"Oh," you say, "that is an extraordinary case." No, not one-half as extraordinary as you dream. Men and women have done the same in other cases. They have asked something of God and have been granted it. They have been to the throne, showed a promise, said they would not come away without its fulfillment, and have come back from God's throne conquerors of the Almighty, for prayer moves the arm that moves the world. "Prayer is the sinew of God," said one, "It moves His arm." And so it is. Truly, in prayer, with the strength of the faithful heart, there is a beautiful fulfillment of the text, "*He would put strength in me.*"

Not only in prayer, but in duty, the man who has great faith in God, and whom God has girded with strength, becomes gigantic! Have you never read of those great heroes who put to flight whole armies and scattered kings like seed that is sown broadcast? Have you never read of those men who were fearless of foes and stalked onward before all their opposers, as if they would as soon die as live?

I read of a case in the old king of Scotland that occurred before King James, who wished to force "the black prelacy" on them. Andrew Melville and some of his associates were deputized to wait upon the king. As they were going with a scroll already written, they were warned to take care and return, for their lives were at stake. They paused a moment, and Andrew said, "I am not afraid, thank God, nor feeble-spirited in the cause and message of Christ. Come what pleases God to send us, our commission will be executed." At these words the delegation took courage and went forward.

On reaching the palace and having obtained an audience, they found his majesty attended by Lennox, Arran, and several other lords, all of whom were English. They presented the scroll with their strong objections. Arran lifted it from the table and glanced over it. He then turned to the ministers and furiously demanded, "Who dares sign these treasonable articles?" "We dare," replied Andrew Melville, "and we will render our lives in the cause." Having thus spoken, he came forward to the table, took the pen, subscribed his name, and was followed by his brethren. Arran and Lennox were confounded. The king looked on in silence, and the nobles in surprise.

Thus did our good forefathers appear before kings, and yet were not ashamed. "*The proud have had* [them] *greatly in derision, yet have* [they] *not declined from thy law*" (Psalm 119:51). Having thus discharged their duty, after a brief conference, the ministers were permitted to depart in peace. The king trembled more at them than if a whole army had been at his gates. Why was this? It was because God had put His own strength into them to make them masters of their duty.

You have some such in your midst now. Despised they may be, but God has made them like the lionly men of David, who would go down into the pit in the depths of winter, take the lion by the throat, and slay him. We have some in our churches—a remnant, I admit—who are not afraid to serve their God, like Abdiel, who was "*found faithful*" (1 Corinthians 4:2) among the faithless. We have some who are superior to the customs of the age and scorn to bow at mammon's knee, who will not use the trim language of too many modern ministers, but stand out for God's gospel and the pure white banner of Christ, unstained and unsullied by the doctrines of men. Then are they mighty! Why they are mighty is because God has put strength in them.

"And will I be able to hold on to the end?" says the believer. Yes, you will, for God's strength is in you. "Will I be able to bear such a trial?" Yes, you will. Cannot Omnipotence stem the torrent? Omnipotence is in you. Like Ignatius of old, you are a God-bearer. You bear God about within you. Your heart is a temple of the Holy Spirit, and you will yet overcome.

"But can I ever stand firm in such an evil day?" Oh, yes you will, for He will put His strength in you!

Some time ago, I was in the company of some other ministers. One of them observed, "Brother, if there were to be stakes in Smithfield again, I am afraid they would find very few to burn among us." "Well," I said, "I do not know anything about how you would burn. But this I know very well, that there never will be any lack of men who are ready to die for Christ." "Oh!" said he, "But they are not the right sort of men." "Well," said I, "but do you think they are the Lord's children?" "Yes, I believe they are, but they are not the right sort." "Ah," said I, "you would find them the right sort, if they came to the test, every one of them. They do not have burning grace yet. What would be the use of it? We do not need the grace until the stakes come, but we should have burning grace in burning moments."

If now a hundred of us were called to die for Christ, I believe there would not only be found a hundred, but five hundred, that would march to death and sing all the way. Whenever I find faith, I believe God will put strength into the man. I never think anything to be impossible to a man with faith in God, while it is written, "*He would put strength in me.*"

Caesar could not swim the Tiber, encumbered as he was. Do you hope to swim the Jordan with your flesh about you? No, you will sink unless Jesus, as Aeneas carried Anchises upon his shoulders from the flames of Rome, would lift you from the Jordan and carry you across the stream. You will never be able to walk across the river or face that tyrant and smile in his face, unless you have something more than mortal flesh to depend on. You will need then to be belted about with the girdle of divinity, or else your loins will be loosed and your strength will fail you when you need it most. Many a man has ventured to the Jordan in his own strength, but how he has shrieked and howled when the first wave touched his feet! But no weakling ever went to death with God in him, except he found himself mightier than the grave. Go on, Christian, for this is your promise, "*He would put strength in me.*"

> Weak, though I am,
> Yet through His might,
> I all things can perform.

Go on. Do not dread God's power, but rejoice in this: He will put His strength in you. He will not use His power to crush you.

3

LIBERTY FROM THE FEAR OF DEATH

Where the Spirit of the Lord is, there is liberty.
—2 Corinthians 3:17

The true child of God serves his Master more than he ever did anyone else. As Erskine penned:

Slight now His loving presence if they can;
No, no; His conquering kindness leads the van.
When everlasting love exerts the sway,
They judge themselves most kindly bound to obey;
Bound by redeeming love in stricter sense,
Than ever Adam was in innocence.

"Where the Spirit of the Lord is, there is liberty" from the fear of death. O death, how many a sweet cup have you made bitter! O death, how many a revel have you broken up! O death, how many a gluttonous banquet have you spoiled!

O death, how many a sinful pleasure have you turned into pain! Take the telescope and look through the vista of a few years. What do you see? Grim death in the distance, grasping his scythe. He is ever coming. What is behind him? It depends upon your own character. If you are the sons of God, there is the palm branch. If you are not, you know what follows death—hell follows him. O death, your specter has haunted many a house where sin otherwise would have rioted. O death, your chilly hand has touched many a heart that was big with lust and made it start, frightened from its crime. Oh, how many are slaves to the fear of death!

Half the people in the world are afraid to die. There are some madmen who can march up to the cannon's mouth. There are some fools who rush with bloody hands before their Maker's tribunal. But most men fear to die.

Who is the man who does not fear to die? I will tell you—the man who is a believer. Fear to die? Thank God, I do not. The cholera may come again. I pray to God it will not, but if it does, it matters not to me. I will toil and visit the sick by night and by day until I drop. If it takes me, sudden death is sudden glory.

And so it is with the weakest saint. The prospect of dissolution does not make you tremble. Sometimes you fear, but more often you rejoice. You sit down and calmly think of dying. What is death? It is a low porch through which you stoop to enter heaven. What is life? It is a narrow screen that separates us from glory, and death kindly removes it!

I recollect a saying of a good old woman, who said, "Afraid to die, sir? I have dipped my foot in Jordan every morning before breakfast for the last fifty years, and do you think I am afraid to die now?" Die? Why, we die hundreds of times. We *"die daily"* (1 Corinthians 15:31). We die every morning; we die each night when we sleep; by faith we die. And so, dying will be old work when we come to it. We will say, "Ah, death, you and I have been old acquaintances. I have had you in my bedroom every night. I have talked with you each day. I have had the skull upon my dressing table. I have often thought of you. Death, you have come at last, but you are a welcome guest. You are an angel of light and the best friend I have had." Why dread death, since there is no fear of God's leaving you when you come to die?

Here I must tell you that anecdote of the good Welsh lady, who, when she lay dying, was visited by her minister. He said to her, "Sister, are you sinking?" She answered him not a word, but looked at him with an incredulous eye. He repeated the question, "Sister, are you sinking?" She looked at him again as if she could not believe that he would ask such a thing. At last, rising a little in bed, she said, "Sinking? Did you ever know a sinner to sink through a rock? If I had been standing on the sand, I might sink; but, thank God, I am on the Rock of Ages, and there is no sinking there."

How glorious to die! O angels, come! O cohorts of the Lord of Hosts, stretch your wide wings and lift us up from earth. O winged seraphim, bear us far above the reach of this inferior plane. But until you come, I'll sing:

> Since Jesus is mine,
>   I'll not fear undressing,
> But gladly put off these garments of clay.
>   To die in the Lord is a covenant blessing,
> Since Jesus to glory,
>   Through death led the way.

There are two sides to propositions such as this. There are some glorious things that we are free to. Not only are we freed from sin in every sense, from the law, and from the fear of death, but we are free to something. *"Where the Spirit of the Lord is, there is liberty."* That liberty gives us certain rights and privileges.

We are free to heaven's charter. The Magna Carta of heaven is the Bible, and you are free to it. There is a choice passage: *"When thou passest through the waters, I will be with thee; and through the rivers, they shall not overflow thee"* (Isaiah 43:2). You are free to that. Here is another: *"Mountains shall depart, and the hills be removed; but my kindness shall not depart"* (Isaiah 54:10). You are free to that. Here is another: *"Having loved his own…he loved them unto the end"* (John 13:1). You are free to that. *"Where the Spirit of the Lord is, there is liberty."*

Here is a chapter touching election; you are free to that if you are elect. Here is another, speaking of the noncondemnation of the righteous and their justification; you are free to that.

You are free to all that is in the Bible. It is a never-failing treasure, filled with boundless stores of grace. It is the bank of heaven: you may draw from it as much as you please without hindrance or abatement. Bring nothing with you except faith. Bring as much faith as you can muster, and you are welcome to all that is in the Bible. There is not a promise, not a word in it, that is not yours. In the depths of tribulation, let it comfort you. Amid waves of distress, let it cheer you. When sorrows surround you, let it be your helper. This is your Father's love-token. Let it never be shut and covered with dust. You are free to it, so use your freedom.

Next, remember that you are free to the throne of grace. It is the privilege of Englishmen that they can always send a petition to Parliament. Likewise, it is the privilege of a believer that he can always send a petition to the throne of God. I am free to God's throne. If I want to talk to God tomorrow morning, I can. If tonight I wish to have conversation with my Master, I can go to Him. I have a right to go to His throne. It matters not how much I have sinned. I go and ask for pardon. It signifies nothing how poor I am. I go and plead His promise that He will provide all things that I need. I have a right to go to His throne at all times, in midnight's darkest hour or in the heat of midday. Wherever I am—if fate commands me to the utmost verge of the wide earth—I have still constant admission to His throne. Use that right, beloved. Use that right on behalf of others as well as yourself.

There is not one of you who lives up to his privileges. Many a gentleman will live beyond his income, spending more than he has coming in. But there is not a Christian who does so—I mean, who lives up to his spiritual income. Oh, you have an infinite income, an income of promises, an income of grace. No Christian ever lived up to his income. Some people say, "If I had more money, I would have a larger house and horses and a carriage and so on." Very well and good, but I wish Christians would do the same. I wish they would set up a larger house and do greater things for God, look happier and take those tears away from their eyes.

With such stores in the bank and so much in hand that God gives you, you have no right to be poor. Rejoice, rejoice! The Christian ought to live up to his income, not below it.

> Turn, then, my soul unto your rest,
>   The ransom of your great High Priest
> Hath set the captive free.
>   Trust to His efficacious blood,
> Nor fear your banishment from God,
>   Since Jesus died for thee.

4

SUFFERING
AND CONSOLATION

For as the sufferings of Christ abound in us,
so our consolation also aboundeth by Christ.
—2 Corinthians 1:5

Just *"as the sufferings of Christ abound in us, so our consolation also abound-eth by Christ."* Here is a blessed proportion. God always keeps a pair of scales; in one side He puts his people's trials, and in the other He puts their consolations. When the scale of trials is nearly empty, you will always find the scale of consolation in nearly the same condition. When the scale of trials is full, you will find the scale of consolation just as heavy.

"As the sufferings of Christ abound in us, so our consolation also aboundeth by Christ." This is a matter of pure experience. Oh, it is mysterious that, when the black clouds gather the most, the light within us is always brightest! When the night lowers and the tempest is coming on, the heavenly captain is always closest to his crew. It is a blessed thing, when we are most cast down, that then it is we are most lifted up by the consolations of Christ.

Trials make more room for consolation. There is nothing that makes a man have a big heart like a great trial. I always find that little, miserable people, whose hearts are about the size of a grain of mustard seed, never have had much to try them. I have found that those people who have no sympathy for their fellows—who never weep for the sorrows of others—very seldom have had any woes of their own.

Great hearts can only be made by great troubles. The spade of trouble digs the reservoir of comfort deeper and makes more room for consolation. When God comes into our heart and finds it full, He begins to break away our comforts and to make it empty. Then there is more room for grace. The humbler a man is, the more comfort he will always have.

I recall walking with a plowman one day, a man who was deeply taught, although he was a plowman. (Really, some plowmen would make better preachers than many college gentlemen.) He said to me, "Depend upon it, if you or I ever get one inch above the ground, we will get just that inch too high." I believe it is true. The lower we lie, the nearer to the ground we are, the more our troubles humble us, and the more fit we are to receive comfort. God always gives us comfort when we are most fit for it. That is one reason why consolations increase in the same ratio as our trials.

Then trouble exercises our graces, and the very exercise of our graces tends to make us more comfortable and happy. Where showers fall most, there the grass is greenest. I suppose the fogs and mists of Ireland make it "the Emerald Isle." Wherever you find great fogs of trouble and mists of sorrow, you always find emerald-green hearts, full of the beautiful verdure of the comfort and love of God. Christian, do not say, "Where have the swallows gone? They are gone. They are dead." Wrong you are. They are not dead. They have skimmed the purple sea and gone to a far-off land, but they will be back again soon.

Child of God, do not say the flowers are dead. Do not say the winter has killed them and they are gone. Ah, no, though winter has coated them with the ermine of its snow, they will put up their heads again and will be alive very soon. Do not say, child of God, that the sun is quenched, because the cloud has hidden it. Oh, no, he is behind there, brewing summer for you. When he comes out again, he will have made the clouds fit to drop in April showers, all of them mothers of the sweet May flowers.

Above all, when your God hides His face, do not say that He has forgotten you. He is but tarrying a little while to make you love Him better. When

He comes, you will have joy in the Lord and will rejoice with joy unspeakable. Waiting exercises our grace and tries our faith. Therefore, wait on in hope, for though the promise may tarry, it can never come too late.

Another reason why we are often most happy in our troubles is this: it is then that we have the closest relationship with God. I speak from heart knowledge and real experience. We never have such close dealings with God as when we are in the midst of tribulation. When the barn is full, man can live without God. When the purse is bursting with gold, we somehow can do without so much prayer. But once your gourds are taken away, you want your God. Once the idols are cleansed out of the house, then you must go and honor Jehovah.

Some of you do not pray half as much as you ought. If you are children of God, you will have the whip. When you have that whip, you will run to your Father. It is a fine day, and the child walks before its father, but there is a lion in the road. Now he comes and takes his father's hand. He could run half a mile before him when all was fine and fair, but once a lion lurks about, it is "Father, Father!" as close as he can be. It is even so with the Christian. Let all be well, and he forgets God. Jeshurun waxed fat and began to kick against God. (See Deuteronomy 32:15.) But when hopes are dashed, joys are blasted, infants lie in the coffin, crops are ruined, the herd is cut off from the stall, the husband's broad shoulder lies in the grave, children are fatherless—then it is that God is a God indeed.

Oh, strip me naked. Take from me all I have. Make me poor—a beggar, penniless, helpless. Dash that cistern in pieces, crush that hope, quench the stars, put out the sun, shroud the moon in darkness, and place me all alone in space without a friend or a helper. Still, *"Out of the depths* [will] *I cry unto thee, O* Lord" (Psalm 130:1). There is no cry so good as that which comes from the bottom of the mountains, no prayer half so hearty as that which comes up from the depths of the soul through deep trials and afflictions. Hence they bring us to God, and we are happier. That is the way to be happy—to live near God. So then, while troubles abound, they drive us to God, and consolations abound.

Some people call troubles "weights." Truly they are so. A ship that has large sails and a fair wind needs ballast. Troubles are the ballast of a believer. The eyes are pumps that fetch out the bilge water of his soul and keep him from sinking. But if trials are weights, I will tell you a happy secret. There is such a thing as making a weight lift you. If I have a weight chained to me, it keeps me down. Yet, give me pulleys and certain appliances, and I can make it lift me up. Yes, there is such a thing as making troubles raise me toward heaven.

A gentleman once asked his friend, concerning the friend's beautiful horse, which was feeding in the pasture with a weight attached to its leg, "Why do you tie down and restrain such a noble animal?" "Sir," replied the man's friend, "I would much sooner confine him than lose him. He is given to leaping hedges." That is why God tethers His people. He would rather restrain them than lose them. If He did not clog them, they would leap the hedges and be gone. They need a tether to prevent their straying. So God binds them with afflictions to keep them near Him, to preserve them, and have them in His presence. It is a blessed fact that as our troubles abound, so our consolations abound also.

5

THE SAINTS ARE KINGS

And hast made us unto our God kings and priests;
and we shall reign on the earth.
—Revelation 5:10

Take the royal office of the saints. They are kings. They are not merely to be kings in heaven, but they are also kings on earth. For if this verse does not say so, the Bible declares it in another passage: *"Ye are a chosen generation, a royal priesthood"* (1 Peter 2:9). We are kings even now. I want you to understand that before I explain the idea.

Every saint of the living God not only has the prospect of being a king in heaven, but positively, in the sight of God, he is a king now. He must say, with regard to his brethren and himself, *"And* [even now Christ] *hast made us unto our God kings and priests; and we shall reign on the earth."* A Christian is a king. He is not simply like a king, but he is a king, actually and truly.

Remember the Christian's royal ancestry. What a fuss some people make about their grandfathers and grandmothers and distant ancestors! I remember seeing depicted at Trinity College the pedigree of some great lord that went back as far as Adam, and Adam was there digging the ground, the first man. It was traced all the way back. Of course I did not believe it. (I have heard of some pedigrees that go back further, but I leave that to your own common sense to believe or not.) Oh, what some would give for a pedigree in which could be found dukes, marquises, kings, and princes!

I believe, however, that it is not what our ancestors were, but what we are that will make us shine before God; that it is not so much in knowing that we have royal or priestly blood in our veins as knowing that we are an honor to our race, walking in the ways of the Lord and reflecting credit upon the church and upon the grace that makes us honorable. But since some men will glory in their descent, I will glory that the saints have the proudest ancestry in all the world. Talk of Caesars or Alexanders or tell me even of our own good Queen, and I say that I am of as proud an ancestry as her Majesty or the greatest monarch in world. I am descended from the King of Kings.

The saint may well speak of his ancestry—he may exult and glory in it—for he is the son of God, positively and actually. His mother, the church, is the bride of Jesus. He is a twice-born child of heaven, one of the blood royal of the universe. The poorest woman or man on earth, born anew in Christ, is of a royal line. Give a man the grace of God in his heart, and his ancestry is noble. I can turn back the roll of my pedigree, and I can tell you that it is so ancient it has no beginning. It is more ancient than all the rolls of mighty men put together because, from all eternity, my Father existed. Thus, I indeed have a royal, ancient ancestry.

The saints, like monarchs, have a splendid retinue. Kings and monarchs can travel only with a great entourage of state. In olden times, they had far more magnificence than they have now, but even in these days we see much of it when royalty is abroad. There must be a select kind of horse, a splendid chariot, and outriders, with all the regalia of gorgeous pomp.

The kings of God—those whom Jesus Christ has made kings and priests unto God—also have a royal retinue. "But," you say, "I see some of them in rags and walking the earth alone, sometimes without a helper or a friend." Ah, but there is a fault in your eyes. If you had eyes to see, you would perceive a bodyguard of angels always attending every one of the blood-bought family.

You remember Elijah's servant could not see anything around Elijah until his master opened his eyes. Only then he could see that there were horses and chariots around Elijah. There are horses and chariots about me. About you also, saint of the Lord, wherever you are, there are horses and chariots. In the bedchamber where I was born, angels stood to announce my birth on high. In seas of trouble, when wave after wave seems to wash over me, angels are there to lift up my head. When I come to die, when sorrowing friends carry me to the grave, angels will stand by my bier. And, when my body is put into the grave, some mighty angel will stand to guard my dust and contend for its possession with the devil. Why should I fear? I have a company of angels about me and glorious cherubim whenever I walk abroad.

Kings and princes have certain things that are theirs by positional right. For instance, her Majesty has Buckingham Palace, her other palaces, her royal crown, her scepter, and so on. But does a saint have a palace? Yes, I have a palace! Its walls are not made of marble, but of gold; its borders are garnets and precious gems; its windows are of agates; its stones are laid with fair colors; around it there is a profusion of every costly thing; rubies sparkle here and there; and pearls are but common stones within it.

Some call it a mansion, but I have a right to call it a palace also, for I am a king. It is a mansion when I look at God. It is a palace when I look at men, because it is a prince's habitation. Mark where this palace is. I am not a prince of India. I have no inheritance in any far-off land that men dream of. I have no El Dorado or Taj Mahal, but yet I have a substantial palace. Over yonder, on the hills of heaven it stands. I do not know its position among the other mansions of heaven, but there it stands. I know that if the earthly house of this tabernacle is dissolved, I have a building of God, a *"house not made with hands, eternal in the heavens"* (2 Corinthians 5:1).

Do Christians have a crown, too? Oh, yes, but they do not wear it every day. They have a crown, but their coronation day has not yet arrived. They have been anointed monarchs, they have some of the authority and dignity of monarchs, but they are not crowned monarchs yet. However, the crown is made. God will not have to order heaven's goldsmiths to fashion it later. It is made already hanging up in glory. God has *"laid up for me a crown of righteousness"* (2 Timothy 4:8). O saint, if you opened some secret door in heaven and went into the treasure chamber, you would see it filled with crowns.

When Cortez entered the palace of Montezuma, he found a secret chamber that was bricked up. So many different things were stowed away, he thought the wealth of all the world was there. If you could enter God's secret treasure house, what wealth you would see! "Are there so many monarchs, so many crowns, so many princes?" you would ask. "Yes," some bright angel would say, "And note that crown! It is yours." If you were to look within, you would read, "Made for a sinner saved by grace, whose name is ___." Then you would hardly believe your eyes, as you saw your own name engraved upon it. You are indeed a king before God, for you have a crown laid up in heaven.

Whatever other insignia belong to monarchs the saints will have. They will have robes of white; they will have harps of glory; they will have all things that become their regal state. We are indeed monarchs, you see, not mock-monarchs, clothed in purple garments of derision and scoffed at with "Hail, king of the Jews." Rather, we are real monarchs. He *"hast made us kings and priests unto our God."*

Kings are considered the most honorable among men. They are always looked up to and respected. A crowd gives way when it is announced, "A monarch is here!" I would not command much respect if I were to attempt to move about in a crowd. By contrast, if anyone should shout, "Here is the Queen!" everyone would step aside to make room for her. A monarch generally commands respect.

We think that worthy princes are the most honorable of the earth, but if you were to ask God, He would reply, "My saints in whom I delight, these are the honorable ones." Do not tell me of tinsel and baubles. Do not tell me of gold and silver. Do not tell me of diamonds and pearls. Do not tell me of ancestry and rank. Do not preach to me of pomp and power. Tell me that a man is a saint of the Lord, for then he is an honorable man. God respects him, angels respect him, and the universe one day will respect him when Christ comes to call him to his account and says, *"Well done, thou good and faithful servant...enter thou into the joy of thy Lord"* (Matthew 25:21). You may despise a child of God now, sinner. You may laugh at him and say he is a hypocrite. You may call him a ninny, an empty talker, and everything you like; but know that those titles will not mar his dignity. He is the honorable of the earth, and God esteems him as such.

But some will say, "I wish you would prove what you affirm, when you say that saints are kings. If we were kings, we would never have any sorrows. Kings are never poor as we are and never suffer as we do." Who told you so? You say if you are kings, you would live at ease. Don't kings ever suffer? Wasn't David an anointed king? Was he not hunted like a partridge on the mountains? Didn't the king himself pass over the brook Kedron and all his people weeping as he went, when his son Absalom pursued him? Was he not a monarch when he slept on the cold ground with no bed except the damp heather? Oh, yes, kings have their sorrows, and crowned heads have their afflictions. For often, "Uneasy lies the head that wears a crown." Do not expect that because you are a king, you are to have no sorrows.

"It is not for kings, O Lemuel, it is not for kings to drink wine; nor for princes strong drink" (Proverbs 31:4). And it is often so. The saints get but little wine here. It is not for kings to drink the wine of pleasure. It is not for kings to have much of the intoxicating drink and the profusion of this world's delight. They will have joy enough up yonder, when they drink it in their Father's kingdom. Poor saint, do dwell on this. You are a king! I beseech you, do not let it slip from your mind. In the midst of your tribulation, still rejoice in it. If you have to go through the dark tunnel of infamy, for Christ's name, if you are ridiculed and reviled, still rejoice in the fact that you are a king, and all the dominions of the earth will be yours!

6

THE HOLY SPIRIT, ANOTHER COMFORTER

The Father…shall give you another Comforter,
that he may abide with you for ever.
—John 14:16

The Holy Spirit is a very loving Comforter. Suppose I am in distress and want consolation. When some bystander hears about my sorrow, he steps in, sits down, and attempts to cheer me. He speaks soothing words, but he loves me not. He is a stranger; he knows me not at all; he has only come in to try his skill. What is the consequence? His words run over me like oil on a slab of marble. They are like the pattering rain upon the rock. They do not break my grief, which stands unmoved, because he has no love for me.

However, let someone who loves me dearly as his own life come and plead with me, then truly his words are music. They taste like honey. He knows the password to the doors of my heart, and my ear is attentive to every word. I catch the intonation of each syllable as it falls, for it is like the harmony of the harps of heaven. Oh, it is a voice in love. It speaks a language that is its own. It is an idiom and an accent that none can mimic. Wisdom cannot imitate it. Oratory cannot attain unto it. It is love alone that can reach the mourning heart. Love is the only handkerchief that can wipe the mourner's tears away.

Is not the Holy Spirit a loving Comforter? Saint, do you know how much the Holy Spirit loves you? Can you measure the love of the Spirit? Do you know how great is the affection of His soul toward you? Go, measure heaven with your span; weigh the mountains in the scales; take the ocean's water and count each drop; count the sand upon the sea's wide shore. When you have accomplished all this, you can tell how much He loves you. He has loved you long, He has loved you well, He loved you ever, and He still will love you. Surely He is the person to comfort you because He loves. Admit Him, then, to your heart, O Christian, that He may comfort you in your distress.

He is a faithful Comforter. Love sometimes proves unfaithful. Oh, sharper than a serpent's tooth is an unfaithful friend! Oh, far more bitter than the gall of bitterness is it to have a friend turn from me in my distress! Oh, woe of woes, to have one who loves me in my prosperity forsake me in the dark day of my trouble! Sad indeed, but such is not God's Spirit. He ever loves, even to the end—a faithful Comforter.

Child of God, you are in trouble. A little while ago you found Him to be a sweet and loving Comforter. You obtained relief from Him when others were but broken cisterns. He sheltered you in His bosom and carried you in His arms. Why do you distrust Him now? Away with your fears, for He is a faithful Comforter.

"But," you say, "I fear I will be sick and will be deprived of His ordinances." Nevertheless, He will visit you on your sickbed and sit by your side to give you consolation. "But I have distresses greater than you can conceive of. Wave upon wave rolls over me. Deep calls unto deep at the sound of the Eternal's waterspouts." (See Psalm 42:7.) Nevertheless, He will be faithful to His promise.

"Oh, but I have sinned." So you have, but sin cannot sever you from His love. He loves you still. Think not, downcast child of God, that because the scars of your old sins have marred your beauty that He loves you less for that blemish. No! He loved you when He foreknew you in your sin. He loved you with the knowledge of what the aggregate of your wickedness would be. He does not love you less now. Come to Him in all boldness of faith. Tell Him you have grieved Him. He will forget your roaming and will receive you again. The kisses of His love will be bestowed on you. The arms of His grace will embrace you. He is faithful, so trust Him. He will never deceive you. Trust Him, for He will never leave you.

He is an unwearied Comforter. Sometimes I have tried to comfort people who have been tried. Now and then, you may meet with the case of a nervous person. You ask, "What is your trouble?" You are told, and you try, if possible, to remove it. However, while you are preparing your artillery to batter the trouble, you find that it has shifted its quarters and is occupying a different position. You change your argument and begin again, but it is again gone. You become bewildered. You feel like Hercules cutting off the ever-growing heads of the Hydra and give up your task in despair. You meet with people whom it is impossible to comfort, bringing to mind the man who locked himself up in fetters and threw the key away so that nobody could free him.

I have found some in the fetters of despair. They cry, "'*I am the man that hath seen affliction*' (Lamentations 3:1). Pity me, pity me, O my friends." The more you try to comfort such people, the worse they get. Therefore, out of all heart, we leave them to wander alone among the tombs of their former joys. But the Holy Spirit is never lacking heart with those whom He wishes to comfort. He attempts to comfort us, but we run away from the sweet cordial He offers. He gives some sweet drink to cure us, but we will not sip it. He gives some wondrous portion to charm away all our troubles, but we put it away from us. Still He pursues us. Even though we say that we will not be comforted, He says we will be. And what He has said, He does. He is not wearied by all our sins, not by all our murmuring.

How wise a Comforter is the Holy Spirit. Job had comforters, and I think he spoke the true when he said, "*Miserable comforters are ye all*" (Job 16:2). But I dare say they esteemed themselves wise. When the young man Elihu rose to speak, they thought he had a world of impudence. Were they not grave and reverend seniors? Didn't they comprehend his grief and sorrow? If they could not comfort him, who could? But they did not find out the cause.

They thought he was not really a child of God and that he was self-righteous, and then offered him the wrong remedy. It is a bad case when the doctor misdiagnoses the disease, gives a wrong prescription, and so, perhaps, kills the patient. Sometimes when we go to visit people, we mistake their disease. We want to comfort them on this point, whereas they do not require any such comfort at all, and they would be better left alone than spoiled by such unwise comforters as we are.

But how wise the Holy Spirit is! He takes the soul, lays it on the table, and dissects it in a moment. He finds out the root of the matter, He sees where the complaint is, and then He applies the knife where something is required to be taken away, or puts a plaster where the sore is. He never makes a mistake. Oh, how wise is the blessed Holy Spirit! From every comforter I turn and leave them all, for You alone give the wisest consolation.

Note how safe a Comforter the Holy Spirit is. Mark that all comfort is not necessarily safe. Over there is a very melancholy young man. You know how he became so. He stepped into the house of God and heard a powerful preacher. The Word was blessed and convicted him of sin. When he went home, his father and the rest found there was something different about him. "Oh," they said, "John is mad. He is crazy." What did his mother say? "Send him into the country for a week. Let him go to the party or to the theater." Later, they asked, "John, did you find any comfort there?" "Ah, no, they made me worse. While I was there, I thought hell might open and swallow me up." "Did you find any relief in the gaieties of the world?" "No," said he, "I thought it was idle waste of time." Alas! This is miserable comfort, but it is the comfort of the worldling.

When a Christian gets into distress, how many will recommend some pat remedy! Go hear Preacher So-and-So. Have a few friends at your house. Read a particularly consoling volume. Very likely it is the most unsafe advice in the world. The devil will sometimes come to men's souls as a false comforter and say to the soul, "What need is there to make all this ado about repentance? You are no worse than other people." He tries to make the soul believe that what is presumption is the real assurance of the Holy Spirit. Thus he deceives many by false comfort.

There have been many, like infants, destroyed by elixirs given to lull them to sleep. Many have been ruined by the cry of *"peace, peace, when there is no peace"* (Jeremiah 6:14), hearing gentle things when they ought to be stirred to the quick. Cleopatra's asp was brought in a basket of flowers, and men's ruin often lurks in fair and sweet speeches. However, the Holy Spirit's comfort is safe, and you may rest on it. Let Him speak the Word, and there is a reality about it. Let Him give the cup of consolation, and you may drink it to the bottom, for in its depth there are no dregs, nothing to intoxicate or ruin. It is all safe.

Moreover, the Holy Spirit is an active Comforter: He does not comfort by words, but by deeds. Some comfort with, *"Be ye warmed and filled; notwithstanding*

[they] *give them not those things which are needful to the body"* (James 2:16). But the Holy Spirit gives. He intercedes for us. He gives us promises, He gives us grace, and so He comforts us. He is always a successful Comforter. He never attempts what He cannot accomplish.

Then He is an ever present Comforter, so that you never have to send for Him. Your God is always near you, and when you need comfort in your distress, behold, *"the word is nigh thee, even in thy mouth, and in thy heart"* (Romans 10:8). He is an ever present help in trouble.

7

PROMISES FOR THE BRUISED AND BROKEN

A bruised reed shall he not break, and smoking flax shall he not quench, till
he send forth judgment unto victory.
—Matthew 12:20

Babbling fame ever loves to talk of one man or another. There are some whose glory she trumpets forth, whose honor she extols above the heavens. Some are her favorites. Their names are carved on marble and heard in every land and every climate. Fame is not an impartial judge. She has her favored ones. Some men she extols, exalts, and almost deifies. Others, whose virtues are far greater and whose characters are more deserving of commendation, she passes by unheeded, putting the finger of silence on her lips.

You will generally find that those persons beloved by fame are men made of brass or iron and cast in a rough mold. Fame caressed Caesar because he ruled the earth with a rod of iron. Fame loved Luther because he boldly and manfully defied the Pope of Rome and with knit brow dared laugh at the thunders of the Vatican. Fame admired Knox, for he was stern and proved himself the bravest of the brave. Generally, you will find her choosing out the men of fire and mettle, who stood before their fellow creatures fearless of them; men who were made of courage, who were consolidated lumps of fearlessness, and who never knew what timidity might be.

But you know there is another class of persons equally virtuous and equally to be esteemed—perhaps even more so—those whom fame entirely forgets. You do not hear her talk of the gentle-minded Melanchthon—she says but little of him—yet he did as much, perhaps, in the Reformation as even the mighty Luther. You do not hear fame talk much of the sweet and blessed Rutherford and of the heavenly words that distilled from his lips; or of Archbishop Leighton, of whom it was said that he was never out of temper in his life.

Fame loves the rough granite peaks that defy the storm cloud. She does not care for the more humble stones in the valley on which the weary traveler rests. She wants something bold and prominent, something that courts popularity, something that stands out before the world. She does not care for those who retreat and stay in the shadows.

Hence it is, that the blessed Jesus, our adorable Master, escaped fame. No one says much about Jesus except His followers. We do not find His name written among the great and mighty men; although, in truth, He is the greatest, mightiest, holiest, purest, and best of men that ever lived. However, because He was "Gentle Jesus, meek and mild," because He was emphatically the Man whose kingdom is not of this world, because He had nothing rough about Him for He was all love, because His words were softer than butter and His utterances more gentle in their flow than oil, because no man spoke so gently as this Man, He is neglected and forgotten.

Jesus did not come to be a conqueror with His sword nor a Mohammed with his fiery eloquence. Rather, He came to speak in a *"still small voice"* (1 Kings 19:12) that melts the rocky heart, that binds up the broken in spirit, and that continually says, *"Come unto me all ye that labor and are heavy laden. Take my yoke upon you, and learn of me; for I am meek and lowly in heart: and ye shall find rest unto your souls"* (Matthew 11:28–29). Jesus Christ was all gentleness. This is why He has not been extolled among men as He otherwise would have been.

The work of God's Holy Spirit begins with bruising. In order to be saved, the fallow ground must be plowed up, the hard heart must be broken, the rock must be split apart. An old divine says there is no going to heaven without passing hard by the gates of hell—without a great deal of soul-trouble and heart-exercise. I take it then that the *"bruised reed"* is a picture of the poor sinner when first God commences his operation upon the soul. He is as a bruised reed, almost entirely broken and consumed. There is but little strength in him.

The *"smoking flax"* I take to be a backsliding Christian, one who has been a burning and shining light in his day, but by neglect of the means of grace, the withdrawal of God's Spirit, and falling into sin, his light has almost gone out. Not quite completely can it go out, for Christ says, "I will not quench it." But it becomes like a lamp when ill-supplied with oil, almost useless. It is not extinguished; it still smokes. It was a useful lamp once, but now it has become as smoking flax.

Thus, I think these metaphors very likely describe the contrite sinner as a bruised reed and the backsliding Christian as smoking flax. However, I do not choose to make such a division, but will put both metaphors together and hope we may draw a few thoughts from them.

What in the world is weaker than the bruised reed or the smoking flax? Just let a wild duck light upon a reed that grows in the fen or marsh, and it snaps. Let but the foot of man brush against it, and it is bruised and broken. Every wind that comes howling across the river shakes it back and forth and nearly tears it up by the roots. I can conceive of nothing more frail or brittle, or whose existence depends more upon circumstances, than a bruised reed. Then look at a smoking flax—what is it? It has a spark within, it is true, but it is almost smothered. An infant's breath might blow it out, or the tears of a maiden quench it in a moment. Nothing has a more precarious existence than the little spark hidden in the smoking flax. Weak things are described here. Well, Christ says of them, "I will not quench the smoking flax; I will not break the bruised reed."

Some of God's children, blessed be His name, are made strong to do mighty works for Him. God has His Samsons here and there who can pull up Gaza's gates and carry them to the top of the hill. He has here and there His mighty Gideons who can go to the camp of the Midianites and overthrow their hosts. He has His mighty men who can go into the pit in winter and slay the lions.

But the majority of God's people are a timid, weak race. They are like starlings that are frightened at every movement—a little, fearful flock. If temptation comes, they fall before it. If trial comes, they are overwhelmed by it. Their frail skiffs dance up and down with every wave. When the wind comes, they are blown along like a sea bird on the crest of the billows—weak things, without strength, without force, without might, without power.

Often you may feel compelled to say, "I would, but cannot sing. I would, but cannot pray. I would, but cannot believe." You are saying that you cannot do anything; that your best resolves are weak and vain; and when you cry, "My strength renew," you feel weaker than before. You are weak, are you? Bruised reeds and smoking flax? I am glad you can come in under the denomination of weak ones, for here is a promise that He will never break or quench them, but will sustain and hold them up.

I have heard of a man who would pick up a pin as he walked along the street on the principle of economy, but I never yet heard of anyone who would stop to pick up bruised reeds. They are not worth having. Who would care to have a bruised reed, a piece of rush lying on the ground? We all despise it as worthless. And smoking flax, what is its worth? It is an offensive and noxious thing, but the worth of it is nothing. No one would give the snap of a finger either for the bruised reed or for smoking flax.

Well, then, there are many of us who are worthless things in our own estimation. There are some, who, if they could weigh themselves in the scales of the sanctuary and put their own hearts into the balance of conscience, would appear to be good-for-nothing, worthless, useless. There was a time when you thought yourselves to be the very best people in the world. If anyone had said that you had more than you deserved, you would have balked at it and said, "I believe I am as good as other people." You thought yourselves to be something wonderful, extremely worthy of God's love and regard. But now you feel yourselves to be worthless. Sometimes you imagine God can hardly know where you are, you are such a despicable creature—so worthless, not worth His consideration. You can understand how He can look upon a minuscule organism in a drop of water or upon a grain of dust in the sunbeam or upon the insect of the summer evening. But you can hardly conceive how He can think of you because you appear so worthless—a dead blank in the world, a useless thing. You say, "What good am I? I am doing nothing. As for a minister of the gospel, he is of some service: as for a deacon of the church, he is of some use; as for a Sunday-school teacher, he is doing some good; but of what service am I?"

You might ask the same question here. What is the use of a bruised reed? Can a man lean on it? Can a man strengthen himself by it? Can it be a pillar in a house? Can you bind it up into the pipes of Pan and make music come from a bruised reed? No! It is of no service. Of what use is smoking flax? The midnight traveler cannot be lighted by it. The student cannot read by its flame. It is of no use: men throw it into the fire to be consumed. Ah! That is how you talk of yourselves. You are good-for-nothing, and so are these things. But Christ will not throw you away because you are of no value. You do not know of what use you may be, and you cannot tell how Jesus Christ values you after all.

There is a good woman—a mother, perhaps—who says, "Well, I do not often go out. I keep house with my children and seem to be doing no good." Mother, do not say so. Your position is a high, lofty, responsible one. In training up children for the Lord, you are doing as much for His name as eloquent Apollos, who so valiantly preached the Word.

And you, poor man, all you can do is to toil from morning until night and earn just enough to enable you to live day by day. You have nothing to give away. When you go to Sunday school, you can barely read and cannot teach much. Well, unto him to whom little is given, of him little is required. (See Luke 12:48.) Do you not know that there is such a thing as glorifying God by sweeping the street crossing? If two angels were sent down to earth, one to rule an empire and the other to sweep a street, they would have no choice in the matter, as long as God ordered them. So God, in His providence, has called you to work hard for your daily bread. Do it to His glory.

8

AGAINST THE WORLD

This is the victory that overcometh the world, even our faith.
—1 John 5:4

We know there have been great battles where nations have met in strife, and one has overcome the other. But who has read of a victory that overcame the world? Some will say that Alexander was its conqueror, but I answer that negatively. He was himself the vanquished man, even when all things were in his possession. He fought for the world and won it. Then note how it mastered its master, conquered its conqueror, and lashed the monarch who had been its scourge. See the royal youth weeping and stretching out his hands with idiotic cries for another world that he might ravage. He seemed, by outward appearances, to have overcome old earth. But in reality, within his innermost soul, the earth had conquered him, had overwhelmed him, had wrapped him in the dream of ambition, and had girdled him with the chains of covetousness, so that when he had all, he was still dissatisfied. Like a poor slave, he was dragged on at the chariot wheels of the world, crying, moaning, lamenting, because he could not win another.

Who is the man who ever overcame the world? Let him step forward. He is a Triton among the minnows. He outshines Caesar. He outmatches our own Wellington, if he can say he has overcome the world. It is so rare a thing, a victory so prodigious, a conquest so tremendous, that he who can claim to have won it may walk among his fellows, like Saul, with head and shoulders far above all. He will command our respect. His very presence will awe us into reverence. His speech will persuade us to obedience. Yielding honor to whom it is due, we will say when we hear his voice, "'Tis even as if an angel shook his wings."

Even so, the Christian overcomes the world. His is a tough battle, not one that tapestry knights might win. No easy skirmish is this that he might win, who dashed to battle on some sunny day, looked at the host, then turned his courser's rein and daintily dismounted at the door of his silken tent. This battle is not one that will be gained by the soldier who, but a raw recruit today, puts on his regimental uniform and foolishly imagines that one week of service will ensure a crown of glory. No, it is a lifelong war—a fight needing all the power of a strong heart and muscles, a contest that needs all our strength if we are to be triumphant.

If we do come off as more than conquerors, it will be said of us, as Hart said of Jesus Christ: "He had strength enough and none to spare." It is a battle at which the most courageous heart might cower, a fight about which the bravest might shake. He must remember that the Lord is on his side, and, therefore, whom should he fear; the Lord is the strength of his life, and so, of whom should he be afraid? (See Psalm 27:1.) This fight with the world is not one of brute force or physical might. If it were, we might soon win it, but it is all the more dangerous from the fact that it is a strife of mind, a contest of heart, a struggle of the spirit, a strife of the soul.

When we overcome the world in one fashion, we are not half done with our work. The world is a Proteus, changing its shape continually. Like the chameleon, it has all the colors of the rainbow. When you have bested the world in one shape, it will attack you in another. Until you die, you will always have fresh appearances of the world to wrestle with.

We rebel against the world's customs. And if we do so, what is the conduct of our enemy? The world changes her facade. "That man is a heretic; that man is a fanatic; he is a hypocrite," says the world directly. She grasps her sword, she puts a frown upon her brow, she scowls like a demon, she girds tempests around her, and she says, "The man dares defy my government; he will not do as others do. Now I will persecute him. Slander, come from the depths of hell and hiss at him! Envy, sharpen up your tooth and bite him!" She fetches up all false things, and she persecutes the man. If she can, she does it with the hand; if not, then by the tongue. She afflicts him wherever he is. She tries to ruin him in business; or, if he stands forth as the champion of the truth, then she laughs, mocks, and scorns. She lets no stone be unturned whereby she may injure him.

What is then the behavior of the Lord's warrior, when he sees the world take up arms against him, and when he sees all earth, like an army, coming to chase him and utterly destroy him? Does he yield? Does he bend? Does he cringe? Oh, no! Like Luther, he writes *cedo nulli* on his banner: "I yield to none." Then he goes to war against the world if the world goes to war against him.

The true child of God cares little for man's opinion. Says he, "Let my bread fail me. Let me be doomed to wander penniless the world over. Let me die. Each drop of blood within these veins belongs to Christ, and I am ready to shed it for His name's sake." He counts all things but loss, in order that he may win Christ and be found in Him. (See Philippians 3:8–9.) When the world's thunders roar, he smiles at the uproar while he hums his pleasant tune. When her sword comes out, he looks at it. "Ah," says he, "just as the lightning leaps from its thunderous lair, splits the clouds, and frightens the stars, but is powerless against the rock-covered mountaineer, who smiles at its grandeur, so now the world can no longer hurt me. In the time of trouble my Father hides me in His pavilion. In the secret of His tabernacle He hides me and sets me up upon a rock." Thus, again, we conquer the world, by not caring for its frowns.

"Well," says the world, "I will try another style," and this, believe me, is the most dangerous of all. A smiling world is worse than a frowning one. She says, "Since I cannot smite the man low with my repeated blows, I will take off my glove of mail, and, showing him a fair hand, I'll bid him kiss it. I will tell him I love him. I will flatter him. I will speak smooth words to him." John Bunyan well describes this Madam Bubble. She has a winning way with her. She drops a smile at the end of each of her sentences. She talks much of fair things, trying to win and woo.

Oh, believe me, Christians are not so much in danger when they are persecuted as when they are admired. When we stand on the pinnacle of popularity, we may well tremble and fear. It is not when we are hissed at and hooted that we have any cause to be alarmed. It is when we are rocked in the lap of fortune and nursed upon the knees of the people. It is when all men speak well of us that woe is on us. It is not in the cold, wintry wind that I take off my coat of righteousness and throw it away. It is when the sun comes, when the weather is warm and the air balmy, that I unguardedly strip off my robes and become naked. How many a man has been made naked by the love of this world! The world has flattered and applauded him. He has drunk the flattery. It was an intoxicating draught. He has staggered, he has reeled, he has sinned, he has lost his reputation. As a comet that flashes across the sky, wanders far into space, and is lost in darkness, so does he. Great as he was, he falls. Mighty as he was, he wanders and is lost.

But the true child of God is never so. He is as safe when the world smiles as when it frowns. He cares as little for her praise as for her scorn. If he is truly praised, he says, "My deeds deserve praise, but I refer all honor to my God." Great souls know what they merit from their critics. To them it is nothing more than the giving of their daily income. Some men cannot live without a large amount of praise. If they have no more than they deserve, let them have it. If they are children of God, they will be kept steady. They will not be ruined or spoiled, but they will stand with feet like hinds' feet upon high places. *"This is the victory that overcometh the world."*

Sometimes, the world turns jailer for a Christian. God allows affliction and sorrow until life is a prison, the world its jailer—and a wretched jailer, too. Have you ever been in trials and troubles, my friends? Has the world never come to you and said, "Poor prisoner, I have a key that will let you out. You are in financial difficulties. I will tell you how you may get free. Put that Mr. Conscience away. He just bothers you by asking whether it is a dishonest act. Never mind about him. Let him sleep. Think about the honesty after you have gotten the money and repent at your leisure." So says the world. But you say, "I cannot do the thing." "Well," says the world, "then groan and grumble. A good man like you locked up in this prison!" "No," says the Christian, "my Father sent me into want, and in His own time He will get me out. But if I die here, I will not use wrong means to escape. My Father put me here for my good, so I will not grumble. If my bones must lie here, if my coffin is to be under these stones, if my tombstone will be in the wall of my dungeon, then here will I die, rather than so much as lift a finger to get out by dishonest means." "Ah," says the world, "then you are a fool." The scorner laughs and passes on, saying, "The man has no brain, he will not do a bold thing. He has no courage. He will not launch upon the sea. He wants to go in the old beaten track of morality." So he does, for thus he overcomes the world.

I might tell of battles that have been fought. There has been many a poor maid who has worked and worked until her fingers were worn to the bone to earn a scanty living by sewing the things that we wear, not knowing that we often wear the blood and tears of poor girls. That poor maid has been tempted a thousand times to sell her purity. The evil one has tried to seduce her, but she has fought a valiant battle. Stern in her integrity, in the midst of poverty she still stands upright, "Clear as the sun, fair as the moon, and terrible as an army with banners," a heroine unconquerable by the temptations and enticements of vice.

In other cases, many a man has had the chance of being rich in an hour, affluent in a moment, if he would but clutch something that he dare not look at because God within him said, "No." The world said, "Be rich, be rich," but the Holy Spirit said, "No! Be honest. Serve your God." Oh, the stern contest and the manly combat carried on within the man's heart! But he said, "No! Could I have the stars transmuted into worlds of gold, I would not for those globes of wealth belie my principles and damage my soul." Thus he walks a conqueror. *"This is the victory that overcometh the world, even our faith."*

9

THE DIVINE REFUGE

The eternal God is thy refuge, and underneath are the everlasting arms.
—Deuteronomy 33:27

The children of Israel, while they were in Egypt and the wilderness, were a visible type of God's church on earth. Moses was speaking primarily of them, but, secondarily, of all the chosen ones of God in every age. Now, as God was the shelter of His ancient people Israel, so is He the refuge of His saints through all time. First, He was eminently their shelter when they were under bondage and the yoke was heavy. When they had to make bricks without straw and the taskmasters oppressed them, the people cried unto the Lord. God heard their cry and sent to them His servant Moses.

Likewise, there often comes a time when men begin to feel the oppression of Satan. I believe that many ungodly men feel the slavery of their positions. Even some of those who are never converted have sense enough to feel at times that the service of Satan is a hard one, yielding but little pleasure and involving awful risks. Some men cannot continue making bricks without straw for long without becoming more or less conscious that they are in a house of bondage. These, who are not God's people, under the mental pressure consequent to a partial discovery of their state, turn to some form of self-righteousness or pleasure in order to forget their burden and yoke.

However, God's chosen people, moved by a higher power, are led to cry out to their God. It is one of the first signs of a chosen soul that it seems to know as if by heavenly instinct where its true refuge is. You may recollect that, although you knew but little of Christ, in doctrinal matters you were very dark, and you did not understand even your own need, yet there was something in you that allowed you to see that only at the mercy seat could you find refuge.

Before you were a Christian, your bedside was the witness to many flowing tears, when your aching heart poured itself out before God, perhaps in strains like these: "O God, I want something. I do not know what it is I want, but I feel a heaviness of spirit. My mind is burdened, and I feel that You alone can unburden me. I know that I am a sinner. Oh, that You would forgive me! I hardly understand the plan of salvation, but one thing I know, that I want to be saved. I arise and go to my Father. My heart pants to make You my refuge." I say that this is one of the first indications that such a soul is one of God's chosen. It is true, just as it was of Israel in Egypt, that God is the refuge of His people, even when they are under the yoke.

When captivity is led captive (see Psalm 68:18), the eternal God becomes the refuge of His people from their sins. The Israelites were brought out of Egypt. They were free. Admittedly, they did not know where they were marching, yet their chains were snapped. They were emancipated and no longer needed to call anyone "Master." Yet, Pharaoh was angry and pursued them. With his horses and chariots, he hastened after them. The enemy said, *"I will pursue, I will overtake, I will divide the spoil; my lust shall be satisfied upon them"* (Exodus 15:9).

Similarly, there is a period in the spiritual life when sin labors to drag back the sinner who has newly escaped from it. Like hosts ready for battle, all the poor sinner's past iniquities hurry after him and overtake him in a place where his way is hedged in. The poor fugitive would escape, but he cannot. What, then, must he do? Remember that at that point Moses cried unto the Lord. When nothing else could be found to afford shelter to the poor escaped slaves, when the Red Sea rolled before them and mountains shut them in on either side, and an angry foe pursued them, there was one road that was not stopped up. That was the king's highway upward to the throne, the way to their God. Therefore, they began at once to travel that road, lifting up their hearts in humble prayer to God, trusting that He would deliver them. You know the story: how the uplifted rod divided the watery deeps, how the people passed through the sea as a horse through the wilderness, and how the Lord brought all the hosts of Egypt into the depths of the sea that He might utterly destroy them, so that not one of them was left, and those who had seen them one day saw them no more.

In this sense, God is still the refuge of His people. Our sins, which pursued us so hotly, have been drowned in the depths of the Savior's blood. They sank to the bottom like stones, the depths have covered them, and not one of them is left. We, standing upon the shore in safety, can shout in triumph over our drowned sins, *"Sing unto the Lord for he hath triumphed gloriously;* [all our iniquities] *hath he thrown into the sea"* (Exodus 15:1).

While God is thus the refuge of His people under the yoke, and when sin seeks to overcome them, He is also their refuge in times of want. The children of Israel journeyed into the wilderness, but there was nothing for them to eat there. The arid sand yielded neither leeks nor garlic nor cucumbers. No brooks or rivers like the Nile were there to quench their thirst. They would have famished if they had been left to depend on the natural productions of the soil. They came to Marah, where the well water was very bitter. At other stations there were no wells at all, even with bitter water. What then? The unfailing refuge of God's people in the wilderness was prayer. Moses, their representative, always took himself to the Most High, at times falling upon his face in agony, and at other seasons climbing to the top of the hill, to plead in solemn communion with God that He would deliver the people.

You have heard often how men ate angels' food in the desert, how Jehovah rained bread from heaven upon His people in the howling wilderness, and how He smote the rock and waters gushed forth. You have not forgotten how the strong wind blew and brought them flesh so that they ate and were satisfied. Israel had no need unsupplied. Their garments did not wear out. Though they went through the wilderness, their feet were not sore. God supplied all their wants. We in our land must go to the baker, the butcher, the clothier, and many others in order to equip ourselves, but the men of Israel went to God for everything. We have to store up our money and buy this in one place and that in the other, but the eternal God was their refuge and their resort for everything. In every time of want, they had nothing to do but to lift up their voices to Him.

Now it is just so with us spiritually. Faith sees our position today to be the same as the children of Israel then: whatever our wants are, "*the eternal God is [our] refuge.*" God has promised you that your bread and water will be given to you. He who supplies spiritual wants will not deny temporal ones. The mighty Master will never suffer you to perish while He has it in His power to succor you. Go to Him, whatever may be the trouble that weighs you down. Do not suppose your case too bad, for nothing is too hard for the Lord.

Do not think that He will refuse to undertake temporal needs as well as the spiritual wants. He cares for you in all things. In everything you are to give thanks, and surely in everything by prayer and supplication, you may make known your wants unto God. (See Philippians 4:6). In times when the cruse of oil is ready to fail and the handful of meal is all but spent, then go to the all-sufficient God. You will find that those who trust in Him will not lack any good thing. (See Psalm 34:10).

Furthermore, our God is the refuge of His saints when their enemies rage. When the host was passing through the wilderness, they were suddenly attacked by the Amalekites. Unprovoked, these marauders of the desert set upon them and smote many, but what did Israel do? The people did not ask to have a strong body of horsemen hired out of the land of Egypt for their refuge. Even if they did wish it, he who was their wise leader, Moses, looked to another arm than that of man, for he cried unto God. How glorious is that picture of Moses, with uplifted hands, upon the top of the hill giving victory to Joshua in the plain below. Those uplifted arms were worth ten thousand men to the hosts of Israel; no, twice ten thousand had not so easily won a victory as did those two extended arms, which brought down Omnipotence Himself from heaven. This was Israel's master weapon of war, her confidence in God. Joshua went forth with mighty men of war, but the Lord, Jehovah-Nissi, is the banner of the fight and the giver of the victory.

Thus, "*the eternal God is [our] refuge.*" When our foes rage, we need not fear their fury. Let us not seek to be without enemies, but let us take our case and spread it before God. We cannot be in such a position that the weapons of our foes can hurt us, while the promise stands true: "*No weapon that is formed against thee shall prosper, and every tongue that riseth against thee in judgment thou shalt condemn*" (Isaiah 54:17). Though earth and hell should unite in malice, the eternal God is our fortress and stronghold, securing to us an everlasting refuge.

10

THE USE OF CHASTISEMENT

My son, despise not thou the chastening of the Lord.
—Hebrews 12:5

God's people can never by any possibility be punished for their sins. God has punished them already in the person of Christ. Christ, their substitute, has endured the full penalty for all their guilt, and neither the justice nor the love of God can ever exact again what Christ has paid. Punishment can never happen to a child of God in the judicial sense. He can never be brought before God as his Judge, charged with guilt, because that guilt was long ago transferred to the shoulders of Christ and the punishment was exacted at the hands of his Surety.

But yet, while the sin cannot be punished, while the Christian cannot be condemned, he can be chastised. While he will never be arraigned before God's bar as a criminal and punished for his guilt, yet he now stands in a new relationship—that of a child to his parent. As a son, he may be chastised because of sin. Foolishness is bound up in the heart of all God's children, and the Father's rod must bring that folly out of them. (See Proverbs 22:15.)

It is essential to observe the distinction between punishment and chastisement. Both may agree as to the nature of the suffering: the suffering under one may be as great as under the other. The sinner, while he is punished for his guilt, may suffer no more in this life than the Christian who is only chastised by his parent. They do not differ as to the nature of the affliction, but they differ in the mind of the one who afflicts and in the relationship of the person who is afflicted. God punishes the sinner on his own account because He is angry with the sinner. His justice must be avenged, His law must be honored, and His commands must have their dignity maintained.

However, God does not punish the believer on his own account. It is on the Christian's account to do him good. He afflicts him for his profit. God lays on the rod for His child's advantage. He has a good intention toward the person who receives the chastisement. In punishment, the design is simply with God for God's glory; in chastisement, it is with the person chastised for his good and his spiritual profit and benefit. Besides, punishment is laid on a man in anger. God strikes him in wrath, but when He afflicts His child, chastisement is applied in love, all of His strokes are put there by the hand of love. The rod has been baptized in deep affection before it is laid on the believer's back. God does not afflict willingly or grieve us for nothing. Rather, His chastising is out of love and affection, because He perceives that if He leaves us unchastised, we will bring upon ourselves misery ten-thousandfold greater than we will suffer by His slight rebukes and the gentle blows of His hand.

Understand this from the very start: whatever your trouble or your affliction, there cannot be anything punitive in it. You must never say, "God is punishing me for my sin." You have fallen from your steadfastness when you talk so. God cannot do that. He has done it once for all: *"The chastisement of our peace was upon him, and with his stripes we are healed"* (Isaiah 53:5).

God is chastising you, not punishing you. He is correcting you in measure, not smiting you in wrath. There is no hot displeasure in His heart. Even though His brow may be wrinkled, there is no anger in His heart. Even though His eye may have closed upon you, He does not hate you. He loves you still. He is not wrathful with His heritage, for He sees no sin in Jacob, neither iniquity in Israel, who are considered in the person of Christ. It is simply because He loves you, because you are sons, that He therefore chastises you.

Why should you murmur against the dispensations of your heavenly Father? Can He treat you harder than you deserve? Consider what a rebel you were, but He has pardoned you. Surely, if He chooses now to lay the rod upon you, you need not cry out. Among the Roman emperors of old, it was the custom when they set a slave at liberty to give him a blow on the head and then say, "Go free!" This blow that your Father gives you is a token of your liberty.

Do you grumble because He smites you rather hardly? After all, are not His strokes fewer than your crimes and lighter than your guilt? Are you smitten as hard as your sins deserve? Consider all the corruption that is in your heart, and then will you wonder that so much of the rod is needed to drive it out? Weigh yourself, and discern how much dross is mingled with your gold. Do you think the fire is too hot to bring up the dross you have? Why, I think the furnace is not hot enough. There is too much dross, too little fire. The rod is not laid on hard enough, for that proud spirit of yours proves that your heart is not thoroughly sanctified. Though your heart may be right with God, your words do not sound like it, and your actions do not portray the holiness of your nature. It is the old Adam within you that is groaning.

Take heed if you murmur, for it will go hard with murmurers. God always chastises His children twice if they do not bear the first blow patiently. I have often heard a father say, "Boy, if you cry for that, you will really have something to cry for by and by." So, if we murmur at a little, God gives us something that will make us cry. If we groan for nothing, He will give us something that will make us groan. Sit down in patience. *"Despise not the chastening of the Lord."* Do not be angry with Him, for He is not angry with you. Do not say that He deals so hardly with you. Let humility rise up and speak, "It is well, O Lord! You are just in Your chastising, for I have sinned. Righteous are You in your blows, for I need them to bring me near to You. If You leave me uncorrected and unchastised, I, a poor wanderer, must pass away to the gulf of death and sink into the pit of eternal perdition." The first sense in which we may despise the chastening of the Lord is that we may murmur under it.

There are certain things that happen to us in life that we immediately set down as a providence. If a grandfather of ours should die and leave us five hundred pounds, what a merciful providence that would be! If by some extraordinary event in business we were suddenly to accumulate a fortune, that would be a blessed providence! If an accident happens, but we are preserved and our limbs are not hurt, that is always a providence.

But suppose we were to lose five hundred pounds, would not that be a providence? Suppose our establishment should break up and business fail, would not that be a providence? Suppose we should break a leg in the accident, would not that be a providence? Here is the difficulty: it is always a providence when it is a good thing, but why is it not a providence when it does not happen to be just as we please? Surely it is so. If the one thing is ordered by God, so is the other. It is written, "*I form the light and create darkness: I make peace and create evil: I, the* LORD, *do all these things*" (Isaiah 45:7). But I question whether it is not despising the chastening of the Lord when we set a prosperous providence before an adverse one, for I do think that an adverse providence ought to be the cause of as much thankfulness as a prosperous one. If it is not, we are violating the command, "*In everything give thanks*" (1 Thessalonians 5:18).

However, we say, "Of what use will such a trial be to me? I cannot see that it can by any possibility be useful to my soul. Here I was growing in grace just now, but there is something that has dampened all my ardor and overthrown my zeal. Just now I was on the mount of assurance, and God has brought me to the valley of humiliation. Can that be any good to me? A few weeks ago I had wealth, and I distributed it in the cause of God. Now I have none. What can be the use of that? All these things are against me." Now, you are despising the chastening of the Lord, when you say that it is of no use.

No child thinks the rod is of much value. Anything in the house is of more use than that rod in his opinion. If you were to ask the child what part of the household furniture could be dispensed with, he would like chairs, tables, and everything else to remain except the rod, which he does not think of any good whatever. He despises the rod, and so do we. We think it cannot benefit us. We want to get rid of the rod and turn it away. "*My son, despise not thou the chastening of the Lord.*"

Let me show you how wrong you are. Does your ignorance intend to say that God is unwise? I thought it was written that He was too wise to err. I did think that you knew that He was too good to be unkind. Does your tiny wisdom assign to itself the chair of honor? Does your finite knowledge stand up before your Maker and tell Him He is unwise in what He does? Will you dare to say that one of His purposes will be unfulfilled, that He does an unwise act? You are impudently arrogant if you speak in such a manner! Do not say so, but bend meekly down before His superior wisdom and say, "O God, I believe that in the darkness You are brewing light, that in the storm clouds You are gathering sunshine, that in the mines You are fashioning diamonds, and in the beds of the sea You are making pearls. I believe that however unfathomable may be Your plans, yet they have a bottom. Though it is in the whirlwind and in the storm, You have a way that is good and righteous altogether. I would not have You alter one atom of your dispensations. It shall be just as You will. I bow before You and give my ignorance the command to hold its tongue and to be silenced while Your wisdom speaks words of right."

"My son, despise not thou the chastening of the Lord" by thinking that it can be of no possible service to you. Many men have been corrected by God, and that correction has been in vain. I have known Christian men—men who have committed some sin. God, by the rod, would have shown them the evil of that sin. They have been smitten and seen the sin, but never afterward did they correct it. That is despising the chastening of the Lord. When a father chastises a son for anything he has done, and the boy does it again directly, it shows that he despises his father's chastening. So also have we seen believers who have had an error in their lives, and God has chastened them on account of it, but they have continued to repeat the error.

You will remember the case of Eli. God chastened him once when He sent Samuel to tell him dreadful news, that because he had not reproved his children, those children would be destroyed. But Eli kept on the same as ever. He despised the chastening of the Lord although his ears were made to tingle. In a little while God did something else for him. His sons were taken away, and then it was too late to mend for the children were gone. The time in which he might have reformed his character had passed away.

How many of you get chastened by God, but do not hear the rod? There are many deaf souls that do not hear God's rod. Many Christians are blind and cannot see God's purposes. When God would take some folly out of them, the folly is still retained.

Not every affliction benefits the Christian, only a sanctified affliction. Not every trial purifies an heir of light, only a trial that God Himself sanctifies by His grace. Take heed if God is trying you, that you search and find out the reason. Are the consolations of God small with you? Then, there is some reason for it. Have you lost that joy you once felt? There is some cause for it.

Many a man would not have suffered half as much if he had looked for the cause of it. I have sometimes walked a mile or two almost limping because there was a stone in my shoe, but I did not stop to check it. Many a Christian goes limping for years because of the stones in his shoe, but if he would only stop to look for them, he would be relieved. What is the sin that is causing you pain? Get it out in the open and repent of it, for if you do not, you have not regarded this admonition that speaks to you as unto sons: "*My son, despise not thou the chastening of the Lord.*"

11

RESPONSIBILITY AND SUCCESS

We are unto God a sweet savor of Christ, in them that are saved,
and in them that perish.
—2 Corinthians 2:15

The minister is not responsible for his success. He is responsible for what he preaches, he is accountable for his life and actions, but he is not responsible for other people. If I but preached God's Word, if there never were a soul saved, the King would say, "*Well done, good and faithful servant!*" (Matthew 25:23). If I only tell my message, even if none listen to it, He would say, "You have fought the good fight. Receive your crown." Truly hear the words of the text, "*We are unto God a sweet savor of Christ, in them that are saved, and in them that perish.*"

This will be apparent if I simply tell you what a gospel minister is called in the Bible. On occasion he is called an ambassador. Now, for what is an ambassador responsible? He goes to a country as a fully authorized diplomat. He carries terms of peace to the conference table. He uses all his talents for his ruler. He

305

tries to show that war is inimical to the prosperity of the differing countries. He endeavors to bring about peace, but the other rulers haughtily refuse it. When he comes home, his governor asks, "Why did you not make peace?" "Why, my lord," he replies, "I told them the terms, but they said nothing." "Well, then," his commander would say, "you have done your duty. I cannot condemn you if the war continues."

Again, the minister of the gospel is called a fisherman. Now a fisherman is not responsible for the quantity of fish he catches, but for the way he fishes. That is a mercy for some ministers, I am sure, for they have not caught fish or even attracted any around their nets. They have been spending their lives fishing with the most elegant silk lines and gold and silver hooks. They always use nicely polished phrases, but the fish do not bite for all that, whereas we of a rougher presentation have put the hook into the jaws of hundreds. However, if we cast the gospel net in the right place, even if we catch none, the Master will find no fault with us. He will say, "Fisherman! Did you labor? Did you throw the net into the sea in the time of storms?" "Yes, my Lord, I did." "What have you caught?" "Only one or two." "Well, I could have sent you a shoal, if it so pleased Me. It is not your fault. I give in My sovereignty where I please, or withhold when I choose. But as for you, you have labored well. Therefore, here is your reward."

Sometimes the minister is called a sower. No farmer expects a sower to be responsible for the harvest. All he is responsible for is this: does he sow the seed, and does he sow the right seed? If he scatters it on good soil, then he is happy. But if it falls by the wayside and the fowls of the air devour it, who will blame the sower? Could he help it? No, he did his duty. He scattered the seed broadcast, and there he left it. Who is to blame? Surely not the sower.

So if a minister comes to heaven with but one sheaf on his shoulder, his Master will say, "O reaper! Once a sower! Where did you gather your sheaf?" "My Lord, I sowed upon the rock, and it would not grow. Only one seed on a chance Sabbath morning was blown a little awry by the wind, and it fell upon a prepared heart, and this is my one sheaf." "Hallelujah!" the angelic choirs resound, "One sheaf from a rock is more honor to God than a thousand sheaves from a good soil. Therefore, let him take his seat as near the throne as that man, who, stooping beneath his many sheaves, comes from some fertile land, bringing his sheaves with him."

I believe that if there are degrees in glory, they will not be in proportion to success, but in proportion to the earnestness of our endeavors. If we, as ministers, mean right and strive to do right with all our hearts (even if we never see any effect), still will we receive the crown.

But how much happier is the man who will have it said about him in heaven, "He shines forever, because he was wise and won many souls unto righteousness." It is always my greatest joy to believe that, when I enter heaven in future days, I will see heaven's gates open. In will come a smiling person who, looking me in the face, will pass along to God's throne and bow down before Him. When he has paid his homage and his adoration to the Almighty, he may come to me and clasp my hand, though unknown to me. If there were tears in heaven, surely I would weep, and he would say, "Brother, from your lips I heard the word. Your voice first admonished me of my sin. Here I am. You were the instrument of my salvation."

As gates open one after another, still will they come in—souls ransomed, souls redeemed—and for each one of these a star, for each one of these another gem in the diadem of glory, for each one of them another honor and another note in the song of praise. *"Blessed are the dead which die in the Lord…saith the Spirit, that they may rest from their labors; and their works do follow them"* (Revelation 14:13).

What will happen to some Christians if crowns in heaven are measured in value by the souls that are saved? Some will have a crown in heaven without a single star in it. I read a little while ago a piece about a starless crown in heaven—a man in heaven with a crown without a star! Not one saved by him! He will sit in heaven as happy as can be because sovereign mercy saved him, but to be in heaven without a single star! Mother, what would you say to be in heaven without one of your children to deck your brow with a star? Minister, what would you say to be a polished preacher and yet have no star? Writer, will it become you to have written as gloriously as Milton if you are found in heaven without a star?

I am afraid we pay too little attention to this. Men will sit down and write huge tomes, so that they may have them put in libraries forever and have their names handed down by fame, but how many are looking to win stars forever in heaven? Toil on, child of God, toil on. If you wish to serve God, your bread that you cast upon the waters will be found after many days. If you *"send forth the feet of the ox and the ass"* (Isaiah 32:20), you will reap a glorious harvest in that day when He comes to gather in His elect. The minister is not responsible for his success.

Still, to preach the gospel is high and solemn work. The minister has been very often degraded into a trade. In these days men are taken and made into ministers who would have made good captains at sea, who could have waited well at the counter, but who were never intended for the pulpit. They are selected by man. They are crammed full with literature. They are educated up to a certain point. They are turned out already dressed. People call them ministers. I wish them all God's blessing, every one of them. As good Joseph Irons used to say, "God be with many of them, if it be only to make them hold their tongues."

Man-made ministers are of no use in this world, and the sooner we get rid of them the better. Their way is this: they prepare their sermon manuscripts very carefully, then read them on Sunday most sweetly in *sotto voce*, and so the people go away pleased. However, that is not God's way of preaching. If it were so, then I am capable of preaching forever. I can buy manuscript sermons for a shilling, provided they have been preached fifty times before. However, if I use them for the first time, the price is a guinea or more. But that is not God's way.

Preaching God's Word is not what some seem to think—mere child's play—a mere business or trade to be taken up by anyone. A man ought to feel first that he has a solemn call to it. Next, he ought to know that he really possesses the Spirit of God and that when he speaks there is an influence upon him that enables him to speak as God would have him. Otherwise, out of the pulpit he should go directly. He has no right to be there, even if the living is his own property. He has not been called to preach God's truth, and unto him God says, "*What hast thou to do to declare my statutes?*" (Psalm 50:16).

What is there difficult about preaching God's gospel? Well, it must be somewhat hard, because Paul asked, "*Who is sufficient for these things?*" (2 Corinthians 2:16). First I will tell you that it is difficult because it is so hard not to be warped by your own prejudices in preaching the Word. You want to say a stern thing, but your heart says, "Master, in so doing you will condemn yourself also!" Then the temptation is not to say it. Another persuasion is that you are afraid of displeasing the rich in your congregations. You think, "If I say this thing, So-and-So will be offended. Such a person does not approve of that doctrine. I had better leave it out." Or, perhaps you will happen to win the applause of the multitude and must not say anything that will displease them, for if they cry "Hosanna" today, they will cry "Crucify, crucify," tomorrow. All these things work on a minister's heart. He is a man, and he feels it.

Then comes again the sharp knife of criticism, along with the arrows of those who hate the minister and hate his Lord. He cannot help feeling it sometimes. He may put on his armor and cry, "I care not about your malice," but there were seasons when the archers sorely grieved even Joseph. Then the minister stands in another danger, lest he should come out and defend himself, because he is a great fool whoever tries to do it. He who lets his detractors alone, and like the eagle cares not for the chattering of the sparrows, or like the lion will not turn aside to rend the snarling jackal—he is the man, and he will be honored. The danger is that we want to set ourselves right.

Who is capable of steering clear of these rocks of danger? "*Who is sufficient for these things?*" Who is able to stand up and to proclaim, Sunday after Sunday, weekday after weekday, "*the unsearchable riches of Christ*" (Ephesians 3:8)?

12

DEVOTIONS IN THE NIGHT

With my soul have I desired thee in the night.
—Isaiah 26:9

Night appears to be a time particularly favorable to devotion. Its solemn stillness helps to free the mind from the perpetual din that the cares of the world will bring around it. Looking down from heaven on us, the stars shine as if they would attract us up to God. I do not know how you may be affected by the solemnities of midnight; however, when I have sat alone musing on the great God and the mighty universe, I have felt indeed that I could worship Him, for night seemed to be spread abroad as a temple for adoration, while the moon walked as high priest amid the stars and the worshippers. I myself joined in the silent song that they sang unto God:

O Lord, how great are thy works!...When I consider thy heavens, the work of thy fingers, the moon and the stars which thou hast ordained; what is man that thou are mindful of him? and the son of man, that thou visitest him?

(Psalm 92:5; 8:3–4)

I find that this sense of the power of midnight not only acts upon religious men, but upon others as well. There is a certain poet, whose character I could scarcely reprove too much, a man very far from understanding true religion. I suppose I might justly classify him an infidel or a libertine of the worst order. Yet he says concerning night in one of his poems:

'Tis midnight on the mountains brown,
The cold round moon shines deeply down;
Blue roll the waters, blue the sky
Spreads like an ocean hung on high,
Bespangled with those isles of light,
So wildly, spiritually bright;
Who ever gazed upon them shining,
And turning to earth without repining,
Nor wish'd for wings to flee away,
And mix with their eternal ray.

Even with the most irreligious person, a man farthest from spiritual thought, it seems that there is some power in the grandeur and stillness of night to draw him up to God. I trust many of us can say, like David and Isaiah, "I have been with You continually, I have meditated upon Your name in the night watches, and with my soul have I desired You in the night." (See Psalm 73:23; 63:6; and Isaiah 26:9.)

The Christian man does not always have a bright shining sun. He has seasons of darkness and night. True, God's Word says: "*Her ways are ways of pleasantness, and all her paths are peace*" (Proverbs 3:17). It is a great truth that religion—the true religion of the living God—is calculated to give a man joy below, as well as bliss above. But notwithstanding, experience tells us that if the course of the just is "*as the shining light, that shineth more and more unto the perfect day*" (Proverbs 4:18), yet sometimes that light may be eclipsed. At certain times, darkness and clouds cover the sun, and the man of God beholds no clear, shining daylight, but walks in darkness and sees no light.

Now, there are many who have rejoiced in the presence of God for a season. They have basked in the sunshine God has been pleased to give them in the earlier stages of their Christian career. They have walked along the "*green pastures*," by the side of "*still waters*," and suddenly—within a month or two—they find that glorious sky is clouded. Instead of *"green pastures,"* they have to tread the sandy desert. In the place of *"still waters,"* they find streams brackish to their taste and bitter to their spirits. They say, "Surely, if I were a child of God, this would not happen." Oh, say not so, you who are walking in darkness!

The best of God's saints have their nights. The dearest of His children have to walk through a weary wilderness. There is not a Christian who has enjoyed perpetual happiness. There is no believer who can always sing a song of joy. Not every lark can always carol, not every star can always be seen, and not every Christian is always happy.

Perhaps the King of saints gave you a season of great joy at first because you were a raw recruit, and He would not put you into the roughest part of the battle when you had first enlisted. You were a tender plant, and He nursed you in the hothouse until you could stand severe weather. You were a young child, and therefore He wrapped you in furs and clothed you in the softest mantle. But now you have become strong, and the case is different. Capuan holidays do not suit Roman soldiers, and they would not agree with Christians. We need clouds and darkness to exercise our faith, to cut off self-dependence, and to make us put more faith in Christ and less in evidence, less in experience, less in mental states and feelings. The best of God's children—I repeat it again for the comfort of those who are suffering with depression—have their nights.

Sometimes it is a night over the whole church at once. There are times when Zion is under a cloud, when the fine gold becomes dim and the glory of Zion is departed. There are seasons when we do not hear the clear preaching of the Word, when doctrines are withheld, when the glory of the Lord God of Jacob is dim, when His name is not exalted, when the traditions of men are taught instead of the inspirations of the Holy Spirit. Such a season is it when the whole church is dark. Of course, each Christian participates in it. He goes about weeping and crying, "O God, how long will Zion be oppressed? How long will her shepherds be as *'dumb dogs, they cannot bark'* (Isaiah 56:10)? Will her watchmen always be blind? Will the silver trumpet sound no more? Will not the voice of the gospel be heard in her streets?"

Oh, there are seasons of darkness to the entire church! God grant that we may not have to pass through another, but that, starting from this time, the sun may rise never to set, until, like a sea of glory, the light of brilliance will spread from pole to pole!

At other times, this darkness over the soul of the Christian rises from temporal distresses. He may have had a misfortune, as it is called: something has gone wrong in his business, or an enemy has done somewhat against him; death has struck down a favored child, or bereavement has snatched away the darling of his bosom; the crops are blighted; the winds refuse to bear his ships homeward; a vessel strikes upon a rock, and another founders. All goes ill with him. Like a gentleman who called to see me, he may be able to say, "Sir, I prospered far more when I was a worldly man than I have done since I have become a Christian, for everything has appeared to go wrong with me since then. I thought," he said, "that religion had the promise of this life as well as of that which is to come." I told him that it had, and so it would be in the end.

However, we must remember there was one great legacy that Christ left His people, and I was glad he had come in for a share of it: *In me ye might have peace [but] in the world ye shall have tribulation* (John 16:33). Yes! You may be troubled about this. You may be saying, "Look at So-and-So. See how he spreads himself like a chestnut tree. He is an extortioner and wicked man, yet everything he does prospers." You may even observe his death and say, "There are no bands in his death." *They are not in trouble as other men, neither are they plagued like other men* (Psalm 73:5). God has set them in slippery places, but He casts them down to destruction.

Better to have a Christian's days of sorrow than a worldling's days of mirth. Better to have a Christian's sorrows than a worldling's joys. Happier it is to be chained in a dungeon with a Paul than reign in the palace with an Ahab. Better to be a child of God in poverty than a child of Satan in riches. Cheer up, then, you downcast spirit, if this is your trial. Remember that many saints have passed through the same, and the best, most eminent believers have had their nights.

Christian men very frequently have their nights, but a Christian man's religion will keep its color in the night. *With my soul have I desired thee in the night.* What a lot of silver-slippered religion we have in this world! Men will follow Christ when everyone cries, "Hosanna! Hosanna!" The multitude will crowd around the Man then, and they will take Him by force and make Him a king when the sun shines and a soft wind blows. They are like the plants upon the rock, which sprang up and for a little while were green, but when the sun had risen with fervent heat straightway withered away.

Demas and Mr. Hold-the-World, and a great many others, are very pious people in easy times. They will always go with Christ by daylight and will keep in company so long as fashion gives religion the doubtful benefit of its patronage. But they will not go with Him in the night. There are some goods whose color you can only see in sunlight—and there are many professing believers whose colors you can only see by the light of day. If they were in the night of trouble and persecutions, you would find that there was very little in them. They are good by daylight, but they are bad by night.

Do you not know that the best test of a Christian is the night? The nightingale, if she would sing by day when every goose is cackling, would be considered no better a musician than the wren. If a Christian remained steadfast only by daylight when every coward is bold, what would he be? There would be no beauty in his courage, no glory in his bravery. But it is because he can sing in the night, sing in times of trouble, sing when he is driven to despair, which proves his sincerity. The testing has its glory in the night. The stars are not visible by daylight, but they become apparent when the sun sets.

There are many Christians whose piety did not evidence itself much when they were in prosperity, but will be shown in adversity. I have marked it in some of my brethren when they were in deep trial. I had not heard them speak much about Christ before, but when God's hand had robbed them of their comfort, I remember that I could discern their true beliefs infinitely better than I could before.

Nothing can bring our religion out better than trials. Grind the diamond a little, and you will see it glisten. Do but put trouble on the Christian, and his endurance of it will prove him to be of the true seed of Israel.

All that the Christian wants in the night is his God. "*With my soul have I desired thee in the night.*" By day there are many things that a Christian will desire besides his Lord, but in the night he wants nothing but his God.

I cannot understand how this happens, unless it is to be accounted for by the corruption of our spirits. When everything is going well with us, we are setting our affection first on this object and then on another; and that burning desire, which is as insatiable as death and as deep as hell, never rests satisfied. We are always wanting something, always desiring a yet-beyond. But if you place a Christian in trouble, you will find that then he does not want gold or carnal honor—then he only wants his God.

I suppose he is like the sailor. When he sails along smoothly, he loves to have fair weather and wants this and that with which to amuse himself on deck. But when the winds blow, all that he wants is the haven. He does not desire anything else. The biscuit may be moldy, but he does not care. The water may be brackish, but he does not care. He does not think of it in the storm. He only thinks about the haven then.

So it goes with the Christian: when he is going along smoothly he wants this and that comfort; he is aspiring after this position or is wanting to obtain that promotion. But let him once doubt his interest in Christ—let him once get into some distress so that it is very dark—and all he will feel then is, *"With my soul have I desired thee in the night."*

When a little girl is put to bed, she may lie quietly while there is light, looking at the trees that shake against the window and admiring the stars that are coming out. But when it gets dark and the child is still awake, she cries for her parent. She cannot be amused by anything else.

So also in daylight will the Christian look at anything. He will cast his eyes around on this pleasure and that. But when the darkness gathers, his cry is, *"My God! my God! why hast thou forsaken me? O why art thou so far from helping me and from the words of my roaring?"* (Psalm 22:1).

13

ALL JOY AND PEACE

Now the God of hope fill you with all joy and peace in believing, that ye may
abound in hope, through the power of the Holy Spirit.
—Romans 15:13

Alarge number of people profess to have believed in the Lord Jesus Christ, but they assert that they have no joy and peace as a consequence thereof. They do not make this profession by union with the Christian church or in any open manner, but when they are hard pushed on the matter of personal salvation, they will sometimes say, "I do believe in Christ, but still I am so unhappy. I am so miserable that I cannot believe I am saved." The statement is tantamount to this: the Word of God declares that whosoever believes in Jesus is not condemned, but they assert that they have believed in Jesus and, nevertheless, are haunted with fears of condemnation that lead them to believe that they cannot have been delivered from the wrath to come.

I speak to tender hearts and to those who desire to have tender hearts, to those who have their faces toward Jerusalem, though as yet they are traveling in the dark. If you are truly desirous to obtain joy and peace through believing, I trust that God may bless you in the obtaining of it.

Take care, while valuing joy and peace, that you do not overestimate them. Remember that joy and peace are, though eminently desirable, not infallible evidences of safety. There are many persons who have great joy and much peace who are not saved, for their joy springs from a mistake, and their peace is the false peace that does not rest upon the rock of divine truth but upon the sand of their own imaginations. It is certainly a good sign that spring has come when you find the weather to be so warm, but there are very mild days in winter. I must not therefore infer because the heat of the sun is at a certain degree, that therefore it is necessarily spring. On the other hand, we have cold days in spring that, if we had to judge by such evidences, might attest that we were in November rather than in May.

And so, joy and peace are like fine sunny days. They come to those who have no faith, who are in the winter of their unbelief. They may not visit you who have believed; or, if they come, they may not abide, for there may be cold weather in May, and there may be some sorrow and some distress of mind even to a truly believing soul.

Understand that you must not look upon the possession of joy and peace as being the absolute consequence of your being saved. A man may be in the lifeboat, but that lifeboat may be so tossed about that he may still feel himself exceedingly ill and think himself to be still in peril. It is not his sense of safety that makes him safe; he is safe because he is in the lifeboat, whether he is aware of this or not.

Understand then that joy and peace are not infallible or indispensable evidences of safety and that they certainly are not unchanging evidences. The brightest Christians sometimes lose their joy. Some of those who stand well in the things of God—and concerning whom you would entertain no doubt—entertain many suspicions, however, about themselves.

Joy and peace are the normal element of a Christian, but he is sometimes out of his element. Joy and peace are his usual state of being, but there are times when, with fightings within and wars without, his joy departs and his peace is broken. The leaves on the tree prove that the tree is alive, but the absence of leaves will not prove that the tree is dead. True joy and peace may be very satisfactory evidences, but the absence of joy and peace during certain seasons can often be accounted for by some other hypothesis than that of there being no faith within.

In the first place, to trust Christ because you just feel happy is irrational. Suppose a man would say during another monetary panic, "I feel sure that the bank my money is in is safe." Why? "Because I feel so easy about my money." Now anybody would say to him, "That is no reason." But suppose he said, "I feel sure that my money is safe," and you had asked, "What is the reason?" "Because I believe the bank is safe." "Oh," you say, "that is right enough; that is good reasoning." In the first case, he put the emotion in the place of the cause and tried to make that a cause, but that cannot be done.

If a man would say, "I have a large estate in India." You ask, "How do you know?" "Why, because I feel so happy in thinking about it." "You fool," you say, "that is no proof whatever, not the slightest." But if he says to you, "I feel very happy," and you ask him why, and he replies, "Because I have an estate in India." "Oh," you say, "that may be right enough." A man may be thankful for what he rightly possesses, but to make joy and peace the evidence of external facts is supremely ridiculous. For a man to say, "I know I am saved because I am happy," is most irrational, while to be happy because you are saved is right. Oh, I pray you, take care that you do not act so irrationally before God!

Consider another view. Suppose I was in fear about the health of some dear friend. "Well," I say, "I would like to have my friend healthy, but I want to feel safe about that friend. I do not know anything about the state of my friend just now, and I am uneasy. Now I tell you, if I could get to feel easy, then I would be convinced that my friend is well." "Why," you would justly reply, "there is no connection between the two things! The proper mode of procedure is to find out whether your friend is well, and then you will feel easy."

You say, "I would believe I am saved if I felt happy." Is there any logic in that? On the contrary! First, believe that you are saved, and then happiness will follow. You cannot believe that you are saved while you persist in doing what God does not tell you to do, namely, looking to your own joy and peace instead of looking to the finished work of Jesus Christ.

Christian men are but men. They may have a bad liver or an attack of bile or some other trial, and then they get depressed about it. I would defy the apostle Paul himself to help it. But what then? Well, then you can get joy and peace through believing.

I am the subject of depressions of spirit so fearful that I hope none of you ever gets to such extremes of wretchedness as I go to. But I always get back again by this: I know I trust Christ. I have no reliance but in Him. If He falls, I will fall with Him; but if He does not, I will not. Because He lives, I will live also, and I spring to my feet again and fight with my depression and my downcast soul and get the victory over them. So may you do, and so you must, for there is no other way of escaping from it. In your most depressed seasons, you are to get joy and peace through believing.

"Ah," says someone, "but suppose you have fallen into some great sin—what then?" Why then all the more reason that you should cast yourself upon Him. Do you think Jesus Christ is only for little sinners? Is He a doctor that only heals headaches? It requires no faith to trust Christ when I do not have any sin, but it is true faith when I am foul, black, and filthy. When during the day I have tripped up and fallen, doing serious damage to my joy and peace, I go back by faith to that dear fountain and say, "Lord, I never loved washing so much before as I do tonight, for today I have made a fool of myself. I have said and done what I ought not to have done, and I am ashamed and full of confusion, but I believe Christ can save me, even me, and I will rest in Him still."

14

MR. READY-TO-HALT
AND HIS COMPANIONS

God hath dealt to every man the measure of faith.
—Romans 12:3

When faith first commences in the soul, it is like a grain of mustard seed, which the Savior said was the least of all seeds. But as God the Holy Spirit is pleased to bedew it with the sacred moisture of His grace, it germinates and grows and begins to spread, until at last it becomes a great tree.

To use another figure, when faith commences in the soul, it is simply looking unto Jesus. Perhaps even then there are so many clouds of doubts and so much dimness of the eye that we have need for the light of the Spirit to shine upon the cross before we are able even so much as to see it.

When faith grows a little, it rises from looking to Christ to coming to Christ. The person who once stood afar off and looked to the cross eventually plucks up courage, and finding heart, runs up to the cross. Perhaps he does not run but has to be drawn before he can so much as creep there, and even then it is with a limping gait that he draws near to Christ the Savior.

But that done, faith goes a little farther: it lays hold of Christ. It begins to see Him in His excellence and appropriates Him in some degree, conceives Him to be the real Christ and the real Savior and is convinced of His suitability. When it has done as much as that, it goes further: it leans on Christ, its Beloved. It casts all the burden of its cares, sorrows, and griefs upon that blessed shoulder and permits all its sins to be swallowed up in the great red sea of the Savior's blood.

Faith can go further still. Having seen and run toward Him, having laid hold of Him and leaned on Him, faith can next put in a humble, but sure and certain, claim to all that Christ is and all that He has done. Then, trusting alone in this, appropriating all this to itself, faith mounts to full assurance. Outside of heaven there is no state more rapturous and blessed.

But this faith is very small, and there are some Christians who never get out of little faith all the while they are here. You may have noticed in John Bunyan's *Pilgrim's Progress* how many Little-Faiths he mentions. There is our old friend Ready-to-Halt, who went all the way to the Celestial City on crutches, but left them when he went into the river Jordan. Then there is little Feeble-Mind, who carried his feeble mind with him all the way to the banks of the river and then left it. He ordered it to be buried in a dunghill so that none might inherit it. Then there is Mr. Fearing, who used to stumble over a straw and was always frightened if he saw a drop of rain, because he thought the floods of heaven were let loose upon him. You remember Mr. Despondency and Miss Much-Afraid, who were so long locked up in the dungeon of Giant Despair that they were almost starved to death, with little left of them but skin and bone. Poor Mr. Feeble-Mind, who had been taken into the cave of Giant Slay-Good, was about to be eaten by him when Great-Heart came to his deliverance.

John Bunyan was a very wise man. He has put a great many of those characters in his book because there are a great many of them. He has not left us with one Mr. Ready-to-Halt, but he has given us seven or eight graphic characters, because he himself in his own time had been one of them and had known many others who had walked in the same path.

Little-Faith is quite as sure of heaven as Great-Faith. When Jesus Christ counts up His jewels at the last day, He will take to Himself the little pearls as well as the great ones. If a diamond is ever so small, still it is precious because it is a diamond. So it is with faith, be it ever so little, if it is true faith. Christ will never lose even the smallest jewel of His crown. Little-Faith is always sure of heaven, because the name of Little-Faith is in the book of eternal life. Little-Faith was chosen by God before the foundation of the world. Little-Faith was bought with the blood of Christ and cost as much as Great-Faith. *"For every man…half a shekel"* (Exodus 38:26) was the price of redemption. Every man, whether great or small, prince or peasant, had to redeem himself with half a shekel.

Christ has bought all, both little and great, with the same precious blood. Little-Faith is sure of heaven, for God has begun the good work in him, and He will carry it on. God loves him, and He will love him to the end. God has provided a crown for him and will not allow it to hang there without a head. He has erected for him a mansion in heaven, and He will not allow the mansion to stand empty forever.

Little-Faith is always safe, but he very seldom knows it. If you meet him, he is sometimes afraid of hell and very often afraid that the wrath of God abides on him. He will tell you that the country on the other side of the flood can never belong to a worm as base as he. Sometimes it is because he feels himself so unworthy, another time it is because the things of God are too good to be true, he says, or he cannot think they can be true for such a one as he. Sometimes he is afraid he is not one of the elect. Another time he fears that he has not been called right, that he has not come to Christ properly. Another time his fears are that he will not hold on to the end, that he will not be able to persevere. If you kill a thousand of his fears, he is sure to have another host by tomorrow, for unbelief is one of those things that you cannot destroy. "It hath," wrote Bunyan, "as many lives as a cat." You may kill it over and over again, but still it lives. It is one of those weeds that sleep in the soil even after it has been burned, and it only needs a little encouragement to grow again.

Now, Great-Faith is sure of heaven, and he knows it. He climbs Pisgah's top and surveys the landscape. He drinks in the mysteries of paradise even before he enters within the pearly gates. He sees the streets that are paved with gold. He beholds the walls of the city, the foundations of which are precious stones, He hears the mystic music of the glorified and begins to smell on earth the perfumes of heaven. But poor Little-Faith can scarcely look at the sun. He very seldom sees the light. He gropes in the valley, and while all is safe he always thinks himself unsafe.

Strong-Faith can well battle with the enemy. Satan comes along and says, *"All these things will I give thee, if thou wilt fall down and worship me"* (Matthew 4:9). "No," we say, "you cannot give us all these things, for they are ours already." "But," says the enemy, "you are poor, naked, and miserable." "Yes," say we to him, "but still these things are ours, and it is good for us to be poor, good for us to be without earthly goods, or else our Father would give them to us." "Oh," says Satan, "you deceive yourselves. You have no portion in these things. But if you will serve me, then I will make you rich and happy here." Strong-Faith says, "Serve you, you fiend? Away! Do you offer me silver? Behold, God gives me gold. Do you say to me, 'I will give you this if you disobey?' Fool that you are! I have wages a thousand times greater for my obedience than you offer for my disobedience."

But when Satan meets Little-Faith, he says to him, *"If thou be [a] son of God, cast thyself down"* (Matthew 4:6). Poor Little-Faith is so afraid that he is not a son of God that he is apt to cast himself down on the supposition. "There," says Satan, "I will give you all this if you will disobey." Little-Faith says, "I am not quite sure that I am a child of God, that I have a portion among those who are sanctified." He is very apt to fall into sin by reason of the littleness of his faith.

Yet at the same time, I must observe that I have seen some Little-Faiths who are far less apt to fall into sin than others. They are so cautious that they dare not put one foot before the other, because they fear they would step awry. They scarcely dare to open their lips, but they pray, "Lord, You open my lips," because they are afraid that they would let a wrong word out if they were to speak. Always alarmed lest they should fall into sin unconsciously, they have very tender consciences.

I like people of this sort. I have sometimes thought that Little-Faith clings more tightly to Christ than any other. A man who is very near drowning is sure to clutch the plank with the grasp of a drowning man, which tightens and becomes more clenched the more his hope is decreased. Little-Faith may be kept from falling, but this is the fruit of tender conscience and not of slight faith. Careful walking is not the result of limited faith. It may go with it, and so may keep Little-Faith from perishing. But small faith is in itself a dangerous thing, laying us open to innumerable temptations and taking away very much of our strength to resist them.

"The joy of the LORD is your strength" (Nehemiah 8:10). If that joy ceases, you become weak and very apt to turn aside. Little-Faiths have many nights and few

days; long winters and short summers; many howlings, but little of shouting; often playing upon the pipe in mourning, but very seldom sounding the trumpet in exultation.

Perhaps the only way in which most men have their faith increased is by great trouble. We don't grow strong in faith on sunshiny days. It is only in rough weather that a man gets faith. Faith is not an attainment that drops like the gentle dew from heaven; it generally comes in the whirlwind and the storm.

Look at the old oaks. How is it that they have become so deeply rooted in the earth? Ask the March winds, and they will tell you. It is not the April shower that did it, or the sweet May sunshine, but it was the rough wind of March, the blustering month of old Boreas, the Greek god of the north wind, shaking the tree back and forth and causing the roots to bind themselves around the rocks.

So must it be with us Christians. We don't make great soldiers in the barracks at home; they must be made amid flying shot and thundering cannon. We cannot expect to become good sailors on the Serpentine; they must be made far away on the deep sea, where the wild winds howl and the thunders roll like drums in the march of the God of armies. Storms and tempests are the things that make men tough and hardy mariners. They see the works of the Lord and His wonders in the deep. So it is with Christians. Great-Faith must have great trials. Mr. Great-Heart would never have been Mr. Great-Heart if he had not once been Mr. Great-Trouble. Valiant-for-Truth would never have put to flight those foes and been so valiant if the foes had not first attacked him. So it is with us; we must expect great trouble before we can attain to much faith.

15

JOY IN LIFE'S HARD TIMES

At evening time it shall be light.
—Zechariah 14:7

I will not notice the particular occasion when these words were uttered or try to discover the time to which they specifically refer. Rather, I will take the sentence as a rule of the kingdom, as one of the great laws of God's dispensation of grace, that *"at evening time it shall be light."* Whenever philosophers wish to establish a general law, they think it necessary to collect a considerable number of individual instances. Putting these together, they then formulate from them a general rule. Happily, this need not be done with regard to God. We have no need, when we look abroad in providence, to collect a great number of incidents and then from them generalize the truth. Since God is immutable, one act of His grace is enough to teach us the rule of His conduct.

Now, in one place I find it is recorded that, on a certain occasion during a certain adverse condition of a nation, God promised that at evening time it would be light. If I found that in any human writing, I would suppose that the thing might have occurred once, that a blessing was conferred in emergency on a certain occasion, but I could not extract a rule from it. But when I find this written in the Word of God—that on a certain occasion when it was evening time with His people, God was pleased to give them light—I feel myself more than justified in inducing from it the rule that to His people at evening time there will always be light.

The church at large has had many evening times. If I might choose a figure to describe her history from anything in this natural world, I would describe her as being like the sea. At times the abundance of grace has been gloriously manifest. Wave upon wave has triumphantly rolled in upon the land, covering the mire of sin and claiming the earth for the Lord of Hosts. So rapid has been its progress that its course could scarcely be obstructed by the rocks of sin and vice. Complete conquest seemed to be foretold by the continual spread of the truth. The happy church thought that the day of her ultimate triumph had certainly arrived, so potent was the Word delivered by her ministers, so glorious was the Lord in the midst of her armies, that nothing could stand against her. She was *"fair as the moon, clear as the sun, and terrible as an army with banners"* (Song of Solomon 6:10). Heresies and schisms were swept away. False gods and idols lost their thrones. God Almighty was in the midst of His church, and upon His white horse He *"went forth conquering and to conquer"* (Revelation 6:2).

Before long, however, it always has happened that there came an ebb tide. Again the stream of grace seemed to recede, as the poor church was driven back either by persecution or by internal decay. Instead of gaining upon man's corruption, it seemed as if man's corruption gained on her. Where once there had been righteousness like the waves of the sea, there was the black mud and mire of the filthiness of mankind. The church had to sing mournful tunes, when by the rivers of Babylon she sat down and wept, remembering her former glories and weeping over her present desolation.

So has it always been—progressing, retrograding, standing still a while, and then progressing once more and falling back again. The whole history of the church has been a history of onward marches and then quick retreats—a history that is, on the whole, a history of advance and growth, but which, read chapter by chapter, is a mixture of success and repulse, conquest and discouragement. So I think it will be, even to the last. We will have our sunrises, our meridian high point, and then the sinking in the west. We will have our sweet dawnings of better days, our Reformations, our Luthers, and our Calvins. We will have our bright noontide, when the gospel is fully preached and the power of God is known. We will have our sunset of ecclesiastical weakness and decay. But just as sure as the eventide seems to be drawing over the church, *"at evening time it shall be light."*

We may expect to see darker evening times than ever before. Let us not imagine that our civilization will be more enduring than any other that has gone before it, unless the Lord preserves it. Perhaps the suggestion will be realized, which has often been laughed at as folly, namely, that one day men will sit on the broken arches of London Bridge and marvel at the civilization that has departed, just as men walk over the mounds of Nimrod and marvel at cities buried there. It is possible that all the civilization of this country may die out in blackest night. It may be that God will repeat the great story that has been so often told: "I looked, and lo, in the vision I saw a great and terrible beast, and it ruled the nations, but it passed away and was not." (See Daniel 7.)

But if ever such things would be and the world would ever have to return to barbarism and darkness, if instead of what we sometimes hope for—a constant progress to the brightest day—all our hopes would be blasted, let us rest quite satisfied that *"at evening time there shall be light,"* that the end of the world's history will be concluded in glory. However red with blood, however black with sin the world may yet be, she will one day be as pure and perfect as when she was created. The day will come when this poor planet will find herself unrobed of those swaddling bands of darkness that have kept her luster from breaking forth. God will yet cause His name to be known *"from the rising of the sun to the going down of the same"* (Psalm 113:3).

> And the shout of jubilee,
> Loud as mighty thunders roar,
> Or the fullness of the sea,
> When it breaks upon the shore,
> Shall yet be heard the wide world o'er.

We know that in nature the very same law that rules the atom also governs the starry orbs.

> The very law that molds a tear,
> And bids it trickle from its source,
> That law preserves the earth a sphere,
> And guides the planets in their course.

It is even so with the laws of grace. "*At evening time it shall be light*" to the church. "*At evening time it shall be light*" to every individual. Christian, let us descend to lowly things. You have had your bright days in temporal matters. You have sometimes been greatly blessed. You can remember the day when the calf was in the stall, when the olive yielded its fruit and the fig tree did not deny its harvest. You can recollect the years when the barn was almost bursting with corn and when the vat overflowed with oil. You remember when the stream of your life was deep and your ship floated softly on, without one disturbing billow of trouble to molest it. You said then, "I will see no sorrow. God has hedged me about. He has preserved me. He has kept me. I am the darling of His providence. I know that all things work together for my good, for I can see it is plainly so."

Well, after that, Christian, you have had a sunset. The sun, which had shone so brightly, began to cast his rays in a more oblique manner every moment, until at last the shadows were long because the sun was setting and the clouds began to gather. Though the light of God's countenance tinged those clouds with glory, yet it was waxing dark. Then troubles lowered over you: your family sickened, your wife died, your crops were meager, your daily income was diminished, your cupboard was empty, and you wondered for your daily bread. You did not know what would become of you.

Perhaps you were brought very low; the keel of your vessel grated upon the rocks; there was not enough of bounty to float your ship above the rocks of poverty. You used both industry and economy, and you added perseverance; but all was in vain. It was in vain that you rose up early, sat up late, and ate the bread of carefulness. You could do nothing to deliver yourself, for all attempts failed. You were ready to die in despair. You thought the night of your life had gathered with eternal blackness. You would not live always, but you would rather depart from this vale of tears.

Was it not light with you at evening time? The time of your extremity was just the moment of God's opportunity. When the tide had run out to its very farthest, then it began to turn. Your ebb had its flow; your winter had its summer; your sunset had its sunrise. At evening time it was light. All of a sudden by some strange work of God, as you thought then, you were completely delivered. He brought "*forth thy righteousness as the light, and thy judgment as the noonday*" (Psalm 37:6). The Lord appeared for you as in the days of old. He stretched out His hand from above. He drew you out of deep waters. He set you upon a rock and established your course.

16

CURE FOR HEARTACHE

Let not your heart be troubled, neither let it be afraid.
—John 14:27

I t is the easiest thing in the world in times of difficulty to let the heart be troubled. It is very natural for us to give up and drift with the stream, to feel that it is of no use "taking arms against [such] a sea of trouble," but that it is better to lie back passively and to say, "If one must be ruined, so be it."

Despairing idleness is easy enough, especially to evil, rebellious spirits who are willing to get into further mischief that they may have the wherewithal to blame God more, against whose providence they have quarreled. Our Lord will not have us be rebellious. He bids us to pluck up our hearts and be of good courage in the worst conditions.

Here is the wisdom of His advice, namely, that a troubled heart will not help us in our difficulties or out of them. It has never been perceived in time of drought that lamentations have brought showers of rain. Doubting, fears, and discouragement have never been observed to produce a thaw in seasons of frost. I have never heard of a man with a declining business who managed to multiply the number of his customers by unbelief in God. I do not remember reading of a person whose spouse or child was sick who discovered any miraculous healing power in rebellion against the Most High.

It is a dark night, but the darkness of your heart will not light a candle for you. It is a terrible tempest, but to quench the fires of comfort and open the doors to admit the howling winds into the chambers of your spirit will not stay the storm. No good comes out of fretful, petulant, unbelieving heart trouble. This lion yields no honey. If it would help you, you might reasonably sit down and weep until the tears had washed away your woe. If it were really to some practical benefit to be suspicious of God and distrustful of His providence, why then, you might have a shadow of excuse. But since this is a mine out of which no one ever dug any silver and an oyster bed from which a diver never brought up a pearl, we would say, "Renounce what cannot be of service to you; for as it can do no good, it is certain that it does much mischief."

A doubting, fretful spirit takes from us the joys we have. You do not have all you could wish, but you have much more than you deserve. Your circumstances are not what they might be, but still they are not even now so bad as the circumstances of some others. Your unbelief makes you forget that your health still remains if poverty oppresses you or that, if both health and abundance have departed, you are a child of God, and your name is not blotted out from the roll of the chosen.

There are flowers that bloom in winter, if we have the grace to see them. Never was there a night of the soul so dark but that some lone star of hope might be discerned, and never a spiritual tempest so tremendous but that there was a haven into which the soul could put if it only had enough confidence in God to head for it. Be assured that though you have fallen very low, you might have fallen lower if it were not that underneath you are the everlasting arms. A doubting, distrustful spirit will wither the few blossoms that remain on your bough. If half the wells are frozen by affliction, unbelief will freeze the other half by its despondency. You will gain no good, but you may get incalculable mischief by a troubled heart. This root bears no fruit except wormwood.

A troubled heart makes that which is bad worse. It magnifies, aggravates, caricatures, and misrepresents. If just an ordinary foe is in your way, a troubled heart makes him swell into a giant. "We were in their sight but as grasshoppers," said the ten spies who gave the evil report, "and we were as grasshoppers in our own sight when we saw them." (See Numbers 13:33.) But it was not so. No doubt the men were very tall, but they were not so big as to make an ordinary six-foot-tall man look as small as a grasshopper. Their fears made them grasshoppers by first making them fools.

If they had possessed ordinary, nominal courage, they would have been men; but being cowardly, they subsided into grasshoppers. After all, what is an extra three, four, or five feet of flesh to a man? Is not the bravest soul the tallest? If he is of shorter stature, but nimble and courageous, he will have the best of it. Little David made short work of great Goliath. Yet so it is. Unbelief makes our difficulties seem to be gigantic. Then it leads us to suppose that no soul had such difficulties before, and so we utter the self-centered cry, "*I am the man that hath seen affliction*" (Lamentations 3:1). We claim to be peers in the realm of misery, if not the emperors of the kingdom of grief.

Yet it is not so. Why? What ails you? The headache is excruciating! It is bad enough, but what would you say if you had seven such aches at once, with cold and nakedness along with them? Twitches of rheumatism are horrible—well can I endorse that statement! But, what then? Why, there have been men who have lived with such tortures all their lives, like Baxter, who could tell all his bones because each one had made itself heard by its own unusual pang. What is our complaint compared with the diseases of Calvin, the man who preached every daybreak to the students in the cathedral and worked on until long past midnight, all the while a mass of disease with a complicated agony? You are poor? Ah, yes! But you have your own room, scanty as it is, and there are hundreds on the streets who find sorry comfort there. It is true you have to work hard. Yes, but think of the Huguenot galley slave in times past, who for the love of Christ was bound with chains to the oar and scarcely knew rest day or night. Think of the sufferings of the martyrs of Smithfield or of the saints who rotted in their prisons. Above all, let your eye turn to the great Apostle and High Priest of your profession, and "*consider him that endured such contradiction of sinners against himself, lest ye be weary and faint in your minds*" (Hebrews 12:3).

> His way was much rougher
>> And darker than mine,
> Did Jesus thus suffer,
>> And shall I repine?

Yet, the habit of unbelief is to draw our picture in the blackest possible colors, to tell us that the road is unusually rough and utterly impassable, that the storm is such a tornado as never blew before, that our name will be written down in the wreck register, and that it is impossible that we will ever reach the haven.

Be of good cheer, soldier, the battle must soon end. That bloodstained banner, when it will wave so high; that shout of triumph, when it will trill from so many thousand lips; that grand assembly of heroes, all of them made more than conquerors; the sight of the King in His beauty, riding in the chariot of His triumph on streets paved with love for the daughters of Jerusalem; the acclamations of spirits glorified; and the shouts and songs of cherubim and seraphim—all these will make up for all the fighting of today:

> And they who, with their Master,
>> Have conquered in the fight,
> For ever and for ever
>> Are clad in robes of light.

17

A WORD TO THE TROUBLED

*Call upon me in the day of trouble: I will deliver thee,
and thou shalt glorify me.*
—Psalm 50:15

Of all things in the world to be dreaded, despair is the chief. Let a man be abandoned to despair, and he is ready for all sorts of sins. When fear unnerves him, action is dangerous; but when despair has loosed his joints and paralyzed his conscience, the vultures hover around him waiting for their prey. As long as a man has hope for himself, you may have hope for him. But the devil's object is to drive out the last idea of hope from men, that then they may give themselves up to be his slaves forever.

Let me just say to those who are in trouble, which I hope every faithful Christian will repeat again and again: *There is hope.* There is hope about your financial difficulties, your sickness, your present affliction. God can help you through it. Do not sit down with your elbows on your knees and cry all day. That will not get you through it. Call upon God who sent the trouble. He has a great design in it. It may be that He has sent it as a shepherd sends his black dog to fetch the wandering sheep to him. It may be He has a design in making you lose temporal things so that you may gain eternal things. Many a mother's soul would not have been saved if it had not been for that dear infant who was taken from her bosom. Not until it was taken to the skies did God give the attracting influence that drew her heart to pursue the path to heaven. Do not say there is no hope. Others have been in as terrible a set of circumstances as you have now. Even if it seems as if it has come to a crisis of bread, yet still there is hope. Go and try again on Monday morning. God's providence has a thousand ways of helping us if we have the heart to pray.

Are you in despair about your character? It may be that there is somewhere a woman who says, "I have fallen. My character is gone. There is no hope for me." My sister, there is lifting up. Some who have fallen as terribly as you have slipped have been restored by sovereign grace. There may be someone who has been a drunkard or who is about to become a thief. No one knows it, perhaps, but he is conscious of great degradation and says, "I will never be able to look my fellow-men in the face." Ah, my dear friend, you do not know what Christ can do for you if you would only rest and trust in Him.

Suppose you could be made into a new creature—would not that alter the matter? "Oh," say you, "but that can never be." "Not true," I respond, "that will be." Christ said, "*Behold, I make all things new*" (Revelation 21:5). "*If any man be in Christ, he is a new creature*" (2 Corinthians 5:17). There was an old fable about a spring at which old men washed their faces and grew young. Now there is a spring that welled up from the heart of the Lord Jesus. If an old sinner washes not only his face there, but also his whole spirit, he will become like a little child and will be clean even in the sight of God. There is still hope.

"Ah," says one, "but you do not know my case." No, my dear friend, and I do not particularly desire to know it, because this sweeping truth can meet it, whatever it is. "*All manner of sin and blasphemy shall be forgiven unto men*" (Matthew 12:31). "*The blood of Jesus Christ, his Son, cleanseth us from all sin*" (1 John 1:7). Noah's ark was not made to hold just a few mites, but the elephant, the lion, and the largest beasts of prey all entered and found room. So my Master, who is the great ark of salvation, did not come into this world to save only a few who are little sinners, but "*he is able also to save them to the uttermost that come unto God by him*" (Hebrews 7:25). See Him over there, see Him on the cross in extreme agony, bearing griefs and torments numberless and sweating in agony, all for love of you who were His enemies. Trust Him. Trust Him, for there is hope and lifting up. However bowed down you may be, there is hope even for you in Jesus Christ.

I feel as if I were walking along a corridor, and I see a number of cells of the condemned. As I listen at the keyhole, I can hear those inside weeping in doleful, dolorous dirges. "There is no hope, no hope, no hope." I can see the warden at the other end, smiling calmly to himself, as he knows that none of the prisoners can come out as long as they say there is no hope. It is a sign that their manacles are not broken and that the bolts of their cells are not removed. Oh, if I could look in! I think I can. I think I can open the gate just a little and cry, "There is hope!"

The fiend who said there is no hope is a liar and a murderer from the beginning, and the father of lies. (See John 8:44.) Yet, there is hope since Jesus died. There is hope anywhere except in the infernal lake. There is hope in the hospital when a man has sickened and is within the last hour before his departure. There is hope, though men have sinned themselves beyond the pale of society; hope for the convict, though he faces execution; hope for the man who has cast himself away. Jesus is still able to save.

"No hope" is not to be said by any member of the mariners' life brigade while he can sight the crew of the sinking vessel. "No hope" is not to be said by any one of the fire company while he knows there are living men in the burning pile. "No hope" is not to be said by any one of the valiant army of the Christian church while the soul is still within reach of mercy. "No hope" is a cry that no human tongue should utter, that no human heart should heed.

May God grant us grace whenever we get an opportunity to go and tell all we meet with who are bowed down, "There is lifting up." And likewise tell them where it is. Tell them it is only at the cross. Tell them it is through the precious blood. Tell them it is to be had for nothing, through simply trusting Christ. Tell them it is of free grace, that no merits of theirs are wanted, that no good things are they to bring, but that they may come just as they are and find lifting up in Christ.

Still, nothing will avail unless there is much prayer. We need to pray that God may give effectiveness to the counsels He has given us and reward our obedience with abundant fruit. Oh, beloved, prayer is the grandest thing for those of us who have no might of ourselves. It is wonderful what prayer can do for us.

A dear friend said the other day, "Look at Jacob. In the early part of his life there was much that was unseemly in his character, and very much that was unhappy in his circumstances. Crafty himself, he was often the victim of craft, reaping the fruit of his own ways. But one night in prayer—what a change it made in him! Why, it raised him from the deep poverty of a cunning supplanter to the noble peerage of a prince in Israel!" Bethel itself is hardly more memorable in Jacob's history than Peniel.

And what might one night spent in prayer do for some of us? Suppose we were to try it instead of the soft bed. We need not go to the brook. It is enough that, like Jacob, we were left alone in some place where sighs and cries would be heard by none but God. One night spent thus in solitary prayer might put the spurs on some of you and make you spiritual knights in God's army, able to do great exploits. Oh, yes! May all other gracious exercises be started in prayer, crowned with prayer, and perfected by much prayer.

18

ALL THINGS WORK TOGETHER FOR GOOD

For we know that all things work together for good to them that love God,
to them who are the called according to his purpose.
—Romans 8:28

We know that all things work." Look around, above, beneath, and all things work. They work, in opposition to idleness. The idle man who folds his arms or lies upon the bed of sloth is an exception to God's rule—for all things work except the lazy sluggard. There is not a star, though it seems to sleep in the deep blue firmament, which does not travel innumerable miles and work. There is not an ocean or a river that is not ever working, either clapping its thousand hands with storms or bearing on its bosom the freight of nations. There is not a silent nook within the deepest forest glade where work is not going on. Nothing is idle.

The world is a great machine, never standing still. Silently all through the watches of the night and through the hours of day, the earth revolves on its axis and works out its predestined course. Silently the forest grows, and eventually it is felled. All the while between its growing and felling, it is at work. Everywhere the earth works. Mountains work. Nature in its inmost bowels is at work. Even the center of the great heart of the world is ever beating. Sometimes we discover its working in the volcano and the earthquake, but even when most still, all things are ever working.

They are ever working, too, in opposition to play. Not only are they ceaselessly active, but they are active for a purpose. We are apt to think that the motion of the world and the different evolutions of the stars are like the turning of a child's windmill, producing nothing. That wise, old preacher Solomon once said as much as that:

> *The sun also ariseth, and the sun goeth down, and hasteth to his place where he arose. The wind goeth toward the south, and turneth about unto the north; it whirleth about continually, and the wind returneth again according to his circuits.* (Ecclesiastes 1:5–6)

But Solomon did not add that things are not what they seem. The world is not at play; it has an object in its wildest movement. Avalanche, hurricane, and earthquake are only order in an unusual form. Destruction and death are progress in veiled attire. Everything that is, and is done, works out some great end and purpose. The great machine of this world is not only in motion, but there is also something weaving in it, which as yet mortal eye has not fully seen, but which our text hints at when it says that it is working out for God's people.

All things work in opposition to Sabbath. We morally speak of work, especially on this day, as being the opposite of sacred rest and worship. At present, all things work. Since the day when Adam fell, all things have had to toil and labor. Before Adam's fall, the world kept high on a perpetual holiday, but now the world has come to its workdays and has to toil. When Adam was in the garden, the world had its Sabbath rest, but it will never have another Sabbath until the millennium dawns. Then, when all things have ceased to work and the kingdoms have been given to God the Father, the world will have her Sabbath rest. But at present, all things do work.

Let us not wonder if we have to work, too. When we have to toil, let us remember, this is the world's week of toil. The 6,000 years of continual labor, toil, and travail have happened not to us alone, but to the whole of God's great universe. The whole world is groaning and travailing. Let us not be backward in doing our work. If all things are working, let us work, too. "*Work…while it is day; the night cometh when no man can work*" (John 9:4). And let the idle and slothful remember that they are a great anomaly. They are blots in the great writings of God on work. They mean nothing. In the entire book of letters where God has written out the great word *work*, the idle are nothing at all. Still, let the man who works, though it be with the sweat of his brow and with aching hands, remember that, if he is seeking to bless the Lord's people, he is in sympathy with all things—not only in sympathy with their work, but in sympathy with their aims.

"*All things work together.*" That is in opposition to their apparent conflicting. Looking upon the world with the mere eye of sense and reason, we say, "Yes, all things work, but they work contrary to one another. There are opposite currents. The wind blows to the north and to the south. The world's sailing vessel, it is true, is always tossed with waves, but these waves toss her first to the right and then to the left. They do not steadily bear her onward to her desired haven. It is true the world is always active, but it is with the activity of the battlefield, where hosts encounter hosts and the weaker are overcome."

Do not be deceived. It is not so. Things are not always what they seem. "*All things work together.*" No opposition exists in God's providence. The raven of war is coworker with the dove of peace. The tempest does not strive with the peaceful calm; they are linked together and work together, although they seem to be in opposition. Look at English history. So many events have seemed to be conflicting in their day, but they have worked out for good! It might have been thought that the striving of barons and kings for mastery was likely to tread out the last spark of British liberty, but instead they kindled the pile. The various rebellions of nations, the heaving of society, the strife of anarchy, the tumults of war—all these things, overruled by God, have made the chariot of the church progress more mightily. They have not failed their predestined purpose, "*for good to them that love God, who are the called according to his purpose.*"

I know it is very hard to believe this. "What?" you say, "I have been sick for such a long time. My wife and children, dependent on my daily labor, are crying for food. Will this work together for my good?" So says the Word, and so will you find it before long.

"I have been in the business world," says another, "This commercial pressure has brought me exceedingly low and distressed me. Is it for my good?" You are a Christian. I know you do not seriously ask the question, for you know the answer. He who said, "*All things work together,*" will soon prove to you that there is a harmony in the most discordant parts of your life. You will find, when your biography is written, that the black page harmonized with the bright one—that the dark and cloudy day only served as a glorious foil to set forth the brighter noontide of your joy.

"*All things work together.*" There is never a clash in the world. Men think so, but it never is so. With much cleverness and art, the charioteers of the Roman circus might avoid each other's glowing wheels. But with skill infinitely consummate, God guides the fiery coursers of man's passion, yokes the storm, and bridles the tempest. Keeping each clear of the other, He still induces good, and even better than that, from seeming evil in infinite progression.

We must understand the word *together* also in another sense. "*All things work together for good.*" That is to say, none of them work separately.

I remember an old minister using a very pithy and homely metaphor: "'*All things work together for good.*' But perhaps, any single one of those '*all things*' might destroy us if taken alone. For example, a physician prescribes some medicine for you. You go to the pharmacist, and he makes it up. There is something taken from this drawer, something from that vial, something from that shelf. Any one of those ingredients, it is very possible, could be a deadly poison and kill you outright if you would take it separately; but the pharmacist puts one into the mortar and then another and another. When he has ground them all up with his pestle and has made a compound, he gives them all to you as a whole, and together they work for your good. But any single one of the ingredients might either have operated fatally or in a manner detrimental to your health."

Learn, then, that it is wrong to ask, concerning any particular act of providence, if it is for your good. Remember, it is not the one thing alone that is for your good; it is the one thing put with another thing, and that with a third, and that with a fourth, and all these mixed together that work for your good. Your being sick very probably might not be for your good, except that God has something to follow your sickness, some blessed deliverance to follow your poverty. He knows that, when He has mixed the different experiences of your life together, they will produce good for your soul and eternal good for your spirit.

We know very well that there are many things that happen to us in our lives that would be the ruin of us if we were always to continue in the same condition. Too much joy would intoxicate us; too much misery would drive us to despair.

But the joy and the misery, the battle and the victory, the storm and the calm, all these compounded make that sacred elixir by which God makes all His people perfect through suffering and leads them to ultimate happiness. *"All things work together for good."*

There are different senses to the word *good*. There is the worldling's sense of the word by which he means transient good, the good of the moment. "Who will put honey into my mouth? Who will feed my belly with hidden treasures? Who will drape my back with purple and make my table groan with plenty?" That is "good" to the world—the vat bursting with wine, the barn full of corn! Now, God has never promised that all things will work together for such good as that to His people. Very likely, all things will work together in a totally contrary way to that. Do not expect, Christian, that all things will work together to make you rich. It is just possible they may all work to make you poor. It may be that all the different providences that will happen to you will come wave upon wave, washing your fortune upon the rocks until it is wrecked. Then waves will break over you, until, in that poor boat of the humble remnant of your fortune, you will be out on the wide sea with none to help you but God Almighty. Do not expect, then, that all things will work together for your material good.

The Christian understands the word *good* in another sense. By good, he understands spiritual good. "Ah!" says he, "I do not call gold good, but I call faith good! I do not think it always for my good to increase in treasure, but I know it is good to grow in grace. I do not know that it is for my good that I should walk in the circles of high society, but I know that it is for my good that I walk humbly with my God.

"I do not know that it is necessarily for my good that my children should be about me, like olive branches around my table, but I know that it is for my good that I flourish in the courts of my God and that I become the means of winning souls from going down into the pit. I am not certain that it is altogether for my good to have kind, generous friends with whom I may have fellowship, but I know that it is for my good that I have fellowship with Christ, that I have communion with Him, even though it is in His sufferings. I know it is good for me that my faith, my love, my every grace grow and increase, and that I would be conformed to the image of Jesus Christ my blessed Lord and Master."

To a Christian, however, the highest good he can receive on earth is to grow in grace. "There!" he says, "I would rather be bankrupt in business than I would be bankrupt in grace. Let my fortune be decreased. Better that than that I would backslide! Let your waves and your billows roll over me. Better an ocean of trouble than a drop of sin. I would rather have your rod a thousand times upon my shoulders, O my God, than I would even once put out my hand to touch that which is forbidden or allow my foot to run in the way of gainsayers." The highest good a Christian has here on earth is spiritual.

All things work together for a Christian's lasting good. They all work to bring him to the Savior's feet. "*So he bringeth them unto their desired haven*" (Psalm 107:30), said the psalmist—by storm and tempest, flood and hurricane. All the waves of troubles in a Christian's life simply wash him nearer heaven's shores. The rough winds only hurry his passage across the straits of this life to the port of eternal peace. All things work together for the Christian's eternal and spiritual good.

Yet sometimes all things work together for the Christian's temporal good. You know the story of old Jacob. "*Joseph is not, Simeon is not, and now ye will take Benjamin away; all these things are against me*" (Genesis 42:36), said the old patriarch. However, if he could have read God's secrets, he might have found that Simeon was not lost, for he was retained as a hostage; that Joseph was not lost, but gone before to smooth the passage of his gray hairs into the grave; and that even Benjamin was to be taken away by Joseph in love for his brother. So what seemed to be against him, even in temporal matters, was for him.

You may have also heard the story of that eminent martyr who habitually said, "*All things work together for good.*" When he was seized by the officers of Queen Mary to be taken to the stake to be burned, he was treated so roughly on the road that he broke his leg. The officers jeeringly said, "'*All things work together for good,*' do they? How will your broken leg work for your good?" "I don't know how it will," said he, "but for my good I know it will work, and you will see it so." Strangely, it proved true that it was for his good. Having been delayed a day or so on the road through his lameness, he arrived in London just in time to hear that Elizabeth was proclaimed queen. So he escaped the stake by his broken leg. He turned to the men who had carried him—as they had thought—to his death and said to them, "Now will you believe that '*all things work together for good*'?"

Though the primary meaning of the text is spiritual good, yet sometimes there may be carried in the main current some rich and rare temporal benefits for God's children, as well as the richer spiritual blessings.

19

AN EVER PRESENT HELP

Fear thou not; for I am with thee: be not dismayed; for I am thy God.
—Isaiah 41:10

We sometimes speak and think very lightly of doubts and fears, but such is not God's estimate of them. Our heavenly Father considers them to be great evils, extremely mischievous to us and exceedingly dishonorable to Himself, for He very frequently forbids our fears and as often affords us the most potent remedies for them. *"Fear not"* is a frequent utterance of the divine mouth. *"I am with thee"* is the fervent, soul-cheering argument to support it.

Unless the Lord had judged our fears to be a great evil, He would not so often have forbidden them or have provided such a heavenly sedative for them. Martin Luther used to say that to comfort a despondent spirit is as difficult as raising the dead. However, we have a God who both raises the dead from their graves and His people from their despair. *"Though ye have lien among the pots, yet shall ye be as the wings of a dove covered with silver, and her feathers with yellow gold"* (Psalm 68:13). *"Weeping may endure for a night, but joy cometh in the morning"* (Psalm 30:5).

More or less, all believers need consolation at all times, because their lifestyle is a very unusual one. The walk of faith is one protracted miracle. The life, the conflict, the support, and the triumph of faith are all far above the vision of the eye of sense. The inner life is a world of mysteries. We see nothing beneath or before us, and yet we stand upon a rock and go from strength to strength. We march onward to what seems destruction, but we find safety blooming beneath our feet. During our whole Christian career, the promises of God must be applied to the heart, or else—such is the weakness of flesh and blood—we are ready to go back to the flesh pots of the Egypt of carnal senses and leave the delights that faith alone can yield us.

There are certain special occasions when the Comforter's work is needed. One of these certainly is when we are racked with physical pain. Many bodily pains can be borne without affecting the mind, but there are certain others whose sharp fangs insinuate themselves into the marrow of our nature, boring their way most horribly through the brain and the spirit. For these, much grace is needed. When the head is throbbing, the heart is palpitating, and the whole system is disarranged, it is natural to say with Jacob, "*All these things are against me,*" to complain of the lack of providence, and to think that we are the ones above all others who have seen affliction. Then is the time for the promise to be applied with power. "*Fear thou not; for I am with thee.*" The Lord has promised to strengthen and sustain you when you are sick. (See Psalm 41:3.) When bodily pain gives every sign of increasing or we expect the dreadful surgeon's knife, then to be sustained under such sufferings— the mere thought of which brings shudders to the flesh—we want the upholding gentleness of God. Like the song of the nightingale, "*Fear thou not; for I am with thee*" is sweetest when heard in the night.

When the trouble comes in our relative sorrows, borne personally by those dear to us; when we see them fading gradually by consumption, like lilies snapped at the stalk; or when suddenly they are swept away as the flowers fall beneath the mower's scythe; when we have to visit the grave again and again, and each time leave a part of ourselves behind; when our garments are the banners of our woe, and we desire to sit down in the dust and sprinkle ashes upon our heads because the desire of our eyes is taken from us—then we require the heavenly Comforter. Then, indeed, skillful counsel is in great request, and sweet to the heart are words like these: "*Fear thou not; for I am with thee: be not dismayed; for I am thy God.*"

When all the currents of providence run counter to us; when, after taking arms against a sea of trouble, we find ourselves unable to stem the boisterous torrent and are being swept down the stream, loss succeeding loss, riches taking to themselves wings and flying away until we see nothing before us but absolute want, and perhaps are brought actually to know what want is—then we require abundant grace to sustain our spirits. It is not so easy to come down from wealth to penury, from abundance to poverty, with perfect resignation. That is a philosophy to be learned only where Paul was taught it, when he said, *"I have learned, in whatsoever state I am, therewith to be content"* (Philippians 4:11).

Some would find it hard to be content in the widow's position, with seven children and nothing to maintain them but the shameful pittance that is wrung out by her for her labors with her needle, at which she sits, stitching far into the dead of the night, sewing her very soul away. You might not find it quite so easy to bear poverty if you were shunned by men who courted you in prosperity, but who now do not know you if they meet you in the street. There are bitter things about the poor man's lot that are not easily rinsed from his cup. Then it is that the gracious soul needs the promise, *"Fear thou not; for I am with thee." "Thy Maker is thine husband"* (Isaiah 54:5). *"A father of the fatherless, and a judge of the widow is God in his holy habitation"* (Psalm 68:5). If you are brought into this condition, may my Lord and Master say to you, *"It is I, be not afraid"* (John 6:20).

Dear reader, did you ever stand, as a servant of God, alone in the midst of opposition? Were you ever called to attack some deadly popular error, and, with rough bold hand, like an iconoclast, to dash down the graven images of the age? Have you heard the clamor of many, some saying one thing and some the other— some saying, "He is a good man," but others saying, "No, he deceives the people"? Did you ever see the rancor of the priests of Baal flashing from their faces and foaming from their mouths? Did you ever read their hard expressions, see their misrepresentations of your speech and of your motives? Did you never feel the delight of saying, "The best of all is that God is with us; and, in the name of God, instead of folding up the standard, we will set up our banners. If this is vile, we purpose to be viler still and throw down the gauntlet once more in the name of the God of truth, against the error of the times"?

If you have ever passed through the ordeal, then you have needed the words, *"Fear thou not; for I am with thee: be not dismayed; for I am thy God." "Who are thou, that thou shouldest be afraid of a man that shall die, and of the son of man which shall be made as grass?"* (Isaiah 51:12). *"I will make thee unto this people a fenced brazen wall: and they shall fight against thee, but they shall not prevail against thee"* (Jeremiah 15:20). *"Fear not: for thou shalt not be ashamed"* (Isaiah 54:4).

But, my dear reader, we will want this word of comfort most of all when we travel down the banks of the final black river, when we hear the booming of its waves, feel the chilling influence of its dark flood, but cannot see to the other side. When the mists of depression of spirit hide from us *"the heavenly Jerusalem"* (Hebrews 12:22), and our eye catches no glimpse of the *"land that floweth with milk and honey"* (Leviticus 20:24), then the soul is occupied with present pain and wrapped in darkness that may be felt. In such a condition:

> We linger shivering on the brink,
>   And fear to launch away.

We talk of death too lightly. It is solemn work to the best of men. It would be no child's play to an apostle to die. Yet if we can hear the whisper, *"Fear thou not; for I am with thee,"* then the mists will sweep away from the river, and that stream, turbid though it was before, will become clear as crystal, and we will see the "Rock of Ages" at the bottom of the flood. Then will we descend with confidence, hear the splash of the death stream, and think it music. It will be music as it melts into the songs of the seraphim, who will accompany us through its depths.

And it will be delightful when those mists have rolled away to see the shining ones coming to meet us, to go with us up the celestial hills to the pearly gates, to accompany us to the throne of God, where we will rest forever. Happy are they who will hear their Lord say to them, *"I am with thee; be not afraid."*

After death, we read in this word of great events, what will happen to us, but we only feebly comprehend the revelation. After death, solemnities will follow that may well strike a man with awe as he thinks upon them. There is a judgment and a resurrection. There is a trumpet that will summon the sons of men to hear from heaven's doomsday book their future destiny. The world will be on fire, and the elements will melt with fervent heat. The time will surely come when there will be a pompous appearing of the great Judge at the dread inquest. There will be the finalization of the dispensation and the gathering together of all things in one that are in Christ. There will be a casting down into hell of the tares bound up in bundles to burn, and the fire that will never be quenched will send up its smoke forever and ever.

What about that future? Why, faith can look forward to it without a single tremor. She does not fear, for she hears the voice of the everlasting God saying to her, "'*I am with thee.*' I will be with you when your dust rises. Your first transporting vision will be the King in His beauty. You will be satisfied when you wake up in His likeness. I will be with you when the heavens are ablaze, your Preserver, your Comforter, your Heaven, your All in All. Therefore, fear you not, but look forward with unmoved delight to all the mystery and the glory of the age unborn."

20

DELIVERANCE FROM SURROUNDING TROUBLES

Thou hast beset me behind and before, and laid thine hand upon me.
—Psalm 139:5

No doubt the children of Israel supposed that all was over. The Egyptians had sent them away, entreating them to depart and loading them with riches. Terror had smitten the heart of Egypt. From the king on the throne to the prisoner in the dungeon, all was dismay and fear on account of Israel. Egypt was glad when they departed.

Thus, the children of Israel said to themselves, "We will now march to Canaan at once. There will be no more dangers, no more troubles, no more trials. The Egyptians themselves have sent us away, and they are too afraid of us ever to molest us again. Now we will tread the desert with quick footsteps. After a few days, we will enter into the land of our possession—the land that flows with milk and honey."

"Not quite so speedily," said God. "The time has not arrived yet for you to rest. It is true I have delivered you from Egypt, but there is much you have to learn before you will be prepared to dwell in Canaan. Therefore, I will lead you about, to instruct you and teach you." And it came to pass that the Lord led the children of Israel through the wilderness of the Red Sea, until they arrived over against Baalzephon, where the craggy mountains shut them in on either side. Pharaoh heard of it. He came upon them to overcome them. They stood in terrible fright and jeopardy of their lives.

Now, it is usually similar with a believer: he marches out of Egypt spiritually at the time of his conversion and says to himself, "Now I will always be happy." He has a bright eye and a light heart, for his fetters have been dashed to the ground. No longer does he feel the lash of conscience upon his shoulder. "Now," says he, "I may have a short life, but it will be a happy one."

> A few more rolling years at most,
>   Will land me on fair Canaan's coast.

The Israelites had a great trial sent by God Himself. There was the Red Sea in front of them. Now, it was not an enemy who put the sea there; it was God Himself. We may therefore think that the Red Sea represents some great and trying providence, which the Lord will be sure to place in the path of every newborn child, in order to try his faith and to test the sincerity of his trust in God.

I do not know whether your experience will back up mine, but I can say this: the worst difficulty I ever met with, or I think I can ever meet with, happened a little time after my conversion to God. And you must generally expect, very soon after you have been brought to know and love Him, that you will have some great, broad, deep Red Sea straight before your path, which you will scarcely know how to pass.

Sometimes it will occur in the family. For instance, if he is an ungodly man, the husband may say, "You will not attend that place of worship. I positively forbid you to be baptized, or to join that church." There is a Red Sea before you. You have done nothing wrong. It is God Himself who places that Red Sea before your path. Or perhaps before that time, you were carrying on a business that now you cannot conscientiously continue. There is a Red Sea that you have to cross in renouncing your means of livelihood. You don't see how it is to be done, or how you will maintain yourself and provide things honestly in the sight of all men. Perhaps your employment calls you among men with whom you lived before on amicable terms, but now suddenly they say, "Come! Won't you do as you used to do?" The Red Sea before you is a hard struggle. You do not like to come out and say, "I cannot, I will not, for I am a Christian." You stand still, half afraid to go forward.

Perhaps the Red Sea is something proceeding more immediately from God. You find that just when He plants a vine in your heart, He blasts all the vines in your vineyard, and when He plants you in His own garden, then it is that He uproots all your comforts and your joys. Just when the Sun of Righteousness is rising upon you, your own little candle is blown out. Just when you seem to need it most, your gourd is withered, your prosperity departs, and your flood begins to ebb.

I say again, it may not be so with all of you, but I think that most of God's people have not long escaped the bondage of Egypt before they find some terrible, rolling sea lashed perhaps by tempestuous winds directly in their path. They stand aghast, and say, "O God, how can I bear this? I thought I could give up all for you, but now I feel as if I could do nothing! I thought I would be in heaven and all would be easy. But here is a sea I cannot ford. There is no squadron of ships to carry me across. It is not bridged even by Your mercy. I must swim it, or else I fear I must perish."

The children of Israel would not have cared about the Red Sea a single atom if they had not been terrified by the Egyptians who were behind them. These Egyptians, I think, may be interpreted by way of parable as the representatives of those sins that we thought were completely dead and gone. For a little while after conversion, sin does not trouble a Christian. He is very happy and cheerful, in a sense of pardon. But before many days are past, he will understand what Paul said, "*I find a law, so that when I would do good, evil is present with me*" (Romans 7:21). The first moment when he wins his liberty, the Christian laughs and leaps in an ecstasy of joy. He thinks, "Oh! I will soon be in heaven. As for sin, I can trample that beneath my feet!"

But, scarcely has another Sunday gladdened his spirit before he finds that sin is too much for him. The old corruptions, which he fancied were laid in their graves, resurrect and start up afresh. He begins to cry, "*O wretched man that I am! who shall deliver me from the body of this death?*" (Romans 7:24). He sees all his old sins galloping behind him like Pharaoh and his host pursuing him to the borders of the Red Sea.

There is a great trial before him. He thinks he could bear that. He thinks he could walk through the Red Sea. But those Egyptians are behind him! He thought he would never see them any more forever. They were the plague and torment of his life when they made him work in the brick kiln. He sees his old master, the very man who habitually laid the lash on his shoulders, riding hastily after him. There are the eyes of that black Pharaoh, flashing like fire in the distance. He sees the horrid scowling face of the tyrant, and how he trembles! Satan is after him, and all the legions of hell seem to be let loose, if possible, to destroy his soul utterly.

At such a time, moreover, our sins are more formidable to us than they were before they were forgiven because, when we were in Egypt, we never saw the Egyptians mounted on horses or in chariots. They only appeared as our taskmasters with their whips. But now these people see the Egyptians on horseback, clad in armor. They have come out with their warlike instruments to slay them.

These poor children of Israel had such faint hearts. They no sooner saw the Egyptians than they began to cry out. When they beheld the Red Sea before them, they murmured against their deliverer. A faint heart is the worst foe a Christian can have. While he keeps his faith firm, while the anchor is fixed deep in the rock, he never need fear the storm. But when the hand of faith is palsied, or the eye of faith is dim, it will go hard with us.

As for the Egyptian, he may throw his spear. While we can deflect it with our shield of faith, we are not terrified by the weapon; but if we lose our faith, the spear becomes a deadly dart. While we have faith, the Red Sea may flow before us, as deep and as dark as it pleases. Like Leviathan, we trust we can snuff up Jordan at a gulp. But if we have no faith, then at the most insignificant streamlet, which Faith could take up in her hands in a single moment and drink like Gideon's men, poor Unbelief stands quivering and crying, "Ah! I will be drowned in the floods, or I will be slain by the foe. There is no hope for me. I am driven to despair. It would have been better for me that I had died in Egypt than that I should come here to be slain by the hand of the enemy."

The child of God, when he is first born again, has very little faith, because he has had but little experience. He has not tried the promises and therefore he does not know their faithfulness. He has not used the arm of faith, and therefore the sinews of it have not become strong. Let him live a little longer and become confirmed in the faith, and he will not care for Red Seas or for the Egyptians. But just then his little heart beats against the walls of his body and he laments, "Ah, me! Ah, me! 'O wretched man that I am!' How will I ever find deliverance?"

Cheer up, then, heir of grace! What is your trial? Has providence brought it upon you? If so, unerring wisdom will deliver you from it. What is it with which you are now disciplined? As truly as you are alive, God will remove it. Do you think God's cloudy pillar would ever lead you to a place where God's right arm would fail you? Do you imagine that He would ever guide you into such a narrow ravine that He could not conduct you out again? The providence that apparently misleads will in truth befriend you. That which leads you into difficulties guards you against foes. It casts darkness on your sins while giving light to you.

How sweet is providence to a child of God when he can reflect upon it! He can look out into this world, and say, "However great my troubles are, they are not as great as my Father's power. However difficult my circumstances are, yet all things around me are working together for good. He who holds up the unpillared arch of the starry heavens can also support my soul without a single apparent prop. He who guides the stars in their well-ordered courses, even when they seem to move in mazelike dances, surely He can overrule my trials in such a way that out of confusion He will bring order and produce lasting good from seeming evil. He who bridles the storm and puts the bit in the mouth of the tempest, surely He can restrain my trial and keep my sorrows in subjection. I need not fear while the lightning is in His hands and the thunders sleep within His lips, while the oceans gurgle from His fist and the clouds are in the hollow of His hands, while the rivers are turned by His foot, and while He digs the channels of the sea. Surely He, whose might wings an angel, can furnish a worm with strength. He who guides a cherub will not be overcome by the trials of an ant like myself. He who makes the most ponderous orb roll in dignity and keeps its predestined orbit, can make a little atom like myself move in my proper course and conduct me as He pleases."

Christian, there is no sweeter pillow than providence! Even when providence seems adverse, believe it still, lay it under your head, because you may depend upon it that there is comfort in its bosom. There is hope for you, child of God! That great trouble that is to come in your way in the early part of your pilgrimage is planned by love, the same love that will interpose itself as your protector.

The children of Israel had another refuge. They knew that they were covenant people of God, and that, even though they were in difficulties, God had brought them there. Therefore, God (let me say it with reverence) was bound by His honor to bring them out of that trouble into which He had brought them. "Well," says the child of God, "I know I am in a predicament, but this is one thing

I also know—I did not come out of Egypt by myself; I know that He brought me out. I know that I did not escape by my own power or slay my firstborn sins myself; I know that He did it. And though I fled from the tyrant, I know that He made my feet mighty for travel, for there was not one feeble in all our tribes. I know that though I am at the Red Sea, I did not run there uncalled, but He bade me go there. Therefore, I give to the winds my fears, for if He has led me here into this difficulty, He will lead me out and lead me through."

The third refuge that the children of Israel had was in a man. Neither of the two others, without him, would have been of any avail. It was the man Moses. He did everything for them. Your greatest refuge in all your trials, O child of God, is in a Man: not in Moses, but in Jesus; not in the servant, but in the Master. He is interceding for you, unseen and unheard by you, even as Moses did for the children of Israel. If you could, in the dim distance, catch the sweet syllables of His voice as they distill from His lips and see His heart as it speaks for you, you would take comfort, for God hears that Man when He pleads. He can overcome every difficulty. He has not a rod, but a cross, which can divide the Red Sea. He has not only a cloudy pillar of forgiving grace, which can dim the eyes of your foes and can keep them at a distance, but He also has a cross that can open the Red Sea and drown your sins in the very midst.

Jesus will not leave you. Look! On yonder rock of heaven He stands, cross in hand, even as Moses did with his rod. Cry to Him, for with that uplifted cross He will cleave a path for you and guide you through the sea. He will make those old floods, which had been friends forever, stand asunder like foes. Call to Him, and He will make you a way in the midst of the ocean and a path through the pathless sea. Cry to Him, and there will not a sin of yours be left alive. He will sweep them all away. And the king of sin, the devil, he too will be overwhelmed beneath the Savior's blood, while you sing:

> Hell and my sins obstruct my path,
> But hell and sin are conquered foes;
> My Jesus nailed them to His cross,
> And sang the triumph as He rose.

21

A HARP'S SWEET NOTE

Fear thou not; I am with thee.
—Isaiah 41:10

This harp sounds most sweetly. Saul was subject to fits of deep despondency. But when David, the skillful harpist, laid his hand among the obedient strings, the evil spirit departed, overcome by the subduing power of melody. Our text is such a harp, and if the Holy Spirit will but touch its strings, its sweet discourse will charm away the demon of despair. *"I am with thee."* It is a harp of ten strings, containing the full chords of consolation. Its notes quiver to the height of ecstasy or descend to the hollow bass of the deepest grief.

All through life, I may picture the saints as marching to its music, even as the children of Israel set out to the notes of the silver trumpets. Israel came to the Red Sea. They might well have been afraid because the Egyptians were behind them. The crack of their whips could be heard. The rolling sea was before them, but Israel marched confidently through its depths, because the word was given, "Fear not; the Lord God is with His people." See the pillar of cloud by day and the pillar of fire by night. How safely the Israelites followed their direction, even through the heart of the sea!

They trod the sand on the other side. It was an arid waste. How would they support themselves or their flocks? *"Fear thou not; for I am with thee."* Oh! The manna dropped from heaven, and the waters rippled from the rock. But, see, they came to Jordan! It was their last difficulty, and then they would reach the land of their inheritance. Jordan divided—what ailed you, O Jordan, that you were driven back? God was with His people. They feared not, but entered into their rest. This is the heritage of all the saints.

As I thought of the life of faith, I saw before my eyes, as in a vision, a lofty staircase of light. Led by an invisible hand, I mounted step by step. When I had ascended long and far, it turned again and again. I could see no supports to this elevated staircase, no pillars of iron, no props of stone. It seemed to hang in air. As I climbed, I looked up to see where the staircase went, but I saw no further than the step on which I stood, except that now and then the clouds of light above me parted asunder and I thought I saw the throne of the Eternal and the heaven of His glory. My next step seemed to be upon the air. Yet when I boldly put down my foot, I found it as firm as pavement beneath me. I looked back on the steps that I had trod and was amazed, but I dared not tarry, for "forward" was the voice that urged me on. I knew, for faith had told me, that the winding stair would end at last, beyond the sun and moon and stars in the excellent glory.

As now and then I gazed down into the depths out of which the stairs had lifted me, I shuddered at my fate, should I slip from my standing or should the next step plunge me into the abyss! Over the edge of the chasm where I stood, I gazed with awe, for I saw nothing but a gaping void of black darkness. Into this I must plunge my foot in the hope of finding another step beneath it. I would have been unable to advance, and would have sat down in utter despair, had I not heard the word from above of one in whom I trusted, saying, *"Fear thou not; for I am with thee."* I knew that my mysterious guide could not err. I felt that infinite faithfulness would not bid me take a step if it were not safe. Therefore, still mounting, I stand at this hour happy and rejoicing, though my faith be all above my own comprehension, and my work above my own ability.

We believe in the providence of God, but we do not believe half enough in it. Remember that Omnipotence has servants everywhere, set in their places at every point of the road. In the old days of the postal horses, there were always relays of swift horses ready to carry onward the king's mails. It is wonderful how God has His relays of providential agents; how, when He is finished with one, there is always another just ready to take his place. Sometimes you have found one friend who failed you. He just died and was buried. "Ah!" you say, "What will I do?" Well, well, God knows how to carry on the purposes of His providence. He will raise up another.

How strikingly punctual providence is! You and I make appointments and miss them by half-an-hour, but God never missed an appointment yet. God never is before His time—although we often wish He were—but He never is behind, not by one tick of the clock. When the children of Israel were to go down out of Egypt, all the Pharaohs in the pyramids, if they had risen to life again, could not have kept them in bondage another half-minute. "*Thus saith the* LORD *God of Israel, Let my people go!*" (Exodus 5:1). It was time, and go they must. All the kings of the earth, and all the princes thereof, are in subjection to the kingdom of God's providence. He can move them just as He pleases. As the showman pulls his string and moves his puppets, so can God move all that are on earth and the angels in heaven, according to His will and pleasure.

And now, trembler, why are you afraid? "*Fear thou not; for I am with thee.*" All the mysterious arrangements of providence work for our good. Touch that string again, you who find yourselves in trouble, and see if there my harp is not a rare instrument.

God well knows how, if He does not interpose openly to deliver us in trouble, to infuse strength into our sinking hearts. "*There appeared an angel unto him from heaven, strengthening him*" (Luke 22:43), it is written of our Lord. I do not doubt but that invisible spirits are often sent by God from heaven to invigorate our spirits when they are ready to sink. Have you never felt it? You sat down an hour ago and wept as if your heart would break, and then you bowed your knee in solemn prayer and spread the case before the Lord. Afterward, when you came down from the chamber, you felt as if you could joyfully encounter the trouble. You were humbled and bowed down under it, as a child under a chastening rod, but you gave yourself up to it. You knew it was your Father that smote. So you did not rebel any longer, but went into the world determined to meet the difficulty that you thought would crush you, feeling that you were quite able to sustain it.

I have read of people who bathe in those baths of Germany that are impregnated with a lot of iron. After bathing, they have felt as if they were made of iron and were able, in the heat of the sun, to cast off the heat as though they were dressed in steel. Happy indeed are they who bathe in the bath of such a promise as this: *"I am with thee!"* Put your whole soul into that consoling element. Plunge into the promise, and you will feel your strength suddenly renewed, so that you can bear troubles that would have overburdened you before.

There is a way by which the Lord can be with His people, which is best of all, namely, by sensible manifestations of His presence, imparting joy and peace that surpass all understanding. I will not venture to explain the exhilaration and the rapture that is caused in a child of God by the consciousness that God is near him. In one sense, He is always near us. In another way, however, there is an opening of our eyes and an unsealing of our ears, a putting away of the external senses and an opening of the inner spiritual awareness by which the inner life of the Christian becomes wondrously conscious of the pervading presence of the Most High.

Describe it, I cannot, for it is not a thing for words. It is like what heaven must be, a stray gleam of the sunlight of paradise fallen upon this sinful world. You are as sure that God is with you as you are sure that you are in the body. Though the walls do not glow, the humble floor does not blaze with light, and no rustle of angels' wings can be heard, yet you are like Moses when he took his shoes from off his feet, for the place where you stand has become holy ground to you. Bowed down, I have felt it, until it seemed as if my spirit would be crushed. Yet at the same time, I felt lifted up until the exceeding weight of glory became so great a joy it was too overwhelming for flesh and blood.

Here is a person who has lost all his worldly goods and is very poor. He is met the next morning by a generous friend who says to him, "Fear not, you will go and share with me. You know that I am a person of considerable property. Fear not, I know your losses, but I am with you." Now, I feel sure that any person so approached would go home and say to himself, "Well, now, I have no need of any anxiety. I am rich, since one half of what my friend has is more than I had before." Yes, but may not the same losses that fell upon you fall upon your friend? May not the same reverses that have made you poor, make him poor? In that case, you are as poor as ever. Besides, your friend may change his mind. He may find you much too expensive a client, and he may shut his door against you one of these days. But, now, God says to you, *"I am with thee."* Now, the Lord has much more than your friend. He is much more faithful. He will never grow weary of you. He cannot change His mind. Surely it is better for you to feel that God is with you than to rely upon an arm of flesh.

Is it not so? Believer, you will never prefer man to God, will you? Will you prefer to rest in a poor, changeable man's promise, rather than to rest upon the immutable covenant of God? You would not dare to say that, though I dare say you have acted as if you would. I am afraid, such is our unbelief, that sometimes we really prefer the poor arm of flesh to the almighty arm of God. What a disgrace to us!

But in our sober senses, we must confess that God's "*I am with thee*," is better than the kindest assurance of the best of friends. You may be engaged in Christian service, working very hard. Would not you feel very happy if God were to raise up a dozen young spirits who would rally round and help? "Oh!" say you, "I could go then to my grave saying, '*Lord, now lettest thou thy servant depart in peace,*' (Luke 2:29), since there are so many others enlisted in the good cause." Well, but is it so? Might they not also grow as weary as you have? And what are they compared with the world's needs? May they not soon be taken away or prove unfaithful? If God says, "*I am with thee,*" is that not better than twenty thousand of the brightest spirits and thousands of the most industrious missionaries? For what would they all be without God? So, the only comfort they can bring you, they have to borrow from Him first of all.

Take the naked promise of God, for it is enough, and more than enough, though all earth's springs were dry.

SOULWINNER

CONTENTS

Preface 363

1. What Is It to Win a Soul? 364

2. Godward Qualities for Soulwinning 384

3. Manward Qualities for Soulwinning 400

4. Messages Likely to Win Souls 411

5. Obstacles to Soulwinning 426

6. How to Induce Our People to Win Souls 433

7. How to Raise the Dead 445

8. How to Win Souls for Christ 457

9. The Cost of Being a Soulwinner 470

10. The Soulwinner's Reward 475

11. The Soulwinner's Life and Work 481

12. Soulwinning Explained 496

13. Saving Souls: Our One Business 510

14. Instruction in Soulwinning 525

15. Encouragement to Soulwinners 540

PREFACE

This volume was planned by Mr. Spurgeon himself. His intention was to deliver to the students of the pastors' college a short course of lectures on what he termed "that most royal employment," soul-winning. Having completed the series, he purposed to collect his previous addresses to other audiences on the same theme and publish the whole for the guidance of all who desired to become soul winners, with the added hope of inducing many more professing Christians to engage in this truly blessed service for the Savior.

This explanation will account for the form in which the topic is treated in the present book. The first six chapters contain the college lectures; then follow four addresses delivered to Sunday-school teachers, open-air preachers, and friends gathered at Monday evening prayer meetings at the Tabernacle; while the rest of the volume consists of teachings in which the work of winning souls is earnestly commended to the attention of every believer in the Lord Jesus Christ.

Thousands will rejoice to read what Mr. Spurgeon spoke and wrote concerning what he called "the chief business of the Christian."

1

WHAT IS IT TO WIN A SOUL?

I purpose, dear ones, if God will enable me, to give you a short course under the general heading of "The Soulwinner." Soulwinning is the chief business of the Christian; indeed, it should be the main pursuit of every true believer. We should each say, with Simon Peter, *"I go fishing"* (John 21:3), and our aim should be, along with Paul, *"That I might by all means save some"* (1 Corinthians 9:22). We will begin our messages on this subject by considering the question: What is it to win a soul?

This question may be instructively answered by describing what it is not. We do not regard it as soulwinning to steal members from other established churches and train them to say our particular creed. We aim to bring souls to Christ rather than to make converts to our churches. Sheep-stealers roam abroad, concerning whom I will say nothing except that they are not brothers, not acting in a brotherly fashion. To their own Master they must stand or fall. We consider it utter meanness to build up our own house with the ruins of our neighbors' mansions. We prefer to quarry for ourselves.

I hope we all sympathize in the bighearted spirit of Dr. Chalmers, who, when it was said that such-and-such an effort would not be beneficial to the special interests of the Free Church of Scotland, although it might promote the general religion of the land, said, "What is the Free Church compared with the Christian good of the people of Scotland?" Indeed, what are all the churches put together, as mere organizations, if they stand in conflict with the moral and spiritual advantage of the nation or if they impede the kingdom of Christ?

It is because God blesses men through the churches that we desire to see them prosper, and not merely for the sake of the churches themselves. There is such a thing as selfishness in our eagerness for the expansion of our own party. May grace deliver us from this evil spirit! The increase of the kingdom is more to be desired than the growth of a clan.

We would do a great deal to make an immature Baptist brother into a mature Baptist simply because we value our Lord's ordinances. We would labor earnestly to raise a believer in salvation by free will into a believer in salvation by grace, for we long to see all religious teaching built upon the solid rock of truth and not upon the sand of imagination. At the same time, our grand object is not the revision of opinions, but the regeneration of natures. We should bring men to Christ, not to our own particular views of Christianity.

Our first care must be that the sheep are gathered to the Great Shepherd. There will be time enough afterward to secure them for our various folds. To make proselytes is a suitable labor for Pharisees. To lead men to God is the honorable aim of all laborers of Christ.

In the next place, we do not consider soul-winning to be accomplished by hurriedly inscribing more names upon our church rolls in order to show a good increase at the year's end. This is easily done, and there are those who use great pains, not to say arts, to effect it. But if this practice is regarded as the epitome of a Christian's efforts, the result will be deplorable.

By all means, let us bring true converts into the church, for it is a part of our work to teach them to observe everything Christ has commanded them. But still, this is to be done with disciples, and not with those who merely profess to have faith. If care is not used, we may do more harm than good at this point. To introduce unconverted persons to the church is to weaken and degrade it. Therefore, an apparent gain may be a real loss.

I am not among those who decry statistics, nor do I think that they produce all manner of evil, for they do much good if they are accurate and if men use them lawfully. It is a good thing for people to see the nakedness of the land through statistics of decrease, that they may be driven on their knees before the Lord to seek prosperity. On the other hand, it is by no means an evil thing for workers to be encouraged by having some account of results set before them. I would be very sorry if the practice of adding up, deducting, and giving the net result were to be abandoned, because it is good to know our numerical condition.

It has been noticed that those who object to the process are often those whose unsatisfactory reports would somewhat humiliate them; this is not always so, but it is suspiciously frequent. The other day, I heard of the report of a church in which the minister, who was well known for having reduced his congregation to nothing, somewhat cleverly wrote, "Our church is looking up." When he was questioned with regard to this statement, he replied, "Everybody knows that the church is on its back, and it can do nothing else but look up."

When churches are "looking up" in that way, their pastors generally say that statistics are very misleading things and that you cannot tabulate the work of the Spirit or calculate the prosperity of a church by figures. The fact is, you *can* calculate very correctly, if the figures are honest and if all circumstances are taken into consideration. If there is no increase, you may calculate with considerable accuracy that there is not much being done. If there is a clear decrease among a growing population, you may reckon that the prayers of the people and the preaching are not of the most powerful kind.

Still, being in a hurry to get people into the church is very damaging, both to the church and to the supposed converts. I remember several young men who were of good moral character and religiously hopeful. However, instead of searching their hearts and aiming at their real conversion, the pastor never gave them any rest until he had persuaded them to make a profession. He thought that they would be under more bonds to holy things if they professed religion; he felt quite safe in pressing them, for "they were so hopeful." He imagined that to discourage them by vigilant examination might drive them away. To secure them, he made them hypocrites. Presently, these young men are much further from the church of God than they would have been if they had been affronted by being kept in their proper places and warned that they were not yet converted.

It is a serious injury to a person to receive him into the number of the faithful unless there is good reason to believe that he is really regenerate. I am sure it is so, for I speak after careful observation. Some of the most glaring sinners known to me were once members of a church and had been, as I believe, led to make a profession by pressure, well meant but ill judged. Do not think that soulwinning is or can be secured by the multiplication of baptisms and the swelling size of your church.

What do dispatches from the battlefield such as the following mean? "Last night fourteen souls were under conviction, fifteen were justified, and eight received full sanctification." I am weary of this public bragging, this counting of unhatched chickens, this exhibition of doubtful spoils. Lay aside such numberings of the people, such idle pretense of certifying in half a minute that which will need the testing of a lifetime. Hope for the best, but in your highest excitements be reasonable. Inquiry rooms are all very well, but if they lead to idle boasting, they will grieve the Holy Spirit and work abounding evil.

Nor is it soulwinning, friends, merely to create excitement. Excitement will accompany every great movement. We may justly question whether the movement was earnest and powerful if it was as serene as a drawing room Bible reading. You cannot very well blast great rocks without the sound of explosions, nor fight a battle and keep everybody as quiet as a mouse. On a dry day, a carriage is not moving much along the roads unless there is some noise and dust. Friction and stir are the natural result of force in motion.

When the Spirit of God is abroad and men's minds are stirred, there must and will be certain visible signs of movement, although these must never be confused with the movement itself. If people imagine that to make dust is the object aimed at by the rolling of a carriage, they can take a broom and very soon raise as much dust as fifty coaches; however, they will, be committing a nuisance rather than conferring a benefit. Excitement is as incidental as dust, and it is not for one moment to be aimed at. When the woman in the biblical parable swept her house, she did it to find her money, not for the sake of raising a cloud of dust. (See Luke 15:8.)

Do not aim at sensation and "effect." Flowing tears and streaming eyes, sobs and outcries, crowded after-meetings and all kinds of confusion may occur, and may be borne with as accompanying genuine feeling. But, I urge you, do not plan their production. It very often happens that the converts who are born in excitement die when the thrill is over. They are like certain insects that are the product of an exceedingly warm day and die when the sun goes down. Some converts live like salamanders—in the fire—but they expire at a reasonable temperature.

I do not delight in religion that creates a hothead. Give me the godliness that flourishes upon Calvary rather than upon Vesuvius. The utmost zeal for Christ is consistent with common sense and reason; raving, ranting, and fanaticism are products of another zeal, which is not according to knowledge. We should prepare men for the communion table, not for a padded room at the insane asylum. No one is more sorry than I that such a caution as this should be needed. However, remembering the whims of certain revivalists, I cannot say less.

What is the real winning of a soul for God? As far as this is done by instrumentality, what are the processes by which a soul is led to God and to salvation? I take it that one of its main operations consists of instructing a person so that he may know the truth of God. Instruction by the gospel is the commencement of all real work upon men's minds.

> *"Go ye, therefore, and teach all nations, baptizing them in the name of the Father, and of the Son, and of the Holy Ghost: teaching them to observe all things whatsoever I have commanded you: and, lo, I am with you alway, even unto the end of the world."* (Matthew 28:19)

Teaching begins the work and crowns it, too.

The gospel according to Isaiah is, *"Incline your ear, and come unto me: hear, and your soul shall live"* (Isaiah 55:3). It is ours, then, to give men something worth their hearing—in fact, to instruct them. We are sent to evangelize, or to *"preach the gospel to every creature"* (Mark 16:15). That is not done unless we teach them the great truths of revelation.

Gospel means "good news." To listen to some preachers, you would imagine that the gospel was a pinch of sacred snuff to make them wake up, or a bottle of strong spirits to excite their brains. It is nothing of the kind.

The gospel is news: there is information and instruction in it concerning matters that men need to know, and statements in it calculated to bless those who hear it. It is not a magical incantation or charm whose force consists in a collection of sounds. It is a revelation of facts and truths that require knowledge and belief. The gospel is a reasonable system; it appeals to men's understanding. A matter for thought and consideration, it appeals to the conscience and reflecting powers.

Hence, if we do not teach men something, we may shout, "Believe! Believe! Believe!" but what are they to believe? Each exhortation requires a corresponding instruction, or it will mean nothing. "Escape!" From what? This question requires for its answer the doctrine of the punishment of sin. "Fly!" But where? To answer this question, you must preach Christ and His wounds, and the clear doctrine of atonement by sacrifice. "Repent!" Of what? Here you must answer such questions as, What is sin? What is the evil of sin? What are the consequences of sin? "Be converted!" But what is it to be converted? By what power can we be converted? What from? What to?

The field of instruction is wide if men are to be made to know the truth that saves. *"That the soul be without knowledge, it is not good"* (Proverbs 19:2). It is ours as the Lord's instruments to make men know the truth so that they may believe it and feel its power. We are not to try to save men in the dark. Rather, in the power of the Holy Spirit, we are to seek to turn them from darkness to light.

Do not believe, dear friends, that when you go into revival meetings or special evangelistic services, you are to leave out the doctrines of the gospel, for then you ought to proclaim the doctrines of grace more, rather than less. Teach gospel doctrines clearly, affectionately, simply, and plainly, especially those truths that have a present, practical bearing upon man's condition and God's grace.

Some enthusiasts seem to have embraced the notion that, as soon as a minister addresses the unconverted, he should deliberately throw away his usual doctrinal messages, because supposedly there will be no conversions if he preaches the whole counsel of God. It comes down to this: supposedly, we are to conceal the truth and utter half-falsehoods in order to save souls. We are to speak the truth to God's people because they will not hear anything else, but we are to wheedle sinners into faith by exaggerating one part of truth and hiding the rest until a more convenient season. This is a strange theory, yet many endorse it. According to them, we may preach the redemption of a chosen number of God's people, but universal redemption must be our doctrine when we speak with the outside world. We are to tell believers that salvation is by grace alone, but sinners are to be spoken with as if they were to save themselves. We are to inform Christians that the Holy Spirit alone can convert, but when we talk with the unsaved, the Holy Spirit is scarcely to be named.

We have not learned Christ thus. Others have done these things, but let them be our warning signals, not our examples. He who sent us to win souls does not permit us either to invent falsehoods or to suppress truth. His work can be done without such suspicious methods.

Perhaps some of you will reply, "But, still, God has blessed half-statements and wild assertions." Do not be quite so sure. I venture to assert that God does not bless falsehood. He may bless the truth that is mixed in with error, but much more blessing would have come if the preaching had been more in accordance with His own Word. I cannot admit that the Lord blesses evangelistic Jesuitism, and the suppression of truth is not too harshly named when I so describe it. The withholding of the doctrine of the total depravity of man has worked serious harm in many who have listened to a certain kind of preaching. These people do not get a true healing because they do not know the disease under which they are suffering. They are never truly clothed because nothing is done to strip them.

In many ministries, there is not enough of probing the heart and rousing the conscience by the revelation of man's alienation from God, and by the declaration of the selfishness and wickedness of such a state. Men need to be told that, unless divine grace brings them out of their enmity to God, they will eternally perish. They must be reminded of the sovereignty of God, that He is not obliged to bring them out of this state, that He would be right and just if He left them in such a condition, that they have no merit to plead before Him and no claims upon Him, and that if they are to be saved, it must be by grace, and by grace alone. The preacher's work is to throw sinners down in utter helplessness, so that they may be compelled to look up to Him who alone can help them.

To try to win a soul for Christ by keeping that soul in ignorance of any truth is contrary to the mind of the Spirit. To endeavor to save men by mere nonsense, excitement, or oratorical display is as foolish as to hope to hold an angel with bird lime or lure a star with music. The best attraction is the gospel in its purity. The weapon with which the Lord conquers men is the truth as it is in Jesus.

The gospel will be found equal to every emergency—it is an arrow that can pierce the hardest heart, a balm that will heal the deadliest wound. Preach it, and preach nothing else. Rely implicitly upon the old, old gospel. You need no other nets when you fish for men; those your Master has given you are strong enough for the great fish and have meshes fine enough to hold the little ones. Spread these nets and no others, and you do not need to fear the fulfillment of His Word, "*I will make you fishers of men*" (Matthew 4:19).

Second, to win a soul, it is necessary not only to instruct our hearer and make him know the truth, but also to impress it upon him so that he may feel it. A purely didactic ministry, which would always appeal to the understanding and leave the emotions untouched, would certainly be a limping ministry. *"The legs of the lame are not equal"* (Proverbs 26:7), said Solomon. The unequal legs of some laborers cripple them. We have seen such a one limping about with a long doctrinal leg, but a very short emotional leg. It is a horrible thing for a man to be so doctrinal that he can speak coolly of the doom of the wicked, so that, if he does not actually praise God for it, it costs him no anguish of heart to think of the ruin of millions of the human race. This is horrible!

I hate to hear the terrors of the Lord proclaimed by men whose hard countenances, harsh tones, and unfeeling spirits betray a sort of doctrinal dehydration: all the milk of human kindness is dried out of them. Having no feeling himself, such a preacher creates none. The people sit and listen while he keeps to dry, lifeless statements. They come to value him for being "sound," and they themselves come to be sound, too. I need not add, sound asleep. What life they have is spent sniffing out heresy and making earnest men offenders for a word. May we never be baptized into this spirit!

Whatever I believe, or do not believe, the command to love my neighbor as myself still retains its claim upon me. God forbid that any views or opinions should so contract my soul and harden my heart as to make me forget this law of love! Love for God is first, but by no means lessens the obligation of love for man. In fact, the first commandment includes the second. We are to seek our neighbors' conversion because we love them. We are to speak to them in terms of God's loving gospel because our hearts desire their eternal good.

A sinner has a heart as well as a head, emotions as well as thoughts. We must appeal to both. A sinner will never be converted until his emotions are stirred. Unless he feels sorrow for sin and a measure of joy in receiving the Word, there is not much hope for him. Truth must soak into the soul and dye it with its own color. The Word must be like a strong wind sweeping through the whole heart and swaying the whole man, even as a field of ripening corn waves in the summer breeze. Religion without emotion is religion without life.

But, still, we must consider how these emotions are caused. Do not play upon the mind by exciting feelings that are not spiritual. Some preachers are very fond of introducing funerals and dying children into their messages. They make the people weep through natural emotion. This may lead to something better, but in itself, what is its value? What is the good of opening up a mother's griefs or a widow's sorrows? I do not believe our merciful Lord has sent us to make men weep over their departed relatives by digging anew their graves or rehearsing past scenes of bereavement. Why would He?

It is true that you may profitably illustrate the deaths of a departed Christian and of a dying sinner as proof of the rest of faith in the one case, and the terror of conscience in the other. But it is out of the fact proved, and not out of the illustration itself, that the good must arise.

Natural grief is of no service in itself. Indeed, we look upon it as a distraction from higher thoughts and as a price too great to exact from tender hearts, unless we can repay them by engrafting lasting spiritual impressions upon the stock of natural emotion. "It was a very splendid oration, full of pathos," says one hearer. Yes, but what is the practical outcome of this pathos? A young preacher once remarked, "Were you not greatly struck to see so large a congregation weeping?" "Yes," said his judicious friend, "but I was more struck with the reflection that they would probably have wept more at a play." Exactly. The weeping in both cases may be equally valueless.

I saw a girl on board a steamboat reading a book and crying as if her heart would break. But when I glanced at the volume, I saw that it was only one of those silly novels that fill our railway bookstalls. Her tears were a sheer waste of moisture, and so are those that are produced by mere pulpit tale-telling and deathbed descriptions.

If our hearers will weep over their sins and after Jesus, let their tears flow in rivers. But if the object of their sorrow is merely natural and not at all spiritual, what good is done by starting them weeping? There might be some virtue in making people joyful, for there is sorrow enough in the world, and the more we can promote cheerfulness, the better. But what is the use of creating needless misery? What right do you have to go through the world pricking everybody with your lancet just to show your skill in surgery? A true physician only makes incisions in order to effect cures, and a wise man only excites painful emotions in men's minds with the distinct object of blessing their souls.

You and I must continue to drive at men's hearts until they are broken. Then we must keep on preaching "*Christ crucified*" (1 Corinthians 1:23) until their hearts are bound up. When this is accomplished, we must continue to proclaim the gospel until their whole nature is brought into subjection to the gospel of Christ. Even in these preliminaries, you will be made to feel the need of the Holy

Spirit to work with you and through you; but this need will be still more evident when you advance a step further to speak of the new birth itself, in which the Holy Spirit works in a style and manner most divine.

I have already insisted upon instruction and impression as necessary for soul-winning, but these are not all that is needed. Indeed, they are only means to the desired end. A far greater work must be done before a man is saved. A wonder of divine grace must be worked upon the soul, far transcending anything that can be accomplished by the power of man. Of all whom we would with pleasure win for Jesus, it is true, *"Except a man be born again, he cannot see the kingdom of God"* (John 3:3). The Holy Spirit must work regeneration in the objects of our love, or they never can become possessors of eternal happiness. They must be quickened into a new life, and they must become new creatures in Christ Jesus. The same energy that accomplishes resurrection and creation must put forth all its power upon them. Nothing short of this can meet the case. They must be born again from above.

At first, this might seem to eliminate human instrumentality altogether; but on turning to the Scriptures, we find nothing to justify such an inference—and much of quite an opposite tendency. We certainly find the Lord to be all in all, but we find no hint that the use of means must therefore be dispensed with. The Lord's supreme majesty and power are seen all the more gloriously because He works by means. He is so great that He is not afraid to put honor on the instruments He employs, by speaking of them in high terms and imputing to them great influence. It is sadly possible to say too little of the Holy Spirit—indeed, I fear this is one of the crying sins of the age. Yet that infallible Word, which always rightly balances truth, while it magnifies the Holy Spirit, does not speak lightly of the men by whom He works. God does not think His own honor to be so questionable that it can be maintained only by depreciating the human agent.

There are two passages in the Epistles which, when put together, have often amazed me. Paul compared himself both to a father and to a mother in the matter of the new birth. He says of one convert, *"Whom I have begotten in my bonds"* (Philemon 1:10); and of a whole church, he said, *"My little children, of whom I travail in birth again until Christ be formed in you"* (Galatians 4:19). This is going very far, much farther than modern orthodoxy would permit the most useful servant to venture. Yet it is language sanctioned, even dictated, by the Spirit of God Himself, and therefore it is not to be criticized. God infuses such mysterious power into the instrumentality which He ordains that we are called *"labourers together with God"* (1 Corinthians 3:9). This is at once the source of our responsibility and the ground of our hope.

Regeneration, or the new birth, works a change in the whole man. As far as we can judge, its essence lies in the implantation and creation of a new principle within the man. The Holy Spirit creates in us a new, immortal nature, which is known in Scripture as "the spirit," by way of distinction from the soul.

Our theory of regeneration is that man in his fallen nature consists only of body and soul, and that when he is regenerated there is created in him a new and higher nature—"the spirit"—that is a spark from the everlasting fire of God's life and love. This spark falls into the heart and abides there, making its receiver a *"partaker[…] of the divine nature"* (2 Peter 1:4). From that moment on, the man consists of three living parts—body, soul, and spirit—and the spirit becomes the reigning power of the three. (See 1 Thessalonians 5:23.)

You will all remember that memorable chapter about the resurrection, 1 Corinthians 15, where the distinction between soul and spirit is well brought out in the original Greek and may even be perceived in our Scripture version. The passage rendered, *"It is sown a natural body"* (verse 44), might be read:

> *It is sown a [soulish] body; it is raised a spiritual body. There is a [soulish] body, and there is a spiritual body. And so it is written, The first man Adam was made a living soul; the last Adam was made a quickening spirit. Howbeit that was not first which is spiritual, but that which is [soulish]; and afterward that which is spiritual.* (1 Corinthians 15:44–46)

We are first in the natural or soulish stage of being, like the first Adam. In regeneration we enter into a new condition and become possessors of the life-giving spirit. Without this spirit, no one can see or enter the kingdom of heaven. It must therefore be our intense desire that the Holy Spirit would visit our hearers and create them anew, that He would come down on those dry bones and breathe eternal life into the dead in sin. Until this is done, they can never receive the truth, for *"the natural man receiveth not the things of the Spirit of God: for they are foolishness unto him: neither can he know them, because they are spiritually discerned"* (1 Corinthians 2:14). *"The carnal mind is enmity against God: for it is not subject to the law of God, neither indeed can be"* (Romans 8:7). A new and heavenly mind must be created by omnipotence, or sinners must abide in death.

You see that we have before us a mighty work, for which we are, in ourselves, totally incapable. No Christian living can save a soul; neither can all of us together—all the saints on earth and in heaven—work regeneration in one single person. The whole business on our part is the height of absurdity unless we regard ourselves as used by the Holy Spirit and filled with His power.

On the other hand, the marvels of regeneration that attend our ministry are the best seals and witnesses of our commission. Whereas the apostles appealed to the miracles of Christ and to those that they performed in His name, we appeal to the miracles of the Holy Spirit, which are as divine and real as those of our Lord Himself. These miracles are the creation of a new life in the human heart and the total change of the whole being of those upon whom the Spirit descends.

As this God-begotten spiritual life in men is a mystery, we will speak more practically if we dwell on the signs following and accompanying it, for these are the things at which we must aim. First, regeneration will be shown in conviction of sin. This we believe to be an indispensable mark of the Spirit's work. As the new life enters the heart, one of its first effects is that it causes intense inward pain. Though now we hear of people being spiritually healed before they have been wounded and brought into a certainty of justification, and without ever having lamented their condemnation, we are very dubious as to the value of such healing and justification. This method is not according to the truth. God never clothes men until He has first stripped them; neither does He quicken them by the gospel until they are first slain by the law. When you meet with people in whom there is no trace of conviction of sin, you may be quite sure that they have not been worked upon by the Holy Spirit, for *"when he is come, he will reprove the world of sin, and of righteousness, and of judgment"* (John 16:8). When the Spirit of the Lord breathes on us, He withers all of man's glory, which is but as the flower, and then He reveals a higher and abiding glory.

Do not be astonished if you find this conviction of sin to be very acute and alarming. On the other hand, do not condemn those in whom it is less intense, for as long as sin is mourned over, confessed, forsaken, and abhorred, you have an evident fruit of the Spirit. Much of the horror and unbelief that go with conviction are not of the Spirit of God, but come from Satan or the corrupt nature. Yet there must be true and deep conviction of sin. This the preacher must labor to produce, for where this is not felt, the new birth has not taken place.

It is equally certain that true conversion may be known by the demonstration of a simple faith in Jesus Christ. You do not need me to speak to you of that, for you yourselves are fully persuaded of it. The production of faith is the very center of the target at which you aim. The proof that you have won a person's soul for Jesus is never before you until he has finished with himself and his own merits, and has closed in with Christ.

Great care must be taken that this faith is exercised upon Christ for complete salvation, and not for just a part of it. Numbers of people think that the Lord Jesus is available for the pardon of past sin, but they cannot trust Him for their preservation in the future. They trust for years past, but not for years to come. No such subdivision of salvation is spoken of in Scripture as the work of Christ. Either He bore all our sins, or none; either He saves us once for all, or not at all. His death can never be repeated, and it must have made sacrifice for the future sin of believers, or they are lost, since no further atonement can be supposed, and future sin is certain to be committed. Blessed be His name, for *"by him all that believe are justified from all things"* (Acts 13:39, emphasis added).

Salvation by grace is eternal salvation. Sinners must commit their souls into the keeping of Christ for all eternity. How else are they saved? Alas! According to the teaching of some, believers are only saved in part, and for the rest must depend upon their future endeavors. Is this the gospel? I think not. Genuine faith trusts a whole Christ for the whole of salvation.

Is it any wonder that many converts fall away, when, in fact, they were never taught to exercise faith in Jesus for eternal salvation, but only for temporary conversion? A faulty presentation of Christ begets a faulty faith. When this "faith" ebbs away in its own weakness, who is to blame for it? According to their faith, so it is unto them: the preacher and believer of a partial faith must together bear the blame of the failure when their poor mutilated trust comes to a breaking point.

I earnestly insist upon this because a semi-legal way of believing is so common. We must urge the trembling sinner to trust wholly and alone upon the Lord Jesus forever, or we will have him inferring that he is to begin in the Spirit and be made perfect by the flesh. He will surely walk by faith as to the past and then by works as to the future, which will be fatal. True faith in Jesus receives eternal life and sees perfect salvation in Him, whose one sacrifice sanctified the people of God once and for all.

The sense of being saved, completely saved in Christ Jesus, is not, as some suppose, the source of carnal security and the enemy of holy zeal, but the very reverse. Delivered from the fear that makes the salvation of self a more immediate object than salvation from self, and inspired by gratitude to his Redeemer, the regenerated believer becomes capable of virtue and is filled with enthusiasm for God's glory.

While trembling under a sense of insecurity, a person gives his chief thought to his own interests. Planted firmly on the Rock, he has time and heart to utter the new song that the Lord has put into his mouth. Then is his moral salvation complete, for self is no longer the lord of his being. Do not rest content until you see clear evidence in your converts of a simple, sincere, decided faith in the Lord Jesus. Together with undivided faith in Jesus Christ there must also be unfeigned repentance of sin. *Repentance* is an old-fashioned word, not much used by modern revivalists. "Oh!" said a Christian to me one day, "it only means a change of mind." This was thought to be a profound observation. Only a change of mind, but what a change! A change of mind with regard to everything! Instead of saying, "It is only a change of mind," it seems to me more truthful to say it is a great and deep change—even a change of the mind itself. But whatever the literal Greek word may mean, repentance is no trifle. You will not find a better definition of it than the one given in the children's hymn:

> Repentance is to leave
> The sins we loved before;
> And show that we in earnest grieve,
> By doing so no more.

True conversion is in all men attended by a sense of sin (which we have spoken of in the discussion of conviction); by a sorrow for sin or holy grief at having committed it; by a hatred of sin, which proves that its dominion is ended; and by a practical turning from sin, which shows that the life within the soul is operating upon the life without. True belief and true repentance are twins. It would be idle to attempt to say which is born first. All the spokes of a wheel move at once when the wheel moves, and thus all the graces commence action when regeneration is worked by the Holy Spirit. However, there must be repentance. No sinner looks to the Savior with a dry eye or a hard heart. Aim, therefore, at breaking up the hardness of the heart, at bringing home the reality of condemnation to the conscience and weaning the mind from sin. Do not be content until the whole mind is deeply and vitally changed in reference to sin.

Another proof of the conquest of a soul for Christ will be found in a real change of life. If a person does not live differently from what he did before, both at home and away from home, his repentance needs to be repented of, and his conversion is mere fiction. Not only action and language, but also spirit and temper must be changed. "But," says someone, "grace is often grafted to a crab apple stem." I know it is, but what is the fruit of the grafting? The fruit will be like the graft, and not like the nature of the original stem.

"But," says another, "I have an awful temper, and it overcomes me suddenly. My anger is soon over, and I feel very penitent. Though I cannot control myself, I am sure I am a Christian." Not so fast, my friend, or I may answer that I am quite as sure the other way. What is the use of your quick cooling off if in two or three moments you scald all around you? If a man stabs me in a fury, it will not heal my wound to see him grieving over his madness. A hasty temper must be conquered, and the whole man renewed, or conversion will be questionable.

We are not to hold up a modified holiness before our people and say, "You will be all right if you reach that standard." The Scripture says, "*He that committeth sin is of the devil*" (1 John 3:8). Abiding under the power of any known sin is a mark of our being the servants of sin, for "*his servants ye are to whom ye obey*" (Romans 6:16).

Idle are the boasts of a person who harbors within himself the love of any transgression. He may feel what he likes and believe what he likes, but he is still "*in the gall of bitterness, and in the bond of iniquity*" (Acts 8:23) while a single sin rules his heart and life. True regeneration implants a hatred of all evil. Where one sin is delighted in, the evidence is fatal to a sound hope. A man need not take a dozen poisons to destroy his life; one is quite sufficient.

There must be a harmony between the life and the profession of faith. A Christian professes to renounce sin. If he does not truly do so, his very name is a pretense. A drunken man came up to Rowland Hill one day and said, "I am one of your converts, Mr. Hill." "I daresay you are," replied that shrewd and sensible preacher, "but you are not one of the Lord's, or you would not be drunk." To this practical test we must bring all our work.

In our converts we must also see true prayer, which is the vital breath of godliness. If there is no prayer, you may be quite sure the soul is dead. We are not to urge men to pray as though it were the great gospel duty and the one pre-scribed way of salvation, for our chief message is, *"Believe on the Lord Jesus Christ"* (Acts 16:31). It is easy to put prayer in the wrong place and make it out to be a kind of work by which men are to live; but this you will, I trust, most carefully avoid.

Faith is the great gospel grace. However, we still cannot forget that true faith always prays, and when a person professes faith in the Lord Jesus and yet does not cry out to the Lord daily, we dare not believe in his faith or his conversion. The Holy Spirit's evidence by which He convinced Ananias of Paul's conversion was not, "Behold, he talks loudly of his joys and feelings," but, *"Behold, he prayeth"* (Acts 9:11). That prayer was earnest, heartbroken confession and supplication. Oh, to see this sure evidence in all who profess to be our converts!

There must also be a willingness to obey the Lord in all His commandments. It is a shameful thing for a man to profess discipleship and yet refuse to learn his Lord's will on certain points, or even dare to decline obedience when that will is known. How can a man be a disciple of Christ when he openly lives in disobedi-ence to Him?

If the professed convert deliberately declares that he knows his Lord's will but does not intend to obey it, you are not to pamper his presumption. Rather it is your duty to assure him that he is not saved. Has not the Lord said, *"Whosoever doth not bear his cross, and come after me, cannot be my disciple"* (Luke 14:27)? Mistakes as to what the Lord's will may be are to be tenderly corrected; but any willful disobedience is fatal: to tolerate it would be treason to Him who sent us. Jesus must be received as King and as Priest. Where there is any hesitancy on this, the foundation of godliness is not yet laid.

> "Faith must obey her Maker's will
>   As well as trust His grace;
> A pardoning God is jealous still
>   For His own holiness."

Thus, you see, my friends, the signs that prove that a soul is won are by no means trifling, and the work to be done before those signs can exist is not to be spoken of lightly.

A soulwinner can do nothing without God. He must cast himself on the Invisible or be a laughingstock to the devil, who regards with utter disdain all who imagine they can subdue human nature with mere words and arguments. To all who hope to succeed in such a work by their own strength, we would address the words of the Lord to Job:

> *Canst thou draw out leviathan with an hook? or his tongue with a cord which thou lettest down?...Wilt thou play with him as with a bird? or wilt thou bind him for thy maidens?...Lay thine hand upon him, remember the battle, do no more. Behold, the hope of him is in vain: shall not one be cast down even at the sight of him?* (Job 41:1, 5, 8–9)

Dependence upon God is our strength and our joy. In that dependence, let us go forth and seek to win souls for Him.

Now, in the course of our ministry, we will meet with many failures in this matter of soulwinning. There are many birds that I have thought I had caught. I have even managed to put salt on their tails, but they have gone flying off, after all.

I remember one man, whom I will call Tom Careless. He was the terror of the village in which he lived. There were many incendiary fires in the region, and most people attributed them to him. Sometimes, he would be drunk for two or three weeks at a spell, and then he raved and raged like a madman. That man came to hear me. I recollect the sensation that went through the little chapel when he came in. He sat there and fell in love with me. I think that was the only conversion that he experienced, but he professed to be converted. He had, apparently, been the subject of genuine repentance, and he became outwardly quite a changed character, gave up his drinking and swearing, and was in many respects an exemplary individual.

I remember seeing him tugging a barge, with perhaps a hundred people on board, whom he was drawing up to a place where I was going to preach. He was glorying in the work and singing as gladly and happily as any one of them. If anybody spoke a word against the Lord or His servant, he did not hesitate a moment, but knocked him over.

Before I left the district, however, I was afraid that there was no real work of grace in him. He was a wild sort of a man. I have heard of him taking a bird, plucking it, and eating it raw in the field. This is not the act of a Christian man. It is not one of the things that are lovely and of good repute. After I left the neighborhood, I asked after him, and I could hear nothing good of him. The spirit that kept him outwardly right was gone, and he became worse than he was before, if that were possible. Certainly, he was no better. He was unreachable by any agency.

That work of mine did not stand the fire. It would not bear even ordinary temptation, you see, after the person who had influence over the man was gone away. When you move from the village or town where you have been preaching, it is very likely that some, who did run well, will go back. They have affection for you, and your words have a kind of mesmerizing influence over them. When you are gone, the dog will run to his vomit, *"and the sow that was washed to her wallowing in the mire"* (2 Peter 2:22). Do not be in a hurry to count these supposed converts. Do not take them into the church too soon. Do not be too proud of their enthusiasm if it is not accompanied by some degree of softening and tenderness to show that the Holy Spirit has really been at work within them.

I remember another case of quite a different sort. I will call this person Miss Mary Shallow, for she was a young lady who was never blessed with many brains, but living in the same house with several Christian young ladies, she also professed to be converted. When I conversed with her, there was apparently everything that one could wish for. I thought of proposing her to the church, but it was judged best to give her a little trial first. After a while, she left the associations of the place where she had lived and went where she had nothing much to help her. I never heard anything more of her except that her whole time was spent in dressing herself as smartly as she could and in frequenting grand society. She is a type of those who do not have much mental furniture; if the grace of God does not take possession of the empty space, they very soon go back into the world.

I have known several like a young man whom I will call Charley Clever, who were uncommonly clever young fellows at anything and everything, very clever at counterfeiting religion when they took up with it. They prayed very fluently. They tried to preach and did it very well. Whatever they did, they did it with ease. It was as easy to them as kissing their hand.

Do not be in a hurry to take such people into the church. They have known no humiliation on account of sin, no brokenness of heart, no sense of divine grace. They cry, "All serene!" and away they go; but you will find that they will never repay you for your labor and trouble. They will be able to use the language of God's people as well as the best of His saints. They will even talk of their doubts and fears and will work up a deep experience in five minutes. They are a little too clever and are likely to do much harm when they get into the church, so keep them out, if you possibly can.

I remember one who was very saintly in his talk. I will call him John Fairspeech. Oh, how cunningly he could act the hypocrite, getting among our young men and leading them into all manner of sin and iniquity; yet he would call to see me and have a half hour of spiritual conversation! An abominable wretch, he was living in open sin at the very time that he was seeking to come to the Lord's Table, joining our societies, and anxious to be a leading man in every good work. Keep your watchful eye open, friends!

They will come to you with money in their hands, like Peter's fish with the silver in its mouth, and they will be so helpful in the work. They speak so softly and are such perfect gentlemen! Yes, I believe Judas was a man exactly of that kind, very clever at deceiving those around him. We must guard that we do not get any of these into the church; we must try to keep them out by any means.

You may say to yourself, at the close of a service, "Here is a splendid haul of fish!" Wait a bit. Remember our Savior's words: "*The kingdom of heaven is like unto a net, that was cast into the sea, and gathered of every kind: which, when it was full, they drew to shore, and sat down, and gathered the good into vessels, but cast the bad away*" (Matthew 13:47–48). Do not number your fish before they are broiled, or count your converts before you have tested and tried them.

This process may make your work somewhat slow, but then it will be sure. Do your work steadily and well, so that those who come after you may not have to say that it was far more trouble to them to clear the church of those who ought never to have been admitted than it was for you to admit them. If God enables you to build three thousand bricks into His spiritual temple in one day, you may do it; but Peter has been the only bricklayer who has accomplished that feat up until now.

Do not go and paint the wooden wall to resemble solid stone. Rather, let all your building be real, substantial, and true, for only this kind of work is worth the doing. Let all your building for God be like that of the apostle Paul:

According to the grace of God which is given unto me, as a wise masterbuilder, I have laid the foundation, and another buildeth thereon. But let every man take heed how he buildeth thereupon. For other foundation can no man lay than that is laid, which is Jesus Christ. Now if any man build upon this foundation gold, silver, precious stones, wood, hay, stubble; every man's work shall be made manifest: for the day shall declare it, because it shall be revealed by fire; and the fire shall try every man's work of what sort it is. If any man's work abide which he hath built thereupon, he shall receive a reward. If any man's work shall be burned, he shall suffer loss: but he himself shall be saved; yet so as by fire. (1 Corinthians 3:10–15)

2

GODWARD QUALITIES FOR SOULWINNING

O ur main business is to win souls. Like the blacksmiths, we need to know a great many things. Just as the smith must know about horses and how to make shoes for them, so we must know about souls and how to win them for God. The subject that I desire to address now is "Godward qualities for soulwinning." I will try to treat the subject in somewhat of a commonsense style, asking you to judge for yourselves what those qualifications would be that God would naturally look for in His servants—what qualifications He would be likely to approve and most likely to use.

You must know that every workman, if he is wise, uses a tool that is likely to accomplish the task he has in mind. There are some artists who have never been able to play except on their own violins, or to paint except with their own favorite brush and palette. Certainly, the great God, the mightiest of all the workers, in His great artistic work of soulwinning, loves to have His own special tools. In the old creation, He used none but His own instruments: *He spake, and it was done* (Psalm 33:9). In the new creation, the efficient agent is still His powerful Word. He speaks through the ministry of His servants. Therefore they must be fit trumpets for Him to speak through, fit instruments for Him to use for conveying His Word to the ears and hearts of men. Judge yourselves whether God will use you.

Imagine yourselves in His place and think about what kind of men those would be whom you would be most likely to use if you were in the position of the Most High God. I am sure you would say, first of all, that a man who is to be a soulwinner must have holiness of character. How few who attempt to preach think sufficiently of this! If they did, it would strike them at once that the Eternal would never use dirty tools, that the thrice-holy Jehovah would select only holy instruments for the accomplishment of His work. No wise man would pour his wine into foul bottles; no kind and good parent would allow his children to go to see an immoral play; and God will not go to work with instruments that would compromise His own character.

Suppose it were well known that, if men were only clever, God would use them, no matter what their character and conduct might be. Suppose it were understood that you could get on as well in the work of God by chicanery and untruthfulness as by honesty and uprightness. What person in the world, with any right feeling, would not be ashamed of such a state of affairs? But, beloved, it is not so.

There are many today who tell us that the theater is a great school for morals. That must be a strange school, where the teachers never learn their own lessons. In God's school, the teachers must be masters of the art of holiness. If we teach one thing by our lips and another by our lives, those who listen to us will say, "*Physician, heal thyself*' (Luke 4:23). You say, 'Repent.' Where is your own repentance? You say, 'Serve God, and be obedient to His will.' Do you serve Him? Are you obedient to His will?"

An unholy ministry would be the derision of the world and a dishonor to God. *"Be ye clean, that bear the vessels of the Lord"* (Isaiah 52:11). God will speak through a fool, if he is but a holy man. I do not, mean, of course, that God chooses fools to be His laborers. But let a man once become really holy, even though he has but the slenderest possible ability, and he will be a fitter instrument in God's hand than the man of gigantic accomplishments who is not obedient to the divine will, or clean and pure in the sight of the Lord God Almighty.

Dear friends, I do beg you to attach the highest importance to your own personal holiness. Do live unto God. If you do not, your Lord will not be with you. He will say of you, as He said of the false prophets of old, *"I sent them not,* nor commanded them: therefore they shall not profit this people at all, saith the Lord" (Jeremiah 23:32). You may preach very fine sermons, but if you yourselves are not holy, there will be no souls saved. The probability is that you will not come to the conclusion that your lack of holiness is the reason for your nonsuccess. You will blame the people, you will blame the age in which you live, you will blame anything except yourself. But there will be the root of the whole trouble.

Do I not know men of considerable ability and industry, who go on year after year without any increase in their churches? The reason is that they are not living before God as they ought to live. Sometimes the evil is in the minister's family: his sons and daughters are rebels against God, bad language is allowed even among his own children, and his reproofs are simply like Eli's mild question to his wicked sons, "Why do ye such things?" (1 Samuel 2:23). Sometimes, the man is worldly, greedy after gain, neglectful of his work. That is not according to God's mind, and He will not bless such a man.

When I listened to Mr. George Müller, as he was preaching at Mentone, it was just such an address as might be given in Sunday school by an ordinary teacher, yet I never heard a sermon that did me more good or more richly profited my soul. It was George Müller in it that made it so useful. There was no George Müller in it, in one sense, for he did not preach himself, but Christ Jesus the Lord. He was there only in his personality as a witness to the truth, but he bore that witness in such a manner that you could not help saying, "That man not only preaches what he believes, but also what he lives." In every word he uttered, his glorious life of faith seemed to fall upon both ear and heart. I was delighted to sit and listen to him. Yet, as for novelty or strength of thought, there was not a trace of it in the whole message. Holiness was the preacher's force; and you may depend on it that, if God is to bless us, our strength must lie in the same direction.

This holiness ought to show itself in communion with God. If a man delivers his own message, it will have such power as his own character gives to it. But if he delivers his Master's message, having heard it from his Master's lips, that will be quite another thing. If he can acquire something of the Master's spirit as He looked upon him and gave him the message, if he can reproduce the expression of his Master's face and the tone of his Master's voice, that also will be quite another thing.

Read the whole of McCheyne's *Memoir*. I cannot do you a better service than to recommend that you read it. There is no great freshness of thought, nothing very novel or striking in it. But as you read it, you will get good out of it, for you are conscious that it is the story of the life of a man who walked with God.

Moody would never have spoken with the force he did if he had not lived a life of fellowship with the Father, and with His Son, Jesus. The great force of any message lies in what has gone before it. You must get ready for the whole service by private fellowship with God and real holiness of character.

You will all confess that, if a man is to be used as a winner of souls, he must have spiritual life to a high degree. Friends, our work, under God, is to communicate life to others. It would be well to imitate Elisha when he stretched himself upon the dead child and brought him back to life. The prophet's staff was not sufficient, because it had no life in it. The life must be communicated by a living instrument; the man who is to communicate the life must have a great deal of it himself. You remember the words of Christ: *"He that believeth on me, as the scripture hath said, out of his belly shall flow rivers of living water"* (John 7:38). When the Holy Spirit dwells within a living child of God, He later rises out of the very midst of him as a fountain or a river, so that others may come and participate in the Spirit's gracious influences.

I do not think there is one of you who would wish to be a dead servant. God will not use dead tools for working living miracles. He must have living servants, and servants who are all alive. There are many who are alive, but they are not altogether alive.

I remember once seeing a painting of the resurrection that was one of the most unusual pictures I have ever seen. The artist had attempted to depict the moment when the event was only half done: there were some who were alive down as far as their waists; some had one arm alive; some had part of their heads alive. The thing is quite possible in our day. There are some people who are only about half alive; they have a living jaw, but not a living heart. Others have a living heart, but not a living brain. Still others have a living eye, so they can see things pretty plainly, but their hearts are not alive; they can give good descriptions of what they see, but there is no warmth of love in them.

There are some people who are half angel, and the other half—well, let us say, maggots. It is an awful contrast, but there are many instances of it. They preach well, and you say, as you listen to one of them, "That is a good man." You feel that he is a good man. You hear that he is going to someone's house for supper, and you think that you will go there for supper, too, so that you may hear what gracious words will fall from his lips. But, as you watch, out they come—maggots! He was an angel in the pulpit, but now come the worms! Often it is so, but it ought never to be. If we are to be witnesses for God, we must be all angel and no worms. May God deliver us from this state of semi-death!

May we be altogether alive from the crowns of our heads to the soles of our feet! I know such Christians. You cannot come into contact with them without feeling the power of the spiritual life that is in them. It is not merely while they are talking about religious topics, but even in the commonplace things of the world, that you are conscious there is something about them that tells you that they are altogether alive to God. Such Christians will be used by God for the quickening of others.

Suppose it were possible for you to be exalted into the place of God. Do you not think, next, that you would employ a person who thought little of himself, a person of humble spirit? If you saw a very proud man, would you be likely to use him as your servant? Certainly, the great God has a predilection for those who are humble. *"For thus saith the high and lofty One that inhabiteth eternity, whose name is Holy; I dwell in the high and holy place, with him also that is of a contrite and humble spirit, to revive the spirit of the humble, and to revive the heart of the contrite ones"* (Isaiah 57:15). God loathes the proud. Whenever He sees the high and mighty, He passes them by; but whenever He finds the lowly in heart, He takes pleasure in exalting them.

He delights especially in humility among His followers. It is an awful sight to see a proud Christian. There are few things that can give the devil more joy than this sight, whenever he takes his walks abroad. He delights in a proud Christian, and he says to himself, "Here are all the preparations for a great fall before long." Some pastors show their pride by their style in the pulpit. You can never forget the way in which they announced their text, *"It is I: be not afraid"* (John 6:20). Others manifest it in their attire, in the vanity of their dress, or in their talk, in which they continually magnify others' deficiencies and amplify their own excellencies.

There are two sorts of proud people. It is difficult sometimes to say which of the two is worse. First is the kind that is full of the vanity that talks about itself and invites other people to talk about it, too. It wants others to pat it on the back and stroke its feathers the right way. It is full of its little morsel of self and goes strutting about, saying, "Praise me, please, praise me, I want it," like a little child who goes to each one in the room and says, "Look at my new dress. Isn't it a beauty?" You may have seen some of these pretty dears. I have met many of them.

The other kind of pride is too big for that sort of thing and does not care for it. This kind despises people so much that it does not condescend to wish for their praises. It is so supremely satisfied with itself that it does not stoop to consider what others think of it. I have sometimes thought it is the more dangerous kind of pride, spiritually, but it is much the more respectable of the two. There is, after all, something very noble in being too proud to be proud. Suppose those great donkeys did bray at you; do not be such a donkey as to notice them.

But this other poor little soul says, "Well, everybody's praise is worth something." So he baits his mousetraps and tries to catch little mice of praise, so that he may cook them for his breakfast. He has a mighty appetite for such things.

Get rid of both kinds of pride if you have anything of either of them about you. The dwarf pride and the ogre pride are both abominations in the sight of the Lord. Never forget that you are disciples o Him who said, *"Learn of me; for I am meek and lowly in heart"* (Matthew 11:29).

Humility is not having a low opinion of yourself. If a man has a low opinion of himself, it is very possible that he is correct in his estimate. I have known some people whose opinion of themselves, according to what they have said, was very low indeed. They thought so little of their own powers that they never ventured to try to do any good. They said they had no self-reliance. I have known some people so wonderfully humble that they have always picked an easy place for themselves. They were too humble to do anything that would bring any blame upon them. They called it humility, but I thought "sinful love of ease" would have been a better name for their conduct.

True humility will lead you to think correctly about yourselves, to think the truth about yourselves. In the matter of soulwinning, humility makes you feel that you are nothing and nobody, and that if God gives you success in the work, you will be driven to ascribe to Him all the glory, for none of the credit for it could properly belong to you. If you do not have success, humility will lead you to blame your own folly and weakness, not God's sovereignty.

Why should God give blessing and then let you run away with the glory of it? The glory of the salvation of souls belongs to Him, and to Him alone. Then why should you try to steal it? You know how many attempt this theft. "When I was preaching at such-and-such a place, fifteen persons came into the vestry at the close of the service and thanked me for the message I had preached." You and your blessed sermon be hanged—I might have used a stronger word if I had liked—for really you are worthy of condemnation whenever you take to yourself the honor that belongs only to God.

You will remember the story of the young prince who came into the room where he thought his dying father was sleeping and put the king's crown on his head to see how it would fit him. The king, who was watching him, said, "Wait a little while, my son; wait until I am dead." So, when you feel any inclination to put the crown of glory on your head, just imagine that you hear God saying to you, "Wait until I am dead before you try on My crown." As that will never be, you had better leave the crown alone and let Him to whom it rightfully belongs wear it. Our song must always be, *"Not unto us, O Lord, not unto us, but unto thy name give glory, for thy mercy, and for thy truth's sake"* (Psalm 115:1).

Some men who have not had humility have been sent adrift from the ministry, for the Lord will not use those who will not ascribe the honor entirely to Him. Humility is one of the chief qualifications for usefulness. Many have passed away from the roll of useful men because they have been lifted up with pride, and so have fallen into *"the snare of the devil"* (1 Timothy 3:7).

Perhaps you feel that, as you are only poor students, there is no fear of your falling into this sin. But it is quite possible that with some of you, there is all the more danger, for this very reason, if God should bless you and put you in a prominent position. A man who is brought up in a high circle of society all his life does not feel the change as much when he reaches a position that to others would be a great elevation.

I always feel that, in the case of certain men whom I could name, a great mistake was made. As soon as they were converted, they were taken out of their former associations and put before the public as popular preachers. It was a great pity that many made little kings of them, and so prepared the way for their fall, for they could not bear the sudden change. It would have been a good thing for them if they had been verbally attacked and abused for ten or twenty years, for it probably would have saved them from much misery later.

I am always very grateful for the rough treatment I received in my earlier days from all sorts of people. The moment I did any good thing at all, they were at me like a pack of hounds. I did not have time to sit down and boast of what I had done, for they were raving and roaring at me continually. If I had been picked up all of a sudden and placed where I am now, it is likely that I would have gone down again just as quickly.

When you leave college, it will be well for you if you are treated as I was. If you have great success, it will turn your head, if God does not permit you to be afflicted in some way or other. If you are ever tempted to say, *"Is not this great Babylon, that I have built?"* (Daniel 4:30), just remember Nebuchadnezzar when he was *"driven from men, and did eat grass as oxen, and his body was wet with the dew of heaven, till his hairs were grown like eagles' feathers, and his nails like birds' claws"* (Daniel 4:33). God has many ways of bringing down proud Nebuchadnezzars, and He can very easily humble you, too, if you are ever lifted up with conceit. This point of the need for deep humility in a soulwinner does not require any proof; everyone can see, with half an eye, that God is not likely to bless any one much unless he is truly humble.

The next essential qualification for success in the work of the Lord—and it is a vital one—is a living faith. You know how the Lord Jesus could not do many mighty works in his own country because of the unbelief of the people. It is equally true that, with some Christians, God cannot do many mighty works because of their unbelief. If you will not believe, neither will you be used by God. *"According to your faith be it unto you"* (Matthew 9:29) is one of the unalterable laws of His kingdom. *"If ye have faith as a grain of mustard seed, ye shall say unto this mountain, Remove hence to yonder place; and it shall remove; and nothing shall be impossible unto you"* (Matthew 17:20). But if the question has to be put, *"Where is your faith?"* (Luke 8:25), the mountains will not move for you, nor will even a sycamore tree be stirred from its place.

You must have faith about your call to the ministry. You must believe without question that you are really chosen by God to be ministers of the gospel of Christ. If you firmly believe that God has called you to preach the gospel, you will preach it with courage and confidence. You will feel that you are going to your work because you have a right to do it. If you have an idea that possibly you are nothing but an intruder, you will do nothing of any account. You will be only a poor, diffident, half-apologetic preacher, for whose message no one will care. You must not begin to preach until you are quite sure that God has called you to the work.

A man once wrote to ask me whether he should preach or not. When I do not know what reply to send to someone, I always try to give as wise an answer as I possibly can. Accordingly, I wrote to this man, "Dear Friend, If the Lord has opened your mouth, the devil cannot shut it; but if the devil has opened it, may the Lord shut it up!" Six months later I met the man, and he thanked me for my letter, which, he said, greatly encouraged him to go on preaching. I said, "How was that?" He replied, "You said, 'If the Lord has opened your mouth, the devil cannot shut it.'" I said, "Yes, I did, but I also put the other side of the question." "Oh!" said he, at once, "that part did not relate to me." We can always have oracles to suit our own ideas if we know how to interpret them. If you have genuine faith in your call to the ministry, you will be ready, with Luther, to preach the gospel even while standing within the jaws of the leviathan, between his great teeth.

You must also believe that the message you have to deliver is God's Word. I would sooner know that you believed half-a-dozen truths intensely than a hundred only feebly. If your hand is not large enough to hold a great deal, hold firmly what you can. In a regular free-for-all, in which all of us were allowed to carry away as much gold as we could take from a heap, it might not be much use to have a very big purse. He who would close his hand tightly on as much as he could conveniently hold and not let it go would come off best in the scuffle.

We may sometimes do well to imitate the boy mentioned in the ancient fable. When he put his hand into a narrow-necked jar and grasped as many nuts as he could hold, he could not get even one of them out; but when he let half of them go, the rest came out easily. We must do the same. We cannot hold everything. It is impossible. Our hands are not big enough. But when we do get a grasp of something, let us hold it fast and grip it tightly.

Believe what you do believe, or else you will never persuade anybody else to believe it. Do not adopt this style, "I think this is a truth, and as a young man I beg to ask your kind attention to what I am about to say. I am merely suggesting," and so on. If this is your mode of preaching, you will go to work the easiest way to breed doubters. I would rather hear you say, "Young as I am, what I have to say comes from God, and God's Word says so-and-so and so-and-so. There it is, and you must believe what God says, or you will be lost." The people who hear you will say, "That young fellow certainly believes something," and very likely some of them will be led to believe, too. God uses the faith of His ministers to breed faith in others. You may depend upon it that souls are not saved by someone who doubts. The preaching of your doubts and questions cannot possibly decide a soul for Christ.

You must have great faith in the Word of God if you are to be winners of souls to those who hear it. You must also believe in the power of that message to save people. You may have heard the story of one of our first students, who came to me and said, "I have been preaching now for some months, and I do not think I have had a single conversion." I said to him, "And do you expect that the Lord is going to bless you and save souls every time you open your mouth?" "No, sir," he replied. "Well, then," I said, "that is why you do not get souls saved. If you had believed, the Lord would have given the blessing." I had caught him very nicely, but many others would have answered me in just the same way as he did. Trembling, they believe that it is possible, by some strange mysterious method, that once in a hundred times God might win a quarter of a soul. They have hardly enough faith to keep them standing in their boots. How can they expect God to bless them?

I like to go to the pulpit feeling, "This is God's Word that I am going to deliver in His name. It cannot return to Him void; I have asked His blessing on it; He is bound to give it; and His purposes will be answered, whether my message is a taste of 'life unto life' (2 Corinthians 2:16), or of 'death unto death' (verse 16) to those who hear it." Now, if this is how you feel, what will be the result if souls are not saved? Why, you will call special prayer meetings to seek to know why the people do not come to Christ. You will have inquirers' meetings for the anxious. You will meet the people with a joyful countenance, so that they may see that you are expecting a blessing. But at the same time, you will let them know that you will be grievously disappointed unless the Lord gives you conversions.

Yet how is it in many places? Nobody prays much about the matter, there are no meetings for crying out to God for a blessing, and the leaders never encourage the people to come and tell them about the work of grace in their souls. "*Verily I say unto you, They have their reward*" (Matthew 6:2). He gets what he asked for; he receives what he expected; his Master gives him his penny, but nothing else. The command is: "*Open thy mouth wide, and I will fill it*" (Psalm 81:10). But here we sit, with closed lips, waiting for the blessing. Open your mouth with full expectation and a firm belief; it will be unto you according to your faith.

The essential point is that you must believe in God and in His gospel if you are to be a winner of souls. Some other things may be omitted, but this matter of faith must never be. It is true that God does not always measure His mercy by our unbelief, for He has to think of other people as well as us. However, looking at the matter in a commonsense way, it does seem that the most likely instrument to do the Lord's work is the one who expects that God will use him and who goes forth to labor in the strength of that conviction. When success comes, he is not surprised, for he was looking for it. He sowed living seed, and he expected to reap a harvest from it. He cast his bread upon the waters, and he intends to search and watch until he finds it again.

Once more, if one is to succeed in his ministry and win many souls, he must be characterized by thorough earnestness. Do we not know some men who preach in such a lifeless manner that it is highly improbable that anybody will ever be affected by what they say? I was present when a good man asked the Lord to bless with the conversion of sinners the message that he was about to deliver. I do not wish to limit omnipotence, but I do not believe that God could bless to any sinner the sermon that was then preached unless He had made the hearer misunderstand what the preacher said.

It was one of those "bright poker sermons," as I call them. You know that there are pokers that are kept in drawing rooms and are meant to be looked at but never used. If you ever tried to poke the fire with them, would you not catch it from the lady of the house? These sermons are just like those pokers—polished, bright, and cold. They might have some relation to people living in outer space, but they certainly have no connection with anyone in this world. What good could come of such messages, no one can tell. I feel sure there is not enough power in them to kill a cockroach. Certainly, there is no power in them to bring a dead soul to life.

It can be truly said about some messages that, the more you think of them, the less you think of them. If any poor sinner goes to hear them with the hope of getting saved, you can only say that the preacher is more likely to stand in the way of his going to heaven than to point him to the right road.

You can depend on it: you will make men understand the truth if you really want to do so; but if you are not in earnest, it is not likely that they will be. If a man were to knock at my door in the middle of the night, and when I put my head out the window to see what was the matter, he were to say in a quiet, unconcerned way, "There is a fire at the back part of your house," I would have little thought of any fire and would feel inclined to empty a jug of water over him. If I am walking along, and a man comes up to me and says, in a cheerful tone of voice, "Good afternoon, sir, do you know that I am starving? I have not tasted food for ever so long: indeed, I have not," I would reply, "Good fellow, you seem to take it very lightly; I do not believe you lack much, or you would not be so unconcerned about it."

Some men seem to preach in this way: "My dear friends, this is Sunday, so here I am. I have been spending my time in my study all week, and now I hope you will listen to what I have to say to you. I do not know that there is anything in it that particularly concerns you. It might have some connection with the man in the moon. But I understand that some of you are in danger of going to a certain place that I do not wish to mention, only I hear that it is not a nice place for even a temporary residence. I have especially to preach to you that Jesus Christ did something or other, which, in some way or other, has something to do with salvation, and if you mind what you do," etc., etc. That is, in a nutshell, the full report of many a message. There is nothing in that kind of talk that can do anybody any good. After the man has kept on in that style for three-quarters of an hour, he closes by saying, "Now it is time to go home," and he hopes that the deacons will give him a couple of dollars for his services. Now, that sort of thing will not do. We did not come into the world to waste our own time, or other people's, in that way.

I hope we were born for something better than to be mere chips in the porridge, like the man I have described. Just imagine God sending a man into the world to try to win souls when that is his way of thinking and the whole spirit of his life. There are some ministers who are constantly worn out from doing nothing. They preach two messages, of a sort, on Sunday and say the effort almost wears them out. They go and give little pastoral visitations, which consist in drinking a cup of tea and talking small gossip. But there is no vehement agony for souls, no "Woe! Woe!" on their hearts and lips, no perfect consecration, no zeal in God's service. If the Lord sweeps them away, if He cuts them down as encumberances, it will not be surprising. Jesus Christ wept over Jerusalem, and you will have to weep over sinners if they are to be saved through you. Dear ones, do be earnest. Put your whole soul into the work, or else give it up.

Another qualification that is essential to soulwinning is great simplicity of heart. I do not know whether I can thoroughly explain what I mean by that, but I will try to make it clear by contrasting it with something else. You know some men who are too wise to be just simple believers. They know so much that they do not believe anything that is plain and simple. Their souls have been fed with such delicacies that they cannot live on anything but Chinese birds' nests and similar luxuries. There is no milk that ever came fresh from a cow that is good enough for them, for they are far too fine to drink such a beverage. Everything they have must be incomparable. Now, God does not bless these celestial dandies, these spiritual aristocrats. No, as soon as you see them, you feel ready to say, "They may do well enough as Lord So-and-So's servants, but they are not the men to do God's work. He is not likely to employ such grand gentlemen as they are."

When they select a text, they never explain its true meaning, but they dig around to discover something that the Holy Spirit never intended to convey by it. When they get hold of one of their precious "new thoughts," oh, dear, what a fuss they make over it! Here is a man who has found a stale herring! What a treat! It is so odoriferous! Now we will hear of this stale herring for the next six months, until somebody else finds another one. What a shout they send up! "Glory! Glory! Here is a new thought!" A new book comes out about it, and all these great men go sniffing around it to prove what deep thinkers and what wonderful men they are. God does not bless that kind of wisdom.

By simplicity of heart, I mean that a man clearly goes into the ministry for the glory of God and the winning of souls—and nothing else. There are some men who would like to win souls and glorify God if it could be done with due regard to their own interests. They would be delighted, certainly very pleased, indeed, to extend the kingdom of Christ, if the kingdom of Christ would give full play to their amazing powers. They would go in for soulwinning if it would induce people to parade them in triumph through the streets. They must be somebody; they must be known. They must be talked about and must hear people say, "What a splendid man that is!"

Of course, they give God the glory after they have sucked the juice out of it, but they first must have the orange themselves. Well, you know, there is that sort of spirit even among church leaders, and God cannot endure it. He is not going to have a man's leftovers. He will have all the glory or none at all. If a man seeks to serve himself, to get honor for himself, instead of seeking to serve God and honor Him alone, the Lord Jehovah will not use that man.

A person who is to be used by God must believe that what he is going to do is for the glory of God, and he must work from no other motive. When outsiders go to hear some preachers, all that they remember is that they were excellent actors, but here is a very different kind of preacher. After they have heard him preach, they do not think about how he looked or how he spoke, but about the solemn truths he uttered. A preacher may keep rolling out what he has to say in such a fashion that those who listen to him say to one another, "Do you not see that he lives by his preaching? He preaches for a living." I would rather hear it said, "That man said something in his message that made many of the people think less of him; he uttered the most distasteful sentiments; he did nothing but drive at us with the Word of the Lord while he was preaching. His one aim was to bring us to repentance and faith in Christ." That is the kind of man whom the Lord delights to bless.

I like to see men, like some before me here, to whom I have said, "Here you are, earning a good salary and likely to rise to a position of influence in the world. If you give up your business and come into the college, you will very likely be a poor Baptist minister all your life." Yet they have looked up and said, "I would sooner starve and win souls than spend my life in any other calling." Most of you are that kind of men—I believe you all are. There must never be an eye to the glory of God and the fat sheep; it must never be God's glory and your own honor and esteem among men. It will not do, not even if you preach to please God and your wife. It must be for God's glory alone, nothing less and nothing else, not even your wife. As the limpet is to the rock, so is she to the minister, but it will not do for him to think of pleasing even her. With true simplicity of heart, he must seek to please God, whether men and women are pleased or not.

Last, there must be a complete surrender of yourself to God, in this sense: that from this time, you wish to think not your own thoughts but God's thoughts, and that you determine to preach nothing of your own invention, but God's Word. Further, you resolve not even to give out that truth in your own way, but in God's way. Suppose you read your sermons, which is not very likely. You desire not to write anything but what is entirely according to the Lord's mind. When you get hold of a fine big word, you ask yourself whether it is likely to be a spiritual blessing to your people. If you think it would not be, you leave it out. Then there is that grand bit of poetry that even you could not understand, but you felt that you could not omit. However, when you asked whether it was likely to be instructive to the rank and file of your people, you were obliged to reject it. If you want to show the people how industrious you have been, then you must stick those gems, found on some literary dust heap, into your message. But if you desire to leave yourself entirely in God's hands, it is probable that you will be led to make some very simple statement, some slight remark, something with which everyone in the congregation is familiar. If you feel moved to put that in the sermon, put it in, by all means, even if you have to leave out the big words, the poetry, and the gems, for it may be that the Lord will bless that simple statement of the gospel to some poor sinner who is seeking the Savior.

If you yield yourself unreservedly to the mind and will of God, eventually, when you get out into the ministry, you will sometimes be impelled to use a strange expression or to offer an odd prayer, which at the time may have a strange sound even to yourself. Later it will be explained, when someone comes to tell you that he never understood the truth until you put it that day in such an unusual way.

You will be more likely to feel this influence if you are thoroughly prepared by study and prayer for your work in the pulpit. I urge you always to make all due preparation and even to write out in full what you think you should say. But do not deliver it memorized like a parrot repeating what it has been taught, for if you do that, you will certainly not leave yourself to the guidance of the Holy Spirit.

I have no doubt you will sometimes feel that there is a passage that you must put in, a fine piece by one of the British poets or a choice extract from some classic author. I do not suppose you would like it to be known, but you read it to a college friend. Of course, you did not ask him to praise it, because you felt sure that he could not help doing so. There was one particular piece in it that you have very seldom heard equaled. You are sure that no one could have done better. You are quite certain that, when the people hear your message, they will be obliged to feel there is something in it.

It may be, however, that the Lord will consider that it is too good to be blessed because there is too much in it. It is like the host of men that were with Gideon: they were too many for the Lord. He could not give the Midianites into their hands lest they would vaunt themselves against Him, saying, "Our own have gotten us the victory." When twenty-two thousand of them had been sent away, the Lord said to Gideon, "*The people are yet too many*" (Judges 7:4), and all of them had to be sent home except the three hundred men who lapped. (See verses 4–7.) Then the Lord said to Gideon, "*Arise, get thee down unto the host; for I have delivered it into thine hand*" (Judges 7:9). Similarly, the Lord says about some of your sermons, "I cannot do any good with them; they are too big." That message with the fourteen subdivisions—leave seven of them out, and perhaps the Lord will bless it.

Some day it may happen, right when you are in the middle of your message, that a thought will come across your mind, and you will say to yourself,

"Now, if I say this, that old deacon will make it hot for me. There is a gentleman who just came in who runs a school; he is a critic and will be sure not to be pleased if I say this. Besides, there is here 'a remnant according to the election of grace' (Romans 11:5) and the hypercritic up in the gallery will give me one of those heavenly looks that are so full of meaning." Now, brother, feel ready to say just anything that God gives you to say, irrespective of all the consequences and utterly regardless of what the hypercritics or the "lowpercritics" or anybody else will think or do.

One of the principal qualifications of a great artist's brush must be its yielding of itself to the artist so that he can do what he likes with it. A harpist will love to play on one particular harp because he knows the instrument, and the instrument almost appears to know him. So, when God puts His hand upon the very strings of your being and every power within you seems to respond to the movements of His hand, you are an instrument that He can use. It is not easy to stay in that condition, to be in such a sensitive state that you receive the impression that the Holy Spirit desires to convey and are influenced by Him at once.

If a great ship is out at sea and a tiny ripple comes on the waters, the ship is not moved by it in the least. A moderate wave comes, but the vessel does not feel it. The ship sits still upon the heart of the deep. But there. If only a fly drops into the water, they feel the motion and dance upon the tiny wave. May you be as mobile beneath the power of God as the cork is on the surface of the sea!

I am sure that this self-surrender is one of the essential qualifications for a preacher who is to be a winner of souls. When there is something that must be said if you are to be the means of saving that man in the corner, woe unto you if you are not ready to say it; woe unto you if you are afraid to say it; woe unto you if you are ashamed to say it; woe unto you if you do not dare to say it lest somebody up in the gallery would say that you were too earnest, too enthusiastic, too zealous!

These seven things, I think, are the Godward qualifications that would strike the mind of any of you, if you tried to put yourself in the position of the Most High and considered what you would wish to have in those whom you employed in the winning of souls. May God give us all of these qualifications, for Christ's sake! Amen.

3

MANWARD QUALITIES FOR SOULWINNING

Previously, I spoke of the Godward qualifications that would equip a person to be a soulwinner. I tried to describe to you the kind of person that the Lord would be most likely to use in the winning of souls. Now I would like to discuss the manward characteristics of a soulwinner.

I might almost mention the very same points that I enumerated earlier as being those that will be most effective manward. I think that those qualities that commend themselves to the notice of God as being most adapted to the end He desires are also likely to be approved by the object acted upon, that is, the soul of man.

There have been many men in the world who have not been at all adapted for this work. First, let me say that an ignorant person is not likely to be much of a soulwinner. A man who knows only that he is a sinner and that Christ is a Savior may be very useful to others in the same condition as himself. It is his duty to do the best he can with the knowledge he possesses. But on the whole, I would not expect such a man to be used to a great extent in the service of God. If he enjoyed a wider and deeper experience of the things of God, if he were, in the highest sense, a learned man because he had been taught by God, he could use his knowledge for the good of others. However, being to a great extent ignorant of the things of God himself, I do not see how he can make them known to other people.

Truly, there must be some light in the candle that is to lighten men's darkness, and there must be some information in one who is to be a teacher of his peers. The person who is almost or altogether ignorant, whatever will he has to do good, must be left out of the race of great soulwinners. He is disqualified from even entering the lists. Therefore, let us all ask that we may be well instructed in the truth of God, so that we may *"be able to teach others also"* (2 Timothy 2:2).

Granted, you are not ignorant, like those to whom I have been referring. But let us suppose that you are well instructed in the best of all wisdom. What are the qualities that you must have toward men if you are to win them for the Lord? I should say, there must be an evident sincerity about us, such that it is manifested at once to anyone who honestly looks for it. It must be quite clear to your hearers that you have a firm belief in the truths you are preaching. Otherwise, you will never make them believe them. Unless they are convinced, beyond all doubt, that you believe these truths yourselves, there will be no effectiveness or force in your preaching. No one must suspect you of proclaiming what you do not fully believe yourself. If this is ever the case, your work will be of no effect.

All who listen to you ought to be conscious that you are exercising one of the noblest callings and performing one of the most sacred functions that ever fell to man. If you have only a feeble appreciation of the gospel you profess to deliver, it is impossible for those who hear your proclamation to be greatly influenced by it. I heard it asked about a certain preacher, "Did he preach a good message?" The reply to the inquiry was, "What he said was very good." "But did you not profit by the message?" "No, not in the slightest degree." "Was it not a good talk?" Again came the first answer, "What he said was very good." "What do you mean? Why did you not profit by the message if what the preacher said was very good?" This was the explanation that the listener gave: "I did not profit by the message because I did not believe in the man who delivered it. He was simply an actor performing a part. I did not believe that he felt what he preached, nor that he cared whether we felt or believed it or not."

Where such a state of things as that exists, the hearers cannot be expected to profit by the sermon, no matter what the preacher may say. They may try to imagine that the truths he utters are precious. They may resolve that they will feed upon the provision, no matter who may set the dish before them. However, it is no use. They cannot separate the spiritless speaker from the message he delivers so carelessly. As soon as a person lets his work become a matter of mere form or routine, it sinks into a performance in which the preacher is simply an actor. He is only acting a part, as he might in a play at the theater, and not speaking from his inmost soul, as a man sent from God.

I do plead with you, speak from your hearts or else not at all. If you can be silent, be silent; if you must speak for God, be thoroughly sincere about it. It would be better for you to go back to the business world and weigh butter, sell reels of cotton, or do anything rather than pretend to be ministers of the gospel, unless God has called you to the work.

I believe that the most damnable thing a person can do is to preach the gospel merely as an actor and turn the worship of God into a kind of theatrical performance. Such a caricature is more worthy of the devil than of God. Divine truth is far too precious to be made the subject of such a mockery. You may depend upon the fact that once the people suspect that you are insincere, they will never listen to you again except with disgust. Also, they will not be likely to believe your message if you give them cause to think that you do not believe it yourselves.

I hope I am not wrong in supposing that all of us are thoroughly sincere in our Master's service. Therefore, I will go on to what seems to me to be the next manward qualification for soulwinning, which is evident earnestness. The command to the one who would be a true servant of the Lord Jesus Christ is, "*Thou shalt love the Lord thy God with all thy heart, and with all thy soul, and with all thy mind, and with all thy strength*" (Mark 12:30). If a person is to be a soulwinner, he must have intensity of emotion as well as sincerity of heart. You may preach the most solemn warnings and the most dreadful punishments in such an indifferent or careless way that no one will be affected by them in the least. You may repeat the most affectionate exhortations in such a halfhearted manner that no one will be moved either to love or fear.

I believe that, for soulwinning, there is more in this matter of earnestness than in almost anything else. I have seen and heard some who were very poor preachers, yet who brought many souls to the Savior through the earnestness with which they delivered their message. There was absolutely nothing to their sermons (until the merchant used them to wrap his butter), yet those feeble messages brought many to Christ. It was not what the preachers said, as much as how they said it that carried conviction to their hearers' hearts. The simplest truth was so driven home by the intensity of the words and emotion of the one from whom it came that it was surprisingly effective.

If any gentleman here would present me with a cannonball—say one weighing fifty or a hundred pounds—for me to roll across the room, and if another would entrust me with a rifle bullet and a rifle out of which I could fire it, I know which would be the more effective of the two. Let no man despise the little bullet, for very often that is the one that kills the sin and the sinner, too. So, it is not the bigness of the words you speak, but the force with which you deliver them that decides the outcome of the what you say.

I have heard of a ship that was fired at by the cannon in a fort, but no impression was made upon it until the general in command gave the order for the balls to be made red-hot. Then the vessel was sent to the bottom of the sea in three minutes. That is what you must do with your messages—make them red-hot. Never mind if men say you are too enthusiastic or even too fanatical; give them red-hot shot. There is nothing else half as good for the purpose you have in view. We do not go out snowballing on Sundays; we go fire-balling. We ought to hurl grenades into the enemy's ranks.

What earnestness our theme deserves! We have to tell of an earnest Savior, an earnest heaven, and an earnest hell. How earnest we ought to be when we remember that in our work we are dealing with souls that are immortal, with sin that is eternal in its effects, with pardon that is infinite, and with terrors and joys that are to last forever and ever! A person who is not in earnest when he has such a theme as this—can he possess a heart at all? Could one be discovered even with a microscope? If he were dissected, probably all that could be found would be a pebble, a heart of stone, or some other substance equally incapable of emotion. I trust that, when God gave us hearts of flesh for ourselves, He gave us hearts that could feel for other people, also.

These things being taken for granted, I would say, next, that it is necessary for one who is to be a soulwinner to have an evident love for his hearers. I cannot imagine someone being a winner of souls when he spends most of his time berating his congregation and talking as if he hated the very sight of them. Such men seem happy only when they are emptying vials of wrath over those who have the unhappiness of listening to them.

I heard of a brother preaching from the text, "*A certain man went down from Jerusalem to Jericho, and fell among thieves*" (Luke 10:30). He began his message thus: "I do not say that this man came to the place where we are, but I do know another man who did come to this place and fell among thieves." You can easily guess what would be the result of such caustic attacks. I know of one man who preached from the passage, "*And Aaron held his peace*" (Leviticus 10:3). One who heard him said that the difference between the preacher and Aaron was that Aaron held his peace, but the preacher did not. On the contrary, he raved at the people with all his might.

You must have a real desire for the good of the people if you are to have much influence over them. Why, even dogs and cats love the people who love them; human beings are much the same as these dumb animals. People very soon get to know when a cold man gets into the pulpit. They sense he is one of those who seem to have been carved out of a block of marble.

There have been one or two from here of that kind, and they have never succeeded anywhere. When I have asked the cause of their failure, in each case, the reply has been, "He is a good man, a very good man; he preaches well, very well; but still we do not get along with him." I have asked, "Why do you not like him?" The reply has been, "Nobody ever did like him." "Is he quarrelsome?" "Oh, dear, no; I wish he would make a row." I try to fish out what the drawback is, for I am very anxious to know. At last someone says, "Well, sir, I do not think he has any heart; at least, he does not preach and act as if he had any." It is very sad when the failure of any ministry is caused by lack of heart.

You ought to have a great big heart, like the harbor at Portsmouth or Plymouth, so that all the people in your congregation could come and cast anchor in it and feel that they were under the shelter of a great rock. Do you not notice that men succeed in the ministry and win souls for Christ in direct proportion as they are men with large hearts? Think, for instance, of Dr. Brook, a mass of a man, one who had a heart of compassion. (What good is a pastor who does not?) I do not hold up the accumulation of flesh as an object worthy of your attainment, but I do say that you must have big hearts if you are to win men to Jesus. You must be Greathearts if you are to lead many pilgrims to the Celestial City. I have seen some very lean men who said that they were perfectly holy. I could almost believe that they could not sin, for they were like old bits of leather. There did not appear to be anything in them that was capable of sinning. I met one of these "perfect" men once: he was just like a piece of seaweed—no humanity in him.

I like to see a trace of humanity somewhere or other about a person, and people in general like it, too. They get on better with someone who has some human nature in him. Human nature, in some aspects, is an awful thing. But when the Lord Jesus Christ took it and joined His own divine nature to it, He made a grand thing of it. Human nature is a noble thing when it is united to the Lord Jesus Christ. Those men who keep to themselves like hermits, living a supposed sanctified life of self-absorption, are not likely to have any influence in the world or to do good to their fellow creatures. You must love people and mix with them if you are to be of service to them.

There are some pastors who really are much better men than others, yet they do not accomplish as much good as those who are more human, those who go and sit down with the people and make themselves at home with them as much as possible. Friends, you know that it is possible for you to appear to be just a tiny bit too good, so that people will feel that you are altogether transcendental beings, more fit to preach to angels, cherubim, and seraphim than to the fallen sons of Adam. Just be men among men, keeping yourselves clear of all their faults and vices, but mingling with them in perfect love and sympathy. Feel that you would do anything in your power to bring them to Christ, so that you might even say, with the apostle Paul:

> Though I be free from all men, yet have I made myself servant unto all, that I might gain the more. And unto the Jews I became as a Jew, that I might gain the Jews; to them that are under the law, as under the law, that I might gain them that are under the law; to them that are without law, as without law, (being not without law to God, but under the law of Christ,) that I might gain them that are without law. To the weak became I as weak, that I might gain the weak: I am made all things to all men, that I might by all means save some.   (1 Corinthians 9:19–22)

The next manward qualification for soulwinning is evident unselfishness. A person ceases to bring men to Christ as soon as he becomes known as selfish. Selfishness seems to be ingrained in some people. You see it at the table at home, in the house of God, everywhere. When such individuals come to deal with a church and congregation, their selfishness soon manifests itself. They intend to get all they can, although in the Baptist ministry they do not often get much. I hope each of you will be willing to say, "Well, let me have but food and clothing, and I will be content." (See 1 Timothy 6:8.)

If you try to put the thought of money away from you altogether, the money will often come back to you doubled; but if you seek to grab and grasp everything, you will very likely find that it will not come to you at all. Those who are selfish in the matter of salary will be the same in everything else. They will not want their people to know anyone who can preach better than they, and they cannot bear to hear of any good work going on anywhere except in their own chapels. If there is a revival at another place, and souls are being saved, they say with a sneer, "Yes, there are many converts, but what are they? Where will they be in a few months' time?" They think far more of their own gain of one new member per year than of their neighbor's hundred at one time.

If your people see that kind of selfishness in you, you will soon lose power over them. If you make up your mind that you will be a great man, no matter who has to be thrust aside, you will go to the cats as sure as you are alive. What are you, my dear friend, that people should all bow down and worship you and think that in all the world there is no one besides you? I will tell you the way it is: the less you think of yourself, the more people will think of you; and the more you think of yourself, the less people will think of you. If any of you have any trace of selfishness about you, I urge you to get rid of it at once, or you will never be fit instruments for the winning of souls for the Lord Jesus Christ.

I am sure that another thing that is desired in a soulwinner is holiness of character. It is no use talking about "the higher life" on Sundays and then living the lower life on weekdays. A Christian pastor must be very careful not only to be innocent of actual wrongdoing, but also not to be a cause of offense to the weak ones of the flock. *"All things are lawful for me, but all things are not expedient"* (1 Corinthians 10:23). We ought never to do anything that we judge to be wrong, but we also ought to be willing to abstain from things that might not be wrong in themselves, but that might be an occasion of stumbling to others. When people see that we not only preach about holiness, but that we are also holy ourselves, they will be drawn toward holy things by our character as well as by our preaching.

I also think that, if we are to be soulwinners, there must be a seriousness of manner about us. Some people are serious by nature. Some time ago, a gentleman in a railway carriage overheard a conversation between two of the passengers. One of them said, "Well, now, I think the Church of Rome has great power and is likely to succeed with the people, because of the evident holiness of her leaders. There is, for instance, Cardinal So-and-So, who is just like a skeleton. Through his long fasting and prayers, he has reduced himself almost to skin and bone. Whenever I hear him speak, I feel at once the force of the holiness of the man. Now, look at Spurgeon; he eats and drinks like an ordinary mortal. I would not give a pin to hear him preach." His friend heard him very patiently, and then said quite quietly, "Did it ever strike you that the Cardinal's appearance was to be accounted for by the fact of his liver being out of order? I do not think it is grace that makes him as lean as he is. I believe it is his liver."

There are some men who are naturally of a melancholy disposition and are thus always very serious. However, in them, it is not a sign of grace, but only an indication that their livers are out of order. They never laugh; they think it would be wicked to do so. They go about the world increasing the misery of humankind, which is dreadful enough without the addition of their unnecessary portion. Evidently, such people imagine that they were predestined to pour buckets of cold water upon all human mirth and joy. So, dear friends, if any of you are very serious, you must not always attribute it to grace, for it may all be due to the state of your liver.

Most of us, however, are far more inclined to the laughter that does *"good like a medicine"* (Proverbs 17:22), and we will need all our cheerfulness if we are to comfort and lift up those who are cast down. But we will never bring many souls to Christ if we are full of the levity that characterizes some men. People will say, "It is all a joke; just hear how those young fellows jest about religion. It is one thing to listen to them when they are in the pulpit, but it is quite another matter to listen to them when they are sitting around the supper table."

I have heard of a man who, when he was dying, sent for the pastor to come and see him. When the pastor came in, the dying man said to him, "Do you remember a young man walking with you one evening, some years ago, when you were going out to preach?" The pastor said that he did not. "I recollect it very well," replied the other. "Do you not remember preaching at such-and-such a village, from such-and-such a text, and after the service a young man walked home with you?" "Oh, yes, I remember that very well!"

"Well, I am the young man who walked home with you that night. I remember your sermon; I shall never forget it." "Thank God for that," said the preacher. "No," answered the dying man, "you will not thank God when you have heard all I have to say. I walked with you to the village, but you did not say much to me on the way there, for you were thinking over your message. You deeply impressed me while you were preaching, and I was led to think about giving my heart to Christ. I wanted to speak to you about my soul on the way home, but the moment you got out, you cracked a joke, and all the way back you made such fun of serious subjects that I could not say anything about what I felt. It thoroughly disgusted me with religion and all who professed it. Now I am going to be damned, and my blood will lie at your door, as sure as you are alive." Just so, he passed out of the world.

One would not like anything of that sort to happen to him. Therefore, take heed, friends, that you give no occasion for it. There must be a prevailing seriousness about our whole lives; otherwise, we cannot hope to lead other men to Christ.

Finally, if we are to be used by God as soulwinners, we must have in our hearts a great deal of tenderness. I like a person to have a certain amount of holy boldness, but I do not care to see him brazen and impudent. A young man goes into a pulpit, apologizes for attempting to preach, and hopes the people will bear with him. He is not sure he has anything particular to say. If the Lord had sent him, he might have had some message for them, but he feels so young and inexperienced that he cannot speak very positively about anything. Such talk will never save a mouse, much less an immortal soul.

If the Lord has sent you to preach the gospel, why should you apologize? Ambassadors do not apologize when they go to foreign courts. They know their monarchs have sent them, and they deliver their messages with all the authority of king and country behind them. Neither is it worthwhile to call attention to your youth. You are only a trumpet of ram's horn, and it does not matter whether you were pulled off the ram's head yesterday or twenty-five years ago. If God blows through you, there will be enough noise, and more than mere noise. If He does not, nothing will come of the blowing.

When you preach, speak out straight, but be very tender about it. If there is an unpleasant thing to be said, take care that you put it in the kindest possible form. Some of our men had a message to deliver to a certain Christian brother, and when they went to him, they put it so awkwardly that he was grievously offended. When I spoke to him about the matter, he said, "I would not have minded your speaking to me; you have a way of putting an unpleasant truth so that a man cannot be offended with you, no matter how much he may dislike the message you bring to him." I said, "But I put the matter just as strongly as the others did." "Yes, you did," he replied, "but they said it in such a nasty way that I would not stand it. Why, sir, I would rather be blown up by you than praised by those other people!"

There is a way of doing such things so that the person reproved feels positively grateful to you. One may kick a man downstairs in such a way that he will rather like it, while another may open a door in such an offensive way that you do not want to go through until he is out of the way. If I have to tell anyone certain unpalatable truths that are necessary for him to know if his soul is to be saved, it is a stern necessity for me to be faithful to him. Yet I will try to deliver my message in such a way that he will not be offended at it. Then, if he does take offense, he must. The probability is that he will not, but rather, that what I say will take effect on his conscience.

I know some men who preach as if they were prizefighters. When they are in the pulpit, they remind me of the Irishman at Donnybrook Fair: all the way through the message, they appear to be calling someone to come up and fight them. They are never happy except when they are pitching into somebody or other. There is a man who often preaches on Clapham Common. He does it so pugnaciously that the infidels whom he assails cannot endure it, and there are frequent fights and rows.

There is a way of preaching that upsets everyone. If some men were allowed to preach in heaven, I am afraid they would set the angels fighting. I know a number of ministers of this kind. There is one who, to my knowledge, has been at over a dozen places during his not-very-long ministerial life. You can tell where he has been by the ruin he leaves behind him. He always finds the churches in a sad state, and he immediately begins to "purify" them—that is, to destroy them. As a general rule, first the principal deacon leaves. Next, all the leading families leave. Before long, the man has purified the place so effectively that the few people who are left cannot afford to keep him. Off he goes to another place and repeats the process of destruction.

He is a spiritual ship-scuttler and is never happy except when he is boring a hole through the planks of some good vessel. He says he believes the ship is unsound. So he bores and bores until, just as she is going down, he slips off and gets on board another vessel, which soon sinks in the same manner.

He feels that he is called to the work of separating "the precious from the vile" (Jeremiah 15:19)—and a preciously vile mess he makes of it. I have no reason to believe it is the condition of the liver with this brother. It is more likely that there is something wrong with his heart. Certainly, there is an evil disease upon him that always makes me get into a bad temper with him. It is dangerous to entertain him for more than three days, for he would quarrel in that time with the most peaceably disposed man in the world. I never intend to recommend him to a pastorate again. Let him find a place for himself, if he can, for I believe that, wherever he goes, the place will be like the spot where the foot of the Tartar's horse is put down—the grass will never again grow there.

If any of you have even a little bit of this nasty, bitter spirit about you, go to sea so that you may get rid of it. I hope it may happen to you according to the legend that is told concerning Muhammad: "In every human being," so the story runs, "there are two black drops of sin. The great prophet himself was not free from the common lot of evil, but an angel was sent to take his heart and squeeze out of it the two black drops of sin." Get those black drops out somehow while you are in college. If you have any malice, ill will, or bad temper in you, ask the Lord to take it out of you while you are here. Do not go into the churches to fight as others have done.

"Still," says a brother, "I am not going to let the people tread on me. I will take the bull by the horns." You will be a great fool if you do. I never felt I was called to do anything of the kind. Why not let the bull alone to go where he likes? A bull is likely to project you into space if you meddle with his horns. "Still," says another, "we must set things right." Yes, but the best way to set things right is not to make them more wrong than they are. Nobody thinks of putting a mad bull into a china shop in order to get the china cleaned. Likewise, no one can, by a display of bad temper, set right anything that is wrong in the church. Take care to speak the truth in love, especially when you are rebuking sin.

I believe, friends, that soulwinning is to be done by men of the character that I have been describing. This will be the case to the greatest degree when they are surrounded by people of a similar character. You need to get the very atmosphere in which you live and work permeated with this spirit before you can rightly expect the fullest and richest blessings. Therefore, may you and all your people be all that I have pictured, for the Lord Jesus Christ's sake!

4

MESSAGES LIKELY TO
WIN SOULS

Friends, I am going to speak I am next going to speak to you about the kind of messages that are most likely to convert people. We will examine the sort of messages we should deliver if we really want our hearers to believe in the Lord Jesus Christ and to be saved. Of course, we are all perfectly agreed that the Holy Spirit alone can convert a soul; no one can enter the kingdom of God unless they are born again from above. All the work is done by the Holy Spirit. We must not take to ourselves any part of the credit for the result of the work, for it is the Spirit who creates and works in man according to the eternal purpose of God. Still, we may be instruments in His hands, for He chooses to use instruments, and He chooses them for wise reasons.

There must be an adaptation of the means to the end, as there was with David when he went forth with the sling and stone to slay Goliath of Gath. Goliath was a tall fellow, but a stone from a sling can rise. Besides, the giant was armed, protected, and scarcely vulnerable except on his forehead, so that was the very place to hit him. Though David took a sling, it was not so much because he had no other weapon but because he had practiced slinging, as most boys do in some form or other. Then he chose a smooth stone because he knew it would fit the sling. David picked the right kind of stone to pierce Goliath's head, so that, when he hurled the stone at the giant, it struck him in the forehead and penetrated his brain.

You will find that this principle of adaptation runs through the whole work of the Holy Spirit. When a man was needed to be the apostle to the Gentiles, the Holy Spirit selected the large-minded, well-trained, highly-educated Paul. He was more adapted for such work than was the somewhat narrow, though strong-minded, Peter, who was better suited for preaching to the Jews and was of far more use to the circumcision than he ever could have been among the uncircumcision. Paul, in his place, was the right man, and Peter, in his place, was the right man.

You may see in this principle a lesson for yourselves and seek to adapt your means to your end. The Holy Spirit can convert a soul by any text of Scripture, apart from your paraphrase, your comment, or your exposition. But you know there are certain Scriptures that are the best to bring to the minds of sinners. If this is true about your texts, it is much more so concerning your messages to your hearers.

As to which messages are most likely to be blessed to the conversion of those to whom they are preached, I would say that first are those sermons which are distinctly aimed at the conversion of the hearers. Some time ago, I heard a prayer from a minister who asked the Lord to save souls by the sermon he was about to deliver. I do not hesitate to say that God Himself could not bless the message to that end unless He made the people misunderstand all that the preacher said to them, because the whole message was apt to harden the sinner in his sin rather than to lead him to renounce it and to seek the Savior. There was nothing in it that could be blessed to any hearer unless he turned it inside out or upside down.

The message did me good through the principle that was applied by a dear old lady to the minister she was obliged to hear. When asked, "Why do you go to such a place?" she replied, "Well, there is no other place of worship to which I can go." "But it must be better to stay at home than to hear such stuff," said her friend. "Perhaps so," she answered, "but I like to go out to worship even if I get nothing by going. Sometimes you will see a hen scratching all over a heap of rubbish to try to find some corn; she does not get any, but it shows that she is looking for it, and using the means she has been given to get it. Then, too, the exercise warms her." The old woman was saying that scratching over the poor sermons she heard was a blessing to her because it exercised her spiritual faculties and warmed her spirit.

There are messages of such a kind that, unless God takes to ripening wheat by means of snow and ice and begins to illuminate the world by means of fogs and clouds, He cannot save souls under them. The preacher himself evidently does not think that anybody will be converted by them. If two hundred or only two were converted by them, nobody would be as astonished as the preacher himself.

In fact, I know a man who was converted, or at least convicted, under the preaching of a minister of that kind. In a certain parish church, as the result of the clergyman's preaching, there was a man who was under deep conviction of sin. He went down to see his minister, but the poor man did not know what to make of him and said to him, "I am very sorry if there was anything in my message that made you uncomfortable; I did not mean it to be so." "Well, sir," answered the troubled man, "you said that we must be born again." "Oh!" replied the clergyman, "that was all done in baptism." The man, who was not to be put off, said, "But, sir, you did not say so in your sermon; you spoke of the necessity of regeneration." "Well, I am very sorry I said anything that made you uncomfortable, for really I think all is right with you. You are a good sort of a fellow; you were never a poacher, or anything else that is bad." "That may be, sir, but I have a sense of sin, and you said we must be new creatures." "Well, my good man," said the perplexed parson, "I do not understand such things, for I never was born again." He sent him to a Baptist minister. The man is now a Baptist minister, partly as a result of what he learned from the preacher who did not himself understand the truth he had declared to others.

Of course, God can convert a soul by such a message, and by such a minister, but it is not likely. It is more probable that, in His infinite sovereignty, He will work in a place where a wholehearted man is preaching to people the truth that he himself has received, all the while earnestly desiring their salvation and ready to guide them further in the ways of the Lord as soon as they are saved. God does not usually lay His newborn children down among people where the new life will not be understood, or where it will be left without any proper nurture or care.

So, if you want your hearers to be converted, you must see that your preaching aims directly at conversion, and that it is such that God will be likely to bless to that end. When that is the case, then look for souls to be saved, and look for a great number of them, too. Do not be satisfied when a single soul is converted.

Remember that the rule of the kingdom is, *"According to your faith be it unto you"* (Matthew 9:29).

In a message at the Tabernacle, I said that I was glad that Scripture was not written, "According to your unbelief be it unto you." If there is in us a great faith, God will give us blessing according to our faith. Oh, that we were altogether rid of unbelief, that we believed great things of God, and with heart and soul preached in such a way that men were likely to be converted by our messages, proclaiming truths likely to convert them, and declaring them in a manner that would be likely to be blessed to the conversion of our hearers! Of course, all the while, we must trust the Holy Spirit to make the work effective, for we are but instruments in His hands.

But coming a little closer to our subject, if the people are to be saved, it must be by messages that correct them. You first have to get them to come where they can hear the gospel, for there is, in London, anyway, a great aversion to places of worship. I am not much surprised that it is so concerning many churches and chapels.

I think, in many instances, the common people do not attend such services because they do not understand the theological "lingo" that is used in the pulpit. It is neither English nor Greek, but gibberish. When a working man goes once and listens to these fine words, he says to his wife, "I will not go there again, Sal; there is nothing there for me, or for you. There may be a good deal for a gentleman that's been to college, but there is nothing for the likes of us." No, friends, we must preach in what Whitefield used to call "market language" if we want all classes of the community listening to our message.

Then, when they do come in, we must preach interestingly. The people will not be converted while they are asleep. If they go to sleep, they should be at home in bed, where they would sleep much more comfortably. We must have the minds of our hearers awake and active if we are to do them real good. You will not shoot your birds unless you get them to fly. You must cause them to start up from the long grass in which they are hiding. I would sooner use a little of what some very proper preachers regard as a dreadful thing, that wicked thing called humor—I would sooner wake the congregation up that way than have it said that I droned at them until we all went to sleep together. Sometimes, it may be quite right to have it said of us, as it was said of Rowland Hill, "What does that man mean? He actually made the people laugh while he was preaching." "Yes," was the wise answer, "but did you not see that he made them cry directly after?" That was good work, and it was well done.

I sometimes tickle my oyster until he opens his shell, and then I slip the knife in. He would not have opened for my knife, but he did for something else. That is the way to do it with people. They must be made to open their eyes, ears, and souls somehow. When you get them open, you must feel, "Now is my opportunity; in with the knife." There is one vulnerable spot in the hides of those rhinoceros sinners that come to hear you. Take care that, if you do get a shot through that weak spot, it is a thorough gospel bullet, for nothing else will accomplish the work that needs to be done.

Moreover, the people must be interested to make them remember what is said. They will not recollect what they hear unless the subject interests them. They forget our fine lectures and cannot recall our pretty pieces of poetry. I do not know that these things would do them any good if they did remember them. However, we must tell our hearers something they will not be likely to forget.

I believe in what Father Taylor calls "the surprise power of a sermon"—that is, something that is not expected by those who are listening to it. Just when they think that you are sure to say something precise and straightforward, say something awkward and crooked. They will remember that. You will have tied a gospel knot where it is likely to remain.

I remember reading of a tailor who, having made his fortune, promised to tell his brother tailors how he had done it. They gathered around his bed when he was dying. As they all listened very attentively, he said, "Now I am to tell you how you tailors are to make your fortunes. This is the way: always put a knot in your thread." I give that same advice to you: always put a knot in your thread. If there is a knot in the thread, it does not come out of the material. Some preachers put in the needle, but there is no knot in their thread, so it slips through, accomplishing nothing. Put a good many knots in your messages so that there may be all the greater probability that they will remain in people's memories. You do not want your preaching to be like the sewing done by some machines, in which, if one stitch breaks, the whole then comes undone.

There ought to be plenty of burrs in a message. Mr. Fergusson will tell you what burrs are. I'll warrant you that he has often found them clinging to his coat in his bonnie Scotland. Put these burrs all over the people: say something that will strike them, something that will stick to them for many days and that will be likely to bless them. I believe that a message, under God's smile, is likely to be the means of conversion if it has this quality about it: it must be interesting to the hearers as well as directly aimed at their salvation.

The third thing in a message that is likely to win souls to Christ is that it must be instructive. If people are to be saved by a message, it must contain at least some measure of knowledge. There must be light as well as fire. Some preachers are all light and no fire, and others are all fire and no light. What we need is both fire and light. I do not judge those men who are all fire and fury, but I wish they had a little more knowledge of what they talk about, and I think it would be well if they did not begin to preach quite so soon what they hardly understand themselves. It is a fine thing to stand up in the street and cry out, "Believe! Believe! Believe!" Yes, my dear soul, but what are we to believe? What is all this noise about?

Preachers of this sort are like the little boy who had been crying, and something happened that stopped him in the middle of his cry. Presently he said, "Ma, please tell me, what was I crying about?" Emotion is doubtless a very proper thing in the pulpit. The feeling, the pathos, and the power of heart are good and grand things in the right place, but do also use your brains a little and tell us something when you stand up to preach the everlasting gospel.

The messages that are most likely to convert people seem to me to be those that are full of truth—truth about the Fall, truth about the law, truth about human nature and its alienation from God, truth about Jesus Christ, truth about the Holy Spirit, truth about the everlasting Father, truth about the new birth, truth about obedience to God and how we learn it, and all such great truths. Tell your hearers something whenever you preach!

Of course, some good may come even if your hearers do not understand you. I suppose it might be so, for there was a very esteemed lady speaking to the Quaker Friends gathered at the Devonshire House meeting. She was a most gracious woman and was addressing the English Friends in Dutch. She asked one of the men to translate for her, but the hearers said there was so much power and spirit about her speaking, even though it was in Dutch, that they did not want it translated, for they were getting as much good out of it as was possible. Now, these hearers were Friends, and they are of a different mold that I am, for I do not care how good a woman the esteemed lady was, I would have liked to have known what she was talking about. I am sure I would not have been in the least degree profited unless it had been translated.

I like ministers always to know what they are talking about, and to be sure that there is something in it worth saying. Do try, therefore, dear friends, to give your hearers something besides a string of moving anecdotes that will set them crying. Tell them something. You are to teach your hearers, to preach the gospel to them, to make them understand, as far as you can, things that should make for their peace. We cannot expect people to be saved by our messages unless we really try to instruct them by what we say to them.

Fourth, people must be impressed upon by our messages if they are to be converted. They must not only be interested and instructed, but they must be impressed upon. I believe, dear friends, that there is a great deal more in impressive sermons than some people think. In order to impress the Word upon those to whom you preach, remember that it must be impressed upon yourself first. You must feel it yourself and speak as a person who feels it—not *as if* you feel it, but *because* you feel it. Otherwise, you will not make it be felt by others.

I wonder what it must be to go up into the pulpit and read somebody else's message to the congregation. We read in the Bible of one thing that was borrowed, and the head of that came off. I am afraid that the same thing often happens with borrowed messages—the heads come off. (See 2 Kings 6:1–7.) Men who read borrowed sermons positively do not know anything about our troubles of mind in preparing for the pulpit, or our joy in preaching with the aid of only brief notes.

A dear friend of mine, who reads his own sermons, was talking to me about preaching. I was telling him how my very soul is moved and my very heart is stirred within me when I think of what I will say to my people, and afterward when I am delivering my message. He said that he never felt anything of the kind when he was preaching. He reminded me of the story of the little girl who was crying because her teeth ached, and her grandmother said to her, "Lilly, I wonder that you are not ashamed to cry about such a small matter." "Well, Grandmother," answered the little girl, "it is all very well for you to say that, for, when your teeth ache, you can take them out, but mine are fixed."

Some men, when the message they have selected will not develop smoothly, can go to their box and take out another. However, when I have a message full of joy, but I myself feel heavy and sad, I am utterly miserable. When I want to beg and persuade men to believe, yet my spirit is dull and cold, I feel wretched to the utmost degree. My teeth ache, and I cannot take them out, for they are my own.

As my sermons are my own, I therefore may expect to find a good deal of trouble, both in the getting of them and in the using of them.

I remember the answer I received one time when I said to my venerable grandfather, "Whenever I have to preach, I always feel terribly sick, literally sick. I mean, I might as well be crossing the Channel." I asked the dear old man whether he thought I would ever get over that feeling. His answer was, "Your power will be gone if you do." So, my friends, when it is not so much that you have taken hold of your subject, but that it has taken hold of you, and you feel its grip with a terrible reality yourself, then that is the kind of message that is most likely to make others feel. If it is not impressed upon you, you cannot expect to impress it upon others. So take care that your sermons always have something in them that will really be impressed upon both yourself and the hearers whom you are addressing.

I also think that the delivery of our messages should make an impression upon our hearers. The delivery of some preachers is very bad. If yours is so, try to improve it in all possible ways. One young man wanted to learn singing, but he was told by the teacher, "You have only one tone to your voice, and that is outside the scale." Similarly, there are some ministers' voices that have only one tone, and there is no music in that one. Do try, as far as you can, to make the very way in which you speak minister to the great end you have in view. Preach, for instance, as you would plead if you were standing before a judge, begging for the life of a friend, or if you were appealing to the Queen herself on behalf of someone very dear to you. Use the kind of tone in pleading with sinners that you would use if a gallows were erected, and you were to be hanged on it unless you could persuade the person in authority to release you. That is the sort of earnestness you need in pleading with men as ambassadors for God.

Try to make every message such that the most flippant person will see, without any doubt, that, if it is an amusement for them to hear you, it is no amusement for you to speak to them, but that you are pleading with them in downright solemn earnest about eternal matters. I have often felt just like this when I have been preaching. I have known what it is to use up all my ammunition; and then I have, as it were, rammed myself into the great gospel gun and fired myself at my hearers—all my experience of God's goodness, all my consciousness of sin, and all my sense of the power of the gospel. There are some people upon whom that kind of preaching has a marked effect when nothing else would have worked, for they see that then you are communicating to them not only the gospel, but also yourself.

The kind of message that is likely to break the hearer's heart is that which has first broken the preacher's heart; and the sermon that is likely to reach the heart of the hearer is the one that has come straight from the heart of the preacher. Therefore, dear ones, always seek to preach so that the people will be impressed upon as well as interested and instructed.

In the fifth place, I think that we should try to take out of our messages everything that is likely to divert the hearers' minds from the object we have in view. The best style of preaching in the world, like the best style of dressing, is that which nobody notices. Somebody went to spend the evening with Hannah More, and when he came home, his wife asked him, "How was Miss More dressed? She must have been dressed very splendidly." The gentleman answered, "Really she was—dear me, how was she dressed? I did not notice at all how she was dressed. Anyway, there was nothing particularly noticeable in her dress. She was herself the object of interest." That is the way a true lady is dressed—so that we notice her and not her garments. She is so well dressed that we do not know how she is dressed. Likewise, that is the best way of dressing a sermon. Let it never be said of you, as it is sometimes said of certain popular preachers, "He did the thing so majestically; he spoke with such lofty diction, etc., etc., etc."

Never introduce anything into your message that would be likely to distract the attention of the hearer from the great object you have in mind. If you take the sinner's mind off the main subject by speaking after the manner of men, there is so much less likelihood of his receiving the impression you desire to convey, and, consequently, the smaller probability of his being converted.

I remember once reading what Mr. Finney said in his book *Revival*. He wrote that a person was on the point of being converted, when just then an old woman wearing clogs came shuffling up the aisle, making a great disturbance. That soul was lost! I know what the evangelist meant, even though I do not like the manner in which he expressed the episode. The noise of the old woman's wooden-soled shoes probably did take the person's mind away from what he should have been thinking about. It is also quite possible that he could not be brought back to exactly the same position again. However, we are to look at all these little things as if everything depended on us, but remember that it is the Holy Spirit alone who can make the Word effective.

Your message should not distract the people's attention through being only very distantly related to the text. There are many hearers still left who believe that there should be some sort of connection between the message and the text. They might begin asking themselves, "How did the minister ever get over there? What does his talk have to do with the text?" Then you will have lost their attention. That wandering habit of yours may be a very destructive one to them.

Keep to your text. If you do not, you will be like the little boy who went out fishing, and his uncle asked him, "Have you caught many fish, Samuel?" The boy answered, "I have been fishing for three hours, Uncle, and I have not caught any fish, but I have lost a lot of worms." I hope you will never have to say, "I did not win any souls for the Savior, but I spoiled a lot of precious texts. I confused and confounded many passages of Scripture, but I did no good with them. I was not supremely concerned with learning the mind of the Spirit as revealed in the text so as to get its meaning into my own mind, although it took a great deal of squeezing and packing to get my mind into the text." That is not a good thing to do.

Stick to your texts, and seek to get from the Scriptures what the Holy Spirit put into them. Never let your hearers have to ask the question, "What does this message have to do with the text?" If you do, people will not benefit from your message, and perhaps they will not be saved.

I would say to you, get all the education that you can, drink in everything that your instructors can possibly impart to you. It will take you all your time to get out of them all that is in them. Endeavor to learn all that you can, because, believe me, a lack of education may hinder the work of soulwinning. That "'orrible" omission of the letter *h* from places where it ought to be, that aspiration of the *h* until you exasperate it altogether—you cannot tell what harm such mistakes may cause. There was a young woman who might have been converted, for she did seem greatly impressed upon by your message. However, she was so disgusted by the dreadful way in which you put in *h*s where they ought not to be, or left them out where they ought to be in, that she could not listen to you with any pleasure. Her attention was distracted from the truth by your errors of pronunciation. That letter *h* has done vast harm. It is *"the letter* [that] *killeth"* (2 Corinthians 3:6) in the case of a great many, and all sorts of grammatical blunders may do more harm than you can imagine.

You may think, perhaps, that I am speaking of trifling matters that are hardly worthy of consideration. But I am not, for these things may cause most serious results. As easy as it is to learn to speak and write correct English, do try to know all you can of it.

Perhaps someone says, "Well, I know such-and-such a successful brother, and he was not an educated man." That is true, but note this: times are changing. One young woman said to another, "I do not see why we girls need to learn so many lessons. Young women before us did not know much, and yet they got married." "Yes," said her companion, "but then, you know, there were no boarding schools in them days, but now the young men will be educated, and it will be a poor future for us as ain't."

A young man might say, "Such-and-such a minister was not grammatical, and yet he did well." But the people of his day were ungrammatical, too, so it did not matter as much. However, now, when people have had more education, if they come and listen to you, it will be a pity if their minds are taken off the solemn things that you wish them to think about because they cannot help noticing your deficiencies of education. Even if you are not an educated man, God may bless you. Wisdom tells us that we should not let our lack of education hinder the gospel from blessing men. Possibly you say, "They must be very hypercritical to find fault like that." But, then, do not hypercritical people need saving just as much as other people? I would not want a hypercritical person to be able to say truthfully that my preaching had jarred on his ears and disturbed his mind so much that he could not possibly receive the doctrine that I was trying to set before him.

Have you ever heard why Charles Dickens would not become a spiritualist? At a séance, he asked to see the spirit of Lindley Murray, the American grammarian. There came in what professed to be the spirit of Lindley Murray, and Dickens asked, "Are you Lindley Murray?" The reply came, "I are." There was no hope of Dickens' conversion to spiritualism after that ungrammatical answer.

You may well laugh at the story, but see to it that you remember the moral of it. You can easily see that, by forgetting when to use the nominative or accusative case of a noun or pronoun, or by using the wrong tense of a verb, you might take the mind of your hearer away from what you are trying to bring before him, and so prevent the truth from reaching his heart and conscience. Therefore, divest your sermons as much as you can of everything that is likely to take the mind of your hearers away from the one object before you. The whole attention and thoughts of the people must be concentrated on the truth we are setting before them if we are to preach so as to save those who come within sound of our voices.

Sixth, I believe that the messages that are most full of Christ are the most likely to be blessed to the conversion of the hearers. Let your sermons be full of Christ—from beginning to end crammed full of the gospel. As for myself, I cannot preach anything but Christ and His cross, for I know nothing else. Long ago, like the apostle Paul, I determined not to know anything else *"save Jesus Christ, and him crucified"* (1 Corinthians 2:2). People have often asked me, "What is the secret of your success?" I always answer that I have no other secret but this: I have preached the gospel—not about the gospel, but the gospel—the full, free, glorious gospel of the living Christ who is the incarnation of the Good News. Preach Jesus Christ, always and everywhere. Every time you preach, be sure to have much of Christ in the message.

Do you remember the story of the old minister who heard a sermon by a young man? When the elder minister was asked by the preacher what he thought of it, he was rather slow to answer, but at last he said, "If I must tell you, I did not like it at all. There was no Christ in your sermon." "No," answered the young man, "because I did not see that Christ was in the text." "Oh!" said the old minister, "But do you not know that from every little town and village and tiny hamlet in England there is a road leading to London? Whenever I get hold of a text, I say to myself, 'There is a road from here to Jesus Christ, and I intend to keep on His track until I get to Him.'" "Well," said the young man, "but suppose you are preaching from a text that says nothing about Christ?" "Then I will go over hedge and ditch until I get to Him."

We must do the same, friends. We must have Christ in all our messages, no matter what else is in them or not in them. There ought to be enough of the gospel in every message to save a soul. Take care that it is so when you are called to preach before Her Majesty the Queen. Whether you are to preach to charwomen or chairmen, always make sure that there is the real gospel in every message. I have heard of a young man asking, when he was going to preach in a certain place, "What kind of church is it? What do the people believe? What are their doctrinal views?" I will tell you how to avoid the necessity of such a question: preach Jesus Christ to them. If that does not suit their doctrinal views, then preach Jesus Christ the next Sunday you go, and do the same thing the next Sabbath, and the next, and the next, and never preach anything else. Those who do not like Jesus Christ must have Him preached to them until they do like Him, for they are the very people who need Him most.

Remember that all the tradesmen in the world say that they can sell their goods when there is a demand for them; but our goods create as well as supply the demand. We preach Jesus Christ to those who want Him, and we also preach Him to those who do not want Him; we keep on preaching Christ until we make them feel that they do want Him and cannot do without Him.

Seventh, friends, it is my firm conviction that the messages that are most likely to convert men are those that really appeal to their hearts—not those that are fired over their heads or aimed only at their intellects. I am sorry to say that I know some preachers who will never do much good in the world. They are good men, have plenty of ability, can speak well, and have a good deal of discernment; but, somehow or other, there is a very sad omission in their nature, for to anyone who knows them, it is quite evident that they do not have any heart. I know one or two men who are as dry as leather. If you were to hang them up on the wall, as you do a piece of seaweed, in order to tell what the weather is going to be like, they would be no guide to you, for scarcely any weather would affect them.

But I also know some men who are the very opposite of that type. They, too, are not likely to win souls, for they are so flippant, frivolous, and foolish that there is nothing serious about them, nothing to show that they are living in earnest. I cannot find any traces of a soul in them. They are too shallow to contain one. It could not live in the inch or two of water that is all that they hold. They appear to have been made without any souls, so they cannot do any good in preaching the gospel. You must have souls. If you are to look after your brothers' and sisters' souls, depend on this: you must have a heart if you are to reach their hearts.

Another kind of preacher cannot weep over sinners. What good is he in the ministry? He never wept over men in his life. He never agonized before God on their behalf. He never said, *"Oh that my head were waters, and mine eyes a fountain of tears, that I might weep day and night for the slain of the daughter of my people!"* (Jeremiah 9:1).

I know a brother like this. In a meeting of ministers, after we had been confessing our shortcomings, he said that he was very much ashamed of us all. Well, no doubt, we ought to have been more ashamed of ourselves than we were. But he told us that, if we had truly meant what we had said in our confessions to God, we were a disgrace to the ministry; perhaps we were. He said he was not like that.

As far as he knew, he never preached a message without feeling that it was the best he could preach, and he did not know that he could do any better than he had done. He always studied the same number of hours every day, always prayed exactly the same number of minutes, always preached a certain length of time. In fact, he was the most regular man I ever knew.

When I heard him say this to us, I asked myself, "What does his ministry show as the result of this perfect way of doing things?" Why, it did not show anything that was satisfactory. He has great gifts of dispersion; if he goes to a full chapel, he soon empties it. Yet he is a good man, in his way.

I sometimes wish that his clock would stop, or strike in the middle of the half hour, or that something extraordinary might happen to him, because some good might come of it. He is so regular and orderly that there is no hope of his doing anything. The fault with him is that he does not have any faults. You will notice, friends, that preachers who do not have any faults do not have any excellencies either. So try to avoid that flat, dead level and everything else that makes people less likely to be converted.

Coming back to the matter of the possession of a heart, of which I was speaking, I asked a young girl, who recently came to join the church, "Do you have a good heart?" She replied, "Yes, sir." I said, "Have you thought over that question? Do you not have an evil heart?" "Oh, yes!" she answered. "Well," I said, "how do your two answers agree?" "Why," responded the girl, "I know that I have a good heart, because God has given me a new heart and a right spirit; and I also know that I have an evil heart, for I often find it fighting against my new heart." She was right, and I would rather feel that a minister had two hearts than that he had none at all. It must be heart work with you, far more than head work, if you are to win many souls. Amid all your studies, never let your spiritual life become dry. There is no need for it to, although with many, study has had that effect. The instructors will bear me witness that there is a very drying influence about Latin, Greek, and Hebrew. That couplet is true:

> Hebrew roots, as known to most,
> Do flourish best on barren ground.

There is a very drying influence about the classics. There is a very drying influence about mathematics. You may get absorbed in any science until your heart is gone. Do not let that be the case with any of you, so that people would have to say of you, "He knows much more than he did when he first came here, but he does not have as much spirituality as he used to have." Take care that this is never the case. Do not be satisfied with merely polishing your fireplaces, but stir the fire in your hearts and get your own souls aflame with love for Christ, or else you will not likely be greatly used in winning the souls of others.

Lastly, friends, I think that messages that have been prayed over are the most likely to convert people. I mean those messages that have had much real prayer offered over them, both in the preparation and the delivery, for there is much so-called prayer that is only playing at praying. Some time ago, I rode with a man who claims to work wonderful cures by the acids of a certain wood. After he had told me about his marvelous remedy, I asked him, "What is in that remedy that effects cures such as you profess to have brought about?" "Oh!" he answered, "it is the way in which I prepare it, much more than the stuff itself. That is the secret of its curative properties. I rub it as hard as I can for a long while, and I have so much vital electricity in me that I put my very life into it."

He was only a quack, yet we may learn a lesson even from him. The way to make sermons is to work vital electricity into them, putting your own life and the very life of God into them by earnest prayer. The difference between a message that has been prayed over and one that has been prepared and preached by a prayerless man is like the difference that Mr. Fergusson suggested in his prayer when he referred to the high priest before and after his anointing. You must anoint your messages, and you cannot do so except by much communion with God.

May the Holy Spirit anoint every one of you, and richly bless you in winning souls, for our Lord Jesus Christ's sake! Amen.

5

OBSTACLES TO SOULWINNING

I have spoken to you, friends, about soulwinning, a most royal employment. May you all become, in this sense, mighty hunters before the Lord and bring many sinners to the Savior! At this time, I want to say a few words about obstacles that lie in our paths as we seek to win souls for Christ.

They are very many of these obstacles, and I cannot attempt to make a complete list of them. But the first obstacle, and doubtless one of the most difficult, is the indifference and lethargy of sinners. All men are not indifferent to the same degree. In fact, there are some people who seem to have a sort of religious instinct that influences them for good, long before they have any real love for spiritual things. But there are districts, especially rural districts, where indifference prevails. The same state of things exists in various parts of London. It is not infidelity. The people do not care enough about religion even to oppose it. They are not concerned about what you preach or where you preach, for they have no interest whatever in the matter. They have no thoughts of God. They care nothing about Him or His service. They use His name only in profanity.

I have often noticed that any place where there is not much business is bad for religious effort. Among the blacks of Jamaica, whenever they did not have much work, there was little prosperity in the churches. I could indicate districts not far from here where business is slack; there you will find that there is very little good being done. All along the valley of the Thames, there are places where a man might preach his heart out and kill himself. But there is little or no good being accomplished in those regions, just as there is no active business life there.

Now, whenever you meet with indifference, as you may do, my dear friend, in the place where you go to preach—indifference that affects your own people and even seems to tinge your own deacons—what are you to do? Well, your only hope of overcoming it is to be doubly in earnest yourself. Keep your own zeal alive; let it be even vehement, burning, blazing, all-consuming. Stir the people up somehow. If all your earnestness seems to be in vain, still blaze and burn. If that has no effect on your hearers, go elsewhere as the Lord may direct you. The indifference or lethargy that possesses the minds of some people is very likely to have a bad influence on our preaching. However, we must strive and struggle against it, and try to wake both ourselves and our hearers up.

I would far rather have a person be an earnest, intense opposer of the gospel than have him be careless and indifferent. You cannot do much with someone if he will not speak about religion or will not come to hear what you have to say concerning the things of God. You might as well have him be a downright infidel, like a very leviathan covered with scales of blasphemy, as have him be a mere earthworm wriggling away out of reach.

Another very great obstacle to soulwinning is unbelief. You know that it is written of the Lord Jesus that when He was in *"his own country…he did not many mighty works there because of their unbelief"* (Matthew 13:57–58). This evil exists in all unregenerate hearts, but in some people it takes a very pronounced form. They do think about religion, but they do not believe in the truth of God that we preach to them. Their opinions are to them more weighty, more worthy of belief, than God's inspired declarations. They will not accept anything that is revealed in the Scriptures. These people are very hard to influence, but I would warn you not to fight them with their own weapons.

I do not believe that infidels ever are won by argument; or, if so, it very seldom happens. The argument that convinces men of the reality of religion is that which they gather from the holiness and earnestness of those who profess to be Christ's followers. As a rule, they barricade their minds against the assaults of reason. If we give our pulpits over to arguing with them, we will often be doing more harm than good. In all probability, only a very small portion of our audience will understand what we are talking about.

While we are trying to do them good, most likely we will be teaching infidelity to others who do not know anything about such things. The first knowledge they ever have of certain heresies will come to them from our lips. Possibly our refutation of the error may not be perfect, and many young minds may become tainted with unbelief through listening to our attempted exposure of it.

I believe that you will rout unbelief by your faith rather than by your reason. By your belief and your living up to your conviction of the truth, you will do more good than by any argument, however strong it may be. There is a friend who sits to hear me generally every Sabbath. "What do you think?" he said to me one day. "You are my only link with better things; but you are a terrible man, in my estimation, for you do not have the slightest sympathy with me." I replied, "No, I do not; or, rather, I do not have the least sympathy with your unbelief." "That makes me cling to you, for I fear that I will always remain as I am. But when I see your calm faith and how God blesses you in exercising it, and know what you accomplish through the power of that faith, I say to myself, 'Jack, you are a fool.'" I said to him, "You are quite right in that verdict, and the sooner you come to my way of thinking, the better, for nobody can be a bigger fool than the man who does not believe in God."

One of these days, I expect to see him converted. There is a continual battle between us, but I never answer one of his arguments. I said to him once, "If you believe that I am a liar, you are free to think so if you like. But I testify to what I know and state what I have seen, tasted, handled, and felt. You ought to believe my testimony, for I have no possible purpose to serve in deceiving you." That man would have beaten me long ago if I had fired at him with the paper pellets of reason. So, I advise you to fight unbelief with belief, falsehood with the truth, and never to cut and pare down the gospel to try to make it fit in with the follies and fancies of men.

A third obstacle in the way of winning souls is the fatal delay that men so often make. I do not know whether this evil is not on the whole more widespread and harmful than the indifference, lethargy, and unbelief of which I have spoken. Many a man says to us what Felix said to Paul, "*Go thy way for this time; when I have a convenient season, I will call for thee*" (Acts 24:25). Such an individual gets near the border; he seems to be within a few steps of Emmanuel's land, and yet he sidesteps our movements toward home and puts us off by saying, "Yes, I will think the matter over; it will not be long before I decide." There is nothing like pressing men for a speedy decision and getting them to settle at once this all-important question. Never mind if they do find fault with your teaching. It is always right to preach what God says, and His word is, "*Behold, now is the accepted time; behold, now is the day of salvation*" (2 Corinthians 6:2).

This leads me to mention another obstacle to soulwinning that is the same thing in another form—carnal security. Many men imagine that they are quite safe. They have not really tested the foundation on which they are building to see that it is sound and firm, but they suppose that all is well. If they are not good Christians, they can at least say that they are rather better than some who are Christians, or who call themselves by that name. Further, if there is anything lacking in them, they can at any time put on the finishing touches and make themselves fit for God's presence. Thus they have no fear; or, if they do fear at all, they do not live in constant dread of the eternal destruction from the presence of the Lord and from the glory of His power that will certainly be their portion unless they repent and believe in the Lord Jesus Christ.

Against these people we ought to thunder day and night. Let us plainly proclaim to them that the unbelieving sinner is "*condemned already*" (John 3:18), and that he is certain to perish everlastingly if he does not trust in Christ. We ought to preach so as to make every sinner tremble in his seat. If he will not come to the Savior, he ought at least to have a hard time of it while he stops away from Him. I am afraid that we sometimes preach smooth things, too soothing and agreeable, and that we do not set before men their real danger as we should. If we hold back in this respect from declaring "*all the counsel of God*" (Acts 20:27) at least part of the responsibility of their ruin will lie at our door.

Another obstacle to soulwinning is despair. The pendulum swings first one way and then the other; the man who yesterday had no fear, today has no hope. There are thousands who have heard the gospel and yet live in a kind of despair of its power ever being exerted upon them. Perhaps they have been brought up among people who taught them that the work of salvation was something of God altogether apart from the sinner. So they say that, if they are to be saved, they will be saved. You know that this teaching contains a great truth, and yet, if it is left by itself, without qualification, it is a terrible falsehood. It is fatalism, not predestination, that makes men talk as if there is nothing whatever for them to do, or that there is nothing that they can do. There is no likelihood of anyone being saved while he gives you as his only hope, "If salvation is for me, it will come to me in due time."

You may meet with people who talk in this way. When you have said all you can, they will remain as if they were encased in steel, with no sense of responsibility, because there is no hope awakened in their spirits. If they would but hope that they might receive mercy by asking for it and so be led to cast their guilty souls on Christ, what a blessing it would be! Let us preach full and free salvation to all who trust in Jesus, so that we may reach these people. If the carnally secure were to be tempted to presume this hope, some who are quietly despairing might pluck up heart and hope, and might venture to come to Christ.

No doubt a great obstacle to soulwinning is the love of sin. *"Sin lieth at the door"* (Genesis 4:7). Many men never get saved because of some secret lust. It may be that they are living in fornication. I remember well the case of a man who I thought would certainly come to Christ. He was fully aware of the power of the gospel and seemed to be impressed upon under the preaching of the Word. But I found out that he had become entangled with a woman who was not his wife, and that he was living in sin while professing to be seeking the Savior. When I heard that, I could easily understand why he could not obtain peace. Whatever tenderness of heart he may have felt, there was this woman always holding him in the bondage of sin.

There are some men who are guilty of dishonest business transactions. You will not see them saved while they continue their dishonesty. If they will not give up their swindling, they cannot be saved. There are others who are drinking to excess. People who drink are often very easily affected under our preaching. They are tearful, their drinking has made them softheaded, and there is a maudlin kind of sensitivity in them. However, as long as a man clings to "the cup of devils," he will not be likely to come to Christ. With others, it is some secret sin or some hidden lust that is the great difficulty. One says that he cannot help flying into a rage; another declares that he cannot give up getting drunk; yet another laments that he cannot find peace, whereas the root of the trouble is that there is a prostitute who stands in his way. In all these cases, we have only to keep on preaching the truth, and God will help us to aim the arrow at the joint in the sinner's harness.

Another obstacle is put in our way by men's self-righteousness. They have not committed any of these sins I have mentioned. They have kept all the commandments from their youth up. What do they still lack? There is no room for Christ in a full heart. When a person is clothed with his own righteousness, he has no need of Christ's righteousness. At least, he is not conscious of his need. If the gospel does not convince him of it, Moses must come with the law and show him what his true state is. That is the real difficulty in many cases: a person does not come to Christ because he is not conscious that he is lost. He does not ask to be lifted up because he does not know that he is a fallen creature. He does not feel that he has any need of divine mercy or forgiveness; thus, he does not seek it.

In addition, there are some with whom all we say has no effect because of their utter worldliness. This worldliness takes two forms. In the poor, it is the result of grinding poverty. When a man has scarcely enough bread to eat and hardly knows how to get clothes to put on, when at home he hears the cries of his little children and looks into the face of his overworked wife, we must preach very wonderfully if we are to secure his attention and make him think about the world to come. *"What shall we eat? or, What shall we drink? or, Wherewithal shall we be clothed?"* (Matthew 6:31) are questions that press very heavily upon the poor. To a hungry man, Christ is very lovely when He has a loaf of bread in His hand. That is the way our Lord appeared when He was breaking the bread and fish for the multitude, for even He did not disdain to feed the hungry. When we can relieve the needs of the destitute, we may be doing a necessary thing for them by placing them where they may be capable of listening with profit to the gospel of Christ.

The other kind of worldliness comes from having too much of this world, or at least of making too much of this world. The gentleman must be fashionable; his daughters must be dressed in the best style; his sons must learn to dance, and so on. This sort of worldliness has been the great curse of our nonconformist churches.

Then there is another kind of man who is from morning to night grinding away at the shop. His one business seems to be to open his shop and to close it again. He will rise early, sit up late, and eat the bread of anxiety, just to make money. What can we do for these covetous people? How can we ever hope to touch the hearts of those whose one aim is to be rich—people who scrape together pennies? Economy is good, but there is an economy that becomes stinginess. That stinginess becomes the habit of these miserly folk. Some will even go to chapel because it is the proper and respectable thing, hoping to gain customers by going. Judas remained unconverted even in the company of the Lord Jesus Christ, and we have some people still among us in whose ears the thirty pieces of silver chink so loudly that the sound of the gospel cannot be heard by them.

I may mention one more obstacle to soul-winning, namely, the obstacle that exists with some men through their habits, resorts, and company. How can we expect a working man to go home and sit all evening in the one room that he has to live and sleep in? Perhaps there are two or three children crying, clothing drying, and all sorts of things to produce discomfort. The man comes in to find that his wife is scolding, his children are crying, and the clothing is drying. What would you do if you were in his place? Suppose you were not Christian men: would you not go somewhere or other? You cannot walk the streets, and you know that there is a cozy room at the tavern with its flashing light, or there is the gin palace at the corner, where everything is bright and cheerful and there are plenty of lighthearted companions.

Well, you cannot hope to be the means of saving men while they go to such places and meet with the company that is found there. All the good that they receive from the hymns that they hear on the Sabbath is driven away as they listen to the comic songs in the drink shop. All remembrance of the services of the sanctuary is obliterated by the very questionable tales that are told in the bar.

Thus is the great mercy of having a place where working men can come and sit in safety, or of having a blue-ribbon meeting, a gathering where it may not be all singing, preaching, or praying, but where there is something of all these things. Here the man is enabled to get out of the former habits that seemed to hold him fast, and before long he does not go to the bars at all. Instead, he has two rooms, or perhaps a little cottage so that his wife can dry the clothing in the backyard. Now he finds that the baby does not cry as much as he used to, probably because his mother has more to give him. Everything gets better and brighter now that the man has forsaken his former resorts.

I think a Christian minister is quite justified in using all right and lawful means to wean people from their evil associations. It may be well sometimes to do that which seems to be extraordinary if thereby we can win men to the Lord Jesus Christ. That must be our one aim in all that we do. Whatever obstacles may be in our pathway, we must seek the aid of the Holy Spirit, so that they may be removed, and so that souls may be saved and God may be glorified.

6

HOW TO INDUCE PEOPLE
TO WIN SOULS

I have spoken to you about the great work of our lives, which is that of winning souls. I have tried to show you various ways in which we win souls, the qualifications both toward God and toward man of those who are likely to be used in winning souls, the kind of messages that are most likely to win souls, and the obstacles in the way of soulwinners. Now I would like to talk to you about another aspect of the subject: How can we induce people to become soulwinners?

You are aspiring, each of you, in due time, to become pastors of churches, unless the Lord calls you to be evangelists or missionaries. You begin at first as single sowers of the good seed of the kingdom and go scattering your own handfuls from your own baskets. You desire, however, to become spiritual farmers and to have a certain acreage that you will not sow entirely yourself; you will have servants who will aid you in the work. Then, to one you will say, "Go," and he will go immediately, or, "Come," and he will come at once. You will seek to lead them into the art and mystery of seed-sowing, so that, after a while, you may have large numbers of people around you doing this good work. Thus, a far greater acreage may be brought into cultivation for the great Father.

There are some of us who have, by God's grace, been so richly blessed that we have all around us a large number of people who have been spiritually quickened through our instrumentality, people who have been awakened under our ministry, who have been instructed and strengthened by us, and who are all doing good service for God. Let me warn you not to look for all this at first, for it is the work of time. Do not expect to get, in the first year of your pastorate, that result which is the reward of twenty years of continuous toil in one place.

Young men sometimes make a very great mistake in the way they talk to those who never saw them until about six weeks earlier. They cannot speak with the authority of one who has been as a father among his people, having been with them for twenty or thirty years. If they do, it becomes a sort of foolish affectation on their part. It is equally foolish to expect the people immediately to be what they might be after they had been trained by a godly minister for a quarter of a century.

It is true that you may go to a church where somebody else has faithfully labored for many years and long sown the good seed. You may find your sphere of labor in a most blessed and prosperous state, and how happy you will be if you can thus jump into a good man's shoes and follow the path he has been treading. It is always a good sign when the horses do not know that they have a new driver. You, my friend, inexperienced as you are, will be a very happy man if that should be your lot.

However, the probability is that you will go to a place that has been allowed to run almost to ruin, possibly to one that has been altogether neglected. Perhaps you will try to get the principal deacon to imitate your earnestness. You are at a white heat; when you find him as cold as steel, you will be like a piece of hot iron dipped in a pail of water. He may tell you that he remembers others who were at first just as hot as you, but they soon cooled down, and he will not be surprised if you do the same. He is a very good man, but he is old and you are young, and we cannot put young heads on old shoulders, even if we were to try.

Perhaps next you will resolve to try some of the young people. Possibly you can get on better with them. But they do not understand you; they are shy and retiring, and they soon fly off on a tangent. You must not be surprised if this is your experience. Very likely, you will have almost everything to do in connection with the work. In any case, expect that it may be so. Then you will not be disappointed if it turns out that way.

It may be otherwise, but you will be prudent if you go into the ministry expecting not to find any great assistance from the people in the work of soul-winning. Anticipate that you will have to do it yourself, and do it alone. Begin alone: sow the seed and tramp up and down the field, looking to the Lord of the harvest to bless your labor. Look forward to the time when, through your efforts under the divine blessing, instead of a plot of land that is apparently covered with nettles, or full of stones, weeds, or thorns, or partly trodden down, you will have a well tilled farm in which you may sow the seed to the best advantage and on which you will have a little army of fellow laborers to aid you in the service.

Yet all that is the work of time. I would certainly say to you: do not expect all this at least for some months after you settle down to work. Revivals, if they are genuine, do not always come the moment we whistle for them. Try to whistle for the wind, and see if it will come. The great rain was given in answer to Elijah's prayers, but not even then the first time he prayed. We must pray again and again and again, and at last the cloud will appear with the showers. Wait a while, work on, plod on, plead on, and, in due time, the blessing will be given. You will find that you have the church after your own ideal, but it will not come to you all at once.

I do not think that Mr. John Angell James, of Birmingham, saw much fruit in his ministry for many years. As far as I remember, Carr's Lane Chapel was not the place of any great renown before he preached there. But he kept on steadily preaching the gospel, and at last he drew around him a company of godly people who helped to make him the greatest power for good that Birmingham had at that time. Try to do just the same. Do not expect to see immediately what he and other faithful ministers have been able to accomplish only after many years.

In order to secure this objective of gathering around you a group of Christians who will themselves be soulwinners, I recommend that you do not go to work according to any set rule. That which would be right at one time might not be wise at another, and that which would be best for one place would not be as good elsewhere.

Sometimes, the very best plan would be to call all the members of the church together, tell them what you would like to see, and plead earnestly with them that each one should become a soulwinner for God. Say to them, "I do not want to be your pastor simply so that I may preach to you; I long to see souls saved, and to see those who are saved seeking to win others for the Lord Jesus Christ.

You know how the Pentecostal blessing was given; when the whole church met with one accord in one place, and continued in prayer and supplication, the Holy Spirit was poured out, and thousands were converted. Can we not get together in like manner and all of us cry mightily to God for a blessing?" That might succeed in rousing them.

Calling them together and earnestly pleading with them about the matter, pointing out what you want them especially to do and to ask of God, may be like setting a light to dry fuel. On the other hand, nothing may come of it because of their lack of sympathy in the work of soul-saving. They may say, "It is a very nice meeting. Our pastor expects a good deal of us, and we all wish he may get it." There it will end, as far as they are concerned.

If that should not succeed, God may lead you to begin with one or two. There is usually some "choice young man" in each congregation. As you notice deeper spirituality in him than in the rest of the members, you might say to him, "Will you come down to my house on such-and-such an evening, so that we may have a little prayer together?" You can gradually increase the number to two or three godly young men, if possible, or you may begin with some gracious matron, who perhaps lives nearer to God than any of the men and whose prayers would help you more than theirs. Having secured their sympathy, you might say to them, "Now we will try and see if we cannot influence the whole church. We will begin with our fellow members before we go to outsiders. Let us always try to be ourselves at the prayer meetings, to set an example for the rest. Let us also arrange to have gatherings for prayer in our own houses and seek to get our brothers and sisters to them. You, good sister, can get half-a-dozen sisters together into your house for a little meeting. You, brother, can say to a few friends, 'Could we not meet together to pray for our pastor?'"

Sometimes, the most effective way to burn a house is to pour petroleum down the middle of it and set fire to it, as the ladies and gentlemen did in Paris in the days of the commune! Sometimes, the shortest method is to light it at the four corners. I have never tried either plan, but that is what I think. I like to burn churches rather than houses, because they do not burn down, they burn up and keep on burning when the fire is of the right sort. When a bush is nothing but a bush, it is soon consumed when set on fire. But when it is a bush that burns on and is not consumed, we know that God is there. It is the same way with a church that is flaming with holy zeal.

Your work is to set your church on fire somehow. You may do it by speaking to all the members, or you may do it by speaking to a few choice spirits, but you must do it somehow. Have a secret group for this sacred purpose. Turn yourselves into a band of celestial Fenians whose aim is to set the whole church on fire. If you do so, the devil will not like it. You will cause him such disquiet that he will seek the utter breakup of the union. That is just what we want: we do not desire anything but war between the church and the world and all its habits and customs.

But again, I say, all this will take time. I have seen some fellows run so fast at first that they have soon become like broken-winded horses, truly a pitiable sight. So take time, and do not look for everything you desire to be secured all at once.

I suppose that, in most places, there is a prayer meeting on Monday nights. If you want your people, as well as yourself, to be soulwinners, keep up the prayer meetings all you can. Do not be like certain ministers in the suburbs of London who say that they cannot get the people out to a prayer meeting and a lecture, too, so they have one weeknight meeting for prayer at which they give a short address. One lazy man said that the weeknight address was almost as bad as delivering a sermon, so he has a prayer meeting and lecture combined in one. It is neither a prayer meeting nor a lecture; it is neither fish, flesh, fowl, nor good red herring. Soon he will give it up because he says it is no good, and I am sure the people think so, too. After that, why should he not give up one of the Sunday services? The same reasoning might apply to that.

Today, I saw in an American paper the following paragraph:

The well known fact is again going the rounds that, in Mr. Spurgeon's church in London, the regular hearers absent themselves one Sunday evening every three months, and the house is given up to strangers. English "boasting is excluded" in this matter. Our American Christianity is of so noble a type that hosts of our people give up their pews to strangers every Sunday night in the year.

I hope it will not be so with your people, either with respect to the Sabbath services or the prayer meetings.

If I were you, I would make that prayer meeting a special feature of my ministry. Let it be such a prayer meeting that there is not the like of it within seven thousand miles. Do not go walking into the prayer meeting, as so many do, to say anything that may occur to you at the moment, but do your best to make the meeting interesting to all who are there. Do not hesitate to tell good Mr. Snooks that, God help you, he will not pray for twenty-five minutes. Earnestly entreat him to cut it short; if he does not, then stop him.

If a man came into my house intending to cut my wife's throat, I would reason with him as to the wrong of it, and then I would effectively prevent him from doing her any harm. I love the church almost as much as I love my dear wife. So, if a man will pray long, he may pray long somewhere else, but not at the meeting over which I am presiding. Tell him to finish it up at home if he cannot pray in public for a reasonable length of time. If the people seem dull and heavy, get them to sing Moody and Sankey hymns. When they can sing them all by heart, do not have any more "Moody and Sankey" for a time, but go back to your own hymnbook.

Keep up the prayer meeting, whatever else fails. It is the great business evening of the week, the best service between Sabbaths. Be sure you make it so. If you find that your people cannot come in the evening, try to have a prayer meeting when they can come. You might get a good meeting in the country at half-past four in the morning. Why not? You would get more people at five o'clock in the morning than you would at five o'clock at the other end of the day. I believe that a prayer meeting at six o'clock in the morning among agricultural people would attract many. They would drop in, just have a few words of prayer, and be glad of the opportunity. Or you might have it at twelve o'clock at night. You would find some people who would attend then whom you could not get at any other time. Try one, two, or three o'clock, or any hour of the day or night, so as, somehow or other, to get the people out to pray.

If they cannot be induced to come to the meetings, go to their houses and say, "I am going to have a prayer meeting in your parlor." "Oh, dear, my wife will be in a state." "Tell her not to trouble, for we can go in the carriage house or garden or anywhere, but we must have a prayer meeting here." If they will not come to the prayer meeting, we must go to them.

Suppose that fifty of us go trudging down the street and hold a meeting in the open air. There might be many worse things than that. Remember how the American women fought the liquor sellers when they prayed them out of the business. If we cannot stir the people without doing extraordinary things, in the name of all that is holy, let us do extraordinary things. Somehow we must keep up the prayer meetings, for they are at the very secret source of power with God and with men.

We must always set an earnest example ourselves. A slow minister will not have a lively, zealous church, I am sure. A man who is indifferent, or who does his work as if he takes it as easily as he can, ought not to expect to have people around him who are in earnest about the salvation of souls.

I know that you desire to have around you a group of Christians who long for the salvation of their friends and neighbors, a set of people who will be always expecting that God will bless the preaching of your messages, who will watch the countenances of your hearers to see if they are being impressed upon, who will be sorely distressed if there are no conversions, and who will be greatly troubled if souls are not saved. Perhaps they would not complain to you if that were the case, but they would cry to God on your behalf.

Possibly, they would also speak to you about the matter. I remember one of my deacons saying to me, as we were going down to communion one Sunday evening when we had only fourteen to receive into the church, "Sir, this won't do." We had been accustomed to having forty or fifty every month, and the good man was not satisfied with a smaller number. I agreed with him that we must have more in the future if it were at all possible. I suppose some men would have felt annoyed to have had anything like that remark made to them, but I was delighted with what my good deacon said, for it was just what I myself felt.

Next, we need Christians around us who are willing to do all they can to help in the work of winning souls. There are numbers of people who cannot be reached by the pastor. You must try to find Christian workers who will "buttonhole" people—you know what I mean. It is pretty close work when you hold a friend by a lock of his hair or by his coat button. Absalom did not find it easy to get away when he was caught in the oak by the his hair. So, try to get close with sinners. Talk gently to them until you have whispered them into the kingdom of heaven, and have told into their ears the blessed story that will bring peace and joy to their hearts. We need in the church of Christ a band of well-trained sharpshooters, who will pick the people out individually and always be on the watch for all who come into the place, not annoying them, but making sure that they do not go away without having had a personal warning, invitation, and exhortation to come to Christ.

We need to train all our people for this service, so as to make Salvation Armies out of them. Every man, woman, or child who is in our churches should be set to work for the Lord. Then they will not relish the fine sermons that the Americans seem to delight in so much, but they will say, "Pooh! Gibberish! We don't want that kind of thing."

What do people who are at work in the harvest field want with thunder and lightning? They want just to rest awhile under a tree, to wipe the sweat from their foreheads, to refresh themselves after their toil, and then to get to work again. Our preaching ought to be like the address of a commander-in-chief to his army: "There is the enemy; do not let me know where they are tomorrow." Something short, something sweet, and something that stirs and impresses upon them is what our people need.

We are sure to get the blessing we are seeking when the whole atmosphere in which we are living is favorable to soulwinning. I remember one of our friends saying to me one evening, "There will be sure to be a blessing tonight; there is such a lot of dew about." May you often know what it is to preach where there is plenty of dew!

The Irishman said that it was no use irrigating while the sun was shining, for he had noticed that, whenever it rained, there were clouds about, so that the sun was hidden. There was a great deal of sense in that observation, more than appears at first sight, as there usually is in Hibernian statements. The shower benefits the plants because everything is suitable for the rain to come down—the shaded sky, the humidity of the atmosphere, the general feeling of everything being damp all around. But if you were to pour the same quantity of water down while the sun was shining brightly, the leaves would probably be turned yellow, and they would shrivel and die in the heat. Any gardener would tell you that he is always careful to water the flowers in the evening when the sun is off them. This is the reason why irrigation, however well it is done, is not as beneficial as the rain: there must be a favorable influence in the whole atmosphere if the plants and flowers are to derive benefit from the moistening.

It is the same way in spiritual things. I have often noticed that when God blesses my ministry to an unusual extent, the people in general are praying. It is a tremendous thing to preach in an atmosphere full of the dew of the Spirit. I know what it is to preach with it. Alas, I also know what it is to preach without it! Then is it like Gilboa, when there was no dew or rain. (See 2 Samuel 1:21.) You may preach, and you may hope that God will bless your message, but it is no use. I hope it will not be so with you. Perhaps your lot will be cast where some dear brother has long been toiling, praying, and laboring for the Lord, where you will find all the people very ready for the blessing.

When I go out to preach, I often feel that no credit is due to me—everything is a gift. The good folk sit with their mouths open, waiting for the blessing. Almost everybody there is expecting me to say something good. Because they are all looking for it, it does them good. When I am gone, they keep praying for the blessing, and they get it. When a man is put on a horse that runs away with him, he must ride; that is just how it has frequently been with me. The blessing has been given because all the surroundings were favorable.

You may often trace the happy results not only to the preacher's message, but also to all the circumstances connected with its delivery. That was the case with Peter's message on the Day of Pentecost, which brought three thousand souls to Christ. Never was a better sermon preached: it was a plain, personal message likely to convince people of the sin in their treatment of the Savior by putting Him to death. But I do not attribute the conversions to the apostle's words alone, for there were clouds about; the whole atmosphere was damp. As my friend said to me, there was "plenty of dew about." Had not the disciples been long continuing in prayer and supplication for the descent of the Spirit, and had not the Holy Spirit descended upon all of them, as well as on Peter? In the fullness of time, the Pentecostal blessing was poured out most plentifully.

Whenever a church gets into the same state as that of the apostles and disciples at that memorable period, the whole heavenly electricity is concentrated at that particular spot. Yet you remember that even Christ Himself could not do many mighty works in some places because of the people's unbelief. I am sure that all His servants who are thoroughly in earnest are at times hampered in the same way. Some of our men who are here have, I fear, a worldly, Christless people. Still, I am not sure that they ought to run away from them. I think that, if possible, they should stop and try to make them more Christlike.

It is true that I have had the other sort of experience, as well as the joyous one I have been describing. I remember preaching one night in a place where they had not had a minister for some time. When I reached the chapel I did not have any kind of welcome. Those in authority there were to receive monetary benefit, if nothing else, from my visit, but they did not welcome me at all. They said, in fact, that a majority at the church meeting had been in favor of inviting me, but the deacons did not approve of it because they did not think I was "sound." Some brothers and sisters from other churches who attended seemed pleased and profited. But the people who belonged to the place did not receive it.

When the service was over, I went into the vestry, where the two deacons were standing, one on each side of the mantelpiece. I said to them, "Are you the deacons?" "Yes," they answered. "The church does not prosper, does it?" I asked. "No," they replied. "I should not think it would with such deacons," I said. "Do you know of anything against the deaconate?" they asked. "No," I said, "but I do not know anything in your favor." I thought that, if I could not get at them as a group, I would try what I could with one or two. I was glad to know that my sermon or my remarks afterward led to an improvement. One of our men is there, doing well to this day.

One of the deacons was so irritated by what I said that he left the place; but the other deacon was irritated the right way, so that he remained there, labored, and prayed until better days came. It is hard when you are rowing against wind and tide, but it is even worse if you have a horse on the riverbank pulling a rope and dragging your boat the other way. If that is your situation, nevermind, just work all the harder and pull the horse into the water.

Remember, once a favorable atmosphere is created, the difficulty is to maintain it. You notice that I said, "When the atmosphere is created." That expression reminds us how little we can do, or rather, that we can do nothing, without God. It is He who has to do with atmospheres; He alone creates and maintains them. Therefore, our eyes must continually be lifted to Him, from whom our help comes. It may happen that some of you preach very earnestly and well, giving messages that are likely to be blessed. Yet you do not see sinners saved. Well, do not quit preaching, but say to yourself, "I must try to gather around me a number of people who will be praying with me and for me; who will talk to their friends about the things of God; who will live and labor in such a way that the Lord will give a blessed shower of grace because all the surroundings are suitable; and who will and help to make the blessing come."

I have heard ministers say that when they have preached in the Tabernacle, there has been something in the congregation that has had a powerful effect on them. I think it is because we have good prayer meetings, because there is an earnest spirit of prayer among the people, and because so many of the people are on the watch for souls. There is one brother, especially, who is always looking after any hearers who have been impressed upon. I call him my hunting dog, and he is always ready to pick up the birds I have shot and bring them to me. I have known him to waylay one after another, so that he might bring them to Jesus.

I rejoice that I have other friends of this kind. When Fullerton and Smith had been conducting some special services for a very eminent preacher who is in the habit of using rather long words, this preacher said that the evangelists had the faculty for "the precipitation of decision." He meant that the Lord blessed them in bringing men to decision for Christ. It is a tremendous thing when a person has the faculty for the precipitation of decision. But it is an equally tremendous thing when he has a number of people around him who say to each hearer after every service, "Well, friend, did you enjoy that message? Was there something in it for you? Are you saved? Do you know the way to salvation?"

Always have your own Bible ready, and turn to the passages you want to quote to the inquirers. I often noticed the method of that friend of mine, of whom I just spoke. He seemed to me to open his Bible at most appropriate passages; he appeared to have them all ready and handy, so that he would be sure to hit on the right texts. You know the sort of texts I mean; exactly those that a seeking soul wants: "*The Son of man is come to seek and to save that which was lost*" (Luke 19:10). "*He that believeth on the Son hath everlasting life*" (John 3:36). "*The blood of Jesus Christ his Son cleanseth us from all sin*" (1 John 1:7). "*Him that cometh to me I will in no wise cast out*" (John 6:37). "*Whosoever shall call upon the name of the Lord shall be saved*" (Romans 10:13). Well, this brother has a number of such passages printed in bold type and fastened inside his Bible, so that he can refer to the right one in a moment. Many troubled souls has he thus led to the Savior. You will not be unwise if you adopt a method such as he has found so exceedingly helpful.

Now, finally, do not be afraid when you go to a place and find it in a very bad condition. It is a fine thing for a young man to begin with a real downright bad prospect, for, with the right kind of work, there has to be an improvement sooner or later. If the chapel is all but empty when you go to it, it cannot be in a much worse state than that. The probability is that you will be the means of bringing some into the church and so making matters better. If there is any place where I would choose to labor, it would be right on the borders of the infernal lake, for I really believe that it would bring more glory to God to work among those who are considered the worst of sinners. If your ministry is blessed to such people as these, they will be likely to cling to you through your whole life.

In reality, the very worst sort of people are those who have long been professing Christians, but who are destitute of grace, who have the name of life and yet are dead. Alas, there are people like that among our deacons and church members, but we cannot get them out. As long as they remain, they exert a very destructive influence. It is dreadful to have dead members where every single part of the body should be instilled with divine life. Yet in many cases it is so. We are powerless to cure the evil. We must let the tares grow until the harvest.

But the best thing to do, when you cannot root up the tares, is to water the wheat, for there is nothing that will keep back the tares like good strong wheat. I have known ungodly men who have had the place made so hot for them that they have been glad to clear out of the church. They have said, "The preaching is too strong for us, and these people are too puritanical and too strict to suit us." What a blessing it is when that is the case! We did not wish to drive them away by preaching the truth. But as they went of their own accord, we certainly do not want them back. We will leave them where they are, praying that the Lord, in the greatness of His grace, will turn them from the error of their ways and bring them to Himself. Then we will be glad to have them back with us to live and labor for the Lord.

7

HOW TO RAISE THE DEAD

Fellow laborers in the vineyard of the Lord, let me call your attention to a most instructive miracle worked by the prophet Elisha, as recorded in 2 Kings 4. The hospitality of the Shunammite woman had been rewarded by the gift of a son. But, alas, all earthly mercies are of uncertain tenure, and after certain days the child fell sick and died. The distressed but believing mother hurried at once to the man of God. Through him, God had originally spoken the promise that fulfilled her heart's desire, and she resolved to plead her case with him, so that he might lay it before his Divine Master and obtain for her an answer of peace.

> Then he said to Gehazi, Gird up thy loins, and take my staff in thine hand, and go thy way; if thou meet any man, salute him not; and if any salute thee, answer him not again: and lay my staff upon the face of the child. And the mother of the child said, As the LORD liveth, and as thy soul liveth, I will not leave thee. And he arose, and followed her. And Gehazi passed on before them, and laid the staff upon the face of the child; but there was neither voice, nor hearing Wherefore he went again to meet him, and told him, saying, The child is not awaked. And when Elisha was come into the house, behold, the child was dead, and laid upon his bed. He went in therefore, and shut the door

upon them twain, and prayed unto the LORD. And he went up, and lay upon
the child, and put his mouth upon his mouth, and his eyes upon his eyes, and
his hands upon his hands; and he stretched himself upon the child; and the
flesh of the child waxed warm. Then he returned, and walked in the house to
and fro; and went up, and stretched himself upon him; and the child sneezed
seven times, and the child opened his eyes. And he called Gehazi, and said,
Call this Shunammite. So he called her. And when she was come in unto him,
he said, Take up thy son. Then she went in, and fell at his feet, and bowed
herself to the ground, and took up her son, and went out.

(2 Kings 4:29–37)

The position of Elisha in this case is exactly your position, friends, in relation to your work for Christ. Elisha had to deal with a dead child. It is true that,
in his instance, it was natural death. But the death with which you have to come
in contact is not a less real death because it is spiritual. The boys and girls in
your Sunday school classes are, as surely as adults, *"dead in trespasses and sins"*
(Ephesians 2:1).

May none of you fail fully to realize the state in which all human beings are
naturally found! Unless you have a clear sense of the ruin and spiritual death of
your children, you will be incapable of being a blessing to them. Go to them, not
as to sleepers whom you corpses who can only be quickened by a divine power.
Elisha's great object was not to cleanse the dead body, embalm it with spices,
wrap it in fine linen, or place it in an appropriate posture, and then leave it still a
corpse. He aimed at nothing less than the restoration of the child to life. Beloved,
may you never be content with aiming at secondary benefits, or even with realizing them. May you strive for the grandest of all ends, the salvation of immortal
souls!

Your business is not merely to teach the children in your classes to read the
Bible, not just to instill the duties of morality, or even to instruct them in the
mere letter of the gospel. Your high calling is to be the means, in the hands of
God, of bringing life from heaven to dead souls. Your teaching on the Lord's Day
will have been a failure if your children remain dead in sin. In the case of the
secular teacher, the child's proficiency in knowledge will prove that the instructor
has done his job. In your case, even though your youthful charges should grow up
to be respectable members of society, though they may become regular hearers
of the means of grace, you will not feel that your petitions to heaven have been

answered, or your desires granted to you, or your highest ends attained, unless something more is done—unless, in fact, it can be said of your children, *"God... hath quickened* [them] *together with Christ"* (Ephesians 2:4–5).

Resurrection, then, is our aim! To raise the dead is our mission! We, like Peter at Joppa or Paul at Troas, have a young Dorcas or Eutychus to bring to life. How is so strange a work to be achieved? If we yield to unbelief, we will be staggered by the evident fact that the work to which the Lord has called us is quite beyond our own personal power. We cannot raise the dead. If asked to do so, each one of us, like the king of Israel, might rend our clothes, and say, *"Am I God, to kill and to make alive?"* (2 Kings 5:7). We are, however, no more powerless than Elisha, for he himself could not restore the Shunammite's son. It is true that, by ourselves, we cannot cause the dead hearts of our students to palpitate with spiritual life; but a Paul or an Apollos would have been equally as powerless. Need this fact discourage us? Does it not rather direct us to our true power by shutting us out from our imagined fancied might?

I trust that all of us are already aware that the person who lives in the region of faith dwells in the realm of miracles. Faith trades in marvels, and her commerce is with wonders.

> Faith, mighty faith, the promise sees,
> And looks to that alone;
> Laughs at impossibilities,
> And cries, It shall be done.

Elisha was no common man when God's Spirit was upon him, calling him to God's work and aiding him in it. And you, devoted, earnest, prayerful teacher, remain no longer a common being. You have become, in a special manner, the temple of the Holy Spirit. God dwells in you, and you, by faith, have entered into the career of a wonder-worker. You are sent into the world not to do the things that are possible to man, but those impossibilities that God works by His Spirit, by the means of His believing people. You are to work miracles, to do marvels. You are not, therefore, to look upon the restoration of these dead children, which you are called by God to bring about, as being something unlikely or difficult when you remember who it is that works by your feeble instrumentality. *"Why should it be thought a thing incredible with you, that God should raise the dead?"* (Acts 26:8).

Unbelief will whisper to you, as you note the wicked giddiness and early obstinacy of your children, *"Can these bones live?"* (Ezekiel 37:3). But your answer must be, *"O, Lord God, thou knowest"* (verse 3). Committing all cases to the Almighty, it is yours to prophesy to the dry bones and to the heavenly wind. Before long you, too, will see in the valley of your vision the triumphant signal of life over death.

Let us take up at this moment our true position, and let us realize it. We have dead children before us, and our souls yearn to bring them to life. We confess that all quickening must be done by the Lord alone. Our humble petition is that, if the Lord will use us in connection with His miracles of grace, He would now show us what He would have us do.

It would have been well if Elisha had recollected that he was once the servant of Elijah, and had studied his master's example so as to have imitated it. If so, he would not have sent Gehazi with a staff, but would have done at once what he was finally constrained to do. In the seventeenth chapter of 1 Kings, you will find the story of Elijah's raising of a dead child. There you will see that Elijah, the master, had left a complete example for his servant. It was not until Elisha followed it in all respects that the miraculous power was manifested. It would have been wise if Elisha had, at the outset, imitated the example of the master whose mantle he wore.

With far more force, may I say to you, my fellow servants, that it will be well for us if, as teachers, we imitate our Master, studying the modes and methods of our glorified Master and learning at His feet the art of winning souls. Just as He came in deepest sympathy into the nearest contact with our wretched humanity and graciously stooped to our sorrowful condition, we must come near to the souls with whom we have to deal, yearn over them with His yearning, and weep over them with His tears, if we would see them raised from the state of sin. Only by imitating the spirit and manner of the Lord Jesus will we become wise to win souls.

Forgetting this, however, Elisha preferred to strike out a course for himself, which would more clearly display his own prophetic dignity. He gave his staff into the hand of Gehazi, his servant, and told him to lay it upon the child, as if he felt that the divine power was so generously upon him that it would work in any way, and, consequently, his own personal presence and efforts might be dispensed with. The Lord's thoughts were not so.

I am afraid that, often, the truth that we deliver from the pulpit—and doubtless it is much the same in your classes—is a thing that is extraneous and outside of ourselves, like a staff that we hold in our hand, but that is not a part of ourselves. We take doctrinal or practical truth as Gehazi did the staff and lay it upon the face of the child, but we ourselves do not agonize for his soul. We try this doctrine and that truth, this anecdote and the other illustration, this way of teaching a lesson and that manner of delivering an address. However, as long as the truth that we deliver is a matter apart from ourselves and unconnected with our innermost beings, it will have no more effect on a dead soul than Elisha's staff had on the dead child.

Alas! I fear I have frequently preached the gospel in this way. I have been sure that it was my Master's gospel, the true prophetic staff, and yet it has had no result. I fear I have not preached it with the zeal, earnestness, and heartiness that ought to have gone with it! Could you not make the same confession, that sometimes you have taught the truth—it was the truth, you know it was—the very truth which you found in the Bible, that has at times been precious to your own soul, and yet no good result has followed from it? While you taught the truth, you did not feel it, or feel for the child to whom the truth was addressed, but were just like Gehazi placing with an indifferent hand the prophetic staff upon the face of the child. It is no wonder that you had to say with Gehazi, "The child is not awaked" (2 Kings 4:31), for the true awakening power found no appropriate medium in your lifeless teaching.

We are not sure that Gehazi was convinced that the child was really dead. He spoke as if he were only asleep and needed waking. God will not bless those teachers who do not grasp in their hearts the truly fallen state of their children. If you think the child is not really depraved, if you indulge foolish notions about the innocence of childhood and the dignity of human nature, it should not surprise you if you remain barren and unfruitful. How can God bless you to work a resurrection when, if He did work it by you, you would be incapable of perceiving its glorious nature? If the lad had awakened, it would not have surprised Gehazi; he would have thought that he was only startled from an unusually sound sleep. If God were to bless to the conversion of souls the testimony of those who do not believe in the total depravity of man, they would merely say, "The gospel is very moralizing and exerts a most beneficial influence," but they would never bless and magnify the regenerating grace by which He who sits on the throne makes all things new.

Observe carefully what Elisha did when thus foiled in his first effort. When we fail in one attempt, we must not therefore give up our work. If you have been unsuccessful until now, my dear brother or sister, you must not infer that you are not called to the work, any more than Elisha might have concluded that the child could not be restored. The lesson of your nonsuccess is not to cease the work, but to change the method. It is not the person who is out of place; it is the plan that is unwise. If you have not been able to accomplish what you wished, remember the schoolboy's song:

> If at first you don't succeed,
> Try, try, try again.

Do not, however, try in the same way, unless you are sure that it is the best one. If your first method has been unsuccessful, improve on it. Examine where you have failed, and then, by changing your mode or your spirit, the Lord may prepare you for a degree of usefulness far beyond your expectations. Elisha, instead of being dispirited when he found that the child was not awake, girded up his loins and hastened with greater vigor to the work before him.

Notice where the dead child was placed: *"And when Elisha was come into the house, behold, the child was dead, and laid upon his bed"* (2 Kings 4:32). This was the bed that the hospitality of the Shunammite woman had prepared for Elisha, the famous bed that, with the table, the stool and the candlestick, will never be forgotten in the church of God. That famous bed had to be used for a purpose that the good woman little thought of when, out of love for the prophet's God, she prepared it for the prophet's rest.

I like to think of the dead child lying on that bed because it symbolizes the place where our unconverted children must lie if we want them to be saved. If we are to be a blessing to them, they must lie in our hearts. They must be our daily and nightly charge. We must take the cases of our children with us to our silent couches. We must think of them in the watches of the night. When we cannot sleep because of care, they must share in those midnight anxieties. Our beds must witness our cries: "Oh, that Ishmael might live before You! (See Genesis 17:18.) May the dear children in my class become the children of the living God!" Elijah and Elisha both teach us that we must not place the child far from us, out-of-doors, or down below us in a vault of cold forgetfulness. If we want him to be raised to life, we must place him in the warmest sympathies of our hearts.

In reading on, we find that *"he went in therefore, and shut the door upon them twain, and prayed unto the Lord"* (2 Kings 4:33). Now the prophet is at his work in real earnest, and we have a noble opportunity of learning from him the secret of raising children from the dead. If you turn to the narrative of Elijah, you will find that Elisha adopted the orthodox method of proceeding, the method of his master Elijah. You will read there:

And he said unto her, Give me thy son. And he took him out of her bosom, and carried him up into a loft, where he abode, and laid him upon his own bed. And he cried unto the Lord, and said, O Lord, my God, have Thou also brought evil upon the woman with whom I sojourn, by slaying her son? And he stretched himself upon the child three times, and cried unto the Lord, and said, O Lord, my God, I pray Thee, let this child's soul come into him again. And the Lord heard the voice of Elijah, and the soul of the child came into him again, and he revived. (1 Kings 17:19–22)

The great secret lies, in a large measure, in powerful supplication. "*He…shut the door upon them twain, and prayed unto the Lord*" (2 Kings 4:33). The old proverb is, "Every true pulpit is set up in heaven," which means that the true preacher is much with God. If we do not pray to God for a blessing, if the foundation of the pulpit is not laid in private prayer, our open ministry will not be a success. It is the same with you; every real teacher's power must come from on high. If you never enter your prayer closet and shut the door, if you never plead at the mercy seat for your child, how can you expect that God will honor you in the child's conversion?

It is a very excellent method, I think, actually to take the children one by one into your room and pray with them. You will see your children converted when God enables you to individualize their cases, to agonize for them, and to take them one by one, with the door closed, to pray both with them and for them. There is much more influence in prayer privately offered with one than in prayer publicly voiced in the class—not more influence with God, of course, but more influence with the child. Such prayer will often be made its own answer. While you are pouring out your soul, God may make your prayer into a hammer to break the heart that mere addresses had never touched. Pray separately with your children, and it will surely be the means of a great blessing.

If this cannot be done, at any rate there must be prayer, much prayer, constant prayer, zealous prayer, the kind of prayer that will not take a denial, like Luther's prayer, which he called the bombarding of heaven—that is to say, the planting of a cannon at heaven's gates to blow them open. In this way, fervent men prevail in prayer. They will not leave the mercy seat until they can cry with Luther, "*Vici*, I have conquered; I have gained the blessing for which I strove." "*The kingdom of heaven suffereth violence, and the violent take it by force*" (Matthew 11:12). Let us offer such violent, God-constraining, heaven-compelling prayers; the Lord will not permit us to seek His face in vain!

After praying, Elisha adopted the means. Prayer and means must go together. Means without prayer—presumption! Prayer without means—hypocrisy! There lay the child, and there stood the venerable man of God! Watch his singular proceeding. He stoops over the corpse and puts his mouth upon the child's mouth. The cold, dead mouth of the child was touched by the warm, living lips of the prophet, and a vital stream of fresh, hot breath was sent down into the chilled, stone-like passages of the dead mouth, throat, and lungs. Next, the holy man, with loving ardor of hopefulness, placed his eyes upon the child's eyes and his hands upon the child's hands. The warm hands of the old man covered the cold palms of the departed child. Then he stretched himself upon the child and covered him with his whole body, as though he would transfer his own life into the lifeless frame. He would either die with him or make him live.

We have heard of the chamois hunter who acted as a guide to a fearful traveler. When they came to a very dangerous part of the road, the hunter strapped the traveler firmly to himself and said, "Both of us or neither," that is to say, "Both of us will live, or neither of us; we are one." So did the prophet effect a mysterious union between himself and the boy; in his own mind, it was resolved that either he would be chilled with the child's death or he would warm the child with his life.

What does this account of Elisha and the dead child teach us? The lessons are many and obvious. We see here, as in a picture, that if we want to bring spiritual life to a child, we must very vividly realize that child's state. It is dead, dead. God wants you to feel that the child is as dead in trespasses and sins as you once were. God wants you, dear teacher, to come into contact with that death by painful, crushing, humbling sympathy.

I told you that, in soulwinning, we should observe how our Master worked; now, how did He work? When He purposed to raise us from death, what was necessary for Him to do? He had to die Himself; there was no other way. It is the same with you.

If you want to raise a dead child, you must feel the chill and horror of that child's death yourself. A dying man is needed to raise dying men. I cannot believe that you will ever pluck a brand from the burning without putting your hand near enough to feel the heat of the fire. You must have, more or less, a distinct sense of the dreadful wrath of God and of the terrors of the judgment to come, or you will lack energy in your work and so lack one of the essentials of success.

I do not think the preacher ever speaks well on such topics until he feels them pressing upon him as a personal burden from the Lord. "I did preach in chains," said John Bunyan, "to men in chains." You can depend upon it. When the death in your children alarms, depresses, and overwhelms you, that is when God is about to bless you.

Thus, realizing the child's state and putting your mouth on the child's mouth and your hands on his hands, you must next strive to adapt yourself as far as possible to the nature, habits, and temperament of the child. Your mouth must discover the child's words, so that the child may know what you mean. You must see things with a child's eyes. Your heart must feel a child's feelings, so as to be his companion and friend. You must be a student of juvenile sin. You must be a sympathizer in juvenile trials. You must be able to enter into childhood's joys and griefs. You must not fret at the difficulty of this matter or feel that it is humiliating, for if you consider anything to be a hardship or a condescension, you have no business in the Sunday school. If anything difficult is required, you must do it and not think it difficult. God will not raise a dead child by you if you are not willing to become all things to that child, if by any possibility you may win his soul.

The prophet, it is written, *"stretched himself upon the child"* (2 Kings 4:34). One would have thought it should be written, "He contracted himself." He was a full-grown man, and the other a mere lad. Should it not be "he contracted himself"? No, *"he stretched himself."* Take note: no stretching is harder than for a man to stretch himself to fit a child. He is no fool who can talk to children. A simpleton is much mistaken if he thinks that his folly can interest boys and girls. It requires our best wits, our most industrious studies, our most earnest thoughts, and our ripest powers to teach our little ones. You will not quicken the child until you have stretched yourself. Though it seems a strange thing, it is so. The wisest man will need to exercise all his abilities if he wants to become a successful teacher of the young.

We see, then, in Elisha, a sense of the child's death and an adaptation of himself to his work. But, above all, we see sympathy. While Elisha himself felt the chill of the corpse, his personal warmth was entering into the dead body. This, in itself, did not raise the child, but God worked through it. The old man's body heat passed into the child and became the medium of quickening. Let every teacher weigh these words of Paul:

But we were gentle among you, even as a nurse cherisheth her children; so,
being affectionately desirous of you, we were willing to have imparted unto
you, not the gospel of God only, but also our own souls, because ye were dear
unto us. (1 Thessalonians 2:7–8)

The genuine soulwinner knows what this means. For my own part, when the Lord helps me to preach, after I have delivered all my matter and have fired off my shot so fast that my gun has grown hot, I have often rammed my soul into the gun and fired my heart at the congregation. This discharge has, under God, won the victory. God will bless by His Spirit our hearty sympathy with His own truth, and make it do that which the truth alone, coldly spoken, would not accomplish.

Here, then, is the secret: You must, teacher, impart to the young your own soul. You must feel as if the ruin of that child would be your own ruin. You must feel that, if the child remains under God's wrath, it is to you as true a grief as if you were under that wrath yourself. You must confess the child's sins before God as if they were your own and stand as a priest before the Lord, pleading on his behalf. The child was covered by Elisha's body, and you must cover your class with your compassion, with the agonizing stretching forth of yourself before the Lord on its behalf. Behold in this miracle the *modus operandi* of raising the dead: the Holy Spirit remains mysterious in His operations, but the way of the outward means is here clearly revealed.

The result of the prophet's work soon appeared: *"the flesh of the child waxed warm"* (2 Kings 4:34). How pleased Elisha must have been. Yet I do not find that his pleasure and satisfaction caused him to relax his exertions. Dear friends, never be satisfied with finding your children in a barely hopeful state. Did a girl come to you and cry, "Teacher, pray for me?" Be glad, for this is a good sign, but look for more. Did you observe tears in a boy's eyes when you were speaking of the love of Christ? Be thankful that the flesh is waxing warm, but do not stop there. Can you relax your exertions now? Think, you have not yet gained your end! It is life you want, not warmth alone. What you want, dear teacher, in your beloved charge is not mere conviction, but conversion. You desire not only impression, but regeneration—life, life from God, the life of Jesus. This your students need. Nothing less must content you.

Again, I must ask you watch Elisha. There was a little pause. *"Then he returned, and walked in the house to and fro"* (2 Kings 4:35). Notice the restlessness of the man of God; he cannot rest easy. The child waxes warm, blessed be God for that, but he does not yet live. So, instead of sitting down in his chair by the table, the prophet walks *"to and fro"* with a restless pace, disquieted, groaning, panting, longing, and ill at ease. He could not bear to look upon the disconsolate mother or to hear her ask, "Is the child restored?" He continued pacing the house as if his body could not rest because his soul was not satisfied.

Imitate this consecrated restlessness. When you see a boy becoming somewhat affected, do not sit down and say, "The child is very hopeful, thank God; I am perfectly satisfied." You will never win the priceless gem of a saved soul in that way. You must feel sad, restless, troubled, if you ever become a parent in the church. Paul's statement is not to be explained in words, but you must know its meaning in your hearts: *"I travail in birth again until Christ be formed in you"* (Galatians 4:19). Oh, may the Holy Spirit give you such inward travail, such unrest, disquietude, and sacred uneasiness, until you see your hopeful students soundly converted!

After a short period of walking to and fro, the prophet *"returned,…went up, and stretched himself upon him"* (2 Kings 4:35). What it is well to do once, it is proper to do a second time. What is good twice is good seven times. There must be perseverance and patience. You were very earnest last Sabbath. Do not be slothful next Sunday. How easy it is to pull down, on any one day, what we have built up the day before! If by one Sabbath's work, God enables me to convince a child that I was in earnest, let me not convince the child the next Sunday that I am not in earnest. If my past warmth has made the child's flesh wax warm, God forbid that my future chilliness should make the child's heart cold again! As surely as warmth went from Elisha to the child, cold may go from you to your class unless you are in an earnest state of mind.

Elisha stretched himself on the bed again with many a prayer, many a sigh, and much believing. At last his desire was granted him: *"The child sneezed seven times, and the child opened his eyes"* (2 Kings 4:35). Any form of action would indicate life and content the prophet. Some say that the child *"sneezed"* because he died with a disease of the head. He had said to his father, *"My head, my head"* (2 Kings 4:19). The sneeze may have cleared the passages of life that had been blocked up. This we do not know. The fresh air entering anew into the lungs might well compel a sneeze. The sound was nothing very articulate or musical, but it spoke of life.

This is all we should expect from young children when God gives them spiritual life. Some church members expect a great deal more, but for my part, I am satisfied if the children sneeze—if they give any true sign of grace, however feeble or indistinct. If the dear child does feel his lost state and rests upon the finished work of Jesus, though we find out that fact only by a very indistinct statement—not such as we would accept from a doctor of divinity or expect from a grown person—should we not thank God, receive the child, and nurse him for the Lord?

If only Gehazi had been there, perhaps he would not have thought much of this sneezing, because he had never stretched himself upon the child; but Elisha was content with it. Similarly, if you and I have really agonized in prayer for souls, we will be very quick of eye to catch the first sign of grace and will be thankful to God if the sign is but a sneeze.

Then the child opened his eyes. We will venture to say that Elisha thought he had never seen such lovely eyes before. I do not know what kind of eyes they were, hazel or blue, but I know that any eye that God helps you to open will be a beautiful eye to you. I heard a teacher talking the other day about a "fine lad" who had been saved in his class, and another spoke of a "dear girl" in her class who loved the Lord. No doubt of it. It would be a wonder if they were not "fine" and "dear" in the eyes of you who have brought them to Jesus, for to Jesus Christ they are finer and dearer still. Beloved friends, may you often gaze into opened eyes that, but for divine grace owning your teaching, would have been dark with the film of spiritual death! Then you will be favored, indeed.

One word of caution. Is there a Gehazi here? If there is among you one who can do no more than carry the staff, I pity him. My friend, may God in His mercy give you life, for how else can you expect to be the means of quickening others? If Elisha had been a corpse himself, it would have been a hopeless task to expect life to be communicated through placing one corpse upon another. It is useless for that little class of dead souls to gather around another dead soul such as you are. A dead mother, frostbitten and cold, cannot cherish her little one. What warmth, what comfort, can come to those who shiver before an empty fireplace? And such are you. May you have a work of grace in your soul first; and then may the blessed and eternal Spirit, who alone can quicken souls, cause you to be the means of quickening many, to the glory of His grace!

Accept, dear friends, my brotherly regards, and believe that my fervent prayers are with you so that you may be blessed and be made a blessing.

8

HOW TO WIN SOULS
FOR CHRIST

I t is a great privilege to speak to so noble a group of preachers. I wish that I were more fit for the task. Silver of eloquent speech and gold of deep thought have I none, but such as I have, give I unto you.

What is it to win a soul? I hope you believe in the old-fashioned way of saving souls. Everything appears to be shaken nowadays and shifted from the old foundations. It seems that we are to evolve out of men the good that is already in them. You will not get much good if you attempt the process! I am afraid that in the process of evolution you will develop devils. I do not know much else that will come out of human nature, for humanity is as full of sin as an egg is full of potential meat. The evolution of sin must be everlasting evil.

We all believe that we must go soulwinning, desiring in God's name to see all things made new. This old creature is dead, corrupt, and must be buried—the sooner, the better. Jesus has come that there may be a passing away of the old things and a making of all things new. In the process of our work, we endeavor to bless men by trying to make them temperate. May God bless all work of that sort!

However, we should think that we have failed if we produced a world of total abstainers, but left them all unbelievers. We drive at something more than just

457

temperance, for we believe that men must be born again. It is good that even a corpse should be clean and that the unregenerate should be moral. It would be a great blessing if they were cleansed of the vices that make this city reek in the nostrils of God and good men. But that is not so much our work as this: that the dead in sin would live, that spiritual life should quicken them, and that Christ would reign where the *"prince of the power of the air"* (Ephesians 2:2) now has sway.

Preach with this object: that men may renounce their sins and run to Christ for pardon, that by His blessed Spirit they may be renovated and become as much in love with everything that is holy as they are now in love with everything that is sinful. Aim at a radical cure. Lay the ax at the root of the tree. Amendment of the old nature would not content you; you seek the imparting, by a divine power, of a new nature, that those who gather around you in the streets may live for God.

Our object is to turn the world upside down, so that *"where sin abounded, grace* [may] *much more abound"* (Romans 5:20). We are aiming at a miracle. It is well to settle this purpose at the beginning. Some men think that they ought to lower what they say to the spiritual ability of the hearer, but this is a mistake. According to them, you ought not to exhort a person to repent and believe unless you believe that he himself is able to repent and believe. My reply is a confession: I command men in the name of Jesus to repent and believe the gospel, though I know they can do nothing of the kind apart from the grace of God. I am not sent to work according to what my private reasoning might suggest, but according to the orders of my Lord and Master.

Ours is the miraculous method that comes of the endowment of the Spirit of God, who chooses His ministers to perform wonders in the name of the holy Christ Jesus. We are sent to say to blind eyes, "See," to deaf ears, "Hear," to dead hearts, "Live," and even to Lazarus rotting in that grave, *"Lazarus, come forth"* (John 11:43). Dare we do this? We will be wise to begin with the conviction that we are utterly powerless for this unless our Master has sent us and is with us. But if He who sent us is with us, *"all things are possible to him that believeth"* (Mark 9:23).

If you are about to stand up to see what you can do, it will be wise of you to sit down quickly; but if you stand up to prove what the Almighty can do through you, then infinite possibilities lie around you! There are no bounds to what God can accomplish if He works by your heart and voice.

Before I entered the pulpit the other Sabbath morning, the dear deacons and elders of my church gathered around me for prayer. One of them said, "Lord, take him as a man takes a tool in his hand when he gets a firm hold of it and then uses it to work his own will with it." That is what all workers need: that God may work through them. You are to be instruments in the hands of God, while you actively put forth all the faculties and forces that the Lord has lent to you. Yet never depend upon your personal power, but rest alone upon the sacred, mysterious, divine energy that works in us, by us, and with us on the hearts and minds of men.

Friends, we have been greatly disappointed, have we not, with some of our converts? We will always be disappointed with them as far as they are our converts. We will greatly rejoice over them when they prove to be the Lord's work. When the power of grace works in them, then it will be, as my brother says, "Glory!" and nothing else but glory. Grace brings glory, but mere oratory will only create sham and shame in the long run.

When we are preaching, and we think of a very pretty, flowery passage or a very neat, poetical paragraph, I wish we could be restrained by the fear that acted upon Paul when he said that he would not use the *wisdom of words, lest the cross of Christ should be made of none effect* (1 Corinthians 1:17). It is the duty of the gospel preacher, indoors or outdoors, to say, "I can say that very prettily, but then they might notice how I said it. I will, therefore, say it in such a way that that they will observe only the intrinsic value of the truth that I want to teach them."

It is not our way of putting the gospel, or even our method of illustrating it, that wins souls, but the gospel itself does the work in the hands of the Holy Spirit. We must look to Him for the thorough conversion of men. A miracle is to be worked, by which our hearers will become the products of the mighty power that God worked in *Christ, when he raised him from the dead, and set him at his own right hand in the heavenly places, far above all principality, and power* (Ephesians 1:20–21). For this glorious power, we must look outside of ourselves to the living God, must we not? We desire thorough conversion, and therefore we must rely upon the power of the Holy Spirit. If it is a miracle, God must work it, that is clear. It is not to be accomplished by our reasoning, persuasion, or warning. It can come only from the Lord.

Since the winning of souls lies in God, in what way can we hopefully expect to be endowed with the Spirit of God and to go forth in His power? I reply that a great deal depends on the condition of the soulwinner himself. I am persuaded that we have never laid enough stress on the work of God within our own selves in its relation to our service for God. A consecrated Christian may be charged with divine energy to the fullest, so that everybody around him will perceive it. They cannot tell what it is, or where it comes from, or, perhaps, where it goes. But they know that there is something about that Christian that is far beyond the common order of things.

At another time, that same Christian may be feeble and dull, and be conscious that he is so. He shakes himself, as at other times, but he cannot do any mighty deed. It is clear that Samson himself must be in a right condition, or he can win no victories. If the champion's locks have been shaved, the Philistines will laugh at him. If the Lord is gone from the person, he has no power left for useful service.

Dear friends, look carefully to your own condition before God. Take care of the home farm. Look well to your own flocks and herds. Unless your walk is close with God, unless you dwell in the clear light that surrounds the throne of God and is only known to those who are in fellowship with the eternal, you will go out and hurry to your work, but nothing will come of it. True, the vessel is but an earthen one, yet it has its place in the divine arrangement. It will not be filled with the divine treasure unless it is a clean vessel and unless in other respects it is a vessel fit for the Master's use.

Let me show you some ways in which in soulwinning, much depends on the soulwinner himself. We win some souls to Christ by acting as witnesses. We stand up and testify for the Lord Jesus Christ concerning certain truths. Now, I have never had the great privilege of being bamboozled by a trial lawyer. I have sometimes wondered what I would do if I were put into the witness box to be examined and cross-examined. I think I would simply stand up and tell the truth as far as I knew it. I would not make an attempt to display my wit, language, or judgment. If I gave straightforward, simple answers to his questions, I would beat any lawyer under heaven. But the difficulty is that so often when a witness is put into the box, he is more conscious of himself than of what he has to say. Thus, he is soon worried, teased, and provoked. By losing his temper, he fails to be a good witness for the cause.

Now, you who witness for Christ are often bamboozled. The devil's lawyers are sure to come to you. He has a great number of them constantly retained in his service. The one thing you have to do is to bear witness to the truth. If you inquire in your own mind, "How can I answer this man cleverly, so as to get a victory over him?" you will not be wise. A witty answer is often a very proper thing. At the same time, a gracious answer is better. Say to yourself: "It does not matter whether that man proves me to be a fool or not, for I already know that I am. I am content to be thought a fool for Christ's sake and not to care about my reputation. I have to bear witness to what I know, and by the help of God, I will do so boldly. If the interrupter questions me about other things, I will tell him that I do not come to bear witness about other matters. I will speak to only one point, and to no other."

Friends, the one who witnesses must himself be saved, and he should be sure of it. I do not know whether you doubt your own salvation. Perhaps I should recommend that you preach even when that is the case, since, if you are not saved yourself, you still desire others to be. You do not doubt that you once enjoyed full assurance. But now, if you have to sorrowfully confess, "Alas! I do not feel the full power of the gospel on my own heart," you can truly add, "Yet I know that it is true, for I have seen it save others, and I know that no other power can save me." Perhaps even that faltering testimony, so truly honest, might bring a tear into your opponent's eye and make him feel sympathy for you. "I preached," said John Bunyan, "sometimes without hope, like a man in chains to men in chains, and when I heard my own fetters rattle, yet I told others that there was deliverance for them, and I bade them look to the great Deliverer." I would not have stopped Mr. Bunyan from preaching so.

At the same time, it is a great thing to be able to declare from your own personal experience that the Lord has *"broken the gates of brass, and cut the bars of iron insunder"* (Psalm 107:162). Those who hear our witness say, "Are you sure of it?" Sure of it? I am as sure of it as I am sure that I am living. They call this dogmatism. Never mind about that. A person ought to know what he is preaching about, or else let him sit down. If I had any doubt about the matters I preach from my pulpit, I would be ashamed to remain the pastor of my church. But I preach what I do know and testify to what I have seen. If I am mistaken, I am heartily and intensely mistaken. I risk my soul and all its eternal interests on the truth of what I preach. If the gospel of what I preach does not save me, I will never be saved, for what I proclaim to others is my own ground of trust. I have no private lifeboat; the ark to which I invite others holds myself and all that I have.

A good witness ought to know all that he is going to say. He should feel himself at home in his subject. Suppose a man is brought up as a witness in a certain case of robbery. He knows what he saw and has to make a declaration of that only. When the lawyers begin to question him about a picture in the house, or the color of a dress that was hanging in the wardrobe. He answers, "You are going beyond what I know; I can only witness to what I saw." What we do know and what we do not know would make two very large books. We may safely ask to be let alone as to the second volume.

Friend, say what you know, and then sit down. But be calm and composed while speaking of that with which you have personal acquaintance. You will never properly indulge your emotions in preaching, so as to feel at home with the people, until you are at home with your subject. When you know what you are about, your mind will be free for earnestness. Unless you know the gospel from beginning to end and know where you are in preaching it, you cannot preach with due emotion. When you feel at home with your doctrine, stand up and be as bold, earnest, and unrelenting as you please. Face the people feeling that you are going to tell them something worth hearing, about which you are quite sure, which to you is your very life. There are honest hearts in every assembly, outdoor or indoor, who only want to hear honest beliefs. They will accept them and be led to believe in the Lord Jesus Christ.

But you are not only witnesses, you are also pleaders for the Lord Jesus Christ. Now, in pleading, much depends on the pleader. It seems as if the sign and symbol of Christianity in some preachers was not a tongue of fire but a block of ice. You would not like to have a lawyer stand up and plead your cause in a cool, deliberate way, never showing the slightest concern about whether you were found guilty of murder or acquitted. How could you endure his indifference when you yourself were likely to be hanged? Oh, no, you wish to silence such a false advocate! So, when a person has to speak for Christ, if he is not in earnest, let him go to bed. You smile, but is it not better that he should go to bed than send a whole congregation to sleep without their going to bed? We must be downright earnest.

If we are to prevail with men, we must love them. There is a genuine love for men that some have, and there is a genuine dislike of men that others have. I know a gentlemen, whom I esteem in a way, who seem to think that the working classes are a shockingly bad lot, to be kept in check and governed with force. With such views they will never convert working men. To win men, you must feel: "I am one of them. If they are a sad lot, I am one of them. If they are lost sinners, I am one of them. If they need a Savior, I am one of them." To the chief of sinners you should preach with this text before you: *"Such were some of you"* (1 Corinthians 6:11).

Grace alone makes us different, and that grace we preach. Genuine love for God and fervent love for man make up the great qualifications of a pleader.

I further believe, although certain people deny it, that the influence of fear is to be exercised over the minds of men, and that it ought to operate on the mind of the preacher himself. *"Noah…moved with fear, prepared an ark to the saving of his house"* (Hebrews 11:7). Through Noah's fears, there was salvation for this world from perishing in the flood. When a Christian fears for others, his heart cries out, "They will perish, they will perish; they will sink to hell; they will be forever banished from the presence of the Lord." When this fear oppresses his soul, weighs him down, and then drives him to go out and preach with tears, then he will plead with men so as to prevail!

Knowing the terror of the Lord, he will persuade men. To know the terror of the Lord is the means of teaching us to persuade without speaking harshly. Some have used the terrors of the Lord to terrify, but Paul used them to persuade. (See 2 Corinthians 25:11.) Let us copy him. Say, "We have come out to tell you that the world is on fire, and you must flee for your lives and escape to the mountain, lest you be consumed." We must give this warning with the full conviction that it is true, or else we will be but as the boy who in foolishness cried, "Wolf !" Something of the shadow of the last tremendous Day must fall upon our spirits to give the accent of conviction to our message of mercy, or we will miss the pleader's true power. We must tell men that there is pressing need of a Savior and show them that we perceive their need and feel for them, or else we will not be likely to turn them to the Savior. He who pleads for Christ should himself be moved with the prospect of Judgment Day.

When I come in the door at the back of the pulpit, and the sight of that vast crowd bursts upon me, I frequently feel appalled. I think of those thousands of immortal souls gazing through the windows of those wistful eyes, and that I am to preach to them all and be responsible for their blood if I am not faithful to them. I tell you, it makes me feel ready to run back through the door. But my fear is not alone. I am borne up by the hope and belief that God intends to bless these people through the Word that He will enable me to deliver. I believe that everybody in that throng is sent there by God for some purpose, and that I am sent to effect that purpose.

When I am preaching, I often think to myself, "Who is being converted now?" It never occurs to me that the Word of the Lord will fail. No, that can never be. I often feel sure that men are being converted, and at all times that God is glorified by the testimony of His truth. You may depend on the fact that your hopeful conviction that God's Word cannot return to Him void is a great encouragement to your hearers as well as to yourself. Your enthusiastic confidence that they will be converted may be like the little finger of a mother held out to her baby, to help it to make its way to her. The fire within your hearts may shoot sparks into their souls by which the flame of spiritual life will be kindled in them. Do let us all learn the art of pleading with the souls of men.

Still, dear Christians, we are not only to be witnesses and pleaders, but we are also to be examples. One of the most successful ways of hunting wild ducks is the use of the decoy bird. The decoy duck enters the net itself, and the others follow it. We need to employ the holy art of the decoy more in the Christian church. That is to say, we need to draw others to Christ through our examples of coming to Christ, of living godly lives in the midst of a perverse generation, of joy and sorrow, and of holy submission to the divine will in the time of trouble. Then our examples, in all manner of gracious ways, will be the means of inducing others to enter the way of life.

You cannot, of course, stand up in the street and tell about your example. However, there is no street preacher who is not known better than he thinks. Someone in the crowd may be in the secret places of the speaker's private life. I once heard of an open-air preacher to whom a hearer cried out, "Ah, Jack, you dare not preach like that at your own door!" It so happened, unfortunately, that Mr. John had offered to fight one of his neighbors a little while before, and therefore it was not likely that he would have done much preaching very near home. This made the interruption an awkward one.

If any man's life at home is unworthy, he should go several miles away before he stands up to preach. When he stands up, he should say nothing. They know us, friends. They know far more about us than we imagine, and what they do not know they make up. At the same time, our walk and conversation should be the most powerful part of our ministries. This is what is called being consistent, when lips and life agree.

I have said that the working of the Holy Spirit depends largely on the soul-winner himself, but I am bound to add that much will also depend on the kind of people who are around him. An open-air preacher, who has to go out quite alone, must be in a very unfortunate position. It is extremely helpful to be connected with an earnest, living church that prays for you. If you cannot find such a church where you labor, the next best thing is to get half-a-dozen brothers or sisters who will back you up, go out with you, and especially pray with you. Some preachers are so independent that they can do without helpers, but they will be wise if they do not seek solitude. May they look at the matter in this way: "By bringing several men to go out with me, I will be doing good to these young men, training them to be workers."

If you can associate with yourself a half-dozen Christians who are not all very young, but somewhat advanced in their knowledge of divine truth, the association will be greatly to your mutual advantage. I confess to you all that, although God has greatly blessed me in His work, none of the credit is due to me at all, but to those dear friends at the Tabernacle, and, indeed, all over the world, who make me the special subject of their prayers.

A man ought to do well with such people around him as I have. My friend and deacon, Mr. William Olney, once said, "Our minister has so far led us forward, and we have followed heartily. Everything has been a success; do you not believe in his leadership?" The people cried, "Yes." Then said my dear friend, "If our pastor has brought us up to a ditch that looks as if it could not be passed, let us fill it up with our bodies and carry him across." This was grand talk: the ditch was filled—no, it seemed to fill itself up at once. If you have a true comrade, your strength is more than doubled.

What a blessing a good wife is! You women, who would not be in your right place if you began to preach in the streets, can make your husbands happy and comfortable when they come home, and that will make them preach all the better! Some of you can even help in another way if you are discreet and gentle. You can tenderly hint that your spouse was a little out of line in certain small matters, and he may take your hint and put himself right. A good brother once asked me to give him some instruction, pleading thus: "The only instructor I have had was my wife, who had a better schooling than fell to my lot. I used to say, 'We was,' and 'Us did it.' She quietly hinted that people might laugh at me if I did not attend to grammar." His wife thus became to him a professor of the English language and was worth her weight in gold to him, which he knew. You who have such helpers ought to thank God daily for them.

Next to this, it is very helpful to join in brotherly league with some earnest Christian who knows more than we do and will benefit us with wise advice. God may bless us for the sake of others when He might not bless us for our own sake. You have heard the story of the man who had preached and won many souls to Christ. He was congratulating himself one night, when it was revealed to him that he would have none of the honor of it at the last great Day. He asked the angel in his dream who, then, would have the credit for it, to which the angel replied, "That deaf old man who sits on the pulpit stairs and prays for you was the means of the blessing." Let us be thankful for that deaf man, or that old woman, or those poor praying friends who bring down a blessing upon us by their intercession.

The Spirit of God will bless two when He might not bless one. Abraham alone did not get one of the five cities saved, although his prayer was like a ton weight in the scale. But nearby was his nephew Lot, who was about the poorest lot that could be found. He did not have more than half an ounce of prayer in him, but that tiny fragment turned the scale, and Zoar was preserved. (See Genesis 14:8–9, 18:17–19:29.) Add, then, your odd half-ounce to the mightier weight of the supplications of eminent saints, for they may need it.

Dear friends, I am not trying to instruct you. Some of you could far better instruct me. Yet I do not know, for I suspect I must be getting rather old, from what I hear. At the beginning of this year, a woman was trying to get some money out of me, and she said, "I remember hearing your dear voice more than forty years ago." I said, "Heard my voice forty years ago! Where was that?" She said, "You were preaching at the bottom of Pentonville Hill, near where Mr. Sawday's chapel is." "Well," I said, "was it not more than forty years ago?" "Yes," she said, "It might be fifty." "Oh," I said, "I suppose I was quite young then?" "Oh, yes!" she said, "you were such a dear young man." That, of course, was a needless assurance; but I do not think she was quite so sure of my dearness when I told her that I never preached at the bottom of Pentonville Hill, that fifty years ago I was only three years old, and that I thought it was shameful for her to suppose that I should give her money for telling falsehoods. However, I will presume upon the woman's statement tonight and imagine that I am that venerable person she described me as being. I will make bold to say to you, dear ones, that if we are going to win souls, we must go in for downright hard labor and work.

First, we must work at our preaching. You are not distrustful of the use of preaching, are you? I hope you do not weary of it, though you certainly sometimes must weary in it. Cobbler, stick to your trade; preacher, stick to your preaching. In the great Day, when the roll is read, all those who were converted through fine music, splendid church decor and architecture, or religious exhibitions and entertainments will amount to the tenth part of nothing. But it will always please God *"by the foolishness of preaching to save them that believe"* (1 Corinthians 1:21).

Keep to your preaching; if you do anything else, do not let it throw your preaching into the background. In the first place preach, and in the second place preach, and in the third place preach. Believe in preaching the love of Christ; believe in preaching the atoning sacrifice; believe in preaching the new birth; believe in preaching the whole counsel of God. The old hammer of the gospel will still break the rock in pieces. The ancient fire of Pentecost will still burn among the multitude. Try nothing new, but go on with preaching.

If we all preach with the *"Holy Spirit sent down from heaven"* (1 Peter 1:12), the results will astound us. After all, there is no end to the power of the tongue! Look at the power of a bad tongue—what great harm it can do! Will not God put more power into a good tongue, if we will but use it right? Look at the power of fire: a single spark might set a city ablaze. Similarly, the Spirit of God being with us, we do not need to calculate how much or what we can do. There is no calculating the potentialities of a flame, and no end to the possibilities of divine truth spoken with the enthusiasm that is born of the Spirit of God.

Have great hope yet, brothers; have great hope yet, despite the shameless midnight streets, despite the flaming gin palaces at the corner of every street, despite the wickedness of the rich, despite the ignorance of the poor. Go on, go on, go on; in God's name, go on. If the preaching of the gospel does not save men, nothing will. If the Lord's own way of mercy fails, then hang the skies in mourning and blot out the sun in everlasting midnight, for there remains nothing for our race but the blackness of night. Salvation by the sacrifice of Jesus is the ultimatum of God. Rejoice that it cannot fail. Let us believe without reserve and then go straight ahead with the preaching of the Word.

Truehearted preachers will be sure to combine with their preaching much earnest private talk. What numbers of people have been converted in the Tabernacle by the personal conversation of certain brothers, whom I will not further indicate! They are all about the place while I am preaching! I remember that a brother was speaking to me one Monday night. Suddenly, he vanished before he finished the sentence that he was whispering. I never quite knew what he was going to say, but I quickly saw him in the left-hand gallery, sitting in the pew with a lady unknown to me. After the service, I said to him, "Where did you go?" and he said, "A gleam of sunlight came in at the window and made me see a face that looked so sad. I hurried upstairs and took my seat in the pew close to the woman with the sad face." "Did you cheer her?" "Oh, yes! She received the Lord Jesus very readily. Just as she did so, I noticed another eager face. Asking her to wait in the pew until after the service, I went after the other —a young man." He prayed with both of these people and would not be satisfied until they had given their hearts to the Lord. That is the way to be on the alert.

We need a body of sharpshooters to pick out their men one by one. When we fire great guns from the pulpit, execution is done, but many are missed. We need loving spirits to go around to deal with individual cases by pointed personal warnings and encouragement. Every preacher should not only address the hundreds, but should also be ready to pounce upon the ones. He should have others with him who have the same happy ability. How much more good would come of preaching in the streets if every open-air preacher were accompanied by a group of people who would drive his nails home for him by personal conversation!

Last Sunday night, my dear brother told us a little story that I will never forget. He was at Croydon Hospital one night, as one of those appointed to visit it. All the porters had gone home, and it was time to shut up for the night. He was the only person in the hospital, with the exception of the physician, when a boy came running in, saying that there was a railway accident, and someone must go to the station with a stretcher. The doctor said to my brother, "Will you take one end of the stretcher if I take the other?" "Oh, yes!" was the cheerful reply. So away went the doctor and the pastor with the stretcher. They brought a sick man back with them.

My brother later said, "I went often to the hospital during the next week or two, because I felt so much interest in the man whom I had helped to carry." I believe he will always take an interest in that man, because he once felt the weight of him. When you know how to carry a person in your heart and feel the burden of his situation, you will have his name engraved upon your soul. So those of you who privately talk to people are feeling the weight of souls. I believe that this is what many preachers need to experience, and then they will preach better. When preaching and private talk are not available, you need to have a tract ready. This is often an effective method. Some tracts would not convert a beetle; there is not enough in them to interest a fly. Get good, striking tracts, or none at all. But a touching gospel tract may be the seed of eternal life. Therefore, do not go out without your tracts.

I suppose, besides giving a tract, if you can, you try to find out where a person who frequently hears you lives so that you may call on him. What a fine thing a visit from an open-air preacher is! "Why," says a man's wife, "there is that man come to see you, Bill—that gentleman who preaches at the corner of the street. Shall I tell him to come in?" "Oh, yes!" is the reply, "I have heard him many times; he is a good fellow." Visit as much as you can, for it will be of use to you as well as to the people.

Also, what power there is in a letter to an individual! Some people still have a kind of superstitious reverence for a letter. When they get an earnest letter from a revered person, they think a great deal of it. Who knows if a note by post may hit the man your message missed. Young people who are not able to preach might do much good if they would write letters to their young friends about their souls. They could speak very plainly with their pens pens, though they might be shy about speaking with their tongues.

Let us save men by all the means under heaven; let us prevent men from going down to hell. We are not half as earnest as we ought to be. Do you not remember the young man, who, when he was dying, said to his brother, "How could you have been as indifferent to my soul as you have been?" He answered, "I have not been indifferent to your soul, for I have frequently spoken to you about it." "Oh, yes!" he said, "you spoke. But somehow, I think, if you had remembered that I was going down to hell, you would have been more earnest with me. You would have wept over me, and, as my brother, you would not have allowed me to be lost." Let no one say this of you.

But I hear it observed that most men, when they grow earnest, do such odd things and say such strange things. Let them say strange things and let them do strange things, if these come out of genuine earnestness. We do not want pranks and performances that are the mere sham of earnestness; real white-heat intensity is the need of the times. Where you see that, it is a pity to be so critical. You must let a great storm rage in its own way. You must let a living heart speak as it can. If you are zealous and yet cannot speak, your earnestness will invent its own method of working out its purpose. As Hannibal is said to have melted the rocks with vinegar, earnestness will one way or another dissolve the rocky hearts of men.

May the Spirit of God rest upon you, one and all, for Jesus Christ's sake! Amen.

9

THE COST OF BEING
A SOULWINNER

I want to say a word to you who are trying to bring souls to Jesus. You long and pray to be useful. Do you know what this involves? Are you sure that you do? Prepare yourselves, then, to see and suffer many things that you would rather be unacquainted with. Experiences that would be unnecessary to you personally will become your portion if the Lord uses you for the salvation of others.

An ordinary person may rest in his bed all night, but a surgeon will be called up at all hours. A farmer may take his ease at his fireside, but if he becomes a shepherd, he must be out among the lambs and endure all kinds of weather for them. Similarly, Paul said, "*Therefore I endure all things for the elect's sakes, that they may also obtain the salvation which is in Christ Jesus with eternal glory*" (2 Timothy 2:10). For this reason we will be made to undergo experiences that will surprise us.

Some years ago, I underwent terrible depression of spirit. Certain troublesome events had happened to me. I was also unwell, and my heart sank within me. Out of the depths, I was forced to cry out to the Lord. Just before I went away to Mentone for rest, I suffered greatly in body, but far more in soul, for my spirit was overwhelmed. Under this pressure, I preached a message from the words,

"My God, my God, why hast thou forsaken me?" (Mark 15:34). I was as much qualified to preach from that text as I ever expect to be; indeed, I hope that few of you could have entered so deeply into those heartbreaking words. I felt to my fullest extent the horror of a soul forsaken by God. Now, that was not a desirable experience. I tremble at the mere idea of passing again through that eclipse of soul. I pray that I may never suffer in that way again unless the same result would come from it.

That night, after the service, a man came into the vestry who was as nearly insane as he could be and still be out of an asylum. His eyes seemed ready to spring from his head. He said that he would have utterly despaired if he had not heard that message, which had made him feel that there was one man alive who understood his feelings and could describe his experience. I talked with him and tried to encourage him. I asked him to come again on Monday night, when I would have a little more time to talk with him. Later, I saw the brother again, and I told him that I thought he was a hopeful patient and was glad that the word had been so suited to his situation. Apparently, he had put aside the comfort that I presented for his acceptance; and yet I had the consciousness within me that the precious truth that he had heard was at work upon his mind and that the storm of his soul would soon subside into a deep calm.

Now, hear the sequel. Last night, of all the times in the year, I was preaching from the words, *"The Almighty…hath vexed my soul"* (Job 27:2). After the service, in walked this same brother who had called on me five years before. This time he looked as different as midday from midnight, or as life from death. I said to him, "I am glad to see you, for I have often thought about you and wondered whether you were brought into perfect peace." I told you that I went to Mentone, and my patient also went into the country, so that we had not met for five years. To my inquiries, this brother replied, "Yes, you said I was a hopeful patient. I am sure you will be glad to know that I have walked in the sunlight from that day until now. Everything is changed and altered with me."

Dear friends, as soon as I saw my poor despairing patient the first time, I blessed God that my terrible experience had prepared me to sympathize with him and guide him. But last night, when I saw him perfectly restored, my heart overflowed with gratitude to God for my former sorrowful feelings. I would go into the depths a hundred times to cheer a downcast spirit. It is good for me to have been afflicted, so that I might know how to speak a word in season to one who is weary.

Suppose that, by some painful operation, you could have your right arm made a little longer. I do not suppose you would care to undergo the operation. But, if you foresaw that, by undergoing the pain, you would be enabled to reach and save drowning men who otherwise would sink before your eyes, I think you would willingly bear the agony and pay a heavy fee to the surgeon to be thus qualified for the rescue of your fellowmen. Realize, then, that to acquire soulwinning power, you will have to go through fire and water, through doubt and despair, through mental torment and soul distress.

It will not be the same with all of you, or perhaps with any two of you, but according to the work allotted you will be your preparation. You must go into the fire if you are to pull others out of it, and you will have to dive into the floods if you are to draw others out of the water. You cannot work a fire escape without feeling the scorch of the blaze, or man a lifeboat without being covered with the waves. If Joseph were to keep his brothers alive, he himself had to go down into Egypt. If Moses were to lead the people through the wilderness, he must first spend forty years there with his flock. Payson truly said, "If anyone asks to be a successful minister, he knows not what he asks. It becomes him to consider whether he can drink deeply of Christ's bitter cup and be baptized with His baptism."

I was led to think of this by the prayer that has just been offered by our brother, Mr. Levinsohn. He is of the seed of Abraham, and he owed his conversion to a city missionary of his own nation. If that missionary had not himself been a Jew, he would not have known the heart of the young stranger, nor have won his ear for the gospel.

Men are usually won to Christ by suitable instruments. This suitability lies in the power to sympathize. A key opens a door because it fits the tumblers of the lock. Likewise, an address touches the heart because it meets the state of that heart. You and I have to be made into all sorts of shapes to suit all forms of mind and heart, just as Paul said:

> *And unto the Jews I became as a Jew, that I might gain the Jews; to them that are under the law, as under the law, that I might gain them that are under the law; to them that are without law, as without law (being not without law to God, but under the law to Christ), that I might gain them that are without law. To the weak became I as weak, that I might gain the weak; I am made all things to all men, that I might by all means save some.*
>
> (1 Corinthians 9:20–22)

These processes must be worked upon us, also. Let us cheerfully bear whatever the Holy Spirit works within our spirits, so that we may thus be even more of a blessing to our fellowmen. Come and lay your all on the altar! Give yourselves up, you workers, into the Lord's hand.

You who have delicacy and refinement may have to be shocked into the power to benefit the coarse and ignorant. You who are wise and educated may have to be made fools of, so that you may win fools to Jesus. Fools need saving, and many of them will not be saved except by means that men of culture cannot admire. How finely some people go to work when what is needed may not be daintiness, but energy! On the other hand, how violent some people are when what is desired is tact and gentleness, not force! This has to be learned. We must be trained in this, as dogs are trained to follow game.

Here is one form of experience. The brother is elegant. He wishes to speak earnestly, but he must be elaborate, too. He has written out a nicely prepared address and has his notes carefully arranged. Alas, he has left the priceless document at home! What will he do? He is too gracious to give up. He will try to speak. He begins nicely and gets through his first point. "Fair and softly, good sir." What comes next? See, he is looking up for the next point. What should be said? What can be said? The good man flounders about, but he cannot swim. He struggles toward land, and as he rises from the flood, you can hear him mentally saying, "That's my last attempt." Yet it is not so. He speaks again. He gathers confidence and grows into an impressive speaker. By such humiliations as these, the Lord prepares him to do his work efficiently.

In our beginnings, we are too fine to be fit, or too great to be good. We must serve an apprenticeship and thus learn our trade. A lead pencil is of no use at all until it is sharpened. The wood must be shaved away, and then the inward metal that marks and writes will have fair play.

The knife of affliction is sharp, but restorative. You cannot delight in it, but faith may teach you to value it. Are you not willing to pass through every ordeal if by any means you may save some? If this is not your spirit, you had better keep to your farm and your merchandise, for no one will ever win a soul who is not prepared to suffer everything within the realm of possibility for a soul's sake.

A good deal may have to be suffered through fear. Yet that fear may assist in stirring the soul, putting it into fit posture for work. At least, it may drive the heart to prayer, and that alone is a great part of the necessary preparation.

A good man thus described one of his early attempts at visitation for the purpose of speaking to individuals about their spiritual condition: "On the way to the person's residence, I was thinking how I would introduce the subject and all that I would say. All the while, I was trembling and agitated. Reaching the door, it seemed as if I would sink through the stones; my courage was gone. As I lifted my hand to the knocker, my hand dropped at my side without touching it. I went partly down the steps from sheer fear. A moment's reflection sent me again to the knocker, and I entered the house. The sentences I spoke and the prayer I offered were very broken. Oh, how very thankful I am that my fears and cowardice did not prevail. The ice was broken." That process of ice-breaking must be gone through, but its result is highly beneficial.

O poor souls, you who wish to find the Savior, Jesus has died for you. And now His people live for you! We cannot offer any atoning sacrifice for you. There is no need that we should. But still we would gladly make sacrifices for your soul's sake. We would do anything, be anything, give anything, and suffer anything if we might but bring you to Christ. I assure you that many of us feel this way. Will you not care for yourselves? Will we be earnest about your souls while you trifle them away? Be wise, I urge you, and may infinite wisdom at once lead you to our dear Savior's feet. Amen.

10

THE SOULWINNER'S REWARD

I observed on the notice board of the police station a striking poster offering a large reward to anyone who can discover and bring to justice the perpetrators of a great crime. No doubt our policemen know that the hope of a huge reward is the only motive that will have power with the companions of assassins. The informer earns so much scorn and hate that few can be induced to stand in his place, even when piles of gold are offered. It is a poor business at best.

It is far more pleasant to remember that there is a reward for bringing men to mercy that is of a higher order than the premium for bringing men to justice. Further, it is much more within our reach, and that is a practical point worthy of our notice. We cannot all hunt down criminals, but we may all rescue the perishing. Let us thank God that assassins and burglars are comparatively few; yet sinners, who need to be sought and saved, swarm around us everywhere. Here is perspective for you. No one needs to think he is shut out from the rewards that love bestows on all who do her service.

At the mention of the word *reward*, some will prick up their ears and mutter, "Legality." Yet the reward we speak of is not of debt, but of grace. It is not enjoyed with the proud conceit of merit, but with the grateful delight of humility. Other friends will whisper, "Is not this a low and mercenary motive?" We reply that it is as mercenary as the spirit of Moses, who *"had respect unto the recompense of the reward"* (Hebrews 11:26). In this matter, everything depends on what the reward is. If it happens to be the joy of doing good, the comfort of having glorified God, and the bliss of pleasing the Lord Jesus, then the ambition to be allowed to endeavor to save our fellowmen from going down into the pit is in itself a grace from the Lord.

Even if we did not succeed in it, the Lord would still say of it, as He did of David's intent to build a temple, *"Thou didst well that it was in thine heart"* (1 Kings 8:18). Even if the souls we seek all persist in unbelief, if they all despise and reject and ridicule us, it will still be a divine work to have at least made the attempt. If no rain comes out of the cloud, it has still screened off the fierce heat of the sun. All is not lost, even if the greater purpose is not accomplished. What if we only learn how to join the Savior in His tears and mourn, *"How often would I have gathered thy children together…and ye would not!"* (Matthew 23:37). It is sublime honor itself to be allowed to stand on the same platform with Jesus and weep with Him. We are the better for such sorrows, if no others are.

But, thank God, our labors are not in vain in the Lord. I believe that the majority of you who have really tried, in the power of the Holy Spirit by scriptural teaching and prayer, to bring others to Jesus, have been successful.

I may be speaking to a few who have not succeeded. If so, I would recommend that they steadily look over their motives, their spirits, their work, and their prayers, and then begin again. Perhaps they may come to work more wisely, more believingly, more humbly, and more in the power of the Holy Spirit. They must act as farmers do who, after a poor harvest, plow again in hope. They ought not to be dispirited, but they ought to be roused.

We should be anxious to find out the reason of failure, if there is any, and we should be ready to learn from all our fellow laborers. But we must steadfastly set our faces, if by any means we may save some, resolving that, whatever happens, we will leave no stone unturned to effect the salvation of those around us. How can we bear to leave the world without sheaves to carry with us rejoicingly?

I believe that the majority of us who are now assembled to pray have been successful beyond our expectations. God has blessed us, not beyond our desires, but yet beyond our hopes. I have often been surprised at the mercy of God toward myself. Poor messages of mine, that I could cry over when I get home, have led scores to the cross. More wonderful still, words that I have spoken in ordinary conversation, mere chance sentences, as men call them, have nevertheless been as winged arrows from God, have pierced men's hearts and laid them wounded at Jesus' feet.

I have often lifted up my hands in astonishment and said, "How can God bless such a weak instrumentality?" This is the feeling of most who addict themselves to the blessed craft of fishing for men. The desire of such success furnishes as pure a motive as could move an angel's heart, as pure, indeed, as that which swayed the Savior when, "*for the joy that was set before him* [He] *endured the cross, despising the shame*" (Hebrews 12:2). "*Doth Job* [serve] *God for nought?*" said Satan (Job 1:9). If Job could have answered the question affirmatively, if it could have been proven that the "*perfect and upright*" (Job 1:1) man found no reward in his holy living, then Satan would have disputed God's justice and urged men to renounce a service so unprofitable.

Truly, there is a reward for the righteous, and in the exalted pursuits of grace there are recompenses of infinite value. When we endeavor to lead men to God, we pursue a business far more profitable than the pearl fisher's diving or the diamond hunter's searching. No pursuit of mortal men is to be compared with that of soulwinning. Think of it as men think of entering a cabinet position in the government or occupying a throne. It is a royal business, and they are true kings who follow it successfully.

The harvest of godly service is not yet reaped: "*Do we with patience wait for it*" (Romans 8:25). But we have deposits on our wages, refreshing pledges of that which is laid up in heaven for us. Partly, this reward lies in the work itself. Men go hunting and shooting for mere love of the sport. Surely, in an infinitely higher sphere, we may hunt for men's souls for the pleasing indulgence of our benevolence. To some of us, it would be an unendurable misery to see men sink to hell and to be making no effort for their salvation. It is a reward to us to have a vent for our inward fires. It is weariness to us to be shut up from the sacred activities that aim at plucking firebrands from the flame. We are in deep sympathy with our fellowmen and feel that in a way, their sin is our sin, their peril our peril.

> If another lose the way,
> My feet also go astray;
> If another downward go,
> In my heart is also woe.

It is therefore a relief to set forth the gospel, so that we may save ourselves from the misery that echoes in our hearts with the crash of a ruined soul.

Soulwinning is a service that brings great benefit to the individual who consecrates himself to it. The person who has watched for a soul, prayed for him, laid his plans for him, spoken with much trembling, and endeavored to make an impression upon him has been educating himself by the effort. Having been disappointed, he has cried to God more earnestly, has tried again, has looked up the promise to meet the case of the convicted one, and has turned to the point of the divine character that seems most likely to encourage trembling faith. In every step he has been benefiting himself.

When he has gone over the old, old story of the cross to the weeping penitent and has at last gripped the hand of one who could say, "I do believe, I will believe, that Jesus died for me," he has found the reward contained in the process through which his own mind has gone. It has reminded him of his own lost state. It has shown him the struggles the Spirit had in bringing him to repentance. It has reminded him of that precious moment when he first looked to Jesus. It has strengthened him in his firm confidence that Christ will save men.

When we see Jesus save another, and that marvelous transfiguration that comes over the face of the saved one, our own faith is greatly confirmed. Skeptics and modern-thought men have little to do with converts. Those who labor for conversions believe in conversions. Those who behold the processes of regeneration see a miracle worked and are certain that "this is the finger of God." It is the most blessed exercise for a soul and the most divine ennobling of the heart to spend yourself in seeking to bring another to the dear Redeemer's feet. If it ended there, you might thank God that He ever called you to a service so comforting, so strengthening, so elevating, so confirming as that of converting others from their evil ways.

Another precious recompense is found in the gratitude and affection of those you bring to Christ. This is a choice blessing—the blessedness of rejoicing in another's joy, the bliss of hearing that you have led a soul to Jesus. Measure the sweetness of this reward by the bitterness of its opposite. Men of God have brought many to Jesus, and all things have gone well in the church until declining years have thrown the good man into the shade. Then the minister's own spiritual children have been eager to turn him out to pasture. The unkindest cut of all has come from those who owed their souls to him. His heart was broken while he has sighed, "I could have borne it, had not the people I brought to the Savior turned against me."

The pang is not unknown to me. I can never forget a certain household in which the Lord gave me the great joy of bringing four employers and several people engaged by them to Jesus' feet. Snatched from the utmost carelessness of worldliness, these who had previously known nothing of the grace of God were joyful confessors of the faith. After a while, they adopted certain opinions differing from mine. From then on, some of them had nothing but hard words for me and my preaching. I had done my best to teach them all the truth I knew. If they had found out more than I had discovered, they might at least have remembered where they learned the elements of the faith. It is years ago now, but I still feel the pain much. I only mention these sharp pricks to show how sweet it is to have those around you whom you have brought to the Savior.

A mother feels great delight in her children, for an intense love comes with natural relationships. But there is a still deeper love connected with spiritual kinship, a love that lasts through life and will continue in eternity. Even in heaven each servant of the Lord will say, "*Behold I and the children which God hath given me*" (Hebrews 2:13). They neither marry nor are given in marriage in the city of our God, but fatherhood and brotherhood in Christ will still survive. Those sweet and blessed bonds that grace has formed continue forever, and spiritual relationships are developed rather than dissolved by translation to the better land.

If you are eager for real joy, such as you may think over and sleep upon, I am persuaded that no joy of growing wealthy, no joy of increasing knowledge, no joy of influence over your fellow creatures, no joy of any other sort, can ever be compared with the rapture of saving a soul from death and helping to restore our lost family to our great Father's house. Talk of a ten-thousand-dollar reward! That is nothing at all. One might easily spend that amount. But one cannot exhaust the unutterable delights that come from the gratitude of souls converted from the error of their ways.

However, the richest reward lies in pleasing God and causing the Redeemer to see the results of the travail of His soul. That Jesus should have His reward is worthy of the eternal Father, but it is marvelous that we would be employed by the Father to give to Christ the purchase of His agonies. This is a wonder of wonders! O my soul, this is an honor too great, a bliss too deep for words! Listen, dear friends, and answer me. What would you give to cause a thrill of pleasure in the heart of the Beloved? Recall the grief you cost Him and the pangs that shot through Him so that He might deliver you from your sin and its consequences. Do you not long to make Him glad?

When you bring others to His feet, you give Him joy, and no small joy, either. Is not this a wonderful text: "*There is joy in the presence of the angels of God over one sinner that repenteth*" (Luke 15:10)? What does that mean? Does it mean that the angels have joy? We generally read it so, but that is not the intent of the verse. It says, "*There is joy in the presence of the angels of God.*" That means there is joy in the heart of God, around whose throne the angels stand. It is a joy that angels delight to behold.

What is this? Is the blessed God capable of greater joy than His own boundless happiness? What a wondrous thought! The infinite bliss of God is more eminently displayed, if it cannot be increased. Can we be the instruments of this? Can we do anything that will make the Ever Blessed glad? Yes, for we are told that the Great Father rejoices beyond measure when His prodigal son, who was dead, is alive again, and the lost one is found.

If I could say this as I ought to say it, it would make every Christian cry out, "Then I will labor to bring souls to the Savior." It would make those of us who have brought many to Jesus "*instant in season,* [and] *out of season*" (1 Timothy 2:4), to bring more to Him. It is a great pleasure to be doing a kindness to an earthly friend; but to be doing something distinctly for Jesus, something that will be of all things in the world most pleasing to Him, is a great delight! It is a good work to build a meetinghouse and give it outright to the cause of God, if it is done with a proper motive. But one living stone, built upon the "*sure foundation*" (Isaiah 28:16) by our instrumentality, will give the Master more pleasure than if we erected a vast pile of natural stones, which might only encumber the ground.

Go, dear friends, and seek to bring your children and your neighbors, your friends and your relatives, to the Savior's feet. Nothing will give Him as much pleasure as to see them turn to Him and live. By your love for Jesus, become fishers of men.

11

THE SOULWINNER'S LIFE AND WORK

The fruit of the righteous is a tree of life, and he that winneth souls is wise.
—Proverbs 11:30

I t seems to me that there is a higher joy in looking at Christians as a body of believers than that which arises from regarding them merely as saved. Yes, there is a great joy in salvation, a joy worthy to stir the angelic harps. Think of the Savior's agony in the ransom of every one of His redeemed; think of the work of the Holy Spirit in every renewed heart; think of the love of the Father as resting upon every one of the regenerate. I could not, if I took up my parable for a month, set forth all the mass of joy that is to be seen in a multitude of believers if we look only at what God has done for them, promised to them, and will fulfill in them.

However, there is a wider field of thought that my mind has been traversing all this day: the thought of the capacities of service contained in a large group of believers, the possibilities of blessing others that lie within the hearts of regenerate persons. We must not think so much of what we already are that we forget what the Lord may accomplish by us for others. Here are the coals of fire, but who will describe the blaze that they may cause?

We ought not to regard the Christian church as a luxurious hotel where each Christian may dwell at his ease in his own inn, but as barracks in which soldiers are drilled and trained for war. We should not regard the Christian church as an association for mutual admiration and comfort, but as an army with banners, marching to the fray to achieve victories for

Christ, to storm the strongholds of the foe, and to add province after province to the Redeemer's kingdom.

We may view converted persons gathered into church membership as so much wheat in the granary. Let us thank God that it is there, and that so far the harvest has rewarded the sower.

Far more soul-inspiring is the view when we regard each believer as likely to be made a living center for the extension of the kingdom of Jesus. Then we see believers sowing the fertile valleys of our land and promising before long to bring forth a crop—some thirty, some forty, some fifty, and some a hundredfold.

The capacities of life are enormous. One becomes a thousand in a marvelously brief space. Within a short time, a few grains of wheat would suffice to seed the whole world, and a few true saints might suffice for the conversion of all nations. Only take that which comes of one year, store it well, sow it all, store it again the next year, and then sow it all again, and the multiplication almost exceeds the power of computation.

Oh, that every Christian were thus year by year the Lord's seed corn! If all the wheat in the world had perished except for a single grain, it would not take many years to replenish all the earth and sow her fields and plains. But in a far shorter time, in the power of the Holy Spirit, one Paul or one Peter would have evangelized all lands. View yourselves as grains of wheat predestined to seed the world. That believer lives sublimely who functions as if the very existence of Christianity depended upon himself, and is determined that to all men within his reach the unsearchable riches of Christ will be made known.

If all we whom Christ is pleased to use as His seed corn were only scattered and sown as we ought to be, and were to sprout and bring forth the green blade and the corn in the ear, what a harvest there would be! It would again be fulfilled, *"There shall be an handful of corn in the earth upon the top of the mountains* [a very bad position for it]; *the fruit thereof shall shake like Lebanon: and they of the city shall flourish like grass of the earth*" (Psalm 72:16). May God grant us to feel some degree of the Holy Spirit's quickening power while we talk together, not so much about what God has done for us as about what God may do by us, and how far we may put ourselves into a right position to be used by Him!

There are two main points in our text, and these are found laid out with much distinctness in its two sentences. The first is that the life of the believer is, or ought to be, full of soul blessing: "*The fruit of the righteous is a tree of life.*" In the second place, the pursuit of the believer ought always to be soulwinning. The second is much the same as the first, only the first sets forth our unconscious influence, and the second, the efforts that we put forth with the objective of winning souls for Christ.

Let us begin at the beginning, because the second cannot be carried out without the first. Without fullness of life within, there cannot be an overflow of life to others. It is of no use for any of you to try to be soulwinners if you are not bearing fruit in your own lives. How can you serve the Lord with your lips if you do not serve Him with your lives? How can you preach His gospel with your tongues when you are preaching the devil's gospel with your feet, hands, and hearts and setting up antichrist by your practical unholiness? We must first have life and bear personal fruit to the divine glory. Then, out of our examples, will spring the conversion of others. Let us go to the fountainhead and see how the believer's own life is essential to his being useful to others.

First, the life of the believer is full of soul blessing. We will consider this fact by means of a few observations growing out of the text. Initially, let us remark that the believer's outward life comes from him as fruit. This is prominent to notice. "*The fruit of the righteous*"—that is to say, his life—is not something fastened onto him, but growing out of him. It is not a garment that he puts on and off, but is inseparable from himself. The sincere believer's religion is the believer himself, not a cloak for his concealment. True godliness is the natural outgrowth of a renewed nature, not the forced growth of greenhouse excitement. Is it not natural for a vine to bear clusters of grapes or a palm tree to bear dates? It is certainly as natural as it is for the apples of Sodom to be found on the trees of Sodom, and for noxious plants to produce poisonous berries.

When God gives a new nature to His people, the life that comes out of that new nature springs spontaneously from it. The person who has a religion that is not part and parcel of himself will soon discover that it is worse than useless to him. The person who wears his piety like a mask at a carnival, so that, when he gets home, he changes from a saint to a savage, from an angel to a devil, from John to Judas, from a benefactor to a bully—such a person knows very well what formalism and hypocrisy can do for him, but he has no vestige of true religion. Fig trees do not bear figs on certain days and thorns at other times, but they are true to their nature at all seasons.

Those who think that godliness is a matter of vestment and has an intimate relationship with blue, scarlet, and fine linen are consistent if they keep their religion to the proper time for the wearing of their sacred pomposity. But he who has discovered what Christianity is knows that it is much more a life than an act, a form, or a profession. Much as I love the creed of Christendom, I am ready to say that true Christianity is far more a life than a creed. It is a creed with its ceremonies, but it is mainly a life. It is a divine spark of heaven's own flame that falls into the human heart and burns within, consuming much that lies hidden in the soul. Then, at last, as a heavenly life, it flames forth, evident to all those around.

Under the indwelling power of the Holy Spirit, a regenerate person becomes like that bush in Horeb, all aglow with Deity. (See Exodus 3:1–6). The God within him makes him shine so that the place around him is holy ground. Those who look at him feel the power of his hallowed life.

Dear ones, we must take care that our religion becomes increasingly an outgrowth of our souls. Many professing believers are hedged about with, "You must not do this or that," and are driven onward with, "You must do this, and you must do that." But there is a doctrine, too often perverted, that is, nevertheless, a blessed truth, and ought to dwell in your hearts: *"Ye are not under the law, but under grace"* (Romans 6:14). Hence, you do not obey the will of God because you hope to earn heaven, or dream of escaping from divine wrath by your own works, but because there is a life in you that seeks after that which is holy and pure, right and true, and cannot endure that which is evil. You are careful to maintain good works, not from either legal hopes or legal fears, but because there is something holy within you, born of God, that seeks, according to its nature, to do that which is pleasing to God.

Look to it more and more that your religion is real, true, natural, vital—not artificial; constrained; superficial; a thing of times, days, places; a fungus produced by excitement; or a fermentation generated by meetings and stirred by oratory. We all need a religion that can live either in a wilderness or in a crowd, a religion that will show itself in every walk of life and company. Give me the godliness that is seen at home, especially around the fireside, for it is never more beautiful than there; the godliness that is seen in the tussle of ordinary business among scoffers and opposers as well as among Christians. Show me faith that can defy the sharp eyes of the world and walk fearlessly where all scowl with fierce eyes of hate, as well as where there are sympathetic observers and lenient friends. May you be filled with the life of the Spirit; may your whole conduct and conversation be the natural, blessed outgrowth of the Spirit's indwelling!

Note, next, that the fruit that comes from a Christian is fruit worthy of his character: *"The fruit of the righteous is a tree of life."* Each tree bears its own fruit and is known by it. The righteous one bears righteous fruit. Do not let us be at all deceived, friends, or fall into any error about this: *"He that doeth righteousness is righteous….Whosoever doeth not righteousness is not of God, neither he that loveth not his brother"* (1 John 3:7, 10).

We are prepared, I hope, to die for the doctrine of justification by faith and to assert before all adversaries that salvation is not of works. But we also confess that we are justified by a faith that produces works, and if any man has a faith that does not produce good works, it is the faith of devils. Saving faith appropriates the finished work of the Lord Jesus, and so saves by itself alone, for we are justified by faith without works. However, the faith that is without works cannot bring salvation to anyone.

We are saved by faith without works, but not by *a* faith that is without works, for the real faith that saves the soul works by love and purifies the character. If you can cheat across the counter, your hope of heaven is a cheat, too. Though you can pray as prettily as anybody and practice acts of outward piety as well as any other hypocrite, you are deceived if you expect to be right in the end. If as a servant you are lazy, lying, and loitering, or if as a master you are hard, tyrannical, and unchristianly, your fruit shows that you are a tree in Satan's own orchard and bear apples that will suit his tooth. If you can use dishonest business practices, and if you can lie—and how many lie every day about their neighbors or about their goods—you may talk as you like about being justified by faith, but *"all liars, shall have their part in the lake which burneth with fire and brimstone"* (Revelation 21:8). You will be among the biggest liars, for you are guilty of the lie of saying, "I am a Christian," whereas you are not. A false profession is one of the worst of lies, since it brings the utmost dishonor upon Christ and His people.

The fruit of the righteous is righteousness: the fig tree will not bring forth thorns; neither can we gather grapes from thistles. *"The tree is known by his fruit"* (Matthew 12:33). If we cannot judge men's hearts and must not try to do so, we can judge their lives. I pray that we may all be ready to judge our own lives and see if we are bringing forth righteous fruit, for if not, we are not righteous men.

However, let it never be forgotten that the fruit of the righteous, though it comes from him naturally, for his newborn nature yields the sweet fruit of obedience, is always the result of grace and the gift of God. No truth ought to be remembered more than this: *"From me is thy fruit found"* (Hosea 14:8). We can bring forth no fruit except as we abide in Christ. *"The righteous shall flourish as a branch"* (Proverbs 11:25), and only as a branch. How does a branch flourish? By its connection with the stem and the consequent inflowing of the sap.

So, though the righteous person's righteous actions are his own, they are always produced by the grace that is imparted to him. He never dares to take any credit for them, but he sings, *"Not unto us, O Lord, not unto us, but unto thy name give glory"* (Psalm 115:1). If he fails, he blames himself. If he succeeds, he glorifies God. Imitate his example. Lay every fault, every weakness, every infirmity at your own door. If you fall in any respect short of perfection—and I am sure you do—take all that to yourself and do not excuse yourself. But if there is any virtue, any praise, any true desire, any real prayer, anything that is good, ascribe it all to the Spirit of God. Remember, the righteous person would not be righteous unless God had made him righteous, and the fruit of righteousness would never come from him unless the divine sap within him had produced that acceptable fruit. To God alone be all honor and glory.

The main lesson of the passage is that this outburst of life from the Christian, this consequence of life within him, this fruit of his soul, becomes a blessing to others. Like a tree, it yields shade and sustenance to all around. It is a *"tree of life,"* an expression that I cannot fully work out as I would like to, but there is a world of instruction compressed in the illustration.

That which to the believer is fruit becomes to others a tree; it is a singular metaphor, but by no means a lame one. From the child of God falls the fruit of holy living, even as an acorn drops from an oak. This holy living becomes influential and produces the best results in others, even as the acorn becomes an oak and lends its shade to the birds of the air. The Christian's holiness becomes a *"tree of* life." I suppose this means a living tree, a tree suited to giving life and sustaining it in others. A fruit becomes a tree! A *"tree of life"* !

Christ in the Christian produces a character that becomes a *"tree of life."* The outward character is the fruit of the inner life. This outer life itself grows from a fruit into a tree. As a tree, it bears fruit in others to the praise and glory of God.

Dear brothers and sisters, I know some of God's saints who live very near to Him. They are evidently *"tree*[s] *of life,"* for their very shadows are comforting, cooling, and refreshing to many weary souls. I have known the young, the tried, and the downcast who go to them, to sit beneath their shade and pour out the tale of their troubles. They have felt it a rich blessing to receive their sympathy, to be told of the faithfulness of the Lord, and to be guided in the way of wisdom.

There are a few good men in this world whom to know is to be rich. Such men are libraries of gospel truth. They are better than books, for the truth in them is written on living pages. Their character is a true and living tree. It is not a mere post of the dead wood of doctrine, bearing an inscription and rotting while it does so. Rather, it is a vital, organized, fruit-producing thing, a plant of the Lord's right-hand planting. (See Psalm 80:15.)

Not only do some saints give comfort to others, but they also give spiritual nourishment to them. Well-trained Christians become nurturing fathers and nursing mothers, strengthening the weak and binding up the wounds of the brokenhearted. So, too, the bold, strong, generous deeds of large-hearted Christians are of great service to their fellow Christians and tend to raise them to a higher level. You feel refreshed by observing how they act: their patience in suffering, their courage in danger, their holy faith in God, their happy faces under trial. All these energize you for your own conflicts. In a thousand ways, the sanctified believer's example acts in a healing and comforting way to other Christians and assists in raising them above anxiety and unbelief. Even as the leaves of the tree of life are for *"the healing of the nations"* (Revelation 22:2), so the words and deeds of saints are medicine for a thousand maladies.

And then what fruit, sweet to the taste of the godly, instructed believers bear! We can never trust in men as we trust in the Lord, but the Lord can cause the members to bless us in their measure, even as their Head is ever ready to do. Jesus alone is the Tree of Life, but He makes some of His servants to be instrumentally to us little trees of life. By them He gives us fruit of the same sort that He bears Himself, for He puts it in them. It is Himself in His saints causing them to bring forth golden apples, with which our souls are gladdened. May every one of us be made like our Lord, and may His fruit be found on our boughs.

We have put into the tomb many of the saints who have fallen asleep. Among them there were some, of whom I will not at this moment speak particularly, whose lives, as I look back on them, are still a *"tree of life"* to me. I pray to God that I may be like them. If you will only recall their holy, devoted lives, the influence they have left behind will still be a *"tree of life"* to you. They *"being dead yet speaketh"* (Hebrews 11:4). Hear their eloquent exhortations! Even in their ashes their continuing fires live. Kindle your souls at their warmth. Their noble examples are the endowments of the church; her children are ennobled and enriched as they remember their walk of faith and labor of love.

Beloved, may every one of us be true benedictions to the churches in whose gardens we are planted! "Oh!" says one, "I am afraid I am not much like a tree, for I feel so weak and insignificant." If you *"have faith as a grain of mustard seed"* (Mathew 17:20), you have the beginnings of the tree beneath whose branches the birds of the air will yet find a lodging. The very birds that would have eaten the tiny seed come and find nesting places in the tree that grows out of it. People who despise and mock you, now that you are a beginner, will one of these days, if God blesses you, be glad to borrow comfort from your example and experience.

But one other thought on this point. Remember that the completeness and development of the holy life will be seen above. There is a city of which it is written, *"In the midst of the street of it, and on either side of the river, was there the tree of life"* (Revelation 22:2). The *"tree of life"* is a heavenly plant, and so the fruit of the Christian is a thing of heaven. Though not transplanted to glory yet, it is being prepared for its final abode.

What is holiness but heaven on earth? What is living unto God but the essence of heaven? What are uprightness, integrity, Christlikeness? Have not these qualities even more to do with heaven than harps and palms and streets of purest gold? Holiness, purity, loveliness of character—these qualitites make a heaven within a person's own heart. Even if there were no place called heaven, the heart that is set free from sin and made like the Lord Jesus would have a heavenly happiness.

See then, dear friends, what an important thing it is for us to be indeed righteous before God. Then the outcome of that righteousness will be fruit that will be a *"tree of life"* to others here on earth, and a *"tree of life"* in heaven above, world without end. O blessed Spirit, make it so, and You will have all the praise!

This brings us to our second point. The pursuit of the believer should be soulwinning. *"He that winneth souls is wise."* The two things are put together—the life first, the effort next. *"What therefore God hath joined together, let not man put asunder"* (Mark 10:9).

It is implied in our text that there are souls that need winning. Ah, me, all souls of men are lost by nature. You might walk through the streets of the city and say, with sighs and tears, about the masses of men you meet on those crowded sidewalks, "Lost, lost, lost!" Wherever Christ is not trusted, the Spirit has not created a new heart, and the soul has not come to the great Father, there is a lost soul. But here is the mercy: these lost souls can be won. They are not hopelessly lost. Not yet has God determined that they will forever abide as they are. It is not yet said, *"He which is filthy, let him be filthy still"* (Revelation 22:11). They are in the land of hope where mercy may reach them, for they are spoken of as capable of being won. They may yet be delivered, but the phrase hints that it will require all our efforts: *"He that winneth souls."*

What do we mean by that word "win"? We use it in courting; we speak of the bridegroom who wins his bride. Sometimes there is a large expense of love, many a pleading word, and many wooing acts before the valued heart is all the suitor's own. I use this explanation because in some respects it is the very best. Souls will have to be won for Christ in this fashion, so that they may be betrothed to Him.

We must woo the sinner for Christ; that is how hearts are to be won for Him. Jesus is the Bridegroom. We must speak for Him and tell of His beauty, as Abraham's servant, when he went to seek a wife for Isaac, acted as a wooer in his stead. Have you never read the story? Then turn to it when you have an opportunity and see how he talked about his master, what possessions he had, and how Isaac was to be heir of it all, and so on, finishing his address by urging Rebecca to go with him. The question was put home to her, *"Wilt thou go with this man?"* (Genesis 24:58). Similarly, the minister's business is to commend his Master and his Master's riches, and then to say to souls, "Will you be wedded to Christ?" He who can succeed in this very delicate business is a wise man.

We also use the term in a military fashion. We speak of winning a city, a castle, or a battle. We do not win victories by going to sleep. Believe me, castles are not captured by men who are only half awake. Winning a battle requires the best skill, the greatest endurance, and the utmost courage. To storm fortresses that are regarded as almost impregnable, men need to burn the midnight oil and study well the arts of attack. When the time comes for the assault, not one soldier must be a dawdler, but all force of artillery and manpower must be brought to bear on the point assailed. To carry man's heart by the main force of grace, to capture it, to break down the bars of brass and dash the gates of iron into pieces, requires the exercise of a skill that only Christ can give. To bring up the big battering rams and shake every stone in the sinner's conscience, to make his heart rock and reel within him for fear of the wrath to come—in a word, to assail a soul with all the artillery of the gospel—requires a wise man, one fully roused to his work. To hold up the white flag of mercy or to use the battering ram of warnings until a breach is made, and then with the sword of the Spirit in his hand to capture the city, tear down the black flag of sin, and run up the banner of the cross, requires all the force the choicest preacher can command, and a great deal more.

Those whose souls are as cold as the Arctic regions and whose energy is reduced to the vanishing point are not likely to take the city of Mansoul for Prince Emmanuel. If you think you are going to win souls, you must throw your soul into your work, just as a warrior must throw his soul into a battle, or victory will not be yours.

We use the words "to win" in reference to making a fortune, and we all know that the man who becomes a millionaire has *"to rise up early, to sit up late, to eat the bread of sorrows"* (Psalm 127:2). It takes much toiling and saving, and I do not know what else besides, to amass immense wealth. We have to go in for winning souls with the same ardor and concentration of our faculties as old Astor of New York went in to build up that fortune of so many millions that he has now left behind him.

Indeed, it is a race. As such, nobody wins unless he strains every muscle and sinew. *"They which run in a race run all, but one receiveth the prize"* (1 Corinthians 9:24). That one is generally he who had more strength than the rest. Certainly, whether he had more strength or not, he gave all he had. We will not win souls unless we imitate him.

In the text, Solomon declared that, *"He that winneth souls is wise."* Such a declaration is all the more valuable as it comes from so wise a man. Let me show you why a soulwinner is wise. First, he must be taught by God before he will attempt it. The man who does not know that, whereas he was once blind, now he sees, had better think of his own blindness before he attempts to lead his friends in the right way. If you yourself are not saved, you cannot be the means of saving others. He who wins souls first must be wise unto salvation for himself.

That being taken for granted, he is a wise man who selects such a pursuit. Are you choosing a purpose worthy to be the great aim of your life? I do hope you will judge wisely and select the most noble of ambitions. If God has given you great gifts, I hope they will not be wasted on any low, sordid, or selfish purposes.

Suppose I am now addressing one who has great talents and has an opportunity of being whatever he wants—of going into the legislature and helping to pass great measures, or of going into business and making himself someone of importance. I hope he will weigh the claims of Jesus and immortal souls as well as other claims. Should I addict myself to study? Should I surrender myself to business? Should I travel? Should I spend my time in pleasure? Should I become the principal fox hunter of the county? Should I spend my time in promoting political and social reforms? Think them all over. But if you are a Christian, my dear friend, nothing will equal in enjoyment, usefulness, honor, and lasting recompense the giving of yourself to the winning of souls.

Oh, it is grand hunting, I can tell you. It beats all the fox hunting in the world in excitement and exhilaration. Have I not sometimes gone with a cry over hedge and ditch after some poor sinner and kept up with him in every twist and turn he took, until I have overtaken him by God's grace? Later, I have been in at the death and rejoiced exceedingly when I have seen him captured by my Master. Our Lord Jesus calls His ministers fishermen. No other fishermen have such labor, such sorrow, and such delight as we have.

What a happy thing it is that you may win souls for Jesus, and may do this even though you continue in your secular callings. Some of you would never win souls in pulpits. It would be a great pity if you tried. But you can win souls in the workshop, in the laundry, in the nursery, and in the drawing room. Our hunting grounds are everywhere: by the side of the road, at home, in a corner, and in the crowd. Among the common people, Jesus is our theme. Among the great ones, we have no other.

You will be wise, my friend, if your one absorbing desire is that you may turn the ungodly from the error of their ways. For you there will be a crown glittering with many stars, which you will cast at Jesus' feet in the day of His appearing.

Further, not only is it wise to make this your aim, but you will also have to be very wise if you are to succeed in it. Because the souls to be won are so different in their constitutions, feelings, and conditions, you will have to adapt yourselves to them all. The trappers of North America have to find out the habits of the animals they wish to catch; in the same way, you will have to learn how to deal with each class of cases.

Some are very depressed; you will have to comfort them. Perhaps you will comfort them too much and make them unbelieving. Therefore, possibly, instead of comforting them, you will sometimes need to administer a sharp word to cure the sulkiness into which they have fallen. Another person may be frivolous, and if you put on a serious face you will frighten your bird away. You will have to be cheerful and drop a word of admonition as if by accident. Some people will not let you speak to them, but will talk to you; you must know the art of putting a word in edgewise.

You will have to be very wise and become *"all things to all men"* (1 Corinthians 9:22). Your success will prove your wisdom. Theories of dealing with souls may look very wise, but they often prove to be useless when actually tried. He who by God's grace accomplishes the work is a wise man, though perhaps he knows no theory whatever. This work will need all your wits and far more. You will have to cry to the great Winner of Souls above to give you of His Holy Spirit.

Note that he who wins souls is wise because he is engaged in a business that makes men wiser as they proceed with it. You will bungle at first, and very likely drive away sinners from Christ by your attempts to draw them to Him. I have tried to move some souls with all my might with a certain passage of Scripture, but they have taken it in an opposite light to what it was intended and have started off in the wrong direction. It is very difficult to know how to act with bewildered inquirers. If you want some people to go forward, you must pull them backward. If you want them to go to the right, you must insist on their going to the left; and then they go to the right. You must be ready for these follies of poor human nature.

I knew a poor elderly Christian woman who had been a child of God for fifty years, but she was in a state of melancholy and distress from which nobody could rouse her. I called several times and endeavored to cheer her up, but, generally, when I left, she was worse than before. So, the next time I called to see her, I did not say anything to her about Christ or religion. She soon introduced those topics herself. I then remarked that I was not going to talk to her about such holy things, for she did not know anything about them. I told her she was not a believer in Christ and had been, no doubt, a hypocrite for many years. She could not stand that! In self-defense, she asserted that the Lord above knew her better than I did, and He was her witness that she did love the Lord Jesus Christ. She scarcely forgave herself afterward for that admission, but she could never talk to me quite so despairingly anymore.

True lovers of men's souls learn the art of dealing with them. The Holy Spirit makes them expert soul surgeons for Jesus. It is not because they have more abilities, or altogether because they have more grace, but because the Lord causes them to love the souls of men intensely. This imparts a secret skill, since, for the most part, the way to bring sinners to Christ is to love them to Christ.

Beloved, I will say once more that he who really wins souls for Jesus, however he wins them, is a wise man. Some of you are slow to admit this. You say, "Well, I suppose So-and-So has been very useful, but he is very rough." What does his roughness matter if he wins souls? "Ah," says another, "but I am not built up under him." Why do you go to hear him to get built up? If the Lord has sent him to pull down, let him pull down. You go elsewhere for edification. Do not grumble at a man who does one work because he cannot do another. We are also too apt to pit one minister against another and to say, "You should hear my minister." Perhaps we should, but it would be better for you to hear the man who edifies you, and let others go where they are instructed.

"He that winneth souls is wise." I did not ask you how he did it. He sang the gospel, and you did not like it. But if he won souls, he was wise. Soulwinners have their own ways. If they do but win souls, they are wise. I will tell you what is not wise, and will not be thought so in the end—namely, to go from church to church, doing nothing yourself and railing at all the Lord's useful servants.

Imagine a dear brother on his deathbed. He has the sweet thought that the Lord enabled him to bring many souls to Jesus and the expectation that when he comes to the gates, many spirits will come to meet him. They will throng the ascent to the New Jerusalem and welcome the man who brought them to Jesus. They are immortal monuments to his labors. He is wise.

Imagine another who has spent all his time in interpreting biblical prophecies, so that everything he read about in the newspapers he could see in Daniel or Revelation. Some say he is wise, but I would rather spend my time in winning souls. I would sooner bring one sinner to Jesus than unravel all the mysteries of the Word, for salvation is the thing we are to live for. I wish to God that I understood all mysteries, yet most of all I want to proclaim the mystery of soul-saving by faith in the blood of the Lamb.

It is comparatively a small matter for a minister to have been a staunch upholder of orthodoxy all his days and to have spent himself in keeping up the hedges of his church. Soulwinning is the main concern. It is a very good thing to contend earnestly for *"the faith which was once delivered unto the saints"* (Jude 3), but I do not think I would like to say in my last account, "Lord, I have lived to fight false religion and the state church, and to put down erroneous sects, but I never led a sinner to the cross." No, we will fight the good fight of faith, but the winning of souls is the greater matter; he who attends to it is wise.

Imagine another brother who has preached the truth, but who so polished up his sermons that the gospel was hidden. A message was never fit to preach, he thought, until he had written it out a dozen times to see whether every sentence was according to the canons of Cicero and Quintilian. Then he delivered the gospel as a grand oration. Was that wise? It takes a wise man to be a thorough orator, but it is better not to be an orator if fine speech prevents your being understood. Let eloquence be flung to the dogs rather than souls be lost. What we want is to win souls. They are not won by flowery speeches. We must have the winning of souls at heart and be red-hot with zeal for their salvation. Then, however much we blunder according to the critics, we will be numbered among those whom the Lord calls wise.

Now, Christian men and women, I want you to take up this matter practically, and to determine that you will try this very night to win a soul. Try the one next to you in the seat if you cannot think of anybody else. Try on the way home. Try with your own children. Have I not told you of what happened one Sunday evening? In my message I said, "Now, you mothers, have you ever prayed with each of your children, one by one, and urged them to take hold of Christ? Perhaps dear Jane is now in bed, and you have never yet pleaded with her about eternal things. Go home tonight, wake her up, and say, 'Jane, I am sorry I have never told you about the Savior personally and prayed with you, but I mean to do it now.' Wake her up, put your arms around her neck, and pour out your heart to God with her."

Well, there was a good sister here who had a daughter named Jane. What do you think? She came on Monday to bring her daughter Jane to see me in the vestry, for when she woke her up and began, "I have not spoken to you about Jesus," or something to that effect, "Oh, dear mother!" said Jane, "I have loved the Savior for six months and wondered why you had not spoken to me about Him." Then there was great kissing and rejoicing. Perhaps you may find that to be the case with a dear child at home. If you do not, so much the more reason why you should begin at once to speak.

Have you never won a soul for Jesus? You will have a crown in heaven, but no jewels in it. You will go to heaven childless. In old times, women dreaded that they would be childless. Let it be so with Christian people: let them dread being spiritually childless. We must hear the cries of those whom God has given to be born unto Himself by our means. We must hear them or else cry out in anguish, *"Give me* [spiritual] *children, or else I die"* (Genesis 30:1).

Young men and old men, and sisters of all ages, if you love the Lord, get a passion for souls. Do you not see them? They are going down to hell by the thousands. As often as the hand on the clock completes its circuit, hell devours multitudes, some of them ignorant of Christ and others willfully rejecting Him. The world lies in darkness. This great city still pines for the light. Your friends and relatives are unsaved, and they may be dead before this week is over. If you have any humanity, let alone Christianity, if you have found the remedy, tell the diseased about it! If you have found life, proclaim it to the dead. If you have found liberty, convince it to the captives. If you have found Jesus, tell others of Him.

My friends in the college, let this be your choice work while studying, and let it be the one object of your lives when you go forth from us. Do not be content when you get a congregation, but labor to win souls. As you do this, God will bless you. As for us, we hope during the rest of our lives to follow Him who is the Soulwinner, and to put ourselves in His hands who makes us soulwinners, so that our lives may not be long follies, but may be proved by results to have been directed by wisdom.

O you souls not won to Jesus, remember that faith in Christ saves you! Trust in Him. May you be led to trust in Him, for His name's sake! Amen.

12

SOULWINNING EXPLAINED

He that winneth souls is wise.
—Proverbs 11:30

The text does not say, "He that wins money is wise," though no doubt such a one would think he was wise. Perhaps, in a certain sense in these days of competition, he is. But such wisdom is earthly and ends with the earth. In another world the currencies of Europe will not be accepted, nor will their past possession be any sign of wealth or wisdom.

In this text, Solomon awards no crown for wisdom to crafty statesmen, or even to the ablest of rulers. He issues no diplomas even to philosophers, poets, or men of wit. He crowns with laurel only those who win souls. He does not declare that he who preaches is necessarily wise. Alas, there are multitudes who preach, gaining much applause, but who win no souls. They will find that it will go hard with them in the end, because they probably have run, but the Master never sent them. Solomon does not say that he who talks about winning souls is wise, since to lay down rules for others is a simple thing, but to carry them out one's self is far more difficult.

He who actually, truly, turns men from the error of their ways to God, and so is made the means of saving them from going down to hell, is wise. That is true of him whatever his style of soulwinning may be. He may be a Paul, deeply logical, profound in doctrine, able to command all fair judgments. If he thus wins souls, he is wise. He may be an Apollos, grandly rhetorical, whose lofty genius soars into the very heaven of eloquence. If he wins souls in that way he is wise, but not otherwise. Or he may be a Cephas, rough and rugged, using uncouth metaphor and stern statements. But, if he wins souls, he is no less wise than his polished brother or his rhetorical friend.

From the text, the great wisdom of soulwinners is proven by their actual success in winning souls. To their Master they are accountable for the ways in which they work, not to us. Let us not be comparing and contrasting this minister and that.

Who are you to judge another man's servants? *"Wisdom is justified of all her children"* (Luke 7:35). Only children argue about incidental methods; men look at successful results. Do these workers of many kinds and diverse ways win souls? Then they are wise. You who criticize them, being yourselves unfruitful, cannot be wise, even though you affect to be their judges. God proclaims soulwinners to be wise, dispute it who dare. A degree from the heavenly college will surely put them in good standing, whatever their fellow mortals say of them.

"He that winneth souls is wise." This can be seen very clearly. He must be wise in even ordinary respects who can by grace achieve so divine a marvel. Great soulwinners never have been fools. A person whom God qualifies to win souls could probably do anything else that Providence might allot him. Take Martin Luther, for instance. The man was not only fit to work a Reformation, but he could have ruled a nation or commanded an army! Think of Whitefield. His thundering eloquence, which stirred all England, was not associated with weak judgment or an absence of brain power; the man was a master orator. If he had applied himself to commerce, he would have become a leading merchant. If he had been a politician, he would have commanded the listeners amid admiring senates. He who wins souls is usually a man who could have done anything else if God had called him to it.

I know that the Lord uses what means He wills, but He always uses means suitable to the end. If you tell me that David slew Goliath with a sling, I answer that it was the best weapon in the world to reach so tall a giant, and the very best weapon that David could have used, for he had been skilled in it from his youth. There is always a propensity in the instruments God uses to produce the ordained result. Though the glory is not to them or the excellence in them, and all is to be attributed to God, yet is there a fitness that God sees, even if we do not.

Assuredly, soulwinners are by no means idiots or simpletons, but such as God makes wise for Himself, even though conceited smart alecks may dub them fools. *"He that winneth souls is wise"* because he has selected a wise objective. I think it was Michelangelo who once carved certain magnificent statues in snow. They quickly were gone; the material that readily compacted in the cold just as readily melted in the heat. He was far wiser when he fashioned the enduring marble and produced works that will last through the ages. But even marble itself is eroded by time. He is wise who selects for his raw material immortal souls, whose existence will outlast the stars. If God blesses us to the winning of souls, our work will remain when the *"wood, hay,* [and] *stubble"* (1 Corinthians 3:12) of earth's art and science have gone to the dust from which they sprang. In heaven itself, the soulwinner, blessed of God, will have memorials of his work preserved forever in the galleries of the skies.

He has selected a wise purpose, for what can be wiser than to glorify God? What can be wiser than in the highest sense to bless our fellowmen—to snatch a soul from the gulf that yawns, to lift it up to the heaven that glorifies, to deliver an immortal from the enslavement of Satan, and to bring him into the liberty of Christ? What is more excellent than this? I say that such an aim would commend itself to all right minds. Angels themselves may envy us poor sons of men that we are permitted to make this our life's object, to win souls for Jesus Christ. Wisdom herself assents to the excellence of the purpose.

To accomplish the work, a man must be wise, for to win a soul requires infinite wisdom. Even God did not win souls without wisdom, for the eternal plan of salvation was dictated by an infallible judgment. In every line of it, infinite skill is apparent. Christ, the great Soulwinner, is *"the power of God, and the wisdom of God"* (1 Corinthians 1:24). There is as much wisdom to be seen in the new creation as in the old. In a sinner saved, there is as much of God to behold as in a universe rising out of nothing.

We, then, who are to be workers together with God, proceeding side by side with Him to the great work of soulwinning, must be wise, too. It is a work that filled the Savior's heart, a work that moved the mind of the eternal Jehovah before the earth was. It is no child's play, nor a thing to be achieved while we are half asleep, nor to be attempted without deep consideration, nor to be carried on without gracious help from *"the only wise God our Savior"* (Jude 25). The pursuit is wise.

Note well, my friends, that he who is successful in soulwinning will prove to have been wise in the judgment of those who see the end as well as the beginning. Even if I were utterly selfish and had no concern for anything but my own happiness, I would choose, if God allowed, to be a soulwinner, for I never knew perfect, overflowing, unutterable happiness of the purest and most ennobling order until I first heard of one who had sought and found a Savior through my means. I remember the thrill of joy that went through me! No young mother ever rejoiced as much over her first-born child, no warrior was ever so exultant over a hard-won victory. Oh, the joy of knowing that a sinner once at enmity with God has been reconciled to Him by the Holy Spirit, through the words spoken by our feeble lips!

Since then, only by the grace given to me, the thought of which prostrates me in self-abasement, I have seen and heard of not only hundreds, but even thousands of sinners who have turned from the error of their ways by the testimony of God in me. Let afflictions come, let trials be multiplied as God wills, still this joy surpasses all others—the joy that we are to God a *"sweet savour of Christ"* (2 Corinthians 2:15). As often as we preach the Word, hearts are unlocked, chests heave with new life, eyes weep for sin, and tears are wiped away as they see the great Substitute for sin and live.

Beyond all argument, it is a joy worth worlds to win souls. Thank God, it is a joy that does not cease with this mortal life. It must be no small bliss, as one soars in flight up to the eternal throne, to find others moving at one's side toward the same glory. What delight it will be to turn around and question them, and to hear them say, "We are entering with you through the gates of pearl; you brought us to the Savior." It must be sheer joy to be welcomed to the skies by those who call us father in God—father in better bonds than those of earth, father through grace, and sire for immortality. It will be bliss beyond comparison to meet in the eternal seats with those begotten by us in Christ Jesus, for whom we travailed in birth, until Christ, *"the hope of glory"* (Colossians 1:27) was formed in them. (See Galatians 4:19.) In this sense, we will have many heavens—a heaven in everyone won for Christ, according to the Master's promise: *"they that turn many to righteousness* [shall shine] *as the stars for ever and ever"* (Daniel 12:3).

I have said enough, friends, I trust, to make some of you desire to occupy the position of soulwinners. But before I further address myself to my text, I would like to remind you that the honor does not belong to ministers only. They may take their full share of it, but it belongs to every one of you who has devoted himself to Christ. Such honor have all the saints. Every man, every women, every child whose heart is right with God may be a soulwinner. No one is placed by God's providence where he cannot do some good. There is not a glowworm under a hedge that does not give a needed light. There is not a working man, a suffering woman, a servant girl, a chimney sweeper, or a street cleaner who does not have some opportunities for serving God. What I have said of soulwinners does not belong to the learned doctor of divinity or to the eloquent preacher alone, but to all who are in Christ Jesus. Each of you can, if grace enables you, be wise and win the happiness of turning souls to Christ through the Holy Spirit.

I am about to dwell on my text, *"He that winneth souls is wise,"* in this way: First, I will make its truth stand out a little clearer by explaining the metaphor used in the text—winning souls. Second, I will give you some lessons in the matter of soulwinning, through which I trust the conviction will be forced on each believing mind that the work needs the highest wisdom.

First, then, let us consider the metaphor used in the text: *"He that winneth souls is wise."* We use the word "win" in many ways. It is sometimes found in very bad company, in those games of chance and sleight of hand that con artists are so fond of winning. I am sorry to say that much deception and trickery can be found in the religious world. Why, there are those who pretend to save souls by curious tricks, intricate maneuvers, and clever postures! A basin of water, half-a-dozen drops, certain syllables, and—presto!—an infant is made a child of God, a member of Christ, and an inheritor of the heavenly kingdom! This aqueous regeneration surpasses belief and understanding. Only the initiated can perform this piece of magic, which excels anything ever attempted by the Wizard of the North.

There is a way, too, of winning souls by laying hands upon heads, only the elbows of the aforesaid hands must be encased in sheer linen. Then the machinery acts, and grace is conferred by blessed fingers! I must confess I do not understand the mysterious science. But at this I need not wonder, for the profession of saving souls by such juggling can be carried out only by certain favored persons who have received apostolic succession directly from Judas Iscariot. This confirmation, when men pretend that it confers grace, is an infamous piece of juggling.

The whole thing is an abomination. Just to think that, in this century, there are men who preach salvation by sacraments, and salvation by themselves—indeed! Why, it is surely too late in the day to come to us with this drivel! Let us hope that these practices are anachronistic and out-of-date.

These things might have done for those who could not read in the days when books were scarce. But ever since the day when the glorious Luther was helped by God to proclaim with thunderclaps the emancipating truth, *"By grace are ye saved through faith; and that not of yourselves: it is the gift of God"* (Ephesians 2:8), there has been too much light for these owls. Let them go back to their ivy-mantled towers and complain to the moon of those who of old spoiled their kingdom of darkness. We cannot save souls in their theatrical way, and do not want to do so. We know that, with such juggling as that, Satan will hold the best hand and laugh at them as he turns the cards against them in the end.

How do we win souls, then? Why, the word "win" has a far better meaning. It is used in *warfare*. Warriors win cities and provinces. Now, to win a soul is a much more difficult thing than to win a city. Observe the earnest soulwinner at his work. How cautiously he seeks his great Captain's directions to know when to hang out the white flag to invite the heart to surrender to the sweet love of the Savior. When is the proper time to hang the black flag of warning, showing that, if grace is not received, judgment will surely follow? When should he unfurl, with dread reluctance, the red flag of the terrors of God against stubborn, impenitent souls?

The soulwinner has to sit down before a soul as a great captain before a walled town: to draw his lines of encirclement, dig his entrenchments, and place his batteries. He must not advance too fast, or he may overdo the fighting. He must not move too slowly, or he may not seem to be in earnest and may do himself harm. Then he must know which gate to attack: how to plant his guns at the Ear Gate and how to discharge them; how, sometimes, to keep the batteries going day and night with red-hot shot, to make, perhaps, a breach in the walls; when, at other times, to cease firing; and when suddenly to open all the batteries with terrific violence, so that perhaps, he may take the soul by surprise or cast in a truth when it was not expected, to burst like a shell in the soul and do damage to the dominions of sin.

The Christian soldier must know how to advance little by little—to sap that prejudice, to undermine that old enmity, to blow into the air that lust, and, finally, to storm the citadel. It is his to throw the scaling ladder up and to have his ears gladdened as he hears a clicking on the wall of the heart, telling him that the scaling ladder has grasped and has gained a firm hold. Then, with his saber between his teeth, he climbs up, springs on the man, slays his unbelief in the name of God, captures the city, runs up the bloodred flag of the cross, and declares, "The heart is won, won for Christ at last."

This requires a well-trained warrior, a master in his art. After many days of attack, many weeks of waiting, many an hour of storming by prayer and battering by entreaty, to capture the enemy's flag of depravity is the difficult work. It takes no fool to do this. God's grace must make a person wise thus to capture Mansoul, to lead its captivity captive, and to open wide the heart's gates, so that Prince Emmanuel may come in. This is winning a soul.

The word "win" was commonly used among the ancients to signify winning in a wrestling match. When the Greek sought to win the laurel or the ivy crown, he was compelled a long time before that to put himself through a course of training. When he came forth at last stripped for the encounter, he had no sooner exercised himself in the first few efforts than you saw how every muscle and every nerve had been developed in him. He had a stern opponent and therefore left none of his energy unused. While the wrestling was going on, you could see the man's eyes, how he watched every motion, every feint of his antagonist, and how his hand, his foot, and his whole body were thrown into the encounter. He feared to meet with a fall; he hoped to give one to his foe.

Now, a true soulwinner often has to come into close quarters with the devil within men. He has to struggle with their prejudices, their love of sin, their unbelief, their pride, and then, all of a sudden, grapple with their despair. At one moment he strives with their self-righteousness, at the next moment with their unbelief in God. Ten thousand arts are used to prevent the soulwinner from being conqueror in the encounter. But if God has sent him, he will never renounce his hold on the soul he seeks until he has given a throw to the power of sin and won another soul for Christ.

Besides that, there is another meaning to the word "win" upon which I cannot elaborate here. We use the word, you know, in a softer sense than these that have been mentioned, when we come to deal with hearts. There are secret and mysterious ways by which those who love win the object of their affection, which are wise in their fitness to the purpose. I cannot tell you how the lover wins his fond one, but experience has probably taught you. The weapon of this warfare is not always the same. Yet where that victory is won, the wisdom of the means becomes clear to every eye. The weapon of love is sometimes a look, or a soft word whispered and eagerly listened to; sometimes it is a tear. But this I know, that most of us, in our turn, have cast around another heart a chain that the other would not care to break, which has linked us both in a blessed captivity that has cheered our life.

This is very nearly the way in which we have to save souls. The illustration is nearer the mark than any of the others. Love is the true way of soulwinning, for when I spoke of storming the walls and of wrestling, those were but metaphors, but this is near the fact. We win by love. We win hearts for Jesus by love, by sympathy with their sorrow, by anxiety lest they should perish, by pleading with God for them with all our hearts that they would not be left to die unsaved, by pleading with them that they would seek God's mercy and grace.

Yes, there is a spiritual wooing and winning of hearts for the Lord Jesus. If you want to learn the way, you must ask God to give you a tender heart and a sympathizing soul. I believe that much of the secret of soulwinning lies in having compassion, in having spirits that can be *"touched with the feeling of* [human] *infirmities"* (Hebrews 4:15). You may carve a preacher out of granite, but even if you give him an angel's tongue, he will convert nobody. You may put him into the most fashionable pulpit and make his elocution faultless and his subject matter profoundly orthodox, but as long as he carries within himself a hard heart, he can never win a soul. Soul-saving requires a heart that beats hard against the ribs. It requires a soul full of the milk of human kindness. This is the *sine qua non* of success. This is the chief natural qualification for a soulwinner, which, under God and blessed of Him, will accomplish wonders.

I have not looked at the original Hebrew of the text, but I find—and you who have marginal references in your Bibles may find—that another translation of it is, He that *taketh* souls is wise. The word *taketh* refers to fishing or to bird catching. Every Sunday, as I leave my house and walk along, I cannot help seeing men with their cages and their captive birds, trying all around the common and in the fields to catch poor little warblers. They understand the method of alluring and entrapping their victims. Soulwinners might learn much from them. We must have our lures for souls, adapted to attract, to fascinate, to grasp. We must go forth with our bird lime, decoys, nets, and baits, so that we may catch the souls of men. Their enemy is a fowler possessed of the basest and most astounding cunning. We must outwit him with the guile of honesty, the craft of grace. But the art is learned only through divine teaching; in this we must be wise and willing to learn.

The one who takes fish must also have some art in him. Washington Irving, I think it was, told of three gentlemen who had read in Izaak Walton all about the delights of fishing. They wanted to enter into the same amusement, and accordingly decided to become disciples of the gentle art. They went into New York and bought the best rods and lines that could be purchased. They found out what the exact fly was for the particular day or month, so that the fish might bite at once and fly into the basket with alacrity, as it were. They fished, and fished, and fished the livelong day, but the basket was empty. They were getting disgusted with a sport that had no sport in it, when a ragged boy came down from the hills, without shoes or stockings, and humiliated them to the last degree. He had a bit of a bough pulled off a tree, a piece of string, and a bent pin. He put a worm on the pin and threw it in; immediately, out came a fish, as if it were a needle drawn to a magnet. In again went the line and out came another fish, until his basket was quite full. They asked him how he did it. He said he could not tell them, but that it was easy enough when you had the knack of it.

It is much the same in fishing for men. Some preachers who have silk lines and fine rods preach very eloquently and exceedingly gracefully, but they never win souls. In contrast, another man comes with very simple language, but with a fervent heart, and, immediately, men are converted to God. Surely, there must be a sympathy between the minister and the souls he wants to win. God gives to those whom He makes soulwinners a natural love for their work and a spiritual fitness for it. There is a sympathy between those who are to be blessed and those who are to be the means of blessing. By this sympathy, under God, many souls are taken. But it is as clear as noonday that, to be a fisher of men, one must be wise. *"He that winneth souls is wise."*

Second, friends—you who are engaged in the Lord's work from week to week and who seek to win men's souls to Christ—I am going to illustrate the text by telling you some of the ways by which souls are won. The preacher himself wins souls best, I believe, when he believes in the reality of his work—when he believes in instantaneous conversions. How can he expect God to do what he does not believe God will do? He succeeds best who expects conversion every time he preaches. According to his faith, so will it be done unto him. To be content without conversions is the surest way never to have them. To drive with a single aim entirely at the saving of souls is the surest method of usefulness. If we sigh and cry until men are saved, saved they will be.

He will best succeed who keeps closest to soul-saving truth. Now, all truth is not soul-saving, though all truth may be edifying. A soulwinner keeps to the simple story of the cross, telling men over and over again that whoever believes in Christ is not condemned, that to be saved nothing is needed but a simple trust in the crucified Redeemer. His ministry is largely made up of the glorious story of the cross, the sufferings of the Lamb, the mercy of God, and the willingness of the great Father to receive returning prodigals. In fact, he cries from day to day, *"Behold the Lamb of God, which taketh away the sin of the world"* (John 1:29). Such a one is likely to be a soulwinner, especially if he adds to this much prayer for souls and much anxious desire that men may be brought to Jesus, and then in his private life seeks as much as in his public ministry to be telling others of the love of the Savior for men.

But I am not talking to ministers, but to you who sit in the pews. Therefore, to you let me turn myself more directly. Brothers and sisters, you have different gifts. I hope you use them all. Perhaps some of you, though members of the church, think you have no gifts. But every believer has his gift and his portion of work. What can you do to win souls?

To those who think they can do nothing, let me recommend the bringing of others to hear the Word. That is a duty that is much neglected. Many of you attend churches that are perhaps not even half filled. Fill them. Do not grumble at the smallness of the congregation, but make it larger. Take somebody with you to the very next service, and at once the congregation will be increased. Go with the prayer that your minister's sermon may be blessed. If you cannot yourselves preach, by bringing others under the sound of the Word, you may be doing what is next best.

This is a very commonplace and simple remark, but let me press it upon you, for it is of great practical value. Many churches and chapels that are almost empty might soon have large audiences if those who profit by the Word would tell others about the blessing they have received and persuade them to attend the same ministry. Persuade your neighbors to come out to the place of worship. Look after them; make them feel that it is wrong to stay at home on Sunday from morning until night. I do not say upbraid them, for that does little good. But I do say entice them, persuade them. Get them under the Word, and who knows what may be the result? Oh, what a blessing it would be to you if you heard that what you could not do—for you could scarcely speak for Christ—was done by your pastor, by the power of the Holy Spirit, through your persuading one to come within gunshot of the gospel!

Next to that, soulwinners, try to talk to strangers after sermons. The preacher may have missed the mark, but you need not miss it. Or the preacher may have struck the mark, and you can help to make the impression deeper by a kind word. I remember several people joining the church who traced their conversion to the ministry in the Surrey Music Hall, but who said it was not that alone, but another agency cooperating with it. They were fresh from the country, and some good man—I think he is in heaven now—met them at the gate, spoke to them, said he hoped they had enjoyed what they had heard, listened to their answer, asked them if they were coming in the evening, and said he would be glad if they would drop by his house for tea. They did, and he had a word with them about the Master. The next Sunday it was the same. At last, those whom the messages had not much impressed were brought to hear with other ears until, by-and-by, through the good old man's persuasive words and the good Lord's gracious work, they were converted to God.

There is indeed a fine hunting ground in every large congregation, for you who really want to do good. How many come into my church every morning and evening with no thought of receiving Christ? Oh, if you would all help me, you who love the Master, if you would all help me by speaking to your neighbors who sit near to you, how much might be accomplished! Never let anybody say, "I came to the church for three months, and nobody spoke to me." Rather, by a sweet familiarity that ought always to be allowable in the house of God, seek with your whole heart to impress on your friends the truth that I can only put into their ears, but that God may help you to put into their heart.

Further, let me commend to you, dear friends, the art of buttonholing acquaintances and relatives. If you cannot preach to a hundred, preach to one. Get with the person alone and, in love, quietly and prayerfully talk to him. "One!" you exclaim. Well, is not one enough? I know your ambition, young man. You want to preach to thousands. Be content, and begin with one. Your Master was not ashamed to sit at the well and preach to one. When He had finished His message, He had really done good work to the whole city of Sychar, for that one woman became a missionary to her friends.

Timidity often prevents our being useful in this direction, but we must not give way to it. It must not be tolerated that Christ be unknown through our silence and sinners unwarned through our negligence. We must school and train ourselves to deal personally with the unconverted. We must not excuse ourselves, but force ourselves to the irksome task until it becomes easy.

This is one of the most honorable modes of soulwinning. If it requires more than ordinary zeal and courage, so much the more reason for our resolving to master it. Beloved, we must win souls; we cannot live and see men damned. We must have them brought to Jesus. Be up and doing, and let none around you die unwarned, unwept, uncared for. A tract is a useful thing, but a living word is better. Your eyes, face, and voice will all help. Do not be so cowardly as to give a piece of paper where your own speech would be so much better. I charge you, attend to this, for Jesus' sake.

Some of you could write letters for your Lord and Master. To far-off friends, a few loving lines may be most influential for good. Be like the men of Issachar, who handled the pen. Paper and ink are never better used than in soulwinning. Much has been done by this method. Could not you do it? Will you not try?

Some of you, at any rate, if you could not speak or write much, could live much. That is a fine way of preaching, that of preaching with your feet—I mean preaching by your life, conduct, and conversation. That loving wife who weeps in secret over an unbelieving husband, but is always so kind to him; that dear child whose heart is broken by his father's blasphemy, but is so much more obedient than he used to be before his conversion; that servant at whom the master swears, but whom he trusts with his purse and the gold uncounted in it; that tradesman who is sneered at for his faith, but who, nonetheless, has integrity and would not be compelled to do a dirty action for any reason—these are the men and women who preach the best messages. These are your practical preachers. Give us your holy living; with it as the leverage, we will move the world.

Under God's blessing, we will find tongues, if we can, but we greatly need the lives of our people to illustrate what our tongues have to say. The gospel is something like an illustrated paper. The preacher's words are the text, but the pictures are the living men and women who form our churches. Just as when people pick up a newspaper, they very often do not read the articles, but they always look at the pictures, so in a church, outsiders may not come to hear the preacher, but they always consider, observe, and criticize the lives of the members. If you want to be soulwinners, then, dear brothers and sisters, see that you live the gospel. *"I have no greater joy than to hear that my children walk in truth"* (3 John 1:4).

One thing more: the soulwinner must be a master of the art of prayer. You cannot bring souls to God if you do not go to God yourself. You must get your battle-ax and your weapons of war from the armory of sacred communication with Christ. If you are much alone with Jesus, you will catch His Spirit. You will be fired with the flame that burned in His breast and consumed His life. You will weep with the tears that fell upon Jerusalem when He saw it perishing. If you cannot speak as eloquently as He did, yet there will be about what you say something of the same power that, in Him, thrilled the hearts and awoke the consciences of men.

My dear friends, especially you members of the church, I am always so anxious lest any of you would begin to rest upon your oars and take things easy in the matters of God's kingdom. There are some of you—I bless you, and I bless God at the remembrance of you—who are in earnest for winning souls in season and out of season. You are the truly wise. However, I fear there are others whose hands are slack, who are satisfied to let me preach, but do not themselves preach. They take these seats, occupy these pews, and hope the cause goes well, but that is all they do. Oh, do let me see you all in earnest! A great host of nearly five thousand members, what could we not do if we are all alive and all in earnest? But such a host, without the spirit of enthusiasm, becomes a mere mob, an unwieldy mass, out of which mischief grows and no good results arise. If you were all firebrands for Christ, you might set the nation ablaze. If you were all wells of living water, how many thirsty souls might drink and be refreshed!

Beloved, there is one question I will ask, and then I will conclude. Are your own souls won? You cannot win others otherwise. Are you yourselves saved? What if this night you have to answer to another greater than I am? What if the bony finger of the last great orator would be lifted up instead of mine? What if his unconquerable eloquence would turn those bones to stone, glaze those eyes, and make the blood chill in your veins? Could you hope, in your last extremity, that you were saved? If not saved, how will you ever be? When will you be saved, if not now? Will any time be better than now?

The way to be saved is simply to trust in what the Son of Man did when He became man and suffered punishment for all those who trust Him. For all His people, Christ was the perfect Substitute. His people are those who trust Him.

If you do, He was punished for your sins. You cannot be punished for them, for God will not punish sin twice—first in Christ and then in you. If you trust Jesus, who lives at the right hand of God, you are this moment pardoned, and you are forever saved. Trust Him now! It may be now or never with you. Let it be now. Trusting in Jesus, dear friends, you will have no need to hesitate when asked, "Are you saved?" You can answer, "Yes, I am, for it is written, '*He that believeth on him is not condemned*' (John 3:18)." Trust Him now. Then, may God help you to be a soulwinner. You will be wise, and God will be glorified!

13

SAVING SOULS:
OUR ONE BUSINESS

I am made all things to all men, that I might by all means save some.
—1 Corinthians 9:22

t is a grand thing to see a person who is thoroughly possessed by one master passion. Such a one is sure to be strong; if the master principle is excellent, he is sure to be excellent, too. The man of one objective is a man indeed. Lives with many aims are like water trickling through innumerable streams, none of which are wide enough or deep enough to float the merest cockleshell of a boat. But a life with one purpose is like a mighty river flowing between its banks, bearing to on either side.

Give me a person who not only has a great objective in his soul, but also is thoroughly possessed by it, his powers all concentrated, and himself on fire with vehement zeal for his supreme aim. You have put before me one of the greatest sources of power that the world can produce. Give me a person who is immersed with holy love in his heart and filled with some masterly celestial thought in his mind. Such a person will be known, whatever his lot may be. I venture to prophesy that his name will be remembered long after the place of his grave is forgotten.

Such a man was Paul. I am not about to set him on a pedestal, so that you may look at him and marvel, much less that you may kneel down and worship him as a saint. I mention Paul because what he was, every one of us ought to be. Even though we cannot share in his office, not being apostles, and even though we cannot share in his talents or his inspiration, we still ought to be possessed by the same Spirit that motivated him. Let me also add that we ought to be possessed by it in the same degree.

Do you take exception to that? I ask you what was there in Paul, by the grace of God, that may not be in you? What did Jesus do for Paul more than He has done for you? He was divinely changed; so have you been changed if you have passed from darkness into marvelous light. He had much forgiven him; so have you also been freely pardoned. He was redeemed by the blood of the Son of God; so have you been—at least, so you profess. He was filled with the Spirit of God; so are you, if you are truly such as your profession of Christianity makes you out to be.

Owing your salvation to Christ, being debtors to the precious blood of Jesus, and being quickened by the Holy Spirit, why should you not bear the same fruit from the same sowing? Why not the same effect from the same cause? Do not tell me that the apostle was an exception and cannot be set up as a rule or model for more common folk, for I will have to tell you that we must be as Paul was if we hope to be where Paul is.

Paul did not think that he had attained perfection, or that he was already perfect. Will we think that he was so to the extent that we regard him as matchless, and thus are content to fall short of what he was? No! Rather, let it be our incessant prayer, as believers in Christ, that we may be followers of Paul as far as he followed Christ. Where he failed to set his feet in his Lord's footprints, may we even outstrip him and be more zealous, more devoted to Christ, than even the Apostle to the Gentiles was. Oh, that the Holy Spirit would bring us to be like our Lord Jesus Himself!

I need to speak to you about Paul's great objective in life; he tells us it was to "save some." I will look into Paul's heart and find a few of the great reasons that made him think it was so important that "some" at least should be saved. Then, I will indicate some of the means that the apostle used to that end. All of this is presented with this aim: that you may seek to "*save some*," that you may seek this because of potent reasons that you cannot withstand, and that you may seek it with wise methods that will succeed.

First, friends, what was Paul's great objective in his daily life and ministry? He says it was to "*save some*." There are ministers of Christ present at this hour, together with city missionaries, Bible women, Sunday school teachers, and other workers in my Master's vineyard. I boldly inquire of each one of you, "Is this your object in all your Christian service? Do you above all things aim at saving souls?" I am afraid that some have forgotten this great aim, but anything short of this is unworthy to be the goal of a Christian's life.

I fear there are some who preach with a view of entertaining men. As long as people can be gathered in crowds, their ears can be tickled, and they can leave pleased with what they have heard; the orator is content, folds his hands, and goes back self-satisfied. But Paul did not spend himself to please the public and gather a crowd. If he did not save them, he felt that it was of no avail to interest them. Unless the truth had pierced their hearts, affected their lives, and made new men of them, Paul would have gone home crying, "*Who hath believed our report? and to whom is the arm of the Lord revealed?*" (Isaiah 53:1).

It seems to be the opinion of a large group of people today that the object of Christian effort should be to educate men. I grant you that education is in itself an exceedingly valuable thing, so valuable that I am sure the whole Christian church rejoices greatly that at last we have a national system of education, which only needs to be carefully carried out so that every child in this land will have the keys of knowledge in his hand. Whatever price others may set on ignorance, we are promoters of knowledge. The more it can be spread, the better we will be pleased.

But if the church of God thinks that it is sent into the world merely to train the mental faculties, it has made a very serious mistake. The object of Christianity is not to educate men for their secular callings, or even to train them in the more refined arts and elegant professions, or to enable them to enjoy the beauties of nature or the charms of poetry. Jesus Christ did not come into the world for any of these things. He came "*to seek and to save that which was lost*" (Luke 19:10). He has sent His church on the same errand. She is a traitor to the Master who sent her if she is so beguiled by the beauties of taste and art as to forget that to "preach Christ, and Him crucified" (see 1 Corinthians 1:23, 2:2) is the only object for which she exists among the sons of men. The business of the church is the salvation of souls.

The minister is to use all means to save some. He is no minister of Christ if this is not the one desire of his heart. Missionaries sink far below their level when they are content to civilize; their first object is to save. The same is true of the Sunday school teacher and of all other workers among children. If they have merely taught the child to read, to repeat hymns, and so forth, they have not yet touched their true vocation. We must have the children saved. At this nail we must drive. The hammer must always come down upon this head, so that we *"might by all means save some,"* for we have done nothing unless some are saved.

Paul does not even say that he tried to moralize men. The best promoter of morality is the gospel. When a person is saved, he becomes moral. He becomes more than moral: he becomes holy. To aim first at morality is to miss the mark totally. If we did attain it—but we will not—we would not have attained that for which we were sent to the world.

Dr. Chalmers' experience is a very valuable one to those who think that the Christian ministry ought to preach mere morality, for he says that, in his first parish he preached morality and saw no good whatever arising out of his exhortations. However, as soon as he began to preach Christ crucified, then there was a buzz, a stir, and much opposition, but grace prevailed.

He who wishes for perfumes must grow the flowers. He who wants to promote morality must have men saved. He who desires motion in a corpse should first seek life for it; and he who longs for a rightly-ordered life should first desire an inward renewal by the Holy Spirit.

We are not to be satisfied when we have taught men their duties toward their neighbors, or even their duties toward God. This would suffice for Moses, but not for Christ. *"The law was given by Moses, but grace and truth came by Jesus Christ"* (John 1:17). We teach men what they ought to be, but we do far more; by the power of the gospel, applied by the Holy Spirit, we make them what they ought to be by the power of God's Spirit. We do not put before the blind the things that they ought to see, but we open their eyes in the name of Jesus. We do not tell the captive how free he ought to be, but we open the door and take away his chains. We are not content to tell men what they must be, but we show them how this character can be obtained, and how Jesus Christ freely presents all that is essential to eternal life to all those who come and put their trust in Him.

Now take note: if you or I, or any or all of us will have spent our lives merely in amusing, educating, or moralizing men, when we come to give in our account at the last great Day, we will be in a very sorry condition. We shall have but a very sorry record to render. Of what avail will it be to a man to be educated when he comes to be damned? Of what service will it be to him to have been amused when the trumpet sounds, heaven and earth are shaking, and the pit opens wide her jaws of fire and swallows up the soul unsaved? Of what avail will it have been even to have moralized a man if he is still on the left hand of the Judge, and if "*Depart from me, ye cursed*" (Matthew 25:41) will still be his portion? Blood red with the murder of men's souls will be the skirts of professing Christians, unless the end and aim of all their work has been to "*save some.*"

Oh! I beseech you, especially you, dear friends, who are working in Sunday schools and elsewhere, do not think that you have done anything unless the children's souls are saved. Settle it that this is the top and bottom of the business. Throw your whole strength in the name of Christ, and by the power of the Eternal Spirit, into this object: if by any means you may "*save some*" and bring some to Jesus that they may be delivered "*from the wrath to come*" (1 Thessalonians 1:10).

What did Paul mean by saying that he desired to "*save some*"? What is it to be saved? Paul meant by that nothing less than that some should be born again, for no man is saved until he is made a new creature in Christ Jesus. The old nature cannot be saved, because it is dead and corrupt. The best thing that can be done with it is to let it be crucified and buried in the sepulcher of Christ. A new nature must be implanted in us by the power of the Holy Spirit, or we cannot be saved. We must be such new creations that it is as if we had never existed before. We must come a second time as fresh from the hand of the eternal God as if we had been molded today by divine wisdom, as Adam was in paradise.

The great Teacher's words are, "*The wind bloweth where it listeth, and thou hearest the sound thereof, but canst not tell whence it cometh, and whither it goeth: so is every one that is born of the Spirit*" (John 3:8). "*Except a man be born again* [from above], *he cannot see the kingdom of God*" (John 3:3). This, then, is what Paul meant: that men must be new creatures in Christ Jesus, and that we may never rest until we see such a change worked in them. This must be the object of our teaching and of our praying, indeed, the object of our lives, that "*some*" may be regenerated.

Besides that, Paul meant that some might be cleansed from their past iniquity through the merit of the atoning sacrifice of the Son of God. No one can be saved from his sin except by the Atonement. Under the Jewish law it was written, "*Cursed is every one that continueth not in all things which are written in the book of the law to do them*" (Galatians 3:10; see Deuteronomy 27:26). That curse has never been reversed, and the only way to escape from it is this: Jesus Christ was "*made a curse for us: for it is written, Cursed is every one that hangeth on a tree*" (Galatians 3:13; see Deuteronomy 21:23).

Now, he who believes in Jesus, who puts his hands upon the head of Jesus of Nazareth, the Scapegoat of His people, has lost his sins. His faith is sure evidence that his iniquities were of old laid upon the head of the great Substitute. The Lord Jesus Christ was punished in our place. We are no longer obnoxious to God, inciting His wrath. Behold, the sin-atoning Sacrifice is slain and offered on the altar. (See Leviticus 16:5–10, 15–22.) The Lord has accepted it and is so well pleased that He has declared that whoever believes in Jesus is fully and eternally forgiven.

We long to see men thus forgiven. We pine to bring the prodigal's head to the Father's bosom, the wandering sheep to the good Shepherd's shoulder, the lost piece of money into the Owner's hands. Until this is done, nothing is done. I mean nothing spiritually, nothing eternally, nothing that is worthy of the agony of a Christian's life, nothing that can be looked upon as deserving of an immortal spirit's spending all its fires upon it. O Lord, our souls yearn to see Jesus rewarded by the salvation of the blood-bought! Help us to lead souls to Him.

When the apostle wished that he "*might…save some*," he also meant that, being pardoned and regenerated, they might be purified and made holy, for a person is not saved while he lives in sin. Let him say what he will, he cannot be saved from sin while he is the slave of it. How is a drunkard saved from drunkenness while he still riots as before? How can you say that the swearer is saved from blasphemy while he is still profane? Words must be used in their true meaning. Now, the great object of the Christian's work should be that some might be saved from their sins, purified, made white, and made examples of integrity, chastity, honesty, and righteousness, as the fruit of the Spirit of God. Where this is not the case, we have labored in vain and spent our strength for nothing.

Now, I do protest before you all that I have in this house of prayer never sought anything but the conversion of souls. I call heaven and earth to witness, and your consciences, too, that I have never labored for anything except this: the bringing of you to Christ, that I might present you at last unto God, *"accepted in the beloved"* (Ephesians 1:6). I have not sought to gratify depraved appetites either by novelty of doctrine or ceremony, but I have kept up the simplicity of the gospel. I have kept back no part of the price of God's Word from you, but I have endeavored to give you the whole counsel of God. I have sought out no fineries of speech, but have spoken plainly and straight to your hearts and consciences. If you are not saved, I mourn and lament before God that, up to this day, though I have preached hundreds of times to you, yet I have preached in vain. If you have not closed in with Christ, if you have not been washed in the fountain filled with blood, you are uncultivated pieces of soil, from which no harvest has yet come.

You tell me, perhaps, that you have been kept from a great many sins, that you have learned a great many truths by coming here. So far, so good. But could I afford to live merely to teach you certain truths or keep you from open sins? How could this content me if I knew all the while that you were still unsaved, and must, therefore, be cast into the flames of hell after death? No, beloved, before the Lord, I consider nothing to be worthy of my life, soul, and energy but the winning of you to Christ. Nothing but your salvation could ever make me feel that my heart's desire is granted.

I ask every Christian worker to see to it that he never turns aside from shooting at this target. His aim should be at the center of this target, too, namely, that he may win souls for Christ and see them born to God and washed in the fountain filled with blood. Let the workers' hearts ache and yearn and their voices cry out until their throats are hoarse. Yet let them judge that they have accomplished nothing whatever until, at least in some cases, men are really saved. As the fisherman longs to take the fish in his net, as the hunter desires to bear home his spoil, as the mother yearns to clasp her lost child to her bosom, so do we faint for the salvation of souls. We must have them, or we are ready to die. Save them, O Lord, save them for Christ's sake!

The apostle had great reasons for electing such an objective in life. Were he here, I think he would tell you that his reasons were something of this kind: To save souls! If they are not saved, God is dishonored! Have you ever thought about the amount of dishonor that is done to the Lord our God in any one hour of the day? Take, if you will, this prayer hour, when we are gathered here ostensibly to pray. If the thoughts of this great assembly could all be read, how many of them would be dishonoring to the Most High?

But outside of every house of prayer, outside of every place of worship of every kind, think of the thousands, the tens of thousands, the hundreds of thousands, who have all this day neglected the very semblance of the worship of the God who has made them and who keeps them alive! Think of how many times the door of the gin palace has swung on its hinges during this holy hour, how many times God's name has been blasphemed at the drinking bar! There are worse things than these, if worse can be, but I will not lift the veil.

Transfer your thoughts to an hour or so from now, when the veil of darkness will have descended. Shame will not permit us even to think of how God's name is dishonored in the persons of those whose first father was made after the image of God, but who pollute themselves to be the slaves of Satan and the prey of bestial lusts! Alas, this city is full of abominations, of which the apostle said, "*It is a shame even to speak of those things which are done of them in secret*" (Ephesians 5:12).

Christian men and women, nothing but the gospel can sweep away social evil. Vices are like vipers, and only the voice of Jesus can drive them out of the land. The gospel is the great broom with which to cleanse the filthiness of the city; nothing else will avail. Will you not, for God's sake, whose name is every day profaned, seek to "*save some*"?

Enlarge your thoughts and take in all the great cities of the continent. Further still, take in all the idolaters of China and India, the worshipers of the false prophet and antichrist—what a mass of provocation! What a smoke in Jehovah's nose this false worship must be! (See Isaiah 65:5.) How He must often put His hand to the hilt of His sword as though He would say, "Ah! I will ease Myself of My adversaries." But He bears it patiently. Let us not become indifferent to His long-suffering, but day and night let us cry to Him and daily labor for Him, if by any means we may "*save some*" for His glory's sake.

Dear friends, also think of the extreme misery of our human race. It would be a very appalling thing if you could get any idea of the sum total of the misery of London at the present moment in the hospitals and workhouses. Now, I would not say a word against poverty, for wherever it comes, it is a bitter evil. But note carefully that, while a few are poor because of unavoidable circumstances, a very large mass of the poverty of London is the sheer and clear result of wastefulness, lack of forethought, idleness, and, worst of all, drunkenness.

Ah, that drunkenness! That is the master evil. If drink could only be gotten rid of, we might be sure of conquering the very devil himself. The drunkenness created by the infernal liquor dens that plague the whole of this huge city is appalling. No, I did not speak in haste or let slip a hasty word. Many of the drink houses are nothing less than infernal. In some respects, they are worse, for hell has its uses as the divine protest against sin, but as for the gin palace, there is nothing to be said in its favor.

The vices of the age cause three-fourths of all the poverty. If you could look at the homes—the wretched homes where women tremble at the sound of their husbands' footsteps as they come home, where little children crouch down with fear upon their little heaps of straw because the human brute who calls himself "a man" comes reeling home from the place where he has been indulging his appetites—if you could look at such a sight and remember that it will be seen ten thousand times tonight, I think you would say, "God help us by all means to '*save some*'!" Since the great ax to lay at the root of the deadly tree is the gospel, may God help us to hold that ax there, to work constantly with it until the huge trunk of the poison tree begins to rock to and fro, and we get it down. Then London will be saved, and also the world, from the misery and wretchedness that now drip from every bough!

Again, dear friends, the Christian has other reasons for seeking to "*save some*": chiefly because of the terrible future of impenitent souls. The veil that hangs before me is not penetrated by every glance, but he who has had his eyes touched with heavenly ointment sees through it, and what does he see? Myriads upon myriads of spirits in dreadful procession passing from their bodies and going—where? Unsaved, unregenerate, unwashed in precious blood, we see them go up to the solemn bar from which the sentence comes forth. They are banished from the presence of God, banished to horrors that are not to be described or even to be imagined. This alone is enough to cause us distress day and night. This decision of destiny has a terrible solemnity about it.

But the resurrection trumpet sounds. Those spirits come forth from their prison. I see them returning to earth, rising from the pit to the bodies in which they lived; and now I see them standing—multitudes upon multitudes—"*in the valley of decision*" (Joel 3:14). He comes, sitting on a "*great white throne*" (Revelation 20:11), with the crown upon His head and the books before Him. There they stand as prisoners at the bar. My vision now perceives them—how they tremble! How they quiver, like aspen leaves in the gale! Where can they flee? Rocks cannot hide them, mountains will not open their bowels to conceal them! What will become of them?

The dreadful angel takes the sickle, reaps them as the reaper cuts up the tares for the oven. As he gathers them, he casts them down where despair will be their everlasting torment. Woe is me, my heart sinks as I see their doom and hear the terrible cries of their too-late awaking. Save some, O Christians! *"By all means save some."* From the flames and outer darkness, and the weeping, wailing, and gnashing of teeth, seek to *"save some"*! Let this, as in the case of the apostle, be your great, ruling object in life, that by all means you may *"save some."*

But if they are saved, observe the contrast. Their spirits mount to heaven, and after the resurrection their bodies ascend, also. There they praise redeeming love. No fingers more nimble on the harp strings than theirs! No notes are sweeter than theirs, as they sing, *"Unto him that loved us, and washed us from our sins in his own blood, and hath made us kings and priests unto God and his Father; to him be glory and dominion for ever and ever"* (Revelation 1:5–6). What bliss to see the once rebellious brought home to God, and heirs of wrath made possessors of heaven! All this is involved in salvation. Oh, that myriads may come to this blessed state!

"Save some!" Oh, *"save some,"* at least. Seek that some may be there in glory. Behold your Master. He is your pattern. He left heaven to *"save some."* He went to the cross and the grave to *"save some."* This was the great object of His life—to lay it down for His sheep. He loved His church and gave Himself for her, so that He might redeem her unto Himself. Imitate your Master. Learn His self-denial and blessed consecration, if by any means you may *"save some."*

My soul yearns that I personally may *"save some,"* but my desire is broader than that. I would have all of you, my beloved friends, associated here in church fellowship, to become spiritual parents of children for God. Oh, that every one of you might *"save some"*! Yes, my venerable friends, you are not too old for service. Yes, my young friends, you young men and women, you are not too young to be recruits in the King's service.

If the kingdom is ever to come to our Lord—and come it will—it will never come through a few ministers, missionaries, or evangelists preaching the gospel. It must come through every one of you preaching it, in the shop and by the fireside, when walking outside and when sitting in your room. All of you must always be endeavoring to *"save some."* I would enlist you all afresh and bind anew the King's colors upon you. I desire that you would fall in love with my Master anew, and enter a second time into the love of your engagement.

There is a line from a hymn of Cowper's that we sometimes sing, "Oh, for a closer walk with God!" May we come to have a closer walk with Him. If we do so, we will also feel a more vehement desire to magnify Christ in the salvation of sinners.

I would like to stress the question for you who are saved: How many others have you brought to Christ? I know you cannot do it by yourself. But I mean, how many has the Spirit of God brought by you? Is it quite certain that you have led any to Jesus? Can you not recollect one? I pity you, then!

The Lord said to Jeremiah about Coniah, "*Write ye this man childless*" (Jeremiah 22:30). That was considered to be a fearful curse. Should I write you childless, my beloved friends? Your children are not saved, your wife is not saved, and you are spiritually childless. Can you bear this thought? I entreat you, wake from your slumbering and ask the Master to make you useful. "I wish the saints cared for us sinners," said a young man. "They do care for you," answered one. "They care very much for you." "Why don't they show it, then?" said he. "I have often wished to have a talk about good things, but my friend, who is a member of the church, never broaches the subject and seems to study how to keep clear of it when I am with him." Do not let them say so. Do tell them about Christ. Make this your resolve, every one of you, that if men perish, they will not perish for lack of your prayers or for lack of your earnest and loving instructions. May God give you grace, each one of you, to resolve by all means to "*save some*," and then to carry out your resolution!

I mention in conclusion the great methods that the apostle Paul used. How did he who so longed to "*save some*" set about it? First, he simply preached the gospel of Christ. He did not attempt to create a sensation by startling statements, nor did he preach erroneous doctrine in order to obtain the assent of the multitude. I fear that some evangelists preach what, in their own minds, they must know to be untrue. They keep back certain doctrines, not because they are untrue, but because they do not give scope enough for their ravings. They make loose statements because they hope to reach more minds.

However earnest a man may be for the salvation of sinners, I do not believe that he has the right to make any statement that his sober judgment will not justify. I think I have heard of things said and done at revival meetings that were not according to sound doctrine, but that were always excused by "the excitement of the occasion." I hold that I would have no right to state false doctrine, even if I knew it would save a soul. The supposition is, of course, absurd, but it makes you see what I mean. My business is to bring to bear upon men not falsehood, but truth. I will not be excused if, under any pretense, I palm a lie upon the people.

Rest assured, to keep back any part of the gospel is not the right or true method for saving men. Tell the sinner all the doctrines. If you hold Calvinistic doctrine, as I hope you do, do not stutter about it or stammer over it, but speak it. Depend upon it, many revivals have been short-lived because a full-bodied gospel was not proclaimed. Give the people every truth, baptized in holy fire, and each truth will have its own useful effect upon the mind.

But the great truth is the cross, the truth that *"God so loved the world, that he gave his only begotten Son, that whosoever believeth in him should not perish, but have everlasting life"* (John 3:16). Beloved, keep to that. That is the bell for you to ring. Ring it, and keep on ringing it. Sound forth that note on your silver trumpet. If you are only a ram's horn, sound it forth, and the walls of Jericho will come down.

Alas, for the fineries of our "cultured" modern ministers! I hear them crying out, denouncing my old-fashioned advice. This talking about Christ crucified is said to be archaic, conventional, antiquated, and not at all suitable for the refinement of this wonderful age. It is astonishing how learned we have all grown lately. We are getting so very wise, I am afraid we will ripen into fools before long, if we have not done so already.

People want "thinking" nowadays, or so it is said. Supposedly, working men will go where science has been deified and profound thought enshrined. I have noticed that, as a general rule, wherever the new thinking drives out the old gospel, there are more spiders than people. However, where there is the simple preaching of Jesus Christ, the place is crowded to the doors. Nothing else will crowd a meetinghouse, after all, for any length of time, but the preaching of Christ crucified.

But as to this matter, whether it is popular or unpopular, our minds are made up, and our feet are put down. We have no question as to our own course. If it is foolish to preach atonement by blood, we will be fools. If it is madness to stick to the old truth, just as Paul delivered it in all its simplicity, without any refinement or improvement, we intend to stick to it, even if we are publicly ridiculed as being incapable of progressing with the age.

We are persuaded that this *"foolishness of preaching"* (1 Corinthians 1:21) is a divine ordinance, and that the cross of Christ, which is a stumbling block to so many and is ridiculed by so many more, is still *"the power of God, and the wisdom of God"* (verse 24). Yes, just the old-fashioned truth—if you believe, you will be saved—we will always adhere to. May God send His blessing upon it according to His own eternal purposes! We do not expect this preaching to be popular, but we know that God will justify it. Meanwhile, we are not staggered, because:

> As childish dotage, and delirious dreams,
> The truths we love a sightless world blasphemes.
> The danger they discern not, they deny,
> Laugh at their only remedy, and die.

Next to this, Paul used much prayer. The gospel alone will not be blessed; we must pray over our preaching. A great painter was asked what he mixed his colors with. He replied that he mixed them with brains. Likewise, if anyone should ask a preacher what he mixes truth with, he ought to be able to answer, "With prayer, much prayer."

When a poor man was breaking granite by the roadside, he was down on his knees while he struck his blows. A minister passing by said, "Ah, my friend, here you are at your hard work; your work is just like mine; you have to break stones, and so do I." "Yes," said the man, "and if you manage to break stony hearts, you will have to do it as I do, down on your knees." The man was right; no one can use the gospel hammer well unless he is much on his knees, but the gospel hammer soon splits flinty hearts when one knows how to pray. Prevail with God, and you will prevail with men.

Let us come straight from the closet to the pulpit, with the anointing oil of God's Spirit fresh upon us. What we receive in secrecy we are cheerfully to dispense in public. Let us never venture to speak for God to men until we have spoken for men to God. Yes, dear friends, if you want a blessing on your Sunday school teaching, or any other form of Christian labor, mix it up with fervent intercession.

And then observe one other thing. Paul always went to his work with an intense sympathy for those he dealt with, a sympathy that made him adapt himself to each case. If he talked to a Jew, he did not begin at once blurting out that he was the Apostle to the Gentiles, but he said he was a Jew, as he was. He raised no questions about nationalities or ceremonies. He wanted to tell the Jew about Him of whom Isaiah said, *"He is despised and rejected of men; a man of sorrows, and acquainted with grief*" (Isaiah 53:3), in order that he might believe in Jesus and be saved. If he met a Gentile, the Apostle to the Gentiles never showed any squeamishness that might have been expected to cling to him on account of his Jewish education. He ate and drank as the Gentile did, sat with him, and talked with him. He was, as it were, a Gentile with him, never raising any question about circumcision or uncircumcision, but solely wishing to tell him of Christ, who came into the world to save both Jew and Gentile and to make them one. If Paul met with a Scythian, he spoke to him in the Barbarian tongue, and not in classic Greek. If he met a Greek, he spoke to him as he did at the Areopagus, with language that was appropriate for the polished Athenian. He was *"all things to all men, that* [he] *might by all means save some."*

So let it be with you, Christian people. Your one business in life is to lead men to believe in Jesus Christ by the power of the Holy Spirit. Every other thing should be made subservient to this one objective. If you can but get them saved, everything else will come right in due time. Mr. Hudson Taylor, a dear man of God, who has labored much in inland China, finds it helpful to dress as a Chinese man and wear his hair braided. He always mingles with the people, and as far as possible lives as they do. This seems to me to be a truly wise policy.

I can understand that we will win a congregation of Chinese by becoming as Chinese as possible. If this is the case, we are bound to be Chinese to the Chinese to save the Chinese. It would not be amiss to become a Zulu to save Zulus, though we must see that we do it in another sense than Colenso did.

If we can put ourselves on a level with those whose good we seek, we will be more likely to effect our purpose than if we remain aliens and foreigners, and then talk of love and unity. To sink myself to save others is the idea of the apostle. To throw overboard all peculiarities and yield a thousand trivial points in order to bring men to Jesus is wisdom if we want to extend our Master's kingdom. May no whim or conventionality of ours ever keep a soul from considering the gospel—that would be horrible, indeed. It is better by far to be personally inconvenienced by compliance with things that are insignificant than to delay a sinner's coming by quarreling about trifles.

If Jesus Christ were here today, I am sure He would not wear a gaudy robe. I cannot imagine our Lord Jesus Christ dressed in that style. Why, the apostle tells our women that they are to dress modestly, and I do not think Christ would have His ministers set an example of nonsense. Even in dress something may be done on the principle of our text. When Jesus Christ was here, what did He wear? He wore the common dress of the countrymen, a garment woven from the top throughout, without seam. I think He would have His ministers wear clothes that are similar to the clothes that their hearers commonly wear. So, even in dress, ministers should associate with their hearers and be one among them.

He would have you teachers, if you want to save your children, talk to them like children, and make yourselves children, if you can. You who want to get at young peoples' hearts must try to be young. You who wish to visit the sick must sympathize with them in their sickness. Learn to speak as you would like to be spoken to if you were sick. Come down to those who cannot come up to you. You cannot pull people out of the water without stooping down and taking hold of them. If you have to deal with bad characters, you must come down to them, not in their sin, but in their roughness and in their style of language, so as to take hold of them. I pray to God that we may learn the sacred art of soulwinning by adaptation. They called Mr. Whitefield's chapel at Moorfields, "The Soul Trap." Whitefield was delighted and said he hoped it would always be a soul trap. Oh, that all our places of worship were soul traps, and every Christian a fisher of men, each one doing his best, as the fisherman does, by every art and artifice, to catch those he fishes for! Well may we use all means to win so great a prize as a spirit destined for eternal wealth or woe. The diver plunges deep to find pearls, and we must accept any labor or hazard to win a soul. Rouse yourselves, my friends, for this Godlike work, and may the Lord bless you in it!

14

INSTRUCTION IN
SOULWINNING

He saith unto them, Follow Me, and I will make you fishers of men.
—Matthew 4:19

When Christ calls us by His grace, we not only ought to remember what we are, but we also ought to think of what He can make us. It is, *"Follow me, and I will make you."* We should repent of what we have been, but rejoice in what we may be. It is not, "Follow Me, because of what you are already." It is not, "Follow Me, because you may make something of yourselves," but "Follow Me, because of what I will make you."

Truly, I might say of each one of us, as soon as we are converted, *"It doth not yet appear what we shall be"* (1 John 3:2). It did not seem likely that lowly fishermen would develop into apostles, that men so handy with the net would be quite as much at home in preaching sermons and in instructing converts. One would have said, "How can these things be? You cannot make founders of churches out of peasants of Galilee." But that is exactly what Christ did. When we are brought low in the sight of God by a sense of our own unworthiness, we may feel encouraged to follow Jesus because of what He can make us.

What did Hannah say with sorrowful spirit when she lifted up her song? *"He raiseth up the poor out of the dust, and lifteth up the beggar from the dunghill, to set them among princes"* (1 Samuel 2:8). We cannot tell what God may make of us in the new creation, since it would have been impossible to have foretold what He made of all the beautiful things that came forth from darkness and chaos by that one creative word, *"Let there be light"* (Genesis 1:3). Who can tell what lovely displays of everything that is divinely fair may yet appear in a man's formerly dark life when God has said, *"Let there be light"*? You who see nothing desirable in yourselves at present, come and follow Christ for the sake of what He can make out of you! Do you not hear His sweet voice calling, *"Follow me, and I will make you fishers of men"* ?

Note, next, we are not made all that we shall be, or all that we ought to desire to be, when we are fished for and caught. "Catching us" is what the grace of God does for us at first, but this is not all. We are like the fish; we make sin our element, just as they live in the sea. The good Lord comes, and, with the gospel net, He takes us and delivers us from the life and love of sin. But He has not worked for us all that He can do, or all that we should wish Him to do, when He has done this. It is a higher miracle to make us who were fish become fishers, to make the saved ones means to the Savior, to make the convert into a converter, to make the receiver of the gospel into an imparter of that gospel to other people.

I think I may say to every person whom I am addressing: if you are saved, the work is only half done until you are employed to bring others to Christ. You are but half-formed in the image of your Lord. You have not attained the full development of Christ's life in you unless you have begun in some feeble way to tell others of the grace of God. I trust that you will find no rest for your feet until you have been the means of leading many to the blessed Savior who is your confidence and hope.

His word is, "Follow Me, not merely that you may be saved, or even that you may be sanctified, but ' *follow Me, and I will make you fishers of men.'*" Be following Christ with that intent and aim. Fear that you are not perfectly following Him unless in some degree He is making use of you to be fishers of men.

The fact is that every one of us must take to the business of man-catching. If Christ has caught us, we must catch others. If we have been apprehended by Him, we must be His policemen to apprehend rebels for Him. Let us ask Him to give us grace to go fishing, and to cast our nets so that we may take a great multitude of fish. Oh, that the Holy Spirit may raise up from among us some master fishermen, who will sail their boats in many a sea and surround great schools of fish!

My teaching at this time will be very simple, but I hope it will be eminently practical. My longing is that not one of you who love the Lord may be reserved in His service. What does the Song of Solomon say concerning certain sheep that come up from the washing? It says, *"Every one beareth twins, and there is not one barren among them"* (verse 6:6). May that be so with all the members of my church, and all the Christian people who read this!

The fact is that the day is very dark. The heavens are lowering with heavy thunder clouds. Men little dream of what tempests may soon shake the city and the whole social fabric of this land, even to a general breaking up of society. So dark may the night become that the stars may seem to fall like blighted fruit from the tree. The times are evil. Now, as never before, every glowworm must show its spark. You with the tiniest candle must take it from underneath the bushel and set it on a candlestick. (See Matthew 5:15.)

There is need of you all. Lot was a poor creature. He was a very, very wretched kind of believer. But still he might have been a great blessing to Sodom had he but pleaded for it as he should have done. Poor, poor Christians, as I fear many are, one begins to value very truly every converted soul in these evil days and to pray that each one may glorify the Lord. I pray that every righteous person, distressed as he is with the conversation of the wicked, may be more resolute in prayer than ever before and return to God to receive more spiritual life, so that he may bless the perishing people around him.

Therefore, I address you first of all on this thought. Oh, that the Spirit of God may make each one of you feel his personal responsibility! Here is something for believers in Christ to do, according to their usefulness: *"Follow me."* Second, here is something to be done by the great Lord and Master: *"I will make you."* You will not, of yourselves, grow into fishers, but that is what Jesus will do for you if you will but follow Him. Last, here is a good illustration, *"fishers of men,"* used according to our great Master's custom, for scarcely without a parable did He speak to the people. He presents us with an illustration of what Christians should be— *"fishers of men."* We may get some useful hints out of this illustration, and I pray the Holy Spirit will bless them to us.

First, then, I will take it for granted that every believer here wants to be useful. If he does not, I take leave to question whether he can be a true believer in Christ. Well, then, if you want to be really useful, here is something for you to do to that end: *"Follow me, and I will make you fishers of men."* What is the way to become an efficient preacher? "Young man," says one, "go to college." "Young man," says Christ, "follow Me, and I will make you a fisher of men." How is a person to be useful? "Attend a training class," says one. Quite right. But there is a surer answer than that: follow Jesus, and He will make you fishers of men. The great training school for Christian workers has Christ at its head; He is at its head, not only as a Tutor, but as a Leader.

We are not only to learn of Him in study, but also to follow Him in action. *"Follow me, and I will make you fishers of men."* The direction is very distinct and plain. I believe that it is exclusive, so that no one can become a fisherman by any other process. This process may appear to be very simple, but assuredly it is most efficient. The Lord Jesus Christ, who knew all about fishing for men, was Himself the Ordainer of the rule, "Follow Me, if you want to be fishers of men. If you want to be useful, keep in My tracks."

I understand this command in this sense: be separate unto Christ. These men were to leave their pursuits. They were to leave their companions. They were, in fact, to quit the world, so that their one business might be, in their Master's name, to be fishers of men. We are not called to leave our daily business or to quit our families. That might be rather running away from the fishery than working at it in God's name. However, we are called most distinctly to come out from among the ungodly, to be separate, and not to touch the unclean thing. (See 2 Corinthians 6:17.)

We cannot be fishers of men if we remain among men in the same element with them. Fish will not be fishers. The sinner will not convert the sinner. The ungodly man will not convert the ungodly man. What is more to the point, the worldly Christian will not convert the world. If you are of the world, no doubt the world will love its own, but you cannot save the world. If you are dark and belong to the kingdom of darkness, you cannot remove the darkness. If you march with the armies of the wicked one, you cannot defeat them.

I believe that one reason why the church of God at this present moment has so little influence over the world is because the world has so much influence over the church. Nowadays, we hear nonconformists pleading that they may do this and do that—things that their Puritan forefathers would rather have died at the stake than have tolerated. They plead that they may live like worldlings. My sad answer to them, when they crave this liberty, is, "Do it if you dare. It may not do you much harm, for you are so bad already. Your cravings show how rotten your hearts are. If you have a hungering after such dog's meat, go, dogs, and eat the garbage!"

Worldly amusements are fit food for mere pretenders and hypocrites. If you were God's children, you would loathe the very thought of the world's evil joys. Your question would not be, "How far may we be like the world?" but your one cry would be, "How far can we get away from the world? How much can we come out from it?" Your temptation would be rather to become sternly severe, and ultra-Puritanical in your separation from sin in such a time as this, than to ask, "How can I make myself like other men and act as they do?"

Friends, the church's use in the world is to be like salt in the midst of putrefaction. But if the salt has lost its savor, what is the good of it? If it were possible for salt itself to spoil, it could but make an increased heightening of the general decay. The worst day the world ever saw was when the sons of God were joined with the daughters of men. (See Genesis 6:1–7.) Then came the Flood. The only barrier against a flood of vengeance on this world is the separation of the saint from the sinner.

Your duty as a Christian is to stand fast in your own place and to stand out for God, *"hating even the garment spotted by the flesh"* (Jude 23). You need to resolve, like one of old, that, no matter what others may do, as for you and your house, you will serve the Lord. Come, children of God, you must stand with your Lord outside the camp. (See Hebrews 13:11–13). Jesus says to you today, *"Follow me."*

Was Jesus found at the theater? Did He frequent the race course? Do you think that Jesus was seen in any of the amusements of the Herodian court? Not He. He was *"holy, harmless, undefiled, [and] separate from sinners"* (Hebrews 7:26). In one sense, no one mixed with sinners as completely as He did when, like a physician, He went among them healing His patients. But, in another sense, there was a gulf fixed between the men of the world and the Savior, which He never attempted to cross, and which they could not cross to defile Him.

The first lesson that the church has to learn is this: follow Jesus into the separated state, and He will make you *"fishers of men."* Unless you take up your cross against an ungodly world, you cannot hope that the holy Lord will make you *"fishers of men."*

A second meaning of our text is very obviously this: abide with Christ, and then you will be made *"fishers of men."* These disciples whom Christ called were to come and live with Him. Every day, they were to be associated with Him. They were to hear Him teach publicly the everlasting gospel. In addition, they were to receive in private choice explanations of the Word that He had spoken. They were to be His body servants and His close friends. They were to see His miracles and hear His prayers. Better still, they were to be with Him and become one with Him in His holy labor. They were given to sit at the table with Him and even to have their feet washed by Him. Many of them fulfilled the word, *"Where thou lodgest, I will lodge"* (Ruth 1:16). They were with Him in His afflictions and persecutions. They witnessed His secret agonies, saw His many tears, and observed the passion and the compassion of His soul. Thus, they caught His spirit, and so they learned to be *"fishers of men."* At Jesus' feet, we must learn the art and mystery of soulwinning; to live with Christ is the best education for usefulness.

It is a great blessing to anyone to be associated with a Christian minister whose heart is on fire. The best training for a young man is that which the Vaudois pastors were desirous to give: each older man had a young man with him who walked with him whenever he went up the mountainside to preach, lived in the house with him, observed his prayers, and saw his daily piety. This was a fine course of instruction, but it will not compare with that of the apostles who lived with Jesus Himself and were His daily companions. Matchless was the training of the Twelve. No wonder they became what they were, with such a heavenly Tutor to saturate them with His own spirit.

His bodily presence is not among us now, but His spiritual power is perhaps more fully known to us than it was to the apostles in those three years of the Lord's physical presence. He is intimately near to some of us. We know more about Him than we do about our dearest earthly friends. We have never quite been able to read our friends' hearts in all their windings, but we know the heart of the Beloved. We have leaned our head upon His chest and enjoyed fellowship with Him such as we could not have with any of our own families. This is the surest method of learning how to do good. Live with Jesus, follow Him, and He will make you *"fishers of men."* See how He does the work, and so learn how to do it yourselves.

A Christian should be a bound apprentice to Jesus to learn the trade of a Savior. We can never save men by offering redemption, for we have none to present. But we can learn how to save men by warning them to *"flee from the wrath to come"* (Matthew 3:7) and by offering them the one great effectual remedy. See how Jesus saves, and you will learn how it is done; there is no learning it any other way. Live in fellowship with Christ, and about you will be an air and a manner as of one who has been made ready to teach and wise to win souls.

A third meaning, however, must be given to this *"Follow me,"* which is: obey Christ, and then you will know what to do to save men. We must not talk about our fellowship with Christ or our being separated from the world unto Him, unless we make Him our Lord and Master in everything. Some teachers are not true to their convictions on all points, so how can they look for a blessing? A Christian who is eager to be useful should be particular about every point of obedience to his Master.

I have no doubt whatever that God blesses our churches even when they are very faulty, for His mercy endures forever. When there is a measure of error in the teaching and a measure of mistake in the practice, He may still choose to use the ministry, for He is very gracious. But a large measure of blessing must necessarily be withheld from all teaching that is knowingly or glaringly faulty. God can set His seal upon the truth that is in it, but He cannot set His seal upon the error that is in it. Out of mistakes about Christian ordinances and other things, especially errors in heart and spirit, there may come evils that we never expected. Such evils may even now be having an effect on the present age and may work worse harm on future generations.

If we desire, as *"fishers of men,"* to be used by God, we must copy Jesus in everything and obey Him in every point. Failure in obedience may lead to failure in labor. Each of us, if he wishes to see his child saved, his Sunday school class blessed, or his congregation converted, must take care that he himself is clean as he bears the vessels of the Lord.

Anything we do that grieves the Spirit of God must take away from us some part of our power for good. The Lord is very gracious and merciful, but yet He is a jealous God. He is sternly jealous toward His people who are living in neglect of known duty or in associations that are not clean in His sight. He will wither their work, weaken their strength, and humble them until, at last, each one says, "My Lord, I will take Your way after all. I will do what You command me to do, or else

You will not accept me." The Lord said to His disciples, "*Go ye into all the world, and preach the gospel to every creature. He that believeth and is baptized shall be saved*" (Mark 16:15–16). He promised them that signs would follow (vv. 17–18); so they did, and so they will.

But we must get back to apostolic practice and to apostolic teaching. We must lay aside the commandments of men and the whimsies of our own minds, and we must do what Christ tells us, as Christ tells us, and because Christ tells us. Definitely and distinctly, we must take the place of servants. If we will not do that, we cannot expect our Lord to work with and by us.

Let us be determined that, as true as the needle is to the pole, so true will we be, as far as our light extends, to the command of our Lord and Master. Jesus says, "*Follow me, and I will make you fishers of men.*" By this teaching, He seems to say, "Go beyond Me or fall back away from Me, and you may cast the net, but it will be night with you, and that night you will take nothing. When you do as I command, you will cast your net on the right side of the ship, and you will find."

Again, I think that there is a great lesson in my text to those who preach their own thoughts instead of preaching the thoughts of Christ. These disciples were to follow Christ so that they might listen to Him, hear what He had to say, drink in His teaching, and then go and teach what He had taught them. Their Lord said, "*What I tell you in darkness, that speak ye in light: and what ye hear in the ear, that preach ye upon the housetops*" (Matthew 10:27). If any are faithful reporters of Christ's message, He will make them "*fishers of men.*"

However, you know that the boastful method nowadays is this: "I am not going to preach this old gospel, this musty Puritan doctrine. I will sit down in my study, burn the midnight oil, and invent a new theory. Then I will come out with my brand new thought and blaze away with it." Many are not following Christ, but following themselves, and of them the Lord may well say, "You will see whose Word will stand, Mine or theirs."

Others are wickedly prudent. They judge that certain truths that are clearly God's Word had better be kept back. You must not be rough, but must prophesy smooth things. To talk about the punishment of sin, to speak of eternal punishment—why, these are unfashionable doctrines. It may be that they are taught in the Word of God, but they do not suit the intelligence of the age and must be pared down! Brothers in Christ, I will have no share in this. Will you?

Certain things not taught in the Bible our enlightened age has discovered. Evolution may be completely contrary to the teaching of Genesis, but that does not matter. We are not going to be believers of Scripture, but original thinkers, is the smug attitude of the period.

Note that, as modern theology is preached, the vice of this generation increases in proportion. To a great degree, I attribute the looseness of the age to the laxity of the doctrine preached by its teachers. From the pulpit, they have taught the people that sin is inconsequential. From the pulpit, these traitors to God and to Christ have taught the people that there is no hell to be feared. There may be a little, tiny hell, perhaps; but nothing is made of just punishment for sin. The precious atoning sacrifice of Christ has been derided and misrepresented by those who were pledged to preach it. They have given the people the name of the gospel, but the gospel itself has evaporated in their hands. From hundreds of pulpits, the gospel is as extinct as the dodo from its old haunts.

Still the preachers take the position and name of Christ's ministers. Well, what comes of it? Why, their congregations grow thinner and thinner, and so it must be. Jesus says, *"Follow me, and I will make you fishers of men."* But if you go in your own way, with your own net, you will make nothing of it, and the Lord promises you no help in it. The Lord's directions make Himself our Leader and Example. It is "Follow Me; follow Me. Preach My gospel. Preach what I preached. Teach what I taught, and keep to that." With the blessed servility that becomes one whose ambition it is to be a copyist and never to be an original, copy Christ even in jots and tittles. Do this, and He will make you *"fishers of men."* But if you do not do this, you will fish in vain.

I close this part of my message by saying that we cannot be *"fishers of men"* unless we follow Christ in one more respect: by striving in everything to imitate His holiness. Holiness is the most real power that can be possessed by men or women. We may preach orthodoxy, but we must also live orthodoxy. God forbid that we should preach anything else. However, it will be all in vain unless there is a life behind the testimony. An unholy preacher may render even truth contemptible.

As any of us draw back from a living and zealous sanctification, we will draw back from the place of power in proportion. Our power lies in this word, *"Follow me."* Be Jesus-like. In all things, endeavor to think, speak, and act as Jesus did, and He will make you *"fishers of men."* This will require self-denial. We must daily take up the cross. This may require willingness to give up our reputations: a readiness to be thought fools, idiots, and the like, as men are apt to call those who are keeping close to their Master. There must be the cheerful resigning of everything that looks like honor and personal glory, in order that we may be wholly Christ's and glorify His name. We must live His life and be ready to die His death, if need be. Brothers and sisters, if we do this and follow Jesus, putting our feet into the footprints of His pierced feet, He will make us *"fishers of men"*!

In some way or other, the Lord will make a holy life to be an influential life. If it pleases Him that we will die without having gathered many souls to the cross, we will speak from our graves. It is not possible that a life characterized as following Christ could be an unsuccessful one in the sight of the Most High. *"Follow me,"* is answered with an *"I will"* such as God can never draw back from: *"Follow me, and I will make you fishers of men."*

Second, and briefly, there is something for the Lord to do. When His dear servants are following Him, He says, *"I will make you fishers of men."* Never let it be forgotten that it is He who makes us follow Him. The following of Him is the step to being made a fisher of men, yet this, too, He gives us. It is all of His Spirit. I have talked about catching His Spirit, abiding in Him, obeying Him, listening to Him, and copying Him; but none of these things are we capable of apart from His working them all in us. *"From me is thy fruit found"* (Hosea 14:8) is a text that we must not forget for a moment. So, if we do follow Him, it is He who makes us follow Him. Thus, He makes us *"fishers of men."*

Further, if we follow Christ, He will make us *"fishers of men"* by all our experience. I am sure that the person who is really consecrated to bless others will be helped in this by all that he feels, especially by his afflictions. I feel very grateful to God that I have undergone terrible depression of spirit. I know the edges of despair and the horrible brink of the gulf of darkness into which my feet have almost gone. But hundreds of times I have been able to give a helpful hand to others who have come into that same condition. I could never have given that grip if I had not known their deep despondency. I believe that the darkest, most dreadful experience of a child of God will help him to be a fisher of men if he follows Christ.

Keep close to your Lord, and He will make every step a blessing to you. If God in providence makes you rich, He will equip you to speak to those ignorant and wicked rich, who so much abound in the city and so often are the cause of its worst sin. If the Lord is pleased to let you be poor, you can go talk to the wicked and ignorant poor people, who so often cause sin in the city and so greatly need the gospel.

The winds of providence will waft you where you can fish for men. The wheels of providence are full of eyes, and all those eyes will help us to be winners of souls. You will often be surprised to find how God has been in a house that you visit. Before you arrive there, His hand is at work in its rooms. When you wish to speak to some particular individual, God's providence has been dealing with that individual to make him ready for just the word that you could say, and which nobody else but you could say. Oh, just follow Christ, and you will find that He will, by every experience you are undergoing, make you *"fishers of men"*!

Further, if you will follow Him, He will make you *"fishers of men"* by distinct admonitions in your heart. There are many warnings from God's Spirit that are not noticed by Christians when they are in a callous condition. But when the heart is right with God and living in communion with God, we feel a sacred sensitivity, so that we do not need the Lord to shout, but His faintest whisper is heard. No, He need not even whisper. He will guide us with His eye. How many mulish Christians there are, who must be bridled and receive a cut of the whip every now and then!

The Christian who follows his Lord will be tenderly guided. I do not say that the Spirit of God will say to you, *"Go near, and join thyself to this chariot"* (Acts 8:29), or that you will hear a word in your ear. Yet in your soul, as distinctly as the Spirit said to Philip, *"Go near, and join thyself to this chariot,"* you will hear the Lord's word. As soon as you see an individual, the thought will cross your mind, "Go and speak to that person." Every opportunity of usefulness will be a call to you. If you are ready, the door will open before you, and you will hear a voice behind you saying, *"This is the way, walk ye in it"* (Isaiah 30:21). If you have the grace to run in the right way, you will never be long without an intimation as to what the right way is. That right way will lead you to river or sea, where you can cast your net and be a fisher of men.

Then, too, I believe that the Lord meant by this illustration that He would give His followers the Holy Spirit. They were to follow Him. Then, when they had seen Him ascend into the holy place of the Most High, they were to tarry at Jerusalem for a little while, until the Spirit would come upon them and clothe them with a mysterious power. This word was spoken to Peter and Andrew. You know how it was fulfilled to Peter. What a host of fish he brought to land the first time he cast the net in the power of the Holy Spirit! *"Follow me, and I will make you fishers of men."*

Friends, we have no conception of what God could do by this company of believers gathered here. If we were now to be filled with the Holy Spirit, there are enough of us to evangelize London. There are enough here to be the means of the salvation of the world. God saves not by many nor by few. Let us seek to be made a benediction to our fellow creatures. And if we seek it, let us hear this directing voice, *"Follow me, and I will make you fishers of men."*

You men and women who sit before me, you are by the shore of a great sea of human life swarming with the souls of men. You live in the midst of millions. But if you will follow Jesus, being faithful and true to Him, doing what He commands you, He will make you *"fishers of men."* Do not ask, "Who will save this city?" The weakest will be strong enough. Gideon's barley cake will strike the tent and make it lie along the ground. (See Judges 7:12–15.) Samson, with the jawbone, taken up from the earth where it was bleaching in the sun, will smite the Philistines. (See Judges 15:14–16.) *"Fear not, neither be dismayed"* (Deuteronomy 31:8). Let your responsibilities drive you closer to your Master. Let horror of prevailing sin make you look into His dear face who long ago wept over Jerusalem and now weeps over London. Clasp Him, and never let go of your hold.

By the strong and mighty impulses of the divine life within you, quickened and brought to maturity by the Spirit of God, learn this lesson from your Lord's own mouth: *"Follow me, and I will make you fishers of men."* You are not fit for it, but He will make you fit. You cannot do it of yourselves, but He will make you do it. You do not know how to spread nets and draw schools of fish to shore, but He will teach you. Only follow Him, and He will make you *"fishers of men."* I wish that I could somehow say this as with a voice of thunder, so that the whole church of God might hear it. I wish I could write in stars across the sky, "Jesus says, 'Follow me, and I will make you fishers of men.'" If you forget the precept, the promise will never be yours. If you follow some other track, or imitate some other leader, you will fish in vain. May God grant us to believe fully that Jesus can do great things in us, and then do great things by us for the good of our fellowmen!

The last point you might work out in full for yourselves in your private meditations with much profit. We have here an illustration full of instruction. I will give you just two or three thoughts that you can use. *"I will make you fishers of* men." Jesus says to all of us, "You have been fishers of fish; but if you follow Me, I will make you fishers of men."

A fisherman is very dependent and needs to be trusting. He cannot see the fish. One who goes deep-sea fishing must cast in the net at only a possibility. Fishing is an act of faith. In the Mediterranean, I have seen men go in boats and enclose acres of sea with vast nets. When they have drawn the net to shore, they have not had as much result as I could put in my hand. A few silvery nothings have made up the whole take. Yet they have gone again and cast their nets several times a day, expecting something to come of it.

Nobody is as dependent upon God as the minister of God. Oh, this fishing from the Tabernacle pulpit! What a work of faith! I cannot tell that a soul will be brought to God by it. I cannot judge whether my sermon will be suitable to the people who are here, except that I do believe that God will guide me in the casting of the net. I expect Him to work salvation, and I depend upon Him for it.

I love this complete dependence. If I could be offered a certain amount of preaching power that would be entirely at my own disposal, and by which I could save sinners, I would beg the Lord not to let me have it, for it is far more delightful to be entirely dependent upon Him at all times. It is good to be a fool when Christ is made wisdom unto you. It is a blessed thing to be weak if Christ becomes your strength. Go to work, you who would be *fishers of men,* and yet feel your insufficiency. You who have no strength, attempt this divine work. Your Master's strength will be seen when your own has all gone. A fisherman is a dependent person; he must look up for success every time he puts the net down. But still he is a trustful person; therefore he casts in the net joyfully.

A fisherman who earns his living by fishing is a diligent and persevering man. The fishers are up at dawn. At daybreak our fishermen off the Doggerbank are fishing, and they continue fishing until late in the afternoon. As long as hands can work, men will fish. May the Lord Jesus make us hardworking, persevering, unwearied *"fishers of men"*! *"In the morning sow thy seed, and in the evening withhold not thine hand: for thou knowest not whether shall prosper, either this or that"* (Ecclesiastes 11:6).

The fisherman is intelligent and watchful in his own craft. It looks very easy to be a fisherman, but you would find that it was no child's play if you were to take a real part in it. There is an art in it, from mending the net right on to pulling it to shore. How diligent the fisherman is to prevent the fish from leaping out of the net! I heard a great noise one night in the sea, as if some huge drum were being beaten by a giant. I looked out and saw that the fishermen of Mentone were beating the water to drive the fish into the net, or to keep them from leaping out once they had surrounded them with it.

You and I will often have to be watching the corners of the gospel net lest sinners who are almost caught would make their escape. They are very crafty, these fish; they use this craftiness in trying to avoid salvation. We need to be always at our business, and to exercise all our wits—even more than our own wits—if we are to be successful *"fishers of men."*

The fisherman is a very hardworking person. It is not at all an easy calling. He does not sit in an armchair and catch fish. He has to go out in rough weathers. If he who looks at the clouds will not sow (see Ecclesiastes 11:4), I am sure that he who looks at the clouds will never fish. If we never do any work for Christ except when we feel up to the mark, we will not do much. If we feel that we will not pray because we cannot pray, we will never pray. If we say, "I will not preach today because I do not feel that I could preach," we will never preach any preaching that is worthwhile. We must be always at it until we wear ourselves out, throwing our whole souls into the work, for Christ's sake.

The fisherman is a daring man. He tempts the boisterous sea. A little brine in his face does not hurt him. He has been wet through a thousand times; it is nothing to him. He never expected to sleep in the lap of ease when he became a deep-sea fisherman.

In the same way, the true minister of Christ, who fishes for souls, will never mind a little risk. He will be bound to do or say many things that are very unpopular. Some Christians may even judge his words to be too severe. He must do and say that which is for the good of souls. It is not his to entertain a question as to what others will think of his doctrine or him. In the name of Almighty God, he must feel, "If the sea roars with all its fullness, still at my Master's command I will let down the net."

Now, in the last place, the one whom Christ makes a fisher of men is successful. "But," says one, "I have always heard that Christ's ministers are to be faithful, but that they cannot be sure of being successful." Yes, I have heard that saying, too. In one way I know it is true, but in another way, I have my doubts about it. He who is faithful is, in God's way and in God's judgment, successful.

For instance, suppose a brother says that he is faithful. I must believe him, yet I never heard of a sinner being saved under him. Indeed, I would think that the safest place for a person to be in if he did not want to be saved would be under this gentleman's ministry, because he does not preach anything that is likely to rouse, impress, or convince anybody.

This brother is faithful, or so he says. Well, if any person in the world said to you, "I am a fisherman, but I have never caught anything," you would wonder how he could be called a fisherman. A farmer who never grew any wheat or any other crop—is he a farmer?

When Jesus Christ says, *"Follow me, and I will make you fishers of men,"* He means that you will really catch men, that you will really save some, for he who never caught a fish is not a fisherman. He who never saved a sinner after years of work is not a minister of Christ. If the result of his lifework is nothing, he made a mistake when he undertook it. Go with the fire of God in your hand and fling it among the stubble, and the stubble will burn. Be sure of that. Go and scatter the good seed. It may not all fall in fruitful places, but some of it will. Be sure of that. Only shine, and some eye or other will be lightened thereby. You must, and you will, succeed. But remember, this is the Lord's word: *"Follow me, and I will make you fishers of men."* Keep close to Jesus, do as He did, and He will make you *"fishers of men."*

Perhaps I speak to an attentive one who is not converted at all. Friend, I have the same thing to say to you. You also may follow Christ, and then He can use you, even you. I do not know but that He has brought you to this place so that you may be saved, and that, in later years, He may make you speak for His name and glory. Recall how He called Saul of Tarsus and made him the Apostle to the Gentiles. Reclaimed poachers make the best gamekeepers, and saved sinners make the ablest preachers. Oh, that you would run away from your old master tonight, without giving him a minute's notice. If you give him any notice, he will hold you. Run to Jesus, and say, "Here is a poor runaway slave! My Lord, I still wear the chains upon my wrists. Will You set me free, and make me Your own?"

Remember, it is written, *"Him that cometh to me I will in no wise cast out"* (John 6:37). Never did a runaway slave come to Christ without His taking him in! And Christ never gave a runaway up to his old master. If Jesus *"shall make you free, ye shall be free indeed"* (John 9:36). Flee to Jesus, then, now. May His good Spirit help you, and He will make you a winner of others, to His praise! God bless you! Amen.

15

ENCOURAGEMENT TO SOULWINNERS

Brethren, if any of you do err from the truth, and one convert him; Let him know, that he which converteth the sinner from the error of his way shall save a soul from death, and shall hide a multitude of sins.
—James 5:19–20

T he author of the book of James was primarily practical. If he was the James who was called "the Just," I can understand how he earned the title, for that distinguishing trait in his character shows itself in his epistle. If he were the Lord's brother, he did well to show so close a resemblance to his great Relative and Master, who commenced His ministry with the practical Sermon on the Mount.

We ought to be very grateful that, in the Holy Scriptures, we have food for all types of believers and employment for all the faculties of the saints. It is fitting that the contemplative person is furnished with abundant subjects for thought: Paul has supplied them. He gave us sound doctrine, arranged in the symmetry of exact order; he gave us deep thoughts and profound teachings; he opened up the *"deep things of God"* (1 Corinthians 2:10). No one who is inclined to reflection and thoughtfulness will be without food as long as the Pauline Epistles are available, for he feeds the soul with sacred manna.

For those whose predominating tendencies incline them to more mystic themes, John has written sentences aglow with devotion and blazing with love. We have his simple but sublime epistles, which, when glanced at, seem in their wording to be fit for children, but when examined, seem to be too sublime to be fully grasped by the most advanced of men. You have from that same apostle the wondrous visions of Revelation, where awe, devotion, and imagination may enlarge their flight and find scope for the fullest exercise.

There will always be, however, some people who are more practical than contemplative, more active than imaginative. It was wise that there should be a James, whose main point is to stir up their pure minds by way of remembrance and help them to persevere in the practical graces of the Holy Spirit.

The text before me is perhaps the most practical part of the whole epistle. The whole letter burns, but this ascends in flames to heaven. It is the culmination as it is the conclusion of the letter. There is not a word to spare in it. It is like a naked sword, stripped of its jeweled scabbard and presented to us with nothing to note but its keen edge.

I wish I could preach in the manner of the text. If I cannot, I will at least pray that you may act in the manner of it. Total living for the Lord is sadly needed in many quarters. We have enough of Christian garnishing, but solid, everyday, actual work for God is what we need. If our lives, however unornamented they may be by leaves of literary or polite attainments, will nevertheless bring forth fruit for God in the form of souls converted by our efforts, it will be well. They will then stand forth before the Lord with the beauty of the olive tree, which consists in its fruitfulness.

I call your attention very earnestly to three matters. First, here is a special case dealt with: *"If any of you do err from the truth, and one convert him."* Then, the apostle declares a general fact: *"He which converteth the sinner from the error of his way shall save a soul from death, and shall hide a multitude of sins."* After I have considered these two points, I then intend to make a particular application of the text—not at all intended by the apostle, but I believe abundantly justified—an application of the text to increased effort for the conversion of children.

First, here is a special case dealt with. Read the verse, and you will see that it must relate to a backslider from the visible church of God. The words, *"If any of you,"* must refer to a professed Christian. The erring one had been named by the name of Jesus, and for a while had followed the truth. But in an evil hour, he had been betrayed into doctrinal error and had lapsed from truth. It was not merely that he was mistaken on some lesser matter, which might be compared to the fringe of the gospel, but he erred in some vital doctrine. He departed from the faith in its fundamentals.

There are some truths that must be believed; they are essential to salvation. If these truths are not heartily accepted, the soul will be ruined. This man had been professedly orthodox, but he turned aside from the truth on an essential point. Now, in those days, the saints did not say, as the sham saints do now, "We must be largely charitable and leave this brother to his own opinion. He sees truth from a different standpoint and has a rather different way of putting it, but his opinions are as good as our own, and we must not say that he is in error." That is at present the fashionable way of trifling with divine truth and making things pleasant all around. Thus the gospel is debased, and *"another gospel"* (2 Corinthians 11:4) is propagated.

I would like to ask Modernistic churchmen whether there is any doctrine of any sort for which it would be worthwhile for a person to burn at the stake or to lie in prison. I do not believe they could give me an answer, for if their general tolerance of divergent viewpoints is correct, the martyrs were fools of the first magnitude.

From what I see of their writings and their teachings, it appears to me that the modern thinkers treat the whole body of revealed truth with entire indifference. Though perhaps they may feel sorry that wilder spirits go too far in freethinking, and though they would rather that such men would be more moderate, yet so large is their liberality that they are not sure enough of anything to be able to condemn the reverse of it as a deadly error. To them black and white are terms that may be applied to the same color when it is viewed from different standpoints. In their estimation, "yea" and "nay" are equally true. Their theology shifts like the Goodwin Sands, and they regard all firmness as so much bigotry. Errors and truths are equally included within the circle of their charity.

It was not in this way that the apostles regarded error. They did not prescribe largehearted charity toward falsehood or hold up the errorist as a person of deep thought, whose views were "refreshingly original." Far less did they utter some wicked nonsense about the probability of there being more faith in honest doubt than in half the creeds. They did not believe in justification by doubting, as our theologians do. They set about the conversion of the erring brother. They treated him as a person who needed conversion, and viewed him as a man who, if he were not converted, would suffer the death of his soul and be covered with a multitude of sins.

The apostles were not such easygoing people as our cultured friends of the school of modern thought, who have come to the conclusion that the deity of Christ may be denied, the world of the Holy Spirit ignored, the inspiration of Scripture rejected, the Atonement disbelieved, and regeneration dispensed with. Yet they also conclude that a man who does all this may be as good a Christian as the most devout believer! O God, deliver us from this deceitful infidelity! While it does damage to the one who errs and often prevents his being reclaimed, it does even more harm to our own hearts by teaching us that truth is unimportant and falsehood is a trifle, and so destroys our allegiance to the God of truth and makes us traitors instead of loyal subjects to the King of Kings!

It appears from our text that this man, having erred from the truth, followed the natural, logical consequence of doctrinal error. He has erred in his life as well, for the twentieth verse, which must of course be read in connection with the nineteenth, speaks of him as a sinner converted *"from the error of his way."* His way went wrong after his thought had gone wrong. You cannot deviate from truth without, before long, in some measure, deviating from practical righteousness. This man had erred from right acting because he had erred from right believing.

Suppose a man embraces a doctrine that leads him to think little of Christ. He will soon have little faith in Him and become little obedient to Him. So he will wander into self-righteousness or licentiousness. If he thinks lightly of the punishment of sin, it is natural that he will commit sin with less compunction and burst through all restraints. If he denies the need of the Atonement, the same result will follow, if he acts out his belief.

Every error has its own outgrowth, as all decay has its associated fungus. It is in vain for us to imagine that holiness will be as readily produced from erroneous as from truthful doctrine. *"Do men gather grapes [from] thorns or figs [from] thistles?"* (Matthew 7:16). The facts of history prove the contrary. When truth is dominant, morality and holiness are abundant; but when error is in the front, godly living retreats in shame.

The point aimed at with regard to this sinner was his conversion in thought and deed—turning him around, bringing him to right thinking and to right acting. Alas! I fear many professed Christians do not look upon backsliders in this light; neither do they regard them as hopeful subjects for conversion. I have known a person who erred to be hunted down like a wolf. He was wrong to some degree, but that wrong was aggravated and dwelt upon until the man was harassed into defiance. The fault was exaggerated into a double wrong by ferocious attacks upon it. The manhood of the man took sides with his error because he had been so severely handled. The man was compelled, sinfully, I admit, to take up an extreme position and to go further into mischief, because he could not brook being denounced instead of being reasoned with.

When a man has been blameworthy in his life, it will often happen that his fault is broadcast, retold from mouth to mouth, and magnified, until the poor erring one has felt degraded. Having lost all self-respect, he gives way to far more dreadful sins. The object of some believers seems to be to amputate the limb rather than to heal it. Justice has reigned instead of mercy. Away with him! He is too foul to be washed, too diseased to be restored. This is not according to the mind of Christ, nor after the model of apostolic churches.

In the days of James, if any one erred from the truth and holiness, there were friends found who sought their recovery, whose joy it was thus to *"save a soul from death; and hide a multitude of sins."* Something is very significant in the phrase, *"Brethren, if **any of you** do err from the truth."* It is similar to the warning, *"Considering thyself, lest thou also be tempted"* (Galatians 6:1), and the exhortation, *"Let him that thinketh he standeth take heed lest he fall"* (1 Corinthians 10:12).

He who has erred was one of yourselves, one who sat with you at the communion table, one with whom you took sweet counsel. He has been deceived, and by the subtlety of Satan, he has been decoyed. But do not judge him harshly. Above all, do not leave him to perish unpitied. If he ever was a saved man, he is still your brother. It should be your business to bring back the prodigal and so make glad your Father's heart. For all his errors, he is still one of God's children. Follow up with him and do not rest until you lead him home again.

If he is not a child of God, if his professed conversion was a mistake or a pretense, if he only made a profession but did not have the possession of vital godliness, still pursue him with sacred insistence of love, remembering how terrible his doom will be for daring to play the hypocrite and to profane holy things with his unhallowed hands. Weep over him all the more if you feel compelled to suspect that he has been a willful deceiver, for there is sevenfold cause for weeping. If you cannot resist the feeling that he never was sincere, but crept into the church under cover of a false profession, sorrow over him, for his doom will be even more terrible. Therefore, greater should be your compassion for him. Seek his conversion still.

The text gives us clear indications as to those who are to aim at the conversion of erring friends. It says, *"If any of you do err from the truth, and one convert him."* *"One"* what? One minister? No, any one among the friends. If the minister is the means of the restoration of a backslider, he is a happy man, and a good deed has been done. But nothing is said here concerning preachers or pastors; not even a hint is given. It is left open to any member of the church. The plain inference, I think, is this: every church member, seeing his brother err from the truth or err in practice, should set himself, in the power of the Holy Spirit, to this business of converting this special sinner from the error of his way.

Look after strangers, by all means, but do not neglect your friends. It is the business, not of certain officers appointed by the vote of the church, but of every member of the body of Jesus Christ to seek the good of all the other members. Still, there are certain members upon whom this may be more imperative in individual cases. For instance, consider the case of a young believer. His father and his mother, if they are believers, are called upon by a sevenfold obligation to seek the conversion of their backsliding child. In the case of a husband, no one should be as earnest for his restoration as his wife. The same rule holds true with regard to the wife. If the connection is that of friendship, he with whom you have had the most acquaintance should lie nearest to your heart. When you perceive that he has gone astray, you, above all others, should act the shepherd toward him with kindly zeal.

You are bound to do this to all your fellow Christians, but doubly bound to do it to those over whom you possess influence that has been gained by prior intimacy, lay relationship, or by any other means. I beseech you, therefore, watch over one another in the Lord. When you see a brother *"overtaken in a fault, ye which are spiritual, restore such an one in the spirit of meekness"* (Galatians 6:1). You see your duty; do not neglect it.

Friends, it ought to cheer us to know that the attempt to convert a man who has erred from the truth is a hopeful one. It is one in which success may be looked for. When the success comes, it will be of the most joyful character. Truly, it is a great joy to capture the wild, wandering sinner. But the joy of joys is to find the lost sheep that was once really in the fold and has sadly gone astray. It is a great thing to transform a piece of brass into silver. However, to the poor woman, it was joy enough to find the piece of silver that was silver already and had the king's stamp on it, even though for a while it was lost. To bring in a stranger and an alien and to adopt him as a son suggests a festival. But the most joyous feasting and the loudest music are for the son who was always a son but had played the prodigal. After being lost, he was found, and after being dead, he was made alive again.

I say, ring the bells twice for the reclaimed backslider. Ring them until the steeple rocks and reels. Rejoice doubly over that which had gone astray and was ready to perish, but has now been restored. John was glad when he found poor, backsliding Peter, who had denied his Master. He cheered, comforted, and consoled him, until the Lord Himself had said, "*Simon, son of Jonas, lovest thou me?*" (John 21:16).

It may not appear so brilliant a thing to bring back a backslider as to reclaim a prostitute or a drunkard, but in the sight of God it is no small miracle of grace. To the instrument who has performed it, it will yield no small comfort. Seek, then, my friends, those who were of us, but have gone from us. Seek those who linger in the congregation, but have disgraced the church and are put away from us (and rightly so, because we cannot sanction their uncleanness). Seek them with prayers, tears, and entreaties, if perhaps God may grant them repentance that they may be saved.

Here I would say to any who are backsliders, let this text cheer you if you have a desire to turn to God. Return, backsliding children, for the Lord has told His people to seek you. If He had not cared for you, He would not have spoken of our search for you. Having put it so and made it the duty of all His people to seek those who err from the faith, God has opened a door before you. There are hundreds who sit waiting like porters at the gate to welcome you. Come back to the God whom you have forsaken. If you never did know Him, this day may His Spirit break your hearts and lead you to true repentance, so that you may in real truth be saved! God bless you, poor backsliders! If He does not save you, a multitude of sins will be upon you, and you will die eternally. May God have mercy upon you, for Christ's sake.

We began with the special case, and we will now dwell upon a general fact. This general fact is important; we are bound to give it special attention, since it is prefaced with the words, *"Let him know."* If any one of you has been the means of bringing back a backslider, it is said, *"Let him know."* That is, let him think about it, be sure of it, be comforted by it, be inspired by it. *"Let him know"* it and never doubt it. Do not merely hear it, beloved fellow laborer, but let it sink deep into your heart. When an apostle, inspired of the Holy Spirit, says, *"Let him know,"* I urge you, do not let any laziness of spirit prevent your ascertaining the full weight of the truth.

What is it that you are to know? To know that *"he which converteth the sinner from the error of his way shall save a soul from death."* This is something worth knowing, is it not? To save a soul from death is no small matter. Why, we have men among us whom we honor every time we look at them, for they have saved many precious lives. They have manned the lifeboat or they have plunged into the river to rescue the drowning. They have been ready to risk their own lives amid burning timbers in order that they might snatch the perishing from the devouring flames. These are true heroes, far worthier of renown than bloodstained men of war. God bless the brave hearts! May England never lack a body of worthy men to make her shores illustrious for humanity!

When we see a fellow creature exposed to danger, our pulses beat quickly, and we are agitated with a desire to save him. Is it not so? But the saving of a soul from death is a far greater matter. Let us think about what that death is. It is not nonexistence. I do not know that I would lift a finger to save my fellow creature from mere nonexistence. I see no great harm in annihilation, certainly nothing that would alarm me as a punishment for sin. Just as I see no great joy in mere eternal existence, if that is all that is meant by eternal life, so I discern no terror in ceasing to be. I would as soon not be as be, as far as mere colorless being or not being is concerned.

However, in Scripture, "eternal life" means a very different thing from eternal existence. It means existing with all the faculties developed in fullness of joy, existing not as the dried herb in the hay, but as the flower in all its beauty. "To die," in Scripture, and indeed in common language, is not to cease to exist. The difference between "to die" and "to be annihilated" is very great. To die, in regard to the first death, is the separation of the body from the soul. It is the resolution of our nature into its component elements. To die the second death means the separation of the man—soul and body—from his God, who is the life and joy of our humanity. This is eternal destruction from the presence of the Lord and from the glory of His power. This is to have the palace of humanity destroyed and turned into a desolate ruin for the howling dragon of remorse and the hooting owl of despair to inherit forever.

The descriptions that Holy Scripture gives of the second death are terrible to the last degree. It speaks of a *"worm* [that] *dieth not, and the fire* [that] *is not quenched,"* of *"the terror of the Lord,"* of *"the smoke of their torment* [that] *ascendeth up for ever and ever,"* and of the *"bottomless pit"* (Mark 9:44; 2 Corinthians 5:11; Revelation 14:11; 9:1–2). I am not about to bring all these terrible things together, but there are words in Scripture that, if pondered, might make one's flesh crawl and one's hair to stand on end at the very thought of the judgment to come.

Our joy is that if any one of us are used in God's hands as the means of converting a man *"from the error of his way,"* we will have saved a soul from this eternal death. That dreadful hell the saved one will not know, that wrath he will not feel, that being banished from the presence of God will never happen to him. Is there not a joy worth worlds in all this?

Remember the addition to the picture. If you have saved a soul from death, you have introduced him into eternal life. By God's good grace, there will be another chorister among the white-robed host to sing Jehovah's praise, another pair of hands to eternally play the harp strings of adoring gratitude, another sinner saved to reward the Redeemer for His sufferings. Oh, the happiness of having saved a soul from death!

Further, it is added that, in such a case, you will have covered a *"multitude of sins."* We understand this to mean that the result of the conversion of any sinner will be the covering of all his sins by the atoning blood of Jesus. How many those sins are, in any case, none of us can tell. But if any man is converted from *"the error of his way,"* the whole mass of his sins will be drowned in the Red Sea of Jesus' blood and washed away forever.

Now, remember that your Savior came to this world with two objectives: He came to destroy death and to put away sin. If you convert a sinner from the *"error of his way,"* you are made like Him in both of these works. After your manner, in the power of the Spirit of God, you overcome death by snatching a soul from the second death, and you also put away sin from the sight of God by hiding *"a multitude of sins"* beneath the propitiation of Jesus Christ.

Do observe here that the apostle offers no other inducement to soulwinners. He does not say, "If you convert a sinner from the error of his way, you will have honor." True philanthropy scorns such a motive. He does not say, "If you convert a sinner from the error of his way, you will have the respect of the church and the love of the individual." Such will be the case, but we are moved by nobler motives.

The joy of doing good is found in the good itself. The reward of a deed of love is found in its own result. If we have saved a soul from death and hidden a multitude of sins, that is payment enough, even though no ear might ever hear of the deed and no pen ever record it. Let it be forgotten that we were the instruments if good is effected. It will give us joy even if we are not appreciated and are left in the shadow of forgetfulness. If others wear the honors of the deed that the Lord has accomplished by us, we will not murmur. It will be joy enough to know that a soul has been saved from death and a multitude of sins has been covered.

Dear friends, let us recollect that the saving of souls from death honors Jesus, for there is no saving souls except through His blood. As for you and for me, what can we do in saving a soul from death? Of ourselves nothing, any more than a pen that lies on a table could write *The Pilgrim's Progress*. Yet let a Bunyan grasp the pen, and the matchless work is written. So you and I can do nothing to convert souls until God's eternal Spirit takes us in hand. Then He can do wonders by us and bring Himself glory by us, while it will be joy enough for us to know that Jesus is honored and the Spirit magnified. Nobody talks of Homer's pen; no one has encased it in gold, or published its illustrious achievements. Neither do we wish for honor among men. It will be enough for us to have been the pen in the Savior's hand with which He has written the covenant of His grace upon the tablets of human hearts. This is golden wages for a man who really loves his Master: Jesus is glorified, and sinners are saved.

Now I want you to notice particularly that all that is said by the apostle in the text is about the conversion of one person. *"If any of you do err from the truth, and one convert him; let him know, that he which converteth the sinner from the error of his way shall save a soul from death."* Have you never wished you were a Whitefield? Have you never felt, in your inmost soul, great aspirations to be another McCheyne, Brainerd, or Moffat? Cultivate the aspiration, but at the same time be happy to bring one sinner to Christ. He who converts only one is instructed to know that no small thing has been done, for he has saved a soul from death and covered a multitude of sins.

It does not say anything about the person who is the means of this work. It is not said, "If a minister converts a man," or "if some noted eloquent clergyman has worked it." If this deed is performed by the humblest Christian in the church, if a little child tells the tale of Jesus to his father, if a servant drops a tract where one poor soul finds it and receives salvation, if the humblest preacher at the street corner speaks to the thief or a prostitute, and such shall be saved, let that witness know that he who turns any sinner from the error of his way, whoever he may be, has saved a soul from death and covered a multitude of sins.

Now, beloved, what comes out of this but these suggestions? Let us long to be used in the conversion of sinners. James does not speak concerning the Holy Spirit in this passage, nor of Jesus Christ, for he was writing to those who would not fail to remember the important truths that concern both the Spirit and the Son of God. Yet it may be appropriate here to remind you that we cannot do spiritual good to our fellow creatures apart from the Spirit of God, nor can we be a blessing to them if we do not preach to them *"Jesus Christ, and him crucified"* (1 Corinthians 2:2). God must use us; but let us long to be used, pray to be used, and yearn to be used!

Dear brothers and sisters, let us purge ourselves of everything that would prevent our being employed by the Lord. If there is anything we are doing or leaving undone, any evil we are harboring, or any grace we are neglecting, which may make us unfit to be used by God, let us ask the Lord to cleanse, mend, and scour us until we are vessels fit for the Master's use. Then let us be on the watch for opportunities of usefulness. Let us go about the world with our ears and our eyes open, ready to avail ourselves of every occasion for doing good. Let us not be content until we are useful, but make this the main desire and ambition of our lives.

Somehow or other, we must and will bring souls to Jesus Christ. As Rachel cried, *"Give me children, or else I die"* (Genesis 30:1), so may none of you be content to be barren in the household of God. Cry and sigh until you have snatched some brand from the burning and have brought at least one sinner to Jesus Christ, so that you also may have saved a soul from death and covered a multitude of sins.

Now, let us turn briefly to the point that is not in the text. I want to make a particular application of this whole subject to the conversion of children. Beloved friends, I hope you do not altogether forget the Sunday school, and yet I am afraid a great many Christians are scarcely aware that there are such things as Sunday schools at all. They know it by hearsay, but not by observation. Probably, in the course of twenty years, they have never visited the school or concerned themselves about it. They would be gratified to hear of any success accomplished, but though they may not have heard anything about the matter one way or the other, they are well content.

In most churches, you will find a group of young and ardent spirits giving themselves to Sunday school work. But there are numbers of others who might greatly strengthen the school who never attempt anything of the sort. In this they might be excused if they had other work to do. Unfortunately, however, they have no godly occupation, but are mere killers of time. Meanwhile, this work is entirely neglected even though it lies ready at hand, is accessible, and demands their assistance. I will not say there are any such sluggards here, but I am not able to believe that we are quite free from them. Therefore, I will ask conscience to do its work with the guilty parties.

Children need to be saved. Children may be saved. Children are to be saved by instrumentality. Children may be saved while they are children. He who said, "*Suffer the little children to come unto me, and forbid them not: for of such is the kingdom of God*" (Mark 10:14), never intended that His church would say, "We will look after the children later when they have grown up to be young men and women." He intended that it should be a subject of prayer and earnest endeavor that children should be converted to God as children.

The conversion of a child involves the same work of divine grace and results in the same blessed consequences as the conversion of the adult. There is the saving of the soul from death in the child's case and the hiding of a multitude of sins. But there is an additional matter for joy, that a great preventive work is done when the young are converted. Conversion saves a child from a multitude of sins. If God's eternal mercy blesses your teaching to a little child, how happy that child's life will be compared with what it might have been if he had grown up in folly, sin, and shame, and had been converted only after many years! It is the highest wisdom and the truest prudence to pray for our children that, while they are yet young, their hearts may be given to the Savior.

> 'Twill save them from a thousand snares,
> To mind religion young
> Grace will preserve their following years,
> And make their virtues strong.

To reclaim the prodigal is good, but to save him from ever being a prodigal is better. To bring back the thief and the drunkard is a praiseworthy action, but so to act that the boy will never become a thief or a drunkard is far better. Hence, Sunday school instruction stands very high in the list of philanthropic enterprises in which Christians ought to be most earnest. He who converts a child from the error of his way prevents, as well as covers, a multitude of sins.

Moreover, this gives the church the hope of being furnished with the best of men and women. The church's Samuels and Solomons are made wise in their youth. David and Josiah were tender of heart when they were tender in years. Read the lives of the most eminent ministers, and you will usually find that their Christian history began early. Though it is not absolutely necessary, yet it is highly advantageous to the growth of a well-developed Christian character, that its foundation be laid on the basis of youthful piety. I do not expect to see the churches of Jesus Christ ordinarily built up by those who have lived in sin throughout much of their lives, but by the bringing up in their midst, in the fear and admonition of the Lord, young men and women who become pillars in the house of our God. If we want strong Christians, we must look to those who were Christians in their youth. Trees must be planted in the courts of the Lord while they are yet young if they are to live long and to flourish well.

Further, I feel that the work of teaching the young has at this time an importance superior to any that it ever had before, for at this time there are those who are creeping into our houses and deluding men and women with their false doctrine. Let the Sunday school teachers teach the children well. Let them not merely occupy their time with pious phrases, but teach them the whole gospel and the doctrines of grace intelligently. Let them pray over the children, and never be satisfied unless they are turned to the Lord Jesus Christ and added to the church.

We have laid aside catechisms, I think with too little reason. But, at any rate, if we do not use godly catechisms, we must bring back decided, plain, simple teaching. There must be pleading and praying for the immediate conversion to the Lord Jesus Christ of the children.

The Spirit of God waits to help us in this effort. He is with us if we are with Him. He is ready to bless the humblest teacher, and even the youngest classes will not be without a blessing. He can give us words and thoughts suitable to our little auditory. He can bless us so that we will know how to speak a word in season to the youthful ear. If not, if teachers are not found, or if they are found but are unfaithful, we will see the children that have been in our schools go back into the world, like their parents, hating religion because of the tedium of the hours spent in the Sunday school. We will produce a race of unbelievers or a generation of superstitious people. The golden opportunity will be lost, and a most solemn responsibility will rest on us!

I pray that the church of God will think much of the Sunday school. I beseech all lovers of the nation to pray for Sunday schools. I entreat all who love Jesus Christ and want to see His kingdom come to be very tender toward all youthful people and to pray that their hearts may be won to Jesus.

I have not spoken as I would like to speak, but this theme lies very near my heart. It is one that ought to press heavily on all our consciences, but I must leave it. May God lead your thoughts fully into it. I leave it, but not until I have asked these questions: What have you been doing for the conversion of children, each one of you? What have you done for the conversion of your own children? Are you quite clear on that matter? Do you ever put your arms around your boy's neck and pray for him and with him? Father, you will find that such an act will exercise great influence over your boy. Mother, do you ever talk to your little daughter about *"Christ, and him crucified"* (1 Corinthians 2:2)? Under God's hands, you may be a spiritual as well as a natural mother to that well-beloved child of yours. What are you doing, you who are guardians and teachers of youth? Are you clear about their souls? You weekday schoolteachers, as well as you who labor on the Sabbath, are you doing all you should that your boys and girls may be brought early to confess the Lord? I leave it with you.

You will receive a great reward if, when you enter heaven, as I trust you will, you find many dear children there to welcome you into eternal habitations. It will add another heaven to your own heaven to meet with heavenly beings who will greet you as their teacher who brought them to Jesus. I would not wish to go to heaven alone—would you? I would not wish to have a crown in heaven without a star in it because no soul was ever saved by my means—would you?

There they go, the sacred flock of blood-bought sheep; the Great Shepherd leads them. Many of them are followed by twins, and others have, each one, their lamb. Would you like to be a barren sheep of the Great Shepherd's flock?

The scene changes. Listen to the tramping of a great host. I hear their war music. My ears are filled with their songs of victory. The warriors are coming home; each one is bringing his trophy on his shoulder to the honor of the great Captain. They stream through the gates of pearl. They march in triumph to the celestial capitol along the golden streets. Each soldier carries with him his own portion of the spoil. Will you be there? And being there, will you march without a trophy and add nothing to the splendor of the triumph? Will you carry nothing that you have won in battle, nothing that you have ever taken for Jesus with your sword and your bow?

Again, another scene is before me. I hear them shout the "harvest home," and I see every one of the reapers carrying his sheaf. Some of them are bowed down with the heaps of sheaves that load their happy shoulders. They went forth weeping, but they have come again rejoicing, bringing their sheaves with them. Here comes one who carries only a little handful, but it is rich grain. He had only a tiny plot and a little seed corn entrusted to him, yet it has multiplied well according to the rule of proportion. Will you be there without so much as a solitary ear, never having plowed or sown, and therefore never having reaped? If so, every shout of every reaper might well strike a fresh pang in your heart as you remember that you did not sow, and therefore could not reap.

If you do not love my Master, do not profess to do so. If He never bought you with His blood, do not lie to Him and come to His table, saying that you are His servant. But if His dear wounds bought you, give yourself to Him. If you love Him, feed His sheep and feed His lambs.

He stands here unseen by my sight, but recognized by my faith. He exhibits to you the marks of the wounds on His hands and feet, and He says to you, "'Peace be unto you: as my Father hath sent me, even so send I you.' 'Go ye into all the world, and preach the gospel to every creature.' Know this: 'He which converteth a sinner from the error of his way shall save a soul from death, and shall hide a multitude of sins' (John 20:21, Mark 16:15)."

Good Master, help us to serve You! Amen.

WHEN CHRIST RETURNS

CONTENTS

1. An Awful Premonition 559

2. The Great White Throne 577

3. The Watchword for Today 594

4. The Final Judgment 613

5. Jesus Glorified in His Saints 629

1

AN AWFUL PREMONITION

Verily I say unto you, There be some standing here, which shall not taste of death, till they see the Son of man coming in his kingdom.
—Matthew 16:28

I confess that I have frequently read this verse with only a vague sense of its poignancy and have passed over it rapidly because I have not understood it clearly. Although I am well acquainted with the usual interpretations, none of them has ever really satisfied me. This text seems to arouse the reader's surprise without suggesting a simple, obvious meaning. Bible commentators have thus invented explanations and offered suggestions that are widely divergent, but all are equally obscure and improbable.

Lately, however, in reading a volume of sermons by Bishop Horsley, I have met with an altogether new view of the passage, which I firmly believe to be the correct one. Though I do not suppose I will be able to convince all of you of this interpretation, yet I will do my best to elicit from our text the terrible charge that I believe the Savior has left here on record.

With His own cross in mind, Jesus had just admonished His disciples to steadfastness and appealed to them to take up their crosses and follow Him at any sacrifice, which He followed with a portrayal of the inestimable value of the soul and the horror of a soul being lost. (See Matthew 16:24–26.) The full force of that doom was (and is) impossible to comprehend until He *"shall come in the glory of his Father with his angels"* (Matthew 16:27). Then He stopped, looked on some of the company, and said something like this: "Certain people are standing here who will never taste of death until they see the Son of Man coming in His kingdom."

Now, what did He mean by this? Obviously, it is either a marvelous promise to some who were His disciples indeed, or else it is a portent of woe to others who would die in their sins. How do the popular interpretations of our learned commentators view this statement of our Lord?

Some say it refers to the Transfiguration. It certainly is remarkable that the account of the Transfiguration immediately follows this verse both in Mark and in Luke, as well as in this record of Matthew. However, can you for a moment convince yourself to believe that Christ was describing His Transfiguration when He spoke of *"the Son of man coming in his kingdom"*? Can you see any connection between the Transfiguration and the preceding verse that says,

> For the Son of man shall come in the glory of his Father with his angels; and then he shall reward every man according to his works.　(Matthew 16:27)

I grant you that Christ was in His glory on Mount Tabor, but He did not *"reward every man according to his works"* there. Neither is it at all fair to call that a "coming of the Son of Man." He did not *"come"* on Mount Tabor because He was already on earth. It is a misuse of language to construe that into an advent.

Besides, what would be the reason for such a solemn introduction as *"Verily I say unto you"*? Does it not raise expectations merely to cause disappointment, if He intended to say no more than this: *"'There be some standing here, which shall not taste of death, till they see'* Me transfigured"? That scene took place only six days later. The next verse tells you so.

> And after six days Jesus taketh Peter, James, and John his brother, and bringeth them up into an high mountain apart.　(Matthew 17:1)

You see, the majesty of the prediction, which carries our thoughts forward to the last days of the world's history, makes us shrink from accepting an immediate fulfillment of it. Thus, I cannot imagine that the Transfiguration is in the slightest degree referred to here. Further, I do not think that anyone would have thought of such a thing unless he had been confused and utterly perplexed in searching for an explanation.

Although it seems almost incredible, some learned scholars endorse this view. Moreover, they say that it also refers to the descent of the Holy Spirit. I am staggered at this thought. I cannot think how any man could find an analogy with Pentecost in the context here. Pentecost took place six months after this event. I really cannot comprehend why Jesus Christ would say, "Truly I say unto you, there are some standing here who will live six months." It seems to me that my Master did not waste people's time by speaking such inanities.

Who, reading this passage, can think it has any reference to the descent of the Holy Spirit?

For the Son of man shall come in the glory of his Father with his angels; and then he shall reward every man according to his works. (Matthew 16:27)

Did Christ come at Pentecost in the glory of His Father? Were there any angels accompanying Him at that time? Did He *"reward every man according to his works"* then? Scarcely can the descent of the Holy Spirit or the appearance of *"cloven tongues like as of fire"* (Acts 2:3) be called *"the Son of man [coming] in the glory of his Father with his angels [to] reward every man according to his works"* without a gross misuse of our language or a strange violation of symbolic imagery.

Both of these theories that I have mentioned are now rejected as unsatisfactory by those modern students who have most carefully studied the subject. However, a third explanation still holds its ground and is currently received, though I believe it to be quite as far from the truth as the others.

Carefully read through the sixteenth chapter of Matthew, and you will find nothing about the siege of Jerusalem there. Yet, this is the interpretation that finds favor at present. According to those who hold this view, Christ was referring to the time when Jerusalem would be destroyed by the Romans. But, why would Jesus have said that some who were standing there would be alive then? Nothing could be more foreign to the entire scope of Christ's narrative or the gospel accounts. There is not the slightest shadow of reference to the siege of Jerusalem. The coming of the Son of Man is spoken of here: "*in the glory of his Father with his angels; [when] he shall reward every man according to his works.*"

Whenever Jesus spoke of the coming siege of Jerusalem, He was accustomed to saying, "*Verily I say unto you, This generation shall not pass, till all these things be fulfilled*" (Matthew 24:34). Never, however, did He single out a select few and say to them, "'*Verily I say unto you, There be some standing here, which shall not taste of death,*' until the city of Jerusalem is besieged and destroyed."

If a child were to read this passage, I know what he would think it meant: he would suppose Jesus Christ is to come again to the earth, and there were some standing there who would not taste of death until really and literally He did so. This, I believe, is the plain meaning.

"Well," I hear someone saying, "I am surprised. Do you think, then, that this refers to the apostle John?" No, by no means. The fable that John was to live until Christ came again was current in early New Testament times, you know. However, John himself repudiated it, for at the end of his gospel, he said,

> Then went this saying abroad among the brethren, that that disciple should not die: yet Jesus said not unto him, He shall not die; but, **if** I will that he tarry till I come, what is that to thee? (John 21:23, emphasis added)

This, you see, was setting forth a hypothetical case, and in no sense was it the language of prediction.

Now, beloved, if you are so far convinced of the unreasonableness of each of these theories to resolve the difficulty of interpretation, I hope that you are in readiness for the explanation that appears to me to harmonize with every aspect of the text. I believe the "*coming*" referred to in our text is the coming of the Son of God to judge at the last great and terrible Day, when He will judge all and separate the wicked from among the righteous.

The next question is, Of whom were the words spoken? Are we warranted in supposing that our Lord intended this sentence as a gracious promise or a kindly expectation that He wanted to kindle in the hearts of His disciples? I trust not. To me it appears to have absolutely no reference to any man who ever had grace in his soul. Such language is far more applicable to the ungodly than to the wicked. The sentence may well have been aimed directly at those followers who would defect from the faith, grasp at the world, endeavor to save their lives but really lose them, and barter their souls.

A True Taste of Death

At the glorious appearing of Christ, there are some who will taste death, but will they be the righteous? Surely, my dear friends, when Christ comes, the righteous will not die. They will be caught up with the Lord in the air. His coming will be the signal for the resurrection of all His saints.

But, at the time of His return, the men who have been without God, without Christ, will begin for the first time to "taste of death." They will have passed the first stage of dissolution when their souls abandon their bodies, but they will have never known the "taste of death." Until Christ's return, they will not have truly known its tremendous bitterness and its awful horror. They will never drink the wormwood and the gall, to really "taste of death," until that time. This tasting of death may be explained, and I believe it is to be explained, as a reference to the second death of which men will not taste until the Lord comes again.

What a dreadful sentence that was when the Savior said (perhaps singling out Judas as He spoke), "Truly I say unto you, there are some who are standing here who will never know what that dreadful word *death* really means until the Lord comes again. You think that if you save your lives, you escape from death. Alas, you do not know what death means! The demise of the body is but a mere prelude to the perdition of the soul. The grave is but the porch of death. You will never understand the full meaning of that terrible word until the Lord comes."

This can have no reference to the saints, because in the gospel of John, you find this passage:

> Verily, verily, I say unto you, If a man keep my saying, he shall never see death. Then said the Jews unto him, Now we know that thou hast a devil. Abraham is dead, and the prophets; and thou sayest, If a man keep my saying, he shall never taste of death. (John 8:51–52)

No righteous man, therefore, can ever "taste of death." Yes, he will fall into that deep, oblivious sleep during which the body sees corruption, but that is another experience, very different from the bitter cup referred to as a "*taste of death."* When the Holy Spirit wanted to use an expression to set forth the equivalent for divine wrath, what wording was used? *"Jesus, who was made a little lower than the angels for suffering of death…by the grace of God should taste death for every man"* (Hebrews 2:9).

The expression "to taste of death" means the reception of the true, essential death that kills both the body and the soul in hell forever. The Savior said, *"Verily I say unto you, There be some standing here, which shall not taste of death, till they see the Son of man coming in his kingdom."* If this is the meaning (and I hold that it is in keeping with the context), it explains the verse, sets forth the reason why Christ invoked breathless attention with the word *verily,* answers both the grammar and the rhetoric, and will not be moved by any argument that I have ever heard. And if so, what amazing indictments are contained in this text! May the Holy Spirit deeply affect our hearts and cause our souls to thrill with its solemnity.

What thoughts this idea stirs up! Compared with the doom that will be inflicted upon the ungodly at Christ's return, the death of the physical body is nothing. Further, compared with the doom of the wicked at His return, even the torment of souls in a separate state is scarcely anything. The startling question then arises: Are there any reading this who will have to taste of death when the Lord comes?

Comparing Physical Death and Final Doom

The sinner's death is only a faint foreshadowing of the sinner's doom at the coming of the Son of Man in His glory. Let me endeavor to show the contrast.

In Regard to Time

We can only make a little comparison between the two as to time. Many men meet with death so suddenly that it can scarcely involve any pain to them. Perhaps they are crushed by machinery, or a shot sends them to find a grave upon the battlefield, or they are poisoned with a quick-acting toxin. Even if they are upon the bed of sickness for hours, days, weeks, or months, yet the real work of dying is short. It is a weary sort of living, rather than an actual process of dying, while hope lingers, though only in fitful dreams. Dying is but the work of a moment. If it is said to last for hours, yet the hours are brief. Misery may count them long, but with what swift wings do they fly. To die, to fall asleep, to suffer, may seem endless, yet to pass away from the land of the living into the realm of shadows takes only a moment!

However, the doom that is to be brought upon the wicked when Christ comes is a death that never dies. Here is a heart that palpitates with eternal misery. Here is an eye that is never clouded over by the kind finger of generous forgetfulness. Here is a body that never will be stiffened in apathy, never will be laid quietly in the grave, rid of sharp pains, wearying disease, and lingering wretchedness. To die, you say, is nature's kind release, because it brings ease. To a man, death becomes a farewell to his woes and griefs—for this world at least.

Yet, there will be no ease, no rest, no pause in the destination of impenitent souls. *"Depart from me, ye cursed"* (Matthew 25:41) will ever ring along the endless aisles of eternity. The thunderbolt of that tremendous word will follow the sinner in his perpetual flight from the presence of God. From its deadly influence he will never be able to escape—no, never. A million years will not make any more difference to the duration of his agony than a cup of water taken from the sea would change the volume of the ocean. When a million years have rolled their fiery orbits over his poor, tormented head, he will be no nearer to the end than he was at first.

Talk about physical death! I might even portray it as an angel of mercy when I compare it to the terrors of the wrath to come. Soon come, soon gone, is death. That sharp scythe gives only one cut, and down falls the flower that withers in the heat of the sun. But, who can measure the wounds of eternity, who can fathom the depths of its gashes? When eternity wields the whip, how dreadfully it falls! When eternity grasps the sword, how deep is the wounding and how terrible the killing!

> To linger in eternal pain,
> Yet death for ever fly.

You are afraid of death, sinner; you are afraid of death. However, were you wise, you would be ten thousand times ten thousand times more afraid of the Second Coming and the Judgment of the Son of Man.

As to Loss

Regarding loss, there is no comparison. When a sinner dies, it is not tasting death in its true sense, for what does he lose? He loses wife and children and friends. He loses all his hearty meat and his sweet desserts. Where are his violin and his lute now? Where are the merry dances and the joyful company? For him there is no more pleasant landscape or gliding stream. For him the light of the sun by day or the light of the moon and stars by night shines no more. At one stroke, he has lost every comfort and every hope. The loss, however, as far as physical death is concerned, is but a loss of earthly things, the loss of material, temporary comforts. It is wretched enough to lose these, but he might put up with that kind of loss.

Nevertheless, let your imagination follow me, faint as my power is to describe the everlasting and infinite loss of the man who is found impenitent at the last great Judgment Day. What does he lose then? The harps of heaven and the songs thereof, the joys of God's presence and the light thereof, the jasper sea and the gates of pearl. He has lost peace and immorality and the crown of life.

Moreover, he has lost all hope. When a man has lost that, what remains for him? His spirit sinks into a terrible depression, more frightening than a madman ever knew in his wildest moods of grief. Never to recover itself, his soul sinks into the depths of dark despair, where not a ray of hope can ever reach him. Lost to God, lost to heaven, lost to time, lost to the preaching of the Gospel, lost to the invitation of mercy, lost to the prayers of the gracious, lost to the mercy seat, lost to the blood of sprinkling, lost to all hope of every sort—lost, lost, forever lost! Compared with this loss, the losses of death are nothing. Thus, the Savior said that lost souls will not even *"taste of death"* until He comes and they receive their sentences.

Concerning Terror

Neither does death bear any comparison with the Judgment concerning terror. I do not like to describe the terrors of the deathbeds of unawakened men. Some, you know, glide gently into their graves. In fact, it is often the mark of the wicked that they have no troubles in dying, but their strength stays firm. They are not distraught as other men are. Like sheep they are laid in the grave. Yet, a peaceful death is no sign of grace. Some of the worst men have died with smiles on their faces, only to have them exchanged for eternal weeping.

However, other men of exquisite sensitivities, educated men, cannot seem to die like brute animals do. They have intense fears and terrors when they are on their deathbeds. Many an atheist has cried out to God when he was experiencing the pangs of death. Many an infidel, who previously bragged and spoke high things against God, has found his cheek turn pale and his throat grow hoarse when he has come to the throes of death. Like the mariner, the boldest man in the great storm of death reels and staggers like a drunkard and is at his wit's end, because he finds that it is no child's play to die.

I try sometimes to picture that hour when we will be propped up in bed, or perhaps lying down with pillows all around us, being diligently watched. As loved ones hush their footfalls and gaze anxiously on, there is a whisper that the solemn time has come. Then there is a grappling of the strong man with one stronger than he. Oh, what must it be to die without a Savior—to die in the dark without a light except the lurid glare of the wrath to come!

Horrors there are, indeed, around the deathbed of the wicked, but these are hardly anything compared with the terrors of the Day of Judgment. When the sinner wakes from his bed of dust, the first thing he will see will be the Great White Throne and the Judge seated upon it. (See Revelation 20:11.) The first sound that will greet his ears will be the trumpet sounding this call:

> Come to judgment, come to judgment,
> Come to judgment, sinner, come.

He will look up to see the Son of Man on His judgment throne with the King's officers arranged on either side, the saints on His right hand and angels round about Him. Then the books will be opened (Revelation 20:12). What creeping horror will come upon the flesh of the wicked man! He knows his turn will arrive in a moment; he stands expecting it. Fear grips him while the eyes of the Judge look him through and through. He cries to the rocks to hide him and the mountains to fall upon him. (See Revelation 6:16.) Happy would he be now to find a friendly shelter in the grave, but the grave has burst its doors and can never be closed upon him again. He would even be glad to rush back to his former state in hell, but he must not. The Judgment has come; the indictment is set. Again the trumpet rings,

> Come to judgment, come to judgment,
> Come to judgment, come away.

Then the Book of Life is opened, and the dreadful sentence is pronounced. We discover this in the words of Scripture:

And death and hell were cast into the lake of fire. This is the second death.
And whosoever was not found written in the book of life was cast into the lake
of fire.   (Revelation 20:14–15)

The condemned sinner never knew what death was before. The first death was just a flea bite, but this is death indeed. The first death he might have looked back upon as a dream compared with this taste of death, now that the Lord has come.

As to Pain

From what we can glean darkly from hints in Scripture, the pains of death are not at all comparable to the pains of the Judgment at the Second Advent. Who could speak in a minimizing manner of the pains of death? If we should attempt to do so, we know that our hearts would contradict us.

In the shades of night, when deep sleep has enveloped you, you sometimes awake abruptly. You are alarmed. The terror by night has come upon you. You expect something—you hardly know what it coming—but you are half-afraid that you are about to die. You know how the cold sweat comes over you suddenly. You may have a good hope through grace, but the very thought of death brings a peculiar shudder.

Again, when death has really come into view, some of us, with terrible grief, have observed the sufferings of our dearest friends. We have heard the belabored gasping for breath. We have seen the face all pallid and the cheeks all hollow and sunken. We have sometimes seen how every nerve has become a road for the hot feet of pain to travel on, and how every vein has become a canal of grief. We have marked the pains, moans, groans, and dying strife that frighten the soul away. These, however, are common to man.

Not so are the pangs that are to be inflicted both on the body and on the soul at the Son of God's return. They are such that I want to veil them, fearful of the very thought. Let the Master's words suffice: *"Fear him, which after he hath killed hath power to cast into hell; yea, I say unto you, Fear him"* (Luke 12:5). Then the body in all its parts will suffer. The members that were once instruments of unrighteousness will now be instruments of suffering. The mind, which has sinned the most, will be the greatest sufferer. The memory, the judgment, the understanding, the will, the imagination, and every power and passion of the soul will become a deep lake of anguish.

I want to spare you these things. Do spare yourself! God knows with what anguish I even touch on these horrors. If they did not have to be addressed (and they must be, or else I must give my account at the Day of Judgment as a faithless servant), and if I did not have to express them now in mercy for your soul, poor sinner, I would just as soon forget them altogether, seeing that my own soul has a hope in Him who saves from the wrath to come.

But, as long as you will not have mercy upon yourself, I must lay this ax at your root. As long as you will make a mockery of sin and consider the terrors of the world to come as nothing, I must sternly warn you of hell. If it is hard to write about these things, what must it be to endure them? If a dream makes you quiver from head to foot, what must it be to endure, really and personally, the wrath to come?

Beloved, if I were to address you now as I should, my knees would be trembling and knocking together. If you were to feel as you should, there would not be an unconverted person reading this who would not cry, "*What must I do to be saved?*" (Acts 16:30). I urge you to remember that death, with all its pangs, is but a drop in a bucket compared with the deep, mysterious, fathomless, shoreless sea of grief that you must endure forever at the coming of the Lord Jesus, unless you repent.

In Regard to Discovery

Death makes great discoveries. The sinner thought himself to be wise, but death drew the curtain, and he saw written in large letters, "You fool!" He thought he was prudent as he hoarded up his gold and silver and kept back the wages of his laborers (see James 5:3–4), but he discovered that he had made a bad bargain when the question was put to him: "What did it profit you to have gained the whole world, but to have lost your soul?" (See Mark 8:36.)

Death is a great revealer of secrets. Many men are not believers at all until they die, but death comes and makes short work of their skepticism. Death deals one blow to the head of doubt, and it is all over. The man believes then, but his belief has come too late. Death gives to the sinner the discovery that there is a God, an angry God, and that punishment is wrapped up in the wrath to come.

Even so, how much greater are the discoveries that await the wayward one on the Day of Judgment! What will the sinner see then? He will see the Man who was crucified, sitting on the throne. He will hear how Satan has been defeated in all of his craftiest undertakings. When those mysterious books are read, the secrets of all hearts will be revealed. Men will understand how the Lord reigned supremely even when Satan roared most loudly. They will finally grasp how the mischief and folly of man brought forth the great purposes of God in the end. All of this will be in the books.

The sinner will stand there defeated, terribly defeated, ruined at every point, baffled, foiled, stultified in every act and every purpose by which he thought to do well for himself. Moreover, he will be utterly confounded in all the hostility and all the negligence of his heart toward the living and true God, who would and who did rule over him. Too late, he will realize the preciousness of the blood he despised, the value of the Savior he rejected, the glory of the heaven that he lost, the terror of the hell to which he is sentenced. How dreadfully wise he will be when fully aware of his terrible, eternal destruction! Thus, sinners will not discover what it truly means to taste of death until the Lord returns.

A Full Taste of Death

In the case of those who have physically died, they have not fully tasted of death, nor will they do so until Christ comes again. The moment a man dies, his spirit goes before God. If he is without Christ, his spirit then begins to feel the anger and the wrath of God. This is like a man being taken before a magistrate. He is known to be guilty, and so he is remanded to prison until his trial is scheduled. Such is the state of souls who are apart from their bodies. They are spirits in prison, awaiting trial.

There is not, in the sense in which the Catholics teach, any purgatory, from which there is a possibility of escape. Yet, there is a place of waiting for lost spirits that in Scripture is called "hell." It is one room in that awful prison in which spirits who die impenitent and without faith in Christ are doomed to dwell forever.

Bodily Suffering

Just consider why those of our departed countrymen who die without Christ have not yet fully tasted of death, and cannot do so until the Second Coming. First, their bodies do not suffer. The bodies of the wicked are still the prey of the worms, but they feel nothing. The atoms are still the sport of the winds, traversing their endless cycles until they will be gathered up again into their bodies at the sound of the last trumpet—at the voice of God.

The ungodly know that their present state is to have an end at the Last Judgment, but afterwards, their state will have no ending. It is then to go on and on, forever unchanged. There may be half a hope at present, an anticipation of some change, for change brings some relief. But, to the finally damned, upon whom the sentence has been pronounced, there is no hope even of a change. Forever and ever there will be the same ceaseless wheel of misery.

The Shame of Public Sentencing

The ungodly, too, in their present state, have not as yet been put to the shame of a public sentence. They have, as it were, merely been cast into prison, the facts being too clear to admit any doubt as to the sentence. They are their own tormentors, vexing and paining themselves with the fear of what is yet to come. They have never yet heard that dreadful sentence: *"Depart from me, ye cursed, into everlasting fire, prepared for the devil and his angels"* (Matthew 25:41).

While studying this subject, I was surprised to find how little is said about the pains of the lost while they are merely souls and how much is said concerning the pains they will have when the Lord returns. In the parable of the rich man and Lazarus, we see that the soul is already being tormented in the flames. (See Luke 16:19–31.) But, if you read the parable of the tares in the thirteenth chapter of Matthew, we find it is at the end of the world that the tares are to be cast into the fire.

The Eternal Lake of Fire

Following the parable of the tares comes the parable of the dragnet in Matthew 13:47–50. When the dispensation comes to an end, the net is to be dragged to shore, and the good are to be put in vessels while the bad are to be cast away. The Lord said,

> *The Son of man shall send forth his angels, and they shall gather out of his kingdom all things that offend, and them which do iniquity; and shall cast them into a furnace of fire: there shall be wailing and gnashing of teeth.*
> (Matthew 13:41–42)

We read in Matthew that memorable description of those of whom Christ will say, "*I was an hungered, and ye gave me no meat: I was thirsty, and ye gave me no drink*" (Matthew 25:42). This event is prophesied to occur "*when the Son of man shall come in his glory, and all the holy angels with him*" (verse 31).

In his second letter to the Thessalonians, Paul, too, tells us plainly that the wicked are to be destroyed at Christ's coming by the radiance of His power. (See 2 Thessalonians 1:7–9.) The recompense of the ungodly, like the reward of the righteous, is anticipated now, but the full reward of the righteous will be at His coming. They will reign with Christ. Their fullness of bliss will be given when the King Himself sits on His throne in all His glory. So, too, the wicked will have the beginning of their heritage at death, but the terrible fullness of it will be thereafter.

At the present moment, death and hell are not yet cast into the lake of fire. Death is still abroad in the world, slaying men. Hell is yet loose. The devil is not yet chained. He still is going "*through dry places, seeking rest, and find*[ing] *none*" (Matthew 12:43). At the Last Day, at the Second Coming, "*death and hell* [will be] *cast into the lake of fire. This is the second death*" (Revelation 20:14). We do not completely understand the symbolism, but if it means anything, one would think it must mean that on that Day the scattered powers of evil, which are to be the tormentors of the wicked but which have hitherto been wandering throughout the world, will all be collected together. Then, indeed, it will be that the wicked begin to "*taste of death*" as they have never tasted of it before!

My soul is bowed down with terror while I write this. I scarcely know how to find suitable words to express the weight of thought that is upon me. Beloved, instead of speculating about these matters, let us try to shun the wrath to come. What can help us to do that better than to weigh the warning words of our loving Savior? He tells us that at His coming such a doom will pass upon impenitent souls that, compared with it, even death itself will be as nothing. Christians swallow death in victory (see 1 Corinthians 15:54) through their faith in the risen Lord; but if you die as an impenitent soul, you swallow death in ignorance. You do not feel its bitterness now. But, unless you repent, that bitter pill has yet to work its way, and that dire potion has yet to be drunk to the dregs.

Examine Your Heart

Does our study of these awful terrors prompt a question in you? Jesus said, "*Verily I say unto you, there be some standing here, which shall not taste of death, till they see the Son of man coming in his kingdom.*" Are there any of you reading this who will taste of death when the Son of Man returns?

O beloved, try your own hearts, and since you may fail in the trial, ask the Lord to search you. As the Lord God lives, unless you search yourselves and find that you are on the right path, you may come to sit at the Lord's table presumptuously. (See Matthew 22:11–14.)

Deceitful Sinners

In that little group addressed by the Savior stood Judas. He had been trusted by his Master, and he was an apostle, but he was a thief and a hypocrite after all. He, "*the son of perdition*" (John 17:12), would not taste of death until Christ should come into His kingdom. Is there a Judas reading these words?

Many of you are members of Christian churches, but are you sure that you have made sound work of it? Is your belief genuine? Do you wear a mask, or are you honest? You may be self-proclaimed among His people here on the earth, but you may have to taste of death when the Lord comes. You may deceive them, but you cannot deceive Him.

Even if you are a preacher, you can reflect that you may be mistaken, that you may be self-deceived. If it is so, may the Lord open your eyes to know the truth of your own state.

Will you offer a prayer of repentance for yourselves, you who profess to know Christ? Do not be too bold or too quick, you who say you are Christ's. Never be satisfied until you are absolutely sure. The best way to be sure is to go again, just as you went at first, and seize eternal life through the power of the blessed Spirit and not by any strength of your own.

Careless Sinners

No doubt, however, there stood in that throng around the Savior some who were careless sinners. He knew that there had been some during His entire ministry and that there would still be some. Thus, they would taste of death at His coming. Are there not some careless, unconcerned people reading this right now?

You who rarely think about religion, you who generally view Sunday as a day of pleasure or who lounge around in your sports clothes the whole day, you who look upon the very name of religion as a monster to frighten children with, you who mock God's servants and condemn the very thought of earnestly seeking after the Most High—will you be among the number of those who taste of death when the Son of Man comes in His kingdom? Must I ring your death knell now? Must my warning be lost upon you? I urge you to recollect that you must either turn or burn. I entreat you to remember this:

> Let the wicked forsake his way, and the unrighteous man his thoughts: and
> let him return unto the LORD, and he will have mercy upon him; and to our
> God, for he will abundantly pardon.   (Isaiah 55:7)

By the wounds of Jesus, sinner, stop and think! Since God's dear Son was slain for human sin, how terrible must that sin be? Since Jesus died for you, how base are you if you are disobedient to the doctrine of faith? I implore you that, if you think of your body, give some thought to your soul.

> Wherefore do ye spend money for that which is not bread? and your labour
> for that which satisfieth not? hearken diligently unto me, and eat ye that which
> is good, and let your soul delight itself in fatness.   (Isaiah 55:2)

Carefully focus on God's Word, and eat of that which is good, real, substantial food. Come to Jesus, so that you may live eternally.

Willful Sinners

Around Jesus were some of another class: the willfully unrepentant Bethsaida and Capernaum sinners. (See Matthew 11:21–24.) Likewise, there are some of you who constantly occupy church pews and sit in services Sunday after Sunday. The same eyes look at the pastor week after week. The same faces salute him often with a smile when Sunday comes. Yet, how many of you are still without God and without Christ?

Have we preachers been unfaithful to you? If we have, forgive us, and pray, both for us and for yourselves, that we all may mend our ways. But, if we have warned you of the wrath to come, why do you choose to walk in the path that leads to it? If we have preached Christ Jesus to you, how is it that His charms do not move you and that the story of His great love does not bring you to repentance? May the Spirit of God deal with you, for man cannot. Our hammers do not break your flinty hearts, but God's arm can do it. May He turn you yet.

Of all sinners over whom a minister ought to weep, you are the worst, for while the careless perish, you perish doubly. You know your Master's will, and yet you do not do it. You see heaven's gate set open, and yet you will not enter. Your vicious free will ruins you. Your base, wicked love of self and sin destroys you. Jesus said, *"And ye will not come to me, that ye might have life"* (John 5:40). You are so stubborn that you will not turn even though Jesus woos you. I do pray that you will let the terror of the Judgment presented here stir you now as you have never been stirred before. May God have pity on you even if you will have no pity on yourselves.

Prostituting Sinners

Among that company perhaps there were some who held to the truth, but who were behaving immorally. Some of you who are reading this may be like those people. You believe in eternal election, as I do, but you make it a cloak for your sin. You hold to the doctrine of the perseverance of the saints, but you still continue in your iniquity. Perhaps there is no worse way of perishing than perishing by making the doctrines of grace an excuse for one's sins. The apostle Paul has well said of such that their *"damnation is just"* (Romans 3:8). God's condemnation of any man is just, but to a sevenfold degree is it just for such a person.

I would not have you forget this doctrine, nor neglect it, nor despise it. But, I beg you, do not prostitute it. Do not turn it to the vile purpose of making it pander to your own carnal desires. Remember, you have no evidence of election except that you are holy, and you have no right to expect you will be saved at the last unless you are saved now. A present faith in a present Savior is the key.

Redeemed Sinners

May my Master bring some of you to trust Him right now. The plan of salvation is simple. Trust Christ, and you are saved. Rely upon Him, and you will live. This faith is the gift of God, but remember that although God gives it, He *"worketh in you both to will and to do of his good pleasure"* (Philippians 2:13).

God does not believe for you; the Holy Spirit does not believe for you; you must believe, or else you will be lost. To say that it is also the act of man is quite consistent with the fact that it is the gift of God. You must, poor soul, be led to trust the Savior, or you can never enter into heaven. Are you saying, "I want to find the Savior now"? Do not go to bed until you have sought Him. Seek Him with sighs and with tears until you find Him.

I think now is a time of grace. I have painted a picture of the law and the terrors of the Lord for you, but now will be a time of grace to the souls of some of you. My Master kills you so that He may make you alive. (See 1 Samuel 2:6.) He wounds you only so that He may make you whole. (See Jeremiah 30:14–17.)

I feel an inward whisper in my heart that there are some of you who even now have begun your flight from the wrath to come. Where should you flee? Run to Jesus. Hurry, sinner, hurry. I trust you will find Him before you retire to your bed. Or, if you lie there, tossing about in doubt and fear, then may He manifest Himself to you before the morning light.

I would freely give my eyes so that you might see Christ, and I would willingly give my hands so that you might lay hold of Him. I implore you, do not put this warning away from you, but let it have its proper work in you and lead you to repentance. May God save you, and may the prayer of my heart be answered, that all of you be found among His elect at His right hand on that great and terrible Day.

Our Father, Save us with Your great salvation. We pray, do not condemn us, Lord. Deliver us from going down to the pit, for You have found the ransom. May we not be among the company that shall taste of death when the Son of Man comes. Hear us, Jesus, through Your blood. God be merciful to us sinners. Amen

2

THE GREAT WHITE THRONE

And I saw a great white throne, and him that sat on it, from whose face the earth and the heaven fled away; and there was found no place for them.
—Revelation 20:11

Many of the visions that the apostle John saw are very obscure. Although a man who is assured of his own salvation may possibly be justified in spending his days endeavoring to interpret them, I am sure that it will not be a profitable task for unconverted people. They have no time to spare on speculations, for they have not yet secured for themselves the absolute certainties. They need not dive into difficulties, for they have not yet laid a foundation of the basic doctrines of faith in Christ Jesus. It is far better to meditate on the Atonement than to be guessing at the meaning of *"a little horn"* (Daniel 8:9). It is far better to know the Lord Jesus in His power to save than to devise an ingenious theory about *"the number of the beast"* (Revelation 13:18).

However, the particular vision in our text is so instructive, so unattended by serious difficulties, that I invite you to consider it. Even more, I do so because it has to do with matters that concern our own eternal prospects. It may be, if the Holy Spirit illuminates the eyes of our faith to look and see the *"great white throne and him that sat upon it,"* that we may reap so much benefit from the sight as to make all of heaven ring with gratitude that we were brought into this world to see the Great White Throne. By seeing it with the eyes of faith, we will not be afraid to look upon it in the Day when the Judge sits and the quick and dead stand before Him. (See Acts 10:42.)

First, I will endeavor to explain what John saw. Secondly, I will set forth the effect that I think would be produced by this sight if the eyes of our faith were now focused there.

John's Vision

First, then, I want to call your very earnest attention to what John saw. It was a scene of the Last Day—that wondrous Day whose coming none can foretell.

> For, as a thief unheard, unseen,
> It steals through night's dark shade.

A Throne of Moral Government

When the eagle-eyed prophet of Patmos, being in the Spirit, looked aloft into the heavens, he saw a throne. From this, I gather that there is a throne of moral government over the sons of men, and that He who sits upon it presides over all the inhabitants of this world. The dominion of this throne reaches from Adam in Paradise down to the last man on earth, whoever he may be. We are not without our Judge, Lawgiver, and King. (See Isaiah 33:22.) This world is not left so that men may do in it as they will, without a governor, without an avenger, without anyone to give reward or to inflict punishment.

In his blindness, the sinner looks, but he sees no throne. Therefore, he cries, "I will live as I desire, for there is none to call me to account." However, John, with illumined eyes, distinctly saw a throne and a personal Ruler, who sat there to call His subjects to account. When our faith looks through the glass of revelation, it sees a throne, too.

It would be good for us if we felt more fully the influence of that ever present throne. Beloved, the fact that *"the LORD reigneth"* (Psalm 93:1) is true now and true at all times. There is a throne on which *"the King eternal, immortal, invisible"* (1 Timothy 1:17) sits. The world is governed by laws made and kept in force by the omniscient Lawgiver. There is one truly moral, righteous Judge. Men are responsible beings and will be brought to account for their actions at the Last Day, when they will all be either rewarded or punished.

"I saw a great white throne." How this invests the actions of men with solemnity! Even if we were left to do exactly as we wanted to without being called to account, it would still be wise to be virtuous. Rest assured, it is best for us to be good. To be evil is enough of a malady in and of itself.

However, we are not left to our own devices. There is a law laid down, the breaking of which involves a penalty. There is a Lawgiver who looks down and sees every action of man and who does not allow one single word or deed to be omitted from His notebook. That Judge is armed with power. He is coming soon to hold His great tribunal, and every responsible agent on the face of the earth must appear at His bar and receive sentencing, as we have been told:

> For we must all appear before the judgment seat of Christ; that every one may receive the things done in his body, according to that he hath done, whether it be good or bad. (2 Corinthians 5:10)

Let it, then, be understood from our text that there is indeed a personal and real moral Governor of the world, an efficient and suitable Ruler, not a mere name, not a myth, not an empty office, but a Person who sits on the throne, who judges righteously, and who will carry out that Judgment before long.

The Right to Rule

Now, brothers and sisters, we know that this moral Governor is God Himself, who has an undisputed right to reign and rule. Some thrones have no right to be, and to revolt from them is patriotism. However, the person who best loves his own race delights the most in the monarchy of heaven.

Doubtless, there are dynasties that are tyrannies and governors who are despots, but none may dispute the right of God to sit upon the Great White Throne or wish that another hand held the *"sceptre of righteousness"* (Hebrews 1:8). He created all; should He not judge all? As Creator, He had a right to set down His laws over His creation. Because those laws are the pattern of everything that is good and true, He had, therefore, an eternal right to govern, in addition to the right that belonged to Him as Creator. He is the Judge of all; He must do right from a necessity of His nature. Who else, then, should sit upon the throne, and who would dare to claim to do so? He may cast down the gauntlet to all His creatures and say, *"I am God, and there is none else"* (Isaiah 45:22). If He reveals the thunder of His power, His creatures must silently admit that He alone is Lord. None can venture to say that this throne is not founded upon right.

Moreover, there are some thrones on which the kings, however right, are deficient in might, but this is not the case with the King of Kings. We often see little princes whose crowns so poorly fit their heads that they cannot keep them on their brows. However, our God has invincible might as well as infallible right.

Who would meet Him in the battle? Will the stubble defy the fire, or will the wax make war with the flame? Jehovah can easily swallow up His enemies when they set themselves in battle array against Him. *"He looketh on the earth, and it trembleth: he toucheth the hills, and they smoke"* (Psalm 104:32). He breaks Leviathan in pieces in the depths of the sea (Psalm 74:13–14). The clouds are His chariots, and He walks on the wings of the wind. (See Psalm 104:3.) At His bidding there is day, and at His will night covers the earth. (See Genesis 1:3–5.) *"Who can hinder him? who will say unto him, What doest thou?"* (Job 9:12). His throne is founded in right and supported by might. Justice and truth have settled it, and omnipotence and wisdom are its guards, so that it cannot be moved.

The Power of His Throne

Additionally, none can escape the power of His throne. At this moment, the sapphire throne of God (see Ezekiel 1:26) is revealed in heaven, where adoring men cast their crowns before it. (See Revelation 4:10.) Its power is felt on earth, where the works of creation praise the Lord. Even those who do not acknowledge the divine government are compelled to feel it, for He does as He wills, not only among those in heaven, but also among the inhabitants of this lower world. Hell feels the terror of that throne. Those chains of fire, those pangs unutterable, are the awful shadow of the throne of Deity. As God looks upon the lost, the torment that flashes through their souls comes from His holiness, which cannot endure their sins.

The influence of that throne, then, is found in every world where spirits dwell. It also rules the realms of inanimate nature. Every leaf that fades in the trackless forest trembles at the Almighty's bidding. Every coral insect that dwells in the unfathomable depths of the sea feels and acknowledges the presence of the all-present King.

No Escape

So then, beloved, if such were the throne that John saw, see how impossible it will be for you to escape from the great tribunal when the Judgment Day is proclaimed and the Judge issues His summons bidding you to appear. Where can the enemies of God flee? If their high-flown impudence could carry them up to heaven, His right hand of holiness would hurl them there. If they could dive under hell's deepest wave, His left hand would pluck them out of the fire to expose them to the fiercer light of His countenance. Nowhere is there a refuge from the Most High. The morning beams cannot convey the fugitive so swiftly that the almighty Pursuer could not follow him. Neither can the mysterious lightning bolt, which annihilates time and space, journey so rapidly as to escape His far-reaching hand. *"If I ascend up into heaven, thou art there: if I make my bed in hell, behold, thou art there"* (Psalm 139:8).

It was said of the Roman Empire under the Caesars that the whole world was only one great big prison, because if any man offended the emperor, it was impossible to escape Caesar's reach. If the man crossed the Alps, could not Caesar find him in Gaul? If he sought to hide himself in the Indies, even there the swarthy monarchs knew the power of the Roman army, so that they would give no shelter to a man who had incurred imperial vengeance. And yet, perhaps, a fugitive from Rome might have prolonged his miserable life by hiding in the dens and caves of the earth.

But, sinner, there is no hiding from God. The mountains cannot cover you from Him, nor can the rocks conceal you. See, then, how this throne strikes our minds with awesome terror at the very outset. Founded in right, sustained by might, and universal in its dominion, look and see the throne beheld by the Beloved Apostle.

Purity of the Throne

This, however, is but the beginning of the vision. Our text tells us that it was a *"white throne,"* and I call your attention to that. *"I saw a great white throne."* Why white? Does this not indicate its immaculate purity? I fear there is no other white throne to be found. The throne of our own country I believe to be as white and as pure as any throne might well be on earth,[1] but there have been years, even in the annals of that throne, when it was stained with blood. Not always was it a throne of excellence and purity. Even now, although our throne possesses a lustrous purity—rare enough among earthly thrones—yet in the sight of God there must be something that is impure in everything that is earthly, and therefore the throne is not white to Him. As for many other thrones that are still in existence, we know all of them are not white.

This is neither the day nor the hour for us to call earthly princes to the bar of God, but some of them will have much to answer for, because, in their self-aggrandizing schemes, they took no account of the blood that would be shed or of the rights that would be violated. Principle seldom moves the royal mind, but the roguish law of policy is the basis of a king's decision—a policy worthy of highwaymen and burglars—and some kings are small-minded. On the continent of Europe, there are more than a few thrones that I might describe as either black or crimson, as I think of the depravity of the conduct of the monarch or of the blood through which he has waded his way to dominion.

However, this is *"a great white throne,"* a throne of holy monarchy that is not stained with blood or defiled with injustice. Why, then, is it white for purity? Is it not because the King who sits on it is pure? Listen to the sacred hymn of the cherubic band and the seraphic choir: *"Holy, holy, holy, is the LORD of hosts"* (Isaiah 6:3). Creatures who are perfectly spotless themselves will unceasingly adore and reverence the superior holiness of the great King. He is too great to need to be unjust, and He is too good to be unkind. This King has done no wrong and can do no wrong, but He is the only king of whom this can be said without fiction. He who sits on this white throne is the essence of holiness, justice, truth, and love. O fairest of all thrones! Who would not be a willing subject of your peerless government?

Moreover, the throne is pure because the law the Judge dispenses is perfect! There is no fault in the Statute Book of God. When the Lord comes to judge the earth, there will be found no decree that bears too harshly upon any one of His creatures. *"The statutes of the LORD are right…the judgments of the LORD are true and righteous altogether"* (Psalm 19:8–9). Who can improve the Book that contains the Ten Commandments, in which you find a summary of the divine

1. This is a reference to Alexandrina Victoria, queen of Great Britain from 1837 to 1901. Her reign was a model of purity and virtue to the world.

will? Who can find anything in excess in it or point out anything that is lacking? *"The law of the LORD is perfect, converting the soul"* (Psalm 19:7), and well may the throne be white from which there emanates such a law.

However, you know that, even with a good law and a good lawgiver, sometimes the throne may make mistakes, and it may be stained by ignorance, if not by willful injustice. Yet, the sentence that will go forth from this Great White Throne will be so consistent with justice that even the condemned culprit himself must give his unwilling assent to it. Christ said of the guilty guest, *"He was speechless"* (Matthew 22:12)—speechless because he could neither bear the sentence nor in any way contradict it.

It is a white throne, since never was a verdict delivered from it of which the culprit had a right to complain. Perhaps there are some who view this as a matter of hope, but to ungodly people it will be the very reverse. Sinner, if you had to be judged before an impure tribunal, you might escape. If the judge were not holy, unholiness might go unpunished. If the law were not perfect, offenses might be condoned. Or, if the sentence were not just, you might escape through partiality. However, where everything is so pure and white,

> Careless sinner,
> What will there become of you?

A Noticeable Throne

I have also thought that perhaps this throne is said to be a white throne to indicate that it will be eminently conspicuous. You may have noticed that a white object can be seen from a very great distance. Perhaps you have observed a white cottage far away on the mountains, standing out noticeably. Often, the residents like to make their cottages intensely white so that, though you would not have perceived it had it been left a stone color, you see it at once, because the bright, whitewashed walls catch your eye. I suppose marksmen prefer white to almost any other color for their targets.

Likewise, this Great White Throne will be so conspicuous that the millions who were dead, but who rise at the last trumpet, will all see it. It will not be possible for a single eye to close itself against the sight. We must see it. It will be so striking a sight that none of us will be able to prevent its coming before us: *"every eye shall see"* (Revelation 1:7).

Possibly it is called a white throne because it is such a convincing contrast to all the colors of this sinful human life. There stand the crowds, and here is the Great White Throne. What can make them see their blackness more thoroughly than to stand there in contrast with the perfection of the law and the Judge? Perhaps that throne, all glistening, will reflect each man's character. As each unforgiven man looks at that throne, its dazzling whiteness will overcome him, covering him with confusion and terror when he sees his own defilement in contrast with it. He will cry, "O God, how can I bear to be judged by You? I could face the judgment seat of my peers, for I could see imperfections in my judges, but I cannot face You, dreadful Supreme, for the pure whiteness of Your throne and the terrible splendor of Your holiness utterly overwhelm me. Who am I, sinner as I am, that I should dare to stand before that Great White Throne?"

The Greatness of the Throne

The other adjective that John used in describing the throne is *"great."* It is a *"great white throne."* You scarcely need me to tell you that it is called a Great White Throne because of the greatness of Him who sits upon it. Have you heard of the greatness of Solomon? He was but a petty prince. Do you speak of the thrones of Rome and Greece, before which multitudes of beings assembled, or of the throne of the Mogul, His Celestial Majesty of China? They are as nothing, mere representatives of associations of the grasshoppers of the world, in the sight of God Almighty.

A throne filled by a mortal is but a shadow of dominion. However, this will be a great throne because on it will sit the great God of the earth, heaven, and hell; *"the King eternal, immortal, invisible"* (1 Timothy 1:17), who will judge the world with righteousness and His people with equity (Psalm 98:9).

Multitudes before the Throne

Beloved, you can see that this will be a *"great white throne"* when you remember the culprits who will be brought before it—not a handful of criminals, but millions upon millions, *"multitudes, multitudes in the valley of decision"* (Joel 3:14). These will not all be of the lesser sort, not just serfs and slaves whose miserable bodies rested from their oppressors in silent graves, but the great ones of the earth will be there. The downtrodden serf who toiled for nothing and felt it sweet to die will not be alone, but his tyrant master who grew fat on his unrewarded toils will be there. The multitudes who marched to battle at their master's bidding and who fell beneath shots and shells will not be alone, but the emperors and kings who planned the conflict will be there, crowned heads no greater than the uncrowned. Men who were demigods among their contemporaries will be mingled with their slaves and will be as vile as they.

What a marvelous procession! With what awe the imagination of it strikes the heart! You who were downtrodden, the great Leveler has put you all upon the same footing now. Death laid you in one equal grave, and now Judgment finds you standing at one equal tribunal, to receive the sentence of One who fears no king and dreads no tyrant, who is *no respecter of persons*" (Acts 10:34), but who metes out justice the same way to all.

Can you picture the sight? Land and sea are covered with the living who once were dead. Hell is empty, and the grave has lost its victims. What a sight that will be! Xerxes, the great king of Persia, with a million parading before him, must have seen a grand spectacle, but what will this be? No flaunting banner, but the colors of eternal majesty. No gaudy courtiers, but assembled angels. No drum beat or cannon roar, but the blast of the archangel's trumpet and the harps of ten thousand times ten thousand holy ones. There will be unrivaled splendor, but not that of heraldry and war. Mere tinsel and baubles will have all vanished. In their place will be the splendor of flashing lightning and the deep bass of thunder. Then, Jesus, the Man of Sorrows, with all His angels, will descend, the pomp of heaven being revealed to the sons of men.

Eternal Judgments from the Throne

It is a Great White Throne because of the matters that will be tried there. These will not be petty quarrels over a suit in litigation or an estate in jeopardy. Our souls will be tried there—our future, not for an age, not for one single century, but forever. Upon those balances will hang heaven and hell. To the right will be distributed triumph without end; to the left, destruction and confusion without pause; and the destiny of every person will be positively declared from that tremendous throne. Can you perceive its greatness? You must comprehend heaven; you must fathom hell; you must measure eternity. Until you do, you will not know the greatness of this Great White Throne.

Remembering the Judgments from the Throne

The throne is great because the transactions of that Day will repeatedly be recalled throughout eternity. Judgment Day will be unto you, you saints, a *"beginning of days"* (Hebrews 7:3), when Christ says to you, *"Come, ye blessed of my Father"* (Matthew 25:34).

That Day will be to you who perish a beginning, too, just as that famous Passover night in Egypt was. When the firstborn were spared in every house where a lamb had shed its blood, it was the first of days to Israel; but to Egypt, the night when the firstborn felt the avenging angel's sword was a dreadful beginning of nights forever. Many a mother counted time from that night when the destroyer came, and throughout eternity, you will likewise calculate from the day when you see the Great White Throne.

The Righteous Judge on the Throne

Do not avert your eyes from the magnificent spectacle until you have seen the glorious Person mentioned in the words, *"and him that sat on it."* I wonder whether anything I have written has made you solemnly ponder the events of that Last Day. I fear I cannot write so as to get at your hearts. But, for a moment, think about Him who sits upon the Great White Throne.

The most fitting One in all the world sits upon that throne. He is God; but, remember, He is also man. *"He will judge the world in righteousness by that man"* (Acts 17:31), wrote Doctor Luke; *"God shall judge by Jesus Christ according to my gospel"* (Romans 2:16), said the apostle Paul. The Judge must be God. Who but God is fit to judge so many and so exactly? The throne is too great for any but Him of whom it is written, *"Thy throne, O God, is for ever and ever: a sceptre of righteousness is the sceptre of thy kingdom"* (Hebrews 1:8).

Christ Jesus, the Son of God, will judge. He will judge as man as well as God. How fitting it is that it should be so! As man, He knows our infirmities (see Hebrews 4:15) and understands our hearts and minds (see 1 Chronicles 28:9), so we cannot object to Him. Our Judge Himself should be like we are. Who could better judge with righteous justice than the One who is *"bone of [our] bones, and flesh of [our] flesh"* (Genesis 2:23)?

And then, there is this rightness about it. He is not only God and man, but He is the Man, the Man of men, of all men the most manly, the type and pattern of manhood. He will be the model in His own person, for if a man is like Christ, that man is righteous, but if a man is other than Christlike, that man deserves to be condemned. That wondrous Judge needs only to look upon His own character to read the law; He needs only to review His own actions to discern whether other men's actions are right or wrong. The thoughts of many hearts were revealed by Christ when He was on earth, and that same Christ will make an open exhibition of men at the great Judgment. He will judge them. He will discern their spirits. He will find out the joints and the marrow of their beings—He will lay bare *the thoughts and intents of the heart* (Hebrews 4:12).

Believer, you will pass before His throne, too. Let no man deceive you with the delusion that you will not be judged. The sheep, as well as the goats, appeared before the Good Shepherd who separated them (see Matthew 25:32–33); those who used their talents were called to account as well as he who buried his (see Matthew 25:14–30); and the disciples themselves were warned that they would account for every idle word at the Judgment (see Matthew 12:36).

You do not need to fear a public trial. Innocence courts the light. You will not be saved by being smuggled into heaven untested and unproved, but you will pass the solemn test with joy in the righteousness of Jesus. The righteous may not be judged at the same time as the wicked (I am not contending about particulars), but I am certain that the righteous will be judged and that Christ's blood has been provided for this very reason, so that they may find the mercy of the Lord in that Day.

O sinner, it is far otherwise for you, for your ruin is sure when the time of testing comes. There will be no witnesses needed to convict you, for the Judge knows all. Jesus Christ, whom you despised, will judge you. The Savior, whose mercy you trampled on, in the fountain of whose blood you would not wash, who was *despised and rejected of men* (Isaiah 53:3)—it is He who will bring righteous justice to you. What will He be able to say but this: *But those mine enemies, which would not that I should reign over them, bring hither, and slay them before me* (Luke 19:27)?

Practical Application of the Vision

At this point, I want to draw the inferences that flow from such a sight as the Great White Throne and thus give John's vision practical relevance.

A Believer's Examination of Self

Believer in Christ, I have a question for you: Can you see the Great White Throne and He who sits upon it? May your response be like this: "I think I see it now. Let me search myself. Whatever profession I may make, I will have to face that Great White Throne. I have been approved by the pastor and the elders. I stand accepted by the church. Still, that Great White Throne is not passed yet. I have borne a reputable character among my fellow Christians. I have prayed in public, and my prayers have been much admired. But, I have not yet been weighed in the last balances. What if I should be found wanting?" (See Daniel 5:27.)

Beloved Christian, what about your private prayers? Can you neglect your prayer closet and yet remember that your prayers will be tried before the Great White Throne? Is your Bible left unread in private? Is your religion nothing but a public show and sham? Remember the Great White Throne, because pretense will not pass there.

Fellow believer, what about your heart and your treasure? Are you merely seeking after material possessions? Do you live as others who are not believers live? Is your delight in the fleeting present? Do you have dealings with the throne of heaven? Have you a stony heart toward divine things? Have you little love for Christ? Do you make an empty profession of faith and nothing more? Oh, think of that Great White Throne!

Some people, when I preach a stirring sermon, feel afraid to come again to hear me. Do searching sermons seem to go through you like a blast of the north wind, chilling you to the marrow and curdling your blood? Friend, if you are afraid of the pastor's voice, how will you bear His voice who will speak in tones of thunder? Oh, what must it be to stand before that dreadful tribunal? Are you doubting now? What will you be then? Can you not bear a little self-examination now? If not, how will you bear that God-examination? If earthly scales tell you that you are wanting, what message will the scales of heaven give you?

I am writing to you as I would address my own heart, and I entreat you, professing Christians, "*Examine yourselves, whether ye be in the faith; prove your own selves. Know ye not your own selves, how that Jesus Christ is in you, except you be reprobates?*" (2 Corinthians 13:5).

Hypocrites

Having directed a word to the Christian, I now write to all of you, in recalling this Great White Throne, to shun hypocrisy. Are you tempted to be baptized, although you are not a believer, in order to please your parents and friends? Beware of that Great White Throne, and think how your insult to God will look at that Last Day! Are you persuaded to put on the cloak of religion and carry on your deceitful masquerade simply because it will help your business or make you seem respectable? Beware, you hypocrite, beware of that Great White Throne.

Of all the terrors that will come forth from it, there will be none more severe than those that will scathe the mere pretender who made a profession of religion for personal gain. If you must be damned, be damned in any way other than as a hypocrite, for they deserve the deepest hell who, for the sake of gain, make a profession of godliness. The ruin of expediency and hypocrisy will be just indeed. O you high-flying professors, whose wings (like those of the mythological Icarus) are fastened on with wax, beware of the sun that will surely pour its heat on you. Fearful will be your fall from so great a height!

Unrepentant Sinners

But there are some of you who say, "I do not make any profession of faith." Nevertheless, our text has a word for you, and I want you to judge your actions by that Last Great Day. O reader, how about that night of sin? "No," you say, "never mind it; do not bring it to my remembrance." But, it will be brought to your remembrance, and that deed of sin will be proclaimed far wider than just from the housetops. It will be spread to all the multitudes who have ever lived since the first man, and your infamy will become *a proverb and a byword among all people* (1 Kings 9:7). What do you think of this, you secret sinners, you lovers of wantonness and debauchery?

Ah, young man, you have commenced by filching, but you will go on to be a downright thief. It is not hidden to all, so *be sure your sin will find you out* (Numbers 32:23). Young woman, you have begun to dally with sin. You think no one has seen you, but the Mighty One has seen your acts and heard your words. There is no curtain between Him and your sin. He sees you clearly, and what will you do with these sins of yours that you think have been concealed? "It was many years ago," you tell me. Yes, but, although buried to you, they are all alive to Him, for everything is present to the all-seeing God. Your forgotten deeds will one day stand out very presently to you, also.

Dear readers, I entreat you to do nothing that you would not do if you thought God was watching you, for He does see you. Look at your actions in the light of the Judgment. That secret drinking of yours, how will that look when God reveals it? That private lust of yours that nobody knows about, how would you dare even think about it if you recollected that God knows it? Young man, it is a secret, a fearful secret, and you would not whisper it in anyone's ear. But, it will be whispered—no, it will be thundered out before the world. I pray that you would think of this. There is an Observer who takes note of all that we do and will publish all to an assembled universe.

As for us all, are we ready to meet that Last Great Day? If tonight the trumpet should be sounded, what would be your state of mind? Suppose that right now every ear should be startled with a loud and dreadful blast, and a voice were heard as it called,

> Come to judgment, come to judgment,
> Come to judgment, come away.

Suppose that some of you could hide in the closets and in the basements, would not many of you rush to find concealment? How few of us might go walking steadily into the open air and saying, "I am not afraid of the Judgment, for '*there is therefore now no condemnation to them which are in Christ Jesus*'" (Romans 8:1)!

Facing Judgment with Assurance

Brothers and sisters, I hope there are some of us who would go gladly to that judgment seat, even if we had to traverse the jaws of death to reach it. I hope there are some of us who can sing this in our hearts:

> Bold shall I stand in that great day;
> For who aught to my charge shall lay?
> While, through thy blood, absolved I am
> From sin's tremendous curse and blame.

Many of us might be very much put out to say that. It is easy to speak of full assurance, but, believe me, it is not quite so easy to have it in absolute earnest in

trying times. If some of you get a finger ache, your confidence oozes out at your joints, and if you have but a little sickness, you think, "Oh, it may be cancer; what will I do?" If you cannot bear to die, how then will you bear to live forever? If you cannot look death in the face without a shudder, then how will you endure the Judgment?

Could you gaze upon death and feel that it is your friend and not your foe? Could you keep a skull on your nightstand and contemplate it as your reminder of death? It may well take the bravest of us to face death so fearlessly. The only sure way to do so is to come as we are to Jesus, with no righteousness of our own to trust in, but finding all we need in Him. (See Philippians 3:9.)

When William Carey[2] was about to die, he ordered this verse to be put on his tombstone:

> A guilty, weak, and helpless worm,
> On Christ's kind arms I fall,
> He is my strength, my righteousness,
> My Jesus, and my all.

I would like to wake up in eternity with such a verse as that in my mind. Likewise, I wish to go to sleep in this world with such a hope as this in my heart:

> Nothing in my hand I bring,
> Simply to the cross I cling.

Time Can Catch You Off Guard

I am referring to themes that you may think are far removed, but just changing your perspective can bring them near to you. A thousand years is a long time, but how soon it flies! While reading English history, we almost seem to go back and shake hands with William the Conqueror. Going further back in time a few more generations quickly brings us to the Flood. As we look backward, millennia seem to be nothing.

You who are approaching the age of fifty, and especially you who are sixty or seventy, must feel how fast time flies. I seem to preach a sermon one Sunday only in time to get ready for the next. Time rushes by with such a whirl that no express train can overtake it, and even a flash of lightning seems to lag behind it.

2. William Carey (1761–1834), missionary to India, called the "father of modern missions."

We will soon be at the Great White Throne. We will soon be at the judgment bar of God. Let us be making ready for it. Let us not live so much in this present time, which is but a dream or an empty shadow, but let us live in the real, substantial future.

Oh, may I reach some heart right now! I have a notion that there is someone reading this who will not have another warning. Who among my readers will it be who will die this week, beyond hope? Ponder the question well! Will you be the one to dwell in the devouring flames if you do not repent right now? Will you abide in everlasting fire? If I knew you, I would willingly cover you with tears. If I knew you who are to die this week, I would find you, kneel down at your side, and urge you to think of eternal things. But I do not know you, and therefore, by the living God, I implore you all to fly to Jesus by faith.

Be Prepared

These are no trifling matters, are they? If they are, I am but a sorry trifler, and you may laugh at me. But, if they are true and real, it suits me to be in earnest, and how much more it will suit you to be so. Prepare to meet your God. He is coming, so prepare now for that Day! *"Behold, now is the accepted time; behold, now is the day of salvation"* (2 Corinthians 6:2). The gates of mercy are not closed. Your sin is not unpardonable. You may yet find mercy. Christ invites you. His blood-drops cry to you:

> Come and welcome,
> Come and welcome, sinner, come.

May the Holy Spirit put life into these simple words of mine, and may the Lord help you to come to Him now. The way to come is just to trust in Christ. It is all done when you trust in Christ. Throw yourselves on Him and His mercy, putting your trust in nothing else.

Just now I am resting my entire weight in a sturdy old chair, but should this chair give way, I would fall. Lean on Christ in that same way. Risk everything with Christ; trust nothing else but Him. If you can get a grip on the cross and stand there beneath the crimson canopy of the atoning blood, God Himself cannot smite you, and the Judgment Day will dawn upon you with splendor and delight, instead of gloom and terror.

Return, O wanderer, to thy home,
Thy Father calls for thee;
No longer now an exile roam
In guilt and misery.
Return, return.

Return, O wanderer, to thy home,
'Tis Jesus calls for thee:
"The Spirit and the bride say, Come,"[3]
Oh, now for refuge flee.
Return, return.

Return, O wanderer, to thy home,
'Tis madness to delay
There are no pardons in the tomb,
And brief is mercy's day.
Return, return.

---

3. Revelation 22:17

3

THE WATCHWORD
FOR TODAY

*For our conversation is in heaven; from whence also we look for the Saviour,
the Lord Jesus Christ: who shall change our vile body, that it may be fashioned
like unto his glorious body, according to the working whereby he is able even
to subdue all things unto himself. Therefore, my brethren, dearly beloved and
longed for, my joy and crown, so stand fast in the Lord, my dearly beloved.*
—Philippians 3:20–4:1

E very doctrine of the Word of God has its practical application. As each
tree bears seed after its kind, so does every truth of God bring forth
practical virtues. Hence, you find the apostle Paul very full of *therefores*—his
therefores being the conclusions drawn from certain statements of divine truth.
I marvel that the early translators who codified the Holy Scriptures divided the
argument from the conclusion by making a new chapter where there is least
reason for it.

I want to remind you of the surest and most certain resurrection of our Lord
Jesus. There is a practical force in that truth, which constitutes part of what is

meant by *"the power of his resurrection"* (Philippians 3:10). Since the Lord has risen, He will surely come a second time, when He will raise the bodies of His people at His return.

That is something to wait for and a grand reason for steadfastness while we are waiting. We are looking for the coming of our Lord and Savior, Jesus Christ, from heaven and anticipating that He will *"change our vile body, that it may be fashioned like unto his glorious body."* Therefore, let us stand fast in the position that will secure us this honor. Let us keep our posts until the coming of the great Captain releases us from our sentinel watch.

Our glorious resurrection will abundantly repay us for all the toil and travail we have to undergo for the Lord in the battle. *"For I reckon that the sufferings of this present time are not worthy to be compared with the glory which shall be revealed in us"* (Romans 8:18). The glory to be revealed even now casts a light upon our path and causes sunshine within our hearts. The hope of this happiness makes us even now *"strong in the Lord, and in the power of his might"* (Ephesians 6:10).

Paul was deeply anxious that those in whom he had been the means of kindling the heavenly hope might be preserved faithful until the coming of Christ. He trembled for fear that any of them should seem to draw back and prove traitors to their Lord. He feared that he might lose, by their turning aside from the faith, what he hoped he had gained. Hence, he urged them to *"stand fast."* Earlier, he had expressed his conviction that He who had begun a good work in them would perform it (Philippians 1:6), but his intense love made him exhort them to *"stand fast in the Lord, my dearly beloved."* In such exhortations, perseverance to the end is promoted and secured.

Paul had fought bravely, and in the case of the Philippian converts, he believed that he had secured the victory, but he feared that it might yet be lost. His words remind me of the death of the British hero, General James Wolfe, who received a fatal wound while commanding his troops from the heights of Quebec, just at the moment when the enemy had begun to flee. When he knew that they were running, a smile was on his face, and he cried, "Hold me up. Let not my brave soldiers see me drop. The day is ours. Oh, do keep it!" His sole anxiety was to make the victory sure. Thus warriors die, and thus Paul lived. His very soul seemed to cry, "We have won the day. Oh, do keep it!"

My beloved, I believe that many of you are *"in the Lord,"* but I entreat you to *"stand fast in the Lord."* In your case, also, the day is won, but, oh, do keep it! That is the essence of all I am about to express to you in this chapter. May the Holy Spirit write it on your hearts!

I entreat those of you who have done all things well so far to obey the exhortation of Jude to *"keep yourselves in the love of God, looking for the mercy of our Lord Jesus Christ unto eternal life"* (Jude 1:21), and to join with me in adoring Him who alone *"is able to keep you from falling, and to present you faultless before the presence of his glory with exceeding joy"* (verse 24). Unto Him be glory forever.

In developing my thoughts on this blessed Scripture passage, I will endeavor to show you certain truths that can easily be discerned. First, it seems to me from the text that Paul perceived that these Philippian Christians were in right relationship with Christ—they were *"in the Lord"*—and in such a position that he could safely bid them to *"stand fast."* Second, he longed that they should maintain their position: *"Stand fast in the Lord, my dearly beloved."* Moreover, he urged them to have the best motives for holding their positions. Finally, I will discuss these motives, which are found in the first two verses of our text.

Start in Right Relationship with Christ

Paul joyfully perceived that his beloved converts were in right relationship with Christ. Indeed, it is very important that we begin well. The beginning is not everything, but it is a great deal. A well-known proverb states, "Well begun is half done." That is certainly so in the things of God. It is vital to *"enter in at the strait gate"* (Matthew 7:13) and to start on the heavenly journey from the right point.

I have no doubt that many slips and falls and apostasies of those professing to be true believers are due to the fact that they were not right at the first. Their foundations were always upon the sand. (See Matthew 7:26–27.) So, it was no more than might have been expected when their houses fell down at last. A flaw in the foundation is pretty sure to be followed by a crack in the superstructure. Do see to it that you lay *"a good foundation against the time to come"* (1 Timothy 6:19). It is better to have no repentance than a repentance that needs to be repented of. It is better to have no faith than a false faith. It is better to make no profession of belief than to make an untruthful one.

May God give us grace that we may not make a mistake in learning the alphabet of godliness, lest in all our learning we continue to blunder and increase in error. We should learn early the difference between grace and merit, between the purpose of God and the will of man, between trust in God and confidence in the flesh. If we do not start correctly, the farther we go, the farther we will be from our desired end, and the more thoroughly in the wrong we will find ourselves. Yes, it is of prime importance that our new birth and our first love should be genuine beyond all question.

The only position, however, in which we can begin correctly is to be "*in the Lord.*" The essential point is that this is the only place to begin from which we may safely proceed. It is a very good thing for Christians to be in the church. However, if you are in the church before you are "*in the Lord,*" you are out of place. It is a good thing to be engaged in holy work. But, if you are doing holy work before you are "*in the Lord,*" you will have no heart for it, and neither will the Lord accept it. It is not essential that you be in this church or in that church, but it is essential that you be "*in the Lord.*" It is not essential that you attend Sunday school or prayer meetings or the missionary society, but it is absolutely essential that you are "*in the Lord.*" Paul rejoiced over those who at Philippi were converted because he knew that they were in the Lord. They were where he desired them to remain. Thus, he urged them, "*Stand fast in the Lord.*"

What does it mean to be "*in the Lord*"? Well, beloved, we are in the Lord vitally and certainly when we come to the Lord Jesus by repentance and faith and make Him our refuge and hiding place. Is it so with you? Have you fled from self? Are you trusting in the Lord alone? Have you come to Calvary and beheld your Savior? As the doves build their nests in the rock, have you likewise made your home in Jesus? There is no shelter for a guilty soul but in His wounded side. Have you come there? Are you in Him? Then stay there. You will never have a better refuge. In fact, there is no other. "*Neither is there salvation in any other: for there is none other name under heaven given among men, whereby we must be saved*" (Acts 4:12).

I cannot tell you to "*stand fast in the Lord*" unless you are in Him. Hence, my first inquiry is, Are you in Christ? Is He your only confidence? In His life, His death, and His resurrection do you find the grounds of your hope? Is He Himself all your salvation and all your desire? If so, "*stand fast in the Lord.*"

In Daily Living

The Philippians, in addition to having fled to Christ for refuge, were now in Christ as to their daily lives. They had heard Him say, "*Abide in me*" (John 15:4), and therefore they remained in the daily enjoyment of Him, in reliance upon Him, in obedience to Him, and in the earnest imitation of His example. They were Christians, that is to say, persons who were identified with the name of Christ. They were endeavoring to realize the power of His death and resurrection as a sanctifying influence, killing their sins and fostering their virtues. They were laboring to reproduce His image in themselves, so that they might bring glory to His name. Their lives were spent within the circle of their Savior's influence.

Are you living as they lived, my dear friends? Then stand fast. You will never find a nobler example. You will never be saturated with a more divine spirit than that of Christ Jesus your Lord. Whatever you eat or drink, or *"whatsoever ye do in word or deed, do all in the name of the Lord Jesus"* (Colossians 3:17), and so live in Him.

In Vital Union with Christ

Moreover, the Philippian believers had realized that they were in Christ by a real and vital union with Him. They had come to feel, not like separated individuals copying a model, but as members of a body, made like their Head. By a living, loving, lasting union they were joined to Christ as their Covenant Head. They could say,

> For I am persuaded, that neither death, nor life, nor angels, nor principalities, nor powers, nor things present, nor things to come, nor height, nor depth, nor any other creature, shall be able to separate us from the love of God, which is in Christ Jesus our Lord. (Romans 8:38–39)

Do you know what it is to experience that the life in you is first in Christ and flows from Him into you, even as the life of the branch is mainly in the stem? *"I live; yet not I, but Christ liveth in me"* (Galatians 2:20). This is what it is to be in Christ. Are you in Him in this sense? Forgive my pressing the question. If your answer is in the affirmative, I entreat you to *"stand fast"* in Him. It is in Him, and in Him only, that spiritual life is to be sustained, even as only from Him can it be received. To be engrafted into Christ is salvation. To abide in Christ is the full enjoyment of it. True union with Christ is eternal life. Paul, therefore, rejoiced over these Philippians, because they were joined to the Lord in one spirit.

Christ, Our Element

The next expression, *"in the Lord,"* is very short, but very full of meaning. Does it not mean that we are in Christ as the birds are in the air, which buoys them up and enables them to fly? Are we not in Christ as the fish are in the sea? Our Lord has become our element, vital and all-surrounding. *"In him we live, and move, and have our being"* (Acts 17:28). He is in us, and we are in Him. We are *"filled with all the fulness of God"* (Ephesians 3:19), because in Christ dwells *"all the fulness of the Godhead bodily"* (Colossians 2:9), and we dwell in Him. Christ to us is all, He is in all, and He is all in all! To us, Jesus is everything in everything. Without Him we can do nothing (see John 15:5), and we are nothing. Thus we are emphatically in Him. If you have attained this kind of relationship, *"stand fast"* in it.

If you dwell in the secret place of the tabernacle of the Most High, abide under the shadow of the Almighty. (See Psalm 91:1.) Do you sit at His table and eat of His banquet? Then prolong the visit, and do not think about leaving. Say in your soul:

> Here would I find a settled rest,
> While others go and come;
> No more a stranger, or a guest,
> But like a child at home.

Has Jesus brought you into His green pastures? Then lie down in them (Psalm 23:2). Go no further, for you will never fare better. Stay with your Lord, however long the night, for only in Him do you have hope of morning.

You see, then, that these people were where they should be, *"in the Lord,"* and that this was the reason why the apostle Paul took such delight in them. See how he loved them and rejoiced over them: *"Therefore, my brethren, dearly beloved and longed for, my joy and crown, so stand fast in the Lord, my dearly beloved."* He heaped titles of love on them! Some dip their morsels in vinegar, but Paul's words were saturated with honey. Here, we not only have sweet words, but they also mean something. His love was real and fervent. Paul's heart is spelled out plainly in this verse.

Spiritual Family

Because they were in Christ, they therefore were Paul's *"brethren."* This was a new relationship, not earthly, but heavenly. What did this Jew from Tarsus know about the Philippians? Many of them were Gentiles. There had been a time when he would have called them dogs and despised them as the uncircumcised, but now he addressed them as *"my brethren."*

Lately, that poor word has become very hackneyed. We talk of "our brethren" without particularly having much brotherly love for them. True brothers have a love for one another that is very unselfish and admirable. Thus, a brotherhood exists between real Christians that they will neither disown nor dissemble nor forget. Scripture says of our Lord:

> *For both he that sanctifieth and they who are sanctified are all of one: for which cause he is not ashamed to call them brethren.*   (Hebrews 2:11)

Surely, therefore, believers should never be ashamed to call one another brethren. Paul, at any rate, looked at the jailer, the jailer who had set his feet in the stocks, and he looked at the jailer's family, at Lydia, and many others—in fact, at the whole company that he had gathered at Philippi— and saluted them lovingly as *"my brethren."* Their names were written in the same family register because they were in Christ, and therefore had one Father in heaven.

Dearly Beloved

Next, Paul called them, *"my dearly beloved."* Philippians 4:1 nearly begins with these words, and the verse quite finishes with them. The repetition imparts the meaning of "my doubly dear ones." Such is the love that every true servant of Christ will have for those who have been begotten into the faith of Christ by the servant's ministry. Yes, if you are in Christ, His ministers love you. How could there be a lack of affection in our hearts toward you, especially if we have been the means of bringing you to Jesus? Without hypocrisy or display, we call you our *"dearly beloved."*

Longed For

Then, the apostle called them his *"longed for,"* that is, his most desired ones. He first desired to see them converted. After that, he desired to see them baptized. Then, he desired to see them exhibiting all the graces of Christians. When

Paul saw holiness in them, he longed to visit and commune with them. Their constant kindness created in him a strong desire to speak with them face to face. He loved them and longed for their company because they were in Christ, so he spoke of them as those for whom he yearned. His delight was in thinking of them and in hoping to visit them.

A Joy and Crown

Following this, Paul called them *"my joy and crown."* Paul had been the means of their salvation. When he thought of that blessed result, he never regretted all that he had suffered. His persecutions among the Gentiles seemed light indeed, since these priceless souls were his reward. Although he was nothing but a poor prisoner of Christ, he talked in a royal style—to him they were his crown.

To Paul, the Philippians were his *stephanos*, which in Greek customs was a special crown given as an honored prize in the public games. Among the Greeks this was usually a wreath of flowers placed around the victor's brow. Paul's crown would never fade. He wrote as if he felt the never-fading amaranth on his temples. Even then, he viewed the Philippians as his wreath of honor. They were his joy and his crown. He anticipated, I do not doubt, that throughout eternity it would be a part of his heaven to see them amid their blessedness and to know that he helped to bring them to that bliss by leading them to Christ.

Beloved, it is indeed the highest joy of an ambassador for Christ that he has *"not run in vain, neither laboured in vain"* (Philippians 2:16). You who *"were as a firebrand plucked out of the burning"* (Amos 4:11) and are now living to the praise of our Lord Jesus Christ, you are the prize, the crown, the joy, of the one who was instrumental in bringing you to Christ.

Stay in Right Relationship

These converts were all this to Paul simply because they were *"in Christ."* They had begun well, they were where they should be, and so he rejoiced in them. For this reason Paul longed that they would stay there, so he exhorted them to remain where they were: *"So stand fast in the Lord, my dearly beloved."*

The beginning of faith is not the whole of it. You must not suppose that the sum of the Christian life is contained within the experience of a day or two, or a week, or a few months, or even a few years. Precious are the feelings that attend conversion, but do not dream that repentance, faith, and so forth, are just for a season, and then all is over and done with. I fear there are some who secretly think, "Everything is now complete. I have experienced the necessary change; I have been to see the elders and the pastor; I have been baptized and received into the church. Thus, everything with me is right forever." That is a false view of your condition.

Finish the Course

In conversion you have started the race, and you must run to the end of the course. In your confession of Christ, you have carried your tools into the vineyard, but the day's work now begins. Remember that *"he that shall endure unto the end, the same shall be saved"* (Matthew 24:13).

Godliness is a lifelong business. It is not a matter for a certain number of hours or for a limited period of life that we are to work out the salvation that the Lord is working in us. (See Philippians 2:12–13.) Salvation is unfolded throughout our entire sojourn here. We continue to repent and to believe, and even the process of our salvation continues as we are changed more and more into the image of our Lord. (See 2 Corinthians 3:18.) Enduring perseverance throughout the life span is the necessary evidence of genuine conversion.

As ministers rejoice over converts, we likewise feel an intense sorrow when any disappoint us and turn out to be merely temporary camp followers. We sigh over the seed that sprang up so speedily but that withered so soon because it had neither root nor depth. (See Matthew 13:20–21.) We were ready to say, "Ring the bells of heaven," but the bells of heaven did not chime because these people talked about Christ and said they were in Christ, but it was all a delusion. After a while, for one reason and another, they turned back to their old ways.

> *They went out from us, but they were not of us; for if they had been of us, they would no doubt have continued with us: but they went out, that they might be made manifest that they were not all of us.* (1 John 2:19)

Our churches suffer most seriously from the great numbers who drop out of their ranks. They either go back to the world or else must be pursuing a very secret and solitary path on their way to heaven, for we hear no more of them. Our joy is turned to disappointment, our crown of laurel becomes a circle of decaying leaves, and we are sorrowful at the remembrance of it. With great earnestness, therefore, we exhort you who are beginning the race: "Continue on your course. Neither turn aside nor slacken your running until you have won the prize."

I heard an expression recently that pleased me very much. I had spoken about the difficulty of keeping in the faith. "Yes," answered my friend, "and it is harder still to keep on keeping on." So it is. There is the hitch. I know lots of fellows who are wonders at the outset. With what a rush they start! But, there is no staying power in them. They soon lose their breath.

The difference between the spurious and the real Christian lies in his ability to stay on the course. The real Christian has a life within him that can never die, an incorruptible seed that lives and abides forever. (See 1 Peter 1:23.) In contrast, the spurious Christian starts the same, but stops almost as soon as he begins. He is esteemed as a saint, but he turns out to be a hypocrite. He makes a show for awhile, but soon he quits the way of holiness and makes his own damnation sure. God save you, dear ones, from anything that looks like apostasy. Hence, I press upon you these two weighty words: "Stand fast."

Hold to the Essential Doctrines

I exhort you to stand fast doctrinally. In this age all the ships in the waters are pulling up their anchors; they are drifting with the tide; they are driven about by every wind. It is wisdom to put down more anchors. I have taken the precaution for myself to cast four anchors out of the stern, as well as to see that the great Anchor at the bow of the ship is in its proper place. I will not budge an inch from the essential doctrines for any man.

Now that the cyclone is triumphant over many a crumbling wall and tottering fence, those who are built upon the one sure Foundation (see 1 Corinthians 3:11) must prove its value by standing fast. We will hearken to no teaching but that of the Lord Jesus. If you see a truth in God's Word, grasp it by your faith. Even if it is unpopular, fasten it to you with hooks of steel. If you are despised as a fool for holding it, grasp it more firmly. Like an oak, take deeper root, because the winds would tear you from your place. Defy reproach and ridicule, and you will have already vanquished it.

"Stand fast," as the British squadrons did in prior times. When fierce assaults were made upon them, every man seemed to have been transformed into rock. In more gleeful times we might have wandered a little from the ranks to look after the fascinating flowers that grow on every side of our march. However, now that we know the Enemy surrounds us, we must keep strictly to the line of march and tolerate no roaming. The watchword of the host of God in these times is, "*Stand fast.*" "*Earnestly contend for the faith which was once delivered unto the saints*" (Jude 1:3). Hold fast to sound words, and deviate not one iota from there. Doctrinally, stand fast!

Stand Fast Practically

Practically, also, abide firm in the right, the true, the holy. This is of the utmost importance. The barriers have been broken down. Some want to intermix the church and the world—yes, even the church and the theater. It has been proposed to prostitute God with the devil in one service. Christ and Belial are to perform on one stage. Surely, now is the time when "*the lion shall eat straw like the ox*" (Isaiah 11:7), and very dirty straw, too.

I caution you: "*Come out from among them, and be ye separate, saith the Lord, and touch not the unclean thing*" (2 Corinthians 6:17). Write "HOLINESS UNTO THE LORD" (Zechariah 14:20) not only on your altars, but upon the bells of the horses. Let everything be done as before the living God. Do all things in holiness and edification. Strive together to maintain the purity of the disciples of Christ, take up your cross, and "*go forth unto him without the camp, bearing his reproach*" (Hebrews 13:13).

If you have already stood apart in your decision for the Lord, continue to do so. "*Stand fast.*" In nothing be moved by the laxity of the age or affected by the current of modern opinion. Just say to yourself, "I will do as Christ bids me, to the utmost of my ability. I will follow the Lamb wherever He leads." In these times of worldliness, impurity, self-indulgence, and error, the Christian is wise to roll up his pant legs and keep his feet and his clothes clean from the pollution that lies all around him. We must be more particular and precise than we have been. Oh, for grace to "*stand fast*"!

Stand Fast Experientially

Also, you need to stand fast as to your experience. Pray that your inward encounter may be a close attachment to your Master. Do not go astray from His presence. Neither climb with those who dream of perfection in the flesh, nor grovel with those who doubt the possibility of present salvation. Take Jesus Christ to be your sole treasure, and let your heart be ever with Him. Stand fast in faith in His Atonement, in confidence in His divinity, and in assurance of His Second Advent.

I yearn to know in my soul *"the power of his resurrection"* (Philippians 3:10) and to have unbroken fellowship with Him, even in sharing His sufferings. In communion with the Father, the Son, and the Holy Spirit, let us *"stand fast."* The person whose heart and soul, affections and understanding, are totally wrapped up in Christ Jesus will fare well. Concerning your inward life, your secret prayer, your walk with God, here is the watchword of the day: *"Stand fast."*

Stand Fast with Complete Trust

To put it very plainly, *"Stand fast in the Lord,"* without looking for another source to trust. Do not desire to have any hope but that which is in Christ. Do not entertain the proposition that you should unite another confidence to your confidence in the Lord. Have no hankering for any other kind of faith except the faith of a sinner in his Savior. All hope but that which is set before us in the gospel and brought to us by the Lord Jesus is a poisoned delicacy, highly flavored, but by no means to be so much as tasted by those who have been fed the bread of heaven.

What do we need other than Jesus? What way of salvation do we seek but that of grace? What security do we have but the precious blood? *"Stand fast,"* and wish for no other *"rock of our salvation"* (Psalm 95:1) except the Lord Jesus.

Stand Fast Unwaveringly

Next, stand fast without wavering. Permit no doubt to worry you. Know that Jesus can save you, and, even more, know that He has saved you. Commit yourself totally into His hands, so that you may be as sure of your salvation as of your existence. This day *"the blood of Jesus Christ his Son cleanseth us from all sin"* (1 John 1:7). His righteousness covers us, and His life quickens us unto *"newness of life"* (Romans 6:4). Tolerate no suspicion, mistrust, doubt, or misgiving. Believe in the Lord Jesus Christ completely.

As for myself, I will yield to be lost forever if Jesus does not save me. I will have no other string to my bow, no second door of hope or way of retreat. I could risk a thousand souls on my Lord's truth and feel no risk. Stand fast, without wavering in the trust you have.

Stand Fast in Purity

Moreover, stand fast without wandering into sin. You are tempted this way and that way, but *"stand fast."* Inward passions rise. Lusts of the flesh rebel. The devil hurls his fearful suggestions. The people of your own household tempt you. Nevertheless, *"stand fast."* Only in this way will you be preserved from the torrents of iniquity. Keep close to the example and spirit of your Master, and *"having done all, [still] stand"* (Ephesians 6:13).

Stand Fast Tirelessly

As I have exhorted you to stand fast without wandering, so next I must encourage you to stand fast without growing weary. (See 2 Thessalonians 3:13.) You are tired. Never mind. Take a little rest and brush up again. You say, "this toil is so monotonous." Do it better, and that will be a change. Your Savior endured His life and labor without this complaint, for zeal had consumed Him. (See John 2:17.) "Alas!" you cry, "I cannot see results." Never mind. Wait for results, even as the husbandman waits for the precious fruits of the earth. "I plod along and make no progress," you say. Never mind. You are a poor judge of your own success. Work on, for *"in due reason we shall reap, if we faint not"* (Galatians 6:9).

Practice perseverance. Remember that if you have the work of faith and the labor of love, you must complete the trio with the addition of the patience of hope. (See 1 Thessalonians 1:3.) You cannot go on without this last thing.

> *Therefore, my beloved brethren, be ye stedfast, unmoveable, always abounding in the work of the Lord, forasmuch as ye know that your labour is not in vain in the Lord.* (1 Corinthians 15:58)

I am reminded of Sir Christopher Wren, the great English architect, when he cleared away old St. Paul's to make room for his splendid new edifice. He was compelled to use battering rams against the massive walls. The workmen kept on battering and battering. An enormous force was brought to bear on the walls for many days and nights, but it did not appear to have made the least impression on the ancient masonry. Yet, the wise architect knew what he was doing. He instructed the workmen to keep on incessantly. Thus, the ram fell again and again against the rocky wall until, at length, the whole mass was disintegrating and coming apart. Then, the results of each stroke began to show. At one blow it reeled, at another it quivered, with the next it moved visibly, and with the final impact it fell over amid clouds of dust. Do you think these last strokes did all the work? No, it was the combination of blows, the first as truly as the last. Keep on with the battering ram.

I hope to keep on until I die. Mark you, I may die without seeing the errors of the hour totter and fall, but I will be perfectly content to sleep in Christ, for I have a sure expectation that this work will succeed in the end. I will be happy to have done my share, even if I personally see little apparent results.

Lord, let Your unseen work be apparent to Your servants, and we will be content that Your glory should be reserved for our children. *"Stand fast,"* my beloved, in incessant labors, for the results are sure.

Stand Fast without Distortion

In addition to standing fast tirelessly, stand fast without allowing your faith to become distorted. Timber, when it is rather green, is apt to bend this way or that. The spiritual weather is very bad just now for green wood. One day it is damp with superstition; another it is parched with skepticism. Rationalism and ritualism are both at work. I pray that you may not warp. Keep straight. Keep to the truth, the whole truth, and nothing but the truth, for in the Master's name we bid you, *"Stand fast in the Lord."*

"Stand fast," for there is great need. *"Many walk, of whom I have told you often, and now tell you even weeping, that they are the enemies of the cross of Christ"* (Philippians 3:18).

Strive to Stand Fast

Paul urged the saints at Philippi to stand fast because, even in his own case, spiritual life was a struggle. Paul had written to them, *"Not as though I had already attained, either were already perfect"* (Philippians 3:12). He was pressing forward. He was straining with all of his energy by the power of the Holy Spirit. He did not expect to be carried to heaven on a feather bed. He was warring and agonizing. You, beloved, must do the same.

What a grand example of perseverance Paul set for us all! Nothing enticed him from his steadfastness. *"None of these things move me, neither count I my life dear unto myself"* (Acts 20:24). He has entered into his rest, because the Lord his God helped him to maintain his stance to the end. Most earnestly, from the depths of my soul, I implore you with this: "*Stand fast in the Lord, my dearly beloved.*"

The Best Motivation for Standing Fast

Paul also urged the Philippians to have the right reasons for standing fast. He knew that no matter how their behavior appeared to others, "*man looketh on the outward appearance, but the LORD looketh on the heart*" (1 Samuel 16:7). Further, he was concerned that they follow the biblical mandate that "*whatsoever ye do, do all to the glory of God*" (1 Corinthians 10:31) and not for personal, fleshly motives.

Heavenly Citizenship

First of all, Paul urged them to stand fast because of their citizenship: "*For our citizenship is in heaven*" (Philippians 3:20 RV). If you are in Christ, you are citizens of the New Jerusalem. (See Revelation 3:12.) Men ought to behave themselves according to their citizenship and not dishonor their country.

When a man was a citizen of ancient Athens, he felt it incumbent upon him to be brave. Xerxes[4] said, "These Athenians are not ruled by kings; how will they fight?" "No, they are not," the reply came, "but every man respects the law, and each man is ready to die for his country."

Xerxes soon learned that the same obedience and respect of law ruled the Spartans, and that they, because they were of Sparta, were all brave as lions. He sent word to Leonidas[5] and his little troop to give up their arms. "Come and take them" was the courageous reply. The Persian king had myriads of soldiers with him, while Leonidas had only three hundred Spartans at his side. Yet, the Spartans held the pass. It cost the Persian despot many thousands of men to force a passage. The sons of Sparta died rather than desert their post. Every citizen of Sparta felt that he must stand fast: it was not for such a man as he to yield.

I like the spirit of Bayard, that sixteenth century French knight who was without fear and without reproach. He did not know what fear meant. In his last battle, his spine was broken, and he said to those around him, "Place me up against a tree, so that I may sit up and die with my face to the enemy."

---

4. Xerxes the Great, king of Persia from 486–465 B.C.
5. Leonidas: Greek hero, king of Sparta from around 490–480 B.C.

Yes, if our backs were broken, if we could no more bear the shield or use the sword, it would be incumbent upon us, as citizens of the New Jerusalem, to die with our faces toward the Enemy. We must not yield, we dare not yield, if we are of *"the city of the great King"* (Psalm 48:2). The martyrs urge us to stand fast; the *"cloud of witnesses"* (Hebrews 12:1), bending from their thrones above, beseech us to stand fast; all the shining, heavenly hosts cry to us, *"Stand fast."* Stand fast for God, the truth, and holiness, and let no man take your crown.

With a View toward Christ's Return

The next matter Paul brought up was their outlook. *"Our conversation is in heaven; from whence also we look for the Saviour, the Lord Jesus Christ."* Beloved, Jesus is coming. He is even now on the way. You have heard the tidings until you scarcely give them credence; but the word is true, and it will surely be fulfilled before long. The Lord is coming indeed. He promised to come to die, and He kept His word. He now promises to come to reign, and you can be sure that He will keep His trust with His people. He is coming. Ears of faith can hear the sound of His chariot wheels approaching. Every moment of time and every event of providence bring Him nearer. Blessed will be those servants who are not sleeping when He returns, nor who are wandering from their posts of duty. Happy will they be whom the Lord finds faithfully watching and standing fast in that Last Day. (See Luke 12:37.)

To us, beloved, Christ is coming, not as Judge and Destroyer, but as Savior. We look for the Savior, the Lord Jesus Christ. Now, if we do look for Him, let us *"stand fast."* There must be no going into sin, no forsaking the fellowship of the church, no leaving the truth, no trying to play fast and loose with godliness, no running with the hares and hunting with the hounds. Let us stand so fast in singleness of heart that, whenever Jesus comes, we can joyously cry, "Welcome, welcome, Son of God!"

Sometimes I wait through the weary years with great comfort. There was a ship some time ago outside a certain harbor. A heavy sea made the ship roll fearfully. A dense fog blotted out all buoys and lights. The captain never left the wheel. He could not make his way into the harbor, and for a long time no pilot could get out to him from the harbor. Eager passengers urged him to be courageous and make a dash for the harbor. He said, "No, it is not my duty to run so great a risk. A pilot is required here, and I will wait for one if I wait a week."

The truest courage is that which can bear to be charged with cowardice. To wait is much wiser than to steam on and wreck your vessel on the rocks when you cannot hear the foghorn and have no pilot. Our prudent captain waited his time, and at last he spied the pilot's boat coming to him over the turbulent sea. When the pilot went to work, the captain's anxious waiting was over.

The church is like that vessel, pitched to and fro in the dark storm, and the pilot has not yet come. The weather is very threatening. All around, the darkness hangs like a pall, but Jesus will come before long, walking on the water. He will bring us safely to the desired haven. Let us wait with patience. *"Stand fast."* Jesus is coming, and in Him is our sure hope.

Great Expectations

Further, Paul supplied another true motive, an expectation. *"Christ shall change our vile body,"* or literally, "the body of our humiliation." Think of it, dear friends! No more headaches or heartaches, no more feebleness and fainting, no more inner tumors or tuberculosis. Rather, the Lord will transfigure this body of humiliation into the likeness of the body of His glory.

Our frames are now made up of decaying substances. These bodies are *"of the earth, earthy"* (1 Corinthians 15:47). Our bodies groan, suffer, become diseased, and die. Blessed be God, we will be wonderfully changed, and then *"there shall be no more death, neither sorrow, nor crying, neither shall there be any more pain"* (Revelation 21:4).

The natural appetites of this body engender sad tendencies to sin, and in this respect it is a *"vile body."* It will not always be so. The great change will deliver it from all that is unseemly and carnal. It will be as pure as the Lord's body! Whatever the body of Christ is now, our bodies will be like it. After His resurrection, He said to His disciples, *"Handle me, and see; for a spirit hath not flesh and bones, as ye see me have"* (Luke 24:39). Each of us will have a real, corporeal body, just as Christ's body now has physical substance. Like His body, it will be full of beauty, full of health and strength. It will enjoy unique immunities from evil and special adaptations for good. That is what is going to happen to us.

Therefore, let us stand firm in our belief, *"which is Christ in you, the hope of glory"* (Colossians 1:27). Let us not willingly throw away our prospects of glory and immortality. What! Relinquish resurrection and glory? Relinquish likeness to the risen Lord? O God, save us from such terrible apostasy! Save us from such immeasurable folly! Do not allow us to retreat in the day of battle, since that would be to turn our backs away from the crown of glory that does not fade away (1 Peter 5:4).

Vast Resources of Strength

The apostle Paul then urged the Philippians (and us) to stand fast because of the resources in Christ. Someone may ask, "How can this body of yours be transformed and transfigured so that it becomes like the body of Christ?" I cannot tell you anything about the process. It will all be accomplished *"in a moment, in the twinkling of an eye, at the last trump"* (1 Corinthians 15:52). But, I can tell you by what power it will be accomplished. The omnipotent Lord will bare His arm and exercise His might, *"according to the working whereby he is able even to subdue all things unto himself."*

Beloved, we may well stand fast, since we have infinite power backing us. The Lord is with us with all His energy, even with His all-conquering strength, which will yet subdue all His foes. Do not imagine that any enemy can be too strong for Christ's arm. Since *"he is able even to subdue all things unto himself,"* He can certainly bear us through all opposition. A single glance of His eye may wither all opposers, or, better still, one word from His lips may turn them into friends.

The army of the Lord is strong in reserves. These reserves have never yet been fully called out. We who are in the field are only a small squadron, holding the fort, but our Lord has at His back ten thousand times ten thousand who will carry war into the Enemy's camp. When the Captain of Salvation comes to the front, He will bring His heavenly legions with Him. Our business is to watch until He appears upon the scene. (See Matthew 24:42.) When He comes, His infinite resources will be put in marching order.

I like that speech of Wellington[6] (who was so calm amid the roar of Waterloo), when an officer had sent this word: "Tell the Commander in Chief that he must move me. I cannot hold my position any longer, because my numbers have been so thinned." The great general replied, "Tell him he must hold his place. Every Englishman today must die where he stands or else win the victory." The officer read the command to hold his position, and he did stand until the trumpet sounded victory.

---

6. Wellington: Arthur Wellesley (1769–1852), British general and statesman, first Duke of Wellington.

So it is with us now. My fellow soldiers, we must die where we are rather than yield to the Enemy. If Jesus tarries, we must not desert our posts. Wellington knew that the heads of the Prussian columns would soon be visible, coming in to ensure the victory. Likewise, by faith we can perceive the legions of our Lord approaching. In staggered ranks, His angels fly through as the heavens open. The air is teeming with them. I hear their silver trumpets. Behold, He comes with clouds! When He comes, He will abundantly recompense all who have stood fast amid the raging battle.

4

THE FINAL JUDGMENT

For we must all appear before the judgment seat of Christ;
that every one may receive the things done in his body,
according to that he hath done, whether it be good or bad.
—2 Corinthians 5:10

I now want to address what follows immediately after the resurrection of the dead, namely, the final Judgment. The dead will be raised on purpose, so that they may be judged in their bodies. Their resurrection will be the immediate prelude to the Judgment.

There is no need for me to try to prove to you from Scripture that this great Judgment will occur, for the Word of God abounds with passages that reveal this truth. You find them throughout the Old Testament. The psalmists anticipated that great Judgment in the Psalms (especially in Psalms 9, 49, 50, 72, 96–98, and 110), for most assuredly the Lord is coming again. *"And he shall judge the world in righteousness, he shall minister judgment to the people in uprightness"* (Psalm 9:8). Because God will judge every secret thing, Solomon issued this very solemn, yet tender warning:

Rejoice, O young man, in thy youth; and let thy heart cheer thee in the days of thy youth, and walk in the ways of thine heart, and in the sight of thine eyes: but know thou, that for all these things God will bring thee into judgment.

(Ecclesiastes 11:9)

In night visions Daniel beheld the Son of Man coming with the clouds of heaven and drawing near to the Ancient of Days. Then he saw that the Messiah was given everlasting dominion over all, and the nations gathered before Him to be judged. (See Daniel 7:13–14.) This was no new doctrine to the Jews. It was received and accepted by them as a most certain fact that there would be a Day in which God would judge the earth in righteousness.

The New Testament is very expressive about the coming Judgment. The twenty-fifth chapter of Matthew contains language, from the lips of the Savior Himself, that could not possibly be more clear and definite:

When the Son of man shall come in his glory, and all the holy angels with him, then shall he sit upon the throne of his glory: and before him shall be gathered all nations: and he shall separate them one from another, as a shepherd divideth his sheep from the goats: and he shall set the sheep on his right hand, but the goats on the left. Then shall the King say unto them on his right hand, Come, ye blessed of my Father, inherit the kingdom prepared for you from the foundation of the world. Then shall he say also unto them on the left hand, Depart from me, ye cursed, into everlasting fire, prepared for the devil and his angels. And these shall go away into everlasting punishment: but the righteous into life eternal. (Matthew 25:31–34, 41, 46)

"Jesus Christ, who is the faithful witness" (Revelation 1:5), "will not lie" (Proverbs 14:5). He said that all nations will gather before Him, and He will divide them one from the other, as a shepherd divides the sheep from the goats.

An abundance of other New Testament passages are plain enough. One that I will quote is the entire passage containing our text verse, found in the apostle Paul's second letter to the Thessalonians:

And to you who are troubled rest with us, when the Lord Jesus shall be revealed from heaven with his mighty angels, in flaming fire taking vengeance on them that know not God, and that obey not the gospel of our Lord Jesus

Christ: who shall be punished with everlasting destruction from the presence of the Lord, and from the glory of his power; when he shall come to be glorified in his saints, and to be admired in all them that believe (because our testimony among you was believed) in that day. (2 Thessalonians 1:7–10)

As we discovered in a previous chapter, Revelation is very graphic in its depiction of the Judgment. The prophet of Patmos wrote:

And I saw a great white throne, and him that sat on it, from whose face the earth and the heaven fled away; and there was found no place for them. And I saw the dead, small and great, stand before God; and the books were opened: and another book was opened, which is the book of life: and the dead were judged out of those things which were written in the books, according to their works. (Revelation 20:11–12)

Space would fail me if I referred you to all the Scriptures that point to the Judgment. You will find that the Holy Spirit, whose word is truth (see John 17:17), repeatedly has asserted that the great Judgment of *"the quick and the dead"* (2 Timothy 4:1; 1 Peter 4:5) will occur.

Besides that direct testimony, it should be remembered there is a cogent argument that it must occur because God, as the Ruler over men, is absolutely just. In all human governments, courts of justice must exist. Government cannot be conducted without its days of session and of trial. Thus, inasmuch as sin and evil are clearly in this world, it might fairly be anticipated that there will be a time when God will sit on the judgment seat. Then He will call the prisoners before Him, and the guilty will receive their condemnation.

But, decide for yourselves: Is this present state the conclusion of all things? If so, what evidence would you cite of divine justice, in face of the fact that the best of men in this world are often the poorest and most afflicted, while the worst acquire wealth, practice oppression, and receive the crowd's homage? Who are they who *"ride upon the high places of the earth"* (Isaiah 58:14)? They must be those who

> Wade through slaughter to a throne
> And shut the gates of mercy on mankind.

Where are the servants of God? They are in obscurity and often suffering. Do they not sit like Job among the ashes, subjects of little pity, objects of much upbraiding? And where are the enemies of God? Are not many of them *"clothed in purple and fine linen and* [faring] *sumptuously every day"* (Luke 16:19)? If there is no hereafter, then those rich men have the best of it, and the selfish man who does not fear God, is, after all, the wisest of men and more to be commended than his fellows. (See Luke 16:8–9.)

However, it cannot be so. Our common sense revolts against the thought. There must be another state in which these anomalies will all be rectified. *"If in this life only we have hope in Christ, we are of all men most miserable"* (1 Corinthians 15:19), wrote the apostle. In those times of persecution, the best of men were driven to the worst of straits for being God's servants. Would you then apply the inscription, *Finis coronat opus*, which means "the end crowns the work"? That cannot be the final issue of life, or justice itself is frustrated. There must be a restitution for those who suffer unjustly. There must be a punishment for the wicked and the oppressor.

Not only can this be affirmed from a general sense of justice, but there is also in the conscience of most men, if not of all, an assent to this fact. As an old Puritan said,

God holds a petty session in every man's conscience, which is the earnest of the assize [judgment] which He will hold by and by; for almost all men judge themselves, and their conscience knows this to be wrong and that to be right. I say "almost all," for there seems to be in this generation a race of men who have so stultified their conscience that the spark appears to have gone out, and they put bitter for sweet and sweet for bitter. The lie they seem to approve, but the truth they do not recognize. But let conscience alone and do not stupefy her, and you shall find her bearing witness that there is a Judge of all the earth who must do right.

Now, this is truly the case when the conscience is fully active. Men who are busy with their work or entertained with their pleasures often keep their consciences quiet. As John Bunyan put it, they shut up Mr. Conscience, blind his windows, and barricade his doors. As for the great bell on the top of the house that the old gentleman loved to ring, they cut the bell rope so that he cannot get at it, for they do not wish him to disturb the town of Mansoul. But when death approaches, it often happens that Mr. Conscience escapes from his prison. Then, I warrant you, he makes such a din that there is not a sleeping head in all of

Mansoul. He cries out and avenges himself for his constrained silence, making the man know that there is a something within him that is not quite dead, which still demands justice, and that sin cannot go unchastised.

There must be a Judgment, then. The fact that Scripture asserts it should be enough to firmly establish that there will be a final Day of Judgment. But, by way of collateral evidence, we find that the natural order of things requires it and, additionally, that our consciences attest to it.

Now we come to consider what our text says about the Judgment. I pray you, beloved, if I write coldly about this momentous truth, or fail to excite your attention and stir your deepest emotions, forgive me. May God forgive me also, because I would have good reason to ask His forgiveness; this topic, above all, should arouse my zeal for the honor of the Lord and for the welfare of my fellow creatures, stirring me to be doubly in earnest. However, if ever there were a theme that did not depend on my ability to write convincingly (which alone should command your attention), it is that which I now bring before you. I feel no need of well-selected words. The mere mention of the fact that such a Judgment is impending and will occur before long might well hold you in breathless silence, arrest the throbbing of your pulse, and choke the utterance of your lips. The certainty of it, the reality of it, the terrors that accompany it, the impossibility of escaping from it, all appeal to us now and demand our vigilance.

Who Must Appear?

Now, we will explore the question, Who will have to appear before the throne of judgment? The answer in our text is plain and allows for no exemption: "*We must all appear before the judgment seat of Christ.*" This is very decisive, even if there were no other reference to it. "*We must all appear,*" that is, everyone of the human race must appear. That the godly will not be exempted from this appearance is very clear, for the apostle is speaking here to Christians. He said, "*We walk by faith, not by sight*" (2 Corinthians 5:7); "*We are confident*" (verse 8); "*We labour*" (verse 9); and then, "*We must all appear.*" So, disregarding all others, it is certain that all Christians must appear there. The text is quite explicit on that point.

If we did not have the Corinthian passage, we still have the one in Matthew, previously cited, in which the sheep are summoned to the judgment seat as certainly as the goats are. (See Matthew 25:31–46.) We also have the passage in Revelation 20:12–13, where all the dead are judged according to the things that are written in God's books.

Right now, someone who is reading this is probably thinking, "I thought that the sins of the righteous, having been pardoned and forever blotted out, would never come into the Judgment." May I remind you, beloved, that if they are so pardoned and blotted out—as they undoubtedly are—the righteous have no reason to fear coming into the Judgment. They are the people who covet the Judgment and will be able to stand there to receive a public acquittal from the mouth of the great Judge. Who among us wishes, as it were, to be smuggled into heaven unlawfully? Who desires to have it said by those who are damned in hell, "You were never tried, or else you might have been condemned as we were."

O beloved, we have a hope that we can stand the trial. The way of righteousness by Christ Jesus enables us to submit ourselves to the most tremendous tests, which even that burning Day will bring forth. We should not be afraid to be weighed in the scales of justice. We even desire that Day when our faith in Jesus Christ is strong and firm. We can say, "*Who is he that condemneth?*" (Romans 8:34). We can challenge the Day of Judgment. "*Who shall lay any thing to the charge of God's elect*" (Romans 8:33) in that Day, or at any other, since Christ has died and has risen again?

It is necessary that the righteous be present so that there is not any partiality in the matter whatsoever, that the verdicts may be all clear and straight, and that the rewards of the righteous may be seen to be without any violation of the most rigorous justice, even though the rewards are all of grace.

Dearly beloved, what a Day it will be for the righteous! For some of them were—perhaps some reading this are—lying under some very terrible accusation of which they are perfectly guiltless. All will be cleared up then, and that will be one great blessing of the Judgment Day. There will be a resurrection of reputations as well as of bodies. In this world, the righteous are called fools; at the Judgment, they will "*shine forth as the sun in the kingdom of their Father*" (Matthew 13:43). Ungodly men have hounded the righteous to death as not being fit to live. In early ages they laid on Christians charges of the most terrible character, which I would be ashamed to mention, but on that Day their reputations will all be cleared.

Those "*of whom the world was not worthy*" (Hebrews 11:38), who were driven and hunted and forced to dwell in caves, will come forth as worthy ones. The world will know her true aristocracy. Earth will acknowledge her true nobility. The men whose names she cast out as evil will then be held in great repute, for they will stand out clear and transparent without spot or blemish. (See Ephesians 5:27.) It is good that there should be a trial for the righteous, for the clearing and vindication of their names, and that it should be public, defying the censure and criticism of all mankind.

"*We must all appear.*" What a vast assembly, what a prodigious gathering—that of the entire human race! As I was meditating on this subject, I wondered what the thoughts of Father Adam will be, as he stands there with Mother Eve and looks upon his offspring. It will be the first time in which he will ever have the opportunity of seeing all his children gathered together. What a sight he will then behold—far stretching, covering all the globe that they inhabit, enough not only to populate all the earth's plains, but to crown her hilltops and cover the waves of the sea. How numberless will the human race be when all the generations that have ever lived, or will ever live, will at once rise from the dead! What a sight that will be! Is it too marvelous for our imagination to picture?

Yet, it is quite certain that the assemblage will be mustered, and the spectacle will be beheld. Everyone from before the Flood, from the days of the Patriarchs, from the times of David, from the Babylonian kingdom, all the legions of Assyria, all the hosts of Persia, all the troops of the Greeks, all the vast armies and legions of Rome, the barbarian, the Scythian, the bond, the free (see Colossians 3:11), men of every color and of every tongue—they will all stand in that Last Day before the judgment seat of Christ.

There come the kings, no greater than the men they call their slaves. There come the princes, but they have removed their coronets, for they must stand like common flesh and blood. Here come the judges to be judged themselves, and the advocates and barristers needing an advocate themselves. Here come those who thought themselves too good and kept to themselves on the street. There are the Pharisees, hustled by the publicans on either side and sunk down to the same level with them. Mark the peasants as they rise from the soil. See the teeming myriad from outside the great cities streaming in, countless hosts that not even Alexander or Napoleon ever beheld!

Observe how the servant is as great as his master. "Liberty, Equality, Fraternity," the great cry of the French Revolution, is truly proclaimed now. No kings, no princes, no nobles, can shelter themselves behind their titles, assert privileges, or claim immunity. Alike on one common level, they stand together to be tried before the last tremendous tribunal.

The wicked of every sort will come. Proud Pharaoh will be there; Senacherib, the haughty; Herod, who would have slain the young Child; Judas, who sold his Master for gold; Demas, who deserted His church for the world; and Pilate, who would gladly have washed his hands in innocence. There will come the long list of infallibles, the whole line of popes, to receive their damnation at the Almighty's hands, with the priests that trod on the necks of nations and the tyrants that used the priests as their tools. They will come to receive the thunderbolts of God that they so richly deserve. Oh, what a scene it will be! These groups, which seem to us to be so large, how they will shrink to the size of a drop in a bucket as compared with the ocean of life that will swell around the throne at the last great Judgment Day! They will all be there.

Now, to me, the most important thought connected with this is that I will be there; to you young ones, that you will be there; to you elderly, that you all will be there. Are you rich? Your finery will be cast off. Are you poor? Your rags will not exempt you from attendance. One will say, "I am too obscure." You must come out from that hiding place. Some will say, "I am too public." You must come down from that pedestal. Everyone must be at that court. Note the words *we* and *all* in "We *must all appear.*"

Still further, note the word *appear* in our text. No disguise will be possible. You cannot come there dressed in the costume of vocation or attired in robes of state, but you must appear. You must be seen through, must be displayed, must be revealed. Off will come your garments, and your spirit will be judged of God, not by outward appearance, but according to the inward heart. (See 1 Samuel 16:7.) What a Day that will be when every man sees himself and his fellowman clearly, and when the eyes of angels, devils, and the Lord on the throne see him thoroughly. Let these thoughts dwell in your mind, while you take this for the answer to our first inquiry, Who is to be judged?

Who Will Judge

Our second question is, Who will be the judge? "*We must all appear before the judgment seat of Christ.*" That Christ has been appointed the Judge of all mankind is most proper and fitting. British law ordains that a man be tried by his peers.

There is justice in that statute. Likewise, God will judge men, but at the same time it will be in the person of Jesus Christ, the Man. Men will be judged by a man. He who was once judged by men will judge men. Jesus knows what man should be; He who is ordained to administer the law with authority was Himself "*made under the law*" (Galatians 4:4) in deep humility. He can hold the scales of justice evenly, for He stood in man's place as He bore and braved man's temptations. (See Hebrews 4:15.) He therefore is the most fit Judge.

I have sometimes heard and read sermons in which the preacher said a Christian ought to rejoice that his Friend will be his Judge. No impropriety may have been intended, but it seems to me a rather questionable suggestion. I would not put it in that way, because I believe any judge who is partial to his friends while on the judicial bench should be removed from the seat immediately. I expect no favoritism from Christ, my Judge. I do expect that when He sits there, He will dispense even- handed justice to all. I cannot see how it is right for anyone to propose that we should find encouragement in the Judge being our Friend.

Friend or no friend, every one of us will have a fair trial, because Christ is "*no respecter of persons*" (Acts 10:34). Of Him whom God has appointed to judge the world, it will not be said, when the Judgment is over, that He winked at the crimes of some and overlooked them, while He searched out the faults of others and convicted them. He will be fair and upright throughout. He is our Friend, I grant you, and He will be our Friend and Savior forever; but as our Judge, we must believe and maintain the thought that He will be impartial to all the sons of men. O man, you will have a fair trial. He who will judge you will not take sides against you.

In the past I thought that certain men have been shielded from the punishment they deserved because they were of a select clerical status or because they occupied a certain official position. A poor laborer who kills his wife is hanged, but when another man of superior station does the same deed of violence and stains his hands with the blood of her whom he had vowed to love and cherish, the capital sentence is not executed upon him.

Everywhere in the world we see that, even with the best intentions, justice somehow or other squints a little. Even in this country, there is just the slightest possible tipping of the scales. May God grant that such a distortion be cured soon. I do not think it is intentional, and I hope the nation will not have to complain about it for long. The same justice ought to exist for the poorest beggar who crawls into a filthy slum as for the titled nobleman who owns the broadest acres in all of the country.

Before the law, at least, all men ought to have an equal standing. We can rejoice that at the final Judgment it will be so with the Judge of all the earth. *Fiat justitia, ruat caelum*—"Let justice be done though the heavens fall." Christ will, by all means, hold the scales even.

You will have a fair trial and a full trial, too. There will be no concealment of anything in your favor and no keeping back of anything against you. No witnesses will be hidden across the sea to keep them out of the way. They will all be there, all testimony will be there, and all that is needed to condemn or to acquit will be produced in full court at that trial. Hence, it will be a final trial. From that court there will be no appeal. If Christ says, "Cursed!" cursed must they be forever. If Christ says, "Blessed!" blessed are they forever. Well, this is what we have to expect then, to stand before the throne of Christ Jesus, the Son of God, and there to be judged.

How Will We Be Judged?

Our third point of inquiry is, What will be the standard of the Judgment? Our text says, *"That every one may receive the things done in his body, according to that he hath done, whether it be good or bad."* Thus, it would appear that our actions will be taken as evidence; not our profession, not our boasting, but our actions will be taken as evidence, and every man will receive a just verdict according to what he has done in his body. The text implies that everything done by us in this body will be known then. It is all recorded. It will all be brought to light.

Hence, in the Day of Judgment every secret sin will be published. What was done in private, what was hidden by the darkness—every secret thing—will be published abroad. With great care you have concealed it; most cleverly you have covered it up; but it will be revealed, to your own astonishment, to form a part of the case against you.

There, hypocritical actions as well as secret sins will be laid bare. The Pharisee who devoured the widow's house and made a long prayer will find that widow's house brought against him and that long prayer, too, for the long prayer will then be understood as having been a long lie from beginning to end. Oh, how fine we can make some things look with the aid of paint and varnish and gilt! But, at the

Last Day, off will come the varnish and veneer, and the true metal, the real substance, will then be seen.

When it is said that everything that is done in the body will be brought up as evidence for us or against us, remember this includes every omission as well as every commission of sin. (See James 4:17.) What was not done that should have been done is as greatly sinful as the doing of that which should not have been done. Have you ever noticed in Christ's account of the Judgment, when the sheep were separated from the goats, how those on the left were condemned, not for what they did, but for what they did not do: *"For I was an hungered, and ye gave me no meat: I was thirsty, and ye gave me no drink"* (Matthew 25:42)? According to this principle, how would some of you stand before God, you who have neglected holiness, faith, and repentance all your days? I urge you to consider your present state.

Remember, too, that all our words will be brought up: *"Every idle word that men shall speak, they shall give account thereof in the day of judgment"* (Matthew 12:36). Add to them all of our thoughts, for these lie at the bottom of our actions and give the true color to them, good or bad. Our motives, our heart sins, our neglect of the gospel, our unbelief, and especially our hatred of Christ—all of these will be read aloud and published unreservedly.

"Well," someone says, "who then can be saved?" Indeed, who then can be saved? Let me tell you. There will come forward those who have believed in Jesus, and even though they have many sins to which they might well plead guilty, they will be able to say, "Great God, You provided a Substitute for us, and You said that if we would accept Him, He would be our Substitute and take our sins on Himself. We did accept Him, and our sins were laid on Him, and we now have no sins to be charged against us. We have been purged of them, because they were transferred from us to the great Savior, Substitute, and Sacrifice."

In that Day none will be able to express an objection to that plea. It will hold, for God has said, *"He that believeth on him is not condemned"* (John 3:18). Then, the gracious actions of the righteous will be brought forth to prove that they had faith, for the faith that never evidences itself by good works is a dead faith and a faith that will never save a soul. (See James 2:14–20.)

If someone were to object to the pardoning of the thief who died on a cross next to our Savior, the thief could say, "My sins were laid on Jesus." Satan might reply, "Yes, but what about your good works? You must have some evidence of your faith." Then the recording angel would say, "The dying thief said to his fellow thief who was dying with him, *'Dost not thou fear God?'* (Luke 23:40). In his last moments he did what he could; he rebuked the thief that was dying with him and made a good confession of his Lord. That was the evidence of the sincerity of his faith."

Friend, will there be any evidence of the sincerity of your faith? If your faith has no evidence before the Lord, what will you do? Suppose you thought you had faith and went on drinking. Suppose you went, as I know some have done, straight from church into the pubs? Or, suppose you joined a church but remained a drunkard? Women have done that as well as men and are not exempt. Suppose you professed to have faith in Christ and yet cheated in your business dealings? Do you think that God will never require justice for these things?

If you are no better than other men in your conduct, you are no better than other men in your character, and you will stand no better than other men in the Judgment Day. If your actions are not superior to theirs, then you may profess what you will about your faith, but you are deceived, and, as such, you will be discovered at the Judgment.

If grace does not differentiate us from other men, it is not the grace that God gives His elect. We are not perfect, but all of God's saints keep their eyes on the great standard of perfection and, with strong desire, aim to walk worthy of God's high calling and to bring forth works that show that they love God. If we do not have these signs following our faith, or if they are not put in as evidence for us, we will not be able to prove our faith at the Last Day.

Oh, you who have no faith in Christ, no faith in Jesus as your Substitute, that treacherous unbelief of yours will be a condemning sin against you! It will be proof positive that you hated God, because a man must hate God indeed who will spurn His counsels, give no heed to His reproof, scorn His grace, and dare the vengeance of Him who points out the way of escape and the path that leads to life. He who will not be saved by God's mercy proves that He hates the God of mercy. God gave His own Son to die to redeem men from their just condemnation. Yet, if a person will not trust in His Son and will not have Him as his Savior, then that one sin, even if he had no other, would at once prove that he was an enemy of God and black at heart.

However, if your faith is in Jesus, if you love Jesus, if your heart goes out to Jesus, if your life is influenced by Jesus, if you make Him your Example as well as your Savior, there will be evidence—you may not see it, but there will be evidence—in your favor. Notice those gracious acts that were mentioned when the evidence was brought forth by Christ:

> *For I was an hungered, and ye gave me meat: I was thirsty, and ye gave me drink: I was a stranger, and ye took me in: naked, and ye clothed me: I was sick, and ye visited me: I was in prison, and ye came unto me.*
>
> (Matthew 25:35–36)

The righteous, for whom Christ was offering evidence, replied, "Lord, we never knew this." (See Matthew 25:37–39.)

Should anyone in my presence declare, "I have plenty of evidence to prove my faith," I would necessarily chastise him with this rebuke: "Hold your tongue! Hold your tongue! I am afraid you have no faith at all, or you would not be talking about your evidence." But, if a person says, "I am afraid I have no evidence that will stand me in good stead at the last," and yet if he had been feeding the hungry and clothing the naked and doing all he could for Christ, I would tell him not to be afraid.

The Master will find witnesses to say, "That man relieved me when I was in poverty. He knew I was one of Christ's, and he came and helped me." And another (perhaps it will be an angel) will come and say, "I saw him when he was alone and heard him pray for his enemies." And the Lord will say, "I saw his heart when he put up with rebuke and slander and persecution and would not respond, for My sake. He did it all as evidence that My grace was in his heart." You will not have to find the witnesses. The Judge will call them, for He knows all about your case.

As Christ calls the witnesses, you will be surprised to find how even the ungodly will be obliged to consent to the just salvation of the righteous. How the secret deeds of the righteous and their true sincerity of heart, when thus unveiled, will make devils bite their tongues in wrath to think that there was so much grace given to the sons of men with which to defeat persecution, to overcome temptation, and to follow on in obedience to the Lord!

Yes, the deeds of men—not their prating, not their profession, not their talk, but their deeds—will be the evidence of the grace given to them (although nobody will be saved by the merits of his deeds), or their deeds will be the evidence of their unbelief. Thus, by their works will men stand before the Lord, or by their works will they be condemned. Their deeds will be evidence for or against them, and nothing more.

What Will Result?

Our last point of inquiry is, What will the consequences of this Judgment be? Will sentences of acquittal and condemnation be handed down, and then the whole thing be over? Far from it! The Judgment will occur with a view toward what follows: *"That every one may receive the things done in his body."* The Lord will grant to His people an abundant reward for all that they have done, not that they deserve any reward. God first gave them grace to do good works, then He took their good works as evidence of a renewed heart, and next He will give them a reward for what they have done.

What joy it will be to hear Him say, *"Well done, good and faithful servant"* (Matthew 25:23)! You who have worked for Christ when nobody else knew will find that Christ took stock of it all. You who served the Lord while being slandered will find that the Lord Jesus cleared the chaff away from the wheat and knew that you were one of His precious ones. What bliss you will know when He says, *"Enter thou into the joy of thy lord"* (Matthew 25:21).

But, how terrible for the ungodly it will be! They are to receive the things that they have done, that is to say, the due punishment. Not every man will receive the same punishment: to the greater sinner, the greater doom; to the man who sinned against light, a greater damnation than to the man who did not have the same light. Sodom and Gomorrah will receive their place; Tyre and Sidon theirs; and then to Capernaum and Bethsaida their place of more intolerable torment, because they had the gospel and rejected it. So the Holy Spirit tells us: *"For we must all appear before the judgment seat of Christ; that every one may receive the things done in his body, according to that he hath done, whether it be good or bad."*

Not only will the punishment be meted out in proportion to the transgression, but the consequences to be endured will also be a development of the evil actions done, for every man *"shall eat the fruit of [his] own way"* (Proverbs 1:31). Sin, in the natural order, ripens into sorrow. This is not blind fate but the operation of a divine law, wise and invariable. How dreadful it will be for the malicious man to gnaw forever on his own envious heart, to find his malice coming back home to him as a bird comes home to roost, to hoot forever in his own soul! How torturous it will be for the lustful man to feel, burning in every vein, lust that he can never gratify; for the drunkard to have a thirst that not even a sea of water could quench, if he could find any water; for the glutton who has fared sumptuously to be perpetually hungry; for the wrathful person to be forever raging, with the fire of anger burning like a volcano in his soul; and for the rebel against God to be forever defiant, cursing God whom he cannot touch and finding his curses coming back on himself.

There is no punishment worse than for a man who is sinfully disposed to gratify his lusts, to satiate his bad propensities, and to multiply and fatten his vices. Let men grow into what they would be, and then see what they have become! Take away the policemen in some parts of London; give the people plenty of money; let them do just as they please; and watch what happens.

For example, recently, at least six men got broken heads in a street brawl, and their wives and children were in one general skirmish. If those people were to be kept together while their vigor continued unimpaired by age or decay and their characters kept on developing, they would act worse than a pack of wolves. Let them give way to their rage and anger, with nothing to check their passions. Let miserly, greedy people go on forever with their greed. It makes them miserable here, but let these things be indulged in forever, and what worse hell could there be? Oh, sin is hell, and holiness is heaven!

Men will receive the things done in their bodies. If God has graced them with love for Him, they will continue loving Him. If God has given them trust for Him, they will keep on trusting Him. If God has made them to be like Christ, they will go on being Christlike, and they will receive, as a reward, the things done in their bodies.

However, if a man has lived in sin, *"he which is filthy, let him be filthy still"* (Revelation 22:11). He who was unbelieving will continue to be unbelieving. The damnation of unrepentant sinners, then, will be *"where their worm dieth not, and the fire is not quenched"* (Mark 9:44), to which will be added the wrath of God forever and ever.

May every one of us be given the grace to flee to Christ, for in Him is our only safety. Simple faith in Jesus is the true basis for the character that will produce the evidence that you are chosen by God. A simple belief in the merits of the Lord Jesus, brought about in us by the Holy Spirit, is the solid rock upon which will be built, by the same divine Builder, the character that will establish the truth that the kingdom was prepared for us from before the foundations of the world. May God form such a character in each of us, for Christ's sake. Amen.

5

JESUS GLORIFIED IN HIS SAINTS

When he shall come to be glorified in his saints,
and to be admired in all them that believe
(because our testimony among you was believed) in that day.
—2 Thessalonians 1:10

What a difference between the first and second comings of our Lord! When Christ comes a second time, it will be to be glorified and admired, but when He came the first time, it was to be *"despised and rejected of men"* (Isaiah 53:3). He is coming a second time to reign with unparalleled splendor, but the first time He came to die in circumstances of shame and sorrow.

Lift up your eyes, you who have received His light, and anticipate the change that will be as great for you as for your Lord. Now you are hidden, even as He was hidden, and misunderstood, even as He was misunderstood, when He walked among the sons of men. *"We know that, when he shall appear, we shall be like him; for we shall see him as he is"* (1 John 3:2). His manifestation will be our manifestation. In that Last Day, when He will be revealed in glory, His saints will be glorified with Him.

In the verses just prior to our text, observe that our Lord is spoken of as follows:

> *And to you who are troubled rest with us, when the Lord Jesus shall be revealed from heaven with his mighty angels, in flaming fire taking vengeance on them that know not God, and that obey not the gospel of our Lord Jesus Christ.* (2 Thessalonians 1:7–8)

Christ will come in His glory and, at the same time, He will take vengeance in flaming fire on those who do not know God and who do not obey the gospel. This should be a note of great terror to all those who are ignorant of God and are wickedly unbelieving concerning Christ. Let them take heed, for the Lord will gain glory by the overthrow of His enemies. Those who would not bow before Him cheerfully will be compelled to bow before Him abjectly. They will crouch at His feet; they will lick the dust in terror; and at the glance of His eyes, they will utterly wither away. As it is written, they *"shall be punished with everlasting destruction from the presence of the Lord, and from the glory of his power"* (2 Thessalonians 1:9).

However, this is not the main reason for which Christ will come, nor is this the matter in which He will find His chief glory. Observe that He does this almost as an aside, when He is coming for another purpose. To destroy the wicked is a matter of necessity in which He takes no delight. According to the whole context, He does this, not because He is coming for that purpose, but as He is returning to the earth *"to be glorified in his saints, and to be admired in them that believe."*

The crowning honor of Christ will be seen in His people. This is the purpose for which He will return to the earth in the latter days, so that He may be exceedingly magnified in His saints. Even now, however, His saints glorify Him. When they walk in holiness, they reflect His light, as it were. Their holy deeds are beams from Him who is *"the Sun of righteousness"* (Malachi 4:2). When they believe in Him, they also glorify Him, for there is no grace that pays more respectful and deeper homage to our Lord than the grace of faith by which we trust Him and so confess Him to be our all in all.

Yes, we do glorify our gracious Lord, but, beloved, we must all confess that we do not do this as we desire. Alas, too often we dishonor Him and grieve the

Holy Spirit. By our lack of zeal and by our many sins, we are guilty of discrediting His gospel and dishonoring His name. Happy will be the time when this will no more be possible. Then we will be rid of the inward corruption that now works itself into outward sin. Then we will never dishonor Christ again. Then we will shine with a clear, pure radiance, as did the moon on the first Passover night, when she looked the sun full in the face and then shone her best on the earth.

Today we are pottery vessels on the wheel. Even though we are now only half fashioned, some of His divine skill can still be seen in us as His handiwork. But, the molded clay is only seen in part, and much remains to be done. How much more of the great Potter's creative wisdom and sanctifying power will be displayed when we are the perfect products of His hand! In the unfolding bud, the new nature brings honor to its Author; it will do far more when its perfection manifests the Finisher. When the days of the new creation are ended and God ushers in the eternal rest by pronouncing His work of grace to be very good, then Jesus will be glorified and admired in all of us.

As God helps me, I first want to address the special glorification of Christ referred to in our text. Secondly, I desire to call your attention to the special considerations that this grand truth suggests.

The Special Glorification of Christ

Let us consider carefully what is entailed in this special glorification of our Lord: *"When he shall come to be glorified in his saints, and to be admired in all them that believe (because our testimony among you was believed) in that day."*

When Christ Will Be Glorified

The first point to note is the time. Our text says, *"When he shall come to be glorified in his saints in that day."* The full glorification of Christ in His saints will occur when He comes the second time, according to the sure word of prophecy. Yes, He is glorified in them at present, for He said, *"All mine are thine, and thine are mine; and I am glorified in them"* (John 17:10). However, as of now, that glory is perceptible to Him rather than to the outside world.

The lamps are being trimmed. (See Matthew 25:1–13.) They will shine before long. These are the days of preparation before that revered moment that will be a high holy Day in an infinite sense. As Esther prepared and purified herself with myrrh and sweet perfumes for so many months (see Esther 2:12) before she entered the king's palace to be espoused to him, so are we now being purified and made ready for that Day when the perfected church will be presented to Christ as a bride is presented to her husband. We will be *"prepared as a bride adorned for her husband"* (Revelation 21:2).

This is our night in which we must watch, but the morning is coming, a morning without clouds. Then we will walk in a sevenfold light because our Well Beloved has come. His Second Advent will be His revelation. He was under a cloud when He was here before: except for a few who *"beheld his glory"* (John 1:14), men perceived Him not. (See Luke 24:16.) But, when He comes a second time, all veils will be removed, and *"every eye shall see"* (Revelation 1:7) the glory of His countenance.

For this He waits, and His church waits with Him. We do not know when that time will arrive, but every hour is bringing it nearer to us. Therefore, let us stand, *"looking for and* [eagerly awaiting] *the coming of the day of God"* (2 Peter 3:12).

In Whom Glorified

Note, secondly, in whom this glorification of Christ is to be found. The text does not say He will be glorified "by" His saints, but *"in his saints."* There is more than a slight shade of difference between those two terms. We endeavor to glorify Christ now by our actions, but when He returns, we will glorify Him in our persons, characters, and conditions. At present, He is glorified by what we do, but at His future coming, He will be glorified in what we are.

Who are these people in whom Jesus is to be glorified and admired? They are spoken of with two descriptions: *"in his saints"* and *"in all them that believe."* First, let us explore *"in his saints."* All those in whom Christ will be glorified are described as holy ones or saints: men and women who have been sanctified and made pure; those whose gracious lives show that they have been under the teaching of the Holy Spirit; those whose obedient actions prove that they are disciples of a Holy Master, even of Him who was *"holy, harmless, undefiled, separate from sinners"* (Hebrews 7:26).

Inasmuch as these saints are also said to be believers, I gather that the holiness that will honor Christ at the Last Day is a holiness based on faith in Him. The root of their holiness is that they first trusted in Christ, and then, being saved, they loved their Lord and obeyed Him. Their faith, brought about by His love, purified their souls, and thus cleansed their lives. It is an inner purity as well as an outward chastity, arising out of the living and operative principle of faith.

If some people think they can attain holiness apart from faith in Christ, they are as mistaken as the person who hopes to reap a harvest without first sowing seed into the furrows. Faith is the bulb, and sainthood is the delightfully fragrant flower that comes from it when it is planted in the soil of a renewed heart.

Beware, I urge you, of any pretense of holiness arising out of yourselves and maintained by the energy of your own unaided wills. You might as well try to gather grapes from thorns or figs from thistles. (See Matthew 7:16.) True sainthood must spring from confidence in the Savior of sinners. If it does not, it is lacking in the first element of truth. How can anyone have a perfect character who finds his basis for it in self-esteem? How could Christ be glorified by saints who refuse to trust in Him?

I call your attention once again to the second description, *"all them that believe."* This is emphasized by the hint that they are believers in a particular testimony, according to the parenthetical clause, *"because our testimony among you was believed."* Now, the testimony of the apostles concerned what they had witnessed of Jesus. They saw Him in the body, and they bore witness that He was God *"manifest in the flesh"* (1 Timothy 3:16). They saw His holy life and attested to it. They saw His grievous death, and they testified that *"God was in Christ, reconciling the world unto himself"* (2 Corinthians 5:19). They saw Him risen from the dead, and they said, "We are witnesses of His resurrection." (See Acts 1:22.) They saw Him rise into heaven, and they bore witness that God had taken Him up to His right hand.

All who believe this witness are saved. *"If thou shalt confess with thy mouth the Lord Jesus, and shalt believe in thine heart that God hath raised him from the dead, thou shalt be saved"* (Romans 10:9). All who, with simple faith, come and cast themselves upon the incarnate Son of God, who died and rose again for men and *"who is even at the right hand of God, who also maketh intercession for us"* (Romans 8:34)—these are the ones in whom Christ will be glorified and admired.

However, since they are first said to be saints, let it never be forgotten that this must be a living faith, a faith that produces a hatred of sin, a faith that renews the character and shapes the life after the noble model of Christ, thus turning sinners into saints. The two descriptions must not be violently torn apart. You must not say that the favored people are sanctified without remembering that they are justified by faith. Neither should you say that they are justified by faith without remembering that without *"holiness no man shall see the Lord"* (Hebrews 12:14), and that, in the end, the people in whom Christ will be admired will be those holy ones who were saved by faith in Him.

By Whom Glorified

So far, then, we are clear, but now a question arises: By whom will Christ be glorified and admired? First of all, I answer that His people will personally do so. Every saint will glorify Christ in himself and admire Christ in himself. Each one will marvel, "What a wonder that a poor creature such as I am should be thus perfected! How glorious is my Lord, who has worked this miracle in me!" Surely our consciousness of having been cleansed and made holy will cause us to fulfill those words of John Berridge:

> He cheers them with eternal smile,
> They sing hosannas all the while;
> Or, overwhelm'd with rapture sweet,
> Sink down adoring at His feet.

This I know, that when I personally enter heaven, I will forever admire and adore the everlasting love that brought me there. Yes, we will all glorify and admire our Savior for what He has done in us personally by His infinite grace.

The saints will also admire Christ in one another. When I see you and you see your brothers and sisters in Christ all perfect, we will be filled with wonder and gratitude and delight. You will be free from all envy there, and therefore you will rejoice in all the beauty of your fellow saints. Their heaven will be a heaven to you, and what a multitude of heavens you will have as you rejoice in the joy of all the redeemed! We will as much admire the Lord's handiwork in others as in ourselves, and each one will praise Him for saving all the rest. You will see your Lord in all your brothers and sisters, and this will make you praise and adore Him, world without end, with a perpetual amazement of ever growing delight.

However, that will not be all. Besides the blood-bought and ransomed of Christ, there will be at His Coming all the holy angels, who will stand by and look on with wonder. They greatly marveled when first He stooped from heaven to the earth, and they desired to look into those things that then were a mystery to them. (See 1 Peter 1:12.) But, when they see their beloved Prince come back with ten thousand times ten thousand of the ransomed at His feet, all of them made perfect by having *"washed their robes, and made them white in the blood of the Lamb"* (Revelation 7:14), how the heavenly beings will admire Him in every one of His redeemed! How they will praise that conquering arm that has brought home all these spoils from the war! How the hosts of heaven will shout His praises as they see Him lead these captives captive with a new captivity (see Ephesians 4:8), in chains of love, joyfully gracing His triumph and showing forth the completeness of His victory!

We do not know what other races of creatures there may be, but I think it is no stretch of the imagination to believe that, as this world is only one speck in the creation of God, there may be millions of other races in the countless worlds around us, and all of these may be invited to behold the wonders of redeeming love as manifested in the saints in the Day of the Lord. I seem to see these other intelligences encompassing the saints as *"a cloud of witnesses"* (Hebrews 12:1), and in rapt attention, beholding in them the love and grace of the redeeming Lord. What songs, what shouts, what hymns, will rise from all these to the praise of the eternal God! What an orchestra of praise the universe will become! From star to star the holy melodies will roll, until all space will ring out the hosannas of wondering spirits. *"Wonderful, Counsellor, The mighty God, The everlasting Father, The Prince of Peace"* (Isaiah 9:6), will have brought home all those who are inspiring such wondrous joy, and they with Himself will be the wonder of eternity.

Then Satan and his defeated legions, along with the lost spirits of ungodly men, will bite their lips with envy and rage and tremble at the majesty of Jesus in that Day. By their confessed defeat and manifest despair, they will glorify Him in His people, in whom they have been utterly overthrown. They will see that there is not one lost whom He redeemed by His blood, not one snatched away of all the sheep His Father gave Him (see John 10:27–30), not one warrior enlisted beneath His banner who fell in battle, but all are *"more than conquerors through him that loved* [them]" (Romans 8:37).

What despair will seize upon diabolic spirits as they discover their entire defeat—defeated in men who were once their slaves! Poor dupes whom they could so easily beguile by their craftiness—defeated even in these! Jesus, triumphant by taking the lambs from between the lion's jaws and rescuing His feeble sheep from their power, will utterly put them to shame in His redeemed. With what anguish they will sink into the hell prepared for them, because now they hear with anger all the earth and heaven and every star ringing with the shout, "*Alleluia: for the Lord God omnipotent reigneth*" (Revelation 19:6), and, "The Lamb has conquered by His blood."

To What Degree Glorified

Since we now know there will be enough spectators to magnify Christ in His saints, let us inquire, To what degree will the Lord Jesus be glorified? My answer is that it will be to the very highest degree. He will come to be glorified in His saints to the utmost, for this is clear from the words, "*to be admired.*" When this translation was made, the word *admire* had, to ordinary Englishmen, a stronger inference of wonder than it has now. We often speak of admiring a thing in the less intense sense of liking or desiring it, but the real meaning of the English word, and of the Greek also, is "wonder." Our Lord will be wondered at "*in all them that believe.*" Those who look upon the saints will suddenly be struck with a feeling of sacred delight and awe. They will be startled with the surprising glory of the Lord's work in them. "We thought He could do great things, but this—this surpasses conception!"

Every saint will be a wonder to himself. "I thought my bliss would be great, but not like this!" All his brothers and sisters will be a startling wonder to the perfected believer. He will exclaim, "I thought the saints would be perfect, but I never imagined that such an excessive transformation of glory would be put upon each of us. I could not have dreamed my Lord would be so good and gracious to His feeble followers."

The angels in heaven will say that they never anticipated such deeds of grace. They knew that He had undertaken a great work, but they did not realize that He would do so much for and in His people. The firstborn sons of light, accustomed to seeing great marvels performed in ancient times, will be entranced with a new, unsurpassed wonder as they see the handiwork of Immanuel's free grace and dying love.

The men who once despised the saints, who called them pious hypocrites and trampled on them (perhaps having slayed them), the kings and princes of the earth who sold the righteous for a pair of shoes, what will they say when they see the lowliest of the Savior's followers become a prince of more illustrious rank than the greatest ones of the world, and Christ shining out in all of these favored beings? For their uplifting, Jesus Christ will be wondered at by those who once despised both Him and them.

In What Ways Glorified

The next question leads us into the very heart of the subject: In what ways will Christ be glorified and wondered at? Do not expect me to cover one tenth of it, for I am unable to do so. I am only going to give you a little sample of what this must mean. Exhaustive exposition is quite impossible for me.

With regard to His saints, I think that Jesus will be glorified and wondered at by virtue of their number: *"a great multitude, which no man could number"* (Revelation 7:9). The apostle John was a great mathematician, and he managed to count up to one hundred and forty-four thousand (see Revelation 14:1) of all the tribes of the children of Israel, but that was only a representative member for the Jewish nation. As for the church of God, comprised of the Gentile nations, he gave up all idea of computation and confessed that he saw *"a great multitude, which no man could number."* When the Beloved Apostle heard them sing, he said, *"I heard a voice from heaven, as the voice of many waters, and as the voice of a great thunder"* (Revelation 14:2). There were so many of them that their song was as the Mediterranean Sea whipped to a fury by a tempest— no, not one great sea in an uproar, but ocean upon ocean, the Atlantic and the Pacific piled upon each other, and the Arctic on these, and other oceans on these, layers of oceans, all thundering out their mightiest roar. Such will be the song of the redeemed, for the crowds that swell the unparalleled hymn will be beyond all reckoning.

You who laughed at His kingdom, behold and see how the One has become thousands! Now look, you foes of Christ, and see the fulfillment of that prophecy, long ago foretold:

> *There shall be an handful of corn in the earth upon the top of the mountains; the fruit thereof shall shake like Lebanon: and they of the city shall flourish like grass of the earth.* (Psalm 72:16)

Who can number the drops of the dew or the sands on the seashore? When he has counted these, still he will not have guessed at the multitude of the redeemed that Christ will bring to glory.

All this harvest will have come from one grain of wheat, which would have remained alone had it not fallen to the ground and died. What did the Word say? *"If it die, it bringeth forth much fruit"* (John 12:24). Was this prophecy not fulfilled? O beloved, what a harvest from the solitary Man of Nazareth! What fruit from that glorious Branch!

Men *"did esteem him stricken, smitten of God and afflicted"* (Isaiah 53:4). Even though men made nothing of Jesus, there still sprang from Him these multitudes that are as many as the stars of heaven. Is He not glorified and wondered at in His saints? The Judgment Day will declare it without fail.

However, there is quality as well as quantity that will draw such glory and admiration. Christ will be admired in His saints because they are, each one of them, proof of His power to save from evil. My eye can hardly bear, even though it is only in my imagination, to gaze on the glittering ranks of the white-robed ones, as each one outshines the sun and all are as if a magnified midday had clothed them. Yet all these, as I look at them, tell me, "We have washed our robes, for they were once defiled. We have made them white, but this whiteness is caused by the blood of the Lamb." (See Revelation 7:14.)

They were *"by nature the children of wrath, even as others"* (Ephesians 2:3). They were *"dead in trespasses and sins"* (Ephesians 2:1). *"All we like sheep have gone astray; we have turned every one to his own way"* (Isaiah 53:6). Yet, look at them, and see how He has saved them, washed them, cleansed them, perfected them! His power and grace are seen in all of them. If your eyes pause here and there, you will discover some that were supremely stubborn, whose necks were like iron sinews, and still He conquered them by love. Some were densely ignorant, but He opened their blind eyes. Some were grossly infected with the leprosy of lust, but He healed them.

Some were under Satan's most terrible power, but He cast the devil out of them. Oh, how Christ will be glorified in special cases! That drunkard has been transformed into a saint. This blasphemer has been turned into a loving disciple. That persecutor, who radiated threats of torture, has been taught to sing a hymn of praise forever! The Lord will be extremely glorified in them.

Beloved in the Lord, in each one of us there was some special difficulty as to our salvation, some impossibility that was possible with God, though it would have been forever impossible with us. (See Mark 10:27.) Thus, Christ will be glorified forever in each of us because He overcame those impossible obstacles in us to bring us unto Himself.

Remember, also, that all those saints made perfect would have been in hell had it not been for the Son's atoning sacrifice. They will remember this most vividly, because they will see other men condemned for the sins with which they also were once polluted. The crush of vengeance upon the ungodly will make the saints magnify the Lord all the more as they see themselves delivered. They will each feel,

> Oh, were it not for grace divine,
> That fate so dreadful had been mine.

In all of the saints, the memory of the horrible pit from which they were drawn and the miry clay out of which they were lifted will make their Savior more glorious and wonderful.

Perhaps the principal point in which Christ will be glorified will be the absolute perfection of all the saints. They will then be without *"spot, or wrinkle, or any such thing"* (Ephesians 5:27). We have not experienced what perfection is, and therefore we can hardly conceive it. Our thoughts themselves are too sinful for us to get a full idea of what absolute perfection must be. But, dear friends, we will have no sin left in us, for we will be *"without fault before the throne of God"* (Revelation 14:5). We will have no remaining propensity to sin. There will be no bias in the flesh toward that which is evil, but our whole beings will be fixed forever upon that which is good. The affections will never be wanton again; instead, they will always be chaste for Christ. The understanding will never make mistakes. We will never again *"put bitter for sweet, and sweet for bitter!"* (Isaiah 5:20). We will be *"perfect, even as [our] Father which is in heaven is perfect"* (Matthew 5:48).

Truly, beloved, He who works this in us will be a wonder. Christ will be admired and adored because of this grand result. O mighty Master, with what strange moral alchemy did You work to turn that morosely dispositioned man into a mass of love! How did You work to lift that selfish lover of mammon up from his hoarded gains to make him find his gain in You? How did You overcome that proud spirit, that fickle spirit, that lazy spirit, that lustful spirit—how did You contrive to take all these away? How did You exterminate the roots of sin, even the fine root hairs, out of Your redeemed, so that not one tiny filament remains?

> *In those days, and in that time, saith the* Lord, *the iniquity of Israel shall be sought for, and there shall be none; and the sins of Judah, and they shall not be found: for I will pardon them whom I reserve.* (Jeremiah 50:20)

Neither the guilt of sin nor the propensity to sin will exist—both will be completely eliminated from His saints. Christ will have done it, and He thus will be *"glorified in his saints, and admired in them that believe."*

This is but the beginning, however. In that wondrous Day, in all of the saints will be seen the wisdom and power and love of Christ in having brought them through every trial of the way. He kept their faith alive when it otherwise would have died out. He sustained them under trials when they would have fainted. He held them fast in their integrity when temptation solicited them and their feet almost slipped. He sustained some of them in prison, on the rack, and at the stake, and He held them faithful still!

One might hardly wish to be a martyr, but I think that the martyrs will be the admiration of us all, or rather Christ will be admired in them greatly. How they could bear such pain as some of them endured for Christ's sake none of us can guess, except that we know that Christ was in them, suffering in His members. Jesus will eternally be wondered at in them as all intelligent spirits see how He upheld them, so that *"tribulation, or distress, or persecution, or famine, or nakedness, or peril, or sword"* (Romans 8:35) could not separate them from His love. These were the faithful who *"wandered about in sheepskins and goatskins; being destitute, afflicted, tormented; (of whom the world was not worthy)"* (Hebrews 11:37–38). However, now arrayed as kings and priests, they stand in surpassing glory forever. Truly, the Lord will be admired in them.

Recollect, dear friends, that we will see in that Day how the blessed Christ, as *"the head over all things"* (Ephesians 1:22), has governed every providence for the sanctification of His people: how the dark days brought showers that made the plants of the Lord grow, how the fierce sun that threatened to scorch them to the root filled them with the warmth of love divine and ripened their choice fruit.

What a tale the saints will have to tell of how that which tried to dampen the fire of grace made it burn more mightily, how the stone that threatened to kill their faith was turned into bread for them, how the rod and staff of the Good Shepherd were ever with them to bring them safely home. I have sometimes thought that if I get into heaven by the skin of my teeth, I will sit down on heaven's shore and forever bless Him who, on a board or on a broken piece of the ship, brought my soul safely to land. Surely they who obtain an abundant entrance, coming into the fair havens like a ship in full sail without danger of shipwreck, will have to praise the Lord that they thus came into the blessed port of peace. In each case the Lord will be especially glorified and admired.

I cannot linger over this, but I beg you to notice that, as a king is glorious in his regalia, so Christ will put on His saints as His personal splendor in that Day when He takes up His jewels. It will be with Christ as it was with a virtuous matron of nobility who, when she called at her friends' homes and saw their baubles, asked them to come the next day to her home so she could exhibit her jewels. They expected to see rubies and pearls and diamonds, but she called in her two boys and said, "These are my jewels." Likewise, Jesus will exhibit His saints instead of emerald and amethyst, onyx and topaz. "These are my choice treasures," He will say, "in whom I am glorified."

Solomon surely was never more full of glory than when he had finished the temple, when all the tribes came together to see the noble structure and confessed it to be *"beautiful for situation, the joy of the whole earth"* (Psalm 48:2). But, what glory Christ will have when all the living stones are put into their places and His church has her agate windows, her carbuncle gates, and all her borders of precious stones! Then, indeed, will He be glorified, when the foundations of His New Jerusalem are courses of stones most precious, the likes of which have never been seen before.

In Believers

Inasmuch as our text puts special emphasis on believing, *"in all them that believe,"* I invite you to consider how, as believers as well as saints, the raised ones will glorify their Lord.

First, it will be wonderful that there are so many from varied walks of life brought to faith in Him: men with no God and men with many gods, men steeped in ignorance and men puffed up with carnal wisdom, great men and poor men, all brought to believe in the one Redeemer and to praise Him for His great salvation. Will He not be glorified in their common faith? It will magnify Him that these will all be saved by faith and not by their own merits. Not one among them will boast that he was saved by his own good works, but all will rejoice to have been saved by that blessedly simple way of "Believe and live," and by sovereign grace through the atoning blood, looked to by the tearful eyes of pure faith.

This, too, will make Jesus glorious: all of them, weak as they were, were made strong by faith; and all of them, as personally unfit for battle as they were, were still made triumphant in conflict because, by faith, they overcame through the blood of the Lamb. (See Revelation 12:11.) All of them will be there to show that their faith was honored, that Christ was faithful to His promise, and that He never allowed them to believe in vain. All of them, standing in heavenly places, saved by faith, will ascribe every particle of the glory only to the Lord Jesus:

> I ask them whence their victory came?
> They, with united breath
> Ascribe their conquest to the Lamb,
> Their triumph to His death.

They believed and were saved, but faith takes no credit for itself. It is a self-denying grace and puts the crown upon the head of Christ. Therefore, it is written that He will *"be glorified in his saints, and [also] be admired in all them that believe."*

In Resurrected Bodies

Next, I would like you to reflect that Jesus will be glorified in the risen bodies of all His saints. Those who have died and are in heaven are pure spirits in their present state, but when He returns, they will be clothed again. Poor body, you must sleep awhile, but what you will be at your awakening does not yet appear. (See 1 John 3:1.) You are now the shriveled seed, but there is a flower to come from you that will be lovely beyond all thought. Though sown in weakness, this body will be raised in power. Though *"sown in corruption; it is raised in incorruption"* (1 Corinthians 15:42).

Weakness, sickness, pain, and death will be banished forever. Infirmity and deformity will be completely unknown. The Lord will raise us up with glorious, eternal bodies:

> For the trumpet shall sound, and the dead shall be raised incorruptible, and we shall be changed. For this corruptible must put on incorruption, and this mortal must put on immortality. (1 Corinthians 15:53)

> Beloved, now are we the sons of God, and it doth not yet appear what we shall be: but we know that, when he shall appear, we shall be like him; for we shall see him as he is. (1 John 3:2)

Oh, what a prospect lies before us! Let us remember that this blessed resurrection will come to us because He rose from the dead, for there must be a resurrection to the members because the Head has risen. Oh, the delight of being a risen man, perfect in body, soul, and spirit! All that beauty will be due to Christ, and therefore He will be admired in us.

In All Who Believe

Next, let us consider the absolute perfection of the church regarding its numbers. All who have believed in Christ will be with Him in glory. Notice the word *all* in our text, which says Christ will be *"admired in all them that believe."* If some of those who have believed in Him somehow perished, He could not be admired in them. But, they will all be there, the little ones as well as the great ones.

You will be there, you poor feeble folk who, when you say, *"Lord, I believe,"* are obliged to add, *"help thou mine unbelief"* (Mark 9:24). He will be admired in all believers, without a single exception. Possibly there will be more wonder at the weak believers going to heaven than at the stronger ones. Mr. Greatheart, when he comes there, will owe his victories to his Master and lay his laurels at Christ's feet. But, when fainting Feeblemind, limping Ready-to- halt with his crutches, and trembling Little- faith enter into rest, they will make heaven ring with notes of even greater admiration because such poor, creeping worms of the earth have won the day by mighty grace.

Suppose that one of them were missing at the Last Great Day. Stop the harps! Silence the songs! There will be no beginning to be merry while one child is shut out. I am quite certain that if, as an earthly family, we were going to sing our evening hymn of joy and thankfulness, but mother said, "Where is the little mite? Where is the baby of the family?" we would pause. If we had to say that the baby was lost, there would be no singing and no resting until she had been found.

It is the glory of Jesus that, as our Shepherd, He has lost none of His flock, and, as the Captain of Salvation, He has brought many sons to glory and has lost none. Hence, He is admired, not in some that believe, nor yet in all but one, but He is *"admired in all them that believe."*

Does this not bring you delight, you who are weak and trembling, that Christ will be admired in you? There is little to admire in you at present, as you penitently confess. But, since Christ is in you now, and will be more fully manifested in you, before long there will be much to admire. May you partake in the excellence of our divine Lord and be conformed to His likeness so that He may be seen and glorified in you.

In Eternal Safety

Another point of admiration will be the eternal safety of all His believing people. There they are safe from fear of harm. You dogs of hell, you howled at their heels and hoped to devour them, but they have deftly escaped from you! What must it be like to be lifted out of range of the Enemy's weapons, where no more guard needs to be kept, for even the roar of the satanic canons cannot be heard? O glorious Christ, to bring them all to such a state of safety, You are to be wondered at forever.

In Reflected Glory

Moreover, all the saints will be so honored, so happy, and so like their Lord that they themselves and everything about them will be themes for endless admiration.

You may have seen a room decorated with mirrors hung all around the walls. When you stood in the middle, you were reflected from every point. You were seen here, and there, and there again, and there once more, so that every part of you was reflected. Heaven will be just like that, with Jesus at the center and all His saints reflecting His glory like mirrors. Is He human? So are they. Is He the Son of God? So are they sons of God. Is He perfect? So are they. Is He exalted? So are they. Is He a prophet? So are they, making known *"unto the principalities and powers in heavenly places the manifold wisdom of God"* (Ephesians 3:10). Is He a priest? So are they. Is He the King? So are they, for He *"hath made us kings and priests unto God"* (Revelation 1:6), and we will reign forever and ever. Look where you might among the ranks of the redeemed, this one thing will be seen: the glory of Christ Jesus, even to your surprise and wonder.

Practical Applications

I have limited space to draw out the text's functional implications, so I will just tell you what they are without much explanation.

Take Stock

First of all, our text suggests that each of us should conduct a self-examination, and that the principal subject for this introspection should be: Am I a saint? Am I holy? Am I a believer in Christ? Now is the time for you to determine whether your answer is yes or no, for on your true word depends your eternal glorification of Christ or your banishment from His presence forever.

Expect Reproach

The next thing we can derive is the small value of human opinion. When Christ was here, the world reckoned Him to be a nobody; while His people are here, they must expect to be judged in the same way. What do worldlings know about it? How soon their petty judgments will be reversed! When our Lord next appears, even those who sneered will be compelled to admire. When they see the glory of Christ in His people, they will be awestricken and will have nothing to say against us—not even the false tongue of malicious slander will dare to hiss out one serpent word in the end. Never mind them, then. Just put up with the reproach that will soon be silenced.

An Encouragement to Sinners

The next suggestion is a great encouragement to inquirers who are seeking Christ. I am specifically urging you, you great sinners, to ponder this: If Jesus is to be glorified in saved sinners, would He not be glorified indeed if He saved you? If He were ever to save such a rebel as you have been, would it not be the astonishment of eternity? You who are known in your neighborhood as wicked Jack or as a common thief, what if my Master were to make a saint of you? Of course, you are bad raw material! Yet, suppose He transformed you into a precious jewel and made you to be as holy as God is holy, what would you say of Him?

"Say of Him?" you reply. "I would praise Him, world without end." Yes, and you will do so if you will come and trust Him. Just put your trust in Him. May the Lord help you to do so at once, and He will be admired even in you forever and ever.

Love One Another

Our text also gives an exhortation to believers. Will Jesus Christ be honored and glorified in all the saints? Then, let us think well of them all and love them all. Some dear children of God do not have beautiful looks, or they are blind or deformed or maimed. Many of them have scanty wallets, and it may be that the church knows most of them from when they come for alms. Moreover, they may have little intellect and little power to please; they may be uncouth in their manners; they belong to what are called the lowest ranks of society. Do not despise them because of these things, for soon our Lord will be glorified in them.

How Christ will be admired in that poor, bedridden woman when she rises from her ghetto cot to sing hallelujah to God and the Lamb, along with the brightest of the shining ones! Why, I think the pain, the poverty, the weakness, and the sorrow of saints below will greatly glorify the Captain of their Salvation as they tell how grace helped them to bear their burdens and to rejoice while enduring their afflictions.

Share Your Testimony

Finally, beloved, this text ought to encourage all of you who love Jesus to go on talking about Him to others and bearing your testimony for His name. You see how the apostle Paul has inserted a few words by way of parentheses. Draw the words out of the brackets, and take them to heart: *"Because our testimony among you was believed."*

Do you see those crowds of idolatrous heathen, and do you see those hosts of saved ones before the throne? What was the medium that linked the two groups? By what visible means did those sinners become saints? Do you see that insignificant-looking man with the weak eyes, that man whose bodily presence is puny and whose speech is contemptible? Do you see his needle case and his sewing instruments? He has been making and mending tents, for he is only a tentmaker.

Now, those bright spirits that shine like suns, beaming forth with the rays of Christ's glory, were made so bright through the addresses and prayers of that tentmaker. The Thessalonians were heathens plunged in sin, and this poor tentmaker came in among them and told them of Jesus Christ and His gospel. They believed his testimony. That belief changed the lives of his hearers and made them holy. Being renewed, they came at length to be perfected in holiness. Thus they became, and Jesus Christ is glorified in them.

Beloved, it will be a delightful thing throughout eternity to contemplate that you went into your Sunday school class, afraid you could not say much, but you talked about Jesus Christ with a tear in your eye, and you brought a dear girl to believe in His saving name through your testimony. In years to come, that girl will be among those that shine out to the glory of Christ forever. Perhaps you will get a chance to talk in a mission to some of those poor, despised tramps. Maybe you will tell one of those poor vagrants or one of the fallen women the story of your Lord's love and blood. Just possibly, the poor broken heart will latch onto the gracious word and come to Jesus. Then a heavenly character will have begun and another jewel will have been secured for the Redeemer's diadem.

I think that you will admire His crown all the more because, as you see certain stones sparkling in it, you will say, "Blessed be His name forever. He helped me to dive into the sea and find that pearl for Him, and now it adorns His sacred brow."

Now, get at it, all of you! You who are doing nothing for Jesus, be ashamed of yourselves, and ask Him to work in you that you may begin to work for Him. Unto God be the glory, forever and ever. Amen.

HOW TO HAVE REAL JOY

CONTENTS

1. All Things New 653

2. This Year Also 669

3. Growing in the Lord 675

4. The Joy of the Lord.. 691

5. The Same Yesterday, Today, and Forever 708

6. Suffering and Reigning with Jesus 726

7. Our Own Dear Shepherd 742

1

ALL THINGS NEW

And he that sat upon the throne said,
Behold, I make all things new.
—Revelation 21:5

How pleased we are with things that are new! Our children's eyes sparkle when we talk about giving them a new toy or a new book. Our human nature loves things that are recent because they are like our fleeting lives—suddenly here for a brief time and then gone. In our love of novelty, we are all children, for we eagerly demand the news of the day and are all too ready to rush after new inventions. The Athenians, who spent their time in nothing else but telling and hearing something new (Acts 17:21), were by no means unusual; novelty still fascinates the crowd.

Therefore, I would not be surprised if the words of our text sound like a pleasant song in your ears, but I am thankful that their deeper meaning is even more joyous. The newness that Jesus brings is bright, clear, heavenly, and enduring.

As Christians, we should not be carried away by a childish love of novelty, for we worship a God who is always the same, and whose years will have no end

(Psalm 102:27). In some matters, *"the old is better"* (Luke 5:39). There are certain old things that are so truly new that to exchange them for anything else would be like exchanging old gold for new dross. The old, old Gospel is the newest thing in the world. In its very essence, it is forever the Good News. In the things of God, the old is always new. If anyone presents what seems to be new doctrine and new truth, it is soon perceived that the new dogma is only worn-out heresy cleverly repaired. The so-called discovery in theology is the digging up of a carcass of error that should have been left to rot in oblivion. In the great matter of truth and godliness, we may safely say, *"There is no new thing under the sun"* (Ecclesiastes 1:9).

Yet, there has been so much evil in ourselves and our old natures, so much sin in our lives and our pasts, so much wickedness in our surroundings and old temptations, that we are not distressed by the belief that old things are passing away. Hope springs up at the first sound of such words as these from the lips of our risen and reigning Lord: "Behold, I make all things new." It is fitting that things so worn-out and defiled be laid aside and that better things take their places.

The words that Christ speaks to us are truly divine. Listen to them: *"Behold, I."* Who is the great *"I"*? Who else but the eternal Son of God? *"Behold, I make."* Who can create but God, the Maker of heaven and earth? It is His prerogative to make and to destroy. *"Behold, I make all things."* What a range of creating power! Nothing stands outside of that all-encompassing power. *"Behold, I make all things new."* What a splendor of almighty goodness shines out upon our souls! Lord, let us enter into this new universe of Yours. Let us be a part of the *"all things"* that are newly created. May others see the marvels of Your renewing love in us!

Let us thank Jesus as we hear these encouraging words that He speaks from His throne. O Lord, we want to rejoice and be glad forever in what You create. The former troubles are forgotten and are hidden from our eyes because of Your ancient promise, *"Behold, I create new heavens and a new earth: and the former shall not be remembered, nor come into mind"* (Isaiah 65:17).

I am going to write a little about the great transformation spoken of in the text: *"I make all things new."* Then I will go on to describe the earnest call in the text to consider that transformation: *"He that sat upon the throne said, Behold."* In other words, He said, "Pay attention to it, consider it, look at it!" *"Behold, I make all things new."* Oh, for an outpouring of the Holy Spirit while I discuss this theme and while you read about it!

The Great Transformation

Here is one of the greatest truths that ever came from the lips of Jesus: "*Behold, I make all things new.*" Let us gaze upon the great transformation.

This renewing work has been in our Lord's hands since long ago. Originally, we were under the old covenant, and when our first father and covenantal head, Adam, broke that covenant, we were ruined by his fatal violation. The substance of the old covenant that God made with Adam was this: "If you keep my command, you will live, and your posterity will live. But if you eat from the tree that I have forbidden you to eat from, you will die, and all your posterity in you will die."

As we know, Adam ate the forbidden fruit, and the tremendous Fall destroyed both our Paradise and ourselves. We were broken in pieces, seriously wounded, and even killed. We died in Adam, as far as spiritual life is concerned, and our state of death revealed itself in an inward tendency to evil that reigned in our members. We were like Ezekiel's deserted infant, unclothed and unwashed, left in our uncleanness to die, but the Son of God passed by and saw us in the greatness of our ruin (Ezekiel 16:1–14). In His wondrous love, our Lord Jesus put us under a new covenant, a covenant in which He became the Second Adam, a covenant in which God said to His Son, "If You will live in perfect obedience and vindicate My justice, then those who are in You will not perish, but they will live because You live."

Now, our Lord Jesus, our Surety and covenantal Head, has fulfilled His portion of the covenant, and the compact stands as a bond of pure promise without condition or risk. Those who are participants in that covenant cannot invalidate it, for it never did depend on them, but only on Him who was and is their covenantal Head and Representative before God. Of Jesus the demand was made, and He met it. By Him, man's side of the covenant was undertaken and fulfilled, and now no condition remains; the covenant is made up solely of promises that are unconditional and sure to all who are in Christ. Today, believers are not under the covenant of "If you do this, you will live," but under the new covenant that says, "*Their sins and their iniquities will I remember no more*" (Hebrews 8:12). The new covenant is not "Do and live," but "Live and do." The new covenant is not of merit and reward, but of free grace producing a holy lifestyle as the result of gratitude. What law could not do, grace has accomplished.

We must never forget this basis of everything, this making all things new by the fashioning of a new covenant. By it, we have been released from the bondage of the law and the ruin of the Fall, and we have entered into the liberty of Christ, into acceptance with God, and into the boundless joy of being saved in the Lord with an everlasting salvation. We *"shall not be ashamed nor confounded world without end"* (Isaiah 45:17).

If you know the Lord, I exhort you to thoroughly study that word *covenant*. If you do not yet know the Lord, I encourage you to study that word as soon as you come to know Him. It is a key word that opens the treasures of revelation. He who properly understands the difference between the two covenants has the foundation of sound theology laid in his mind. This understanding is the clue to many perplexities, the "open sesame" of many mysteries. Jesus makes *"all things new,"* beginning with the bringing in of a better hope through a better covenant.

The foundation having been made new, the Lord Jesus Christ has set before us a new way of life, which grows out of that covenant. The old way of life was this: "If you want to enter into life, keep the commandments." The commandments are perfect, holy, just, and good (Romans 7:12). But, alas, dear friend, you and I have broken the commandments. We dare not say that we have kept the Ten Commandments our whole lives; on the contrary, our consciences compel us to confess that in spirit and in heart, if not in act, we have continually broken the law of God. Therefore, we are under sin and condemnation, and there is no hope for us to be saved by the works of the law.

For this reason, the Gospel sets before us another way, and says, *"It is of faith, that it might be by grace"* (Romans 4:16), and *"Believe on the Lord Jesus Christ, and thou shalt be saved"* (Acts 16:31). Therefore, we read of being *"justified by faith"* (Romans 3:28), and being made acceptable to God by faith. To be *"justified"* means to be made truly righteous. Though we were guilty in ourselves, we are regarded as just because of what the Lord Jesus Christ has done for us. Thus, we fell into condemnation through another, and we rise into justification through Another. It is written, *"By his knowledge shall my righteous servant justify many; for he shall bear their iniquities"* (Isaiah 53:11), and this verse is fulfilled in all those who believe in the Lord Jesus and receive eternal life.

Our path to eternal glory is the road of faith: *"The just shall live by faith"* (Romans 1:17). We are *"accepted in the beloved"* (Ephesians 1:6) when we believe in the One whom God has set forth to be our righteousness. *"By the deeds of the law there shall no flesh be justified in his sight"* (Romans 3:20), but we are *"justified freely by his grace through the redemption that is in Christ Jesus"* (v. 24).

What a blessing it is for you and for me that Jesus has made all things new in this respect! I am glad that I do not have to say, "My dear reader, do this and do that, and you will be saved." You would not do as you were commanded, for your fallen nature is weak and wicked. But I can say to you,

> Lay your deadly doing down,
>> Down at Jesus' feet;
> Stand in Him, in Him alone,
>> Gloriously complete.

I trust that you will accept this most gracious way of salvation. It is most glorious to God and safe for you. Do not *"neglect so great [a] salvation"* (Hebrews 2:3). After you have believed and have received life, you will do all kinds of holy deeds as the result of your new life, but do not attempt them with a view to earning life. No longer prompted by the servile and selfish motive of saving yourself, but by gratitude for the fact that you are saved, you will rise to virtue and true holiness. Faith has given us an irreversible salvation, and now, because of the love that we have for our Savior, we must obey Him and become *"zealous of good works"* (Titus 2:14).

By grace, every believer is brought into a new relationship with God. Let us rejoice in this: *"Thou art no more a servant, but a son; and if a son, then an heir of God through Christ"* (Galatians 4:7). Oh, you who are now a believing child, you were an unbelieving servant a little while ago! Or, perhaps you are still an unbelieving servant; if you are, I tell you to expect your wages. Alas, your service has not been true service, but rebellion; and if you get no more wages than you deserve, you will be cast away forever. You ought to be thankful to God that He has not paid you yet, that *"he hath not dealt with [you] after [y]our sins; nor rewarded [you] according to [y]our iniquities"* (Psalm 103:10).

Don't you know, you unbelieving servant, what is likely to happen to you as a servant? What would you yourself do with a bad servant? You would say to him, "There are your wages. Go." *"The servant abideth not in the house for ever"* (John 8:35). You, too, will be driven from your hypocritical profession of faith. Your period of probation will end, and where will you go? The wilderness of destruction lies before you!

"Behold, I make all things new," says Jesus. Indeed, He makes His people into sons. When we are made sons, do we work for wages? We have no desire for any present payment, for our Father says to us, *"Son, thou art ever with me, and all that I have is thine"* (Luke 15:31). Furthermore, we have the inheritance given to us by the covenant. We cannot demand a servant's wages, because we already have all that our Father possesses. He has given us Himself and His all-sufficiency for our everlasting portion; what more can we desire? He will never drive us from His house. Never has our Father disowned one of His sons. It cannot be. His loving heart is too closely involved with His own adopted ones. That near and dear relationship that is manifested in adoption and regeneration binds the child of God to the great Father's heart in such a way that He will never cast him away or allow him to perish. I rejoice in the fact that we are no longer servants, but sons. *"Behold,"* says Christ, *"I make all things new."*

The Holy Spirit has put within us a new life, with all the new feelings, the new desires, and the new works that go with it. The tree has been made new, and the fruits are new as a result. The same Spirit of God who taught us that we were ruined in our old state of sin led us gently by the hand until we came to the new covenantal promise, looked to Jesus, and saw in Him the full atonement for sin. Happy discovery for us! It was the kindling of new life in us. The moment that we trusted in Jesus, a new life darted into our spirits.

I am not going to say which comes first: the new birth, faith, or repentance. When a wheel moves, no one can say which spoke moves first; it moves as a whole. The moment the divine life comes into the heart, we believe; the moment we believe, the eternal life is there. Then we no longer live according to the lusts of the world, but we live by faith in the Son of God, who loved us and gave Himself for us. (See Galatians 2:20.)

Our spiritual life is a newborn thing, the creation of the Spirit of life. We have, of course, the natural life that is sustained by food and that is evidenced by the fact that we are breathing, but there is another life within us that is not seen by others and is not fed by earthly provisions. We are conscious of having been spiritually awakened. We were dead once, and we know it; but now we have passed from death into life (John 5:24), and we know this just as certainly. A new and higher motive sways us now, for we do not seek self, but God. A new hand steers our ship in a new course. We feel new desires, to which we were strangers in our former state. New fears are mighty within us—holy fears that once we would have ridiculed. New hopes are in us, bright and sure, such as we did not even desire to have when we lived a mere carnal life. We are not what we were; we are new, and we have begun a new life. I admit that we are not what we will be, but assuredly, we are not what we used to be.

As for myself, my consciousness of being a new man in Christ Jesus is often as sharp and crisp as my consciousness of being in existence. I know that I am not solely what I was by my first birth. I feel within myself another life—a second and a higher vitality—that often has to contend with my lower self, and by that very contention makes me conscious of its existence. This new life is, from day to day, gathering strength and winning the victory. It has its hand on the throat of the old sinful nature, and it will eventually trample it like dust beneath its feet. I feel this new life within me; do you? If you feel it, I know that you can say that Jesus Christ, who sits on the throne, makes all things new. Blessed be His name. We needed the Lord Himself to make people such as we are new. No one but a Savior on the throne could accomplish it; therefore, let Him have the glory for it.

Perhaps Jesus Christ has not only made you new, but has made everything new to you. "Oh," one woman said when she was converted, "either the world is greatly changed, or else I am." Why, either you and I are turned upside down, or the world is. We used to think that the world is wise, but we think that it is very foolish now! We used to think of it as a brave, glad world that showed us real happiness, but we are no longer deceived. "The world is crucified unto me," Paul said in Galatians 6:14, and perhaps you can say the same. To believers, the world is like a vile criminal who is taken out and hanged. Meanwhile, there is no love lost, for the world thinks much the same of us, and we can agree with Paul when he added, "…and I [am crucified] unto the world."

Grace greatly transforms everything in our little world! In our hearts, there is a new heaven and a new earth. What a change in our joys! We blush to think about what we used to enjoy, but we enjoy heavenly things now. We are equally ashamed of our former hates and prejudices, but these have vanished once and for all. Why, now we love the very things we once despised, and our hearts run after the things that they once detested.

How different the Bible seems to us now! This blessed book is exactly the same in its wording, but how differently we read these precious words! The mercy seat of God, what a different place it is now! Our wretched, formal prayers—if we bothered to pray at all—what a mockery they were! But now we draw near to God and speak to Him with delight. We have access to Him by the "*new and living way*" (Hebrews 10:20). The house of God, how different it is from what it used to be! We love to be found within its walls, and we feel delighted to join in the praises of the Lord.

After a recent church service, I shook the hand of a man who does not often hear me preach. He expressed to me his boundless delight in listening to the doctrine of the grace of God, and he added, "Surely your congregation must be made of stone." "Why?" I asked. He replied, "If they were not, they would all get up and shout 'hallelujah' when you are preaching such a glorious Gospel. I wanted very much to shout, but since everybody else was quiet, I held my tongue." I thought he was wise for remaining silent, yet I am not surprised if men who have tasted God's grace do feel like crying out for joy.

Why shouldn't we lift up our voices in His praise? We will. He has put a new song into our mouths (Psalm 40:3), and we must sing it. "*The mountains and the hills…break forth before* [us] *into singing*" (Isaiah 55:12), and we cannot be silent. Praise is our ever new delight. In praise, we will compete with angels and archangels, for they are not so indebted to grace as we are.

> Never did angels taste above
> Redeeming grace and dying love.

Still, we have tasted these precious things, and unto God we will lift up our loudest song forever.

The process that I have roughly described as taking place in believers is going on in the physical world in other forms. All time is groaning, providence is working, grace is striving, the whole creation is giving birth, and all for one end—the bringing forth of the new and better age. It is coming. It is coming. It is ever nearer to us. And the Beloved Apostle did not write the following in vain:

And I saw a new heaven and a new earth: for the first heaven and the first earth were passed away; and there was no more sea. And I John saw the holy city, new Jerusalem, coming down from God out of heaven, prepared as a bride adorned for her husband. And I heard a great voice out of heaven saying, Behold, the tabernacle of God is with men, and he will dwell with them, and they shall be his people, and God himself shall be with them, and be their God. And God shall wipe away all tears from their eyes; and there shall be no more death, neither sorrow, nor crying, neither shall there be any more pain: for the former things are passed away. And he that sat upon the throne said, Behold, I make all things new. And he said unto me, Write: for these words are true and faithful. (Revelation 21:1–5)

What a prospect all this opens up to the believer! Our future is glorious; we must not let our present be gloomy.

An Earnest Call

Next, in the text, there is an earnest call for us to consider this work of our Lord. He who sits on the throne says, *"Behold, I make all things new."* Why should He call on us to behold this? All His works deserve study. *"The works of the LORD are great, sought out of all them that have pleasure therein"* (Psalm 111:2). Whatever the Lord does is full of wisdom, and the wise will look into His works. But when the Lord Himself sets up a light and calls us to pause and look, we cannot help but respond.

I think that the Lord Jesus Christ specifically calls us to consider the fact that He makes all things new, so that we may be comforted, regardless of our condition.

To the Unsaved

First, this verse is a comfort to the unsaved. If the Lord Jesus makes all things new, then a new birth is possible for you, dear friend, even though you have a wrong state of heart and your sins are upon you, clutching you tightly. There is enough light in your soul for you to know that you are in darkness, and you are saying to yourself, "Oh, if only I could attain better things! I hear people praise God for what Christ has done for them. Can He do the same for me?" Listen! He who sits on the throne says in infinite graciousness to you on the trash heap, *"Behold, I make all things new."* There is nothing so old that He cannot make it new, and nothing so ingrained and habitual that He cannot change it.

Don't you know, dear heart, that the Spirit of God has regenerated men and women just as far gone as you are? They were as deep in sin and as hardened by habit as you could ever be. They thought that they were hopeless, just as you think that you are. Yet the Spirit of God carried out the will of the Lord Christ and made them new. Why shouldn't He make you new? May every thief know that the dying thief entered heaven by faith in Jesus. May everyone who has been a great sinner remember how Manasseh received a new heart and repented of his evil deeds. (See 2 Chronicles 33:1–13.) Let everyone who has left the paths of purity remember how the woman who was a sinner loved much because she had been forgiven much. (See Luke 7:37–48.)

I cannot doubt the possibility of your salvation, my friend, whenever I think of my own. A more determined, obstinate rebel could scarcely have existed. Because I was a child and was kept from gross outward sin by holy restraints, I had a powerful inner nature that would not tolerate control. I rebelliously strove hard. I labored to win heaven by self-righteousness, and this is as real a rebellion as open sin. But, oh, the grace of God, how it can tame us! How it can turn us! With no bit or bridle, but with a blessed tenderness, it turns us according to its pleasure. Oh, anxious one, it can turn you! Therefore, I want to drop this truth into your mind (and may the Spirit of God drop it into your heart): you can be born again. The Lord can work a radical change in you. He who sits on the throne can do for you what you cannot do for yourself. He made you once, and even though you became marred by sin, He can make you new again. He says, "*Behold, I make all things new.*"

To Those Who Want a New Life

This verse is also a comfort to those who desire to lead a new life. To have a new life, you must be new yourself; for as the man is, so his life will be. If the fountain is contaminated, the streams cannot be pure. Renewal must begin with the heart.

Dear friend, the Lord Jesus Christ is able to make your life entirely new. I have seen many people transformed into new parents and new children. Friends have exclaimed in amazement, "What a change in John! What a difference in Ellen!" I have seen men become new husbands and women become new wives. They are the same people, yet not the same. Grace works a very deep, striking, and lasting change. Ask someone who has seen a member of his household converted whether the transformation has not been marvelous. Christ makes new employees, new supervisors, new friends, new brothers, new sisters. The Lord can so change us that we hardly know ourselves.

He can change you who now despair of yourself. Oh, dear heart, it is not necessary for you to go downward in evil until you descend to hell. There is a hand that can pull you in the opposite direction. It would be an amazing thing if Niagara Falls were to flow backward, ascending instead of descending. It would be an incredible thing if the St. Lawrence River were to run backward to Lake Ontario. Yet, God could do even these things.

Likewise, God Almighty can reverse the course of your fallen nature and make you act like a new person. He can stop the tide of your raging passion. He can make someone who is like a devil become like an angel of God, for He says this from the throne of His eternal majesty: "Behold, I make all things new." Come and lay yourself down at His feet, and ask Him to make you new. I implore you, do this at once!

"Well, I am going to mend myself," some people say. "I have taken a pledge that I will be honest, moral, and religious." This is a commendable decision, but what will come of it? You will break your resolutions; you will not be made any better by your attempts at reform. If you go into the business of mending yourself, you will be like the man who had an old gun. He took it to the gunsmith, and the gunsmith said, "Well, this would make a very good gun if it had a new lock, a new stock, and a new barrel." Likewise, mending would make you a very good person, if you could get a new heart, a new life, and an altogether new self, so that there was not one bit of the old self left.

You can depend on it that it is a great deal easier for God to make you new than to mend you, for the fact is that *the carnal mind is enmity against God* (Romans 8:7). The carnal mind is not reconciled to God; indeed, it cannot be. Therefore, mending will not do; you must be made new. *"Ye must be born again"* (John 3:7). What is needed is for you to be made a new creation in Christ Jesus. You must be dead with Christ, buried with Christ, and risen again in Him (Romans 6:4). Then all will be well, for He will have made all things new. I ask God to bless these feeble words of mine and use them to help some of His chosen out of the darkness of their fears.

To the Weary Christian

There are children of God who need this text, *"Behold, I make all things new."* They sigh because they often grow dull and weary in the ways of God and therefore need daily renewing. A fellow believer said to me some time ago, "Dear pastor, I frequently grow very sleepy in my walk with God. I seem to lose the freshness of it. By about Saturday I feel especially dull." Then he added, "But as for you, whenever I hear you, you seem to be alive and full of fresh energy." "My dear brother," I said, "that is because you do not know much about me." That was all I was able to say just then.

I thank God for keeping me near Himself. But I am as weak, as stale, and as unprofitable as any other believer. I say this with much shame—shame for myself and shame for the brother who led me to make the confession. We are both wrong. Since all our fresh springs are in God (Psalm 87:7), we ought to be full of new life all the time. Every minute, our love for Christ ought to be as if it were newborn. Our zeal for God ought to be as fresh as if we had just begun to delight in Him. "Yes, but it is not," most Christians would say, and I am sorry I cannot contradict them. After a few months, a vigorous young Christian begins to cool down. Likewise, those who have walked in the ways of God for a long time find that final perseverance must be a miracle if it is ever to be accomplished, because they tire and grow faint.

Well now, dear friend, why do you and I ever get stale and flat? Why do we sing,

> Dear Lord, and shall we ever live
> At this poor dying rate?

Why do we have to cry,

> In vain we tune our formal songs,
> In vain we strive to rise;
> Hosannas languish on our tongues,
> And our devotion dies?

Why, it is because we stray away from the One who says, *"Behold, I make all things new."* The way to perpetual newness and freshness is to keep going to Christ, just as we did when we were first saved.

An even better way is never to leave Him, but to stand forever at the foot of the cross, delighting in His all-sufficient sacrifice. Those who are full of the joy of the Lord never grow weary of life. Those who walk in the light of His countenance can say of the Lord Jesus, *"Thou hast the dew of thy youth"* (Psalm 110:3), and that dew falls on those who dwell with Him. I am sure that if we would maintain perpetual communion with Him, we would enjoy a perpetual stream of delights.

> Immortal joys come streaming down,
> Joys, like His griefs, immense, unknown.

Still, these joys come only from Him. We will remain young if we stay with the ever young Beloved, whose hair is black as a raven (Song 5:11). He says, and He fulfills the saying, *"Behold, I make all things new."*

He can make that next sermon of yours, my fellow minister, quite new and interesting. He can make that prayer meeting no longer a dreary affair, but quite a new thing to you and all the people. My dear sister, the next time you go to your Sunday school class, the Lord can cause you to feel as if you had just started teaching yesterday. Then you will not be at all tired of your godly work; instead, you will love it better than ever. And you, my dear brother, preaching at the street corner, where you are often interrupted, perhaps with foul language, you will feel pleased with your position of self-denial. Getting near to Christ, you will partake of His joy, and that joy will be your strength, your freshness, the newness of your life. May God grant to us that we may drink of the eternal fountains, so that we may forever overflow.

There may be someone reading this who knows that he is living on a very low plane of spiritual life, but he also understands that the Lord can raise him to a new level. Many Christians seem to dwell in the marshlands. If you ever travel through the valleys of Switzerland, you will find yourself getting feverish and heavy in spirit, and you will see many who are mentally or physically afflicted. However, if you climb the sides of the hills, ascending into the Alps, you will not see that kind of thing in the pure, fresh air. Unfortunately in this present era, too many Christians are of the sickly valley breed. Oh, that they could get up to the high mountains and be strong!

If you have been in bondage all your life, I declare that you do not need to stay there any longer. Jesus has the power to make all things new and to lift you into new delights. It might seem like a resurrection from the dead to you, but it is within the power of that pierced hand to lift you right out of doubt, fear, despondency, spiritual lethargy, and weakness, and to make you now, from this day forward, *"strong in the Lord, and in the power of his might"* (Ephesians 6:10).

Now breathe a prayer, dear brother, dear sister, to the One who makes all things new: "Lord, make Your poor, spiritually sick child strong and spiritually healthy." Oh, what a blessing it would be for some Christian workers if God would make them strong! The whole church would be better because of the way in which the Lord would help them to do their work. Why should you be living on pennies and starving yourself when your Heavenly Father would cause you to live like a prince of royal blood if you would only trust Him? I am persuaded that most of us are beggars when we could be millionaires in spiritual things. And here is our strength for rising to a nobler state of mind: *"Behold, I make all things new."*

To the Afflicted Christian

There is another application of this truth. Someone may be saying to himself, "Oh, I do not know what to make of myself. I have had a hard time lately. Everything seems to have gone wrong. My family causes me great anxiety. My business is a thorny maze. My own health is precarious. I dread this year. In fact, I dread everything." We will not go on with that lamentation, but we will hear the encouraging word, *"Behold, I make all things new."* The Lord, in answer to believing prayer, and especially in answer to your full submission to His will, is able to make all your surroundings new. I have known the Lord to turn darkness into light all of a sudden, and to take away the sackcloth and the ashes from His dear children, for *"he doth not afflict willingly nor grieve the children of men"* (Lamentations 3:33).

Sometimes all our worry is mere discontentment, and when the child of God gets himself right, these imaginary troubles vanish like the morning mist. But when the troubles are real, God can just as easily change your condition, dear child of God, as He can turn His hand. He can make your harsh and ungodly husband become gentle and gracious. He can bring your children to the place where they will bow at the family altar and rejoice with you in Christ. He can cause your business to prosper. Or, if He does not do that, He can strengthen your back to bear the burden of your daily cross.

Oh, it is wonderful how different a thing becomes when it is taken to God. But you want to make it all new yourself, and you fret and worry; you torture, trouble, and burden yourself. Why not stop that, and in humble prayer, take the matter to the Lord and say, "Lord, come to my aid, for You have said, *'I make all things new.'* Make my circumstances new"? He is certainly able to free you from your captivity.

To Those Anxious about Unsaved Loved Ones

There is one more application, and that is that the Lord can convert those dear unsaved loved ones about whom you have been so anxious. The Lord who makes all things new can hear your prayers. At a prayer meeting that I attended recently, a dear brother prayed that God would save his relatives. Then another prayed with great tenderness for his children. I know that his prayer came from an aching heart. Some of you have heartbreakers at home; may the Lord break their hearts—humbling and softening them so that they will come to Him. You are grieved and troubled because you hear the person you hold the dearest blaspheming the God you love. You know that your loved ones are Sabbath-breakers, and utterly godless, and you tremble for their eternal fate.

Certain people attend my church who are not saved. I can say of them that I never stand behind the pulpit without looking to their pews to see whether they are there and without praying to God for them. I forget a great many who are saved, but I always pray for these unsaved ones. And they will be brought in, I feel assured. Oh, may it be soon!

I liked what one man said at a recent service when his brother was introduced to the church. Wondering about his brother's conversion, I asked, "Were you surprised to see him converted?" He said, "I would have been very much surprised if he had not been." "But why, my dear brother?" I asked. "Because I asked the Lord to convert him, and I kept on praying that he would be converted. I would have been very surprised if he had not been." That is the right sort of faith. I would be very surprised if some of the unsaved who attend my church, time after time, are not converted. They will be, blessed be God. I will give Him no rest until He answers me.

But if you are unsaved, aren't you praying for yourself? Don't you agree with the prayers of your Christian friends and relatives who are praying for you? Oh, I trust that you do. But, even if you do not, they will still pray for you. Even if you are opposed to their intercessions and are even angry with them, they will undoubtedly pray all the more. They intend to have you won for Jesus, by the grace of God, and you may as well come sooner rather than later. They are determined to see you in the church confessing your faith in Jesus. They will never let you go, neither will they cease from their persistent prayers, until they get an answer from the throne, and see you saved. Oh, that you would yield to the One who can make a new creation out of you (2 Corinthians 5:17). May God grant that you will!

May the Lord answer my prayers now, for Jesus' sake, for I seek the salvation of every reader of this book.

2

THIS YEAR ALSO

He spake also this parable; a certain man had a fig tree planted in his vineyard; and he came and sought fruit thereon, and found none. Then said he unto the dresser of his vineyard, Behold, these three years I come seeking fruit on this fig tree, and find none: cut it down; why cumbereth it the ground? And he answering said unto him, Lord, let it alone this year also, till I shall dig about it, and dung it: and if it bear fruit, well: and if not, then after that thou shalt cut it down.
—Luke 13:6–9

The interceding vinedresser pleaded for the fruitless fig tree, "*Let it alone this year also,*" securing for it another year. During that year, it would have to bear fruit, or else it would be cut down. Unlike people, trees and fruit-bearing plants have a natural way of marking a year. Evidently the tree's year came to its close when it was time to seek fruit on it, and another year commenced when the vinedresser began once again his digging and pruning. But men are such barren things that their fruit-bearing marks no particular periods, and it becomes necessary to make artificial divisions of time for them. There seems to be no set period for man's spiritual harvest or vintage, or if there is, the sheaves and the clusters do not come in their season. Thus, it is necessary for us to say to one another, "Let us make this the beginning of a new year."

A Look at the Past

Look back over the past year of your life and examine it, deliberately and honestly. In the parable of the fig tree, there had been prior years of grace. It was not the first time that the vine-dresser was made aware of the fig tree's failure. It was not the first time the owner came seeking figs in vain. In the same way, God, who gives us *"this year also,"* has given us others before it. His sparing mercy is no novelty; His patience has already been taxed by our provocations.

First came our youthful years, when even a little fruit for God is especially sweet to Him. How did we spend them? Did we spend all of our strength on sinful pleasures? If so, we should mourn that wasted vigor, that life misspent, that sin exceedingly multiplied. Nevertheless, He who saw us misuse those golden months of youth gives us *"this year also."* We should enter it with a holy jealousy, lest the strength and fervency that are left to us be allowed to flow into the same wasteful avenues as before.

Upon the heels of our youthful years came the years of young adulthood, when we started a family and put out roots. Fruit yielded during that time also would have been precious. Did we bear any? Did we present unto the Lord a basket of summer fruit? Did we offer Him the firstfruits of our strength? If we did so, we should adore the grace that saved us so early; but if not, the past chides us, and, lifting an admonishing finger, it warns us not to let *"this year also"* follow the same path as the rest of our lives. The person who has wasted both youth and early adulthood has surely been foolish enough; he has spent enough time following the desires of his flesh. It would be an overflow of wickedness to allow *"this year also"* to be trodden down in the service of sin.

Many of you are now in the prime of life; many years of your lives are already spent. Do you still need to confess that your years are being eaten up by the grasshopper and the cankerworm (Joel 1:4)? Have you reached midlife and still do not know where you are going? Are you fools at forty? Are you half a century old by the calendar and yet far away from the years of wisdom? How unfortunate that there are men over fifty years old who are still without knowledge!

Unsaved at sixty, unregenerate at seventy, unawakened at eighty, unrenewed at ninety— each and every one of these phrases is startling! Perhaps their wording will startle and awaken someone who is reading this, but, on the other hand, that person might just gloss over them. Continuance in evil breeds hardness of heart, and when the soul has been sleeping in indifference for a long time, it is hard to arouse it from its deadly slumber.

The sound of the words *"this year also"* makes some of us remember years of great mercy, sparkling and flashing with delight. Were those years laid at the Lord's feet? Were they like the horses' silver bells that were engraved with the words, "HOLINESS UNTO THE LORD" (Zechariah 14:20)? If not, how will we explain our neglect if *"this year also"* is musical with joyful mercy and yet spent in the ways of carelessness?

"This year also." These words cause some of us to recall our years of sharp affliction, when we were indeed dug around and fertilized. What were those years like? God was doing great things for us, cultivating carefully and expensively, caring for us very much and very wisely. Did we give back to God according to the benefits we received from Him? Did we rise from the bed of affliction with more patience and gentleness, weaned from the world and welded to Christ? Did we produce clusters of grapes to reward the Vinedresser?

Let us not refuse to answer these questions of self-examination, for this year may be another of those years of trial, another season of the furnace and the crucible. May the Lord grant that the coming tribulation take more chaff out of us than any tribulation before it, leaving the wheat cleaner and better.

A new year reminds us of opportunities for usefulness that have come and gone, and of unfulfilled resolutions of the past that have blossomed, only to fade. Will *"this year also"* be like those that have gone before it? Shouldn't we hope for more grace so that we may build upon grace already gained? And shouldn't we seek power to turn our poor sickly promises into robust action?

Looking back on the past, we lament our foolish actions. We do not want to be held captive by them *"this year also."* At the same time, we adore God's forgiving mercy, His preserving providence, His boundless generosity, and His divine love; and we hope to be partakers of them *"this year also."*

A Gift of Mercy

The text also mentions a mercy. Because of the vinedresser's great goodness, the tree that was merely taking up space was allowed to stand for another year.

Prolonged life should always be regarded as a gift of mercy. We must view *"this year also"* as a grant from infinite grace. It is wrong to speak as if we cared nothing for life, as if we looked upon our being here on earth as torture or punishment. We are here *"this year also"* as the result of love's pleadings and to pursue love's purposes.

The wicked individual should consider that the Lord's longsuffering points to his salvation, and he should permit the cords of love to draw him to it. Oh, that the Holy Spirit would make the blasphemer, the Sabbath-breaker, and the openly immoral to feel what a wonder it is that their lives are prolonged *"this year also"*! Are they spared to curse and to riot and to defy their Maker? Should this be the only fruit of the Lord's patient mercy? Shouldn't the procrastinator who has put off the messenger of heaven with his delays and half promises be amazed that he is allowed to see *"this year also"*? How is it that the Lord has borne with him and has put up with his vacillations and hesitations? Is this year of grace to be spent in the same manner? Short-lived convictions, hasty commitments, and speedy apostasies—are these to be the tiresome story over and over again? The startled conscience, the tyrant passion, the smothered emotion—are these to be the tokens of yet another year?

May God forbid that any one of us should hesitate and delay throughout *"this year also."* Infinite pity holds back the ax of justice. Will His mercy be insulted by the repetition of the sins that caused wrath's instrument to be raised? What can be more tormenting to the heart of goodness than indecision? May the Lord's prophet become impatient and cry, *"How long halt ye between two opinions?"* (1 Kings 18:21). May God Himself push for a decision and demand an immediate reply. Oh, undecided soul, will you swing much longer between heaven and hell, and act as if it were hard to choose between the slavery of Satan and the liberty of the great Father's home of love? *"This year also,"* will you delay in defiance of justice, and pervert the generosity of mercy into a license for still further rebellion? *"This year also,"* must divine love be made an occasion for continued sin? Oh, do not act so wickedly, so contrary to every noble instinct, so injuriously to your own best interests.

The believer, on the other hand, is kept out of heaven *"this year also"* because of God's love, not His anger. There are people who need him to remain on earth: some need him to guide them on their way to heaven, and others need his help and instruction to lead them to the Redeemer's feet. Many saints do not have their heaven prepared for them yet, because their nearest companions have not yet arrived there, and their spiritual children have not yet gathered there in sufficient numbers to give them a thoroughly heavenly welcome. They must wait *"this year also,"* so their rest may be even more glorious and the additional souls that they win to Christ may give them greater joy. Surely, for the sake of souls, for the delight of glorifying our Lord, and for the increase of the jewels in our heavenly crowns, we may be glad to wait below *"this year also."*

The Limitations of Mercy

I want to emphasize that the expression *"this year also"* implies a limit. The vinedresser asked for a reprieve of no longer than one year. If his digging and fertilizing should prove unsuccessful, he would plead no more, and the tree would be cut down.

Even when Jesus is the pleader, the request of mercy has its boundaries and limits. We will not be left alone and allowed to needlessly take up space forever. If we will not repent, we must perish. If we will not be benefited by the spade, we must fall by the ax.

There will be a last year for each one of us. Therefore, let each one say to himself, "Is this year my last?" If it were to be the last for me, I would prepare to deliver the Lord's message with all my soul and to tell my fellowmen to be reconciled to God. Dear friend, is this year to be your last? Are you ready to see the curtain rise upon eternity? Are you now prepared to hear the midnight cry and to enter into the marriage supper (Matthew 25:6; Revelation 19:7–9)? The Judgment and all that will follow it are most surely the heritage of every person. Blessed are they who by faith in Jesus are able to face the judgment seat of God without a thought of terror.

Even if we live to be counted among the oldest inhabitants of the earth, we must depart at last. There must come an end, and we will hear the Lord say, *"Thus saith the LORD…this year thou shalt die"* (Jeremiah 28:16). So many have gone before us, and are going every hour, that no man should need any other reminder that we must die. Yet, man is so eager to forget his own mortality, and thereby to forfeit his hopes of bliss, that we cannot bring it too often before the mind's eye. Oh, mortal man, think! *"Prepare to meet thy God"* (Amos 4:12), for you must meet Him. Seek the Savior; yes, seek Him before another sunset.

"*This year also*"—and this may be the last year—the Cross is once again uplifted as the lighthouse of the world, the one light to which no eye can look in vain. Oh, that millions would look that way and live. Soon the Lord Jesus will come a second time, and then the blaze of His throne will replace the mild radiance of His cross. The Judge will be seen rather than the Redeemer. Now He saves, but then He will destroy. Let us hear His voice at this moment. Let us be eager to avail ourselves of this gracious season. Let us believe in Jesus this day, since it may be our last. Hear these pleadings for your soul's sake, and live.

3

GROWING IN THE LORD

But grow in grace, and in the knowledge of our Lord and Saviour Jesus Christ. To him be glory both now and for ever. Amen.
—2 Peter 3:18

Beloved friends, we are perpetually in danger. Where can we go to escape from peril? Where can we go to avoid temptation? If we venture into business, worldliness is there. If we retire to our homes, trials await us there. One would imagine that in the green pastures of the Word of God, there would be perfect security for God's sheep. Surely no lion is there; surely no ferocious beast can walk there! Unfortunately, it is not so. Even while we are reading the Bible, we are still exposed to peril. It is not that the truth is dangerous, but that our corrupt hearts can find poison in the very flowers of paradise.

Notice what Peter said about the writings of the apostle Paul: *"In which are some things hard to be understood"* (2 Peter 3:16). Also, mark the danger to which we are exposed: *"Which they that are unlearned and unstable wrest, as they do also the other scriptures, unto their own destruction"* (2 Peter 3:16). We can distort even the Word of God to our own destruction. With the Bible before our eyes, we

675

can still commit sin. Pondering over the holy words of inspired Scripture, we can receive a deadly wound from *"the error of the wicked"* (2 Peter 3:17). Even at the horns of the altar (Exodus 27:1–2; 1 Kings 1:50), we still need God to cover us with the shadow of His wings (Psalm 17:8).

How wonderful that our gracious Father has provided a shield to shelter us from every evil. For example, our text will help to prevent us from falling into the evil of unorthodox doctrines, for we are in danger of misinterpreting Scripture to make God say what He does not. If we depart from the teaching of the Holy Spirit, we are in danger of distorting the letter of the Word and losing its spirit, and of deriving from the letter a meaning that can ruin our souls.

How can we escape this? Peter, speaking by the Holy Spirit, pointed out our safeguard in the words of our text: *"But grow in grace, and in the knowledge of our Lord and Saviour Jesus Christ. To him be glory both now and for ever. Amen."* While you search the Scriptures and become acquainted with them, see to it that you *"grow in grace."* While you desire to learn and understand doctrine, long, above all, to grow in *"the knowledge of our Lord and Saviour Jesus Christ."*

However, let both your study of Scripture and your growth in grace and in the knowledge of Christ still be subservient to a higher objective: that you may live to bring *"glory both now and for ever"* to Him who has loved you and has bought you with His blood. Let your heart forever say *"Amen"* to this doxology of praise. In this way, you will be kept from all destructive errors, and you will not *"fall from your own stedfastness"* (2 Peter 3:17). It appears, then, that our text is a heavenly remedy for certain diseases to which even students of Scripture are exposed.

We see in our text two "trumpets." One is blown from heaven to earth: *"Grow in grace, and in the knowledge of our Lord and Saviour Jesus Christ."* The other resounds from earth to heaven: *"To him be glory both now and for ever."*

Another way to look at our text is to divide it into two matters. First, there is a matter of theology: *"Grow in grace."* Second, there is a matter of doxology: *"To him be glory both now and for ever."*

A third way to look at our text, and the way that we will look at it in this chapter, is this: first, we have a divine command with a special direction; and second, a grateful doxology with a significant conclusion.

Growing in Grace

I will begin at the beginning. We have here a divine command with a special direction: "*Grow in grace, and in the knowledge of our Lord and Saviour Jesus Christ.*"

Who Can Grow in Grace?

"*Grow in grace.*" What does this mean? We see in the very outset of this verse that it was written to those who have been awakened by grace. This verse does not apply to the unsaved at all. Dead things cannot grow. Those who are alive unto God by the resurrection of Jesus Christ are the only ones who have any power or ability to grow. The great Life-giver must first implant the seeds of life, and then afterward, those seeds can germinate and grow. Therefore, this text does not apply to you who are "*dead in trespasses and sins*" (Ephesians 2:1). You cannot grow in grace, because you are still under the curse of the law, and the wrath of God remains on you (John 3:36). Tremble, repent, believe; and may God have mercy on you.

However, if you are alive from the dead, if you have been awakened by the Spirit of God who is now in you, you are instructed to grow, for growth will prove that you are spiritually alive. A post planted in the earth does not grow, but a tree rooted there increases from a sapling to a forest king. Drop a pebble into the richest soil, and many years from now, it will still be a pebble of the same size. However, plant a seed, and it will sprout and develop.

Growing in Every Virtue

You who are alive unto God, see to it that you grow in all the graces. Grow in your roots—that is, in your faith. Seek to believe God's promises better than you do now. From that trembling faith that says, "*Lord, I believe; help thou mine unbelief*" (Mark 9:24), grow upward to the faith that "*stagger[s] not at the promise of God*" (Romans 4:20). Like Abraham, believe that "*what he [has] promised, he [is] able also to perform*" (v. 21). Permit your faith increase in extent; believe more truth. Let it increase in constancy; do not allow it to be feeble or wavering, always tossed about with every wind of false doctrine (Ephesians 4:14). Let your faith daily increase in simplicity, resting more fully on the finished work of your Lord Jesus Christ.

In addition to faith, see to it that your love also grows. If your love has been a spark, pray that the spark may become an all-consuming flame. If you have brought to Christ only a little, pray that you may bring your all. Pray that you may offer your all in such a way that, like Mary's broken alabaster box, the King Himself may be satisfied with the perfume (Matthew 26:7–13). Ask that your love may become more extended—that you may have love for all the saints. Ask that it may be more practical, that it may move your every thought, every word, and every deed. Ask that it may be more intense, that you may become like a burning and shining light whose flame is love for God and man.

In addition to love, pray that you may grow in hope. Along those lines, pray that *"the eyes of your understanding being enlightened…ye may know what is the hope of his calling, and what [are] the riches of the glory of his inheritance in the saints"* (Ephesians 1:18). Pray that you will continually look *"for that blessed hope, and the glorious appearing of the great God and our Saviour Jesus Christ"* (Titus 2:13). Pray that the hope not yet realized may enable you to wait patiently (Romans 8:25). Pray that you may, by hope, enter into the joys of heaven while you are on earth. Pray that hope may give you immortality while you are still mortal, may give you resurrection before you die, may allow you to see God clearly where otherwise you could see only a dim reflection.

Ask that you may grow in humility, until you can say, "[I] *am less than the least of all saints"* (Ephesians 3:8). Ask that you may grow in consecration, until you can cry, *"For to me to live is Christ, and to die is gain"* (Philippians 1:21). Ask that you may grow in contentment, until you can say, *"I have learned, in whatsoever state I am, therewith to be content"* (Philippians 4:11). Advance in likeness to the Lord Jesus, so that your very enemies may notice that you have been with Jesus and have learned from Him (Acts 4:13).

In short, if there is any virtue, if there is anything that is praiseworthy, if there is anything that is true and pure, if there is anything that is lovely and of good report (Philippians 4:8), if there is anything that can increase your usefulness, that can add to your happiness, that can make you more useful to man and more glorious toward God, grow in it. Growth is necessary, for we have not *"already attained,"* nor are we *"already perfect"* (Philippians 3:12).

As a Tree Grows

I want to remind you, faithful believer in Christ, that the Bible compares you to a tree—a tree of the Lord's planting (Isaiah 61:3). Seek to grow as a tree grows.

Pray that this year you may grow downward, that you may know more of your own vileness, more of your own nothingness, and so be rooted in humility. Pray that your roots may penetrate below the mere topsoil of truth into the great rocks that underlie the uppermost layer, so that you may grasp the doctrines of eternal love, God's unchangeable faithfulness, complete satisfaction, union with Christ, and the eternal purpose of God. These deep things of God will yield a rich and abundant sap, and your roots will drink from the hidden fountains of *"the deep that lieth under"* (Genesis 49:25).

This growth of your roots will be a growth that will not add to your fame or your vanity, but it will be invaluable during the storms of life. It will be a growth the value of which no heart can conceive when the hurricane is tearing up the hypocrite and hurling into the sea of destruction the *"trees whose fruit withere[d], without fruit, twice dead, plucked up by the roots"* (Jude 12).

As you root downward, seek to grow upward. Send out the top shoot of your love toward heaven. The trees send out their spring shoots and their midsummer shoots. You can see, at the top of the fir tree, that new green child of spring—the fresh shoot that lifts its hand toward the sun. In the same way, you should also long for more love and greater desires for God, a closer communion with Him in prayer, a sweeter spirit of adoption as His child, a more intense and intimate fellowship with the Father and with His Son Jesus Christ. This act of mounting upward will add to your beauty and to your delight.

In addition, pray to grow on either side. Stretch out your branches. Let the shadow of your holy influence extend as far as God has given you opportunities. But see to it also that you grow in fruitfulness, for to increase the bough without adding to the fruit is to diminish the beauty of the tree. Labor this year, by God's grace, to bring forth more fruit for Him than you have ever done. Lord, give to each reader more of the fruits of penitence for sin, faith in the great sacrifice of Jesus, love for the Savior, and zeal for the conversion of souls. We do not want to be like the gleanings of the vintage, when there is only here and there a cluster on the uppermost bough. We want to be like the valley of Eshcol in the Promised Land (Deuteronomy 1:24–25), whose presses burst with new wine.

This is what it means to grow in grace: to root downward, to shoot upward, to extend your influence like far-reaching branches, and to bring forth fruit for the Lord's glory.

As a Child Grows

I will borrow another comparison from Scripture. Fellow believer, we are not only compared to trees, but to children. Let us grow as babes do, nourished by unadulterated milk (1 Peter 2:2). Like babes, let us grow steadily, slowly, but surely and certainly. In this way, we will grow a little each day, but much through the years. Oh, that we may grow in strength as a child does, until the little, wobbling limbs of our faith are firm, muscular legs—the legs of a young man who runs without weariness. May we have untiring feet—the feet of a strong man who walks without fainting. (See Isaiah 40:31.) So far, our wings are unfledged, and we can hardly leave the nest. Lord, command our growth to proceed until we can mount as with the wings of eagles toward You, surmounting clouds and storms, and dwelling in the serene presence of the Most High. Let us develop all our powers. Let us ask that we may no longer be little infants, but that many inches may be added to our height until we become mature in Christ Jesus.

Let us especially pray that we may grow as healthy children—uniformly. Beloved, it is a bad sign if a child's head enlarges but not the rest of his body, or if his arm or foot is swollen disproportionately. Beauty consists in every part having the correct proportion. A vigorous judgment should not be yoked with a cold heart, nor a clear eye with a withered hand. A giant's head looks odd on a dwarf's shoulders. A virtue nourished at the expense of others is like a fattened cannibal fed on the flesh and blood of its murdered relatives; it is not fitting for a Christian to harbor such a monster. Let us pray that faith and love and every grace may be developed, that not one power may be left unnurtured or ungrown. Only in this way can we truly *"grow in grace, and in the knowledge of our Lord and Saviour Jesus Christ."*

Reasons to Grow in Grace

Do you ask why we should grow in grace? Let us say, beloved, that if we do not advance in grace, it is a sorrowful sign. It is a mark of unhealthiness. It is a sickly child who does not grow, an unhealthy tree that sends forth no fresh shoots. Furthermore, it may be a sign not only of unhealthiness but of deformity. If a man's shoulders have grown to a certain breadth, but his lower limbs refuse to lift him to a proportionate height, we call him a dwarf, and we somewhat pity him because he is malformed. O Lord, let us grow, for we do not want to be ill-formed.

We want to be children like God our Father; we want to be pleasing in appearance, every one of us like the sons of a king.

Not to grow may be, moreover, the sign of death. Our lack of growth may say to us, "To the extent that you do not grow, you do not live." If you are not increasing in faith, love, and grace; if you are not ripening for the harvest, fear and tremble. Perhaps you have only a reputation for being alive while you are actually destitute of life (Revelation 3:1). Perhaps you are a painted counterfeit—a lovely picture of a flower, drawn by the artist's skillful hand, but lacking life, lacking the power that makes the flowers germinate, blossom, and bring forth fruit. Advance in grace, because not to progress foretells many evil things and might indicate the worst of all things: lack of spiritual life.

Grow in grace, because, beloved, to increase in grace is the only pathway to lasting nobility. Oh, don't you wish to stand with that noble host who have served their Master well and have entered into their eternal rest? Who does not wish to have his name written with the great missionaries—with Judson and with Carey, with Williams and with Moffat? What Christian has no ambition to find his name written among those servants of God—Whitefield, Grimshaw, Newton, Romaine, Toplady, and others who preached the Word with power? Do you wish to go back to the vile dust from where we sprung up, unwept, unhonored, and unsung? If so, then remain as you are; stop marching forward. Littleness and lowness lie at your door; be small and ignoble, if you desire. But if you want to be a prince in God's Israel, if you want to be a mighty warrior for the Cross of Christ, then pray this prayer: "Lord, help me grow in grace, so I may be a faithful servant and receive Your commendation in the end."

To grow is not only to be noble; it is to be happy. The man who stops growing refuses to be blessed. With most businessmen, if they do not win, they lose. With the warrior, if he does not gain in the battle, his enemy is getting an advantage. The wise man who gets no wiser grows more foolish. The Christian who does not learn more about his Lord and become more like Him, knows less about his Lord and becomes less like Him. If our armor is unused, it will tarnish. If our arms are not strengthened by effort, they will be weakened by laziness. Our happiness declines as our spirituality fades.

To be happy, I say, we must go forward. Ahead is sunlight. Ahead is victory. Ahead is heaven. Ahead is Christ! To stand still is danger; no, it is death. O Lord, for the sake of our happiness, help us to advance; for the sake of our usefulness, let us ascend. Oh, if only we would grow in grace, if only we would grow stronger in faith, mightier in prayer, more fervent in heart, holier in life, who can tell how much we might accomplish? Men who walk lightly leave faint footprints, but men who have the tread of Roman soldiers stamp their footprints on the sands of time, never to be erased. Let us live in such a way that, in our own time and in the future, the world may be better and Christ's church more prosperous for our having lived. For this reason, if for no other, let us grow in grace.

Oh, I want to fire you with holy ambition today! If I could snatch from some ancient altar a live coal such as that which fell on the lips of Isaiah, I would say to you, "'Lo, this hath touched thy lips' (Isaiah 6:7). Go forth in the spirit and power of God, even the Most High, and live as those who did not count their lives dear unto themselves (Acts 20:24) so that they could serve their Master and 'be found in him' (Philippians 3:9). I point you to the redeemed who have entered 'within the veil' (Hebrews 6:19) and who rest in eternal glory, and I say that they won the victory by grace, and growth in grace was the means of their triumph. Imitate them. Press forward just as they did, and through grace you also will inherit the same rest, will share in their triumph, and will sit down with them forever."

Ways to Grow in Grace

Do you ask *how* you will grow in grace? The answer is simple. The One who gave you grace must give you more of it. Where you first received grace, there you must receive the increase of that grace. The One who made the cattle and created man is the same One who afterward said, "*Be fruitful, and multiply, and replenish the earth*" (Genesis 1:28). So the One who has given you grace must speak in your heart with His omnipotent decree, and say to that grace, "'*Be fruitful, and multiply, and replenish*' the soul until its inherent emptiness is filled, until the natural desert rejoices and blossoms like a rose (Isaiah 35:1)."

At the same time, you should use all the spiritual means available, and those means are much more prayer, a more diligent search of the sacred Scriptures, a more constant fellowship with the Lord Jesus Christ, greater activity in His cause, a devout reception of all revealed truth, and so forth. If you do these things, you will never be dwarfed or stunted in your growth as a child of God, because the One who has given you life will thus enable you to fulfill the word that He spoke to you by His apostle: "*Grow in grace, and in the knowledge of our Lord and Saviour Jesus Christ.*"

Growing in Knowledge

I have explained the divine exhortation of our text. However, notice that our text also contains a special direction: *"And in the knowledge of our Lord and Saviour Jesus Christ."*

My fellow believer in the Lord Jesus, we must see to it that we ripen in the knowledge of Him. Oh, that we may know more of Him in His divine nature and in His human relationship to us. Oh, that we may know more of Him in His finished work, in His death, in His resurrection, in His present glorious intercession, and in His future royal advent. To know more of Christ in His work is, I think, a blessed means of enabling us to work more for Christ.

We also must study in order to know more of Christ in His character—in that divine combination of perfection, faith, zeal, deference to His Father's will, courage, meekness, and love. He was the Lion of the tribe of Judah, yet the Man on whom the dove descended in the waters of baptism. Let us thirst to know Him of whom even His enemies said, *"Never man spake like this man"* (John 7:46), and of whom His unrighteous judge said, *"I find no fault in him"* (John 19:4).

Above all, let us long to know Christ in His person. Endeavor to become better acquainted with the Crucified One. Study His hands and His feet. Stay close to the Cross. Let the sponge, the vinegar, and the nails be subjects of your devout attention. Seek to penetrate into His very heart. Search those deep, far-reaching caverns of His undiscovered love, that love that can never find a rival and can never know a parallel.

If you can add to this a personal knowledge of His sufferings, you will do well. Oh, if you can grow in the knowledge of fellowship, if you drink of His cup and are baptized with His baptism, if you abide in Him and He in you, you will be blessed. This is the only growth in grace that is true growth. All growth that does not lead us to increase in the knowledge of Christ is only the puffing up of the flesh and not the building up of the Spirit.

Grow in the knowledge of Christ, then. And do you ask why? Oh, if you have ever known Him, you will not ask that question. He who does not long to know more about Christ, knows nothing about Him yet. Anyone who has ever sipped this new wine will thirst for more, for although Christ satisfies, it is such a satisfaction that we want to taste more and more and more. Oh, if you know the love of Jesus, I am sure that *"as the hart panteth after the water brooks"* (Psalm 42:1), so you will pant after Him. If you say you do not desire to know Him better, then I tell you that you do not love Him, for love always cries, "Nearer, nearer, nearer." To be absent from Christ is hell, but to be present with Christ is heaven. As we get nearer to Him, our heaven becomes more heavenly, and we enjoy it more and feel more that it is of God.

Oh, may you come to the very well of Bethlehem, and not merely to receive a pitcherful from it, as David did, at the risk of the lives of three mighty men (1 Chronicles 11:17–19). May you come to the well and drink—drink from the well itself, from that bottomless wellspring of eternal love. Oh, may the secret of the Lord be with you, and may you be in the secret place of the Most High! My Master, if you would permit me to ask You one thing as a special favor, it would be this, that I may *"know him, and the power of his resurrection...being made conformable unto his death"* (Philippians 3:10). Nearer to You, blessed Lord, nearer to You; this is my cry! The Lord grant that our cry may be heard, that we may grow in the knowledge of Christ!

We wish to know Christ as our Lord—Lord of every thought and every desire, of every word and every act. We want to know Him as our Savior, too, our Savior from every indwelling sin, our Savior from every past evil deed, our Savior from every future trial. All hail Jesus! We salute You as Lord. Teach us to feel Your kingship over us, and to feel it every hour. All hail the Crucified One! We acknowledge You as Savior. Help us to rejoice in Your salvation and to feel the plenitude of that salvation in all and every part of spirit, soul, and body, being wholly saved by You.

Beloved, may you *"grow in grace, and in the knowledge of our Lord and Saviour Jesus Christ."*

Praising the Lord

In the second part of the text, we have a grateful thanksgiving with a significant conclusion: *"To him be glory both now and for ever. Amen."*

The apostles, I must remark, very frequently suspended their writing in order to lift up their hearts in praise. Praise is never out of season. It is no interruption to interrupt any task in order to praise and magnify our God. *"To him be glory."*

Let every heart joyously feel this doxology. *"To him,"* the God who made the heavens and the earth, without whom *"was not any thing made"* (John 1:3). *"To him*" who in His infinite compassion became the surety of the covenant. "*To him*" who became a baby. "*To him*" who was "*despised and rejected of men; a man of sorrows, and acquainted with grief*" (Isaiah 53:3). "*To him*" who on the bloody tree poured out His heart's life so that He could redeem His people. "*To him*" who said, "*I thirst*" (John 19:28), and, "*It is finished*" (v. 30). "*To him*" whose lifeless body slumbered in the grave. "*To him be glory.*"

"*To him*" who burst the bonds of death. "*To him*" who "*ascended up on high,* [and] *led captivity captive*" (Ephesians 4:8). "*To him*" who sits at the right hand of the Father and who will soon come to be our Judge. "*To him be glory both now and for ever.*"

Yes, "*to him,*" you atheists, who deny Him. "*To him,*" you kings who vaunt your splendor and will not have this Man to reign over you (Luke 19:14). "*To him,*" you people who stand up against Him, and you rulers who take counsel against Him (Psalm 2:2). "*To him*"—the King whom God has set on His holy hill of Zion (v. 6)—"*to him be glory.*"

"*To him be glory*" as the King of Kings and Lord of Lords. "*Wonderful, Counsellor, the mighty God, the everlasting Father, the Prince of Peace*" (Isaiah 9:6). Again, "*hosanna in the highest*" (Matthew 21:9)! Hallelujah! King of Kings and Lord of Lords! "*To him be glory*" as Lord. "*To him be glory*" as Savior. He alone has redeemed us unto God by His blood. He alone has "*trodden the winepress*" (Isaiah 63:3); He has come "*from Edom, with dyed garments from Bozrah…glorious in his apparel, travelling in the greatness of his strength*" (v. 1). "*To him be glory.*"

Hear it, you angels: "*To him be glory.*" Clap your wings. Cry, "Hallelujah! '*To him be glory.*'" Hear it, you "*spirits of just men made perfect*" (Hebrews 12:23). Play the strings of your celestial harps and say, "Hallelujah! Glory to Him who has redeemed us unto God by His own blood." "*To him be glory.*" Church of God, respond! Let every godly heart say, "*To him be glory.*" Yes, "*to him be glory,*" you fiends of hell, as you tremble at His presence and see the key of your prison swinging on His belt. Let heaven and earth and hell, let things that are and were and will be, cry, "*To him be glory.*"

Peter added, "*Now.*" "*To him be glory… now.*" Beloved, do not postpone the day of His triumph; do not put off the hour of His coronation. Now,

> Bring forth the royal diadem,
> And crown Him Lord of all.

"To him be glory...now," for now, today, God *"hath raised us up together, and made us sit together in heavenly places in Christ Jesus"* (Ephesians 2:6). *"Beloved, now are we the sons of God"* (1 John 3:2). Now our sins are forgiven; now we are clothed in His righteousness. Now our feet are on a rock, and our steps are established (Psalm 40:2). Who would defer the time of singing hosannas? *"To him be glory...now."* Oh, seraphim above, *"To him be glory...now,"* for you continually cry, *"Holy, holy, holy, is the* Lord *of hosts"* (Isaiah 6:3). Adore Him yet again, for, *"To him be glory...now."*

Notice the last part of the doxology: *"And for ever."* Never will we cease our praise. Time, you will grow old and die. Eternity, your unnumbered years will speed their everlasting course. But forever, forever, forever, *"to him be glory."* Is He not a *"priest for ever after the order of Melchizedek"* (Psalm 110:4)? *"To him be glory."* Is He not King forever—King of Kings and Lord of Lords, the Everlasting Father? *"To him be glory...for ever."*

Never will His praises cease. That which was bought with blood deserves to last as long as immortality endures. The glory of the Cross must never be eclipsed. The luster of the grave and of the Resurrection must never be dimmed. Oh, my beloved, my spirit begins to feel the ardor of the immortals. I anticipate the songs of heaven. My tongue, if it only had celestial liberty, would begin even now to join in those *"melodious sonnets sung by flaming tongues above."* O Jesus, You will be praised forever. As long as immortal spirits live, as long as the Father's throne endures, forever, forever, forever, unto You be glory.

Saying Amen

Now, there is a very significant conclusion to this verse: *"Amen."* Beloved, I want to work this amen out—not as a matter of doctrine, but as a matter of blessed ecstasy. Join your heart with mine in affirming this doxology. *"To him be glory both now and for ever. Amen."*

By the way, the Puritans pointed out—and it is a very remarkable thing— that under the old law, there was no amen to the blessings; the only amen was to the curses. When they pronounced the curses, all the people said amen. (See Deuteronomy 27:9–26.) Under the old law, there was never an amen to the blessings.

Now, it is an equally remarkable and more blessed thing that under the Gospel there is no amen to the curses; the only amen is to the blessings. For example, 2 Corinthians 13:14 says, "*The grace of the Lord Jesus Christ, and the love of God, and the communion of the Holy Ghost, be with you all. Amen.*" On the other hand, 1 Corinthians 16:22 says, "*If any man love not the Lord Jesus Christ, let him be Anathema* [accursed]." No amen. There is no amen to the curse under the Gospel, but "*all the promises of God in him* [Christ] *are yea, and in him Amen*" (2 Corinthians 1:20).

Our Hearts' Desire

What does this amen in our text mean? *Amen* has four meanings in Scripture. First, it is the desire of the heart. Jesus said, "*Surely I come quickly*" (Revelation 22:20). The apostle John responded, "*Amen. Even so, come, Lord Jesus*" (v. 20). We say amen at the end of a prayer to signify, "Lord, let it be so"—it is our hearts' desire.

Now, beloved, join your heart with mine, then, for it is all a heart matter here. "*To him be glory both now and for ever. Amen.*" Is that your heart's desire? If not, you cannot say amen to it. Does your heart long, pant, thirst, groan, and cry out after Christ, so much that you can say, every time you bend your knee in prayer, "*Thy kingdom come. Thy will be done in earth, as it is in heaven....For thine is the kingdom, and the power, and the glory, for ever. Amen*" (Matthew 6:10, 13)? Can you say, "Amen, Lord, let Your kingdom come"? Oh, if you can say it in this sense, if it is your heart's desire that Christ's glory be extended and that His kingdom come, say amen. My heart glows with this amen. The Judge of all knows how my heart longs to see Jesus magnified.

> Amen, with joy divine, let earth's
> Unnumber'd myriads cry;
> Amen, with joy divine, let heaven's
> Unnumber'd choirs reply.

Our Hearts' Belief

However, the word *amen* signifies more than this; it means the affirmation of our faith. We only say amen to that which we really believe to be true. We add our affidavit, as it were, to God's promise, affirming that we believe Him to be faithful and true.

Do you have any doubts that Jesus Christ is glorious now and will be forever? Do you doubt His being glorified by angels, cherubim, and seraphim today? Don't you believe, my beloved, that *"they that dwell in the wilderness shall bow before him; and his enemies shall lick the dust"* (Psalm 72:9)? If you do believe this, if you have faith today amid the world's obstinacy and the sinner's pride, amid abounding superstition and dominant evil, if you still have faith to believe that Christ will be glorious forever and ever, then say amen. *"To him be glory both now and for ever. Amen."*

There are more who can desire these things than there are who believe them. Nevertheless, God remains faithful.

> This little seed from heaven
>> Shall soon become a tree;
> This ever blessed leaven
>> Diffused abroad must be:
> Till God the Son shall come again,
>> It must go on. Amen! Amen.

Our Hearts' Joy

There is yet a third meaning to this amen. It often expresses the joy of the heart. When in ancient times they crowned a Jewish king, the high priest took a horn of oil and poured it on his head. Then came forward a herald, and the moment he sounded the trumpet, someone said in a loud voice, "God save the king! God save the king!" and all the people said amen, and one shout went up to heaven. With joyful hearts, they welcomed the king; they hoped that he would be a prosperous ruler whom God would use to bless them and make them victorious.

Now, as you see King Jesus sitting on Mount Zion with death and hell underneath His feet, as today you anticipate the glory of His advent, as today you are expecting the time when you will reign with Him forever and ever, doesn't your heart cry out amen?

In a season of my life when I was in great darkness of mind and weakness of body, I remember one text that encouraged me beyond all measure. There was nothing in the text about me; it was no promise to me, but it was something about Christ. It was this:

God also hath highly exalted him, and given him a name which is above every name: that at the name of Jesus every knee should bow, of things in heaven, and things in earth, and things under the earth.   (Philippians 2:9–10)

Oh, it seemed so joyous that He was exalted! What did it matter what became of me? What did it matter what became of all believers? King Jesus is worth ten thousand of us. Let our names perish, but let His name last forever. Beloved, I bring forth the King to you. I bring Him before the eyes of your faith today. I proclaim Him King again. If you desire Him to be King and if you rejoice in His reign, say amen. Crown Him! Crown Him! *"To him be glory both now and for ever."* Joyous heart, lift up your voice and say amen.

> Yea, amen, let all adore Thee,
>> High on Thine exalted throne!
> Savior, take Thy power and glory;
>> Claim the kingdoms for Thine own:
>> O come quickly!
> Hallelujah! Come, Lord, come.

Our Hearts' Resolution

Finally, here is a very solemn truth: amen is sometimes used in Scripture as an amen of determination and resolution. It means, "I, in the name of God, solemnly pledge myself that I, in His strength, will seek to make it so; 'to him be glory both now and for ever.'"

Last week I walked through the long galleries that vanity has dedicated to all the glories of France. I passed through room after room, where especially I saw the triumphs of Napoleon. Surely, as you walk through the pages of Scripture, you walk through a much more marvelous picture gallery, in which you see the glories of Christ. This Book contains the memorials of His honors.

In another place in Paris, there stands a column made with the cannons taken by the Emperor in battle. A mighty trophy, certainly. O Jesus, you have a better trophy than this—a trophy made of souls forgiven; of eyes that wept, but whose tears have been wiped away; of broken hearts that have been healed; and of saved souls that rejoice evermore. What wonderful trophies Christ has to make Him glorious, *"both now and for ever"*—trophies of living hearts that love and adore Him; trophies of immortal spirits who find their heaven in gazing upon His beauties!

What glories will be Christ's forever when you and I and all the millions upon millions He has bought with His blood are in heaven! Oh, when we have been there thousands of years, we will feel as fresh an ecstasy as when we first came there. If our spirits should be sent on any errand and we have to leave our Master's presence for a moment, oh, with what wings of a dove we will fly back to behold His face again! When we all surround that throne, what songs will come forth from these lips of mine, the chief of sinners saved by blood! What hymns you will give Him, you who have had your iniquities cleansed and are saved today! What praise all those multitudes who have been partakers of His grace will give Him!

But this has more to do with "*for ever.*" What do you say about our glorifying Him "*now*"? Oh, beloved, do make this your prayer today: "Lord, help me to glorify You. I am poor; help me to glorify You by contentment. I am sick; help me to give You honor by patience. I have talents; help me to extol You by using them for You. I have time, Lord; help me to redeem it, so that I may serve You. I have a heart to feel, Lord; let that heart feel no love but Yours and glow with no flame but affection for You. I have a head to think, Lord; help me to think of You. You have put me in this world for something, Lord; show me what it is, and help me to work out my life's purpose, for I do desire to say amen. I cannot do much; my amen is only a weak one. Yet, as the widow put in her two mites, which was all she had to live on, so, Lord, I put my time and eternity into Your treasury. It is all Yours. Take it, and thus I say amen to Peter's doxology."

And now, will you say amen to this? I pray that you will do so. You who do not love Christ cannot say amen. Remember that you are under the law. There is an amen for all the curses to you; there is none for the blessings while you are under the law. Oh, poor sinner under the law, may this be the day when your slavery under the law will come to an end! "How can this be?" you ask. By faith in Christ. *"He that believeth on him is not condemned"* (John 3:18). Oh, believe on Him, and then your joyful heart will say amen. Then you will say, "Loudest of all the saints in heaven, I will shout amen when I see the royal crown brought forth, and Jesus is acknowledged Lord of all."

I trust that as long as I live it may be mine to give my amen to that doxology: *"To him be glory both now and for ever. Amen."*

4

THE JOY OF THE LORD

The joy of the LORD is your strength.
—Nehemiah 8:10

And the singers sang loud, with Jezrahiah their overseer.
Also that day they offered great sacrifices, and rejoiced:
for God had made them rejoice with great joy: the wives also and the children
rejoiced: so that the joy of Jerusalem was heard even afar off.
—Nehemiah 12:42–43

I would like to consider with you the subject of joy. Perhaps as we think about joy and remark on the many reasons for its existence, some of those reasons may operate on our hearts, and we may lay this book down as recipients of tremendous joy. I will consider this a beneficial book if it causes the people of God to rejoice in the Lord, and especially if those who have been weighed down and burdened in their souls will receive the oil of joy in exchange for their mourning (Isaiah 61:3). It is a significant thing to comfort the Lord's mourners. It is a work especially dear to the Spirit of God, and it is, therefore, not to be taken lightly.

Holy sorrow is precious before God and is not a hindrance to godly joy. Carefully note, in connection with our first text, Nehemiah 8:10, that the fact that there is great mourning is no reason why there should not soon be great joy, for the very people who were told by Nehemiah and Ezra to rejoice were, at the time, weeping for their sins. "*For all the people wept, when they heard the words of the law*" (v. 9). The vast congregation that had gathered before the water gate to hear the teaching of Ezra was awakened and cut to the heart. The people felt the edge of God's law like a sword opening up their hearts— tearing, cutting, and killing. They had good reason to cry. However, as they were crying, it was time to let them feel the Gospel's balm and hear the Gospel's music; therefore, Nehemiah and Ezra changed their tune and consoled them, saying,

> *This day is holy unto the* Lord *your God; mourn not, nor weep....Go your way, eat the fat, and drink the sweet, and send portions unto them for whom nothing is prepared: for this day is holy unto our Lord: neither be ye sorry; for the joy of the* Lord *is your strength.*   (Nehemiah 8:9–10)

Now that they were penitent and had sincerely turned to God, they were told to rejoice. Even as certain fabrics need to be dampened before they will absorb the bright colors with which they are to be dyed, so our spirits need the rain of repentance before they can receive the radiant coloring of delight. The glad news of the Gospel can only be printed on wet paper. Have you ever seen the world around you shine more than after a rain shower? Then the sun transforms the raindrops into gems, the flowers look up with fresher smiles and glitter with the droplets of their refreshing bath, and the birds among the dripping branches sing with notes more rapturous because they have paused awhile. In the same way, when the soul has been saturated with the rain of penitence, the clear shining of forgiving love makes the flowers of gladness blossom all around.

The steps by which we ascend to the palace of delight are usually moistened with tears. In *The Pilgrim's Progress*, by John Bunyan, grief for sin is the porch of the House Beautiful, in which the guests are full of the joy of the Lord. I hope, then, that the mourners who read this book will discover and enjoy the meaning of that divine blessing in the Sermon on the Mount: "*Blessed are they that mourn: for they shall be comforted*" (Matthew 5:4).

From our texts, I will draw several themes for consideration. First, there is a joy of divine origin—*"the joy of the* LORD.*"* Second, that joy is a source of strength for all who share in it—*"the joy of the* LORD *is your strength."* Third, I will show that such strength always reveals itself practically—our second text will help us there. I will close this chapter by noticing, in the fourth place, that this joy, and, consequently, this strength, are within our reach today.

Our Joy Comes from the Lord

First, there is a joy of divine origin. Since the source of this joy is the Lord, it will necessarily be a high and sublime joy.

From the time that man fell in the Garden, he has too often sought enjoyment where the Serpent finds his. God said to the Serpent, *"Upon thy belly shalt thou go, and dust shalt thou eat all the days of thy life"* (Genesis 3:14). This was the Serpent's doom, and man, with foolish ambition, has tried to find his delight in his sensual appetites. Man has tried to content his soul with earth's poor dust. But the joys of time cannot satisfy an undying nature. Once a soul is awakened by the eternal Spirit, it cannot fill itself with worldly pleasure. It cannot even fill itself with the common delights of this life. To try to do so would be like trying to store up wind and eat it for breakfast.

However, beloved, we do not have to search for joy. It is brought to us by the love of God our Father—joy refined and satisfying, suitable for immortal spirits. God has not left us to wander among those unsatisfactory things that mock the chase that they invite. No, He has given us appetites that carnal things cannot gratify, and He has provided suitable satisfaction for those appetites. He has stored up at His right hand pleasures forevermore (Psalm 16:11), which He reveals by His Spirit to those chosen ones whom He has taught to long for them.

In the pages that follow, let us endeavor to analyze that special pleasure that our text calls *"the joy of the* LORD.*"*

The Source and Object of Our Joy

First, our joy springs from God and has God for its object. The believer who is in a spiritually healthy state rejoices mainly in God Himself. He is happy because there is a God, and because God, in His person and character, is what He is. All the attributes of God become continual sources of joy to the thoughtful, contemplative believer, for such a person says within his soul, "All these attributes of my God are mine. His power is my protection. His wisdom is my guidance. His faithfulness is my foundation. His grace is my salvation."

He is a God who cannot lie, who is faithful and true to His promise. He is all love, and, at the same time, infinitely just and supremely holy. Why, to one who knows that this God is his God forever and ever, the contemplation of God is enough to make the eyes overflow with tears because of the deep, mysterious, unspeakable bliss that fills the heart.

There was nothing in the character of Jupiter, or any of the false gods of the heathen, to make a pure and holy spirit glad. But there is everything in the character of Jehovah both to purify the heart and to thrill it with delight. How wonderful it is to think about all the Lord has done, how He has revealed Himself since long ago, and especially how He has displayed His glory in the covenant of grace and in the person of the Lord Jesus Christ. How precious is the thought that He has revealed Himself to me personally and has caused me to see Him as my Father, my Friend, my Helper, my God.

If there is one phrase from heaven that cannot be excelled, even by the brightness of heaven itself, it is this phrase: "My God, my Father," along with that precious promise: "*I will be to them a God, and they shall be to me a people*" (Hebrews 8:10). There is no richer comfort to be found. Even the Spirit of God can reveal nothing more delightful to the Christian's heart.

How marvelous it is when the child of God admires God's character and marvels at His acts and at the same time thinks, "He is my God. I have taken Him to be mine, and He has taken me to be His. He has grasped me with the hand of His powerful love. Having loved me with an everlasting love, with lovingkindness He has drawn me to Himself (Jeremiah 31:3). My Beloved is mine, and I am His (Song 6:3)." Why, then his soul would gladly dance like David before the ark of the Lord, rejoicing in the Lord with all its might (2 Samuel 6:14).

Reconciliation, Acceptance, and Adoption

The Christian who is living near to God finds a further source of joy in a deep sense of reconciliation to God, of acceptance with God, and yet, beyond that, of adoption and close relationship to God. Doesn't it make a person glad to know that his sins, which had once provoked the Lord, are all blotted out and that not one of them remains? Isn't he delighted to know that though he was once alienated from God, and far away from Him because of his wicked works, he is brought near by the blood of Christ? The Lord is no longer an angry Judge pursuing him with a drawn sword, but a loving Father with whom he can share his sorrows and find comfort for every heartfelt grief.

Oh, to know, beloved, that God actually loves us! I have often said I cannot preach on that theme, for it is a subject to muse on in silence, a matter to sit and meditate on for hours. The fact that the Infinite loves an insignificant creature, a fleeting moth, a declining shadow—isn't this amazing? That God pities me I can understand. That God reaches down and has mercy on me I can comprehend. But for Him to love me, for the pure to love a sinner, for the infinitely great to love a worm, is matchless, a miracle of miracles! Such thoughts do indeed comfort the soul.

Then add to this the fact that divine love has brought us believers into actual relationship with God, so that we are His sons and daughters—this again is a river of sacred pleasure. *"Unto which of the angels said he at any time, Thou art my Son?"* (Hebrews 1:5). No angel, no ministering spirit, though perfect in obedience, has received the honor of adoption. To us, even to us frail creatures of the dust, is given a gift denied to Gabriel. Through Jesus Christ the Firstborn, we are members of the family of God! Oh, the depths of joy that lie in being God's child and Christ's joint-heir! Words are useless here.

The joy springing from the Spirit of adoption is very much a portion of the believer's bliss. There cannot be an unhappy man who can cry, *"Abba, Father"* (Romans 8:15). The Spirit of adoption is always attended by love, joy, and peace, which are fruits of the Spirit, for we have not received the spirit of bondage again to fear, but we have received the Spirit of liberty and joy in Christ Jesus (v. 15). "My God, my Father"— oh, how sweet the sound!

You may be thinking, "But all of God's people do not experience this joy." Sad to say, I agree, but I also add that it is their own fault. It is the right of every believer to live in the assurance that he is reconciled to God, that God loves him, and that he is God's child. If he does not live this way, he has only himself to blame. If there is any starving at God's table, it is because the guest cheats himself, for the feast is superabundant. If, however, a believer begins to consistently live with a sense of pardon through the sprinkling of the precious blood, and with a delightful sense of perfect reconciliation with the great God, he will possess a joy unspeakable and full of glory (1 Peter 1:8). I pray that you will begin to live this way.

Fearlessness about the Future

But, beloved, this is not all. The joy of the Lord in our spirits springs also from an assurance that our entire future, regardless of what may happen, is guaranteed by divine goodness. We are joyful when we know that, as children of God, the love of God toward us never changes. The believer feels complete satisfaction in leaving himself in the hands of eternal and unchangeable love.

However happy I may be today, if I am in doubt about tomorrow, there is a worm at the root of my peace. Although the past may now be pleasant in retrospect, and the present satisfying and enjoyable, if the future looks gloomy and frightening, my joy is shallow. If my salvation is still a matter of chance and uncertainty, unmingled joy is not mine, and deep peace is still out of my reach. But my outlook changes when I know that He in whom I have rested has enough power and grace to complete what He has begun in me and for me (Philippians 1:6). I see my future differently when I see the work of Christ as no halfway redemption, but a complete and eternal salvation. Peace comes when I perceive that the promises are established on an unchangeable basis, and are *"yea"* and *"Amen"* (2 Corinthians 1:20) in Christ Jesus, confirmed by oath and sealed by blood. When I realize all this, my soul has perfect contentment.

It is true that as I look forward I may see long avenues of tribulation, but glory is at the end of them. Battles may be foreseen, and woe to the believer who does not expect them, but the eye of faith perceives the crown of victory. Deep waters appear on the maps of our journeys, but faith can see Jehovah fording these rivers with us, and she anticipates the day when we will ascend the banks of the nearby shore and enter into Jehovah's rest.

When we have received these priceless truths into our souls, we are satisfied with God's grace and are full of the goodness of the Lord. There is a theology that denies believers this comfort. I will not enter into controversy over it, but I sorrowfully hint that those who believe the errors of that doctrinal system will be heavily punished by losing the comfort that the truth would have brought into their souls. For my part, I value the Gospel not only for what it has done for me in the past, but for the guarantee that it gives me of eternal salvation. *"I give unto [my sheep] eternal life; and they shall never perish, neither shall any man pluck them out of my hand"* (John 10:28).

Close Fellowship with God

Now, beloved, I have not yet taken you into the great depths of joy, though these streams are certainly by no means shallow. However, there is a deepness of delight for every Christian when he comes into actual fellowship with God. I spoke of the truth that God loves us, and the fact that we are related to Him by ties most near and dear. But, when these doctrines become experiences, then we are indeed anointed with the oil of gladness. When we enter into the love of God and it enters into us, when we walk with God consistently, then our joy is like the Jordan River at harvesttime, when it overflows all its banks.

Do you know what it means to walk with God and to experience the joy that Enoch had? Do you know what it means to sit at Jesus' feet and to experience the joy that Mary had? Do you know what it means to lean your head on Jesus' chest and to experience the joy that John had? Oh, yes, communion with the Lord is not a matter of mere words for some of us. We have known it in the midst of affliction. We have known it in the solitude of many a night of interrupted rest. We have known it when experiencing discouragements and sorrows and defamations, and all sorts of problems. We also know that one teaspoon of fellowship with Christ is enough to sweeten an ocean of tribulation. Only to know that He is near us, and to see the sparkle in His dear eyes, would transform even hell itself into heaven, if it were possible for us to enjoy His presence there.

However, you do not and cannot know this bliss, you who spend your time greedily consuming alcohol. You do not know what this bliss means—you have not dreamed of it, nor could you comprehend it even if someone were to tell you about it. As the beast in the field does not know the far-reaching thoughts of the One who reads the stars and threads the spheres in the heavens, so the carnal man cannot even imagine the joys that God has prepared for those who love Him (1 Corinthians 2:9). But any day and every day, when our hearts seek to know them, He reveals them to us by His Spirit (v. 10).

This is *"the joy of the LORD"*—fellowship with the Father and with His Son Jesus Christ. Beloved, if we reach this point, we must work to maintain our standing, for our Lord says to us, *"Abide in me"* (John 15:4). The habit of communion is the life of happiness.

The Privilege of Serving Christ

Another form of *"the joy of the LORD"* will visit us in a practical way every day; it is the honor of being allowed to serve Him. It is a joy worth worlds to be allowed to do good. To teach a little child the alphabet in Christ's name will give a true heart a taste of the joy of the Lord, if it is consciously done for the Lord's sake alone. To give a meal to the hungry, to visit the sick, to comfort the mourner, to aid the poor, to instruct the ignorant—any and all of such Christian works, if done in Jesus' name, will, in their measure, clothe us in Jehovah's joy.

Moreover, happy are we if, when we cannot work, we are enabled to lie still and suffer, for submission is another silver pipe through which the joy of the Lord will come to us. It is satisfying to smart beneath God's rod and to feel that, if God would have us suffer, it is happiness to do so. It is precious to fall back with the faintness of our nature, but at the same time with the strength of God's grace, and say, *"Thy will be done"* (Matthew 6:10). It is joy, when we are crushed like an olive, to yield nothing but the oil of thankfulness. It is delight, when bruised beneath the flail of tribulation, to lose nothing but the chaff and to yield to God the precious grain of entire submissiveness. Why, this is a little heaven on earth. For us to also exult in tribulations is equal to more than a few steps of ascent toward the likeness of our Lord.

Perhaps the usual times of communion that we have with our Beloved, though exceedingly precious, will never equal those that we enjoy when we have to break through thorns and briers to be with Him. When we follow Him into the wilderness, then we feel that the love of our marriage to Christ is doubly sweet (Jeremiah 2:2). It is a joyous thing when, in the midst of mournful circumstances, we still feel that we cannot mourn because the Bridegroom is with us. Blessed is that believer who, in the most terrible storm, is not driven away from his God, but instead rides nearer to heaven on the crest of the enormous waves. Such happiness is the Christian's lot.

I am not saying that every Christian possesses such happiness, but I am sure that every Christian ought to. There is a highway to heaven, and all on it are safe. But in the middle of that road there is a special way, an inner path, and all who walk on it are happy as well as safe. Many professing Christians are barely on the right path; they walk in the ditch by the roadside. Because they are safe there, they are content to put up with all the inconveniences of their walk. But the believer who walks in the very center of the road that God has constructed will find that no lion will be there, nor will any ferocious beast go up on it. There the Lord Himself will be his companion and will manifest Himself to him.

You shallow Christians whose faith in Christ is barely alive, whose Bibles are unread, whose prayer times are few, whose communion with God is inconsistent—you do not have the joy of the Lord, nor are you strong. I implore you, do not rest as you are, but let your weakness motivate you to seek the means of strength. That means of strength is to be found in a pleasant medicine, as sweet as it is profitable—the delicious and effective medicine of *"the joy of the* Lord.*"*

Meditating on God Brings Joy and Strength

Too many pages would be required for me to fully share my remarks on this very fruitful subject. Therefore, I will turn to my second topic, which I began to explain in the previous section: this joy is a source of great strength.

Very briefly let us consider this thought. Joy is a source of strength because joy arises from meditations that always strengthen the soul. Much of the depth of our godliness will depend on our contemplativeness. Many people, after receiving a doctrine, put it on the shelf. They are orthodox, they have received the truth, and they are content to keep that truth on hand as dead weight. Reader, how can you be benefited if you store your granary with wheat but never grind the wheat for bread, or sow it in the furrows of your fields? He is a joyful Christian who uses the doctrines of the Gospel for spiritual meat, as they were meant to be used.

Some people might as well have an unorthodox creed instead of an orthodox one for all the difference that it makes to them. Having the notion that they know the truth and imagining that simply knowing it is sufficient, they do not consider, contemplate, or regard the truths that they profess to believe. Consequently, they derive no benefit from them.

Now, to contemplate the great truths of divine election, eternal love, justification by faith through the blood of Christ, and the indwelling and perpetual abiding of the Holy Spirit in His people—to think over these thoughts—is to extract joy from them, and doing so also strengthens the mind. To press the heavenly grapes by meditation, and make the red wine flow forth in torrents, is an exercise as strengthening as it is exhilarating. Joy comes from the same truths that support our strength, and it comes by the process of meditation.

Again, *"the joy of the* Lord*"* within us is always the sign and symbol of strong spiritual life. Holy joyfulness is evidence of spiritual vigor. I said earlier that he who has spiritual joy has gained it by communion with God, but communion with God is also the surest fosterer of strength. You cannot be with a strong God without getting strength yourself, for God is always a transforming God. As we regard and look upon Him, we change until we become, in our measure, like our God.

The warmth of southern France, which perhaps you have heard a little bit about, does not come from soft, balmy winds. No, it comes from the sun, for at sunset, the temperature falls. Also, in Italy, you might be on one side of the street and think it is May, and then cross the street into the shade and find it as cold as January. The sun makes all the difference.

Even so, a man who walks in the sunlight of God's countenance is warm and strong for that very reason. The sunlight of joy usually goes with the warmth of spiritual life. As the light of joy varies, so does the warmth of holy strength. He who dwells in the light of God is both happy and strong. He who goes into the shade and loses the joy of the Lord becomes weak at the same time. In this way, the joy of the Lord becomes our strength because it is an indicator of its rise or fall. When a soul is really vigorous and active, it is like a torrent that dashes down the mountainside, scorning to be bound by frost in wintertime. In just a few hours of cold weather, the stagnant pools and slowly moving streams are enchained in ice; but the snow king must bring forth all his strength before he can restrain the rushing torrent. So, when a soul dashes on with the sacred force of faith, it is hard to freeze it into misery. Its vigor secures its joy.

Strength for Suffering and Service

Furthermore, the believer who possesses *"the joy of the LORD"* finds it his strength in another respect: it fortifies him against temptation. What is there that he can be tempted with? He already has more than the world could ever give him as a reward for treachery. He is already rich; who can entice him with the wages of unrighteousness? He is already satisfied; who can seduce him with pleasing baits? He simply says, *"Should such a man as I flee?"* (Nehemiah 6:11).

The rejoicing Christian is equally fortified against persecution. Someone who wins at the rate that a joyful believer wins can well afford to be laughed at. "You may scoff," he says, "but I know within my soul what true faith is, and your scoffing will not make me relinquish the pearl of great price." Moreover, such a person is made strong to bear affliction, for all the sufferings put on him are only a few drops of bitterness flung into his cup of bliss, to give a deeper tone to the sweetness that absorbs them.

Such a believer also becomes strong for service. What can a person who is happy in his God not do? By his God, he leaps over a wall or breaks through a troop (2 Samuel 22:30). He is strong, too, for any kind of self-sacrifice. To the God who gives him everything and is his perpetual portion, the joyful believer gives up all that he has and does not think of it as a sacrifice. He is simply storing his treasure in his own special treasure-house—the God of his salvation.

Portrait of a Strong Christian

A joyous Christian, such as I am now picturing in my mind's eye, is strong in a calm, restful manner. Regardless of what happens, he is not upset or disturbed. He is not afraid of bad news; his heart is steadfast, trusting in the Lord (Psalm 112:7). The fretful person, on the other hand, is always weak. He is in a hurry and does things poorly.

In contrast, the joy-filled believer is quiet; he bides his time and is full of strength. Such a believer, though he is humble, is firm and steadfast. He is not carried away with every wind, or blown over by every breeze (Ephesians 4:14). He knows what he knows, and he believes what he believes. The golden anchor of his hope enters within the veil and holds him tightly (Hebrews 6:19). His strength is not feigned—it is real.

The happiness that comes from communion with God does not cause him to be boastful. He does not talk of what he can do, but he simply does it. He does not say what he could endure, but he endures all that comes.

He himself does not always know what he can do; his weakness is more apparent to him because of the strength that the Holy Spirit puts in him. However, when the time comes, his weakness only illustrates the divine mightiness within him, while he goes calmly on, conquering and to conquer.

The inner light of the joy-filled believer makes him independent of the outward sun. His secret granaries make him independent of the outward harvest. His inner fountains keep him safe from dread, even though the brook Cherith may dry up. (See 1 Kings 17:1–9.) He is independent of men and of angels, and fearless of devils. All people may turn against him if they please, but since God Himself is his exceeding joy, he will not miss their love or mourn their hate. He stands where others fall. He sings where others weep. He wins where others flee. He glorifies his God where others bring dishonor on themselves and on the sacred name.

May God grant us the inner joy that arises from real strength, the kind of joy that is so linked with strength that it is partly its cause.

Joy Brings Results

But now I must go on to notice that this joy and this strength lead to practical results. Please read our second text again:

And the singers sang loud, with Jezrahiah their overseer. Also that day they offered great sacrifices, and rejoiced: for God had made them rejoice with great joy: the wives also and the children rejoiced: so that the joy of Jerusalem was heard even afar off. (Nehemiah 12:42–43)

In these verses, we observe some of the fruits of holy joy and godly strength.

Enthusiastic Praise

First, strength and joy lead to great praise. "*The singers sang loud*"; their singing was hearty and enthusiastic. Sacred song is not a minor matter. Someone once said, "Praying is the end of preaching." Couldn't we go further and say, "Praising is the end of praying"? After all, preaching and praying are not the chief end of man; it is the glorifying of God, of which praising God vocally is one form. Preaching is sowing, prayer is watering, but praise is the harvest. God aims at His own glory, and so should we. The Lord says, "*Whoso offereth praise glorifieth me*" (Psalm 50:23). Be diligent then to sing His praises with understanding.

It is shocking to me to be present in places of worship where not a tenth of the people ever venture to sing at all, and these do it through their clenched teeth so very softly that one needs to have a special hearing aid to enable him to hear the dying strain. Out with such mumbling and murdering of the praises of God! If people's hearts were joyous and strong, they would scorn such miserable worship.

Let us be glad when we come together and unite in singing. Let us all sing to the Lord. Let us not rely on musical instruments to do our praising for us. The human voice is the greatest musical instrument that exists, by far. There is certainly no melody or harmony like those created by living tongues. Let us not rely on a choir or paid musicians to praise for us. God wants to hear the voices of all of His people united in praise.

Couldn't our churches have more praise services? In the church that I pastor, we have had a praise meeting every now and then. Shouldn't our churches hold praise meetings every week? Shouldn't prayer meetings be made more joyous than ever by praise? The singing of God's people should be—and if they were more full of divine strength it would be—more constant and universal. How sinners chant pagan praises in the streets! Some of us can hardly rest in the middle of the night without crude sounds of revelry startling us. Should the worshipers of wine sing so enthusiastically, and we be silent? We are not often guilty of disturbing the world with our music. The days in which Christian zeal interfered with the wicked seem to have gone by. We have settled down into more orderliness, and I am afraid into more lukewarmness as well. Oh, to be free to shout our praises!

Beloved, wake up your singing again. May the Lord help us to sing to Him more, and make us all to praise Him with heart and with voice, until even our adversaries say, "The Lord has done great things for them," and we reply, "Yes, you speak the truth. *'The LORD hath done great things for us; whereof we are glad'* (Psalm 126:3)."

Perhaps there has not been great blessing on our churches because they have not given God the thanksgiving of which He is worthy. During all the times in which we are in trouble, we are anxious and prayerful. When the leader of our country is sick, news of his progress is issued every hour or so. But, oh, when God's mercy comes, very little news is put out to call on us to bless and praise the name of God for His mercies. Let us praise the Lord *"from the rising of the sun unto the going down of the same"* (Psalm 113:3). *"For great is the LORD, and greatly to be praised"* (1 Chronicles 16:25).

Great Sacrifices

The next result of strength and joy is great sacrifice. *"That day they offered great sacrifices, and rejoiced."* What day does the church of God now set aside to make great sacrifices? I have not seen it on the calendar lately. Unfortunately, if people make any sacrifice, they very often do so in a way that indicates that they would avoid making it if they could. Few make great sacrifices and rejoice. You can persuade a person to give a considerable amount of money; a great many arguments overcome him at last, and he gives because he would be ashamed not to. But in his heart, he wishes you had not come that way but had gone to some other donor.

The most acceptable gift given to God is the gift that is given joyfully. It is wonderful to feel that whatever good your gift may do for the church or the poor or the sick, it is twice as beneficial to you to give it. It is good to give because you love to give, even like the flower that scents the air with its perfume because it never dreamed of doing otherwise; or like the bird that quivers with song because it is a bird and finds pleasure in its notes; or like the sun that shines, not by constraint, but because, being a sun, it must shine; or like the waves of the sea that flash back the brilliance of the sun because it is their nature to reflect the light and not to hoard or absorb all of it.

Oh, to have such grace in our hearts that we joyfully make sacrifices to our God! May the Lord grant that we may have much of this grace, for the bringing of the tithes into the storehouse is the way to blessing, as the Scripture says:

> *Bring ye all the tithes into the storehouse, that there may be meat in mine*
> *house, and prove me now herewith, saith the* LORD *of hosts, if I will not open*
> *you the windows of heaven, and pour you out a blessing, that there shall not*
> *be room enough to receive it.* (Malachi 3:10)

Happiness in Everyday Life

They *"rejoiced: for God had made them rejoice with great joy."* Singing and giving are not the only signs of the joy of God's people. In addition to these, other expressions of joy are sure to follow. When the wheels of a machine are well oiled, the whole machine runs easily; and when a man has the oil of joy, then in his business, and in his family, he glides along smoothly and harmoniously because he is a happy man.

On the other hand, there are some professing Christians who imagine that the sorrow of the Lord is their strength. They glory in the spirit of bondage and in an unbelieving experience, having great acquaintance—too much so—with the corruption of their hearts. They try to say that believers' deformities are their beauty, and their faults are their virtues. Such men denounce all who rejoice in the Lord; they tolerate only the unbelieving. Their strength lies in being able to take you through all the catacombs of nature's darkness, and to show you the rottenness of their evil hearts.

Well, let those who want to have such strength have it, but I am persuaded that our text is closer to wisdom: *"The joy of the* LORD *is your strength."* While we know a little about our corruption and mourn over it, while we know a little about the world's troubles and sometimes lament as we bear them, there is a joy in the perfect work of Christ, and a joy in our union with Him, that lifts us far above all other considerations. God becomes to us such a strength that we cannot help showing our joy in our ordinary lives.

Joy Shared with Family and Friends

The text also tells us that holy joy leads to family happiness. *"The wives also and the children rejoiced."* It is so in my own church. I have lately noticed several households that God has blessed, and I have rejoiced to see that father and mother know the Lord, and that even the youngest of the family has been brought to Jesus. Oh, households are happy indeed when the joy is not confined to one person but all partake of it. I greatly dislike that Christianity that makes a person feel, "My only concern is that *I* make it to heaven." Why, a person concerned only about himself is like a furnace that heats itself but does not heat the house.

Too many need all the religion they can acquire to encourage their own hearts, while their poor families and neighbors sit shivering in the cold of ungodliness. Do not be like that. Be like those well-built furnaces that send out all the heat into the house. Send out the heat of godliness into your house, and let all the neighbors participate in the blessing, for our text finishes with, *"The joy of Jerusalem was heard even afar off."* The joy of the Lord should be observed throughout our neighborhoods, and many who might otherwise have been indifferent to true religion will then ask, "What makes these people glad and creates such happy households?" In this way, your joy will be God's missionary.

You Can Have Joy and Strength

This joy and this strength are both within our reach! *"For God had made them rejoice with great joy."* God alone can give us this great joy. It is within the reach of anyone, for God can give it to one as well as to another. If it depended on our good works or our natural abilities, we could never reach it. But if God is the source and giver of it, He may give it to me as well as to you, and to you as well as to someone else.

According to our texts, what were the conditions under which God gave this joy? First, He gave it to these people because they were attentive hearers (Nehemiah 8:3). They were not passive hearers, but they listened intently as the Word was read. As it was read to them, they absorbed it, receiving it into their souls. An attentive hearer is on his way to being a joyous receiver.

Having heard the Word, they felt the power of it, and they wept (v. 9). Does that seem like the way to joy? No, but it was. They received the threats of the Law, with all their terrors, into their souls. They allowed the hammer of the Word to break them in pieces. They submitted themselves to the words of reproof. Oh, that God would incline you to do the same thing, for this, again, is the way in which God gives joy. The Word is heard; the Word is felt.

After they had felt the power of the Word, we see that they worshiped God devoutly (v. 6). They bowed their heads. Their postures indicated what they felt within. Worshipers who truly adore God with penitent hearts will never complain of boring Sundays. Adoration helps to bring us into joy. He who can bow low enough before the throne will be lifted as high before that throne as his heart can desire.

We read also that these hearers and worshipers understood clearly what they heard (v. 8). Never be content with hearing a sermon unless you can understand it. If there is a truth that is above you, strain after it; strive to know it. Bible reader, do not be content with going through the words of a chapter of Scripture. Ask the Holy Spirit to tell you the meaning, and use the proper means for finding out that meaning. Ask those who know, and use your own enlightened judgment to discover the meaning.

When will we be done with formalism in worship and come into living adoration? Sometimes, for all the true singing that there is, the song might as well be in Latin or in Greek. Oh, to know what we are singing, to know what we are saying in prayer, to know what we are reading, to get at it, to come right into it, to understand it—this is the way to holy joy.

I need to make one other point. These people, when they had understood what they had devoutly heard, were eager to obey (Nehemiah 8:14–17). They obeyed not only the common points of the Law that had been observed and demonstrated by former generations of Israelites, but they discovered an old institution that had long been buried and forgotten. It did not matter to them that it had not been observed for a lengthy period of time. God had commanded it, and they celebrated it, and in so doing, a special joy came to them.

Oh, for the time when all believers will search the Word of God, when they will not be content with saying, "I have joined myself with a certain body of believers. They do such and such; therefore, I do the same." May no one say to himself any longer, "This is the rule of my church," but may each of us say, "I am God's servant, not the servant of man, not the servant of man-made rules and regulations, not the servant of the prayer book or the catechism. To my own Master I stand (Romans 14:4), and the only law book I acknowledge is the book of His Word, inspired by His Spirit." Oh, it will be a blessed day, when every person will say, "I want to know what I am wrong about. I desire to know what I am supposed to do. I am eager to follow the Lord fully." If your joy in God leads you to practical obedience, you may rest assured that it has made you strong in the very best manner.

May we be a strong people, and consequently a joyous people, in the strength and joy of the Lord. May sinners in great numbers look unto Jesus and be saved.

THE SAME YESTERDAY, TODAY, AND FOREVER

Jesus Christ the same yesterday, and to day, and for ever.
—Hebrews 13:8

I have written on this text before, but I do not need to be at all afraid of writing on the same text twice. God's Word is inexhaustible. It may be trodden in the winepress many times and still generously yield wine. We should not hesitate to write a second time from the same passage, any more than anyone going to a well would be ashamed to put down the same bucket twice, or any more than anyone would feel at all distressed about sailing down the same river twice. There is always a freshness about gospel truth. Although the subject matter may be the same, there are ways of putting it in fresh light in order to bring new joy to those who meditate on it.

Is it unnecessary for me to repeat my teachings concerning Christ? Is it useless for you to read over and over again the same things about the King? No, we can afford to give and receive the same teachings again. Repetitions concerning Jesus are better than varieties on any other subject. As the French monarch declared that he would sooner hear the repetitions of Louis Bourdaloue, the famous French Jesuit, than the novelties of another, we may declare the same concerning our Lord Jesus. We would sooner hear again and again the precious truths that glorify Him than listen to the most eloquent orations on any other theme in all the world.

There are a few works of art and wonders of creation that you could gaze upon every day of your life and yet not tire of them. Everyone who has ever looked at the ocean or at Niagara Falls knows that, look as often as you may, though you see precisely the same object, there are new tints, new motions of the waves, and new flashes of light that forbid the least bit of monotony and that give to the waters an ever enduring charm. This is the way it is with that sea of all delights that is found in the dear Lover of our souls.

Thus, we come to the old subject of this old text, and may the blessed Spirit give us new anointing while we meditate on it. We will see that our text provides us with three main themes. First, note our Lord's personal name: Jesus Christ. Second, notice His memorable attribute: He is *the same yesterday, and to day, and for ever.*" Third, examine His claims, which are derived from the possession of such a character.

The Personal Names of Our Lord

Jesus

"Jesus" is the first name for our Lord that is mentioned in the text. That is our Lord's Hebrew name, "Joshua," or *"Jesus."* The word signifies a Savior: *"Thou shalt call his name Jesus: for he shall save his people from their sins"* (Matthew 1:21). The name was given to Him while He was still in His cradle.

> Cold on His cradle the dewdrops are shining;
>   Low lies His head with the beasts of the stall;
> Angels adore Him, in slumber reclining,
>   Maker, and Monarch, and Savior of all.

While He was still an infant feeding at His mother's breast, He was recognized as Savior, for the fact of God's becoming incarnate was the pledge, guarantee, and commencement of human salvation. At the very thought of His birth, the Virgin sang, *"My spirit hath rejoiced in God my Saviour"* (Luke 1:47). There was hope that man would be lifted up to God when God came down to man. Jesus in the manger deserved to be called the Savior, for when it can be said that *"the tabernacle of God is with men, and he...dwell[s] with them"* (Revelation 21:3), there is hope that all good things will be given to the fallen race.

He was called Jesus in His childhood—the holy child Jesus. It was as Jesus that He went up with His parents to the temple and sat down with the teachers, hearing them and asking them questions. Yes, Jesus, as He taught the very first principles of His doctrine, was a Savior, liberating the minds of men from superstition and setting them loose from the traditions of their ancestors. Even as a child, He scattered the seeds of truth, the elements of a glorious liberty that would emancipate the human mind from the iron bondage of false philosophy and ritualism.

It was so evident in His active life that Jesus was the Savior that He was commonly called by that name by both His friends and foes. It was as Jesus the Savior that He healed the sick, raised the dead, delivered Peter from sinking, and rescued from shipwreck the ship tossed on the Sea of Galilee. In all the teachings of His midlife, in those laborious three years of diligent service, both in His public ministry and in His private prayer, He was still Jesus the Savior; for by His active, as well as by His passive obedience, we are saved. All during His earthly life, He made it clear that the Son of Man had come *"to seek and to save that which was lost"* (Luke 19:10). If His blood redeems us from the guilt of sin, His life shows us how to overcome its power. If by His death upon the cross He crushed Satan for us, by His life of holiness He teaches us how to break the Dragon's head within us.

He was the Savior as a babe, the Savior as a child, the Savior as the toiling, laboring, tempted man. But He was most clearly Jesus the Savior when dying on the cross. Even Pilate called Him *"Jesus,"* or Savior, when he wrote His title on the cross, which read, *"Jesus of Nazareth the King of the Jews"* (John 19:19). When Pilate was asked to change this title, he said, *"What I have written I have written"* (v. 22).

Preeminently on the cross, He was the Savior, being made a curse for us so that *"we might be made the righteousness of God in him"* (2 Corinthians 5:21). In fact, it was after beholding the dying agonies of his Master that the Beloved Apostle wrote, *"We have seen and do testify that the Father sent the Son to be the Saviour of the world"* (1 John 4:14). At Calvary, it was remarked that the Son of

Man *"saved others"* (Matthew 27:42), but, through blessed incapacity prompted by love, *"himself he [could not] save"* (v. 42). When He was made to feel the wrath of God on account of sin, and pains unknown were suffered by Him as our Substitute, when He was made to pass through the thick darkness and burning heat of divine wrath, then He was, according to Scripture, *"the Saviour of all men, specially of those that believe"* (1 Timothy 4:10).

Yes, it was on the cross that Christ was especially a Savior. If He were nothing better than our example, how unfortunate we would be! We might be grateful for the example if we could imitate it, but without the pardon that spares us, without the grace that gives us power for holiness, the brightest example would only increase our grief. To be shown a picture of what we ought to be, without being given a method to attain that standard, would only mock our misery. But Jesus first pulls us out of the horrible pit into which we are fallen, taking us out of the mud and mire by the power of His atoning sacrifice. Then, having set our feet on a rock by virtue of His merits, He Himself leads the way onward to perfection. Therefore, He is a Savior both in life and in death.

> That Jesus saves from sin and hell,
> Is truth divinely sure;
> And on this rock our faith may rest
> Immovably secure.

Still bearing the name of Jesus, our Lord rose from the dead. Evangelists delight in calling Him Jesus when they speak of His appearance to Mary Magdalene in the garden or His appearance to the disciples when they were gathered together behind locked doors. When He is spoken of as the Risen One, He is always spoken of as Jesus the Savior. Beloved, since we are justified by His resurrection, it is fitting that we regard Him as Savior when speaking of His resurrection. Salvation is strongly linked with a risen Christ, because we see Him, by His resurrection, destroying death, breaking down the prison of the tomb, carrying away, like another Samson, the gates of the grave. He is our Savior because He has already vanquished the enemy that will be the last to be completely destroyed—Death. He rose so that we, having been saved from sin by His death, can be saved from death through His resurrection.

Jesus is the title by which He is called in glory, since *"him hath God exalted with his right hand to be a Prince and a Saviour, for to give repentance to Israel, and forgiveness of sins"* (Acts 5:31). He is today *"the saviour of the body"* (Ephesians 5:23). We adore Him as *"the only wise God our Saviour"* (Jude 25). *"He is able also to save them to the uttermost that come unto God by him, seeing he ever liveth to make intercession for them"* (Hebrews 7:25). As Jesus, He will come again, and we are *"looking for that blessed hope, and the glorious appearing of the great God and our Saviour Jesus Christ"* (Titus 2:13). Our daily cry is, *"Even so, come, Lord Jesus"* (Revelation 22:20).

Yes, Jesus is the name by which He is known in heaven at this hour. By the name of Jesus, the angel spoke of Him before He was conceived by the Virgin. By the name of Jesus, the angels serve Him and do His bidding, for He said to John on Patmos, *"I Jesus have sent mine angel to testify unto you these things"* (Revelation 22:16). The angels prophesied His second coming using that sacred name. They came to Jesus' followers who stood looking up into heaven after His ascension, and they said, *"Ye men of Galilee, why stand ye gazing up into heaven? this same Jesus, which is taken up from you into heaven, shall so come in like manner as ye have seen him go into heaven"* (Acts 1:11). Under this name, the devils fear Him, for didn't an evil spirit say, *"Jesus I know, and Paul I know; but who are ye"* (Acts 19:15)?

The name of Jesus is the spell that binds the hearts of cherubim in chains of love, and it is the name that makes the hosts of hell tremble and cower. This name is both the joy of the church on earth and the joy of the church above. It is a household name for our dear Redeemer among the family of God below, and up there they still sing it.

> Jesus, the Lord, their harps employs:
> > Jesus, my Love, they sing!
> Jesus, the life of both our joys,
> > Sounds sweet from every string.

The Meaning of "Jesus"

Henry Craik of Bristol, a man of God, wrote a little book on the study of the Hebrew language. In it, he used the word *Jesus* as an example of how much may be gathered from a single Hebrew word, for the name of Jesus is particularly rich and meaningful to the mind of the Hebrew scholar. Its root word means "amplitude, spaciousness." It later came to mean "setting at large, setting free, delivering." Then it came to mean what it commonly means today, namely, "Savior."

There are actually two words in the name *Jesus*. The one is a contraction of the word *Jehovah*; the other is the word that I have just now explained to you as ultimately coming to mean "salvation." Broken down to its simplest terms, the word *Jesus* means "Jehovah–Salvation." The first part of His name declares the glorious essence and nature of Christ as Jehovah, "*I Am That I Am*" (Exodus 3:14). The second part of His name reveals His great work for us in setting us free and delivering us from all distress.

Think, beloved believer, of the amplitude, the spaciousness, the breadth, the depth, the abundance, the boundless all-sufficiency laid up in the person of the Lord Jesus Christ. "*It pleased the Father that in him should all fulness dwell*" (Colossians 1:19). You do not have a limited Christ; you do not have a narrow Savior. Oh, the infinity of His love, the abundance of His grace, the exceeding greatness of the riches of His love toward us! There are no words in any language that can sufficiently describe the unlimited, infinite extent of the riches of the glory of Christ Jesus our Lord.

The word that lies at the root of this name *Jesus*, or *Joshua*, sometimes has the meaning of riches, and who can tell what a wealth of grace and glory is laid up in our Emmanuel?

According to Henry Craik, another form of the same word signifies "a cry." The psalmist said, "*Hearken unto the voice of my cry, my King, and my God*" (Psalm 5:2). Thus, salvation, riches, and a cry are all derived from the same root, and all are found in our "Joshua," or Christ. When His people cry out from their prisons, then He comes and sets them free. He comes with all the fullness and wealth of His eternal grace, with all the plenitude of His overflowing power. Delivering His people from every form of bondage, He enables them to enjoy the riches of the glory treasured up in Himself.

If this interpretation makes the name of Jesus a little bit more dear to you, I greatly rejoice. Just think, if there is so much wealth stored up in His name, what must be stored up in His very self! And, if we can honestly say that it would be difficult to give the full meaning of this one Hebrew name that belongs to Christ, how much more difficult would it be to give the full meaning of all His character? If His name alone is such a mine of excellence, what must His person be? If His name, which is only a part of Him, smells so sweetly of myrrh, aloes, and cassia (Psalm 45:8), oh, what must His blessed person be but *"a bundle of myrrh"* (Song 1:13) that we will forever wear around our necks to be the perfume of our lives and the delight of our souls?

> Precious is the name of Jesus,
>   Who can half its worth unfold?
> Far beyond angelic praises,
>   Sweetly sung to harps of gold.

> Precious when to Calvary groaning,
>   He sustain'd the cursed tree;
> Precious when His death atoning,
>   Made an end of sin for me.

> Precious when the bloody scourges
>   Caused the sacred drops to roll;
> Precious when of wrath the surges
>   Overwhelm'd His holy soul.

> Precious in His death victorious,
>   He the host of hell o'erthrows;
> In His resurrection glorious,
>   Victor crowned o'er all His foes.

> Precious, Lord! beyond expressing,
>   Are Thy beauties all divine;
> Glory, honor, power, and blessing,
>   Be henceforth forever Thine.

Christ

I have written about the Hebrew name of God's Son. Now let us reverently consider the second title given to Him in our text—*"Christ."* That is a Greek name, a Gentile name, meaning "anointed." In our text, we have the Hebrew name *Joshua*, or *Jesus*, then the Greek name *Christos*, or *Christ*, so that we may see that there is no longer Jew or Gentile, but that all are one in Jesus Christ (Galatians 3:28). The word *Christ*, as I have mentioned, means "anointed," and as such, our Lord is sometimes called *"the Christ"* (Matthew 16:16), or *"the very Christ"* (John 7:26). At other times, He is called *"the Lord's Christ"* (Luke 2:26) and sometimes *"the Christ of God"* (Luke 9:20). He is the Lord's Anointed, our King, and our Shield.

This word *Christ* teaches us three great truths. First, it indicates His offices. He exercises offices in which anointing is necessary; there are three of them: the office of king, the office of priest, and the office of prophet.

Christ is King in Zion, anointed *"with the oil of gladness above [His] fellows"* (Psalm 45:7), even as it was said long ago,

> *I have found David my servant; with my holy oil have I anointed him: with whom my hand shall be established: mine arm also shall strengthen him....I will set his hand also in the sea, and his right hand in the rivers....Also I will make him my firstborn, higher than the kings of the earth.*
> (Psalm 89:20–21, 25, 27)

Saul, the first king of Israel, was anointed with only a vial of oil, but David was anointed with a horn of oil, as if to signify his greater power and his greater kingdom. But as for our Lord Jesus Christ, He has received the Spirit of anointing without measure (John 3:34). He is the Lord's Anointed, for whom an unquenchable lamp is ordained. The Scripture says, *"There will I make the horn of David to bud: I have ordained a lamp for mine anointed"* (Psalm 132:17).

Beloved, as we think about the name *Christ*, let us reverently yield our souls up to the One whom God has anointed to be King. Let us stand up for His rights over His church, for He is King of Zion, and none have a right to rule there except under and in subjection to the great Head over all, who in all things will have the preeminence (Colossians 1:18). Let us stand up for His rights within our own hearts, seeking to thrust out anything that competes with Him for our affections, desiring to keep our souls chaste for Christ. Let us compel every member of our bodies, although previously they might have surrendered themselves to sin, to be subservient to the anointed King who has an absolute right to rule over them.

Next, the Lord Christ is Priest. Priests had to be anointed. Israelites were not supposed to take this office upon themselves, nor could they become priests without going through the ceremony that set them apart. Jesus Christ our Lord has had grace given to Him that no priest ever had. The outward anointing of the priest was only symbolical, while His anointing was true and real. He has received what their oil only portrayed in type and shadow; He has the real anointing from the Most High.

Beloved, let us always look at Christ as the anointed Priest. My friend, you can never come to God except through the ever living and truly anointed High Priest of your faith's profession. Oh, never for a moment seek to come to God without Him, or through any pretender who may call himself a priest. High Priest of the house of God, we see You thus ordained, and we give our cause into Your hands. Offer our sacrifices for us; present our prayers. Take our praises, put them into the golden censer (Revelation 8:3), and offer them Yourself before Your Father's throne. Rejoice, beloved, every time you hear the name *Christ*, knowing that He who wears it is anointed to be Priest.

Regarding the prophetic office, the Scriptures reveal that Elisha was anointed to prophesy, and likewise Jesus Christ is the Prophet anointed among His people. Peter told Cornelius of *"how God anointed Jesus of Nazareth with the Holy Ghost and with power: who went about doing good, and healing all that were oppressed of the devil; for God was with him"* (Acts 10:38). He was anointed to preach the Good News and to sit as Master in Israel. We should consider no man's teaching to be authoritative except the testimony of the Christ. The teaching of Christ is our creed, and nothing else.

I thank God that in my church we do not have to divide our allegiance between some venerable set of articles and the teaching of our Lord. We have one Master, and we do not acknowledge the right of any man to bind another's conscience. Even if a man is great in piety and deep in learning, like Augustine and Calvin, whose names we honor, for God honored them, still he has no dominance over the private judgment of God's people. Jesus Christ is the Prophet of Christendom. His words must always be the first and the last appeal.

This, then, is the meaning of the word *Christos*: He is anointed as King, Priest, and Prophet. But it means more than that. The name *Christ* declares His right to those offices. He is not King because He sets Himself up as such. God has set Him up as King upon His holy hill of Zion and has anointed Him to rule. He is also Priest, but He has not taken the priesthood upon Himself, for He is the atoning sacrifice that God has set forth for human sin. The Lord God has appointed Christ to be the mediator; He has chosen Christ to be the only mediator between God and man. And as for His prophesying, Christ does not speak on His own; on the contrary, He has revealed to us the things that He has learned from the Father. He does not come as a prophet who assumes office; God has anointed Him to preach the Good News to the poor and to come among His people with the welcome news of eternal love.

Moreover, this anointing signifies a third thing. Even as He has the office, and as it is His by right, so He has the qualifications for the work. He is anointed to be King. God has given Him royal power, wisdom, and government; He has made Him fit to rule in the church and to reign over the world. There is no better king than Christ—none as majestic as He who wore the crown of thorns—for He will one day wear the crown of universal monarchy.

He has the qualifications of a priest, too—qualifications that even Melchizedek did not have (Hebrews 7:1–3, 15–17), qualifications that cannot be found in the long lineage of the house of Aaron. Blessed Son of God, You are perfect in Yourself, and You do not need a sacrifice for Your own sake. Yet, You have presented unto God an offering that has perfected forever those whom You have set apart (Hebrews 10:14). Now, You do not need to make a further offering. You have forever put away sin.

It is the same way with our Lord's prophesying; He has the power to teach. *"Grace is poured into thy lips: therefore God hath blessed thee for ever"* (Psalm 45:2). All the words of Christ are wisdom and truth. The substance of true philosophy and sure knowledge is to be found in the One who is the wisdom and the power of God (1 Corinthians 1:24).

Oh, that word *Christ*! It seems to grow on us as we think it over. It shows us the offices of Christ, His right to those offices, and His qualifications for them.

> Christ, to Thee our spirits bow!
> Prophet, Priest, and King art Thou!
> Christ, anointed of the Lord,
> Evermore be Thou adored.

Now, put the two titles together and ring out the harmony of the two melodi-ous notes: Jesus Christ—Anointed Savior! Oh, how blessed! Don't you see that our Beloved is a Savior appropriately appointed, a Savior abundantly qualified? My friends, if God has appointed Christ to be the Savior of sinners, why do you question His decision? God presented Christ as a sinner's Savior. Come, then, sinners; take Him, accept Him, and rest in Him. Oh, how foolish we are when we begin raising questions, objections, and difficulties! God declares that Christ is a Savior to all who trust in Him. My poor heart trusts Him; it has peace. But why do some of you imagine that He cannot save you? Why do you ask, "How can it be that this man would save me?" God has appointed Him. Take Him; rest in Him.

Moreover, God has qualified Him and given Him the anointing of a Savior. What? Do you think that God has not given Him enough power or furnished Him with enough merit with which to save such as you are? Will you limit what God has done? Will you think that His anointing is imperfect and cannot qualify Jesus to remedy your condition? Oh, do not slander the grace of heaven! Do not insult the wisdom of the Lord! Honor the Savior of God's anointing by coming now, just as you are, and putting your trust in Him.

His Memorable Attribute

Jesus Christ is said to be *"the same."* Now, as far as His circumstances are concerned, He has not been the same at all times, for He was once adored by angels but afterward spit on by men. He exchanged the heavenly splendors of His Father's court for the poverty of the earth, the degradation of death, and the humiliation of the grave.

Jesus Christ is not, and will not, always be the same in regard to His occupation. Once He came *"to seek and to save that which was lost"* (Luke 19:10), but we truly sing, "The Lord will come, but not the same as once in lowliness He came." He will come again with a very different purpose. He will come to scatter His enemies and to break them as with a rod of iron (Psalm 2:9).

Therefore, we are not to interpret the expression *"the same"* in the strictest sense imaginable. Looking at the original Greek, I notice that our text might be read this way: "Jesus Christ Himself, yesterday and today and forever." The anointed Savior is always Himself. He is always Jesus Christ. The word *same* seems to me to have the most intimate relationship with the two titles of the text. Jesus Christ is always Jesus Christ, yesterday and today and forever. Jesus Christ is always Himself. At any rate, if that is not the correct translation, it is a very correct and blessed statement. It is sweetly true that Jesus Christ is always Himself.

The Same Yesterday

An unchangeable nature is ascribed to Christ, and He was always to His people what He is now, for He was *"the same yesterday."*

Some men who are extremely wise (at least in their own opinion) have drawn distinctions between the people of God who lived before the coming of Christ and those who lived afterward. I have even heard it said that those who lived before the coming of Christ do not belong to the church of God. We never know what we will hear next, and perhaps it is a mercy that these absurdities are revealed one at a time, so that we may be able to endure their stupidity without dying of amazement.

Why, every child of God in every place stands on the same footing. The Lord does not have some children whom He loves the best, some who are second-rate, and others whom He hardly cares about. Those who saw Christ's day before it came differ greatly from us as far as what they knew, and perhaps to that extent, they differ as far as what they enjoyed in meditating on Christ while they were on earth. But they were all washed in the same blood, all redeemed with the same ransom price, and all made members of the same body. In the covenant of grace, the Israel of God is not natural Israel, but all believers from all ages.

Before the First Advent, all the types and shadows pointed one way—to Christ. To Him all believers looked with hope. Those who lived before Christ were not saved with a different salvation than the eternal salvation that will come to us. They exercised faith just as we must. Their faith struggled as ours struggles, and their faith obtained its eternal reward just as ours will. Comparing the spiritual life of the believer now with the spiritual life of David is like comparing a man's face with a reflection of that face.

Sometime, when you are reading the book of Psalms, forget for an instant that you are reading about the life of someone who lived a long time ago. You might suppose that David wrote only yesterday. Even in what he wrote about Christ, it seems as though he lived after Christ, instead of before. Furthermore, both in what he saw of himself and of his Savior, he sounds more like a New Testament believer who has found his Messiah than an Old Testament Israelite still awaiting the Christ. What I am saying is that, living before Christ, he had the same hopes and the same fears, the same joys and the same sorrows. He had the same impression of his blessed Redeemer that you and I have in these times. Jesus was the same yesterday as He is today, as far as being an anointed Savior to His people. They received from Him similar precious gifts. If the good prophets could be here today, they would all testify that in every office, He was the same in their time as He is today.

The Same Today

Jesus Christ is the same now as He was in the past, for the text says, "*The same yesterday, and to day.*" He is the same today as He has been from eternity. Before all the worlds existed, He planned our salvation, and He entered into covenant with His Father to undertake it. His "*delights were with the sons of men*" (Proverbs 8:31) who would one day inhabit the earth, and now today He is as faithful to that covenant as ever. He will not lose those who were then given to Him (John 18:9), nor will He fail or be discouraged, for every stipulation of that covenant will be fulfilled. The same infinite love that was in the heart of Christ before the stars began to shine is there today.

Jesus is the same today as He was when He was here on earth. There is much comfort in this thought. When He lived among men, He was most willing to save. "*Come unto me, all ye that labour and are heavy laden*" (Matthew 11:28) was His cry. He is still calling to the weary and the burdened to come to Him. When He was on earth, He would not curse the woman caught in adultery, nor would He reject the tax collectors and sinners who gathered to hear Him. He is still merciful to sinners, and He still says to them, "*Neither do I condemn thee: go, and sin no more*" (John 8:11). That delightful sentence that so graciously came from His lips—"*[Your] sins, which are many, are forgiven*" (Luke 7:47)—is still His favorite utterance to human hearts.

Oh, do not think that Christ in heaven has become distant and reserved, so that you may not approach Him. He is the same now as He was when He lived here—a Lamb, gentle and meek, a Man to whom men drew near without a moment's hesitation. Come boldly to Him, you lowliest and guiltiest ones. Come near to Him with broken hearts and weeping eyes. Though He is King and Priest, surrounded with inconceivable splendor, yet He has the same loving heart and the same generous sympathy for the sons of men.

He is still the same in His ability as well as in His willingness to save. He is still Jesus Christ, the anointed Savior. In His earthly days, He touched the leper and said, *"I will; be thou clean"* (Matthew 8:3). He called Lazarus from the tomb, and Lazarus came. Sinner, Jesus is still just as able to heal or enliven you as He was able to do for others then. *"He is able also to save them to the uttermost that come unto God by him, seeing he ever liveth to make intercession for them"* (Hebrews 7:25). Now that His blood has been shed indeed, and the sacrifice has been fully offered, there is no limit to the ability of Christ to save. Oh, come and rely on Him, and find salvation in Him now.

Believer, it will encourage you also to remember that when our Lord was here on earth, He showed great perseverance in His art of saving. He could say, *"Of them which thou gavest me have I lost none"* (John 18:9). Rejoice that He is the same today. He will not cast one of you away or allow His little ones to perish. He kept all safe in the days of His earthly sojourn; He takes care to keep all safe now in the days of His heavenly glory. He is the same today as He was while on earth.

Blessed be His name; Jesus Christ is the same today as in apostolic days. Then He gave the fullness of the Spirit; then, *"when he ascended up on high, he… gave gifts unto men"* (Ephesians 4:8)—apostles, preachers, teachers of the Word (v. 11). Do not think that we will never see days as good as the Day of Pentecost. He is the same Christ. He could just as readily convert three thousand after one sermon today as in Peter's time. His Holy Spirit is not exhausted, for *"God giveth not the Spirit by measure unto [Christ]"* (John 3:34).

We ought to pray that God would raise up among us prominent men to proclaim the Gospel. We do not pray enough for the ministry. The ministry is the particular gift of the Ascension. When Jesus Christ ascended on high, He received gifts for men, and He gave what? Why, apostles, teachers, preachers. When we ask for salvation, we plead the blood of Jesus; why don't we ask for ministers and plead the Ascension? If we would do this more, we would see raised up among us more Whitefields and Wesleys, more Luthers and Calvins, more men of the apostolic kind. Then the church would be revived. Jesus Christ, being the same, is able to enrich His people with all spiritual gifts this year just as in the year when He ascended to His throne. He is *"the same yesterday, and to day."*

He is the same today as He was to our forefathers in the faith. They have gone to their rest, but they testified before they went of what Christ had been to them, how He had helped them in their time of peril, how He had delivered them in their hour of sorrow. He will do for us just what He did for them. Some who lived before us were burned at the stake for their faith, but Christ was very precious to them as they went to heaven in chariots of fire. We read the stories of Christian martyrs with wonder. How sustaining the presence of Christ was to those who lay in prison, to those who were thrown to the lions, to those who wandered around in sheepskins and goatskins! England, Scotland—all the countries where Christ has been preached—have been dyed with the blood and ennobled with the testimonies of the faithful. Whatever Jesus was to these worthy believers who have now departed, He is to His people still. We only have to ask God, and we will receive the very same benefits.

"Jesus Christ the same...to day," says the text. Therefore, He is the same today as He has been to us in the past. We have greatly enjoyed God's presence. We remember the love of our first days of salvation, and if we do not have the same joys today, it is no fault of His. The same water is still in the well; if we have not drawn it, it is our own fault. We have walked away from the fire, and therefore we are cold. We have walked contrary to Him, and therefore He walks contrary to us (Leviticus 26:23–24). Let us return to Him, and He will be as glad to receive us now as in our first moment of repentance. Let us return to Him. His heart is just as full of love, and He is just as ready to tearfully embrace us as when we first came and sought pardon from His hands.

There are many precious truths in the text, but I cannot linger any longer on this part of the subject. It is enough for us to remember that Jesus Christ is the same today as He always has been.

The Same Forever

Lastly, Christ will be tomorrow what He was yesterday and is today. Our Lord Jesus Christ will be changed in no respect throughout the duration of our lives. It may be a long time before we descend to our graves. Let these hairs of mine all turn gray, and these legs of mine begin to wobble, and these eyes of mine grow dim, for Jesus Christ will have the dew of His youth upon Him (Psalm 110:3), and the fullness of His love will still flow to me. And after death, or, if we do not die, at the coming of Christ and in His glorious reign, Jesus will be the same to His people as He is now.

It seems that an idea is being circulated that after His coming, Christ will deal differently with His people than now. I have been informed by a contemporary school of inventors of religion, who invent newfangled ideas, that some of us will be shut out of the kingdom when Christ comes. Saved by precious blood and brought near to God, adopted into the family, our names written on the breast-plate of Christ, we will be shut out from the kingdom? Nonsense! I see nothing about this in the Word of God, although there might be a great deal of it in the imaginations of people.

The people of God, equally bought with blood and equally dear to Jesus' heart, will be treated on the same scale and footing. They will never be put under the law; they will never come to Christ in a future state and find Him ruling them as a legal Judge, beating them with many lashes, or shutting them out of His estate of millennial majesty. He will not reward some by giving them rule and authority and at the same time exclude others of His redeemed family. His entire family will find that He always treats them as unchanging love and immutable grace dictate.

The rewards of the millennial state will always be those of grace; they will not be such that they will exclude even the very least of God's family. In fact, all believers will receive rewards from the dear Savior's hand.

I know He will not love me today, giving me glimpses of His face and allowing me to delight in His name, and yet, when He comes again, tell me I cannot enter His kingdom but must stand out in the cold. I do not have a tinge of faith in this "purgatory" of banishment, which certain despisers of the ministry have chosen to set up. I marvel that in any Protestant denomination there should arise a dogma as villainous as the dogma of purgatory. These teachers say that everyone else is wrong but that they have been taught deep things and can discover what the best theologians have never seen.

I know this: Jesus will love His people in times to come as strongly as He does now. The destruction or denial of this doctrine would cast sorrow into the whole family of God. Throughout eternity, in heaven, there will still be the same Jesus Christ, with the same love for His people. They will have the same intimate communion with Him—no, they will see Him face-to-face. They will rejoice forever in Him as their unchangeably anointed Savior.

Our Lord's Claims upon Us

Since our Lord is *"the same yesterday, and to day, and for ever,"* then, according to the verse preceding our text, He is to be followed to the end. Observe the seventh verse: "*Remember them which have the rule over you, who have spoken unto you the word of God: whose faith follow, considering the end of their conversation*" (Hebrews 13:7). The meaning of the verse is this: these holy men ended their lives with Christ; their exit out of this life meant going to Jesus and reigning with Him. Beloved, if the Lord is still the same, follow Him until you reach Him. Your exit out of this life will bring you where He is, and you will find Him to be then what He always was. You will "*see him as he is*" (1 John 3:2). If He were a delusive hope, forever changing, it would be dangerous to follow Him. But since He is always equally worthy of your admiration and imitation, follow Him forever.

Henry VI of France gave an eloquent speech on the eve of a certain battle. He said to his soldiers, "Gentlemen, you are Frenchmen. I am your king. There is the enemy!" Similarly, Jesus Christ says, "You are my people. I am your leader. There is the foe!" How dare we do anything unworthy of such a Lord as He is, or of such a citizenship as that which He has given us? If we are indeed His, and He is indeed immutable, let us by His Holy Spirit's power persevere to the end, so that we may obtain the crown.

The next claim of Christ upon us is that we should be steadfast in the faith. Notice the verse after our text: "*Be not carried about with divers* [various] *and strange doctrines*" (Hebrews 13:9). There is nothing new in theology except that which is false. All that is true is old, though I am not saying that all that is old is true. Some speak of new developments as though we had not discovered the whole Christian religion yet. But the religion of Paul is the religion of every person who is taught by the Holy Spirit. We must not, therefore, indulge for a moment the idea that something has been discovered that might correct the teaching of Christ, that some new philosophy or scientific discovery has arisen to correct the declared testimony of our Redeemer. Let us hold tightly to what we have received; let us never depart from "*the faith which was once delivered unto the saints*" (Jude 3) by Christ Himself.

Moreover, since Jesus Christ is immutable, He has an obvious claim to our most solemn worship. Immutability can be the attribute of no one but God. Whoever is "*the same yesterday, and to day, and for ever*" must be divine. Forever, then, believer, bring your adoration to Jesus. At the feet of Him who was crucified, cast your crown. Give royal and divine honors to the One who stooped to the ignominy of crucifixion. Let no one prevent you from glorying in Christ, for you boast in the Son of God made man for you. Worship Him as God over all, blessed forever.

Next, He has a claim to our trust. If He is always the same, here is a rock that cannot be moved. Build on it! Here is a haven. Cast your anchor of hope into it, and hold on in times of storm. If Christ were changeable, He would not be worthy of your confidence. But, since He is forever unchanged, rest on Him without fear.

Lastly, if He is always the same, rejoice in Him, and rejoice always. If you have ever had cause to rejoice in Christ, you always have cause, for He never changes. If yesterday you could sing of Him, today you may sing of Him. If He were subject to change, your joy might change. But if the stream of your gladness springs solely out of this great deep of the immutability of Jesus, then it never needs to stop flowing. Beloved, let us *"rejoice in the Lord alway: and again I say, Rejoice"* (Philippians 4:4). Until the day breaks and the shadows flee away, until the blessed hour arrives when we will see Him face-to-face and be made like Him, let this be our joy, that He is *"the same yesterday, and to day, and for ever."*

6

SUFFERING AND REIGNING
WITH JESUS

*If we suffer, we shall also reign with him: if we
deny him, he also will deny us.*
—2 Timothy 2:12

O ur text is the second part of one of Paul's faithful sayings. If I remember correctly, Paul had four of these. The first occurs in 1 Timothy 1:15, that famous, that foremost of all faithful sayings: *"This is a faithful saying, and worthy of all acceptation, that Christ Jesus came into the world to save sinners; of whom I am chief."* Paul himself had most marvelously proved the value of this golden saying. What should I say about this verse except that, like the light of a lighthouse, it has darted its ray of comfort through miles of darkness and has guided millions of tempest-tossed spirits to the port of peace?

The next faithful saying is in the same epistle:

Godliness is profitable unto all things, having promise of the life that now is, and of that which is to come. This is a faithful saying and worthy of all acceptation. (1 Timothy 4:8–9)

This, too, the apostle knew to be true, since he had learned "*in whatsoever state* [he was], *therewith to be content*" (Philippians 4:11).

Our chosen text, "*If we suffer, we shall also reign with him,*" is a portion of the third faithful saying. The last of the four you will find in Titus:

> *This is a faithful saying, and these things I will that thou affirm constantly, that they which have believed in God might be careful to maintain good works. These things are good and profitable unto men.* (Titus 3:8)

There is a connection between these faithful sayings. The first one, which speaks of Jesus Christ coming into the world to save sinners, lays the foundation of our eternal salvation, which is the free grace of God. This grace was shown to us in the mission of the great Redeemer. The next faithful saying affirms the double blessedness that we obtain through this salvation—the blessings of both the lower and upper springs—of both time and eternity. The third faithful saying shows one of the duties to which the chosen people are called: we are ordained to suffer for Christ with the promise that "*if we suffer, we shall also reign with him.*" The last faithful saying describes the active form of Christian service, instructing us to diligently maintain good works.

Thus you have, first, the root of salvation in free grace; next, the privileges of that salvation in the present life and in the life to come; and, lastly, the two great branches of suffering with Christ and service to Christ, loaded with the fruits of the Spirit of all grace.

Treasure up, dear friend, these faithful sayings. "*Lay up these my words in your heart and in your soul, and bind them for a sign upon your hand, that they may be as frontlets between your eyes*" (Deuteronomy 11:18). Let these choice sayings be printed in letters of gold and posted on the doorposts of our houses and on our gates (v. 20). Let them be the guides of our lives, as well as our comfort and our instruction. The Apostle to the Gentiles proved them to be faithful. They are faithful still. Not one word will fall to the ground. They are worthy of full acceptance. Let us accept them now and prove their faithfulness.

This chapter will focus on a part of the faithful saying that deals with suffering. Let us look at the verse preceding our text: "*It is a faithful saying: for if we be dead with him, we shall also live with him*" (2 Timothy 2:11). All the elect were virtually dead with Christ when He died on the cross; they were on the cross, crucified with Him (Galatians 2:20). In Him, who is their Representative, they rose from the tomb, and they live in *"newness of life"* (Romans 6:4). Because He lives, they will live also (John 14:19).

In due time, the chosen are drawn to God by the Spirit of God. When they are saved, they are made dead with Christ unto sin, unto self-righteousness, unto the world, unto the flesh, and unto the powers of darkness. Then it is that they live with Jesus; His life becomes their life. As He was, so are they also in this world (1 John 4:17). The Spirit of God breathes the quickening grace into those who were once dead in sin, and thus they live in union with Christ Jesus. A believer may be sawed in half or burned at the stake. Yet, since he sleeps in Jesus, he is preserved from the destruction of death by Him; he is made a partaker of Christ's immortality. May the Lord root us and ground us in the mysterious but most comforting doctrine of union with Christ Jesus.

Let us now focus on our text: *"If we suffer, we shall also reign with him: if we deny him, he also will deny us."* The words naturally divide themselves into two parts: first, suffering with Jesus and its reward; second, denying Jesus and its penalty.

Suffering with Jesus and Its Reward

To suffer is the common lot of all people. It is not possible for us to escape from pain. We come into this world through the gate of suffering, and we leave it through the same gate. We suffer if we live, regardless of what kind of lives we lead. The wicked individual may cast off all respect for virtue; he may live riotously in excessive vice. Yet, he must not expect to avoid the well-directed shafts of sorrow. No, rather let him expect a tenfold share of bodily pain and remorse of soul. *"Many sorrows shall be to the wicked"* (Psalm 32:10). Even if a person could so completely degrade himself as to lose his intellectual powers and become like an animal, even then he could not escape from suffering, for we know that the animal is the victim of pain as much as more lordly man. In fact, the animals have the additional misery that they have no mind endowed with reason or encouraged by hope to fortify them in their pain.

Oh, man, don't you see that however you may degrade yourself, you are still under the yoke of suffering? The loftiest men bow beneath it, and the lowest men cannot avoid it. Every acre of humanity must be furrowed with this plow. There may be a sea without a wave, but never a man without a sorrow. He who was God as well as man, had His full measure of pain; in fact, His share was pressed down and running over. Let us be assured that if the Sinless One was not spared the rod, the sinful will not go free. *"Man that is born of a woman is of few days, and full of trouble"* (Job 14:1). *"Man is born unto trouble, as the sparks fly upward"* (Job 5:7).

Suffering That Does Not Ensure a Reward

If, then, a man has sorrow, it does not necessarily mean that he will be rewarded for it, since it is the common lot brought upon all by sin. You may ache under the lashes of sorrow in this life, but your sadness will not deliver you from the wrath to come. Remember, you may live in poverty and lead a wearisome life of unrewarded toil. You may be placed on a sickbed and be made to experience agony in every part of your body. Your mind, too, may be depressed with fears or plunged into the depths of despair. Yet, by all this, you may gain nothing of any value to your immortal spirit. *"Except a man be born again, he cannot see the kingdom of God"* (John 3:3), and no amount of affliction on earth can alter that unchanging rule to admit an unsaved person into heaven.

To suffer is not unique to the Christian. Nor does suffering necessarily bring with it any reward. The text clearly implies that we must suffer *with Christ* in order to reign with Him. The structure of our text plainly requires such a reading. The words *"with him"* may be as accurately placed at the end of the one clause as the other: *"If we suffer* [with Him], *we shall also reign with him."* The suffering that brings the reigning with Jesus must be a suffering with Jesus.

There is a misconception among many poor people who are ignorant of true Christianity, that all poor and afflicted people will be rewarded for their suffering in the next state. I have heard workingmen refer to the parable of the rich man and Lazarus (Luke 16:19–31) with a cruel sort of satisfaction at the pains of the rich man. They have imagined that, in the same manner, all rich people will be cast into the flames of hell without a drop of water to cool their tongues, while all poor people like Lazarus will be triumphantly carried into Abraham's bosom.

A more fearful mistake could not be made. It was not the suffering of Lazarus that entitled him to a place in Abraham's bosom. He might have been licked by all the dogs on earth and then dragged off by the dogs of hell. Many a man goes to hell a pauper. A drunkard's hovel is very wretched; is he to be rewarded for bringing himself to rags? Very much of the poverty we see around us is the result of vice, extravagance, or folly. Are these things so meritorious as to be passports to glory? Let no man deceive himself so horribly.

On the other hand, the rich man was not cast into hell because he was rich and lived luxuriously. Had he been rich in faith, holy in life, and renewed in heart, his purple and fine linen would have done him no harm. Lazarus was carried above by the angels because his heart was in heaven, and the rich man lifted up his eyes from hell because he had never lifted them up toward God and heavenly things.

It is a work of grace in the heart and character that will decide the future, not poverty or wealth. Suffering here does not imply happiness hereafter. Let sensible people combat this false idea whenever they encounter it. It is only a certain type of suffering to which a reward is promised—the suffering that comes to us from fellowship with the Lord Jesus and conformity to His image.

The Necessity of Being in Christ

Let me add a few words here to help you in making the distinction between these two types of suffering. We must not imagine that we are suffering for Christ, and with Christ, if we are not in Christ. If a person is not a branch of the Living Vine, you may prune and cut until the branch bleeds and the sap flows, but he will never bring forth heavenly fruit. Prune the bramble as long as you like—use the knife until the edge is worn away—but the brier will be as sharp and fruitless as ever. No process of pruning will transform the brier into one of the vines of Eshcol (Numbers 13:23).

In the same way, if a person remains in a fallen state, he is a member of the earthly Adam. He will not therefore escape suffering, but ensure it. He must not, however, dream that because he suffers, he is suffering with Christ. He is plagued with the old Adam. He is receiving, with all the other heirs of wrath, the sure heritage of sin. Let him consider these sufferings of his to be only the first drops of the awful shower that will fall upon him forever, the first tingling cuts of that terrible whip that will lacerate his soul forever.

However, if a person is in Christ, he may then claim fellowship with the Second Man, who is the Lord from heaven. He may expect to bear the image of the heavenly in the glory to be revealed. Oh, my reader, are you in Christ by a living faith? Are you trusting in Jesus alone? If not, regardless of what you may have to mourn over on earth, you have no hope of reigning with Jesus in heaven.

Suffering Caused by Our Own Mistakes

Even when a man is in Christ, it does not mean that all his sufferings are sufferings with Christ, for it is essential that he be called by God to suffer. If a good man were, out of mistaken views of dying to self and self-denial, to mutilate his body or to flog his flesh, as many a sincere enthusiast has done, I might admire the man's fortitude, but I would not believe for an instant that he was suffering with Christ. Who called men to such severities? Certainly not the God of love. If, therefore, they torture themselves at the command of their own inclinations, inclination must reward them, for God will not.

If I am rash and imprudent and run into situations for which neither providence nor grace has prepared me, I ought to question whether I am not sinning rather than communing with Christ. Peter drew his sword and cut off the ear of Malchus. (See John 18:3–5, 10–11.) If somebody had cut off Peter's ear in return, what would you say? You would say that Peter used the sword, and therefore he felt the sword. He was never commanded to cut off the ear of Malchus, and it was his Master's gentleness that saved him from the soldiers' rage. If we let passion take the place of judgment, if we let self-will reign instead of scriptural authority, we will fight the Lord's battles with the Devil's weapons, and we must not be surprised if we cut off our own fingers.

On several occasions, excited Protestants have rushed into Catholic cathedrals, knocked down the priest, dashed the wafer to the ground, trod on it, and in other ways exhibited their hatred of idolatry. Now, when the law has intervened to punish such outrages, the offenders are hardly to be considered as suffering with Christ.

I give this as an example of a kind of action to which overheated brains sometimes lead people, under the supposition that they will join the noble army of martyrs. The martyrs were and are all chosen to their honorable estate. I may say of martyrdom, as of priesthood, "*No man taketh this honour unto himself, but he that is called of God, as was Aaron*" (Hebrews 5:4). Let's be careful that we make proper distinctions, that we do not pull a house down on our heads and then ask the Lord to console us under the trial.

Again, in troubles that come upon us as the result of sin, we must not think that we are suffering with Christ. When Miriam spoke evil of Moses and leprosy polluted her, she was not suffering for God. When Uzziah went into the temple to burn incense and became a leper all his days, he could not say that he was afflicted for righteousness' sake. If you speculate and lose your property, do not say that you are losing all for Christ's sake. When you invest in shaky companies and are duped, do not whine about suffering for Christ—call it the fruit of your own folly. If you put your hand into the fire, do not complain if you get burned; why, it is the nature of fire to burn you or anybody else. Do not be so silly as to boast as though you were a martyr. If you do wrong and suffer for it, what thanks do you have (1 Peter 2:20)? Hide your face and weep for your sin, but do not come forth in public to claim a reward.

Many a hypocrite, when he has had his just deserts and has been called by his proper name, has cried out, "I am persecuted." However, it is not, as some believe, an infallible sign of excellence to have a bad reputation. Who feels any esteem for a cold-blooded murderer? Doesn't every man condemn the offender? Is he, therefore, a Christian because he is spoken against and rejected? Assuredly not; he is a heartless villain and nothing more.

Beloved, honesty should stop us from making false claims. We must not talk as if we are suffering nobly for Jesus when we are only troubled as the result of sin. Oh, to be kept from transgression! Then it does not matter how rough the road of obedience may be; our journey will be pleasant because Jesus walks with us.

The Right Motives and Attitudes

Observe, moreover, that the suffering that God accepts and rewards, for Christ's sake, must have God's glory as its goal. If I suffer so that I may earn a name or win applause from others, if I undergo a trial merely so that I may be respected for it, I will get my reward, but it will be the reward of the Pharisee and not the crown of the sincere servant of the Lord Jesus.

I must be careful, too, that love for Christ and love for His elect are always the mainspring of all my patience in suffering. Remember the apostle's words: "*Though I give my body to be burned, and have not charity, it profiteth me nothing*" (1 Corinthians 13:3). If I suffer in bravado, filled with proud defiance of my fellowmen; if I love the dignity of singularity, and out of dogged obstinacy hold to an opinion—not because it is right and I love God too much to deny His truth, but because I choose to think as I like—then I do not suffer with Jesus. If there is no love for God in my soul, if I do not endure all things for the elect's sake, I may bear many a slap and beating, but I miss the fellowship of the Spirit and have no reward.

Also, I must not forget that I must manifest the attitude of Christ or else I do not suffer with Him. I once heard about a certain minister who, having had a disagreement with several members in his church, preached from this text: *"And Aaron held his peace"* (Leviticus 10:3). He preached the sermon with the intention of portraying himself as an astonishing example of meekness, but since his previous words and actions had been quite violent, a witty hearer observed that the only likeness he could see between Aaron and the preacher was: "'Aaron held his peace,' and the preacher did not." It is easy enough to discover some parallel between our situations and those of departed believers, but not so easy to carry out the parallel by holy patience and Christlike forgiveness.

If I have brought upon myself shame and rebuke; if I am quick to defend myself and to punish the slanderer; if I am irritated, unforgiving, and proud, I have lost a noble opportunity of fellowship with Jesus. If I do not have Christ's attitudes in me, I do not suffer acceptably. If, like a sheep before her shearers, I can be silent (Isaiah 53:7); if I can bear insult and love the man who inflicts it; if I can pray with Christ, *"Father, forgive them; for they know not what they do"* (Luke 23:34); if I submit my whole situation to Him who judges righteously; if I consider it my joy to suffer reproach for the cause of Christ, then, and only then, have I truly suffered with Christ.

These remarks may seem very cutting. They may take away much false but highly prized comfort from you. It is not my intention to take away any true comfort from the humblest believer who really suffers with my Lord. But may God grant that we may have enough honesty not to pluck flowers out of other men's gardens or wear other men's honors. Only truth will be desired by true men.

The Sufferers Who Will Receive a Reward

I will now very briefly discuss the ways in which we may suffer for Jesus in our day. It is not our lot now to rot in prisons, to wander around in sheepskins and goatskins, to be stoned, or to be sawed in half, though we ought to be ready to bear all this if God wills it. The days of Nebuchadnezzar's furnace are past, but the fire is still on earth.

Some, for instance, suffer in their finances. I admit that many Christians gain financially rather than lose financially when they become believers in Christ. But I encounter many cases—cases that I know to be genuine—in which Christians have had to suffer severely for conscience' sake. I know people who were once in very comfortable circumstances, but they lived in a neighborhood where most of the business was done on Sundays. When they became Christians and closed their shops on Sundays, their customers left them. I know that some of them are working very hard for their bread, though once they earned abundance without any great toil. They do it cheerfully for Christ's sake, but the struggle is a hard one.

I know other people who were once employed in lucrative jobs, but their jobs involved sin. When they became Christians, they were obliged to resign. Now they do not have anything like the apparent prosperity they used to have. Their incomes have been significantly reduced.

I could point to several cases of people who have truly suffered greatly in financial matters for the Cross of Christ. If this is your situation, you may possess your soul by patience (Luke 21:19) and expect as a reward of grace that you will reign with Jesus, your Beloved.

Those featherbed soldiers who are brokenhearted if fools laugh at them, should blush when they think of those who endure real hardship as good soldiers of Jesus Christ. Who can waste his pity over the small griefs of faint hearts, when cold, hunger, and poverty are cheerfully endured by the true and the brave? Cases of persecution are by no means rare. We who live in a more enlightened society little know the terrorism exercised in some places over poor men and women who endeavor conscientiously to carry out their convictions and walk with Christ. To all saints who are oppressed, this sweet sentence is directed: "If we suffer, we shall also reign with him."

More often, however, the Christian's suffering takes the form of enduring personal contempt. It is not pleasant to be pointed at in the streets and have disgraceful names shouted after you by vulgar tongues. Nor is it a small trial to be greeted in the workplace by reproachful names, or to be looked upon as an idiot or a madman. Yet this is the lot of many people of God every day of the week. Many of those who are of the humbler classes have to endure constant and open reproach, and those who are richer have to put up with the cold shoulder, neglect, and sneers as soon as they become true disciples of Jesus Christ. There is more sting in this than some imagine. I have known strong men who could have borne the whip but were brought down by jeers and sarcasm. Indeed, a lion may be more troubled by the irritations of a wasp than by the attack of the noblest beast of prey.

Believers also have to suffer slander and falsehood. Undoubtedly, it is not profitable for me to boast, but I know a man who scarcely ever speaks a word that is not misrepresented, or performs an action that is not misconstrued. At certain seasons, the press, like a pack of hounds, will get on his trail, harassing him with the vilest and most undeserved abuse. Publicly and privately, he is accustomed to being sneered at. The world whispers, "Oh, he pretends to be zealous for God, but he makes a fine show of it!" Mind you, when the people of the world do learn what he makes of it, maybe they will have to eat their words.

However, I will not focus on myself, for such is the portion of every servant of God who publicly testifies to the truth. Every motive but the right one will be imputed to him. His good will be spoken of as evil; his zeal will be called imprudence; his courage, impertinence; his modesty, cowardice; his earnestness, rashness. It is impossible for the true believer in Christ who is called to any prominent service to do anything right in the eyes of the world. He had better learn right now to say with Luther, "The world hates me, and there is no love lost between us, for as much as it hates me, so heartily do I hate it." He did not mean that he hated the people in the world, for never was there a more loving heart than Luther's. But he meant that he hated the fame, the opinion, the honor of the world. If, in your measure, you bear undeserved rebuke for Christ's sake, comfort yourself with these words: *"If we suffer, we shall also reign with him: if we deny him, he also will deny us."*

If, in your service for Christ, you are enabled to sacrifice yourself in such a way that you bring upon yourself inconvenience and pain, labor and loss, then I think you are suffering with Christ. The missionary penetrating into unknown regions among savages, the teacher going wearily to class, the village preacher walking many toilsome miles, the minister starving on a miserable pittance, the evangelist content to deteriorate in health—all these, and those like them, suffer with Christ.

We are all too occupied with taking care of ourselves. We shun the difficulties of excessive labor. Frequently, because we are too concerned about caring for our health, we do not do half as much as we ought. A minister of God must spurn the suggestion to take it easy; it is his calling to labor. If he destroys his health, I, for one, only thank God that He permits us the high privilege of making ourselves living sacrifices. If earnest ministers bring themselves to the grave, not by imprudence, for that I would not advocate, but by the honest labor that their ministries and their consciences require of them, they will be better in their graves than out of them. What? Are we never to suffer? Are we to be summer soldiers? Are God's people to be pampered—perfumed with fragrances and indulged with quiet softnesses? Certainly not, unless they want to lose the reward of true saints!

In addition, let us not forget that war with our own lusts, denials of proud self, resistance of sin, and agony against Satan, are all forms of suffering with Christ. We may, in the holy war within us, earn as bright a crown as in the wider battlefield beyond us. Oh, for grace to be always dressed in full armor, fighting with principalities and powers, as well as spiritual wickedness of every sort.

I will mention one more type of suffering, that is, friends forsaking us or becoming our foes. Father and mother sometimes forsake their children. The husband sometimes persecutes the wife. I have even known the children to turn against the parents. *"A man's foes [are] they of his own household"* (Matthew 10:36). This is one of Satan's best instruments for making believers suffer, and those who have to drain this cup for the Lord's sake will reign with Him.

Beloved, if you are called to suffer for Christ in this way, will you quarrel with me if I say, in adding up all your sufferings, what very little they are compared with reigning with Jesus? *"For our light affliction, which is but for a moment, worketh for us a far more exceeding and eternal weight of glory"* (2 Corinthians 4:17). When I contrast our sufferings of today with the sufferings of Christians in pagan Rome, why, ours are scarcely a thimbleful! Yet what is our reward? We will reign with Christ. There is no comparison between the service and the reward. Therefore, it is all of grace. We do only a little and suffer only a little, and it is grace that gives us that little bit. Yet the Lord grants us *"a far more exceeding and eternal weight of glory."*

We will not merely sit with Christ; we will reign with Christ. All the royal splendor of His kingship, all the treasure of His wide dominions, all the majesty of His everlasting power—all this is to belong to you. It will be given to you by His rich, free grace as the sweet reward of having suffered for a little while with Him.

Who would draw back, then? Who would flinch? Young man, have you thought about running from the cross? Young woman, has Satan whispered to you to shun the thorny pathway? Will you give up the crown? Will you miss the throne? Beloved, it is so blessed to be in the furnace with Christ, it is such an honor to be publicly humiliated with Him, that if there were no reward, we could consider ourselves happy. But when the reward is so rich, so superabundant, so eternal, so infinitely more than we had any right to expect, will we not take up the cross with songs and go our way rejoicing in the Lord our God?

Denying Christ and Its Penalty

"*If we deny him, he also will deny us.*" That is a dreadful "*if,*" yet an "*if*" that is applicable to every individual. The apostles, in response to Christ's statement that one of them would betray Him, asked, "*Lord, is it I?*" (Matthew 26:22). In the same way, surely we may ask, "Lord, will I ever deny You?" You who say most loudly, "*Though all men shall be offended because of thee, yet will I never be offended*" (v. 33)—you are the most likely to deny Christ.

Ways That People Deny Christ

In what ways can we deny Christ? Scoffers overtly deny Him: "*They set their mouth against the heavens, and their tongue walketh through the earth*" (Psalm 73:9). Others deny Him willfully and wickedly in a doctrinal way. Take, for example, those who deny His deity. Also, those who deny His atonement and those who speak against the inspiration of His Word come under the condemnation of those who deny Christ.

In addition, there is a way of denying Christ without even saying a word, and this is more common. When blasphemy and rebuke are encountered, many hide their heads. They are in company where they ought to speak up for Christ, but they put their hands over their mouths. They do not come forward to profess their faith in Jesus. They have a kind of faith, but it is one that yields no obedience. Jesus instructs each believer to be baptized, but they neglect His ordinance. Neglecting that, they also despise "*the weightier matters of the law*" (Matthew 23:23).

They go to the house of God because it is fashionable to go there, but if it were a matter of persecution, they would forsake "*the assembling of* [themselves] *together*" (Hebrews 10:25). In the day of battle, they are never on the Lord's side. If there is a parade and the banners are flying and the trumpets are sounding, if there are decorations and medals to be given away, they are there. But if shots are flying, if trenches have to be dug, if fortresses have to be stormed, where are they? They have gone back to their dens, and there they will hide themselves until fair weather returns.

Pay attention, for I am giving a description, I am afraid, of many people. Pay attention, I say, you silent one, lest you stand speechless at the judgment seat of Christ.

Some who have been practically denying Christ for a long time by their silence go even further. They apostatize altogether from the faith they once had. No one who has a genuine faith in Christ will lose it, for the faith that God gives will live forever. But hypocrites and formalists have a reputation for being alive while they are yet dead (Revelation 3:1), and after a while they return like the dog to its vomit and like the sow that was washed to her wallowing in the mire (2 Peter 2:22).

Some do not go this far, yet they practically deny Christ by their lives, though they make a profession of faith in Him. Some are baptized and receive communion, but what is their character? Follow them home. I strongly wish that they had never made a profession, because in their own houses they deny what in the house of God they have avowed. If I see a man drunk; if I know that a man indulges in immorality; if I know a man to be harsh, overbearing, and tyrannical to his employees; if I know another who cheats his customers; and if I know that such men profess allegiance to Jesus, which am I to believe, their words or their deeds? I will believe what speaks the loudest. Since actions always speak louder than words, I will believe their actions. I believe that they are deceivers whom Jesus will deny in the end.

Many people belong in one of these categories of those who deny Jesus. Perhaps you are one of them. If so, do not be angry with me, but stand still and hear the Word of the Lord. Understand that you will not perish even if you have denied Christ, if you now run to Him for refuge. Peter denied, yet Peter is in heaven. A transient forsaking of Jesus under temptation will not result in everlasting ruin, if faith steps in and the grace of God intervenes. However, if you continue in a denial of the Savior and persevere in it, this terrible text will come upon you: "*He also will deny* [you]."

Ways That Jesus Will Deny People

In musing over the very dreadful clause that closes our text, "*He also will deny us,*" I was led to think of various ways in which Jesus will deny us. He does this sometimes on earth. Perhaps you have read about the death of Francis Spira. If you have ever read about it, you can never forget it to your dying day. Francis

Spira knew the truth—he was a religious reformer of no low standing. But when threatened with death, out of fear he recanted. In a short time, he fell into despair and suffered hell on earth. His shrieks and exclamations were so horrible that their record is almost too terrible for print. His doom was a warning to the age in which he lived.

Another instance is told of one who was very earnest for Puritanism. But when times of persecution arose, he forsook his profession of faith. The scenes at his deathbed were shocking and terrible. He declared that though he sought God, heaven was shut against him; gates of brass seemed to be in his way. He was given up to overwhelming despair. At intervals he cursed, at other intervals he prayed, and so he perished without hope.

If we deny Christ, we may be delivered to such a fate. If we have stood highest in God's church yet have not been brought to Christ, or if we become apostates, our high soar will end in a deep fall. High pretensions bring down sure destruction when they come to nothing. Christ will deny such people even on earth.

There are remarkable instances of people who sought to save their lives and lost them. Richard Denton was a very zealous follower of the English reformer John Wycliffe and had been the means of the conversion of a prominent believer. But when he came to the stake, he was so afraid of the fire that he renounced everything he held and joined the Church of Rome. A short time afterward, his own house caught on fire. Going into it to save some of his money, he perished miserably, being utterly consumed by the fire that he had denied Christ in order to escape.

If I must be lost, let it be in any other way than as an apostate. If there is any distinction among the damned, it is given to those who are trees *"twice dead, plucked up by the roots"* (Jude 12), who are *"wandering stars, to whom is reserved the blackness of darkness for ever"* (v. 13). Reserved! As if nobody else were qualified to occupy that place but themselves. They are to inhabit the darkest, hottest place, because they forsook the Lord. Let us, my dear friend, prefer to lose everything than to lose Christ. Let us sooner suffer anything than lose our ease of conscience and our peace of mind.

Marcus Arethusus was commanded by Julian the Apostate to give a large contribution toward the rebuilding of a heathen temple that his people had torn down after being converted to Christianity. Arethusus refused to obey. Though he was an elderly man, he was stripped naked and then pierced all over with lancets and knives. The old man stood firm. He was told that if he would give one halfpenny toward the building of the temple, he could be free. If he would cast one grain of incense into the censer devoted to the false gods, he could escape. But he would not approve of idolatry in any degree. As a result, he was smeared with honey, and while his innumerable wounds were still bleeding, the bees and wasps attacked him and stung him to death. He could die, but he could not deny his Lord. Arethusus entered into the joy of his Lord, for he nobly suffered with Him.

A long time ago, when the Gospel was preached in Persia, a courtier of the king named Hamedatha embraced the faith. He was then stripped of his position, driven from the palace, and compelled to feed camels. This he did with great contentment. The king, passing by one day, saw his former favorite at his humble work, cleaning out the camels' stables. Taking pity on him, he took him into his palace, clothed him with luxurious apparel, restored him to all his former honors, and made him sit at the royal table. In the midst of the delicious feast, he asked Hamedatha to renounce his faith. The courtier, rising from the table, tore off his garments with haste, left all the delicacies behind him, and said, "Did you think that for such silly things as these I would deny my Lord and Master?" Away he went to the stable to his lowly work.

How honorable was his reaction! But how I detest the lowness of the apostate. Because of his detestable cowardice, he forsakes the bleeding Savior of Calvary to return to the miserable principles of the world that he once despised. In his fear, he bows his neck once again to the yoke of bondage. Oh, follower of the Crucified One, will you do this? You will not. You cannot. I know you cannot if the spirit of the martyrs dwells in you, and it must dwell in you if you are a child of God.

What will be the doom of those who deny Christ when they reach another world? Perhaps they will come with a sort of hope in their minds and appear before the Judge and say, "Lord, Lord, open to me."

"Who are you?" He will ask.

"Lord, I once took the Lord's Supper. Lord, I was a member of the church, but there came very hard times. Mother told me to give up religion. Father was angry. Business went poorly. I was so ridiculed that I could not stand it. Lord, I had evil acquaintances, and they tempted me. I could not resist. I was Your servant—I did love You—I always had love for You in my heart. But I could not help it. I denied You and went back to the world."

What will Jesus say? "I do not know you."

"But Lord, I want You to be my advocate."

"I do not know you!"

"But Lord, I cannot get into heaven unless You open the gate. Open it for me."

"I do not know you. I do not know you."

"But Lord, my name was in the church's membership book."

"I do not know you. I deny you."

"But won't You hear my cries?"

"You did not hear Mine. You denied Me, and I deny you."

"Lord, I will take the lowest place in heaven, if I may only enter and escape from the wrath to come."

"No, you would not take the lowest place on earth, and you will not enjoy the lowest place here. You had your choice, and you chose evil. Stick with your choice. You were filthy; be filthy still. You were unholy; be unholy still."

Oh, friend, if you do not want to see the angry face of Jesus; oh, friend, if you do not want to behold the lightning flash from His eye and hear the thunder boom from His mouth when He judges the fearful, the unbelieving, and the hypocrite; if you do not want to have your part in the lake that burns with fire and brimstone (Revelation 21:8), mightily cry to God today. Say, "Lord, hold me fast. Keep me; keep me. Help me to suffer with You, so that I may reign with You. But do not, please do not, let me deny You, lest You also deny me."

7

OUR OWN DEAR SHEPHERD

I am the good shepherd; and I know mine own,
and mine own know me, even as the Father
knoweth me, and I know the Father; and
I lay down my life for the sheep.
—John 10:14–15 RV

The Bible version used for the above verses is the Revised Version. As the passage stands in the King James Version, it reads like a number of short sentences with hardly any apparent connection:

I am the good shepherd, and know my sheep, and am known of mine. As the Father knoweth me, even so know I the Father: and I lay down my life for the sheep. (John 10:14–15)

In that form it is still precious, for our Lord's pearls are priceless even when they are not threaded together. But when I point out that the translators left out one of the *ands* in the verse, you will see that they were not too accurate in this case. Admittedly, it was John's style to use many *ands*, but there is usually a true and natural connection between his sentences. With him, the *and* is usually a golden link, not a mere sound. We need a translation that treats it this way.

It is also helpful to know that the word *sheep*, which appears in verse fourteen in the King James Version, is not in the original; it was added by the translators. However, there is no need for this alteration if the passage is more closely rendered.

Again, the Revised Version gives the text in its natural form:

I am the good shepherd; and I know mine own, and mine own know me, even as the Father knoweth me, and I know the Father; and I lay down my life for the sheep.

I admit that I do not care much for the Revised Version of the New Testament in general, and consider it to be by no means an improvement on the King James Version. It is a useful thing to have for private reference, but I trust it will never be regarded as the standard English translation of the New Testament. However, the Revised Version of the Old Testament is so excellent that I am half afraid it might carry the Revised New Testament upon its shoulders into general use. I sincerely hope that this will not happen, for the result would be a decided loss.

However, that is not my point. Returning to our subject, I believe that, on this occasion, the Revised Version is true to the original. We will therefore use it in this instance, and we will find that it makes good sense. "*I am the good shepherd; and I know mine own, and mine own know me, even as the Father knoweth me, and I know the Father; and I lay down my life for the sheep.*"

He who speaks to us in these words is the Lord Jesus Christ. To my mind, every word of Holy Scripture is precious. When God speaks to us by priest or prophet, or in any way, we are glad to hear. When, in the Old Testament, I come across a passage that begins with "Thus saith the Lord," I feel especially blessed to have the message directly from God's own mouth. Yet I make no distinction between one Scripture and another. I accept it all as inspired, and I do not join the dispute about different degrees and varying modes of inspiration, and all that. The matter would be plain enough if learned unbelievers did not mystify it:

All scripture is given by inspiration of God, and is profitable for doctrine, for reproof, for correction, for instruction in righteousness. (2 Timothy 3:16)

Still, there is to my mind a special sweetness about words that were actually spoken by the Lord Jesus Christ Himself. These are like honey to me. The words of our text were not spoken by a prophet, a priest, or a king, but by one who is Prophet, Priest, and King in one, even our Lord Jesus Christ. He opens His mouth and speaks to us. You will open your ears and listen to Him, if you are indeed His own.

In addition, notice that not only do we have Christ for the speaker, but we also have Christ for the subject. He speaks, and He speaks about Himself. It would not be proper for you or for me to extol ourselves, but there is nothing more pleasing in the world than for Christ to commend Himself. He is different than we are. He is infinitely above us, and He is not under rules that apply to us fallible mortals. When He speaks about His own glory, we know that His words are not prideful. Rather, when He praises Himself, we thank Him for doing so, and we admire the humble graciousness that permits Him to desire and accept honor from such poor hearts as ours.

It would be prideful for us to seek honor from men, but it is humility for Christ to do so. He is so great that the esteem of inferior beings like us cannot be desired by Him for His own sake, but for ours. Of all our Lord's words, the sweetest are those that He speaks about Himself. Even He cannot find another theme that can excel that of Himself.

Beloved, who can speak fully of Jesus but Jesus? He masters all our eloquence. His perfection exceeds our understanding. The light of His excellence is too bright for us; it blinds our eyes. Our Beloved must be His own mirror. None but Jesus can reveal Jesus. Only He can see Himself, know Himself, and understand Himself; therefore, none but He can reveal Himself. We are very glad that in His tenderness to us He describes Himself with many helpful metaphors and instructive symbols. By these, He wants us to know a little of that love that surpasses knowledge. With His own hand, He fills a golden cup out of the river of His own infinity and hands it to us so that we can drink and be refreshed.

Take these words, then, as being doubly refreshing, because they come directly from the Well Beloved's own mouth, and they contain rich revelations of His own all-glorious self. I feel that I must quote them again: *"I am the good shepherd; and I know mine own, and mine own know me, even as the Father knoweth me, and I know the Father; and I lay down my life for the sheep."*

In this text, there are three matters that I want to explain. First, I see here complete character: *"I am the good shepherd."* Christ is not a half shepherd, but a shepherd in the fullest possible sense. Second, I see complete knowledge: *"And I know mine own, and mine own know me, even as the Father knoweth me, and I know the Father."* Third, I see complete sacrifice. How preciously that last part concludes the two verses: *"And I lay down my life for the sheep"*! He goes the full length to which sacrifice can go. Let me say that He lays down His *soul* in the place of His sheep; this is the correct translation. He goes the full length of self-sacrifice for His own.

Complete Character

First, then, our text reveals the complete character of our Lord. Whenever the Savior describes Himself by any symbol, that symbol is exalted and expanded, yet it is not able to convey all of His meaning. The Lord Jesus fills every type, every figure, and every character; and when the vessel is full, there is an overflow. There is more in Jesus, the Good Shepherd, than you could ever discover from studying a human shepherd. He is the Good, the Great, the Chief Shepherd; but He is much more.

Symbols to describe Him may be multiplied as the drops of dew in the morning, but this multitude will fail to reflect all His brightness. Creation is too small a frame in which to hang His likeness. Human thought is too small, human speech too insufficient, to adequately describe Him. When all the symbols in earth and heaven will have described Him to their utmost, there will remain aspects not yet described. You can force a square to become a circle before you can fully describe Christ in the language of mortal men. He is inconceivably above our ideas, unspeakably above our words.

The Owner of the Flock

Let us think about what Jesus was actually referring to when He described Himself as a shepherd. The shepherd He was talking about is not the type of shepherd that comes to our minds: someone to look after the sheep for a few months until they are large enough to be slaughtered. No, the shepherd in an Oriental society (biblical examples are Abraham, Jacob, and David) is quite another person. The Eastern shepherd is generally the owner of the flock, or at least the son of their owner and therefore their prospective proprietor. The sheep are his own.

On the other hand, Western shepherds seldom, or never, own the sheep they tend. They are employed to take care of them, and they have no other interest in them. In spite of this, the English shepherds I have known are a very excellent set of men as a rule; they have been admirable examples of intelligent workingmen.

Yet, they are not at all like the Eastern shepherd, and cannot be, for he is usually the owner of the flock. The Eastern shepherd remembers how he came into possession of the flock, and when and where each of his sheep were born, and where he has led them, and what trials he has gone through with them. He remembers all this with the added emphasis that the sheep are his own inheritance. The sheep are his wealth. He very seldom has much of a house, and he does not usually own much land. He takes his sheep over a good stretch of country, which is open to everyone in his tribe. But his flocks are his possession. If you were to ask him, "How much are you worth?" he would answer, "I own this many sheep." In Latin, the word for money is related to the word *sheep*, because wool was the wealth of many of the first Romans; their fortunes lay in their flocks.

The Lord Jesus is our Shepherd; we are His wealth. If you ask Him what His heritage is, He will tell you about *"the riches of the glory of his inheritance in the saints"* (Ephesians 1:18). Ask Him what His jewels are, and He will reply, "[The believers] *shall be mine...in that day when I make up my jewels"* (Malachi 3:17). If you ask Him where His treasures are, He will tell you, *"The LORD's portion is his people; Jacob is the lot of his inheritance"* (Deuteronomy 32:9). The Lord Jesus Christ has nothing that He values as much as He does His own people. For their sakes, He gave up all that He had and died naked on the cross. Not only can He say, *"I gave...Ethiopia and Seba for thee"* (Isaiah 43:3), but He *"loved the church, and gave himself for it"* (Ephesians 5:25). He regards His church as being His own body, *"the fulness of him that filleth all in all"* (Ephesians 1:23).

The Caregiver of the Flock

The Eastern shepherd, the owner of the flock, is generally also the caregiver. He takes care of the sheep continuously. There is a fireman in my congregation who lives at the fire station; he is always on duty. I asked him whether he was off duty during certain hours of the day, but he said, "No, I am never off duty." He is on duty when he goes to bed, while he is eating his breakfast, and if he walks down the street. At any time the alarm may sound, and he must do his job and rush to the fire.

In the same way, our Lord Jesus Christ is never off duty. He takes care of His people day and night. He has declared, *"For Zion's sake will I not hold my peace, and for Jerusalem's sake I will not rest"* (Isaiah 62:1). He can truly say what Jacob did: *"In the day the drought consumed me, and the frost by night"* (Genesis 31:40). He says about His flock what He says about His garden: *"I the Lord do keep it; I will water it [or watch over it] every moment: lest any hurt it, I will keep it night and day"* (Isaiah 27:3).

I cannot tell you all the cares a shepherd has concerning his flock, because he has many different anxieties. Sheep have about as many complaints as people. Perhaps you do not know much about them, and I am not going to go into detail, because I do not know much about them myself! But the shepherd knows, and the shepherd will tell you that he leads an anxious life. All the flock is seldom well at one time. One sheep or another is sure to be hurt or sick, and the shepherd spies it out and has eye and hand and heart ready to help and to give relief. There are many varieties of complaints and needs, and all these are laid on the shepherd's heart. He is both possessor and caregiver of the flock.

The Provider for the Flock

Then, he has to be the provider, too, for there is not a woolly head among the flock that knows anything about selecting good pastures. The season may be very dry, and where there once was grass, there may be nothing but dust. It may be that grass is only to be found beside the rippling brooks, here a little and there a little. But the sheep do not know anything about that; the shepherd must know everything for them. The shepherd is the sheep's provider.

Both for time and for eternity, for body and for spirit, our Lord Jesus supplies all our needs out of His riches in glory (Philippians 4:19). He is the great storehouse from which we derive everything. He has provided, He does provide, and He will provide. Every believer may therefore sing, *"The Lord is my shepherd; I shall not want"* (Psalm 23:1).

Dear friend, we often dream that we are the shepherds, or that we, at any rate, have to find some of the pasture. I could not help saying at a recent prayer meeting, "There is a passage in Psalms that says the Lord will do for us what one would have thought we could do for ourselves: *'He maketh me to lie down in green* pastures' (Psalm 23:2)." Surely, if a sheep can do nothing else, it can lie down. Yet, to lie down is the very hardest thing for God's sheep to do. The full power of the rest-giving Christ has to come in to make our fretful, worrying, doubtful natures lie down and rest. Our Lord is able to give us perfect peace, and He will do so if we will simply trust in His abounding care. It is the shepherd's business to be the provider; let us remember this and be very happy.

The Leader of the Flock

Moreover, the shepherd has to be the leader. He leads the sheep wherever they have to go. I was often astonished at where the shepherds in southern France, which is very much like Palestine, take their sheep. Once every week, I saw a shepherd come down to Menton and conduct his whole flock to the beach. Honestly, I could see nothing for them but big stones. Folks jokingly said that perhaps this is what made his mutton so hard. But I have no doubt that the poor creatures got a little taste of salt or something that did them good.

At any rate, sheep follow the shepherd, and away he goes up the steep hillsides, taking long strides, until he reaches points where the grass is growing on the sides of the hills. He knows the way, and the sheep have nothing to do but to follow him wherever he goes. Theirs is not to make the way; theirs is not to choose the path; but theirs is to keep close to his heels.

Don't you see our blessed Shepherd leading your own pilgrimage? Can't you see Him guiding your way? Don't you say, "Yes, He leads me, and it is my joy to follow"? Lead on, O blessed Lord; lead on, and we will follow Your footprints!

The Defender of the Flock

The shepherd in the East also has to be the defender of the flock, for wolves still prowl in those regions. All sorts of wild beasts attack the flock, and the shepherd must run to their aid. So it is with our Shepherd. No wolf can attack us without finding our Lord in arms against it. No lion can roar at the flock without arousing One greater than David. *"He that keepeth Israel shall neither slumber nor sleep"* (Psalm 121:4).

The Good Shepherd

Jesus is our Shepherd, then, and He completely possesses a shepherd's character—much more completely than I can describe.

Notice that the text adds an adjective to the word *shepherd*, adorning our Shepherd with a chain of gold. The Lord Jesus Christ Himself says, "*I am the good shepherd*." He is "*the good shepherd*." He is not a thief; moreover, He is not a shepherd who deals with the sheep only when he takes them from the fold to the slaughter. He is not a hireling; He does not do only what He is paid or commanded to do. Jesus does everything with tender love, with a willing heart. He throws His soul into it. There is a goodness, a tenderness, a willingness, a powerfulness, a force, an energy in all that Jesus does. He is the best possible shepherd.

Again, He is no hireling, nor is He a loafer. Even shepherds that own their own flocks have neglected them, just as there are farmers who do not cultivate their own farms. But it is never so with Christ. He is the Good Shepherd, good up to the highest point of goodness, good in all that is tender, good in all that is kind, good in all the roles in which a shepherd can be needed. He is good at fighting, good at ruling, good at watching, and good at leading. He is surpassingly good in every way.

Notice how Christ puts it: "*I am the good shepherd*." This is the truth that I want to bring out: we can say about other shepherds, "He is a shepherd," but Jesus is *the* Shepherd. All other shepherds in the world are mere shadows of the true Shepherd; Jesus is the substance. After all, what we see in the world with our physical eyes is not the substance, but the type, the shadow. What we do not see with our physical eyes, what only our faith perceives, is the real thing. I have seen shepherds, but they are only pictures to me. The Shepherd—the truest, the best, the surest example of a shepherd—is Christ Himself.

Moreover, you and I are the sheep. The sheep that we may see grazing on the mountainside are just types or symbols of us, but we are the true sheep, and Jesus is the true Shepherd. If an angel were to fly over the earth to find the real sheep and the real Shepherd, he would say, "The sheep of God's pasture are men, and Jehovah is their Shepherd. He is the true and real Shepherd of the true and real sheep." All the possibilities that lie in a shepherd are found in Christ. Every good thing that you can imagine to be, or that should be, in a shepherd, can be found in the Lord Jesus Christ.

Now, I want you to notice that, according to the text, the Lord Jesus Christ greatly rejoices in being our Shepherd. He says, "*I am the good shepherd*." He does not confess the fact as if He were ashamed of it, but He repeats it in the tenth chapter of John so many times that it almost reads like the refrain of a song: "*I am the good shepherd.*" He evidently rejoices in the fact. He rolls it over His tongue as a sweet morsel. Clearly, this fact brings great contentment to His heart. He does not say in this passage, "I am the Son of God," or, "I am the Son of Man," or, "I am the Redeemer." But this He says, and He congratulates Himself on it: "*I am the good shepherd.*"

This should encourage you and me to firmly grasp the word *shepherd*. If Jesus is so pleased to be my Shepherd, let me be equally pleased to be His sheep. Let me avail myself of all the privileges that are wrapped up in His being my Shepherd, and in my being His sheep. I see that He is not worried about my being His sheep. I see that my needs will not cause Him any perplexity. I see that He will not be inconvenienced by attending to my weakness and troubles. He delights to dwell on the fact, "*I am the good shepherd.*" He invites me to come and bring my needs and problems to Him, and then to look up to Him and be fed by Him. Therefore, I will do so.

Doesn't it make you feel truly happy to hear your own Lord Himself say, and say it to you out of His precious Book, "*I am the good shepherd*"? Don't you reply, "Indeed, You are a good shep-herd. You are a good shepherd to me. My heart puts emphasis on the word *good* and says about You, 'There is no one who is good but One, and You are that good One.' You are the Good Shepherd of the sheep"?

We have now looked at the complete character of the Good Shepherd.

Complete Knowledge

May the Holy Spirit bless our text even more, while I explain the next idea as best as I can.

The knowledge of Christ toward His sheep, and of the sheep toward Him, is wonderfully complete. I must repeat the text again: "*I know mine own, and mine own know me, even as the Father knoweth me, and I know the Father.*"

Christ's Knowledge of Us

First, then, consider Christ's knowledge of His own, and the comparison by which He explains it: "*As the Father knoweth me.*" I cannot imagine a stronger comparison. Do you know how much the Father knows the Son, who is His glory, His beloved, His other self—yes, one God with Him? Do you know how intimate the knowledge of the Father must be of His Son, who is His own wisdom, yes, who is His own self? The Father and the Son are one spirit. We cannot describe how intimate that knowledge is, yet that is how intimately, how perfectly, the great Shepherd knows His sheep.

He knows their number. He will never lose one. He will count them all in that day when the sheep will *"pass again under the hands of him that telleth* [or counts] *them"* (Jeremiah 33:13), and then He will total them up. *"Of them which thou gavest me,"* He says, *"have I lost none"* (John 18:9). He knows the number of those for whom He paid the ransom price.

He knows everything about them. He knows the age and character of every one of His own. He assures us that the very hairs on our heads are all numbered (Luke 12:7). Christ does not have a sheep of which He is unaware. It is impossible for Him to overlook or forget one of them. He has such an intimate knowledge of all who are redeemed with His most precious blood that He never mistakes one of them for another or misjudges one of them. He knows their constitutions—those who are weak and feeble, those who are nervous and frightened, those who are strong, those who are presumptuous, those who are sleepy, those who are brave, those who are sick, sorry, worried, or wounded. He knows those who are hunted by the Devil, those who are caught between the jaws of the lion and are shaken until the very life is almost driven out of them. He knows their feelings, fears, and terrors. He knows the secret ins and outs of every one of us better than any one of us knows himself.

He knows your trials—the particular trial that now weighs heavily on you. He knows your difficulties—that special difficulty that seems to block your way. All the ingredients of our lives are known to Him. *"I know mine own…as the Father knoweth me."* It is impossible to have a more complete knowledge than that which the Father has of His only begotten Son. It is equally impossible to have a completer knowledge than that which Jesus Christ has of every one of His chosen.

He knows our sins. I often feel glad to think that He always did know our evil natures and what would come of them. When He chose us, He knew what we were and what we should be. He did not buy His sheep in the dark. He did not choose us without knowing all the devious ways of our past and future lives.

> He saw us ruined in the fall,
>   Yet loved us notwithstanding all.

Oh, the splendor of His grace! *"Whom he did foreknow, he also did predestinate"* (Romans 8:29). His election of us implies foreknowledge of all our evil ways. People say that human love is blind. But Christ's love has many eyes, and all its eyes are open, and yet He loves us still.

It ought to be very comforting to you that you are known by your Lord in this way, especially since He knows you not merely with the cold, clear knowledge of the intellect, but with the intimate knowledge of love and affection. He knows you in His heart. You are especially dear to Him. You are approved by Him. You are accepted by Him. He knows you by acquaintance, not by hearsay. He knows you by communion with you. He has been with you in sweet fellowship. He has read you as a man reads a book, and He remembers what He has read. He knows you by sympathy with you, for He is a man like yourself.

> He knows what sore temptations mean,
>   For He has felt the same.

He knows your weaknesses. He knows the places where you suffer most, for

> In every pang that rends the heart
>   The Man of Sorrows had a part.

He gained this knowledge in the school of sympathetic suffering. *"Though he were a Son, yet learned he obedience by the things which he suffered"* (Hebrews 5:8). In all points, He was made like us, and by being made like us, He has come to know us. He knows us in a very practical and tender way.

Suppose that you have a watch, and it will not work, or it works very poorly. Now, suppose that you give your watch to someone who knows nothing about watches, and he says, "I will clean it for you." He will do more harm than good. But then you meet the very person who made the watch. He says, "I put every wheel into its place. I made the whole thing, from beginning to end." You think to yourself, "I have great confidence in this man. I can trust him with my watch. Surely he can repair it, for he made it."

It often encourages my heart to think that, since the Lord made me, He can repair me and keep me repaired to the end. My Maker is my Redeemer. He who first made me has made me again, and will continue to make me perfect, for His own praise and glory. That is the first part of this complete knowledge: Christ's knowledge of us.

Our Knowledge of Christ

The second part is our knowledge of Christ. *"And mine own know me, even as…I know the Father."* You may be thinking, "I do not see much meaning in that. I can see a great deal more meaning in Christ's knowing us." Beloved, I see a great deal in our knowing Christ. That He should know me is great condescension, but it must be easy for Him to know me. Being divine, having such a piercing eye as His, it is not difficult for Him to know me. It is amazingly kind and gracious, but not difficult. The marvel is that I could ever know Him. That such a blind, deaf, dead soul as mine could ever know Him, and could know Him as He knows the Father, is ten thousand miracles in one.

Oh, this is a wonder so great that I do not think you and I have fully realized it yet, or else we would sit down in glad surprise and say, "This proves Him to be the Good Shepherd indeed—not only that He knows His flock, but that He has taught them so well that they know Him!" With such a flock as Christ has, that He should be able to train His sheep so that they are able to know Him, and to know Him as He knows the Father, is miraculous!

Oh, beloved, if this is true of us, that we know our Shepherd, we can clap our hands for joy! I think it is true even now. At any rate, I know enough about my Lord Jesus that nothing gives me so much joy as to hear more about Him. I am not boasting by saying this. It is only the truth. You can say the same, can't you? If someone were to preach to you the finest sermon that was ever delivered, would it please you if there were no Christ in it? No. But you open this book and read about Jesus Christ in words as simple as I can find, and you are satisfied.

> Thou dear Redeemer, dying Lamb,
>   We love to hear of Thee:
> No music's like Thy charming name,
>   Nor half so sweet can be.

Take note that this is the way in which Jesus knows the Father. Jesus delights in His Father, and you delight in Jesus. I know you do, and in this the comparison holds true.

Moreover, doesn't the dear name of Jesus stir your very soul? What is it that makes you desire to be involved in holy service for the Lord? What makes your very heart awake and feel ready to leap out of your body? What but hearing of the glories of Jesus? Play on whatever string you please, and my ear is deaf to it. But once you begin to tell of Calvary, and sing the song of free grace and dying love, oh, then my soul opens all her ears and drinks in the music. Then my blood begins to stir, and I am ready to shout for joy! Right now I want to sing,

> Oh, for this love let rocks and hills
> 　Their lasting silence break,
> And all harmonious human tongues
> 　The Savior's praises speak.
> Yes, we will praise Thee, dearest Lord,
> 　Our souls are all on flame,
> Hosanna round the spacious earth
> 　To Thine adored name.

Yes, we know Jesus. We feel the power of our union with Him. We know Him, beloved, so that we will not be deceived by false shepherds. There is a way nowadays of preaching Christ against Christ. It is a new device of the Devil to set up Jesus against Jesus, His kingdom against His atonement, His precepts against His doctrines. The half Christ is preached to frighten people away from the whole Christ, who saves the souls of men from guilt as well as from sin, from hell as well as from folly.

However, these false shepherds cannot deceive us in that way. No, beloved, we can distinguish our Shepherd from all others. We can tell Him apart from a statue dressed in His clothes. We know the living Christ, for we have come into living contact with Him, and we could not be deceived any more than Jesus Christ Himself could be deceived about the Father. *"Mine own know me, even as…I know the Father."*

We know Him by our union with Him and by our communion with Him. *"We have seen the Lord"* (John 20:25). *"Truly our fellowship is with the Father, and with his Son Jesus Christ"* (1 John 1:3).

We know Christ by our love for Him. Our souls cling tightly to Him, even as the heart of Christ cleaves to the Father. We know Him by trusting Him. He is *"all my salvation, and all my desire"* (2 Samuel 23:5).

I remember a certain time when I had many questions and doubts as to whether I was a child of God or not. I went to a little chapel, and there I heard a good man preach. I made my hand-kerchief wet with tears as I heard this simple workingman talk about Christ and His precious blood. Even while I had been preaching the same message to others, I had been wondering whether this truth was mine. But there in that chapel, hearing it for myself, I knew it was mine, for my very soul lived on it. I went to that good man and thanked him for the sermon. He asked me who I was. When I told him, he turned all kinds of colors. "Why, sir," he said, "that was your own sermon." I said, "Yes, I know it was, and it was good of the Lord to feed me with food that I had prepared for others." I perceived that I had a true taste for what I myself knew to be the Gospel of Jesus Christ. Oh yes, we do love our Good Shepherd! We cannot help it!

And we know Him also by our shared desires, for what Christ wants to do, we also long to do. He loves to save souls, and we love to see them saved. Wouldn't we win all the people on a whole street if we could? Yes, in a whole city and in the whole world! Nothing makes us as glad as the fact that Jesus Christ is a Savior. "Have you read the news in the paper?" people ask. That news is often of small importance to our hearts when compared with news of a spiritual nature.

I happened to hear that a poor servant girl had heard me preach the truth and had found Christ, and I confess that I felt more interest in that fact than in all the rise and fall of our political parties. What does it matter who is in the government, as long as souls are saved? That is the main thing. If the kingdom of Christ grows, all the other kingdoms are of small consequence. That is the one kingdom for which we live, and for which we would gladly die. Even as there is a boundless similarity of desires between the Father and the Son, so there is between Jesus and us.

We know Christ as He knows the Father, because we are one with Him. The union between Christ and His people is as real and mysterious as the union between the Son and the Father.

We have a beautiful picture before us. Can you imagine it for a minute? Picture the Lord Jesus with you. He is the Shepherd. Then, around Him are His own people, and wherever He goes, they go. He leads them to green pastures and beside still waters. And there is this specialness about His people: He knows them as He looks on every one of them, and every one of them knows Him. There is a deeply intimate and mutual knowledge between them. As surely as He knows them, they know Him.

The world does not know the Shepherd or the sheep, but they know each other. As surely, as truly, and as deeply as God the Father knows the Son, so does this Shepherd know His sheep. And as God the Son knows His Father, so do these sheep know their Shepherd. Thus, in one company, united by mutual communion, they travel through the world to heaven. *"I know mine own, and mine own know me, even as the Father knoweth me, and I know the Father."* Isn't that a blessed picture? May God help us to be a part of it!

Complete Sacrifice

Lastly, our text reveals the complete sacrifice of our Lord. His complete sacrifice is described in this way: *"I lay down my life for the sheep."*

These words are repeated in John 10 in other forms some four times. The Savior kept on saying, *"I lay down my life for the sheep."* Read the eleventh verse: *"The good shepherd giveth his life for the sheep."* The fifteenth verse: *"I lay down my life for the sheep."* The seventeenth verse: *"I lay down my life, that I might take it again."* The eighteenth verse: *"I have power to lay it down, and I have power to take it again."* It looks as if this is another refrain of our Lord's personal hymn. I call this passage His pastoral song. The Good Shepherd sings to Himself and to His flock, and this comes in at the end of each stanza: *"I lay down my life for the sheep."*

Did He not mean, first of all, that He was continually doing so? All His life He was, as it were, laying it down for them; He was divesting Himself of the garments of life until He came to be fully disrobed on the cross. All the life He had, all the power He had, He was always giving for His sheep. This is the first meaning of our text.

It also means that the sacrifice was actively performed. It was always occurring as long as He lived, but He did it actively. He did not just die for the sheep, but He laid down His life, which is a whole other thing. Many a man has died for Christ; it was all that they could do. But we cannot lay down our lives, because they are due already as a debt of nature to God. We are not permitted to die at our own will. That would be suicide and would be wrong. But the Lord Christ's situation was totally different. He was, as it were, actively passive. *"I lay down my life for the sheep.…I have power to lay it down, and I have power to take it again. This commandment have I received of my Father"* (John 10:15, 18).

I like to think of our Good Shepherd not merely as dying for us, but as willingly dying—laying down His life. While He had that life, He used it for us, and when the time came, He gave up that life on our behalf. He actually did this for us. When Jesus spoke the words of our text, He had not yet given His life. But now the deed has been done. *"I lay down my life for the sheep"* may now be read, "I have laid down My life for the sheep." For you, beloved, He has given His hands to the nails and His feet to the cruel iron. For you, He has borne the fever and the bloody sweat. For you, He has cried, *"Eloi, Eloi, lama sabachthani?"* meaning, *"My God, my God, why hast thou forsaken me?"* (Mark 15:34). For you, He has breathed His last.

And the beauty of it is that He is not ashamed to declare the object of His sacrifice. *"I lay down my life for the sheep."* Whatever Christ did for the world—and I am not one who would limit the implications of the death of Christ for the world—His particular glory is, *"I lay down my life for the sheep."*

Great Shepherd, do You mean to say that You have died for such as these? What? For these sheep? You have died for them? What? The Shepherd dying for sheep? Surely You have other objects for which to live and die besides sheep. Don't You have other loves, other joys? We know that it would grieve You to see the sheep killed, torn by the wolf, or scattered, but do You really love these poor creatures so much that You would lay down Your life? "Ah, yes," He says, "I would, and I have!"

Carry your wondering thoughts to Jesus. What? Son of God, infinitely great and inconceivably glorious Jehovah, would You lay Your life down for men and women? They are no more in comparison with You than so many ants and wasps—pitiful and pathetic creatures. You could make millions of them with a word, or crush them out of existence by one blow of Your hand. They are weak things. They have hard hearts and wandering wills, and the best of them are no better than they are obligated to be. Savior, did You die for such? He looks and says, "Yes, I did. I laid down My life for the sheep. I am not ashamed of them, and I am not ashamed to say that I died for them."

No, He is not ashamed of His dying love. He has told it to His brothers and sisters up in heaven and has made it known to all the servants in His Father's house. This has become the song of that house: *"Worthy is the Lamb that was slain!"* (Revelation 5:12). Let's join in and sing, *"For thou wast slain, and hast redeemed us to God by thy blood"* (v. 9).

Whatever people may say about particular redemption, Christ is not ashamed of it. He glories that He laid down His life for the sheep. Note well, it was for the sheep. He does not say "for the world." The death of Christ has an influence on the world. However, in this verse, He boasts and glories in the particular object of His sacrifice: *"I lay down my life for the sheep."*

The verse could even be read, "I lay down my life *instead* of the sheep." He glories in His substitution for His people. When He speaks of His chosen, He makes it His boast that He suffered in their stead—that He bore, so that they would never have to bear, the wrath of God on account of sin. What He glories in, we also glory in. *"God forbid that I should glory, save in the cross of our Lord Jesus Christ, by whom the world is crucified unto me, and I unto the world"* (Galatians 6:14).

Oh, beloved, what a blessed Christ we have who knows us so, who loves us so—whom we also know and love! May others be taught to know Him and to love Him. Yes, may they come and put their trust in Him, as the sheep put their trust in the shepherd! I ask it for Jesus' sake.

THE FULLNESS OF JOY

CONTENTS

1. Special Thanksgiving to the Father 763

2. Jesus, Our Example of Holy Praise.. 781

3. Marvelous Things..797

4. Christ's Joy and Ours.. 811

5. A Wonderful Transformation...827

6. A Harp of Ten Strings 845

1

SPECIAL THANKSGIVING
TO THE FATHER

*Giving thanks unto the Father, which hath made us meet to be partakers of
the inheritance of the saints in light: who hath delivered us from the power
of darkness, and hath translated us into the kingdom of his dear Son.*
—Colossians 1:12–13

O ur first text is a mine of riches. I anticipate the difficulty I may experience in expressing the depths of these verses and the regret I may feel in concluding this chapter because I am not able to dig out all the gold that lies in this precious vein. I admit that I lack the power to truly grasp, as well as the ability to present, the volume of truths that has been condensed into these few sentences.

We are exhorted to give *"thanks unto the Father."* This counsel is simultaneously needed and advantageous for each and every one of us.

My friends, I think we scarcely need to be told to give thanks to the Son. The remembrance of His bleeding body hanging upon the cross is ever present to our faith. The nails and the spear, His griefs, the anguish of His soul, and His agonizing sweat make such tender, touching appeals to our gratitude that they will always prevent us from ceasing our songs and will often fire our hearts with rekindling rapture in praise of Christ Jesus. Yes, we will bless You, dearest Lord. Our souls are all on fire. As we survey the wondrous cross, we cannot but shout,

> O for this love let rocks and hills
> Their lasting silence break,
> And all harmonious human tongues
> The Savior's praises speak.

It is very much the same with the Holy Spirit. I think we are made to feel our dependence on His constant influence every day. He abides with us as a present, personal Comforter and Counselor. Thus, we praise the Spirit of Grace who has made our hearts His temple and who works in us all that is gracious, well-pleasing, and virtuous in the sight of God.

The Praiseworthy Father

If there is any one Person in the Trinity whom we are more apt to forget than the others in our praises, it is God the Father. In fact, some people even get a wrong idea of Him, a slanderous idea of our God whose name is Love. They imagine that love dwells in Christ, rather than in the Father, and that our salvation is due more to the Son and to the Holy Spirit, rather than to our Father God.

Let us not be numbered with the ignorant, but may we receive this truth for ourselves: we are as much indebted to God the Father as we are to any Person of the Sacred Three. Our heavenly Father loves us as much and as truly as any of the worthy Three Persons does. God the Father is as truly worthy of our highest praise as either the Son or the Holy Spirit is.

The Source of God's Works

A remarkable fact, which we should always bear in mind, is this: in the Scriptures most of the operations that are described as being the works of the Holy Spirit are ascribed to God the Father in other passages. Do we not say that God the Holy Spirit quickens (John 6:63) the sinner who is dead in sin? It is true, but you will find in another verse that it is said, "*The Father raiseth up the dead, and quickeneth them*" (John 5:21). Do we say that the Spirit is the Sanctifier and that the sanctification of the soul is a work of the Holy Spirit? Yes, but you will find a phrase in the opening of Jude's epistle in which he wrote, "*To them that are sanctified by God the Father*" (Jude 1:1).

Now, how are we to account for this? I think it may be explained this way. God the Spirit comes to us by the direction of God the Father. Therefore, whatever acts are performed by the Holy Spirit are truly done by the Father, because He sends forth the Spirit. The Spirit is often the instrument—although I do not say this in any way to detract from His glory—by which the Father works. It is the Father who says to the dry bones, "*live*" (Ezekiel 37:5); it is the Spirit who, going forth with the divine word, makes them live. The quickening is due as much to the Father's word as to the Spirit's influence that went with the word. Since the word came with all the bounty of free grace and goodwill from the Father, the quickening is due to Him.

It is true that the Holy Spirit is the seal upon our hearts:

In whom ye also trusted, after that ye heard the word of truth, the gospel of your salvation: in whom also after that ye believed, ye were sealed with that holy Spirit of promise. (Ephesians 1:13)

And grieve not the holy Spirit of God, whereby ye are sealed unto the day of redemption. (Ephesians 4:30)

The Holy Spirit is the seal, but it is the Eternal Father's hand that stamps the seal. God the Father gives His Spirit to seal our adoption:

But when the Comforter is come, whom I will send unto you from the Father, even the Spirit of truth, which proceedeth from the Father, he shall testify of me. (John 15:26)

Ye have received the Spirit of adoption, whereby we cry, Abba, Father. (Romans 8:15)

I repeat, many of the works of the Spirit can ultimately be attributed to the Father because He works in, through, and by the Spirit.

I ought to make the observation here that the works of the Son of God are, every one of them, intimately connected with the Father. The Son came into the world because His Father sent Him. The Son calls His people because His Father already gave them into His hands. When the Son redeemed the chosen race, was not the Son Himself the Father's gift? Did not God send His Son into the world so that we might live through Him? So then, the Father, the great Ancient of Days, is ever to be extolled; and we must never omit the full homage of our hearts to Him when we sing that sacred doxology:

Praise Father, Son, and Holy Ghost.

In order to stimulate your gratitude to God the Father, I want to discuss this glorious passage in Colossians in detail, as God enables me. If you look at the text, you will see two blessings in it. The first has to do with the present; it concerns our fitness to receive *"the inheritance of the saints in light."* The second blessing, which must go with the first, for indeed it is the effective cause of the first, is related to the past. Here we read of our deliverance from the power of darkness. Let us meditate a little upon each of these blessings. Then, I will endeavor to show the relationship that exists between the two.

A Present Blessing

The first blessing that comes to our notice is this: God the Father has qualified us as partakers of the inheritance of the saints in light. It is a present blessing. This is not one of the mercies laid up for us in the covenant that we have not yet received. Rather, it is a blessing that every true believer already has in his hand. Those future mercies in the covenant, of which we now have a down payment while we wait for their full possession, are just as rich and just as certain as those that have already been bestowed on us with abundant lovingkindness. However, they still are not so precious in our enjoyment. The mercy we have in hand is, after all, the main source of our present comfort.

Already Qualified

Besides, what a blessing this is! *"Made meet to be partakers of the inheritance of the saints in light."* The true believer is fit for heaven; he is qualified to be a partaker of the inheritance—and that is right now, at this very moment.

Does this mean that the believer is perfect, that he is free from sin? No, my friends, where could you ever find such perfection in this world? If no man but a perfect man could be a believer, then what would the perfect man have to believe? Could he not walk by sight? When he became perfect, he might cease to be a believer. No, it is not such perfection that is meant, although perfection is implied and assuredly will be given as the result.

In no way does this mean that we have a right to eternal life from any doings of our own. We have a fitness for eternal life, a suitability for it, but we have not earned it by our works. Even now, in ourselves we deserve nothing from God except His eternal wrath and His infinite displeasure.

The Bride to Be

What, then, does this phraseology mean? It means just this: we are so far qualified that we are *"accepted in the beloved"* (Ephesians 1:6), adopted into the family, and enabled by divine favor to dwell with the saints in light. For example, a woman is chosen to be a bride. She is qualified to be married and fit to enter into the honorable state and condition of matrimony, but at present she does not have on the bridal garment and is not like the bride adorned for her husband. You do not yet see her robed in her elegant attire and wearing her finest jewels, but you know she is fit to be a bride, because she has been received and welcomed as such into the family of her fiancé.

Likewise, Christ has chosen His church to be married to Him. She has not yet bathed herself and lain in the bed of spices for a little while. She has not yet put on her bridal garment and all the beautiful array in which she will stand before the Father's throne. Notwithstanding, however, there is a fitness in her to be the bride of Christ. There is such a fitness in her character, such a grace-given adaptation in her to become the royal bride of her glorious Lord and a partaker of the enjoyments of bliss, that it may be said of the church as a whole, and of every member of it, that they are *"meet to be partakers of the inheritance of the saints in light."*

Of Infants and Acorns

The original Greek word *hikanoo*, which was translated as *"meet,"* bears some of the meaning of suitability, although I cannot give the exact idiom. It is always difficult when a word is not used often. I am aware of this word being used only twice in the New Testament. The words *suitable, fit,* or *sufficient* may often be substituted for the word *meet*. God the Father *"hath made us meet* [sufficient, suitable, worthy, fit] *to be partakers of the inheritance of the saints in light."*

I cannot express my idea of the meaning of this phrase without giving another illustration. When a child is born, it is at once endowed with all the faculties of humanity. If those powers are lacking at birth, they will not appear later on. The baby has eyes, hands, feet, and all its physical organs. Of course, these are rather undeveloped at birth. The senses, although perfect from the first, must be gradually refined, and the understanding gradually matured. The infant can see only a little; it cannot discern distances. The newborn can hear, but it cannot hear distinctly enough at first to know from what direction the sound comes. However, you never find a new leg, a new arm, a new eye, or a new ear growing on that child. Each of these powers will expand and enlarge, but still there is a complete person there at birth. Thus, the child is sufficiently equipped to become an adult. Let God in His infinite providence cause the infant to be nourished and give it strength and increase, and the babe has a sufficient, inherent ability to reach adulthood. It does not lack arm or leg, nose or ear—you cannot make it grow a new member—nor does it require a new member, either, because all are there.

In a similar manner, the moment a man is regenerated, there is every faculty in his new creation that there will be, even when he gets to heaven. His faculties only need to be developed and brought out. He will not gain a new power; he will not get a new grace. Rather, those abilities that he had previously will be developed and brought out.

We are told by the careful botanist that in an acorn there is every root and every bough and every leaf of the future tree in embryo, which only require being developed and brought out in their fullness as the parts of an oak tree. Similarly, in the true believer, there is a sufficiency or meetness *"to be partakers of the inheritance of the saints in light."* The believer does not require that a new thing be implanted in him, but rather that what God has instilled in the moment of regeneration would be cherished and nurtured and made to grow and increase, until it comes unto perfection and he enters into *"the inheritance of the saints in light."* This is, as near as I can give it to you, the meaning and interpretation of the text, as I understand it.

Equipped by the Father

However, you may ask me, "In what sense is this fitness for eternal life the work of God the Father? Have we already been made meet for heaven? How is this the Father's work?" Looking at the text, I will answer you in three ways: First, what is heaven? We read that it is an inheritance. Secondly, who are fit for an inheritance? Sons are. *"If a son, then an heir"* (Galatians 4:7). Thirdly, who makes us sons? God the Father does. *"Behold, what manner of love the Father hath bestowed upon us, that we should be called the sons of God"* (1 John 3:1).

A son has the capacity for an inheritance. The moment the son is born, he is qualified to be an heir. All that is needed is for him to grow up and be able to manage the possession. However, he is fit for an inheritance from the first. If he were not a son, he could not inherit as an heir. Now, as soon as we become sons of God, we are suited to inherit. There is in us the capacity, the power, and the potential to have an inheritance. The prerogative of the Father is to adopt us into His family.

> *Blessed be the God and Father of our Lord Jesus Christ, which according to his abundant mercy hath begotten us again unto a lively hope by the resurrection of Jesus Christ from the dead, to an inheritance incorruptible, and undefiled, and that fadeth not away, reserved in heaven for you.*
>
> (1 Peter 1:3–4)

Do you not see that, since being adopted is really the meetness for inheritance, it is the Father who has made us *"meet to be partakers of the inheritance of the saints in light"*?

Sanctified by the Father to Inherit

Heaven is an inheritance, but whose inheritance is it? It is an inheritance of the saints. It is not an inheritance of sinners, but of saints—that is, of the holy ones—of those who have been made saints by being sanctified. Turn to the Epistle of Jude, and you will see at once who it is that sanctifies. You will observe the moment you fix your eyes upon the passage that it is God the Father. In the first verse you read, *"Jude, the servant of Jesus Christ, and brother of James, to them that are sanctified by God the Father"* (Jude 1:1).

It is an inheritance for saints, and who are saints? The moment a man believes in Christ, he may know himself to have been truly set apart by the covenant decree. He finds this consecration, if I may use that word, verified in his own experience, for he has now become *"a new creature"* (2 Corinthians 5:17) in Christ

Jesus, separated from the rest of the world. Then it is manifest and made known that God has taken him to be His son forever.

The meetness that I must have, in order to enjoy the inheritance of the saints in light, is my becoming a son. God has made me and all believers sons; therefore, we are meet for the inheritance. So then, that meetness has come from the Father. Therefore, how justly the Father claims and deserves our gratitude, our adoration, and our love!

From the Father of Lights

You will observe, however, it is not merely said that heaven is the inheritance of the saints, but that it is the inheritance of the saints *"in light."* So the saints dwell in light—the light of knowledge, the light of purity, the light of joy, the light of love, pure ineffable love, the light of everything that is glorious and ennobling. There they dwell, and if I am to appear fit for that inheritance, what evidence must I have? I must have light shining into my own soul.

But, where can I get it? Do I not read that *"every good gift and every perfect gift is from above, and comes down"*? Yes, but from whom? From the Spirit? No, *"from the Father of lights, with whom is no variableness, neither shadow of turning"* (James 1:17). The preparation to enter into the inheritance in light is light, which comes *"from the Father of lights."* Therefore, my fitness, if I have light in myself, is the work of the Father, and I must give Him praise.

Qualified Three Ways

Do you see then, that as there are three nouns used here—*"the inheritance of the saints in light"*—so we have a threefold meetness? We are adopted and made sons so that we are qualified to inherit. God has sanctified us and set us apart. And then, He has put light into our hearts. All this is the work of the Father, and in this sense, we are *"meet to be partakers of the inheritance of the saints in light."*

Let me make a few general observations here. Beloved, I am persuaded that if an angel from heaven were to come right now and single out any one believer, there is not one believer who is unfit to be taken to heaven. You may not be ready to be taken to heaven at this time; by this I mean that, if I foresaw that you were going to live, I would tell you that you were in a certain sense unfit to die. But if you were to die now where you are, you are fit for heaven if you believe in Christ.

You have a meetness even now that would take you there at once, without being committed to purgatory for a season. You are even now fit *"to be partakers of the inheritance of the saints in light."* You have but to gasp your last breath, and you would be in heaven. There would not be one spirit there more fit for heaven than you, nor one soul more adapted for the place than you are. You will be just as fitted for heaven's element as those who are nearest to the eternal throne.

This should make the heirs of glory think much of God the Father. When we reflect, my friends, on our state by nature and how fit we are to be firebrands in the flames of hell—yet to think that we are, at this very moment, if God Almighty willed it, fit to sweep over the golden harpstrings with joyful fingers, that our heads are fit this very night to wear the everlasting crown, that our bodies are fit to be girded with those fair white robes throughout eternity—I say, this makes us think gratefully of God the Father. This makes us clap our hands with joy and say, *"Thanks [be] unto the Father, which hath made us meet to be partakers of the inheritance of the saints in light."*

Do you not remember the penitent thief? Just a few minutes before his conversion, he had been cursing Christ. I do not doubt that he had joined with the other, for it is written, *"They that were crucified with him reviled him"* (Mark 15:32). Not one, but both—they both reviled Him. And then, a gleam of supernatural glory lit up the face of Christ, and the thief saw and believed. *"Jesus said unto him, Verily I say unto thee, To day* [though the sun is setting] *shalt thou be with me in paradise"* (Luke 23:43). No long preparation was required, no sweltering in purifying fires.

It will be the same with us. We may have been in Christ Jesus, to our own knowledge, only seven days, or we may have been in Him for seven years or seven decades—the date of our conversion makes no difference in our fitness for heaven, in a certain sense. It is true, indeed, that the longer we live, the more grace we have tasted, the riper we are becoming, and the more fit we are to be housed in heaven. However, that is a different sense of the word; that quality is the meetness that the Holy Spirit gives. In contrast, regarding the fitness God the Father gives, I repeat that the tiny blade of corn, the tender growth of gracious wheat that has just appeared above the surface of conviction, is as fit to be carried up to heaven as the fully grown corn in the ear. The sanctification by which we are sanctified by God the Father is not progressive; it is complete at once. We are now adapted for heaven, now fitted for it; by and by we will be completely ready for it and will enter into the joy of our Lord (Matthew 25:21).

I might have entered more fully into this subject, but I am short of space. I am sure I have left some knots still tied, but you must untie them yourselves, if you can. Let me recommend that you untie them on your knees—the mysteries of the kingdom of God are studied best when you are in prayer.

A Past Mercy

The second mercy is mercy that looks backward. We sometimes prefer the mercies that look forward, because they unfold such a bright prospect: "Sweet fields beyond the swelling flood."

However, here is a mercy that looks backward. It turns its back, as it were, on the heaven of our anticipation and looks back on the gloomy past and the dangers from which we have escaped. Let us read the account of it: "*Who hath delivered us from the power of darkness, and hath translated us into the kingdom of his dear Son.*" This verse is an explanation of the preceding one, as I will show you shortly. But just now let us survey this mercy by itself.

Under the Power of Darkness

My friends, what a description we have here of the manner of men we used to be! We were under "*the power of darkness.*" Since I have been musing on this text, I have turned these words over and over in my mind: "*the power of darkness.*" It seems to me one of the most awful expressions that man ever attempted to expound. I think I could deliver a discourse about it, if the Holy Spirit helped me, which might make every bone in your body shake.

"*The power of darkness!*" We all know that a moral darkness weaves its awful spell over the mind of the sinner. Where God is unacknowledged, the mind is void of judgment. Where God is not worshipped, the heart of man becomes a ruin. The chambers of that dilapidated heart are haunted by ghostly fears and degrading superstitions. The dark places of the reprobate mind are tenanted by vile lusts and noxious passions, like vermin and reptiles, from which we turn with disgust in open daylight.

Even the force of natural darkness is tremendous. With the solitary confinement that is practiced in some of our penitentiaries, the very worst results are produced if the treatment is prolonged.

If one of you were to be taken right now, led into some dark cavern, and left there, I can imagine that, for a moment, not knowing your fate, you might feel a childlike kind of interest about it. There might be, perhaps, a laugh as you found yourself in the dark. There might, from the novelty of the surroundings, be some momentary kind of curiosity excited. You might even feel a flush of silly joy.

In a little time you might endeavor to compose yourself to rest. Possibly you would even go to sleep. But, if you should awake and still find yourself down deep in the bowels of earth, where never a ray of sun or candle light could reach you, do you know the next feeling that would come over you? It would be a kind of idiotic thoughtlessness. You would find it impossible to control your desperate imagination; your heart would say, "O God, I am alone, so terribly alone, in this dark place." How you would look frantically all around! Since you would never catch a glimmer of light, your mind would begin to fail. Your next stage would be one of increasing terror. You would fancy that you saw something, and then you would cry, "If only I could see something, anything, whether friend or foe!" You would feel the dark sides of your dungeon. You would begin to scratch and scribble on the walls, as David did before king Achish (1 Samuel 21:13). Agitation would seize you.

If you were kept there much longer, delirium and death would be the consequence. We have heard of many who have been taken from the penitentiary to the lunatic asylum. The lunacy is produced partly by the solitary confinement and partly by the darkness in which they are placed. In a recent report written by the chaplain of Newgate Prison, there are some striking observations about the influence of darkness as a method of discipline. Its first effect is to shut the culprit up with his own reflections and make him realize his true position in the iron grasp of the outraged law. I think the defiant man, who has come in cursing and swearing, when he has found himself alone in darkness, where he cannot even hear the sound of passing traffic from the streets and can see no light whatsoever, is quickly subdued. He gives in and grows tame.

"*The power of darkness*" literally is something awful. If I had time, I would enlarge upon this subject. We cannot properly describe what "*the power of darkness*" is, even in this world. The sinner is plunged into the darkness of his sins, and he sees nothing, he knows nothing. Let him remain there a little longer, and his joy of curiosity—the hectic joy that he now has in the path of sin—will die away. A spirit of slumber will then come over him. Sin will make him drowsy, so that he will not hear the voice of the Spirit, crying to him to escape for his life. Let him continue in his life of sin, and by and by it will make him spiritually an idiot. He will become so set in sin that common reason would be lost on him. All the arguments that a sensible man could receive would only be wasted on him. Let him go on, and he will proceed from bad to worse, until he acquires the raving mania of a desperado in sin. Let death step in, and the darkness will have produced its full effect: he will come into the delirious madness of hell. Only the power of sin is needed to make a man more truly hideous than human thought can realize or language can express. Oh, "*the power of darkness!*"

Now my friends, all of us were under this power once. It is but a few months or years—a few weeks with some of you—since you were under the power of darkness and of sin. Some of you had only gotten as far as the curiosity of sin; others had gone as far as the sleepiness stage; a good many of you had gone as far as the apathy of it; and some of you may have been almost caught up in the terror of it. You had so cursed and sworn, you had so yelled out your blasphemies, that you seemed to be ripening for hell. But, praised and blessed be the name of the Father, He has "*delivered* [you] *from the power of darkness, and hath translated* [you] *into the kingdom of his dear Son.*"

Translated by the Father

Having thus explained this term "*the power of darkness*" to show you what you were, I want to examine the next phrase, "*and hath translated us.*" What a unique word this *translated* is. You probably think it means the process by which a word is interpreted to retain the original meaning when the expression is rendered in another language. That is one meaning of the word *translation*, but it is not the meaning here. The word is used by Paul in this sense: the taking away of a people who have been dwelling in a certain country and planting them in another place. This is called *translation*. We sometimes hear of a bishop being translated or transferred from one jurisdiction or district to another.

Now, if you would like to have this concept explained, let me give you an overview of an amazing instance of a great translation. The children of Israel were in Egypt under taskmasters who oppressed them very severely and brought them into iron bondage. What did God do for these people? There were over two million of them. He did not temper the tyranny of the tyrant; He did not influence the pharaoh's mind to give them a little more liberty. Instead, God translated His people. With a high hand and an outstretched arm, He took every one of His chosen men, women, and children bodily out of Egypt, led them through the wilderness, and translated them into the kingdom of Canaan, where they were settled. What an achievement that was! With their flocks and their herds and their little ones, the whole host of Israel went out of Egypt, crossed the Jordan, and came into Canaan!

My dear friends, the whole of the Exodus was not equal to the achievement of God's powerful grace when He brings one poor sinner out of the region of sin into the kingdom of holiness and peace. I believe it was easier for God to bring Israel out of Egypt, to split the Red Sea, to make a highway through the pathless wilderness, to drop manna from heaven, to drive out the giant inhabitants—it was easier for Omnipotence to do all this than to translate a man *"from the power of darkness into the kingdom of his dear Son."* This is the grandest achievement of God Almighty.

I believe that the sustenance of the whole universe is even easier than the changing of a bad heart and the subduing of an iron will. But, thanks be to the Father, He has done all that for you and for me. He has brought us out of darkness. He has translated us by taking up the old tree, which had struck its roots ever so deep—taking it up roots and all—and then planting it in good soil. He had to cut the top off, it is true—the high branches of our pride—but the tree has grown better in the new soil than it ever did before. Who ever heard of transplanting as huge a tree as a man who has grown for fifty years in sin?

Oh, what wonders our Father has done for us! He has taken the wild leopard, tamed it into a lamb, and purged away its spots. He has regenerated the poor sinner—oh, how black we were by nature! Our blackness permeated our beings to the center of our hearts. But, blessed be His name, He has washed us white and is still carrying on the divine operation, and He will yet completely deliver us from every taint of sin and will finally bring us *"into the kingdom of his dear Son."* Here then, in this second mercy, we discern from what and how we were delivered—God the Father has *"translated us."*

Into the Kingdom

But where are we now? Into what place is the believer brought when he is brought out from under the power of darkness? He is brought into the kingdom of God's dear Son. Into what other kingdom would a Christian desire to be brought? Friends, a republic may sound very good in theory, but in spiritual matters, the last thing we want is a republic.

We need a kingdom. I love to have Christ as the absolute Monarch in my heart. I do not want to have a doubt about it. I want to give up all my liberty to Him, because I feel that I will never be free until I abdicate the throne to Him, and that I will never have my will truly free until it is bound in the golden fetters of His sweet love. We are brought into a kingdom where Christ is Lord and Sovereign. He has *"made us kings and priests unto God"* (Revelation 1:6), and we *"shall reign with him"* (Revelation 20:6).

The proof that we are in this kingdom must consist in our obedience to our King. Here, perhaps, we may raise many causes and questions, but surely we can say that, although we have offended our King many times, yet our hearts are loyal to Him after all. "Oh, precious Jesus, we would obey You and yield submission to every one of Your laws; our sins are not willful or beloved sins. Although we fall, we can truly say that we want to be holy as You are holy; our hearts are true toward Your statutes. Lord, help us to *'run the way of thy commandments'"* (Psalm 119:32).

Thus, you see, this mercy that God the Father has given to us, this second of these present mercies, is that He has *"translated us into the kingdom of his dear Son."* This is the Father's work. Will we not love God the Father from this day forth? Will we not give Him thanks, sing our hymns to Him, exalt His great name, and triumph in His merciful love?

Making the Connection

Now, I would like to show you how these two verses relate to each other. When I get a passage of Scripture to meditate upon, I like, if I can, to see its overall meaning. Then I like to examine its various parts to see if I can understand each one separately, and then I go back again to see what one clause has to do with another. I repeatedly looked at this text and wondered what connection there could be between the two verses. *"Giving thanks unto the Father, which hath made us meet to be partakers of the inheritance of the saints in light."* Well, that is good. We can see how making us meet to go to heaven is the work of God the Father. But, does the next verse, *"Who hath delivered us from the power of darkness, and hath translated us into the kingdom of his dear Son,"* have anything to do with our fitness?

Well, I read it again, and I decided to view it this way. The twelfth verse tells me that the inheritance of heaven is the inheritance of light. Is not heaven light?

Then I can see my fitness for it as described in the thirteenth verse: "*Who hath delivered [me] from the power of darkness.*" Is that not the same thing? If I am delivered from the power of darkness, is that not being suited to dwell in the light? If I am now brought out of darkness into the light, and if I am walking in the light, is not that the very suitability which is spoken of in the verse before?

Then I continue to read. The Scripture says that we are saints. Well, saints are people who obey the Son. Here is my meetness then in the thirteenth verse, where it says, "*Who hath delivered us from the power of darkness, and hath translated us into the kingdom of his dear Son.*" So, I not only have the light, but the sonship also, for I am in "*the kingdom of his dear Son.*"

A Heavenly Inheritance

But, what about the inheritance? Is there anything about that in the thirteenth verse? The entire thing is an inheritance. Do I find anything about a fitness for it there? Yes, I find that I am in "*the kingdom of his dear Son.*" How did Christ come to have a kingdom? Why, by inheritance. Then, it seems that I am in His inheritance; and if I am in His inheritance here, then I am fit to be in it above, for I am in it already. I am even now part of it and partner to it, since I am in the kingdom that He inherits from His Father. Therefore, there is the meetness.

I do not know whether I have expressed this plainly enough, so I will summarize. You see, heaven is a place of light. Our having been brought out of darkness is, of course, our meetness for light. Heaven is a place for sons. When we are brought into the kingdom of God's dear Son, we are adopted as sons, so that there is the meetness for it. Heaven is an inheritance. When we are brought into the inherited kingdom of God's dear Son, we enjoy the inheritance now and, consequently, are suited to enjoy it forever.

Life Lessons

Having shown the connection between these verses, I want to make a few general observations. I like to explain the Scripture so that we can draw some practical inferences from it. I think I have stated some of these lessons many times already. I am repeating them so often so that we may never forget them. Martin Luther said that even though he preached upon justification by faith every day in the week, the people still would not understand. There are some truths, I believe, that need to be said over and over again, either because our silly hearts will not receive them or our treacherous memories will not hold them.

Praise the Father

Of course, the first inference we can draw from this Scripture is this: let us, from this time on, never omit God the Father in our praises. I implore you to habitually sing the praises of the Father in heaven, just as you do the praises of the Son hanging upon the cross. Love God, the eternal Father God, as truly as you love the God-man, Jesus, the Savior who once died for you. That is the greatest lesson.

Be Certain of Your Position in Christ

Yet another inference arises. Beloved, are you conscious that you are not now what you once were? Are you sure that the power of darkness does not now rest upon you, that you love divine knowledge, that you are panting after heavenly joys? Are you sure that you have been *"translated into the kingdom of* [God's] *dear Son"*?

If you can answer those questions in the affirmative with certainty, then you never need to be troubled about thoughts of death. Whenever death may come, you have been made ready to be a partaker *"of the inheritance of the saints in light."* Let no thought distress you about death's coming to you at an unseasonable hour. Should it come tomorrow, should it come now, if your *"faith is fixed on nothing less than Jesus' blood and righteousness,"* you will see the face of God with acceptance.

I have the consciousness in my soul, by the witness of the Holy Spirit, of my adoption into the family of God. I feel that, even if I never preached again, but would lay down my body and my ministry before I could even reach my home and take my final rest in bed, *"I know that my redeemer liveth"* (Job 19:25), and that I would be a partaker *"of the inheritance of the saints in light."* It is not always that one feels this way. However, may you never be satisfied until you do, until you know your fitness for heaven; until you are conscious of it; until, moreover, you are longing to be gone, because you feel that you have powers that never can be satisfied short of heaven—powers that only heaven can employ.

Adapted for Your Eternal Abode

One more reflection lingers. Some of you cannot be thought, by the utmost charity of judgment, to be *"meet to be partakers of the inheritance of the saints in light."* If a wicked man should go to heaven without being converted, heaven would be no heaven to him. Heaven is not adapted for sinners. It is not a place for them.

If you were to take someone who has long lived near the equator up to where the Eskimos dwell, telling him that you would show him the aurora and all the glories of the North Pole, the poor wretch could not appreciate them. He would say, "It is not the element for me; it is not the place where I could be happy!" On the other hand, if you were to take some northern dweller down to a tropical region where trees grow to a stupendous height and where the spices give their balmy odors to the gale, and if you were to tell him to live there in that torrid zone, he could enjoy nothing. He would say, "This is not the place for me, because it is not adapted to my nature." Or, if you were to take a vulture, which has never fed on anything but carrion, put it into the noblest dwelling you could make for it, and feed it the daintiest meals, it would not survive because it is not adapted to that kind of food.

Likewise, you sinner, you are nothing but a carrion vulture. Nothing makes you happy but sin. You do not like too much hymn singing, do you? Sunday is a dull day for you. You want to have all the Sabbath activities over and done with. You do not care about your Bible. You would prefer that there were no Bible at all. You find that going to church is very dull work indeed. Oh, then, you will not be troubled with that in eternity, so do not agitate yourself. If you die as you are and do not love God, you will go to join your own company. You will be with your jolly mates, your good fellows. Those who have been your friends and companions on earth will be your mates forever.

Unless you repent and are converted, you will go to the domain of the Prince of those good fellows. Where God is, you cannot come. It is not an element suited to you. You might as well place a bird at the bottom of the sea, or put a fish in the air, as place an ungodly sinner in heaven.

How to Be Suited for Heaven

What is to be done then? You must have a new nature. I pray that God may give it to you. Remember, if you now feel your need of a Savior, that is the beginning of the new nature. *"Believe on the Lord Jesus Christ, and thou shalt be saved"* (Acts 16:31). Throw yourself totally on His mercy, trust in nothing but His blood, and then you will be filled with a new nature. You will be made ready by the Holy Spirit's operations to partake in *"the inheritance of the saints in light."*

Many a man has come into my church as a rollicking fellow, fearing neither God nor the Devil. Many a man has come from a bar and entered into our services. If he had died at that moment, where would his soul have been? Yet, the Lord met him as he walked through our doors. Many trophies of that grace are now in my congregation. They can say, *"Thanks [be] unto the Father, who hath delivered us from the power of darkness, and hath translated us into the kingdom of his dear Son."*

If God has done that for some, why cannot He do it for others? O poor sinner, why do you need to despair? If you are the worst sinner outside of hell, remember, the gate of mercy stands wide open, and Jesus bids you to come in. Conscious of your guilt, flee. Flee to Him. Look to His cross, and you will find pardon in His veins and life in His death.

2

JESUS, OUR EXAMPLE OF HOLY PRAISE

I will declare thy name unto my brethren:
in the midst of the congregation will I praise thee.
Ye that fear the LORD, praise him; all ye the
seed of Jacob, glorify him; and fear him,
all ye the seed of Israel.
—Psalm 22:22–23

W e greatly esteem the dying words of good men, but what must be the value of their departing thoughts! If we could pass beyond the gate of speech and could see the secret things that are transacted in the silent chambers of their souls in the moment of departure, we might greatly value the revelation. There are thoughts that the tongue cannot and must not utter, and there are deep searchings of heart that cannot be expressed by syllables and sentences. If we could somehow read the innermost thoughts of holy men as they near death, we might be privileged indeed.

781

The Ruling Passion of Jesus

Now, in the Psalm before us and especially in the words of our text verses, we have the last thoughts of our Lord and Master. They beautifully illustrate the fact that He was governed by one ruling passion: that ruling passion, which was most strong in death, was the glorification of God. When Jesus was but a child, He declared, "*I must be about my Father's business*" (Luke 2:49). Throughout His ministry Jesus could have constantly said, "*The zeal of thine house hath eaten me up*" (John 2:17), and "*My meat is to do the will of him that sent me, and to finish his work*" (John 4:34). Then, at the last, as He expired, with His hands and His feet nailed to the cross and His body and soul in extreme anguish (Psalm 22:14–16), His one thought was that God would be glorified. In that last interval before He actually gave up His soul into His Father's hands, His thoughts rushed forward and found a blessed place of rest in the prospect that, as the result of His death, "*all the kindreds of the nations shall worship before thee*" (v. 27), and that the Most High should be honored by a chosen seed (v. 30).

May we have the same concentration upon one thing, and may that one thing be the glory of God! May we be able to say with Paul, "*This one thing I do*" (Philippians 3:13), and may this one thing be the chief end of our being—the glorifying of our Creator, our Redeemer, the Lord of our hearts!

My immediate objective is to arouse in you the spirit of adoring gratitude. Most of us see Christ as our example of how to pray, but I would like to exhibit Him to you as our model for grateful praising. Then I want to ask you to follow Him as your leader in the delightful practice of magnifying the name of God Almighty.

> Far away be gloom and sadness;
> Spirits with seraphic fire,
> Tongues with hymns, and hearts with gladness,
> Higher sound the chords and higher.

In considering our text, we will begin with our Lord's example: "*I will declare thy name unto my brethren: in the midst of the congregation will I praise thee.*" And then, we will examine our Lord's exhortation: "*Ye that fear the* LORD, *praise him; all ye the seed of Jacob, glorify him; and fear him, all ye the seed of Israel.*"

Christ's Example in Declaring God's Name

The praise that Jesus as our Exemplar rendered unto the eternal Father was twofold. First, we have His praise of declaration, *"I will declare thy name unto my brethren,"* which is followed by His more direct and immediate thanksgiving, *"In the midst of the congregation will I praise thee."*

Through His Teaching

The first form of praise that our blessed Mediator rendered unto the eternal Father is that of declaring God's name. My dear friends, you know that Christ repeatedly did this in His teaching.

Some characteristics of God had been revealed to men throughout history. God had spoken to Noah and Abraham, Isaac and Jacob, and especially to His servant Moses. He had been pleased to display Himself in diverse types and ceremonies and ordinances. He was known as Elohim, El Shaddai, and Jehovah, among others. However, never until Christ came did men begin to say, *"Our Father which art in heaven"* (Matthew 6:9). This was the loving word by which the Well Beloved declared His Father's name unto the Israelites. The sterner attributes of God had been discovered amid the thunders of Sinai, the waves of the Red Sea, the smoke of Sodom, and the fury of the Deluge. The splendor of the Most High had been seen and wondered at by the prophets who spoke as they were moved by the Holy Spirit.

By Declaring God As Father

The full radiance of a Father's love, however, was never seen until it was beheld as it beamed through the Savior's face. Christ said, *"He that hath seen me hath seen the Father"* (John 14:9), but until they had seen the Son, they could not see God as Father. Jesus said, *"No man cometh unto the Father, but by me"* (John 14:6). Just as no man can come to God affectionately in the yearnings of his heart or credibly in the actions of his faith, so neither can any man come to God in the enlightenment of understanding except by Jesus Christ, the Son.

The person who understands Christianity has a far better idea of God than he who only comprehends Judaism. When you read the Old Testament through, you will value every sentence and prize it *"above fine gold"* (Psalm 119:127). Yet, you still will feel unrest and dissatisfaction, because the vision is veiled and the light is dim. Turn then to the New Testament, and you discern that in Jesus of Nazareth *"dwelleth all the fulness of the Godhead bodily"* (Colossians 2:9). The bright light of knowledge is around you, and the vision is open and distinct. Jesus is the express image of His Father, and in seeing Him, you have seen God manifest in the flesh. You will assuredly see this sight of God if you are one of those to whom, through the Spirit, Jesus Christ declares the name of the Father.

By His Acts

Our Lord, however, revealed the Father perhaps more by His acts than by His words, for the life of Christ is a discovery of all the attributes of God in action. If you want to know the gentleness of God, perceive Jesus receiving sinners and eating with them. If you would like to know His condescension, behold the loving Redeemer taking little children into His arms and blessing them. If you want to know whether God is just, hear the words of the Savior as He denounces sin, and observe His own life: He *"is holy, harmless, undefiled, separate from sinners"* (Hebrews 7:26). Would you know the mercy of God as well as His justice? Then see it manifested in the thousand miracles of the Savior's hands and in the constant sympathy of the Redeemer's heart.

I cannot belabor this to bring out all the incidents in the Redeemer's life, nor even to give you a brief sketch of it. But, suffice it to say, the life of Christ is a perpetual unrolling of the great mystery of the divine attributes. Be assured that what Jesus is, so the Father is. You need not be startled by the Father, as though He were something strange and unrevealed. You have seen the Father if you have seen Christ. If you have studied well and taken the history of the Man of Sorrows deeply into your spirit, you understand, as well as you need to, the character of God over all, blessed forever.

In His Suffering

Our Lord made a grand declaration of the Godhead through His suffering.

> Here His whole name appears complete,
> Nor wit can guess, nor reason trace,
> Which of the letters best is writ—
> The power, the wisdom, or the grace.

There at Calvary, where Christ suffered—the just for the unjust—to bring us to God, we see the Godhead, resplendent in noonday majesty, although it seems to be eclipsed in midnight gloom to the natural eye. Do you desire to see the justice that the Righteous Judge perpetually exhibits? *"Shall not the Judge of all the earth do right?"* (Genesis 18:25). Would you see the kind of justice that will not spare the guilty, which smites at sin with determined enmity and will not endure it? Then, behold the hands and feet and side of the Redeemer, welling up with crimson blood! Behold His heart, broken as with an iron rod, dashed to slivers as though it were a potter's vessel! Hearken to His cries. Mark the lines of grief that mar His face. Behold the turmoil, the confusion, the whirlwinds of anguish that seethe like a boiling cauldron within the soul of the Redeemer! In all of these things, the vengeance of God is revealed to men, so that they may see it and not die, so that they may behold it and weep, but not with the tears of despair.

In His Death

Similarly, if you desire to see the grace of God, where else could you discover it as you do in the death of Jesus? God's bounty gleams in the light, flashes in the rain, and sparkles in the dew. It blossoms in the flowers that decorate the meadows, and it ripens in the golden sheaves of autumn. All of God's works are full of goodness and truth. The steps of the beneficent Creator are on the sea itself. Yet, all this does not meet the need of guilty, condemned man. Thus, to the eye of him who has wept for sin, nature does not reveal the goodness of God in a more glorious light than that which gleams from the cross.

God is seen best of all as He who *"spared not his own Son, but delivered him up for us all"* (Romans 8:32). *"Herein is love, not that we loved God, but that he loved us"* (1 John 4:10). *"God commendeth his love toward us, in that, while we were yet sinners, Christ died for us"* (Romans 5:8).

Your thoughtful minds will readily discover every one of the great qualities of deity in our dying Lord. You have only to linger long enough amid the wondrous scenes of Gethsemane and Gabbatha and Golgotha to observe how power and wisdom, grace and vengeance, strangely join.

> Piercing His Son with sharpest smart
> To make the purchased blessing mine.

Beloved, "*in the midst of the congregation,*" a dying Savior declares the name of the Lord, and thus He magnifies the Lord as no other can. None of the harps of angels nor the fiery, flaming sonnets of cherubs can glorify God as did the wounds and pangs of the great Substitute when He died to make His Father's grace and justice known.

In His Resurrection

Our Lord continued to declare God's name among His people when He rose from the dead. He literally did so. Among the very first words He said were, "*Go to my brethren,*" and His message to them was, "*I ascend unto my Father, and your Father; and to my God, and your God*" (John 20:17). After His resurrection, Christ's life on earth was very brief, but it was very rich and instructive. In itself it was a showing forth of divine faithfulness.

Christ further revealed the faithfulness and glory of God "*when he ascended up on high, [and] led captivity captive*" (Ephesians 4:8). It must have been a magnificent day when the Son of God actually passed through the pearly gates to remain within the walls of heaven, enthroned until His Second Advent! How must "*the spirits of just men made perfect*" (Hebrews 12:23) have risen from their seats of bliss to gaze on Him! They had not seen a risen one before. Two had passed into heaven without death, but none had entered into glory as risen from the dead. He was the first instance of immortal resurrection, "*the firstfruits of them that slept*" (1 Corinthians 15:20). How angels adored Him! How holy beings wondered at Him while

> The God shone gracious through the man,
> And shed sweet glories on them all!

Celestial spirits saw the Lord that day as they had never seen Him before! They had worshipped God, but the excessive brilliance of absolute Deity had forbidden the sacred familiarity with which they hailed the Lord as He was arrayed in flesh. They were never so near Deity before, for in the Son of Man the Godhead veiled its unapproachable splendor and wore the aspect of a fatherhood and brotherhood most near and dear. The magnificent whole was sweetly shrouded in humanity. Still, enough was seen of glory, as much as finite beings could bear, that God was declared in a new and more delightful manner, and heaven rang out with newborn joy.

In Heaven

What if I say that I think a part of the occupation of Christ in heaven is to declare to perfect spirits what He suffered and how God sustained Him; to reveal to them the covenant and all its solemn bonds, how the Lord ordained it, how He made it firm by His guarantee, and how He based it upon an eternal settlement, so that everlasting mercy might flow from it forever?

What if, contrary to popular opinion, there is preaching in heaven? What if Christ is the Preacher there, speaking as man never spoke before? What if He is forever instructing His saints that they may make known unto principalities and powers yet more fully the manifold wisdom of God as revealed truth in them and in Him—in them, the members, and in Him, the Head! I think that if it is so, it is a sweet fulfillment of this dying vow of our blessed Master, "*I will declare thy name unto my brethren.*"

Through Spreading the Gospel

But, beloved, it is certain that at this time our Lord Jesus Christ continues to fulfill His vow by the spreading of His Gospel on earth. Do not tell me that the Gospel declares God, but that Jesus does not do so. I would remind you that the Gospel does not declare God apart from the presence of Jesus Christ with it. "*Lo, I am with you alway, even unto the end of the world*" (Matthew 28:20) is the Gospel's true life and power. If you take Christ's presence away, all the doctrines and precepts and the invitations of the Gospel would not declare God to this blind-eyed generation, this hard-hearted multitude. But, where Jesus is by His Spirit, there the Father is declared by the Word.

Moreover, my friends, this great process will go on. All through the present dispensation, Christ is declaring God to the sons of men, especially to the elect sons of men, His own family. Then will come the latter days of which we know so little, but of which we hope so much. In that noble period, there will be a declaration, no doubt, of God in brilliant light, for it will be said, "*The tabernacle of God is with men, and he will dwell with them*" (Revelation 21:3). Jesus will be the Sun of that age of light. The great Revealer of Deity will still be the Son of Mary, the Man of Nazareth, the "*Wonderful, Counsellor, the mighty God, the everlasting Father, the Prince of Peace*" (Isaiah 9:6). Each one of us will spread abroad the sweet sound of His name until He comes again. Then we will have no need to say to one another, "*Know the Lord: for all shall know [Him], from the least to the greatest*" (Hebrews 8:11). All will know the Lord for this reason: because they know Christ and have seen God in the person of Jesus Christ His Son.

Unto His Brethren

For both he that sanctifieth and they who are sanctified are all of one: for which cause he is not ashamed to call them brethren. Forasmuch then as the children are partakers of flesh and blood, he also himself likewise took part of the same. (Hebrews 2:11, 14)

I cannot leave this passage without urging you to treasure that precious word of our Master: "*I will declare thy name unto my brethren.*"

> Our next of kin, our brother now,
> Is He to whom the angels bow;
> They join with us to praise His name
> But we the nearest interest claim.

The Savior's brothers are all to know God in Christ. You who are one with Jesus, you who have been adopted into the same family, have been regenerated and quickened with His life. You who are joined together by an indissoluble union—you are to see the Lord. Yes, an indissoluble union, for a wife may be divorced from her husband, but there is no divorce of brothers. I never heard of any law, human or divine, that could ever unbrother a man; that cannot be done. If a man is my brother, he is now and will be my brother, even when heaven and earth pass away. Am I Jesus' brother? Then I am joint heir with Him (Romans 8:17). I share in all He has and all that God bestows upon Him: His Father is my Father; His God is my God. Feast, my brothers and sisters, on this rich morsel, and go your way in the strength of it to bear the trials of earth with more than mere patience.

Following Christ's Example

Our Lord's example, in this instance, I can only hint at. It is this: if the Lord Jesus Christ declares God, especially to His own brethren, it must be your business and mine to proclaim what we know of the excellence and surpassing glories of our God. In this way we may praise God Almighty. Especially let us speak of Him to our immediate families, our relatives, our neighbors, and—since all men are our brothers, in a sense—let us speak of the Father wherever we find ourselves. Dear friends, I truly desire that we talk more about our God.

> But, ah, how faint our praises rise!
> Sure 'tis the wonder of the skies,
> That we, who share His richest love,
> So cold and unconcerned should prove.

How many times this week have you praised the dear Redeemer to your friends? Have you done it once? I do it often officially as a pastor, but I wish I did it more often, spontaneously and personally, to those with whom I may come in contact. Undoubtedly, this week you have murmured and complained, spoken against your neighbors, spread abroad some small amount of scandal, or just talked carelessly and without integrity. It is even possible that impurity has been in your speech; even a Christian's language is not always as pure as it should be.

Oh, if we saved our breath to praise God, how much wiser we would be! If our mouths were filled with the Lord's praise and with His honor all the day, how much holier! If we would but speak of what Jesus has done for us, what good we might accomplish! Why, every man speaks of what he loves. Men can hardly hold their tongues about their inventions and their delights. Speak well, you faithful ones, of the Lord's name. I urge you, do not be silent concerning the One who deserves so much from you, but make this your resolve right now: *"I will declare thy name unto my brethren."*

A Direct Model of Praise

Our Master's second form of praise in the text is of a more direct kind: *"In the midst of the congregation will I praise thee."* Is this just my imagination, or does the text really mean that the Lord Jesus Christ, as man, adores and worships the eternal God in heaven and is, in fact, the great Leader of the adoration in the skies? Would I err if I say that they all bow when He as Priest adores the Lord and that all join their voices with the lifting up of His sacred psalm? Is He the Chief Musician of the sky, the Master of the sacred choir? Does He beat time for all the hallelujahs of the universe? I think so. I think that is the meaning of these words: *"In the midst of the congregation will I praise thee."*

As God, Christ is and will be forever praised. Far above all worshipping, He Himself is forever worshipped. But as Man, the Head of redeemed humanity, the ever living Priest of the Most High God, I believe that He praises Jehovah in heaven. Surely it is the office of the Head to speak and to represent the holy joys and devout aspirations of the whole body that He represents.

"In the midst of the congregation[s]" of earth, too, is not Jesus Christ the sweetest of all singers? I like to think that when we pray on earth, our prayers are not alone, but our great High Priest is there to offer His own petitions with ours. When we sing on earth, it is the same. Is not Jesus Christ *"in the midst of the congregation,"* gathering up all the notes that come from sincere lips, to put them into the golden censer and to make them rise as precious incense before the throne of the infinite Majesty? Thus, He is the great Singer, rather than we. He is the chief Player on our stringed instruments, the great Master of true music. The worship of earth comes up to God through Him, and He is the accepted channel of all the praise of all the redeemed universe.

I am anticipating the day—I hope we are all longing for it—when *"the dead in Christ shall rise"* (1 Thessalonians 4:16), when the sea and land will give up the treasured bodies of the saints, when glorified spirits will descend to enliven their renovated frames, when *"we which are alive and remain"* (v. 17) will be changed and made immortal, and the King Himself will be revealed. Then, all the ashes of our enemies will be trodden under our feet; Satan, bound, will be held under the foot of Michael, the great archangel; and victory will be on the side of truth and righteousness.

What a "Hallelujah Chorus" will peal from land and sea and far-off islands: *"Alleluia: for the Lord God omnipotent reigneth"* (Revelation 19:6)! Who will lead that song? Who will be the first to praise God in that day of triumph? Who first will wave the palm of victory? Who but He who was first in the fight and first in the victory, He who trod the winepress alone and stained His garments with the blood of His enemies, He who *"cometh from Edom, with dyed garments from Bozrah"* (Isaiah 63:1)? Surely it is He who, in the midst of the exulting host, once militant and then triumphant, will magnify and adore Jehovah's name forever and ever. Has He not Himself said, *"My praise shall be of thee in the great congregation"* (Psalm 22:25)?

What do these dark sayings, so hard to understand, really mean?

Then cometh the end, when he shall have delivered up the kingdom to God, even the Father. And when all things shall be subdued unto him, then shall the Son also himself be subject unto him that put all things under him, that God may be all in all. (1 Corinthians 15:24, 28)

Whatever those words may mean, they seem to teach us that the intermediate crown and government are temporary, that they are intended to last only until all rule and all authority and power are put down by Jesus and until the rule of God is universally acknowledged. Jesus cannot renounce His Godhead, but His temporary sovereignty will be yielded up to Him from whom it came. That last solemn act, in which Christ hands back to His Father the all-subduing scepter, will be a praising of God to such a wonderful extent that it is beyond human conception. We wait and watch for it, and we will behold it in the appointed time.

Beloved friends, we also have an example in this second part of our text: let us endeavor to praise our God in a direct manner. We ought to spend at least a little time every day in adoring contemplation. Our private devotions are scarcely complete if they consist only of prayer. They need the element of praise, too. If possible, during each day, sing a hymn or a chorus. Perhaps you are not in a position to sing it aloud—very loud, at any rate—but I would hum it over, if I were you. Many of you laborers find time enough to sing a silly song; why can you not find time for the praise of God? Every day let us praise Him, when the eyelids of the morning first are opened, and when the curtains of the night are drawn. And, yes, if we awaken at the midnight hour, let our hearts put fire to the sacred incense and present it unto the Lord who lives forever and ever.

"In the midst of the congregation" also, whenever we come up to God's house, let us take care that our praise is not merely lip service, but that of the heart. Let us all sing, and so sing that God Himself hears. We need more than the sweet sounds that die upon mortal ears. We want the deep melodies that spring from the heart and that enter into the ears of the immortal God. Imitate Jesus, then, in this twofold praise, the declaring of God and the giving of direct praise to Him.

Our Lord's Exhortation to Praise

Follow me earnestly, my friends, and then follow me practically also. In the second verse of our text, our Lord is exhorting us to praise God Almighty: *"Ye that fear the LORD, praise him; all ye the seed of Jacob, glorify him; and fear him, all ye the seed of Israel."*

This appeal is directed to those who fear God, who have respect for Him, who tremble lest they offend Him, who carry with them the consciousness of His presence into their daily lives, who act toward Him as obedient children toward a father. The exhortation is further addressed to *"the seed of Jacob"*: to those in covenant with God; to those who have despised the pottage and chosen the birthright; to those who, if they have had to sleep with stones for their pillows, have nevertheless seen heaven opened and enjoyed a revelation of God; to those who know what prevailing in prayer means; to those who, in all their trouble, have yet found that all these things are not against them, but work together for their everlasting good; to those who know that Jesus is yet alive and that they will see Him when they die. It is, moreover, directed to *"the seed of Israel"*: to those who once were in Egypt and in spiritual bondage; to those who have been brought out of slavery, who are being guided through the wilderness, fed with heaven's manna, and made to drink of the living Rock; to those who worship the one God and Him only, who put away their idols, and who desire to be found obedient to the Master's will.

Vocal Praise

Now, to them it is said, first of all, *"Praise him."* Praise the Lord vocally. I wish that in every congregation every child of God would take pains to praise God with his mouth as well as with his heart. I have noticed something in my own congregation, which I have jotted down in the pages of my memory, and which I believe to be generally true: you always sing best when you are most spiritually focused. There are definitely times of worship when your singing is very much better than it is at other times. You keep better time and better tune, not because the tune is any easier, but because you desire to worship God with more solemnity than usual. Thus, there is no slovenly singing such as that which sometimes pains the ear and heart. Why, some of you care so little to give the Lord your best music that you fall half a beat behind the rest, others of you are singing quite off-key, and a few make no sound of any kind! I hate to enter a place of worship where half a dozen sing to the praise and glory of themselves, while the rest stand and listen.

I like that good old plan of everybody singing, singing his best, singing carefully and heartily. If you cannot sing artistically, never mind, you will be right enough if you sing from the heart and pay attention to it. Just do not drawl out like a musical machine that has been set agoing and therefore runs on mechanically. With a little care the heart brings the art, and the heart desiring to praise will train the voice to the time and tune by and by.

I would like our worship services to be the best. I personally do not care for the fineries of music and the excellencies of chants and anthems. As for instrumental music, I fear that it often destroys the singing of the congregation and detracts from the spirituality and simplicity of worship. If I could crowd a house twenty times as big as my church with the fine music that some churches delight in, God forbid I should touch it. Rather, let us have the best and most orderly harmony we can make—let the saints come with their hearts in the best of moods and their voices in the best tune, and let them take care that there be no slovenliness or discord in the public worship of the Most High.

Mental Praise

Take care to mentally praise God also. The grandest praise that floats up to the throne is that which arises from silent contemplation and reverent thought. Sit down and think of the greatness of God, His love, His power, His faithfulness, His sovereignty, and as your mind bows prostrate before His majesty, you will have praised Him, though not a sound will have come from you.

Active Praise

Praise God also by your actions. Your sacrifice to Him of your property, your offering to Him week by week of your substance, your giving of your time and energy to "the least of these [His] brethren" (Matthew 25:40) is true praise, and far less likely to be hypocritical than mere words of thanksgiving. "Ye that fear the Lord, praise him."

Glorifying Praise

Our text adds, "All ye the seed of Jacob, glorify him." This is another form of the same thing. Glorify God; let others know of His glory. Let them know of it from what you say, but especially let them know of it from what you are and how you act. Glorify God in your business, in your recreations, in your shops, and in your households. *"Whether therefore ye eat, or drink, or whatsoever ye do, do all to the glory of God"* (1 Corinthians 10:31). In the commonest actions of life, wear the vestments of your sacred calling, and act as a royal priesthood, serving the Most High.

Glorify your Creator and Redeemer. Glorify Him by endeavoring to spread abroad the Gospel that glorifies Him. Magnify Christ by explaining to men how, by believing, they will find peace in Him. Glorify God by boldly relying on His word for yourself, in the teeth of afflicting providence, and over the head of all suspicions and mistrust. Nothing can glorify God more than an Abrahamic faith that *"stagger[s] not at the promise of God through unbelief"* (Romans 4:20). O you wrestling seed of Jacob, see to it that you do not falter in the matter of glorifying your God.

Awesome, Sinless Praise

The last thing mentioned in our text is to *"fear him,"* as if this were one of the highest methods of praise. Walk in His sight; constantly keep the Lord before you; let Him be at your right hand. Sin not, for in sinning you dishonor Him. Suffer rather than sin. Choose the burning fiery furnace rather than bow down before the golden image. Be willing to be despised yourself rather than that God should be despised. Be content to bear the cross rather than allow Jesus to be crucified afresh (Hebrews 6:6). Be put to shame rather than allow Jesus to suffer any more shame. Thus, you will truly praise and magnify the name of the Most High.

The Practice of Praise

I must close this chapter with a few remarks that are meant to assist you in carrying out the practice of this teaching. Beloved brothers and sisters, this morning I felt, before I began to write, very much in the spirit of adoring gratitude. I cannot communicate that to you, but the Spirit of God can. The thoughts that helped me to praise God were something like these (let me give them to you as applied to yourselves): glorify and praise God, for He has saved you, saved you from hell, saved you for heaven. Oh, how much is encompassed by the fact that you are saved! Think of the election that ordained you to salvation, the covenant that assured salvation to you. Think of the incarnation by which God came to you. Consider the precious blood by which you now have been *"made nigh"* (Ephesians 2:13) to God.

Do not hurry over those thoughts, even though I must shorten my words. Linger at each one of these sacred fountains and drink. When you have seen what salvation involved in the past, think of what it means in the future. You will be preserved to the end. You will be educated in the school of grace. You will be admitted into the home of the blessed in the land of the hereafter. You will have a resurrection most glorious and an immortality most illustrious. When days and years will have passed, a crown will adorn your brow, and a harp of joy will fill your hand. All of this is yours, believer. Will you not praise Him?

Make any one of these blessings stand out in your mind, as personally real to you, and I think you will say, "Should I refuse to sing, surely the very stones would cry out" (Luke 19:40).

Your God has done more than this for you. You are not barely saved, like a drowning man just dragged to the bank; you have had more given to you than you ever lost. You have gained by Adam's fall. You might almost say, as one of the fathers did, "O *felix culpa*, O happy fault, that put me into the position to be so richly endowed as now I am!" Had you stood in Adam, you would never have been able to call Jesus "Brother," for there would have been no need for Him to become incarnate. You would never have been washed in His precious blood, for then it had no need to be shed.

Jesus has restored to you what He did not take away in the first place. He has not merely lifted you from the trash heap to set you among men, but to set you among princes, even the princes of His people, and to make you inherit the throne of glory (1 Samuel 2:8). Think of the bright roll of promises, of the rich treasure of covenant provision, of all that you have already had and all that Christ has guaranteed to you of honor and glory and immortality. Will you not praise the Lord *"in the midst of the congregation"*?

Beloved brothers and sisters, some of us have special cause for praising God in the fact that we have recently seen many saved, and among them those dear to us. Mothers, can you hear this fact without joy? Your children are saved! Brothers, your sisters are saved! Fathers, your sons and daughters are saved! How many has God brought in lately that you have been privileged to know about? You Sunday school teachers who have been the instruments of this, you conductors of classes who have been honored by God to be spiritual parents, you elders and deacons and intercessors who have prayed so willingly with these converts—all of you who now share the joy in these conversions, will you not bless God? *"Not unto us, O LORD, not unto us, but unto thy name* [we] *give glory, for thy mercy, and for thy truth's sake"* (Psalm 115:1). Oh, we cannot be silent! Not one tongue must be silent; we will all magnify and bless the Most High.

Beloved friends, if these facts do not suffice to make us praise Him, I would say, think of the glorious God! Think of Father, Son, and Spirit, and what the triune Jehovah is in His own person and attributes. If you do not praise Him then, how far must you have backslidden!

Remember the host who now adore Him. When we bless Him, we do not stand alone: angels and archangels are at our right hand; cherubim and seraphim are in the same choir. The notes of redeemed men do not sound alone; they are united to, and swollen by, the unceasing flood of praise that flows from the hierarchy of angels.

Think, beloved, of how you will praise Him soon and how, before much time has passed, many of us will be with the glorious throng! Recently you have probably seen some of your friends and relatives having been translated to the skies: more links to heaven, fewer bonds to earth. They have gone before you, and to this you have almost said, "Would God it were me instead of them!" They have now seen what eye has not seen, and heard what ear has never heard, and their spirits have drunk in what they could not otherwise have conceived.

We will soon join that heavenly choir! Meanwhile, let each one of us sing:

> I would begin the music here,
> And so my soul should rise:
> Oh, for some heavenly notes to bear
> My passions to the skies!

> There ye that love my Savior sit,
> There I would fain have place
> Among your thrones, or at your feet,
> So I might see His face.

3

MARVELOUS THINGS

O sing unto the Lord a new song; for he hath done marvellous things: his right hand, and his holy arm, hath gotten him the victory. The Lord hath made known his salvation: his righteousness hath he openly showed in the sight of the heathen.
—Psalm 98:1–2

The invitations of the Gospel are invitations to happiness. In delivering God's message, we do not ask men to come to a funeral, but to a wedding feast. If our errand were one of sorrow, we might not marvel when people refuse to listen to us. But, it is one of gladness, not sadness. In fact, you might condense the gospel message into this joyous invitation: "O come, and learn how to *"sing unto the Lord a new song"*! Come, and find peace, rest, joy, and all else that your soul can desire. Come, and *'eat ye that which is good, and let your soul delight itself in fatness'"* (Isaiah 55:2). When the coming of Christ to the earth was first announced, it was not with sad, sonorous sounds of evil spirits, driven from the nethermost hell, but with the choral symphonies of holy angels who joyfully sang, *"Glory to God in the highest, and on earth peace, good will toward men"* (Luke 2:14).

The Gospel, Our Source of Joy

As long as the Gospel is preached in this world, its main message will be one of joy. The Gospel is a source of joy to those who proclaim it, for unto us, "*who* [are] *less than the least of all saints, is this grace given, that* [we] *should preach among the Gentiles the unsearchable riches of Christ*" (Ephesians 3:8). The Gospel is also a source of joy to all who really hear it and accept it, for its very name means "glad tidings of good things."

I feel that if I am not able to witness as I would like, still I am overjoyed in being permitted to proclaim the Gospel at all. If the style and manner of my words are not such as I desire them to be or such as you endorse, yet it matters little, for the simplest telling of the Gospel is a most delightful thing in itself. If our hearts are in a right condition, we would not only be glad to hear of Jesus over and over again, but the story of the love of God Incarnate, and of the redemption brought about by Immanuel, would be the sweetest music that our ears ever heard.

In the hope that our hearts may thus rejoice, I am going to address many points about two general areas: the marvelous things God has done in the person of His Son, and some marvelous things in reference to ourselves, which are almost as marvelous as those that God has done in Christ.

I call your attention to the marvelous tidings mentioned in our text. If you read it carefully, you will notice that, first, there are some marvelous things that are amazing in themselves: "*He hath done marvellous things.*" Secondly, there are some that are wonderful in the way in which they were done: "*His right hand, and his holy arm, hath gotten him the victory.*" Then, there are some that are marvelous as to the way in which they were made known: "*The* LORD *hath made known his salvation: his righteousness hath he openly showed in the sight of the heathen.*"

Simply Marvelous Things

Let us consider the things that are wonderful in themselves: "*He hath done marvellous things: his right hand, and his holy arm, hath gotten him the victory.*" You know the story. We were enslaved by sin; we were in such bondage that we were liable to be forever in chains. However, our great Champion undertook our cause, entered the lists, and pledged to fight for us until the end; and He has done it. It would have been a cause of great joy if I could have said to you, "The Lord Jesus Christ has undertaken to fight our battles for us," but I have something much better than that to say. He has fought the fight, and "*his holy arm, hath gotten him the victory.*"

It must have required more faith to believe in the Christ who was to come than to believe in the Christ who has come. It must have required no little faith to believe in Christ as victorious while He was in the midst of the struggle; for instance, when His bloody sweat was falling amid the olive trees, or when He was hanging upon the cross and moaning out that awful cry: "*My God, my God, why hast thou forsaken me?*" (Matthew 27:46). But the great crisis is past. No longer does the issue of the conflict tremble in the balance: Christ has forever accomplished His warfare, and our foes are all beneath His feet.

> Love's redeeming work is done;
> Fought the light, the battle won.

Christ Overcame Sin

What foes has Christ overcome? Our main foe, our sin, both as to the guilt of it and as to the power of it. As to the guilt of it, there was the law, which we have broken and which must be satisfied. Christ has kept the positive precepts of that law in His own perfect life, and He has vindicated the honor of that law by His sacrificial death on the cross. Therefore, the law being satisfied, the strength of sin is gone.

Now, believers, the sins that you saw in the time of your conviction you will never see again! As Moses triumphantly sang of the enemies of the chosen people, "*the depths have covered them: they sank into the bottom as a stone*" (Exodus 15:5), so can you say of your sins, "There is not one of them left; they have been cast '*into the depths of the sea*'" (Micah 7:19).

Even in God's great Book of Remembrance there is no record of sin against any believer in the Lord Jesus Christ. "*By him all that believe are justified from all things*" (Acts 13:39). Try to realize this, brothers and sisters in Christ. Let the great army of your sins pass before you in review, each one like a son of Anak, a giant (Numbers 13:33) armed to the hilt for your destruction. They have gone down into the depths, and the red sea of Christ's blood has drowned them. Thus, He has gained a complete victory over all the guilt of sin.

As for the power of sin within us, we often groan concerning it, but let us groan no longer. Or, if we do, let us also *"sing unto the* Lord *a new song."*

The experience of a Christian is summed up in Paul's utterance, *"O wretched man that I am! who shall deliver me from the body of this death? I thank God through Jesus Christ our Lord"* (Romans 7:24–25). If you take the whole quotation, I believe you have a summary of a spiritual man's life: a daily groaning and a daily boasting, a daily humbling and a daily rejoicing, a daily consciousness of sin and a daily consciousness of the power of the Lord Jesus Christ to conquer it.

We do believe, beloved, that our sin has received its deathblow. It still lingers within us, for its death is by crucifixion, and crucifixion is a lingering death. Its heart is not altogether fastened to the cross, but its hands are, so that we cannot sin as we once did. Its feet, too, are fastened, so that we cannot run in the way of transgressors as we once did. And one of these days, the spear will pierce its heart, and it will utterly die. Then, with the faultless ones before the throne of God, we will be unattended by depravity or corruption any longer. Therefore, let us *"sing unto the* Lord *a new song,"* because *"his right hand, and his holy arm, hath gotten him the victory"* over sin within us.

> His be the victor's name,
> Who fought our fight alone;
> Triumphant saints no honor claim;
> His conquest was His own.

Christ Conquered Death

In connection with sin came death, for death is the daughter of sin and follows closely upon sin. Jesus has conquered death. It is not possible for believers to die eternally, for Jesus said, *"Because I live, ye shall live also"* (John 14:19). Even the character of the natural death is changed for believers. It is not now a penal infliction, but a necessary way of elevating our nature from the bondage of corruption into the glorious liberty of the children of God, for *"flesh and blood cannot inherit the kingdom of God"* (1 Corinthians 15:50). Even those who will be living at the coming of the Lord must be bodily changed in order that they may be fit to enter glory. Death, therefore, to believers, is but a putting off of our weekday garments so that we may put on our Sunday best, the laying aside of the travel-stained clothes of earth so that we may put on the pure garments of joy forever.

Thus, we do not fear death now, for Christ has conquered it. He has torn away the iron bars of the grave; He has left His own shroud and napkin in the sepulcher so that there might be suitable furniture in what was once a grim, cold, empty tomb; and He has gone up into His glory and left heaven's gate wide open to all believers. Unless He first comes again, we, too, will descend into the grave where He went; but we will also come up again as He did, and we will rise, complete in the perfection of our redeemed humanity. Then, when we awake in the likeness of our Master, we will be satisfied. So let us *"sing unto the LORD a new song; for he hath done marvellous things."*

> Hosannah to the Prince of light,
> Who clothed Himself in clay,
> Entered the iron gates of death,
> And tore the bars away!

> Death is no more the king of dread
> Since our Immanuel rose.
> He took the tyrant's sting away,
> And spoiled our hellish foes.

> See how the Conqueror mounts aloft,
> And to His Father flies,
> With scars of honor in His flesh
> And triumph in His eyes.

Christ Defeated Satan

Just as Christ has conquered sin and death, so has He conquered the Devil and all his hosts of fallen spirits. This monster of iniquity, this monster of craft and malice, has striven to hold us in perpetual bondage. However, Christ met him in the wilderness and vanquished him there. Also, I believe, Christ met him in personal conflict in the Garden of Gethsemane, where He vanquished him once and for all. And now, He has *"led captivity captive"* (Ephesians 4:8). Inferior spirits were driven away by Christ when He was here upon earth, and they fled at the bidding of the King. And now, although Satan still worries and vexes the saints of God, *"the God of peace shall bruise Satan under [our] feet shortly"* (Romans 16:20).

Therefore, dearly beloved in Christ, this is the joyous news we have to bring to sinners: sin and death and the Devil have all been vanquished by the great Captain of our salvation. For this reason, let us so rejoice that we *"sing unto the* Lord *a new song."*

> In hell, He laid hell low;
> Made sin, He sin o'erthrew:
> Bowed to the grave, destroyed it so,
> And death, by dying, slew.

> Sin, Satan, death appear
> To harass and appall;
> Yet since the gracious Lord is near,
> Backward they go, and fall.

The Marvelous Ways of the Lord

According to our text, what the Lord did is not only marvelous in itself, but the way in which He did it was also amazing. Observe that He did it alone: *"His [own] right hand, and His holy arm, hath gotten him the victory."* No one was associated with the Lord Jesus Christ in the conquest that He achieved over sin and death and the Devil, and nothing is more abhorrent to a believing soul than the idea of giving any bit of glory to anyone but the Lord Jesus Christ. He trod *"the winepress alone"* (Isaiah 63:3), so let Him alone wear the crown.

Sinner, you do not have to look for any secondary savior, for Christ is the only Savior you need: He has done it all. You do not need to pay reverence to any saints or martyrs or priests. Christ has done it all, so seek Him for all you want, and honor Him as the one true source of all you need. Christ alone has accomplished the salvation of His people; no other hand has been raised to help Him in the fight. Look then to Jesus alone for salvation. Trust in Him with your whole heart. Throw your weight entirely upon Him, my poor lost soul, if you have not yet done so, and you will find rest and salvation in Him.

The Wisdom of His Ways

Another wonder is that He did it all so wisely: *"His right hand hath gotten him the victory."* You know that today the word *dexterous* is used to signify a thing that is skillfully done. However, its original Latin root word means something that is done with the right hand and is thus done with adeptness and mastery. Thus, when Christ fought our battle with His right hand, He did it with ease, with strength, and with infinite wisdom.

The design of salvation is the very perfection of wisdom, because all the attributes of God are equally glorified in it. There is as much justice as there is mercy in a sinner's salvation by the atoning sacrifice of Christ. Salvation reveals God's complete mercy as well as His total justice: God fulfilled His threatenings against sin by smiting Christ and gave the love of His heart full expression in saving even the chief of sinners through the death of His dear Son.

The more I consider the doctrine of substitution, the more my soul is enamored with the matchless wisdom of God that devised this system of salvation. As for a hazy atonement that atones for everybody in general and for nobody in particular—an atonement made equally for Judas and for John—I care nothing for it. But a literal, substitutionary sacrifice—Christ vicariously bearing the wrath of God on my behalf—this calms my conscience with regard to the righteous demands of the law of God and satisfies the instincts of my nature, which declare that, since God is just, He must exact the penalty of my guilt.

Dear believers, in suffering, bleeding, and dying, Jesus Christ has gotten us the victory. The hand that was pierced by the nails has conquered sin; the hand that was fastened to the wood has fastened up the accusation that was written against us; the hand that bled has brought salvation to us, so that we are Christ's forever. Infinite wisdom shone through in our Lord's conquest of sin and death and the Devil.

The Holiness of His Ways

But, holiness was also involved: *"His holy arm, hath gotten him the victory."* The psalmist seemed, as he progressed in his worship, to fall more and more in love with the matchless holiness of God. The holiness of the victory of Christ is a wonderful thing to glorify, for there is never a sinner so saved as to make God's eyes seem to wink at sin. Since the creation of this world, there was never an act of mercy performed by God that was not in perfect harmony with the severest justice. God, although He has loved and saved unholy men, has never stained His holy hands in the act of saving them. He remains the *"holy, holy, holy, Lord God Almighty"* (Revelation 4:8), although He is still very full of pity and compassion as He passes by transgression, iniquity, and sin, and presses prodigal children to His heart.

The Atonement through the shed blood of Jesus Christ is the answer to these great questions: How can God be just and yet the Justifier of those who believe? How can He be perfectly holy and yet, at the same time, receive into His love and adopt into His family those who are unrighteous and unholy? O Calvary, you have solved the problem. In the bleeding wounds of our Savior, *"righteousness and peace have kissed each other"* (Psalm 85:10).

May God grant you, unconverted sinner, the grace to understand how He can save you, yet be perfectly holy; how He can forgive your sins, yet be perfectly just! I know this is the difficulty that troubles you: How can you be received while God is what He is, *"the Judge of all"* (Hebrews 12:23)? He can receive you because the Lord Jesus Christ took the sins of His people and bore them *"in his own body on the tree"* (1 Peter 2:24). Thus, being the appointed Head of all believers, Christ has vindicated in His own person the inflexible justice of God. Here is the Man who has kept the whole law of God—not Adam, for he failed to keep it. However, the Second Adam, the Lord from heaven, and all whom He represented are now *"accepted in the beloved"* (Ephesians 1:6); they are made acceptable to God because of what Jesus Christ has done. So let us magnify *"his holy arm, [which] hath gotten him the victory."*

The Lord's Marvelous Grace

I now want to look at the marvelous grace that has revealed all this to us. It is a very familiar thing today for us to hear the Gospel, but will you just carry your minds back some two or three thousand years to the period when Psalm 98 was written? What was then known concerning salvation was known almost exclusively by the Jews. Here and there, a proselyte was led into the bonds of the covenant; but for the most part, the whole world lay in heathen darkness. Where there was the seal of circumcision, there were the oracles of God; but the Gentile sinners knew nothing whatever concerning the truth. And it might have been that way until this day if the Lord had not *"made known his salvation: [and] his righteousness in the sight of the heathen.*" Our present privileges are greater than the privileges of the ancient Israelites, of those whom, I am afraid, we sometimes despise—or at least forget—of those whom we have for a moment supplanted. They were the favored people of God. Through their unbelief, they have been set aside for a while, but Israel is yet to be restored to even greater blessings than it formerly experienced.

> The hymn shall yet in Zion swell
> That sounds Messiah's praise,
> And Thy loved name, Immanuel!
> As once in ancient days.

> For Israel yet shall own her King,
> For her salvation waits.
> And hill and dale shall sweetly sing
> With praise in all her gates!

Do we value as we ought the privilege we now have of hearing in our own language the wonderful works of God? My dear unconverted reader, how grateful you ought to be that you ware not born in Rome or Babylon or the far-off Indies, in those days when there was no Christian missionary to seek you out and care for your soul, but when all of the light that shone was shed upon that little land of Israel! Jesus Christ has *"broken down the middle wall of partition"* (Ephesians 2:14). Now it makes no difference whether we are *"Barbarian, Scythian, bond [or] free"* (Colossians 3:11). The Gospel is to be preached to every creature in all the world (Mark 16:15). Moreover, *"he that believeth and is baptized shall be saved"* (v. 16), no matter what the person's previous character may have been or to what race he may have belonged.

The Holy Spirit's Wonderful Revelation

Yet, let us never forget that, in order to accomplish this great work of salvation, it was necessary that the blessed Son of God descend to this world. It was also necessary that the Spirit of God be given to rest upon the church, to be the inspiration by which the Gospel should be preached among the heathen. Again let me ask a question: Do we sufficiently reverence the Holy Spirit and love Him as we should for all that He has done?

The incarnation of the Son of God is no greater mystery than the indwelling of the Spirit of God in the hearts of men. It is truly marvelous that the Holy Spirit, who is equally God with the Father and the Son, should come and reside in these bodies of ours and make them His temple. Yet, remember that, if it had not been so, there would have been no effective preaching of the Gospel. Further, unless the Holy Spirit blesses the Word right now, there will be no open showing of Christ's righteousness to you and no making known of His salvation to your heart. All the victories of Christ, for which I urge your grateful songs, would be unknown to you if the Holy Spirit did not touch men's lips so that they might tell what the Lord has done and publish abroad His glorious victories.

Remember, too, that, in connection with the work of the Holy Spirit, there has had to be an unbroken chain of divine providence to bring the Gospel to you and to your land. Look back through the past ages, and see what wonderful revolutions of the wheels full of eyes (Ezekiel 10:12) there have been. Empires have risen and have fallen, but their rise and fall have had a close connection with the preaching of the Gospel. There have been terrific persecutions of the saints of God. Satan has seemed to summon all the forces of hell to attack the church of Christ, yet he could not destroy its life. There came the dark night of the dogmatic popes, dense as the nights of Egypt's darkness; but old Rome could not put out the light of the Gospel.

Since then, in what marvelous ways has God led His chosen people! He has raised up His servants, one after another, so that the testimony concerning the victories achieved by Christ might be continued among us and might be spread throughout all the nations of the earth. Thus, it has come to pass that you can now have an open Bible in your hands and that I can freely explain the teaching of that Bible to you. How wonderfully has the history of our own country been working toward this happy result! Glorify God and bless His holy name that we live in such golden days as these, when "*the* LORD *hath made known his salvation,*" and "*his righteousness hath he openly showed in the sight of the heathen.*"

A Greater Revelation of Grace

Further, let us more sweetly praise the Lord that we not only live where the Gospel is made known, but that God has made it known to some of us in a still deeper sense. Some of us now understand, as we did not at one time, the righteousness of God—His way of making man righteous through Jesus Christ. We understood it in theory long before God made it savingly known in our souls.

This is another work of the Holy Spirit for which we have good reason to *"sing unto the LORD a new song."*

Sinner, God has sent the Gospel to you to tell you that His Son, Jesus Christ, has conquered sin and death and the Devil, and that, if you believe in Jesus, you will be a partaker in His victory. There is nothing for you to do but to believe in Him. Even the power to understand His truth is God's gift to you; even the faith that receives His truth He works in you according to His Spirit. You are to be nothing so that God may be everything. It is for you to fall at His feet, with confusion of face and contrition of heart. Then, when He bids you do so, you need to rise up and say, "I will sing a new song unto the Lord. 'O LORD, *I will praise thee: though thou wast angry with me, thine anger is turned away, and thou comfortedst me'* (Isaiah 12:1) through Him who won the victory on my behalf."

Amazing Things in Reference to Mankind

The second part of this subject, which I will touch on very briefly, is this: there are some astonishing things in reference to ourselves.

Man's Astounding Indifference

The first of these marvelous things is that after all that Christ has done, and after the mercy of God has made His salvation known, so many people are utterly careless and indifferent concerning it. Tens of thousands will not even cross the threshold of a church to go and hear about it. Bibles are in many of their houses, yet they do not take the time to read them. If they are going on a railway journey, they consult their train schedule, but they do not search God's own Guidebook to find the way to heaven or to learn where and when they must start if they intend to reach that place of eternal happiness and bliss. We can still ask, *"Who hath believed our report? and to whom is the arm of the LORD revealed?"* (Isaiah 53:1).

To me, the most astonishing sight is an unconverted man outside of hell. It is a marvel of marvels that the Son of God Himself left all the glories of heaven and came to earth to bleed and die, in man's shape for man's sake, and yet that there could be anyone in the shape of a man who would not care even to hear the story of His wondrous sacrifice. It is a wonder that anyone, upon hearing the story, could disregard it as if it were of no interest to him. Yet, see how men rush to buy a newspaper when there is some little bit of news! With what eagerness do some young people—and some old people, too, who ought to know better—await the next episode of a foolish serial story of a lovesick maid! How freely their tears flow over imaginary griefs! However, the Lord Jesus Christ, bleeding to death in unconditional love for His enemies, does not move them to tears, and their hearts remain untouched by the story of His sufferings as if they were made of marble.

The Astonishing Depravity of Mankind

The depravity of mankind is a miracle of sin; it is as great a miracle, from one point of view, as the grace of God is from another. Jesus Christ neglected! Eternal love slighted! Infinite mercy disregarded! I have to confess, with great shame, that even the preacher of the Gospel is not always affected by it as he ought to be; not only must I confess this, but so must others, I fear, who preach the Word of God. Why, it ought to make us dance for joy to tell our congregations that there is mercy in the heart of God, that there is pardon for sinners, that there is life for the dead, that the great heart of God yearns over sinners. Our hearts ought to be ready to break when we find that men disregard all this good news and are not affected by it. It is an astounding calamity that men should have fallen so terribly that infinite love is imperceptible by them. May God grant that His grace show to you, unconverted sinners, in what a horrible state your hearts must be, because, after all that Christ has done, you still give Him no token of gratitude, no song of praise for the wonders He has performed.

The Marvel That Any Are Saved

Looking from this point of view, we see another marvelous thing: that some of us have been so enabled to recognize the work of Christ that we are saved by it. To confess the truth, there are some of us who were very unlikely candidates for salvation. Probably, each saved individual reading this has thought himself to be the most unlikely person ever to be saved. I know that I thought so concerning myself.

I recall the story of a Scotsman who went to see Mr. Rowland Hill. For a long while he sat, staring at Rowland in the face, until the good old minister asked him, "What are you looking at?" The Scotsman replied, "I have been studying the lines of your face." "What do you make of them?" asked Rowland. The answer was, "I was thinking what a great vagabond you would have been if the grace of God had not met with you." "That thought has often struck me," replied Rowland.

A similar thought has often struck most of us. If we had not been converted, would we have led others into sin? Would we have invented fresh pleasures of vice and folly? Who would have stopped us? We had daring enough for anything, enough even to have defied the very Devil himself, if we had thought that some new vice could have been invented or some fresh pleasure of sin could have been discovered. But now that God has made us yield, has subdued us by His sovereign grace, has brought us to His feet, and has put on us the chains that now we gladly welcome, and that we long to wear forever, "O [let us] *sing unto the* Lord *a new song; for he hath done marvellous things* [for us]: *his right hand, and his holy arm, hath gotten him the victory.*"

Dear child of God, if there has been special grace in your case, as I know you feel that there has been, you ought to give special honor to Christ. Everyone who is saved ought to live a very special life—an extraordinary life. If you were an extraordinary sinner, or have been an extraordinary debtor to divine love in some way or other, may there be some extraordinary devotion, some extraordinary consecration, some extraordinary faith, some extraordinary liberality, some extraordinary lovingkindness, or some other extraordinary thing about you in which the traces of that marvelous right hand of God and His holy arm will be plainly manifested!

The Marvelous Joy of the Believer

The last thing I want to address is this: there is something marvelous in the joy that we, who have believed in the victory secured by Christ, have received. Probably all of you have sung that song with the refrain, "I am so glad that Jesus loves me." That refrain is very monotonous, yet I think I would like to sing it all night and would not want to stop, even when the morning sun arose.

> I am so glad that Jesus loves me;
> I am so glad that Jesus loves me;
> I am so glad that Jesus loves me,
> I'm singing, glory, hallelujah,
> Jesus loves me.

"I am so glad that Jesus loves me." You may turn it over and over and over and over, as long as you like, but you will never find anything that makes you so glad as the realization that Jesus loves you. You will never find that the sweetness of the thought, "Jesus loves me," will ever be exhausted.

Sinner, if you only knew the blessedness of the life of Christ, you would be overjoyed to run away from your own life and run to share ours in Him! We have peace like a river. We can leave all our cares and our burdens with our God. We are just where we love most to be—in the bosom of our heavenly Father— and the Spirit of adoption makes us feel perfectly at home with Him. We can all say, "*Return unto thy rest, O my soul; for the* LORD *hath dealt bountifully with thee*" (Psalm 116:7). We are in perfect safety, for who can destroy those whom Christ protects? We have a perfect peace even with our own conscience. We have also a blessed prospect for the future: we will be borne along upon the wings of divine providence until we reach the golden shores of our eternal home. We have a heaven below, and we are looking for a still better heaven above.

> All that remains for me
> Is but to love and sing,
> And wait until the angels come
> To bear me to the King.

This is the lower, earthly part of the choir. Some of the singers are up in the galleries, and we are learning here the notes that we will sing above. Come, beloved, let us make these sinners yearn to share our joys. If any of you saints have been moaning and groaning of late, get into a proper attitude of mind. Begin to tune up and to praise the Lord with all your might until the ungodly shall say, "After all, there is something sweeter and brighter and better in the lives of these Christians than we have ever known in ours."

However, whether you will rejoice or not, "*my soul doth magnify the Lord, and my spirit hath rejoiced in God my Saviour*" (Luke 1:46–47); and I will continue, by His help, until death suspends these mortal songs or blends them into the immortal melodies before the throne.

4

CHRIST'S JOY AND OURS

These things have I spoken unto you, that my joy might remain in you,
and that your joy might be full.
—John 15:11

A common saying has crept in among our proverbs, which is being repeated as if it were altogether true: "Man was made to mourn." There is an element of truth in that sentence, but there is also a falsehood in it. Man was not originally made to mourn; he was made to rejoice. The Garden of Eden was his place of happy abode, and as long as he continued in obedience to God, nothing grew in that Garden that could cause him sorrow. For his delight, the flowers breathed out their perfume. For his pleasure, the landscapes were full of beauty, and the rivers rippled over golden sands. God made human beings, as He made His other creatures, to be happy. They are capable of happiness. They are in their right element when they are happy.

Now that Jesus Christ has come to restore the ruins of the Fall, He has come to bring back to us the old joy—only it will be even sweeter and deeper than it could have been if we had never lost it. A Christian has never fully realized what Christ came to make him until he has grasped the joy of the Lord. Christ wants His people to be happy. When they are perfect, as He will make them in due time, they will also be perfectly happy. As heaven is the place of pure holiness, so is it the place of sheer happiness. In proportion to our increasing readiness for heaven, we will have some of the joy that belongs to heaven.

Our Full Joy Is Christ's Will

My first observation about our text is this: all that Jesus spoke in the past and all that He speaks today through His Word is meant to produce joy in His people: *"These things have I spoken unto you, that my joy might remain in you, and that your joy may be full."* It is our Savior's will that, even now, we should dwell and abide in the fullness of His joy.

Words of Instruction

If you will read through the fifteenth chapter of John, from which our text is taken, and also the chapter that precedes it, you will see the nature of the words that Jesus Christ speaks to His people. Sometimes they are words of instruction. He talks to us in order that we may know the truth and the meaning of the truth. However, His objective is that, in knowing the truth, we may have joy in it.

I will not say that the more a Christian knows, the more joy he has, but I can truly say that ignorance often hides from us many wells of delight of which we might otherwise drink. Generally, all other things being equal, the best instructed Christian will be the happiest person. He will know the truth, and the truth will make him free (John 8:32). The truth will kill a thousand fears that ignorance would have fostered within him.

The knowledge of the love of God, the knowledge of the full Atonement made on Calvary, the knowledge of the eternal covenant, the knowledge of the immutable faithfulness of Jehovah—indeed, all knowledge that reveals God in His relationship to His people—will tend to create comfort in the hearts of His saints. Therefore, do not be careless about scriptural doctrine. Study the Word, and seek to understand the mind of the Spirit as revealed in it, for this blessed Book was written for your learning, that *"through patience and comfort of the scriptures [you] might have hope"* (Romans 15:4). If you are diligent students of the Word, you will find that you have good reason to rejoice in the Lord in all circumstances.

Words of Warning

Sometimes our Lord speaks words of warning to us, as He did while He was on earth. In the fifteenth chapter of John, we discover that He told His disciples that they were branches of a vine, and that branches bearing no fruit had to be cut off and cast into the fire. At first, it seems to us that nothing is consoling in such words as those. They sound sharply in our ears, startling us, making each of us fearfully ask himself, "Am I bearing fruit?" Well, beloved, such soul-searching as that is exceptionally beneficial, because it tends to deepen in us true joy. Christ would not have us rejoice with the false joy of presumption, so He takes the sharp knife and cuts that mistaken joy away. Joy on a false basis would prevent us from having true joy. Therefore, the Master gives us the sharp, cutting word so that we will be sound in our faith, so that we will be sound in the life of God, and so that the joy we receive will be worth having—not the mere foam of a wave that is driven with the wind and tossed, but the solid foundation of the Rock of Ages.

Our Lord also tells us that even branches that are bearing fruit have to be pruned in order for them to bring forth more fruit (John 15:2). "What an unpleasant truth!" somebody might say. "It gives me no joy to know that I have to endure the knife of correction and affliction." Yes, dear one, but remember this:

> *And not only so, but we glory in tribulations also: knowing that tribulation worketh patience; and patience, experience; and experience, hope: and hope maketh not ashamed; because the love of God is shed abroad in our hearts by the Holy Ghost which is given unto us.*   (Romans 5:3–5)

Thus, beginning rather low on this chain, you arrive at joy at last, and you get to it by the only right approach. To try to sail up to joy by the balloon of imagination is dangerous work; but to mount up to it by Jacob's ladder, every rung of which God has placed at the proper distance, is to climb to heaven by His appointed, safe road. There is nothing that the Lord Jesus says to us by way of warning that does not guard us against sorrow, conduct us away from danger, and point us to the path of safety. If we will but listen to these words of warning, they will guide us to the truest happiness that mortals can ever find either here or hereafter.

Words of Humbling

You will notice, as you read the chapter, that our Lord, in addition to words of instruction and words of warning, utters some very humbling words. I think that is a very humbling verse in which He says, "*As the branch cannot bear fruit of itself, except it abide in the vine; no more can ye, except ye abide in me*" (John 15:4). But it is good for us to be humbled and brought low. The Valley of Humiliation has always struck me as being the most beautiful place in the whole of the pilgrimage that John Bunyan described in *The Pilgrim's Progress*. What a beautiful experience it is to envision that shepherd boy, sitting down among the sheep, and to hear him playing his pipe and singing something like this:

> He that is down need fear no fall,
> He that is low no pride;
> He that is humble ever shall
> Have God to be his Guide.

This teaches us that to be brought down to our true condition of nothingness before God, to be made to feel our entire dependence upon the power of the Holy Spirit, is the true way to promote in us a joy that angels themselves might envy.

Therefore, beloved, be thankful whenever you read Scripture, whether it instructs you or warns you or humbles you. Say to yourself, "Somehow or other, this leads to my present and eternal joy, and therefore I will give more earnest heed to it, lest by any means I should lose the blessing it is intended to convey to me."

Words of Promise

The fifteenth chapter of John also abounds in gracious words of promise such as this: "*If ye abide in me, and my words abide in you, ye shall ask what ye will, and it shall be done unto you*" (v. 7). There are other promises here, every one of which is full of consolation to the children of God. Are any of you lacking in joy at this time? Do you feel dull and heavy of heart? Are you depressed and tried? Then listen to what Jesus Christ says here: "*These things have I spoken unto you, that my joy might remain in you, and that your joy might be full.*"

What are the things that He says to you in other parts of His Word? "*Take therefore no thought for the morrow: for the morrow shall take thought for the things of itself*" (Matthew 6:34). "*Let not your heart be troubled: ye believe in God, believe also in me*" (John 14:1). "*My sheep hear my voice, and I know them, and they follow*" *me: and I give unto them eternal life; and they shall never perish, neither shall any man pluck them out of my hand"* (John 10:27–28). In this way our Lord graciously talks to us. Do not let Him speak in vain.

My friends, do not allow His precious promises to fall upon your ears as the good seed fell upon the rocky or stony soil. The promise of harvest gives joy to the earth. Do not rob your Lord of the sheaves that He deserves to gather from your heart and life, but believe His Word, rest upon it, and rejoice in it, realizing that His words of promise are meant to bring you great joy.

Words of Precept

Christ's words of precept also bring great joy. The fifteenth chapter of John contains many of them. Jesus told us that it is His command that we should *"love one another"* (v. 12), and also that we should continue in His love (v. 9). He gave us many principles of that kind, and every precept in God's Word is a signpost pointing out the road to joy. The commandments on the tablets of stone seemed very hard, even though etched by the finger of God Himself, and the granite on which they were engraved was hard and cold. But the precepts of the Lord Jesus are tender and gracious; they bring us joy and life.

As you read these precious decrees, you may be quite sure of two things: if Christ denies you anything, it is not good for you; and if Christ commands you to do anything, obedience will promote your highest welfare.

O child of God, never quibble about any precept of your Lord! If your proud flesh should rebel, pray it down. Rest assured that, if you were so selfish as only to wish to do that which would promote your own happiness, it would be the path of wisdom to be obedient to your Lord and Master. I repeat what I wrote just above: the precepts of Christ are signposts indicating the only way to true joy. If you keep His commandments, you will abide in His love. If you carefully keep your full attention on Him in order to immediately do all that He bids you do, you will have the peace of God flowing into your soul like a river, and that peace will never fail to bring you solid and lasting joy.

Pleasing the Lord Brings Joy

The next thing I gather from our text is that when our Lord Jesus Christ takes joy in us, then we also have joy. This meaning of the text is the interpretation given to it by several of the early church fathers. They have expanded our text verse, "*These things have I spoken unto you, that my joy might remain in you,*" to mean, "that I may rejoice over you, rejoice in you, and be pleased with you; thus your joy may be full." I am not certain that this is the complete meaning of the text, nor am I sure that it is not; but either way, it is a very blessed truth. Let me give you some instances to illustrate this.

A child knows that his father loves him; but while he is quite sure that his father will never cease to love him, he also knows that if he is disobedient, his father will be displeased and grieved. The obedient child gives pleasure to his father by his obedience. Moreover, when he has done so, he receives pleasure from that very fact itself.

There used to be servants in much earlier times—and I suppose there are some now—who were so attached to their masters that, if they gave satisfaction to them, they were perfectly satisfied. However, the least word of displeasure from their masters wounded them to the very heart.

Perhaps a better illustration may be found in the nearer and dearer relationship of husband and wife. The wife, if she has pleased her husband, is delighted in the joy that she has given to him; but if she has displeased him in any way, she is unhappy until she has removed the cause of his displeasure and has again given him joy.

Now, I know that my Lord Jesus loves me and that He will never do anything else but love me. Yet, He may not be always pleased with me. When He has no joy in me, my joy also dissipates if I have a heart that is true toward Him. But when He has joy in me, when He can rejoice in me, then my joy is also full. Every one of you whom the Lord has loved will find this to be true: in as much as Jesus Christ can look upon you with joy as obedient and faithful to Him, in that same proportion your conscience will be at ease, and your mind will find joy in the thought that your life is acceptable to Him.

By Abiding in Him

What are the ways in which we can really please Christ Jesus and thus have joy in Christ's pleasure? According to the chapter before us, we please Him when we abide in Him: "*If ye abide in me, and my words abide in you, ye shall ask what ye will, and it shall be done unto you*" (John 15:7). If you sometimes abide in Christ, but sometimes turn away from Him, you will give Him no pleasure. However, if

He is the indispensable Companion of your daily life, if you are unhappy should the slightest cloud come between you and your Lord, if you feel that you must be as closely connected with Him as the tree limb is with the trunk or as the branch is with the stem, then you will please Him, and He will take delight in your fellowship.

Fervent love for Christ is very pleasing to Him, but the chilly, lukewarm love of Laodicea is nauseous to Him. Thus, He said, *"Because thou art lukewarm, and neither cold nor hot, I will spue thee out of my mouth"* (Revelation 3:16). Day by day, if you continue to walk with God carefully and prayerfully and to abide in Christ continually, He will look upon you with eyes of satisfaction and delight. He will see in you the reward of His sufferings. And you, being conscious that you are giving joy to Him, will find that your own cup of joy is also full to overflowing.

What greater joy can a man have than to feel that he is pleasing Christ? My fellow creatures may condemn what I do, but if Christ accepts it, it matters nothing to me how many may condemn it. They may misrepresent and misjudge me; they may impute wrong motives to me; they may sneer and snarl at me. However, if I can keep up constant and unbroken communion with the Son of God, what cause have I for sorrow? No, if He is joyful in us, then our joy will remain and will be full.

By Bringing Forth Much Fruit

Our Lord Jesus has also told us that He has joy in us when we bring forth much fruit: *"Herein is my Father glorified, that ye bear much fruit; so shall ye be my disciples"* (John 15:8). This is to say, "I will recognize in you the evidence of true discipleship with satisfaction and delight."

Beloved in Christ, are you bringing forth much fruit for God's glory? Are you called to suffer? Then, in your suffering, do you bring forth the fruit of patience? Are you strong and in robust health? Then, with that health and strength, are you rendering to the Lord the fruit of holy activity? Are you doing all you can for the Lord Jesus, who has done so much for you? You have received so much from Him; are you yielding an adequate return to Him? It is little enough when your effort is what we call very much, but how tiny it is when it is small in our own estimation!

When our Lord Jesus Christ sees us doing much for God, He is pleased with us, just as the gardener is when, having planted a tree and dug around it and fertilized it and pruned it, he sees the tree at last covered with golden fruit.

The gardener is pleased with his fruitful tree, and Christ is pleased with His fruit-bearing disciples. Are we making Christ glad in this fashion? If so, our own joy will be full.

I am not surprised that some Christians have so little joy, when I remember what little pleasure they are giving to Jesus because they are producing such a sparse crop of fruit for His praise and glory. Beloved, see to this matter, I urge you. If I cannot enforce this truth with the strength that it deserves, may the power of the Holy Spirit cause the truth to come home to your hearts!

By Keeping His Commandments

In this beautiful fifteenth chapter of John, our Lord also tells us that He has joy in us when we keep His commandments:

> *If ye keep my commandments, ye shall abide in my love; even as I have kept my Father's commandments, and abide in his love. These things have I spoken unto you, that my joy might remain in you, and that your joy might be full. This is my commandment, That ye love one another, as I have loved you.*
> (John 15:10–12)

The person who walks carefully in the matter of obedience to Christ's commands, wishing never to do anything offensive to Him, asking for a tender conscience so that he may be immediately aware when he is doing wrong, and earnestly desiring to leave no duty undone—such a man as that must be happy. He may not laugh much and may have very little to say when in frivolous company, but he has found a joy that foolish laughter can but mock. He has a sacred mirth within, compared to which the merriment of fools is but *"the crackling of thorns under a pot"* (Ecclesiastes 7:6). The man with a tender conscience has that joy; the careful walker has that joy. The man who, when he puts his head upon his pillow at night, can say to himself, "I have not been all that I want to be, but I have aimed at holiness; I have tried to curb my passions; I have sought to find out my Master's will and to do it in everything," sleeps sweetly. If he awakens, there is music in his heart. Whatever the trials of life may be, such a man has an abundant source of joy inside. He is pleasing to Christ. Christ has joy in him, and his joy is full.

By Loving One Another

This is especially the case with those who love others in the body of Christ. There are some who do not love others at all; or if they do, they love themselves a great deal more. They are very apt to judge and to condemn one another. If they can find a little fault, they magnify it; and if they can find none, they invent some.

I know some people who seem to be, by nature, qualified to be monks or hermits, living quite alone. According to their idea of things, they are much too good for society. No church is pure enough for them; no ministry can profit them; no one else can reach as high as the wonderful position to which, in their self-conceit, they imagine that they have attained. Let none of us be of that sort. Many of the children of God are far better than we are, and the worst one in God's family has some points in which he is better than we are.

Sometimes I feel as though I would give my eyes to be as sure of heaven as the most obscure and the least in all the family of God. I think that such times may also come to some of you, if you imagine yourselves to be so great and good. You fat cattle, who have pushed the lean ones with your horns and with shoulders until the weak were scattered (Ezekiel 34:20–21), the Lord may say to you, "Go, you do not belong to Me, for My people are not so rough and boastful, not so proud and haughty; instead, I look to the man who is humble, who trembles at My Word, and who has a contrite spirit."

Did you ever try to pray to God under the influence of an awareness of possessing the higher life? Did you ever try to pray to God that way? If you ever did, I do not think you will do it a second time. I tried it once, but I am not likely to repeat the experiment. I thought I would try to pray to God in that fashion, but it did not seem to come naturally from me. When I had done so, I thought I heard somebody at a distance saying, "God be merciful to me a sinner" (Luke 18:13), and then I saw him go home to his house justified (v. 14). Thus, I had to tear off my Pharisaic robes and get back to where the poor publican had been standing, for his place and his prayer suited me admirably.

I cannot make out what has happened to some of my family in Christ, who mistakenly believe themselves to be so wonderfully good. I wish the Lord would strip them of their self-righteousness and let them see themselves as they really are in His sight. Their fine notions concerning the higher life would soon vanish then. Beloved, the highest life I ever hope to reach, this side of heaven, is to say from my very soul,

I the chief of sinners am,
But Jesus died for me.

I do not have the slightest desire to suppose that I have advanced in the spiritual life many stages beyond anyone else. As long as I trust simply to the blood and righteousness of Christ and think nothing of myself, I believe that I will continue to be pleasing to the Lord Jesus Christ, that His joy will be in me, and that my joy will be full.

Christ's Joy Is Ours

Now, in the third place, I think we may surmise from our text verse that the joy Jesus gives to His people is His own joy: *"That my joy might remain in you."* I venture to say that you have noticed that a man cannot communicate to another any joy except that of which he is himself conscious. A man who is rich can tell you the joy of riches, but he cannot give that joy to a poor man. Another man, who takes delight in all sorts of tomfoolery, can tell you the joy of nonsense, but he cannot make another enjoy it.

Abiding in the Father's Love

When Jesus gives us joy, He gives us His own joy. So, what do you think His joy is? First, Jesus' joy is the joy of abiding in His Father's love. He knows that His Father loves Him, that He never did anything else but love Him, that He loved Him before the earth existed, that He loved Him when He was in the manger, and that He loved Him when He was on the cross. Now, that is the joy that Christ gives to you, the joy of knowing that your heavenly Father loves you with the same kind of love.

You who really are believers in the Lord Jesus Christ ought to pause a moment and just roll that sweet morsel over your tongue—the everlasting God loves you! I have known times when I have felt as if I could leap up at the very thought of God's love for me. That He pities you and cares for you, you can understand; however, that He loves you—well, if that does not make your joy full, there is nothing that can! It ought to fill us with delight to know that we are loved by God the Father with an everlasting and infinite love, even as Jesus Christ is loved. *"The Father himself loveth you"* (John 16:27), Christ declares down through the ages.

Therefore, surely you share Christ's joy, and that fact should make your own joy full.

Intimate Friendship

Christ's joy is also the joy of blessed friendship. He said to His disciples, *"Henceforth I call you not servants; for the servant knoweth not what his lord doeth: but I have called you friends; for all things that I have heard of my Father I have made known unto you"* (John 15:15). The friends of Jesus are those who are received by Him into a most intimate fellowship—to lean upon His breast and to become His constant companions. Our Lord Jesus Christ has great joy in being on the friendliest terms with His people. Do you not also have great joy in being on such friendly terms with Him? What higher joy do you want or could you possibly have?

I have heard a man very boastfully say that he once dined with Lord So-and-So. Another, just for the sake of showing off, spoke of his friend, Sir John Somebody-or-Other. However, you have the Lord Jesus Christ as your personal Friend, your Divine Companion. Soon you are going to sit and feast with Him at His own table. He no longer calls you His servant, but His friend. Does that fact not make you rejoice with exceeding joy? What is your heart made of, if it does not leap with joy at such an assurance as that? You are beloved of the Lord and a friend of the Son of God! Kings might well be willing to give up their crowns if they could have such bliss as this.

Glorifying the Father

Moreover, our Lord Jesus feels an intense delight in glorifying His Father. It is His constant joy to bring glory to His Father. Have you ever felt the joy of glorifying God, or do you now feel joy in Christ because He has glorified His Father? I solemnly declare that if Christ would not save me, I must still love Him for what He has done to exhibit the character of God. I have sometimes thought that if He were to shove me outdoors in the snow, I would stand there in the cold and say, "Do what You will with me; crush me if You will; but I will always love You, for there never was another such as You are, never one who so well deserved my love, and so fully won my affection and admiration as You have done."

How gloriously Christ rolled away the great load of human sin, adequately recompensed the claims of divine justice, magnified the law, and made it honorable!

He took the greatest possible delight in doing this. *"For the joy that was set before him [He] endured the cross, despising the shame"* (Hebrews 12:2). Let that joy be yours also. Rejoice that the law is honored, that justice is satisfied, and that free grace is gloriously displayed in the atoning work of our Lord Jesus Christ.

It was Christ's joy that He glorified His Father by finishing the work that the Father had given Him to do (John 17:4). He has finished it, and therefore He is glad. Will you not also rejoice in His finished work? You do not have to sew a single stitch of the robe of righteousness that He has made. It is woven from the top throughout and absolutely perfect in every respect. You do not have to contribute even a penny to the ransom price for your redemption, for it has been paid down to the last mite.

The great redemptive work is forever finished, and Christ has done it all. He is *"Alpha and Omega, the beginning and the end"* (Revelation 21:6). He is the Author and the Finisher of our faith (Hebrews 12:2). Sit down, my brothers and sisters in Christ, and just feed on this precious truth. Surely, this is the *"feast of fat things, a feast of wines on the lees, of fat things full of marrow, of wines on the lees well refined"* (Isaiah 25:6), of which the prophet Isaiah wrote long ago.

I see You, Lord Jesus, with Your foot upon the Dragon's neck. I see You with death and hell beneath Your feet. I see the glory that adorns Your triumphant brow as You wait until the whole earth will acknowledge You as King. You have once and for all declared, *"It is finished"* (John 19:30), and finished it certainly is. My poor heart rejoices because You have finished it, and finished it for me.

Christ's Gift of Full, Lasting Joy

My last observation is that, when Christ communicates His joy to His people, it is a joy that remains and a joy that is full. *"These things have I spoken unto you, that my joy might remain in you, and that your joy might be full."*

A Steadfast Joy

No other joy remains like Christ's does. There is a great deal of happiness in many families when children are born, yet how many little coffins are followed by weeping mothers! There is joy when God fills the barn, and very properly so, for a bountiful harvest should make men glad; but the winter soon comes, with its cold, dark, dreary weather. But, beloved, when we receive the joy of the Lord, it stays. Why? Because the cause of it remains. The brook will continue only as long as the spring runs, but the joy of a Christian is one that can never alter, because the cause of it never changes. God's love never changes toward His people. The Atonement never loses its efficacy. Our Lord Jesus Christ never ceases His intercession. His acceptability with God on our behalf never varies. The promises do not change. The covenant is not like the moon, sometimes waxing and sometimes waning. Oh, no, if you rejoice with Christ's joy today, you will have the same cause for rejoicing tomorrow and forever and forevermore, for He promises that His joy will remain in you.

A Fulfilling Joy

Next, this joy is full joy. Dear friends, if our joy is full, two things should be very clear to us: first, we have no room for any more joy; and, secondly, we have no room for any sorrow. When we get to know the love of God for us, we become so full of delight that we do not need or want any more joy. The pleasures of this world lose all their former charm for us.

When a man has eaten all he can eat, you may set whatever you like before him, but he has no appetite for it. "Enough is as good as a feast," we say. When a person is forgiven by God and knows that he is saved, the joy of the Lord enters his soul. That one says, "You may take all other joys and do what you like with them. I have my God, my Savior, and I want no more." Then ambition ceases, lust is quiet, covetousness is dead, and desires that once roamed abroad now stay at home. The saved one says, "My God, You are enough for me; what more can I require? Since You have said to me, 'I love you,' and my heart has responded, 'My God, I love You, too,' I have more true wealth at my disposal than if I had all the riches of the world under my control."

There is also no longer any room for sorrow, for if Christ's joy has filled us, where can sorrow exist? "But, the man has lost all his money." "Yes," he says, "but if the Lord likes to take it from me, let Him have it." "But, the man is bereaved of those who are very dear to him, as Job was." Still, he says, *"The Lord gave, and the Lord hath taken away; blessed be the name of the Lord"* (Job 1:21). When a man consciously realizes the love of God in his soul, he cannot want more than that. I wish that all of us had that realization, because our joy would then be so great that we would have no room left for sorrow.

Now, dearly beloved, as you come to the table of your Lord in this disposition, you will feel so full of joy that you will be too full for words. People who are really full of joy do not usually talk much. A person who is carrying a glass that is full to the brim does not go dancing along like one who has nothing to carry. He is very quiet and steady, for he does not want to spill the contents of the glass. Likewise, the man who has the joy of the Lord filling his soul is often quiet; he cannot say much about it.

I have even experienced that joy to become so full that I could scarcely tell whether I was "*in the body, or out of the body*" (2 Corinthians 12:3). Pain, sickness, depression of spirit—all seem to have been taken away. I have had so clear a view of Christ, and my mind has been so separated from everything else that, afterwards, it has almost seemed like a dream to me to have felt the love of God in its almighty power, lifting me above all the surrounding circumstances.

An Unforgettable Joy

Then, dear friend, if it is so with you, the joy of the Lord will be much too full for you ever to forget it. If, at this very moment, your soul is filled with Christ's joy, it is possible that, many years from now, you may be able to say, "I remember that night twenty-three and a half years ago when I was engrossed in a book. My Lord then met with me, looked into my soul, and saw there was a void there; so He poured His own heart's joy into me until my soul could not hold any more." And, perhaps, in some dark time in the future, your present experience will be a great source of comfort to your soul. You will recall David's words in a similar circumstance: "*O my God, my soul is cast down within me: therefore will I remember thee from the land of Jordan, and of the Hermonites, from the hill Mizar*" (Psalm 42:6). You will add, "Although, now, '*deep calleth unto deep at the noise of thy waterspouts*' (v. 7), the remembrance of that bright season causes me to know that You do not forsake those on whom Your love has once been set."

An Intimate Joy

Beloved, come close to your Lord. I delight to come very near to Him. To touch the hem of His garment is enough for sinners, but it is not enough for saints. We want to sit at His feet with Mary and to lay our heads upon His bosom as John did. O you unconverted ones, look to Jesus; if you look to Him, you will live! Yet, for you who are converted, a look will not be enough for you. You want to keep on gazing at Him. You desire Him to keep gazing at you, until He says to you, *"Thou hast ravished my heart, my sister, my spouse; thou hast ravished my heart with one of thine eyes, with one chain of thy neck"* (Song 4:9). To this you will respond, *"He brought me to the banqueting house, and his banner over me was love. Stay me with flagons, comfort me with apples: for I am sick of love"* (Song 2:4).

Oh, may there now be such sweet fellowship between Christ and all His blood-besprinkled ones that, if we cannot pass the portals of heaven, we will be very near them; if we cannot hear the songs of the angels, they will at least hear ours; if we cannot look within to behold their joys, let us at least tempt them to look without to see ours. May our closeness be so dear that the angels would wish that they might be allowed to sit with us at this communion table, even though this is an honor reserved for sinners saved by sovereign grace.

> Never did angels taste above
> Redeeming grace and dying love.

May the Master smile on you, my dearly beloved, and make you to be such eminent saints that He can have great joy in you. Then, His joy will remain in you, and your joy will truly be full.

How I wish that everyone reading this knew my dear Lord and Master! I tell you who do not know Christ, and who do not experientially know what true religion is, that five minutes of the realization of the love of Christ would be better for you than a million years of your present choicest delights. There is more brightness in the dark side of Christ than in the brightest side of this poor world. I would sooner linger month after month on my bed, aching in every limb, with the sweat of death on my brow, persecuted, despised, forsaken, poor, and naked, with dogs licking my sores and demons tempting my soul, and yet have Christ for my Friend, than I would sit in the palaces of wicked kings with all their wealth and luxury and pampering and sin. Even in our lowliest state, it is better to be God's dog than the Devil's darling; it is better to have the crumbs and the moldy crusts that fall from Christ's table for the dogs than to sit at the head of princely banquets with the ungodly. *"A day in thy courts is better than a thousand* [outside]. *I had rather be a doorkeeper in the house of my God, than to dwell in the tents of wickedness"* (Psalm 84:10).

May God bless you richly. If you are still unconverted, may God have mercy on you and save you. And He will do so if you trust in Jesus Christ, His dear Son. As soon as you trust in Jesus, you are saved. May God grant that you do so this very hour, for His dear name's sake!

5

A WONDERFUL
TRANSFORMATION

Verily, verily, I say unto you, That ye shall weep and lament,
but the world shall rejoice: and ye shall be sorrowful,
but your sorrow shall be turned into joy.
—John 16:20

At the time Jesus said these words, our Lord was referring to His death, which He knew would cause the deepest grief to His own people, while the ungodly world would rejoice and laugh them to scorn. Thus, He implored them to look beyond the immediate present into the future and to believe that, ultimately, the cause of their sorrow would become a fountain of perpetual joy to them.

It is always wise to look a little ahead. Instead of deploring the dark clouds, let us anticipate the fruits and the flowers that will follow the descent of the needed showers. We might always be miserable if we lived only in the present, for our brightest time is yet to come. As believers in the Lord Jesus Christ, we are now only in the faint dawning of our day; the high noon will come to us by and by.

Although our Savior's words immediately related to His death, He was such a prophetic speaker that everything He said had a broader and deeper meaning than one might at first gather. Just as the fruit of the Tree of Life in the Garden of Eden foreshadows the leaves of the tree in heaven that are "*for the healing of the nations*" (Revelation 22:2), so the words of Christ, which in the past had a specific reference, now have a further living power about them. They may be applicable to present occasions instead of strictly limited to the one when they were first uttered.

Sorrow, Our Common Experience

I think I may fairly say that our Lord did not merely mean that only when He died, His children would have sorrow, but that we may take His words as a prophecy that all who truly follow Him will have their seasons of darkness and gloom. Nowhere has our Lord Jesus Christ promised to His people immunity from trial. On the contrary, He said to His disciples, "*In the world ye shall have tribulation*" (John 16:33). I cannot imagine a better promise for the wheat than that it will be threshed, and this is the promise that is made to us if we are the Lord's wheat and not the Enemy's tares:

> [Christ's] *fan is in his hand, and he will thoroughly purge his* [threshing] *floor, and gather his wheat into the garner; but he will burn up the chaff with unquenchable fire.*   (Matthew 3:12)

As His wheat, you will have the threshing that will fit you for the heavenly granary. You need not mourn, beloved, that it is to be so. If you do, it will make no difference, for your Lord has declared, "*In the world ye shall have tribulation.*" Be assured of that. If you could ask those believers who are now in heaven, they would tell you that they came there through great trials and tribulation. Many of them not only washed their robes in the blood of the Lamb, but they sealed their faithfulness to Him with their own blood.

Earthly Sorrow Is God's Intention for Us

Our Lord intended His disciples to feel the sorrow that was to come upon them, for He said to them, "*Ye shall weep and lament*," and He did not express any blame for their doing so. I would not have any of you even consider that there is any virtue in stoicism. I once heard a woman, wishing to show the wonders brought about in her by the grace of God, say that when her infant son died, she was so resigned to His divine will that she did not even shed a tear. However, I do not believe that it was ever God's divine will that mothers should lose their babies without shedding tears over them. I thank God that I did not have a mother who could have acted like that. I believe that as Jesus Himself wept, there can be no virtue in our saying that we do not weep.

God intends for you to feel the rod, beloved. He expects you sometimes to weep and lament, as Peter said, "*Though now for a season, if need be, ye are in heaviness through manifold temptations*" (1 Peter 1:6). That we should be in heaviness is a necessary part of our earthly discipline. Unfelt trial is no trial; certainly, it would be an unsanctified trial. Christ never meant Christians to be stoics. There is a vast difference between a gracious submission to God's divine will and a callous steeling of your heart to endure anything that happens to you without any feeling whatever. "*Ye shall be sorrowful,*" said our Lord to His disciples, and "*ye shall weep and lament.*" It is through the weeping and the lamenting, oftentimes, that the very essence of the blessing comes to us.

Enduring the World's Laughter

Our Savior mentions one aggravation of our grief, which some of us have often felt: "*the world shall rejoice.*" That is the old story. David found his own trials all the harder to bear when he saw "*the prosperity of the wicked*" (Psalm 73:3). He had been plagued "*all the day long*" and "*chastened every morning*" (v. 14); he could have endured all of that if he had not seen that the ungodly had more than any heart could wish. Sometimes he found himself even troubled with the fear of death, but as for the wicked, he said,

> *There are no bands in their death: but their strength is firm. They are not in trouble as other men; neither are they plagued like other men.*
>
> (Psalm 73:4–5)

It makes our bitterness all the more bitter when the saints of God are afflicted, yet the enemies of God are allowed to dwell in ease. I venture to say that when you were a child, you may have fallen and hurt yourself; while you were smarting from your bruises, the other children around you were laughing at you. The pain was all the sharper because of their laughing. Likewise, the righteous are wounded to the quick when they see the ungodly prospering—prospering, apparently, because of their ungodliness. These ungodly persons will even point the finger of scorn at the righteous and ask, "Where is your God now? Is this the result of serving Him?" (Psalm 115:2).

When this is your lot, remember that your Savior told His disciples that it would be so, and He has told you the same. While you are sorrowing, you will hear their shouts of revelry. You will be up in your own room weeping, and you will hear the sound of their merry feet dizzily dancing. The very contrast between their circumstances and your own will make you feel your grief even more. Well, if this is to be our lot, we must not think it strange when it comes (1 Peter 4:12), but we may hear our Master say to us, *"But these things have I told you, that when the time shall come, ye may remember that I told you of them"* (John 16:4), and, *"If it were not so, I would have told you [that also]"* (John 14:2). When it happens to you, beloved, may you be able to respond, "This is just as Jesus Christ said it would be."

Christ's first disciples, if they ventured out into the streets of Jerusalem after their Savior's crucifixion while His body was in Joseph's tomb, must have found it very trying to hear the jests and jeers of those who had put the Nazarene to death. "That is the end of Him now," they cheered. "His deception is exposed, and His disciples—those poor, foolish fanatics—will soon come to their senses now, and the whole thing will collapse." That was exactly what Jesus said would happen: *"Ye shall weep and lament, but the world shall rejoice."*

God's Remedy for Our Sorrow

Now, what was the Savior's cure for all this? It was the fact that this trial was to last only for a little while—for a very little while. In the case of His first disciples, it was only to last for a few days, and then it would be over, for they would hear the joyful announcement, *"The Lord is risen indeed, and hath appeared to Simon"* (Luke 24:34).

So is it to be with you and with me, dear brothers and sisters in Christ. Our sorrows are all, like ourselves, mortal. There are no immortal sorrows for immortal saints. They come, but, blessed be God, they also go. Like birds of the air, they fly over our heads, but they cannot make their abode in our souls. We suffer today, but we will rejoice tomorrow. *"Weeping may endure for a night, but joy cometh in the morning"* (Psalm 30:5).

However, for that laughing sinner, what weeping and wailing will be his portion unless he repents and weeps in penitence over his many sins! The prosperity of the wicked is like a thin layer of ice on which they always stand in peril. In a moment, they may be brought down to destruction, and the place that knew them will know them no more forever. Our weeping is soon to end, but their weeping will never end. Our joy will be forever, but their joy will speedily come to an end. Look a little ahead, Christian pilgrims, for you will soon have passed through *"the valley of the shadow of death"* (Psalm 23:4). You will then come into the land where even that shadow can never fall across your pathway again.

In speaking these comforting words to His disciples, Jesus made use of this memorable sentence: *"Your sorrow shall be turned into joy."* As I read the whole passage, I pondered over those words and tried to find out their meaning. Perhaps you think, as you glance at them, that they mean that the man who was sorrowful would be joyous. That is a portion of their meaning, but they mean much more than that. They literally and actually mean exactly what is stated—your sorrow itself will be turned into joy—not your sorrow is to be taken away and joy put in its place, but rather the very sorrow that now grieves you so will be turned into joy.

God's Transformation of Sorrow into Joy

This is a very wonderful transformation. Only the God who works great marvels could possibly accomplish it and could, somehow, not only take away the bitterness and give sweetness in its place, but also turn the bitterness itself into sweetness.

That glorious conversion is to be the subject of our present study. I am glad to have an apt illustration of this theme in the observance of Communion, which is the highest act of Christian fellowship and unity for many of us. You know that the Lord's Supper is not at all a funeral gathering, but it is a sacred festival, in which we restfully sit, relaxing and enjoying ourselves as at a banquet. But, what are the provisions for this feast, and what do they represent? That bread, that wine—what do they mean? My friends, they represent sorrow—sorrow even unto death. The bread, apart from the wine, represents the flesh of Christ separated from His blood, and thus they set forth death. The broken bread represents the flesh of Christ bruised, marred, suffering, full of anguish. The wine represents Christ's blood poured out upon the cross, amid the agony that ended only with His death. Yet, these emblems of sorrow and suffering furnish us with our great feast of love. This is indeed joy arising out of sorrow! The festival is itself the ordained memorial of the greatest grief that was ever endured on earth. As you gather around the Lord's table, you can see in these outward emblems that sorrow is turned into joy.

Our Sorrow over the Lord Turned into Joy

If you will keep that picture in your mind's eye, it will help me to bring out the full meaning of the text. My first point is this: our sorrow about our blessed Lord is now turned into joy. The very things that make us grieve concerning Him are the things that make us rejoice concerning Him.

Sorrow over His Testing

This first comes to pass when we look upon Him as tempted, tried, and tested in a thousand ways. No sooner did He rise from the waters of baptism than He was led into the desert to be tempted by the Devil. We grieve to think that, for our sakes, He had to bear the brunt of a fierce duel with the Prince of Darkness. We see that He was tempted and tried and tested all His life, this way and that—sometimes by a Pharisee, sometimes by a faithless disciple. All kinds of temptations were brought to bear upon Him, for He "*was in all points tempted like as we are, yet without sin*" (Hebrews 4:15).

Joy in His Sinless Character

Yet, oh, how thankful we are to know that Christ was thus tempted, for those very temptations helped to prove the sinlessness of His character. How could we know what is in a man who has never been tested and tried? However, our Lord was tested at every point, and at no point did He fail. It is established, beyond all question or doubt, that Jesus Christ is the Lamb of God, "*without blemish and without spot*" (1 Peter 1:19).

You cannot tell what a man's strength of character is unless he is tried; there must be some process to develop the excellence that lies hidden in his nature. We ought to rejoice and bless God that our Savior was passed, like silver, through the furnace seven times (Psalm 12:6); and, like gold, He was tried again and again in the crucible, in the hottest part of the furnace. Yet, no impurity was found in Him, only precious metal, without a particle of alloy. In this we rejoice. He *"was in all points tempted like as we are, yet without sin."* He was assailed by Satan and repudiated by sinners, yet He was found faultless to the end. Thus, our joy arises out of what would otherwise have made us mourn.

Sorrow over His Sufferings

Further, beloved, remember that the griefs and trials of our Lord not only manifested His sinless character, but they also made Him fit for the priestly office that He has undertaken on our behalf. The Captain of our salvation was made *"perfect through sufferings"* (Hebrews 2:10). It is necessary that He, who would truly be a benefactor to mankind, should know and understand men thoroughly. How can He sympathize with us in our sorrows unless He has, at least to some extent, felt as we do? So, our merciful and faithful High Priest is one who can be *"touched with the feeling of our infirmities"* (Hebrews 4:15), seeing that He was tempted and tried even as we are.

Joy in His Sympathetic Understanding

I think that, if I had been alive at the time and if it had been in my power, I would have spared my Lord many of his griefs, and many of you would say the same. He should have never needed to say, *"Foxes have holes, and the birds of the air have nests; but the Son of man hath not where to lay his head"* (Matthew 8:20), for you would gladly have given Him the best room in your house. Oh, but then, the poor would have missed that gracious word, which, I have no doubt, has often comforted them when they have been homeless and forlorn.

You would not have allowed Christ, if you could have helped it, to be weary and worn and hungry and thirsty. You would have liberally supplied all His needs to the utmost of your power. But, then, He would not have been so fully in sympathy as He now is with those who have to endure the direst straits of poverty, since He has passed through an experience similar to theirs. What joy it is to a hurting soul to know that Jesus has gone that way long before!

I had a great grief that struck me down to the very dust, but I looked up and saw His face, which was marred more than any other. I rose to my feet in hope and joyful confidence, and I said, "Are You, my Lord, here where I am? Have You suffered thus, and did You endure far more than I can ever know of grief and brokenness of heart? Then, Savior, I rejoice and bless Your holy name." I know that you, dear friend, must have often grieved over your Savior's suffering, though you have been, at the same time, glad to remember that He passed through it all. He thus became our matchless Comforter, *"who can have compassion on the ignorant, and on them that are out of the way"* (Hebrews 5:2). Because of the very experience through which He passed, *"for in that he himself hath suffered being tempted, he is able to succour them that are tempted"* (Hebrews 2:18).

Sorrow over His Death

The meaning of our text verse comes out even more clearly when we think of the sorrows to which our Lord had been referring, which ended in His death. Oh, the griefs of Jesus when He laid down His life for His sheep! Have you not sometimes said, or at least thought, that the ransom price was too costly for such insignificant creatures as we are? Think of the agony and bloody sweat, the scourging, the spitting, the shame, the hounding through the streets, the piercing of the hands and feet, the mockery, the vinegar, the gall, the *"Eloi, Eloi, lama sabachthani?"* (Mark 15:34), and all the other horrors and terrors that gathered around the cross.

Joy in Our Salvation

We wish that they might never have happened, and yet the fact that they did happen brings to us bliss unspeakable. Our greatest joy is to know that Jesus bled and died upon the tree. How else could our sin be put away? How else could we, who are God's enemies, be reconciled and brought near to Him? How else could heaven be made for us? We might, from one aspect of Christ's sufferings, chant a mournful dirge at the foot of the cross. Yet, before we have done more than just commence the sad strain, we perceive the blessed results that come to the children of men through Christ's death. So we lay down our instruments of mourning, take up the harp and the trumpet, and sound forth glad notes of rejoicing and thanksgiving.

Joy in Christ's Wondrous Victory

Our sorrow about Christ's death is also turned into joy, not only because we derive the greatest possible benefit from it, but also because Jesus Himself, by His death, achieved such wonders.

His precious body—that fair lily, all stained with crimson stripes, from which flowed His heart's blood—must have been a pitiful sight for anyone to see. I wonder how an artist could ever paint the scenes of Christ's body being taken down from the cross or being prepared for the sepulcher. Such sorrowful sights for artists to spend themselves upon: Jesus, the final Conqueror, lying in the grave, the shroud of death wrapped about Him who once wore the purple of the universe!

However, we scarcely have time to sorrow over these facts before we recollect that the death of Christ was the death of sin; the death of Christ was the overthrow of Satan; the death of Christ was the death of death, and out of His tomb we hear that pealing trumpet note,

> O death, where is thy sting? O grave, where is thy victory? The sting of death is sin; and the strength of sin is the law. But thanks be to God, which giveth us the victory through our Lord Jesus Christ.   (1 Corinthians 15:55–57)

I am glad that Jesus fought with Satan in the garden and vanquished him. I am glad that He fought with sin upon the cross and destroyed it. I am glad that He fought with grim death in that dark hour, and that He seized it by the throat and held it captive. I am glad that He entered the gloomy sepulcher, because He rifled it of all its terrors for His loved ones, tore its iron bars away, and set His people free. So, you see, it is all gladness, even as He said to His disciples, "*Your sorrow shall be turned into joy.*"

Joy in His Glory

Whatever else there may be of sorrow that comes out of Christ's cross, we may all be glad of it, for now, Christ Himself is the more glorious because of it. It is true that nothing could add to His glory as God. However, seeing that He assumed our nature and became man as well as God, He added to His glory by all the shame He bore. There is not a reproach that pierced His heart that did not make Him more beautiful. There is not a line of sorrow that furrowed His face that did not make Him more lovely. His marred countenance is more to be admired by us than all the magnificence of earthly beauty.

The Son of God was always superlatively beautiful; His beauty was such that it held the angels spellbound as they looked upon Him. The sun and moon and stars were dim compared with the brightness of His eyes. Heaven and earth could not find His equal. If all heaven had been sold, it could not have purchased this precious diamond. Yet, the setting of the diamond has made Christ appear even brighter than before—the setting of His humanity, His sufferings, His pangs, His shameful death—this setting has made His deity shine all the more resplendent. The plant that sprang from *"a root of Jesse"* (Isaiah 11:10) is now the Plant of renown. He who was despised at Nazareth is now glorified in heaven, and all the more glorified because, between Nazareth and paradise, He was *"despised and rejected of men; a man of sorrows, and acquainted with grief"* (Isaiah 53:3). Blessed Savior, we rejoice that You have gained glory by all Your sorrows, for *"wherefore God also hath highly exalted [You], and given [You] a name which is above every name"* (Philippians 2:9).

The Sorrows of the Church Turned to Joy

Now I want to remind you that, not only has Christ's suffering been turned into joy, but the sorrows of the whole church have also been turned into joy. Collectively, the members of the body of Christ have suffered greatly in order that the Gospel might be disseminated down through the ages.

The Sorrows of Persecution

In speaking of the sorrows of the persecuted church of Christ, I will not compare them to the sorrows of her Lord; but if anything could be comparable to the suffering of the Bridegroom, it would be the suffering of His bride. Think of the early ages of the church of God under the Roman persecutions. Think of the church of Christ in England during the Marian persecution. My blood runs cold as I read of what the saints of God have suffered. I have often set *Foxe's Book of Martyrs* upon the shelf and thought that I could not read it any longer, because it is such an accurate account of what human nature can bear when faith in Christ sustains it.

The Joys of Honoring Christ

Yet, friends, you should not grieve that the martyrs suffered as they did. Or, if you are sorrowful, that very sorrow is turned into joy at the remembrance of how Christ has been glorified through the sufferings of His saints.

Even our poor humanity looks more lovely when we recall what it has endured for Christ's sake. When I think of the honor of being a martyr for the truth, I confess that I would sooner be in that position than be the angel Gabriel. I think it would be far better to go to heaven from the stakes than to have always been in heaven.

What honor it has brought to Christ that poor, feeble men could love Him so much that they could bleed and die for Him! Yes, and women, too, like brave Anne Askew, who, after they had racked her until they had put every bone out of joint, was still courageous enough to argue on behalf of her dear Lord. When they thought that her womanly weakness would make her back down, she seemed stronger than any man might have been. She defied them to do their worst as she said to her persecutors,

> I am not she that lists
> My anchor to let fall
> For every drizzling mist;
> My ship is substantial.

The church of God may well rejoice as she thinks of the noble army of martyrs who praise the Lord on high. Among the sweetest notes that ascend even in heaven are the songs that come from the white-robed throng who shed their blood rather than deny their Lord.

The Sorrows of Heretical Opposition

The church of Christ has also passed through fierce fires of opposition, as well as of persecution. Heresy after heresy has raged. Men have arisen who have denied one or another of the doctrines taught in the Scriptures. Every time these oppositions have come, certain feeble folk in the church have been greatly alarmed.

The Joys of the Victorious Truth

However, in looking back upon all of the heresies up to the present, I think that they are causes for joy rather than sorrow. Whenever what is supposed to be a new heresy comes up, I say to myself, "Oh, I know you; I remember reading about you. You are just an old pair of shoes, worn by heresy many hundreds of years ago, which were thrown on the trash heap. You have been picked up and cleaned up a little, and brought forth as if you were new."

I bless the Lord that, at this moment, there scarcely remains any doctrine to be defended for the first time. They have all been fought over so fiercely in the past that there is hardly any point of doctrine that our noble forefathers did not defend. Moreover, they did their work so well that we can frequently use their weapons for the defense of the truth today.

Who would wish to have kept the Word of God from going through this furnace of opposition? It is *"as silver tried in a furnace of earth, purified seven times"* (Psalm 12:6). Philosophers have tried you, O precious Book, but you were not found wanting! Atheists have tried you; sneering skeptics have tried you. They have all passed you through the fire, but not even the smell of fire is upon you to this day. In this we rejoice now and will rejoice. The day will come when the present heresies and opposition will only be recorded on the page of history as things for our successors to rejoice over, just as we now rejoice over the past victories of the truth of God.

The Sorrows and Joys of Difficult Obstacles

Once again, dear friends, not only is it so with the persecutions and oppositions of the church of Christ, but the church's difficulties have also become themes of rejoicing. As I look at the world at the present time, it does seem an impossible thing that the nations of the earth should ever be converted to Christ. It is impossible as far as man alone is concerned, yet God has commanded the Christian church to evangelize the world: *"Go ye therefore, and teach all nations"* (Matthew 28:19). Someone complains that the church is too feeble and that its adherents are too few to accomplish such a task as this. The fewer the fighters, the greater their share of glory when the victory is won. In order to overcome indifference, idolatry, legalism, atheism, occultism, Hinduism, and Islam, the battle must be a very stern one, but who wants Christ's followers to fight only little battles? My friends, let us thank God that our foes are so numerous. It matters not how many there may be of them; there are only the more to be destroyed. What did David say concerning his adversaries? *"They compassed me about; yea, they compassed me about: but in the name of the LORD I will destroy them"* (Psalm 118:11).

When the Last Day finally comes and Jehovah's banner is at last unfurled, because the book of the wars of the Lord has reached its last page, it will be a grand thing to tell the story of the whole campaign. Then it will be known to everyone that the fight for the faith was not a mere skirmish against a few feeble folk, nor was it a brief battle that began and ended in an hour, but it was a tremendous conflict *"against principalities, against powers, against the rulers of the darkness of this world, against spiritual wickedness in high places"* (Ephesians 6:12). They will have gathered together, thick as the clouds in the day of tempest, but out of heaven our Lord Himself will have thundered; He will have battled and scattered them, and they will have flown before Him *"as chaff before the wind"* (Psalm 35:5).

Our Personal Sorrows Turned into Joy

Now, to come down from those high themes to minor matters, our own personal *"sorrow shall be turned into joy."* When I think of the sorrows of Christ and the sorrows of His church as a whole, I say to myself, "What tiny pinpricks are our griefs compared with the great gash in the Savior's side and the many scars that adorn His church today!" But, dear friends, whatever our own sorrows may be, they will also be turned into joy.

Sometimes we are allowed to witness this wonderful transformation for ourselves. Poor old Jacob sorrowed greatly when he thought that he had lost his favorite son Joseph. When Jacob saw Joseph's coat of many colors, all torn and bloodied, he said, *"An evil beast hath devoured him; Joseph is without doubt rent in pieces"* (Genesis 37:33), and he wrung his hands and wept bitterly for many a day over his lost son. Then came the famine, and the poor old man was dreadfully alarmed concerning his large family. Jacob needed to send some of his sons into Egypt to buy food. When he sent them there, they did not all come back; Simeon had been detained as a hostage. Further, the lord of the land had said that they would not see Simeon's face again unless they brought Benjamin back with them—Benjamin, Jacob's dear and only remaining child of his beloved Rachel. He could not bear the thought of parting with Benjamin only to lose him, too. For that reason, Jacob said to his sons, *"Me have ye bereaved of my children: Joseph is not, and Simeon is not, and ye will take Benjamin away: all these things are against me"* (Genesis 42:36).

Poor Jacob, how mistaken he was! Why, all of these circumstances were as favorable for him as they could possibly be. His dear Joseph, down in Egypt, was sitting next to Pharaoh on the throne, ready to provide for his father and all of the family during the time of famine. Then, there was the famine itself that made Jacob send down to Egypt. Because of the famine, Jacob found out that Joseph was still alive, journeyed and saw his face again, and confessed that the Lord had dealt graciously with him (Genesis 33:11). You dear children of God, who fret and are troubled, should carry out Cowper's good advice:

> Judge not the Lord by feeble sense,
> But trust Him for His grace;
> Behind a frowning providence
> He hides a smiling face.

You have quite enough to cry over without fretting concerning things that you will rejoice over someday. The Lord will put your tears into His bottle (Psalm 56:8); when He shows them to you by and by, I think you will say, "How foolish I was ever to shed them, because the very thing I wept over was really a cause for rejoicing, if I could have only seen a little way ahead." It is like that sometimes in God's providence, as you will discover over and over again between here and heaven.

Our Sorrows Drive Us to God

Our sorrows, dear friends, are turned into joy in many different ways. For instance, there are some of us who are such independent, thoughtless children that we never seem to come close to our heavenly Father unless some sorrow drives us to Him. We ought to be more with Him in days of sunshine, if possible, than in days of storm, but it is not always so. It is said that the more you whip some dogs, the more they love you. I should not like to try that plan even on a dog, but I fear that some of us are very much like dogs in that respect, if the saying is true. When we have a great trouble or get a sharp cut, we seem to wake up and say, "O Lord, I forgot You when all was going smoothly; I wandered from You then, but now I must come back to You."

We often develop a special softness of heart and mellowness of spirit only through being tried and troubled. When that is the case, you and I have great cause to rejoice in our sorrows. They draw us nearer to God and bring us into a closer and more careful walk with Him. When they draw us away from self-complacency and self-sufficiency and worldliness, our sorrows are immediately turned into joy—if we are wise men and women.

Our Sorrows Reveal God's Promises

Again, there is no doubt that, to many, sorrow is a great means of opening the eyes to the preciousness of the promises of God. I believe that we will never get to know the meaning of some of God's promises until we have been placed in the circumstances for which those promises were written. Certain objects in nature can only be seen from certain points of view, and there are precious things in the covenant of grace that can only be perceived from the deep places of trouble. Well, then, if your trouble brings you into a position where you can understand more of the lovingkindness of the Lord, you will be very thankful that you were ever put there, for you will thus find your sorrow turned into joy.

Sorrow Brings Us into Deeper Fellowship

Again, sorrow often gives us further fellowship with Christ. There are times when we can say, "Now, Lord, we can sympathize with You better than we ever did before, for we have felt somewhat as You did in Your agony here below." We have sometimes felt as though that prophecy had been fulfilled to us, "*Ye shall drink indeed of my cup, and be baptized with the baptism that I am baptized with*" (Matthew 20:23). For instance, if friends forsake you, if he who eats bread with you turns against you, you can say, "Now, Lord, I know a little better what You felt when Judas so basely betrayed You." You cannot so fully comprehend the griefs of Christ unless, in your humble measure, you have to pass through a somewhat similar experience. However, when you perceive that you can sympathize more with Christ because of your own sorrow, then, certainly your sorrow is turned into joy.

Sorrows Make Us Partners with Christ

Sorrow also gives us fellowship with our Lord in another way: we feel as if we have become partners with Christ in our trials. Here is a cross, and I have to carry one end of it. However, I look around and see that my Lord is carrying the heavier end of it. Then it is a very sweet sorrow to carry the cross in partnership with Christ. Rutherford wrote in one of his letters, "When Christ's dear child is carrying a burden, it often happens that Christ says, 'Halves, My love,' and carries half of it for him." It is indeed sweet when it is so.

If there is a ring of fire on your finger, and that ring means that you are married to Christ, you may well be willing to wear it no matter what suffering it may cause you. Those were blessed nails that fastened you to the cross, even though they were nails of iron that went right through your flesh, for they kept you all the closer to your Lord.

Our motto must be, "Anywhere with Jesus; nowhere without Jesus." Anywhere with Jesus? Yes, even into Nebuchadnezzar's furnace. When we have the Son of God with us, the glowing coals cannot hurt us. They become a bed of roses to us when He is there. Where Jesus is, our sorrow is turned into joy.

Sorrows of Death Swallowed Up in Victory

I must not fail to remind you that there is a time coming when *"the sorrows of death"* (Psalm 18:4) will get a grip on us. I want you, brothers and sisters, to understand that, unless the Lord comes first, we will not escape the sorrow of dying, but it will be turned into joy. It has been my great pleasure to see many Christians in their last moments on earth, and I am sure that the merriest people I have ever seen have been dying saints. I have been to wedding feasts. I have seen the joy of young people in their youth. I have seen the joy of the merchant when he has made a prosperous venture. I have myself experienced joys of various kinds, but I have never seen any joy that I have so envied as that which has sparkled in the eyes of departing believers.

Just now, there rises up in my mind's eye a vision of the two eyes of a poor consumptive girl—oh, how bright they were! I heard that she was close to death's door, so I went to try to comfort her. To comfort her? Oh, dear, she needed no comforting from me! Every now and then, she would burst forth into a verse of sacred song; and when she stopped, she would tell me how precious Jesus was to her, what loving visits He had already paid her, and how soon she expected to be forever with Him. There was not, in all the palaces of Europe or in all the mansions of the wealthy or in all the ballrooms of the affluent, such a merry and joyous spirit as I saw shining through the bright eyes of that poor shadow of a girl, who had very little here below, but who had so much laid up for her in heaven that it did not matter what she had here. Yes, beloved, your sorrow will be turned into joy.

Many of you will not even know that you are dying. You will shut your eyes on earth and open them in heaven. Some of you may be dreading death, for there is still a measure of unbelief remaining in you. But, in your case also, "*death* [will be] *swallowed up in victory*" (1 Corinthians 15:54). Just as when some people have to take very bitter medicine, it is put into some sweet liquid, and they drink it down without tasting the bitterness, so will it be with all of us who are trusting in the Lord Jesus Christ when we have to drink our last potion. In a few more days or weeks or months or years—it does not matter which, for it will be a very short time at the most—all of us who love the Lord will be with Him where He is, to behold His glory and to share it with Him forever.

Have any of you any sorrows that you still wish to talk about? Some of you are very poor, and others of you are very much tried and troubled in many ways. But, my dear friends, when you and I get to heaven—and we will all do so before long—I think you will have the best of it. If there is any truth in that line, "The deeper their sorrows, the louder they'll sing," the more sorrows you have had, the more you will sing. Nobody enjoys wealth like a man who has been poor. Nobody enjoys health like a man who has been sick. I think that the most pleasant days I ever spend are those that follow a long illness, when I at last begin to go outside and drink in the sweet, fresh air again. And, oh, what joy it will be to you poor ones and you sick ones and you tried ones to get into the land where all is plentiful, where all is peaceful, where all is joyful, where all is holy! You will be there soon—some of you will be there very soon. Dr. Watts penned it this way:

> There, on a green and flowery mount,
> Our weary souls shall sit,
> And with transporting joys recount
> The labors of our feet.

This simply means that the very sorrows we pass through in our earthly pilgrimage will constitute topics for joyful conversation in heaven. I do not doubt that it will be so. In heaven, we will be as glad of our troubles as of our mercies. Perhaps then it will appear to us that God never loved us so much as when He chastened and tried us. When we get home to glory, we will be like children, having grown up and matured, who sometimes say to a wise parent, "Father, I have forgotten about the holidays you gave me; I have forgotten about the pocket money you gave; I have forgotten about a great many sweet things that I very much liked when I was a child; but I have never forgotten the whipping that you gave me when I did wrong, for it altogether saved me from turning out badly. Dear father, I know you did not like to do it, but I am very grateful to you for it now—more grateful for that whipping than for all the candy and treats that you gave me." Likewise, when we get home to heaven, I have no doubt that we will feel, and perhaps say, "Lord, we are grateful to You for everything, but most of all for our sorrows. We see that had You left us unchastised, we would never have been what we now are. Thank You, for You have turned our sorrows into joy."

As for you who are not believers in the Lord Jesus Christ, I want you to ponder most solemnly these few words and to carry them with you in your heart. If you remain as you are, your joys will be turned into sorrows. God grant that they may not be, for Jesus Christ's sake!

6

A HARP OF TEN STRINGS

And Mary said, My soul doth magnify the Lord, and my spirit hath rejoiced in God my Saviour. For he hath regarded the low estate of his handmaiden: for, behold, from henceforth all generations shall call me blessed.For he that is mighty hath done to me great things; and holy is his name. And his mercy is on them that fear him from generation to generation. He hath showed strength with his arm; he hath scattered the proud in the imagination of their hearts. He hath put down the mighty from their seats, and exalted them of low degree. He hath filled the hungry with good things; and the rich he hath sent empty away. He hath holpen his servant Israel, in remembrance of his mercy; as he spake to our fathers, to Abraham, and to his seed for ever.
—Luke 1:46–55

It seems very clear in this passage that Mary was not beginning a new behavior, for she spoke in the present tense, in a tense that seems to have been present for some time in her life: "*My soul doth magnify the Lord.*" Ever since she had received the wonderful tidings that God had chosen her for the high position of being the mother of the Messiah, she had begun to magnify the Lord.

When once a soul has a deep sense of God's mercy and begins to magnify Him, there is no end to his worship. It grows by what it feeds upon: the more you magnify God, the more you can magnify Him. The higher you live, the more you can see. Your view of God is increased in its extent. Where before you praised Him a little at the bottom of the hill, when you get nearer to the top of His exceeding goodness, you lift up the strain still more loudly, and your soul more fully and exultantly magnifies the Lord.

The Meaning of Magnification

"*My soul doth magnify the Lord.*" What does it mean? The usual signification of the word *magnify* is to make great or to make to appear great. We say that when we use a microscope, it magnifies so many times. The insect is the same small, tiny thing, but it is increased in size in our apprehension.

The word *magnify* is also very suitable in our present situation. We cannot make God greater than He is, nor can we have any conception of His actual greatness. He is infinitely above our highest thoughts. When we meditate upon His attributes,

> Imagination's utmost stretch
> In wonder dies away.

We magnify our Lord by having higher, larger, truer conceptions of Him— by making known His mighty acts and praising His glorious name—so that others, too, may exalt Him in their thoughts. This is what Mary was doing: she was a woman who was given to pondering. Those who heard what the shepherds said concerning the holy child Jesus wondered, but "*Mary kept all these things, and pondered them in her heart*" (Luke 2:19). They wondered; Mary pondered. It is only the change of a letter, but it makes a great difference in the attitude of the soul, a change from a vague flash of interest to a deep attention of heart. She pondered: she weighed the matter; she turned it over in her mind; she thought about it; she estimated its value and result. She was like that other Mary, a meditative woman who quietly waited at her Lord's feet to hear His gracious words and to drink them in with yearning faith.

It is no idle occupation thus to get alone, and in your own heart, to magnify the Lord: to make Him great to your mind, to your affections; great in your memory, great in your expectations. It is one of the grandest exercises of the renewed nature. You need not, at such a time, think of the deep questions of Scripture. You may leave the complex doctrines to wiser minds, if you will.

However, if your very soul is bent on making God great in your own comprehension, you will be spending time in one of the most profitable ways possible for a child of God. Depend upon it, there are countless holy influences that flow from the habitual maintenance of great thoughts of God, just as there are incalculable mischiefs that flow from our small thoughts of Him. The root of false theology is belittling God, and the essence of true divinity is enhancing God, magnifying Him, and enlarging our concepts of His majesty and His glory to the utmost.

Yet, Mary did not mean, by magnifying the Lord, merely to extol Him in her own thoughts. Being a true poetess, she intended to magnify the Lord by her words. No, I must correct that—she did not intend to do it, she had been doing it all along. She was doing it when she came, panting and breathless, into her cousin Elizabeth's house. She said, *"My soul doth magnify the Lord."* I am now in such a favored condition that I cannot open my mouth to talk to you, Elizabeth, without speaking of my Lord. My soul now seems filled with thoughts of Him. I must speak, first of all, about Him, and say such things of His grace and power as may help you, my godly older sister, still to think even grander thoughts of God than you have ever before enjoyed. *'My soul doth magnify the Lord.'"*

Mary's Humility

We must recall the fact that Mary was highly distinguished and honored. No other woman was ever blessed as she was; perhaps no other could have borne the honor that was put upon her—to be the mother of the human nature of our Savior. It was the highest possible honor that could be put upon mortal flesh. At the appointed time, the Lord knew where to find a guileless, lowly woman who could be entrusted with such a gift and yet not seek to pilfer away His glory. She was not proud; no, it is a false heart that steals the revenues of God and buys the intoxicating cup of self-congratulation with the looted gain.

The more God gives to a true heart, the more that heart gives back to Him. Like Peter's boat, which sank more deeply in the water, the more fully it was laden with fish, God's true children sink in their own esteem as they are honored by their Lord. God's gifts, when He gives grace with them, do not puff us up; rather, they build us up.

A humble and lowly estimate of ourselves is added when we have a greater esteem of our Lord. The more God gives you, the more you should magnify Him and not yourself. This should be your rule: *"He must increase, but I must decrease"* (John 3:30). Become less and less. Be the Lord's humble servant, yet be bold and confident in your praise of Him who has done great things for you. Henceforth and forever, let this be the one description of your life: *"'My soul doth magnify the Lord.'* I have nothing else to do anymore but to magnify Him and to rejoice in God my Savior."

Mary's Song

An entire book might be profitably produced were I to attempt to teach about each part of Mary's song; but with quite another purpose in mind, I am going to present it to you as a whole. As I put before you this instrument of ten strings, I will ask you, just for a moment or two, to place your fingers on each of the strings as they are indicated. See if you can wake some melody to the praise of the great King, some harmony in His honor. Discover if you can, right now, how to magnify the Lord and rejoice in God your Savior.

Martin Luther used to say that the glory of Scripture was to be found in the pronouns; this is certainly true of our text. Look at the personal touch of them, how it comes over and over again! *"My soul doth magnify the Lord, and my spirit hath rejoiced in God my Saviour."* At a festival at our orphanage, I gave our many friends who were gathered there several reasons why everyone should contribute to the support of the children. "Indeed," I said, "no-body ought to go off the grounds without giving something." I was struck with one brother, who had no money with him, but who brought me his watch and chain. "Oh," I said, "do not give me these things, for they will sell for so little compared with their value." However, he insisted upon my keeping them and said, "I will redeem them tomorrow, but I cannot go away without giving something now."

How glad I would be if every child of God should be as earnest in adoration! As we enter our churches to worship, if only we could say, "I am going to give some praise to God at this service: out of some of those strings I will get music, perhaps out of them all. I will endeavor with my whole heart to say, at some portion of the service and from some point of view, '*My soul doth magnify the Lord*'!"

Do I hear you whisper, "My soul is very heavy"? Lift it up, then, by praising the Lord; begin a psalm, even if at first the tune must be in a minor key. Soon the strain will change, and the "Miserere" will become a "Hallelujah Chorus."

The First String of Joy

The first string that Mary seemed to touch—and that, I trust, we may also reach with the hand of faith—is that of the great joy to be found in the Lord. "*My soul doth magnify the Lord, and my spirit hath rejoiced in God my Saviour.*" Let us bless God that our religion is not one of gloom. I do not know of any commandment anywhere in Scripture that says, "Groan in the Lord always, and again I say, Groan." From the morose conduct of some Christians, we might surmise that they must have altered their New Testaments in that particular passage and thus woefully changed the glory of the original verse: "*Rejoice in the Lord alway: and again I say, Rejoice*" (Philippians 4:4).

The first I ever truly knew of my Master was when I found myself at the foot of His cross, with the great burden that had crushed me effectually gone. I looked around for it, wondering where it could be, and, behold, it was tumbling down into His sepulcher. I have never seen it since, blessed be His name, nor do I ever want to see it again! Well do I remember the leaps of joy I did when I first found that all my burden of guilt had been borne by Him and was buried in the depths of His grave.

Many days have passed since then;
Many changes I have seen!

I have been to many different wells to find water, but when I have drawn and tasted from them, the liquid has been as brackish as the waters of Marah. Yet, whenever I have gone to this well—"*God my Saviour*"—I have never drawn one drop that was not sweet and refreshing. He who truly knows God must be glad in Him. To abide in His house is to be praising Him continually. Yes, we may rejoice in Him all the day long.

A very notable word is that which was found in the mouth of David: *"God my exceeding joy"* (Psalm 43:4). Other things may give us pleasure; we may be happy in the gifts of God and in His creatures, but God Himself, the Spring of all our joys, is greater than them all. Therefore, *"Delight thyself also in the Lord"* (Psalm 37:4). This is His command, and is it not a lovely one? Let no one say that the faith of the Christian is not to be exultant. It is to be a delight. So greatly does God desire us to rejoice in Him that to the command is added a promise: *"and he shall give thee the desires of thine heart."*

What a faith is ours, in which delight becomes a duty, in which to be happy is to be obedient to a command! Heathen religions exact not only self-denials of a proper kind and form, but tortures that men invent to accustom themselves to misery. However, in our holy faith, if we keep close to Christ, while it is true that we bear the cross, it is also true that the cross ceases to be a torture. In fact, it often bears us as we bear it. We discover in the service of our Master that His *"yoke is easy, and [His] burden is light"* (Matthew 11:30), and that, strange to say, His burden gives us rest, and His yoke gives us liberty. We have never had anything from our Master that has not ultimately led to our joy. Even when His rod has made us wince, He has intended it to work for our good, and such good it has produced. Praise Him, then, for such goodness.

Our faith is one of holy joy, especially regarding our Savior. The more we understand that glorious word *Savior*, the more are we ready to dance with delight. *"My spirit hath rejoiced in God my Saviour."* The good tidings of great joy have reached us; as we, by His grace, have believed them, He has saved us from sin and death and hell. He has not simply promised to do it someday, but He has already done it; we have been saved. Moreover, so many of us have entered into rest by faith in Him; salvation is to us a present experience at this very hour, although we still wait for the fullness of it to be revealed in the world to come.

Oh, come, let us rejoice in our Savior. Let us thank Him that we have so much for which to thank Him. Let us praise Him that there is so much that we may rejoice in, so much that we *must* rejoice in. Let us adore His dear name. Let us delight in the knowledge that He has so arranged the whole plan of salvation, that it is calculated to bring heaven to us while we are here and to bring us who are here into heaven hereafter. Therefore, we lift up our hearts because of the great joy that is laid up for us in God.

This is the first string of your heavenly harp. Touch it now. Think of all the joy you have had in God. Praise Him for all the holy mirth He has given you in His house, the bliss of communion with Him at His table, the delights of fellowship with Him in secret. Sing to Him with a grateful heart, saying, *"My soul doth magnify the Lord."*

The Second String of Christ's Deity

The second string we desire to lay our fingers upon is the Godhead of our Savior. *"My soul doth magnify the Lord."*

I do not have a little Lord. *"And my spirit hath rejoiced in God my Saviour."* I know that Jesus Christ is a man, and I rejoice in His humanity. But I will contend to the death for this truth: He is more than man, He is our Savior. One human being could not redeem another or give to God a ransom for his brother. An angel's arm could not bear the tremendous load of the disaster of the Fall, but Christ's arm is more than angelic. He whom we magnify as our Savior, *"being in the form of God, thought it not robbery to be equal with God"* (Philippians 2:6). When He undertook the wondrous task of our redemption, He brought the Godhead with Him to sustain Him in that more than Herculean labor: *"For in him dwelleth all the fulness of the Godhead bodily"* (Colossians 2:9).

Our trust is in Jesus Christ, very God of very God. We will never cease, not only to believe in Him, but also to speak of Him, rejoice in Him, and sing of Him as the incarnate Deity. What a frozen religion it is that does not have the Godhead of Christ in it! Surely, men who can pretend to receive any comfort out of a faith that does not have the divine Savior as its very center must be of a very self-assured and imaginative temperament. I would just as soon consider going to an iceberg to warm myself as to a religion of that kind to find comfort. Nobody can ever magnify Christ too much for me, nor can they say too much in praise of His wisdom or of His power. Every divine attribute ascribed to Christ makes me lift up a new song to Him; for, whatever He may be to others, to me He is God *"who is over all, God blessed for ever"* (Romans 9:5).

I wish that I could sing these words instead of writing them—words about God the Son who was with the Father before all worlds began; whose delights, even then, were with the sons of men in the prospect of their creation. I wish that I could tell the wonderful story of how our Savior entered into covenant with God on the behalf of His people and pledged Himself to pay the debts of those His Father gave to Him. He undertook to gather into one fold all the sheep whom He promised to purchase with His own precious blood. He con-tracted to bring them back from all their wanderings and draw them together to graze on the hilltops of the Delectable Mountains at His Father's feet. This He vowed to do, and He has gone about His task with a zeal that has clothed him as a cloak. Moreover, He will achieve the divine purpose before He delivers up the kingdom to God, even the Father. *"He shall not fail nor be discouraged"* (Isaiah 42:4).

It is our delight to hear this Son of God, this wondrous Being in His com-plex nature as our Mediator, exalted and extolled and very highly elevated. Have you not sometimes felt that if your minister preached more about Jesus Christ, you would be very glad to hear him? I hope that is your inclination, yet I am afraid that we talk a great deal about many things rather than about our Master. Come, let me hear of Him; sing to me or talk to me of Jesus, whose name is honey in the mouth, music in the ear, and heaven in the heart. Oh, for more praise of His holy name! Yes, some of us can touch this string and sing with Mary, *"My soul doth magnify the Lord, and my spirit hath rejoiced in God my Saviour."*

The Third String of Jesus' Condescension

The third string has softer, sweeter music in it, and it may suit some of us better than the more sublime themes that we have already touched. Let us sing and magnify the Lord's loving condescension, just as Mary did when she went on to say, *"For he hath regarded the low estate of his handmaiden."* Here is some-thing to sing about, for ours was not only a low estate, but perhaps some would have had to say, like Gideon, *"My family is poor and I am the least in my father's house"* (Judges 6:15). Like him, you would have been passed over by most people. Possibly even in your own family, you were considered a nobody: if someone uttered a jest, you were sure to be the butt of it; and generally you were misun-derstood and your actions misinterpreted. This was a trying experience for you, but from this you have been gloriously delivered. It may have been that, like Joseph, you were a little dreamy, and perhaps you were a trifle too fond of telling your dreams. Yet, though you were much ridiculed because of this, the Lord at length raised your head up above those around you. It may have been that your lot in life was cast among the very poorest and lowest of mankind, yet the Lord has looked upon you in infinite compassion and saved you. Will you not, then, magnify Him?

If Christ wanted a special people, why did He not choose the kings and princes and nobles of the earth? Instead of them, He takes the poor and makes them to know the wonders of His dying love. Instead of selecting the wisest men in the world, He takes even the most foolish and instructs them in the things of the kingdom.

> Wonders of grace to God belong,
> Repeat His mercies in your song.

All of us who have been saved by grace must strike an even tenderer note, for we were sinful as well as lowly. We went astray like lost sheep; we therefore magnify the Lord, who bought us and sought us and brought us back to His fold. It may be painful to remember what we once were, but it is good sometimes to go back in our thoughts to the time past when we lived in sin, in order that we may better appreciate the favor of which we have been made partakers.

When the apostle Paul wrote out a register of those who will not inherit the kingdom of God, he added, *"And such were some of you: but ye are washed, but ye are sanctified, but ye are justified in the name of the Lord Jesus, and by the Spirit of our God"* (1 Corinthians 6:11). Oh, let us bless the name of the Lord and magnify Him for this! Who else could have cleansed us from our sin? In what other fountain except the one open to the house of David could we have plunged to rid us of our awful defilement?

Christ stoops very low, for some of God's elect were once the most contemptible outcasts. Even when converted, many remained so in the estimate of the world, which sneers at humble Christians. If the followers of Christ happen to meet in some fine building and worship God with grand music and gorgeous ritual, then the people of the world put up with them. They may go even so far as to patronize them, although, even then, their respect is chiefly aroused, not on behalf of the people, but because of the fine building, the artistic music, and the caliber of the transportation. Quality vehicles are especially important to the world, for without a certain number of them parked in front of the church edifice, it is deemed utterly impossible to have a proper display of cultured Christianity.

The more God's people cling to the Lord, the less likely they are to be esteemed highly in the vulgar judgment of unholy men. Yet, the Lord has chosen people of such lowly estate, blessed be His name! It is a great wonder to me that the Lord ever chose some of you, but it is a far greater wonder that He should ever have chosen me! I can somehow understand His love for you, when I look at the gracious points in your character—although I am fully aware that they are only wrought by His grace—but I cannot begin to comprehend the love that He has displayed *"unto me, who am less than the least of all saints"* (Ephesians 3:8). You are probably thinking, "Oh! That is what I was going to say about myself." Yes, I know. I am trying to put it into your mind, so that we may all join in adoring gratitude. It is a miracle of mercy that He should have loved any of us, or that He stooped in His grace to raise such beggars from the dunghill to set us among the princes at His right hand (1 Samuel 2:8).

> Why was I made to hear Thy voice,
> And enter while there's room;
> When thousands make a wretched choice,
> And rather starve than come?

The Fourth String of God's Goodness

The next string, however, is the greatness of God's goodness, for Mary continued to sing: *"He hath regarded the low estate of his handmaiden: for, behold, from henceforth all generations shall call me blessed."* Oh, the Lord has done great things for His people! *"He that is mighty hath done to me great things; and holy is his name."*

God has made you blessed. You were once under the curse, but *"there is therefore now no condemnation [for you who] are in Christ Jesus"* (Romans 8:1). If He had allowed the curse to wither you like some lightning-blasted oak, you could not have questioned it. However, the gracious Lord has instead planted you by the rivers of water; He causes you to bring forth fruit in your season and your leaf not to wither (Psalm 1:3). *"The LORD hath done great things for us; whereof we are glad"* (Psalm 126:3).

To be lifted up from that *"horrible pit, out of the miry clay"* (Psalm 40:2), is such a great thing that we cannot measure it, but to be set upon that throne of mercy in Christ Jesus exceeds our highest thought. Who can measure that? Take your measuring line, and see if you can fathom the depth of such grace or gauge the height of such mercy. Will we be silent when we behold such marvelous lovingkindness? God forbid it! Let us break forth in our hearts now with joyous hallelujahs to Him who has done such wonderful things for us!

Think, beloved! You were blind, but He has made you see. You were lame, but He has made you leap. Worse than that, you were dead, but He has made you live. You were in prison, but He has set you free. Some of us were in the dungeon, with our feet fast in the stocks. Can I not well remember when I was bound in that inner prison, moaning and groaning, without any voice to comfort me or even a ray of light to cheer me in the darkness? And now that He has brought me out, will I forget to utter my deepest thanks? No, I will sing *"songs of deliverance"* (Psalm 32:7), so that others may hear and fear and turn unto the Lord.

Yet, that is not all our Lord has done. He has not only released us from the prison, but He has also seated us in heavenly places (Ephesians 2:6). You and I could go into heaven tonight, if God called us there, and every angel would treat us with respect. If we entered into paradise, even though we had come from the poorest home in the city, we would find that the highest angels are only ministering servants to the chosen people of God. Oh, He has done wonders for us!

I am very much attempting to awaken your memories, so that you may think of the goodness of the Lord's grace and say, "Yes, it is so, and *'my soul doth magnify the Lord'*!"

Not one of the wonders of divine grace has been produced for us without deep necessity for its manifestation. If the very least grace, which may have escaped your attention previously, were taken from you, where would you be? I often meet with people of God who used to be very happy and joyful, but who have fallen into despondency, and who now talk about the mercies of God's covenant love in such a way as to make me blush. They say, "I thought I once had that blessing, but I am afraid I do not have it now, although there is nothing I long for more. Oh, what a precious thing it would be to be able to have access to God in prayer! I would give my eyes to be able to know that I am really a child of God."

Yet, those of us who have these blessings do not often value them; no, dear friends, we do not value them a thousandth part as much as we ought. Our constant song should be: *"Blessed be the Lord, who daily loadeth us with benefits, even the God of our salvation"* (Psalm 68:19). Instead of that, we often take the gifts thoughtlessly and ungratefully from His hand. When a man has plunged himself underwater to the depths of the sea, he may have a great deal of water over his head and not feel it. Yet, when he comes out, if you then put a little pail of water on his head, it becomes quite a burden to him as he carries it. Likewise, some of you are swimming in God's mercy. You are diving into it, and you do not recognize the weight of the glory that God has bestowed upon you. But, if you should once get out of this ocean of joy and fall into a state of sadness of heart, you would begin to appreciate the weight of any one of the mercies, which now do not seem to be of much consequence or to make any claim upon your gratitude. Without waiting to lose the sense of God's grace, in order that we may know the value of it, let us bless Him who has done such inconceivably great things for us. Let us declare, *"My soul doth magnify the Lord."*

The Fifth String of His Grace and Holiness

The fifth string that I would touch is the combination of grace and holiness that we find in what God has done for us: *"He that is mighty hath done to me great things; and holy is his name."* I may not even hint at the particular delicacy of Mary's case, but she knew that it was wholly holy and pure. Now, when the Lord has saved us who did not deserve saving, He did a very wonderful act of sovereign grace in changing us, but the mercy is that He did it all justly.

Nobody can ever say that our salvation ought not to have been bestowed on us. At the Last Great Day, what God has done in His grace will stand the test of justice, for He has never, in the splendor and lavishness of His love, violated the principles of eternal righteousness, even to save His own elect. *"He that is mighty hath done to me great things; and holy is his name."* Sin must be punished: it has been punished in the person of our glorious Substitute. No man can enter into heaven unless he is perfectly pure. They who are redeemed can take no unclean thing within the gates. Every rule and mandate of the divine empire must be observed. The Lawmaker will not be a lawbreaker even to save the sinner. His law will be honored as surely as the sinner will be saved.

Sometimes I feel that I could play on this harp string for hours. Here we have justice, magnified in grace and holiness, rejoicing in the salvation of sinners. The attributes of God are like the clear white light shining through a crystal prism, which may yet be divided into all the colors of the spectrum, each different and all beautiful. The dazzling radiance of God is too glorious for our mortal eyes, but each revelation teaches us more of His beauty and perfectness. In the ruby light of Christ's atoning sacrifice, we are enabled to see how God is just and yet the Justifier of him who believes in Jesus. Glory be to His name for the power of grace mingled with holiness!

"My soul doth magnify the Lord" for this wonderful salvation, in which God's every attribute has its glory—justice as well as mercy, wisdom as well as might. *"Mercy and truth are met together; righteousness and peace have kissed each other"* (Psalm 85:10). Who could have invented such a plan, and who could have carried it out when it was thought of? Only our wonderful Savior and Lord. *"My soul doth magnify the Lord, and my spirit hath rejoiced in God my Saviour."*

The Sixth String of God's Mercy

The sixth string is one that should be sweet in every way. Mary went on to touch the string of God's mercy. *"And his mercy is on them that fear him."* The saints of old often touched this string in the temple. They often sang it, lifting up the refrain again and again: *"His mercy endureth for ever"* (Psalm 136:1).

> For His mercy shall endure,
> Ever faithful; ever sure.

Mercy! Sinner, this is the silver bell for you: *"It is of the Lord's mercies that [you] are not consumed, because his compassions fail not"* (Lamentations 3:22). Listen to the heavenly music that calls you to repent and live. God delights in mercy. He waits to be gracious. Mercy! Saint, this is the golden bell for you, for you still need mercy. Standing with your foot upon the jasper doorstep of paradise, with the pearly gate just before you, you will still need mercy to help you over the last step. When you enter the choir of the redeemed, mercy will be your perpetual song. In heaven you will chant the praises of the God of grace, whose *"mercy endureth for ever."*

Do you mourn over your own backsliding? God will have mercy upon you, dear child, even though you have wandered since you have known Him. Come back to Him this very hour. He wants to woo you again. He wants to press you to His bosom. Have you not often been restored? Have you not often had your iniquities put away from you in the years gone by? If so, again touch this string—a child's finger can make it bring forth its music—touch it now. Say, "Yes, concerning mercy, mercy to this very chief of sinners, *'my soul doth magnify the Lord, and my spirit hath rejoiced in God my Saviour.'"*

The Seventh String of God's Immutability

Space would fail me if I tried to dwell at any length upon any one these wondrous themes, and so I will pass to the next string, number seven, God's immutability. In the verse we have already touched upon, there are two notes, one of His mercy and one of this melody. Mary said, *"His mercy is on them that fear him from generation to generation."* He who had mercy in the days of Mary has mercy today: *"from generation to generation."* He is eternally the same God. *"I am the LORD, I change not; therefore ye sons of Jacob are not consumed"* (Malachi 3:6). You that once delighted in the Lord, do not suppose that He has altered. He still invites you to come and delight in Him. He is *"Jesus Christ the same yesterday, and to day, and for ever"* (Hebrews 13:8).

What a poor foundation we would have for our hope if God could change! But He has confirmed His word by an oath, *"that by two immutable things, in which it was impossible for God to lie, we might have a strong consolation, who have fled for refuge to lay hold upon the hope set before us"* (Hebrews 6:18). The God of my grandfather, the God of my father, is my God this day. The God of Abraham, Isaac, and Jacob is the God of every believer. He is the same God; He is prepared to do the same and to be the same to us as to them. Look back into your own experience; have you not found God always the same? Come, protest against Him if you have ever found Him to change. Is the mercy seat altered? Do the promises of God fail? Has God forgotten to be gracious? Will He be favorable no more? Even *"if we believe not, yet he abideth faithful: he cannot deny himself"* (2 Timothy 2:13). When everything else melts away, this one eternal Rock abides.

Therefore, *"my soul doth magnify the Lord, and my spirit hath rejoiced in God my Saviour."* It is a blessed string to touch. Take the time right now to play it and to evoke such harmonies that will make the angels want to join you in the chorus.

The Eighth String of God's Power

The next string that will awaken a responsive echo in your hearts is God's power: *"He hath showed strength with his arm; he hath scattered the proud in the imagination of their hearts."* This string gives us deep bass music and requires a heavy hand to make it pour forth any melody. What wonders of power God has produced on behalf of His people, from the days of Egypt, when He threw the horse and his rider into the Red Sea (Exodus 15:1), even until now! How strong is His arm to defend His people!

In these days some of us have been driven to look to that power, for all other help has failed. You know how it was in the Dark Ages: it seemed as if the darkness of popery could never be removed; but how soon it was gone when God called forth His men to bear witness to His Son! What reason we have to rejoice that He *"scattered the proud in the imagination of their hearts"*! They thought that they could readily burn up the heretics and put an end to this Gospel of theirs, but they could not do it. Even today there is a dark conspiracy to stamp out the evangelical faith on the part of some who promote their superstitions, set up the crucifix to hide the cross, and point men to sacraments instead of to the Savior. Worse than those are the people who undermine our faith in Holy Scripture, tear from the Book this chapter and that, deny this great truth or another, and try to bring the inventions of man into the place that ought to be occupied by the truth of God.

However, the Lord lives: Jehovah's arm has not waxed short (Numbers 11:23). Depend upon it, before many years have passed, He will take up the quarrel of His covenant and will bring the gospel banner to the forefront again. We will yet rejoice to hear the Good News preached in plainest terms, accentuated by the Holy Spirit Himself upon the hearts of His people.

Let us touch this string again. God Almighty, the Eternal One, is not dead. *"Behold, the Lord's hand is not shortened, that it cannot save; neither his ear heavy, that it cannot hear"* (Isaiah 59:1).

The Ninth String of God's Sovereignty

The next string is one that some friends do not like—at least, they do not say much about it. It is divine sovereignty. Listen to it. You know how God thunders it out. *"I will have mercy on whom I will have mercy, and I will have compassion on whom I will have compassion"* (Romans 9:15). God's will is supreme. Whatever the wills of men may be, God will not be driven from the throng, nor will His scepter be made to quiver in His hands. After all the rebellious acts of men and devils, He will still be eternal and supreme, with His kingdom ruling over all. Thus, Mary sang, *"He hath put down the mighty from their seats, and exalted them of low degree. He hath filled the hungry with good things; and the rich he hath sent empty away."*

Who can speak of the wonders of His sovereign grace? Was it not strange that He should ever have chosen you?

> What was there in you that could merit esteem,
> Or give the Creator delight?
> "'Twas even so, Father," you ever must sing,
> "Because it seemed good in Thy sight."

Do you think it is strange that the Lord should not take the kings and mighty ones, but should so order it that the poor have the Gospel preached to them? God is King of Kings and Lord of Lords, and He acts like a king. *"He giveth not account of any of his matters"* (Job 33:13). But He lets us see very clearly that He has no respect for the greatness and fancied goodness of man, that He does as He pleases, and that He chooses to give His mercy to those who fear Him and bow before Him. He dispenses His favors to those who tremble at His presence, who come humbly to His feet and take His mercy as a free gift; who look to His dear Son because they have nothing else to look to; and who, as poor, guilty worms, find in Christ their life, their wisdom, their righteousness, their all. Oh, the splendor of this great King!

The Tenth String of God's Faithfulness

The tenth string is God's faithfulness: *"He hath holpen his servant Israel, in remembrance of his mercy; as he spake to our fathers, to Abraham, and to his seed for* ever." God remembers what He has said. Take those three words, *"as he spake."* Whatever He said, though it was thousands of years ago, it stands fast forever and ever. God cannot lie.

Friends, are any of you in trouble? Search the Scriptures until you find a promise that suits your case, and when you find it, do not say, "I hope that this is true." That is an insult to God. Believe it, believe it up to the hilt. Do as I have seen boys do in the swimming pool: dive headfirst, and plunge right into the stream of God's mercy. Dive as deeply as you can. There is no drowning there. These are waters to swim in. The more you can lose yourself in this blessed crystal flood of promised mercy, the better it will be. You will rise up out of it as the sheep come from being washed. You will feel refreshed beyond measure in having cast yourself upon God.

When God's promises fail, let your pastor or your elders know of it. Some of us have lived so long on those promises that we do not care to live on anything else; and if they can be proved to be false, we had better give up living altogether. But, we delight to know that they are all absolutely true: what God said to our fathers stands good for their children, and it will stand good even to the end of time and to all eternity.

If any of you have not been able to touch even one of these strings, I would urge you get to your knees and cry out to God, "Why is it that I cannot magnify You, O Lord?" I should not be surprised if you discovered the reason to be that you are too big yourself. He who magnifies himself never magnifies God. Thus, belittle yourself, and greaten your God. Down with self to the lowest depths, and up—higher and still higher—with your thoughts of God.

Poor sinner, you who have not yet grasped the mercy and grace of God, there is sweet music even for you in Mary's song. Perhaps you are saying, "I am nothing but a lump of sin and a heap of misery." Very well, leave your pile of sin and your heap of misery, and let Christ be your All in All. Give yourself up to Christ. He is the Savior. Let Him do His business.

If I were being sued in court, I would not think of hiring an attorney to represent me, but then going into court and meddling with the case for myself. If I did, my attorney would say, "I must drop your case if you do not let it alone." Likewise, the idea may come into your mind that you will do something about saving yourself and have some share in the glory of your salvation. If you do not get rid of that idea, you will be forever lost. Surrender yourself to Christ, and let Him save you. Afterwards, He will work *"in you both to will and to do of his good pleasure"* (Philippians 2:13), while you make melody in your heart unto the Lord for all that He has done on your behalf. Then such delightful melodies will resound from your harp of ten strings that many will listen with such rapture that they will go to your Master and take lessons in this heavenly music for themselves.

The Lord bless you, beloved, and give you a grateful heart for all of His tender mercies to you!

ABOUT THE AUTHOR

C harles Haddon Spurgeon (1834–1892) was born on June 19, 1834, at Kelvedon, Essex, England, the firstborn of eight surviving children. His parents were committed Christians, and his father was a preacher. Spurgeon was converted in 1850 at the age of fifteen. He began to help the poor and to hand out tracts, and was known as "The Boy Preacher."

His next six years were eventful. He preached his first sermon at the age of sixteen. At age eighteen, he became the pastor of Waterbeach Baptist Chapel, preaching in a barn. Spurgeon preached over six hundred times before he reached the age of twenty. By 1854, he was well-known and was asked to become the pastor of New Park Street Chapel in London. In 1856, Spurgeon married Susannah Thompson; they had twin sons, both of whom later entered the ministry.

Spurgeon's compelling sermons and lively preaching style drew multitudes of people, and many came to Christ. Soon, the crowds had grown so large that they blocked the narrow streets near the church. Services eventually had to be held in rented halls, and he often preached to congregations of more than ten thousand. The Metropolitan Tabernacle was built in 1861 to accommodate the large numbers of people.

Spurgeon published over two thousand sermons, which were so popular that they literally sold by the ton. At one point his sermons sold twenty-five thousand copies every week. An 1870 edition of the English magazine *Vanity Fair* called him an "original and powerful preacher...honest, resolute, sincere; lively, entertaining." He appealed constantly to his hearers to move on in the Christian faith, to allow the Lord to minister to them individually, and to be used of God to win the lost to Christ. His sermons were scripturally inspiring and highlighted with flashes of spontaneous and delightful humor. The prime minister of England, members of the royal family, and Florence Nightingale, among others, went to hear him preach. Spurgeon preached to an estimated ten million people throughout his life. Not surprisingly, he is called the "Prince of Preachers."

In addition to his powerful preaching, Spurgeon founded and supported charitable outreaches, including educational institutions. His pastors' college, which is still in existence today, taught nearly nine hundred students in Spurgeon's time. He also founded the famous Stockwell Orphanage.

In his later years, Spurgeon often publicly disagreed with the emergence of modern biblical criticism that led the believer away from a total dependence on the Word of God.

Charles Spurgeon died at Menton, France, in 1892, leaving a legacy of writings to the believer who seeks to know the Lord Jesus more fully.